# Advances in Information Systems Development

## New Methods and Practice for the Networked Society

**Volume 2**

# Advances in Information Systems Development

## New Methods and Practice for the Networked Society

## Volume 2

Edited by

### Gabor Magyar and Gabor Knapp

*Budapest University of Technology*
*Budapest, Hungary*

### Wita Wojtkowski and W. Gregory Wojtkowski

*Boise State University*
*Boise, Idaho USA*

### Jože Zupančič

*University of Maribor*
*Kranj, Slovenia*

 Springer

Gabor Magyar
Budapest University of Technology
    and Economics
Budapest 1111
Muegyetem rkp. 1-3.
Hungary
magyar@mail.bme.hu

Gabor Knapp
Budapest University of Technology
    and Economics
Budapest 1111
Muegyetem rkp. 1-3.
Hungary
knapp@nava.hu

Wita Wojtkowski
Boise State University
1910 University Drive
Boise, Idaho 83725
USA
wwojtkow@boisestate.edu

W. Gregory Wojtkowski
Boise State University
1910 University Drive
Boise, Idaho 83725
USA
gwojtkow@boisestate.edu

Jože Zupančič
University of Maribor
Systems Development Laboratory
SI-6400 Presernova 11
Slovenia
joze.zupancic@fov.uni-mb.si

Proceedings of the 15th International Conference on Information Systems Development—New Methods and Practice for the Networked Society (ISD 2006), held in Budapest, Hungary, August 31–September 2, 2006.

Volume (2): Part 2 of a two-volume set.

ISBN-13 978-1-4419-4359-0          e-ISBN-13 978-0-387-70802-7

Printed on acid-free paper.

9 8 7 6 5 4 3 2 1

springer.com

# Preface

This book is the outcome of the Fifteenth International Conference on Information Systems Development, ISD'2006, held in Budapest, Hungary between 31$^{st}$ August – 2$^{nd}$ September 2006. The theme of the 2006 conference was "New Methods and Practice for the Networked Society".

This theme expresses that we are living in a new era when practically all of our information resources are organized and managed in a networked environment. Information technology has reformed and restructured the workflows of companies and other organizations over the past several decades, and will continue to do so well into the future. This is particularly important now, as we see the emergence of complex networked information systems. "Being digital" by Nicholas Negroponte was the watchword at the dawn of the information society. "Being online" is now at the very heart of our everyday life. New postulates and requirements are stemming from this nature of society of today and tomorrow. The convergence of IT and infocommunication technologies has presented a challange for the ISD profession in terms of accomodating mobility, interoperability, the "always connected" state of information systems, the evolving distributed nature of information resources and the growing volume and diversity of information. IS development, both as a professional and academic discipline, has responded to this challenge through methodologies, tools and theory development. Progress in ISD comes from research as well as from practice. The aim of the Conference was to provide an international forum for the exchange of ideas and experiences between academia and industry, and to stimulate exploration of new solutions.

The ISD Conference evolved from the first Polish-Scandinavian Seminar on Current Trends in Information Systems Development Methodologies, held in Poland in 1988. It was a great honour and responsibility for us to organize the fifteenth event within this fine series of conferences.

Putting together a book of this magnitude requires the cooperation and assistance of many professionals with muchexpertise. We would like to express our gratitude to all the authors and participants for contributing to the conference that we believe to have been successful and memorable. The conference call for papers attracted a great number of very high quality papers. All papers were double-blind refereed by at least two independent reviewers and an Associate Editor. They provided detailed reviews on all papers submitted. We would like to thank the IPC members for their essential work.

Many thanks are due also to the assistance in organization of ISD 2006, especially to the Scientific Association for Infocommunications (HTE) and to the Conference Secretary, Mr. Sándor Szaszkó. We are also grateful to the National Office for Research and Technology (NKTH) the financial support of the Conference.

Gabor Magyar,
Gabor Knapp
Conference co-Chairs,
ISD 2006

# International Science Committee

| | | |
|---|---|---|
| Witold Abramowicz | Economic University | Poland |
| Gary Allen | University of Huddersfield | UK |
| Erling S. Andersen | Norwegian School of Management | Norway |
| Karin Axelsson | Linköping University | Sweden |
| Juris Borzovs | Riga Technical University | Latvia |
| Frada Burstein | Monash University | Australia |
| Rimantas Butleris | Kaunas University of Technology | Lithuania |
| Albertas Caplinskas | Institute of Mathematics and Informatics | Lithuania |
| Sven Carlsson | Lund University | Sweden |
| Dubravka Cecez-Kecmanovic | University of NSW | Australia |
| Antanas Cenys | Semiconductor Physics Institute | Lithuania |
| Rodney Clarke | University of Wollongong | Australia |
| Heitor Augustus Xavier Costa | Universidade Federal de Lavras | Brazil |
| Darren Dalcher | Middlesex University | UK |
| Gert-Jan de Verde | University of Nebraska at Omaha | USA |
| Vitalijus Denisovas | Klaipeda University | Lithuania |
| Dalé Dzemydiene | Law University | Lithuania |
| Jorgen Fischer Nilsson | Technical University of Denmark | Denmark |
| Julie Fisher | Monash University | Australia |
| Guy Fitzgerald | Brunel University | UK |
| Marko Forsell | SESCA Technologies Oy | Finland |
| Odd Fredriksson | Odd Fredriksson | Sweden |
| Chris Freyberg | Massey University | New Zealand |
| Edwin Gray | Glasgow Caledonian University | UK |
| Shirley Gregor | Australian National University | Australia |
| Janis Grundspenkis | Riga Technical University | Latvia |
| G. Harindranath | University of London | UK |
| Igor Hawryszkiewycz | University of Technology Sydney | Australia |
| Haav Hele-Mai | Institute of Cybernetics at Tallinn Technical University | Estonia |
| Alfred Helmerich | Research Institute for Applied Technology | Germany |

| | | |
|---|---|---|
| Karel Richta | Czech Technical University | Czech Republic |
| Kamel Rouibach | Kuwait University | Kuwait |
| Timothy K. Shih | Tamkang University | Taiwan |
| Klaas Sikkel | Universiteit Twente | Netherlands |
| Guttorm Sindre | Norwegian University of Science and Technology | Norway |
| William Song | University of Durham | UK |
| Ioannis Stamelos | Aristotle University | Greece |
| Larry Stapleton | Waterford Institute of Technology | Ireland |
| Eberhard Stickel | Bonn University of Applied Sciences | Germany |
| Uldis Suskovskis | Riga Technical University | Latvia |
| Istvan Szakadat | Budapest University of Technology and Economics | Hungary |
| Sandor Szaszko | Budapest University of Technology and Economics | Hungary |
| Janis Tenteris | Riga Technical University | Latvia |
| John Traxler | University of Wolverhampton | UK |
| Jacek Unold | Wroclaw University of Economics | Poland |
| Olegas Vasilecas | Vilnius Gediminas Technical University | Lithuania |
| W. Gregory Wojtkowski | Boise State University | USA |
| Wita Wojtkowski | Boise State University | USA |
| Carson C. Woo | University of British Columbia | Canada |
| Stanislaw Wrycza | University of Gdansk | Poland |
| Ilze Zigurs | University of Nebraska at Omaha | USA |
| Joze Zupancic | University of Maribor | Slovenia |
| Jozef Zurada | University of Louisville | USA |

# Contents

Preserving Semantics of the Whole-Part Relationships in the Object-Relational
Databases................................................................................................................1
*Erki Eessaar*

Directing and Enacting the Information System.....................................................13
*Björn Abelli*

Several Outlines of Graph Theory in Framework of MDA.....................................25
*Natalja Pavlova*

Designing Software Components for Database Consistency – An Enterprise
Modeling Approach.................................................................................................37
*Lars Jakobsson and Peter Bellström*

Trust-Related Requirements: A Taxonomy.............................................................49
*Guttorm Sindre*

Design of a Peer-to-Peer Information Sharing MAS Using MOBMAS
(Ontology-Centric Agent Oriented Methodology) .................................................63
*N. Tran, G. Beydoun, G. Low*

Recognition and Resolution of Linguistic Conflicts: The Core to a Successful
View and Schema Integration .................................................................................77
*Peter Bellström, Jürgen Vöhringer and Alexander Salbrechter*

Contextual Method Integration ..............................................................................89
*Mauri Leppänen*

A Framework for Situational and Evolutionary Language Adaptation in
Information Systems Development .........................................................................103
*Jörg Becker, Christian Janiesch, Stefan Seidel and Christian Brelage*

Towards Estimating Quality of Experience with Passive Bottleneck Detection
Metrics...................................................................................................................115
*Pál Varga, Gergely Kún, Gábor Sey*

Socio-Technical Perspectives on Design Science in IS Research ...................... 127
*Jörg Becker, Björn Niehaves, Christian Janiesch*

Modeling Objects Dynamics in Conceptual Models ......................................... 139
*Vaclav Repa*

An Interoperability Classification Framework for Method Chunk
Repositories ................................................................................................ 153
*Per Backlund, Jolita Ralyté, Manfred A. Jeusfeld, Harald Kühn*
*Nicolas Arni-Bloch, Jan B.M. Goossenaerts, and Frank Lillehagen*

Configurable Satisfiability Propagation for Goal Models Using Dynamic
Compilation Techniques ................................................................................ 167
*Elena Navarro, Patricio Letelier, David Reolid  and Isidro Ramos*

Cookie-Chain Based Discovery of Relation between Internet Users and Real
Persons ......................................................................................................... 181
*Csaba Legány, Attila Babos, Sándor Juhász*

Requirements Modeling and MDA – Proposal for a Combined Approach ......... 191
*Christian Kop, Heinrich C. Mayr and Nataliya Yevdoshenko*

Moral Problems in Industry-Academia Partnership – The Viewpoint of
Clients on a Project Course .......................................................................... 203
*Tero Vartiainen*

Outlining "Data Track": Privacy-friendly Data Maintenance for End-users ....... 215
*John Sören Pettersson, Simone Fischer-Hübner, Mike Bergmann*

Improving Trust in E-Government Through Paralingual Web Design ................ 227
*Roy Segovia and Murray E. Jennex*

A Study of E-mail Marketing: Why Do People
Read and Forward E-mail? ............................................................................ 239
*Hsi-Pen Lu, Hsin-Chiau Fu, Chia-Hui Yen*

Key Issues in Information Systems Management in Companies in Slovenia ...... 251
*Stanislav Sotlar, Jože Zupančič*

Enterprise Information Systems – Eight Significant Conditions ........................ 263
*Anders G. Nilsson*

Success Factors Across ERP Implementation Phases: Learning from
Practice ....................................................................................................... 275
*Piotr Soja*

Building the Enterprise Architecture: A Bottom-Up Evolution? ........................287
*Hakan P. Sundberg*

Contract Type and PricinStructure and the Practice of Information Systems
Development – An Economical Perspective ......................................................299
*Karlheinz Kautz, Bjarke Nielsen*

An Approach of the Knowledge Management for the Development
of the Organisational Commitment ..................................................................313
*Adriana Schiopoiu Burlea*

Educational Management Information Systems: An Example for Developing
Countries ..........................................................................................................325
*John Traxler*

Management Support Systems Design:
A Competing Values Approach.........................................................................335
*Sven A. Carlsson and Jonas Hedman*

Activity Based Costing System
for a Medium-sized Trade Company.................................................................347
*Arkadiusz Januszewski*

Managing a Software Development Organization with a TQM Approach
for Balance in a Period of Rapid Growth .........................................................359
*Mirja Pulkkinen and Marko Forsell*

Knowledge Management in Higher Education: A Case Study in a Large
Modern UK University ......................................................................................371
*Anne Slater and Robert Moreton*

Creating Value-Adding IT Solutions for SMEs. A Field Study from Poland......383
*Przemysław Lech*

How is Project Success Affected by Replacing
the Project Manager?.........................................................................................397
*Tero Vartiainen, Maritta Pirhonen*

Virtual Organisation Governance by Example
of Virtual University .........................................................................................409
*Malgorzata Pankowska*

Practical Experiences in Web Engineering.........................................................421
*M.J. Escalona, J.J. Gutierrez, D. Villadiego, A. León, J. Torres*

Derivation of Test Objectives Automatically ..................................................... 435
*J. J. Gutiérrez, M. J. Escalona, M. Mejías, J. Torres*

Examining OSS Sucess: Information Technology Acceptance by
FireFox Users ................................................................................................ 447
*Andrzej Slomka, Tomasz Przechlewski, and Stanislaw Wrycza*

Ontology-based User Modeling for Web-based
Information Systems ..................................................................................... 457
*Anton Andrejko, Michal Barla and Mária Bieliková*

IT-Supported Inter-Organizational Services – The Case of a Swedish E-business
Portal for Electronic Invoicing for Regional SMEs ........................................ 469
*Odd Fredriksson*

What Makes a Good Diagram? Improving the Cognitive  Effectiveness
of Diagrams in IS Development ...................................................................... 481
*Daniel Moody*

Searching The Deep Web: The WOW project ................................................. 493
*Domonkos Tikk, Zsolt T. Kardkovács, and Gábor Magyar*

Formal Grammars for Conformance Testing ................................................... 505
*Csaba V. Rotter*

Index ............................................................................................................. 515

# Preserving Semantics of the Whole-Part Relationships in the Object-Relational Databases

Erki Eessaar

Department of Informatics, Tallinn University of Technology, Raja 15, 12618 Tallinn, Estonia. eessaar@staff.ttu.ee

## 1 Introduction

A conceptual data model that is created for example in UML (OMG 2003) can contain aggregation and composition relationships between entity types. This article describes how to preserve the semantics of this kind of relationships in a database that is created by an Object-Relational Database Management System, which implements the prescriptions, proscriptions and suggestions of The Third Manifesto (Date and Darwen 2000).

A lot of research about the semantics of the aggregation and composition relationships has been done by different authors. Examples of the recent research are works of Barbier et al. (2003) and Guizzardi (2005). Their view is that UML (at least prior to the version 2.0) doesn't define the semantics of this kind of relationships precisely enough. Therefore, we use instead the concept "whole-part relationship" in this article. Barbier et al. (2003) list and explain primary and secondary characteristics of the whole-part relationships. We use the values of some of the secondary characteristics in order to choose between the database design alternatives.

A Database Management System (DBMS) can't "understand" semantics of a relationship the same way as humans do - based on the names of a relationship and its participants (Date and McGoveran 1994). However, a DBMS is able to understand and enforce structural and operational properties of the relationships and objects, which participate in these relationships (Zhang et al. 2001). Underlying data model of a DBMS determines the extent of these abilities. Therefore, properties of the data model determine how well a DBMS can preserve semantics of a reality in a database.

*Relational data model* was introduced to a wide audience by Codd (1970) and has been extensively studied since that. Codd's work influenced strongly the design of SQL, but not all original principles of the relational model where taken into an account. SQL became a standard and many DBMSs (RDBMS$_{SQL}$s) started to use it. However, the language had many shortcomings that hampered its usage in the complex systems. An example of this kind of system is a repository system for the management of system specifications. Some examples of the deficiencies of an early SQL are:

1. Impossible to declare new data types.
2. Too big distinction between base- and derived tables.
3. Limited means for presenting missing information.
4. Complex language structure that allows to solve some problems in many different ways but at the same time doesn't help to solve some other problems at all. For example, options for making queries based on the hierarchic or networked data are limited.

SQL:1999 (Gulutzan and Pelzer 1999) and SQL:2003 (Melton 2005) standards try to resolve some problems of SQL. For example, they permit the creation of new data types. The DBMSs that conform to SQL:1999 or SQL:2003 standards are called Object Relational Database Management Systems (ORDBMS$_{SQL}$). Unfortunately, problems of SQL standards and systems have not been completely solved and new problems have emerged (Pascal 2000; Date 2003). In addition, DBMSs that use SQL don't completely follow the standard. Such gap between the *principles* and *practice* makes database design even more difficult. For example, possibilities to declare constraints are limited and updatable views have additional restrictions. Therefore, researchers have the question: "Can we replace SQL and its underlying data model with some language and model which have better design and usability than SQL do?"

One notable revision of the relational data model is The Third Manifesto (Date and Darwen 2000), (Date 2003). The relational data model consists of relation type generators, facilities for defining relation variables (relvars) of such types and assignment operations for assigning relation values (relations) to the relvars (Date 2003). In addition, it consists of the *extensible* collections of scalar types, operators for dealing with the values that have these types and generic relational operators for deriving relations from other relations (Date 2003).

Some principles that are introduced in The Third Manifesto start to appear step by step to SQL standard. Therefore, this manifest can be seen as a compilation of principles of Object-Relational DBMS (ORDBMS$_{TTM}$) that is free from the burdens of SQL. Many researchers have studied how to use standardized and proprietary features of ORDBMS$_{SQL}$s in order to implement structural and operational properties of the aggregation and composition relationships (Soutou 2001; Zhang et al. 2001; Marcos et al. 2001; Pardede et al. 2004). We are not aware of any study about the ORDBMS$_{TTM}$s in this regard.

We evaluate a set of ORDBMS$_{TTM}$ database designs in terms of some of the secondary characteristics of whole-part relationships. Some designs make use of attributes with *complex data types* (user defined scalar types, and generated tuple and relation types) in base relvars. *The main goal* of this article is to investigate whether the usage of complex data types in base relvars simplifies database design. Our *additional goal* is to demonstrate that relational data model as described

in The Third Manifesto has the necessary means for preserving relationship semantics in a database. We also want to raise awareness about the problems of the
ORDBMS$_{SQL}$s in order to stress the need to *improve* or even *replace* them.

The rest of the paper is organized as follows. Firstly, we propose the set of designs that one could use in order to implement a whole-part relationship in an
ORDBMS$_{TTM}$ database. Secondly, we evaluate these designs in terms of some of
the secondary characteristics of the whole-part relationships in order to find out
when it is suitable to use them and when it is not. We present expressions in *Tutorial D* relational language that is proposed in The Third Manifesto. We have tested
these expressions by using the experimental ORDBMS$_{TTM}$ *Rel* that allows to use a
dialect of Tutorial D (Voorish 2006). We haven't tested outer join because *Rel*
doesn't support it fully yet. Thirdly, we discuss our results and refer to some of the
problems of the ORDBMS$_{SQL}$s. Finally, we present conclusions and refer to the
future work.

## 2 Possible Designs

In this section, we present some possible designs of an ORDBMS$_{TTM}$ database
structure in case of a whole-part relationship between entity types.

For the illustrative purposes, we assume that we have the conceptual data
model with the entity types *Whole* and *Part*. They are associated with a generic
binary whole-part relationship. The entity type *Whole* has the attributes *a* and *b*
and *Part* has the attributes *c* and *d*. Values of the attributes *a* and *c* are unique
identifiers of the Wholes and Parts, respectively. We also assume that the attributes *a*, *b*, *c* and *d* have the type INTEGER (INT).

Declarations of the relvar types (see Table 1) consist of the pairs of attribute
and type identifiers. Phrase "part TUPLE {c INT, d INT}" in Table 1 means that
the relvar has the attribute *part* with the generated tuple type. Phrases "part
RELATION {c INT, d INT}" and "part RELATION{part ST}" mean that the relvar has the attribute *part* with the generated relation type. Type ST is a scalar type
that is created based on the entity type *Part*. Its possible representation contains
components that correspond to the attributes *c* and *d*. All relvars that are presented
in Table 1 are *base* relvars.

Table 1 contains illustrations of the values of the relvars. The reader must bear
in mind that the designs are different because they use the different kind of types,
although some designs have the same illustration.

Designs 1 and 6 are similar to the ones that Rahayu et al. (1998) propose to use
in the RDBMS$_{SQL}$ databases in case of the collection type *set* in an object-oriented
conceptual model. Designs 2-5 use complex types - user defined scalar types and
generated tuple- and relation types. They are similar to some of the designs that
the researchers (Marcos et al. 2001; Soutou 2001; Zhang et al. 2001; Pardede et al.
2004) recommend to use in the ORDBMS$_{SQL}$ databases.

**Table 1.** Design alternatives for implementing a whole-part relationship

| ID | Types of the base relvars (*relvar name* : relvar type) | Pictures that illustrate values of the relvars |
|----|---------------------------------------------------------|------------------------------------------------|
| 1 | *Whole* : RELATION {a INT, b INT} <br> *Part* : RELATION {c INT, d INT, a INT} | Whole: a b / 1 2 / 2 4    Part: c d a / 1 5 1 / 2 5 2 |
| 2 | *Whole* : <br> RELATION {a INT, b INT, part ST} | Whole: a b part / 1 2 1, 5 / 2 4 2, 5 |
| 3 | *Whole* : RELATION {a INT, b INT, part TUPLE {c INT, d INT}} | |
| 4 | *Whole* : RELATION {a INT, b INT, part RELATION {c INT, d INT}} | Whole: a b part / 1 2 1, 5 |
| 5 | *Whole* : RELATION {a INT, b INT, part RELATION{part ST}} | 2 4 2, 5 / 3, 6 |
| 6 | *Whole* : RELATION {a INT, b INT} <br> *Part*: RELATION {c INT, d INT } <br> *PartOfWhole*: RELATION {a INT, c INT} | PartOfWhole: a c / 1 1 / 2 2 / 2 3 / 1 3   Whole: a b / 1 2 / 2 4   Part: c d / 1 5 / 2 5 / 3 6 |

# 3 Choosing Between the Designs

In this section, we evaluate the designs (1-6) in terms of some of the secondary characteristics of the whole-part relationships (see Table 2): shareability (SH), lifetime dependency (LD), existential dependency (ED) and separability (SP). We reference to these characteristics in the column *"Values of the characteristics"* in Table 2 by using the abbreviations that are in the brackets. Semantics of these characteristics are explained for example by Barbier et al. (2003) and Guizzardi (2005). Pictograms in the column *"Relationship constraints"* in Table 2 illustrate the participation and cardinality constraints of the relationships that are imposed by the values of the secondary characteristics. "[W]" and "[P]" denote "Whole" and "Part", respectively.

We give marks (0-4) to these designs based on the possible values of the characteristics. Each mark depends on the participation and cardinality constraints and characterizes whether it is reasonable to use a design and how much effort it requires. *Mark 0* means that it is unreasonable to use a design because it would cause data redundancy. For example, in case of: [W]$\diamond$-*0..n*----*0..n*-[P], we could use designs 4 or 5. Pardede et al. (2004) propose to use similar designs in case of the shareable parts. However, in this case data about some part instances would be repeatedly recorded and it will cause *update anomalies*. *Mark 2* means that the design can be used, but besides candidate key and foreign key constraints one has to create additional relvar and database constraints. *Mark 3* means that a database designer has to ensure that attributes can have special values for dealing with the "missing information". Additional constraints like in case of mark 2 are not needed. For example, we could use design 1-5 in case of the following relationship: [W]<>-0..1-----0..n-[P]. In this case, the relation *Whole* must contain exactly one tuple with the special values. This tuple corresponds to a missing whole instance. The Third Manifesto envisages that declarations of the scalar types can be accompanied by the declarations of the special values which represent information that is missing or unknown for some reasons (Date and Darwen 2000). We can use an empty relation as a special value in case of a generated relation type. In case of a generated tuple type, we have to declare that scalar types of attributes of the tuple type permit special values. *Mark 1* means that we have to use additional constraints (mark 2) as well as special values (mark 3). *Mark 4* means that the design can be used by just creating relvars. Each relvar has by definition one or more candidate keys and can have foreign keys – additional constraints (mark 2) and special values (mark 3) are unnecessary.

In the description of lifetime dependency, we use nine cases proposed by Barber et al. (2003) (see Fig. 1) that compare lifetime of the part to the lifetime of the whole. We don't give marks in case of this characteristic (see Table 2) because cardinality constraints are not specified. However, possibility of using one or another design (designs 1-6) and necessary additional constraints depend on these constraints.

**Table 2.** Comparison of the designs

| ID | Values of the characteristics | D 6 | e 1 | s 2 | i 3 | g 4 | n 5 | Grp | Relationship constraints |
|----|------|---|---|---|---|---|---|---|------|
| 1 | LD: lifetime dependency – cases 1, 2, 4, 5. | - | - | - | - | - | - | 5 | [W]<>-1..------[P] |
| 2 | LD: lifetime dependency – cases 3, 6, 7, 8, 9. | - | - | - | - | - | - | 5 | [W]<>-0..------[P] |
| 3 | SH, SP: locally exclusive part with optional wholes. | 4 | 3 | 3 | 1 | 1 | 1 | 4 | [W]<>-0..1----[P] |
| 4 | SP: whole with no more than one optional part. | 4 | 4 | 3 | 3 | 1 | 1 | 4 | [W]<>----0..1-[P] |
| 5 | SH: globally exclusive (non-shareable) part. | 4 | 4 | 4 | 4 | 4 | 4 | 4 | - |
| 6 | SH: globally shareable part. | 4 | 4 | 0 | 2 | 2 | 0 | 3 | - |
| 7 | SH, SP: locally exclusive part with mandatory wholes. ED, SH: inseparable and locally exclusive part. | 2 | 4 | 4 | 2 | 2 | 2 | 3 | [W]<>-1..1----[P] |

| | | | | | | | | | |
|---|---|---|---|---|---|---|---|---|---|
| 8 | SP: whole with exactly one mandatory part. ED: whole with exactly one essential part. | 2 | 2 | 4 | 4 | 2 | 2 | 3 | [W]<>----1..1-[P] |
| 9 | SP: whole with more than one mandatory part. ED: whole with more than one essential part. | 2 | 2 | 0 | 0 | 2 | 2 | 2 | [W]<>----1..n-[P] $n>1$ |
| 10 | SP: whole with more than one optional parts. | 2 | 2 | 0 | 0 | 1 | 1 | 2 | [W]<>----0..n-[P] $n>0$ |
| 11 | SH: locally shareable part. | 2 | 0 | 0 | 0 | 0 | 0 | 1 | [W]<>-m..n---[P] $n>1$ $n>=m$ |
| 12 | SP, SH: mandatory whole with locally shareable parts. ED, SH: inseparable and locally shareable part. | 2 | 0 | 0 | 0 | 0 | 0 | 1 | [W]<>-1..n----[P] $n>1$ |
| 13 | SP, SH: optional whole with locally shareable parts. | 2 | 0 | 0 | 0 | 0 | 0 | 1 | [W]<>-0..n----[P] $n>0$ |
| Σ | | | 30 | 25 | 18 | 16 | 15 | 13 | |

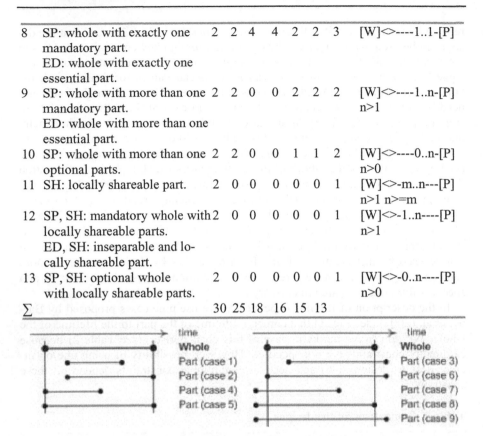

**Fig. 1.** The cases of lifetime dependency (Barber et al. 2003)

If the notation of the cardinality constraint value is n (see Table 2), then we assume that it is some finite number that a designer can specify.

We used "minus technique" algorithm (Võhandu et al. 2006) for ordering the data table (see Table 2) in order to see typical and fuzzy parts of the data. This algorithm *reorders* rows and columns in a table based on the frequencies of the data values (marks in this case). It also finds groups of the relationship characteristic values that have a similar usability (marks) in terms of the designs (1-6) (see column *Grp* in Table 2).

Next, we give examples of the *integrity constraints* that are necessary in case of the designs (1-6) in the context of the values of the characteristics.

Firstly, we investigate the case where the cardinality constraint of the relationship determines that the whole must have at most one part (ID=4 in Table 2). In case of designs 1 and 6 we don't need additional relvar and database constraints besides candidate key and foreign key constraints. In case of design 1, attribute *a* of the relvar *Whole* must be the candidate key. Relvar *Part* must have two candidate keys – attribute *c* as well as the foreign key attribute *a*. In case of design 6, the attribute *a* of the relvar Whole, the attribute *c* of the relvar *Part* and the foreign key attribute *a* of the relvar *PartOfWhole* must be candidate keys. In case of designs 2-5 the attribute *part* of the relvar *Whole* can have the values that represent missing information. In addition, in case of designs 4 and 5 we have to limit the amount of tuples that can be part of a value of the attribute *part*. We could create the relvar constraint with the expression (1):

```
IS_EMPTY((SUMMARIZE (Whole UNGROUP part) PER          (1)
Whole {a} ADD Count AS card) WHERE NOT
(card<=1));
```

IS_EMPTY (<relational expr.>) is the scalar operator with the declared type "boolean", that evaluates to *true* if the body of the relation which is the result of the <relational expr.> contains no tuples (Date 2003).

If the cardinality constraint of the relationship requires that the whole must have exactly one part (ID=8 in Table 2), then attribute *part* can't have a value that represents missing information in case of designs 2-5. In addition, relvar constraint (1) must have the condition card=1 in case of designs 4 and 5. In case of designs 1 and 6 we have to *additionally* create the database constraints with the expressions (2) and (3), respectively:

```
IS_EMPTY(Whole SEMIMINUS Part);                       (2)
```

```
IS_EMPTY(Whole SEMIMINUS PartOfWhole);                (3)
```

A SEMIMINUS B is the relational operation which result contains tuples of A that have no corresponding tuple in B (Date 2003).

Next, we investigate the case where the part must have exactly one associated whole (ID=7 in Table 2). Attribute *c* must be the candidate key of the relvar *PartOfWhole* in case of design 6 and we need similar constraint to the constraint (3), which references to the relvar *Part* instead of the relvar *Whole*. In case of designs 2-5 we have to prevent the possibility that the data about the same part is recorded repeatedly – as part of the different tuples in the relation *Whole*. For example, in case of design 3 we could create relvar constraint with the expression (4) in order to assure that the value of the attribute *c* is not recorded repeatedly in the relation. The attribute *c* is the unique identifier attribute of the entity type *Part*.

```
IS_EMPTY((SUMMARIZE (Whole UNWRAP part) PER           (4)
Whole UNWRAP part {c} ADD COUNT AS cnt) WHERE
cnt>1);
```

UNWRAP is the relational operator that forms a relation which heading contains attributes that correspond to the attributes in the heading H of the tuple type, instead of one attribute with the type TUPLE{H} (Date 2003). In case of design 2, we have to declare that the attribute *part* with a scalar type is a candidate key. It is not enough to declare that the attribute *part* is a candidate key in case of designs 4 and 5. Two distinct values with the same relation type can contain the same tuple. Therefore, in case of designs 4 and 5 we have to use similar constraint to (4) where the operator UNWRAP is replaced with the operator UNGROUP. UNGROUP is the operator that "unnests" an attribute that has a relation type.

In case of designs 1 and 6 we can use the virtual relvars (views) that have attributes with the complex types, in order to present data the same way as in case of designs 2-5. The expression (5) is an example of the relational expression of the virtual relvar that can be used in case of design 1. Virtual relvar with such relational expression has the relation type: RELATION {a INT, b INT, part RELATION {c INT, d INT}}.

```
(Whole LEFT JOIN Part FILL {c "?", d "?"})        (5)
GROUP {c, d} AS part;
```

"A mandatory FILL clause specifies the contents for non-matching tuples, thus avoiding the need for NULLs" (Voorish 2006). We assume that "?" is the special value for unknown data in case of type INT. Date (2003, p. 301) describes *The Principle of Interchangeability* according to which there must be no arbitrary and unnecessary distinctions between the base and virtual relvars. Therefore, an ORDBMS$_{TTM}$ allows to change the values of base and virtual relvars the same way. If we delete tuple from the value of the virtual relvar (5), then system must change the values of the underlying base relvars by deleting corresponding tuples from the relations *Whole* and *Part*. This is the behavior that is needed in case of the inseparable parts (see Table 2).

Next, we draw some conclusions based on Table 2. Designs that have attributes with complex data types in *base* relvars are unsuitable to use in case of the relationship characteristic values which impose restriction that the cardinality constraint at the relationship end connected to the whole is *bigger than one*. It is traditionally seen as property of the aggregation relationship. In addition, designs 2 and 3 that use an attribute with a generated tuple type or user defined scalar type are not usable if the cardinality constraint at the relationship end connected to the part is *bigger than one*. Designs 2 and 3 are well usable and don't require additional constraints if the multiplicity at the both ends of the relationship is 1..1. Design 6 is usable in case of any characteristic value but requires sometimes additional constraints. Design 1 is not usable only in case of the relationship characteristic values, which impose restriction that the cardinality constraint at the relationship end connected to the whole is *bigger than one*.

We summarize marks by designs (see row $\sum$ in Table 2). Generally, the bigger the sum is, the smaller are the usage restrictions of the design and the need for the accompanying constraints and special values. As we can see in Table 2, designs 1 and 6 have bigger results than designs 2-5.

# 4 Discussion

Previous section demonstrates that the relational data model as described in The Third Manifesto has means for implementing properties of the whole-part relationships.

Many researchers have studied how to design an ORDBMS$_{SQL}$ database in case of the aggregation and composition relationships (Marcos et al. 2001; Soutou

2001; Zhang et al. 2001; Pardede et al. 2004). The present work is different, because it is based on the systems (ORDBMS$_{TTM}$) that are an alternative to the ORDBMS$_{SQL}$s. Researchers and developers have already in their disposal experimental open source (Voorish 2006) as well as commercial (Alphora 2006) ORDBMS$_{TTM}$s. One could say that an ORDBMS$_{SQL}$ allows to achieve the same results as an ORDBMS$_{TTM}$ if the database designers bear in mind good database design principles and that much of the ORDBMS$_{TTM}$ features are implemented in the current ORDBMS$_{SQL}$s. However, our study shows that the existing ORDBMS$_{SQL}$s like Oracle 10g (Oracle 2005) don't allow to implement many aspects of the designs that are presented in sections 2 and 3. Next are some examples of the problems:

1. It is not possible to use row type constructor in Oracle and therefore we can't use design 3 (see Table 1).
2. It is not possible to declare that a column with an user-defined structured type or a constructed table type has a key constraint.
3. Possibilities to *declare* constraints to the values of a table type (nested tables in Oracle's terminology) are limited. We can only declare that column in a nested table has some data type. It is also impossible to *declare* minimum and maximum cardinality of a nested table.
4. It is not possible to create *declarative* database constraints like (2, 3) and relvar constraints (1, 4), because system doesn't allow to use assertions and subqueries in the CHECK constraints.
5. Views can be used in order to implement behavioral aspects of a whole-part relationship (see the expression (5)). In Oracle, a DML statement must affect only one underlying table of a updatable join view that uses "one-to-many join". We must program an instead-of trigger by using proprietary imperative language in order to change it.
6. There is no builtin IS_EMPTY scalar operator or SEMIMINUS relational operator in the Oracle SQL dialect.

Other researches have noticed similar problems. For example, Pardede et al. (2004), who try to implement whole-part relationship in an ORDBMS$_{SQL}$ database by using the collection data types, write: "At present, we cannot use SQL to embed integrity constraint checking in ORDB collection." Our research result supports this finding and brings attention to the *practical* need to improve the existing standards and systems.

Barbier et al. (2003) and Guizzardi (2005) have shown that specification of the aggregation and composition relationships in UML has deficiencies. They have proposed improvements to UML metamodel and definitions of relationships. One difference between our work and work of Marcos et al. (2001) and Pardede et al. (2004) is that we don't use this quite simplifying classification to aggregation and composition relationships. Instead, we evaluate proposed designs in terms of some of the secondary characteristics of a general whole-part relationship.

## 5 Conclusions

The Third Manifesto is a thorough specification of the relational data model. Model that it describes can be seen as a kind of object-relational data model because it envisages many features that are also proposed in the SQL:1999 and SQL:2003 standards. We have demonstrated that such data model is powerful enough for implementing properties of the whole-part relationships in a database in order to preserve semantics of the relationships. Database designer can choose between design alternatives, some of which make use of user defined and generated data types in *base* relvars (see Table 1). We evaluated the alternatives in terms of some of the values of the whole-part relationship secondary characteristics, constructed the comparison table and reorganized it (see Table 2). Such evaluation method about implementing complex relationships in a database is also novel result of our work. We have found the cases when to use and when not to use these designs. Existing research mainly focuses on the positive aspects of using complex data types in base tables (relvars). But our research shows that the "traditional" designs (without using complex data types in base relvars) together with the *special values, integrity constraints* and *views* which use complex data types offer actually more freedom and flexibility to the designers. Widespread view is that it is possible to preserve whole-part relationship at the logical database level by having containment hierarchy within a *base* relation. However, a DBMS could also have information about the existence of the whole-part relationship if a database contains certain virtual relvars (see expression (5)) and constraints.

We have also pointed to some of the shortcomings of one current ORDBMS$_{SQL}$. Data types, views and constraints are not supported as well as they could in this system. Therefore, we point to the areas of the existing systems that need improvement. This can also be seen as a result because existing researches focus on the advantages of the ORDBMS$_{SQL}$s and demonstrate usage of their features.

In this article, we didn't consider some secondary characteristics of the whole-part relationships: transitivity, configurationality, mutability. Future work about this topic must also consider these characteristics. We must also study how transition constraints help to implement operational properties of the relationships.

## References

Alphora. Dataphor 2.0 Retrieved April 08, 2006 from http://alphora.com./tiern.asp?ID=DATAPHOR2

Barbier F, Henderson-Sellers B, Le Parc-Lacayrelle A, Bruel J (2003) Formalization of the Whole-Part Relationship in the Unified Modeling Language. IEEE Trans. Softw. Eng. 29(5):459-470

Codd EF (1970) A relational model of large shared data banks. Comm. ACM 13(6):377-387

Date CJ, McGoveran D (1994) The Principle of Orthogonal Design. Database Programming & Design 7, No. 6 (June 1994)

Date CJ, Darwen H (2000) Foundation for Future Database Systems: The Third Manifesto, 2nd edn. Addison-Wesley

Date CJ (2003) An Introduction to Database Systems. 8th edn. Pearson/Addison Wesley, Boston

Guizzardi G (2005) Ontological Foundations for Structural Conceptual Models. Telematica Instituut Fundamental Research Series No. 15. Ph.D. thesis, University of Twente

Gulutzan P, Pelzer T (1999) SQL-99 Complete, Really. Miller Freeman, USA

Marcos E, Vela B, Cavero JM, Caceres P (2001) Aggregation and composition in object-relational database design. In: Caplinskas A, Eder J (eds) Research Communications of ADBIS'01(1). pp 195-209

Melton J (2005) ISO/IEC 9075-2:2003 (E) Information technology — Database languages — SQL — Part 2: Foundation (SQL/Foundation). August, 2003. Retrieved December 26, 2004, from http://www.wiscorp.com/SQL Standards.html

Oracle® Database SQL Reference 10g Release 1 (10.1) Part Number B10759-01. Oracle Corp., Retrieved October 4, 2005, from http://download-west.oracle. com/docs/cd/B14117_01/server.101/b10759/toc.htm

Pardede E, Rahayu JW, Taniar D (2004) Mapping Methods and Query for Aggregation and Association in Object-Relational Database using Collection. In Proc. of the ITCC(1)'2004. IEEE Computer Society, pp 539-543

Pascal F (2000) Practical issues in Database Management. A Reference for the Thinking Practioner, Addison-Wesley. Boston, Mass, 1st edition

Rahayu W, Chang E, Dillon TS (1998) Implementation of Object-Oriented Association Relationships in Relational Databases. In: Eaglestone B, Desai BC, Shao J (eds) Proc. of the IDEAS'1998. IEEE Computer Society, pp 254-263

Soutou C (2001) Modeling relationships in object-relational databases. Data and Knowledge Engineering 36(1):79-107

OMG Unified Modeling Language Specification. March 2003. Version 1.5. formal/03-03-01

Voorish D (2006) An Implementation of Date and Darwen's "TutorialD" http:// dbappbuilder.sourceforge.net/Rel.html (26.03.2006)

Võhandu L, Kuusik R, Torim A, Aab E, Lind G (2006) Some Monotone Systems Algorithms for Data Mining, WSEAS Transactions on Information Science & Applications 3(4):802-809

Zhang N, Ritter N, Härder T (2001) Enriched Relationship Processing in Object-Relational Database Management Systems. In: Lu H, Spaccapietra S (eds) Proc. of the CODAS'01. IEEE Computer Society, pp 53-62

# Directing and Enacting the Information System

Björn Abelli

School of Business at Mälardalen University, Box 883, SE-72123
Västerås, Sweden. bjorn.abelli@mdh.se.

## 1 Information Systems – Not only with Computers

Information existed long before the development of computers and software. Systems for handling this information existed as well, with different technologies in use (cuneiform, petroglyphs, Gutenberg's printing press, etc). Even further back in time, long before humans could use written language, they could communicate information and knowledge through myths and rituals. These rituals may be some of the first constructed information systems. Hunting stories and other extraordinary events became part of the stories told, and when they were acted out in a drama separated from all ceremonial concerns, a first significant step had been taken toward theatre as a specialized activity. The development process of a theatre production could hence be seen as one of the most genuine models for development of manual information systems. (Brocket 1987; Abelli and Révay 2004)

Modern models for development of Information Systems such as RUP or DSDM don't include explicit directions on how to develop manual systems or even manual routines, while OPEN even explicitly is aimed towards computer based systems only. Other models, such as the Swedish models MBI/SAK and SIS:RAS, acknowledge the need for manual routines to a greater extent, such as it would not be possible or not appropriate to computerize everything, but they still don't contain explicit directions for development of all aspects of manual processes. (Révay 1977; Wigander et al. 1979; Hugoson et al. 1983; DSDM Consortium 2002; Firesmith and Henderson-Sellers 2002; Rational Software Corporation 2003)

The current models in use tend to miss less computer-biased aspects, e.g. the role of members in an organization as developers, users and functions of the information system itself. As most computer based systems originates from formalizing and automating existing manual processes, it should be useful to see what an analysis from a theatre perspective could bring. (Abelli 2006)

Abelli and Révay (2004) presented a development model of theatre with some comparisons to what we traditionally see as system development models, and with some results possible to use in other contexts. This paper presents some of the results of a case study where the model has been used to analyze the information processing within an organization from another context than theatre. The theatre model is not a modeling technique, but a model for conceptual analysis of issues not captured by other methods such as structured analysis, data flow modeling or use case-driven analysis (Jacobson 1992; Wieringa 1995). Even though all of those techniques focus on capturing the process rather than only functions of the system, they don't take into consideration all aspects of the context. Individual traits, emotions and behaviors have a great impact on how the information is received. Even the ethnographically informed analysis proposed by Villers and Sommerville (2000) tend to reduce the individuals to actors in a use case sense, instead of acknowledging that individuals can act differently even in the same situation depending on contextual and behavioral factors.

## 2 A Development Model for Theatre Productions

Abelli and Révay (2004) presented the development model of modern theatre productions as performed in a sequence of distinct phases where some activities are performed iteratively. When a theatre production is stripped down to the bare necessities to create a performance, we have dug out "the core processes of theatre production". Input is the message or knowledge the producers of theatre want to pass over to the audience; output is the information and/or experience of emotions the performance in itself mediates to the audience. The core processes of theatre productions maps to the developer roles defined as playwright, director, actor and audience (fig. 1), though any individual can have many roles.

- **The playwright's process – defining what information to mediate.** The playwright creates a manuscript which later on will be evolved into a performance with addition of visual, audial and other elements. The core concept of a play is the "premise", which can be seen as more than the "information" in an IS. In dramatic writing, the premise can often be expressed as a "statement", "sentence", "proverb" or "maxim" that the writer has intended to mediate to the audience. The further work of the playwright, to create characters, a story, a plot, writing dialogue and stage directions, is done through iterative analysis and design in order to enhance the premise. (Abelli and Révay 2004)

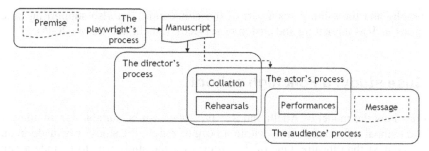

**Fig. 1.** From premise to a message for the audience (Abelli and Révay 2004)

- **The director's process – designing the mediation of information.** The director looks for alternative interpretations of the play, and chooses one to be the premise for the actual production. The play is deconstructed into acts, scenes and action sections, in order to analyze each section for possible actions and reactions for each character. The director then reconstructs the play to see how the sections, scenes and acts work together e.g. regarding tempi and rhythm, entrances and exits. From this work a revised and more detailed manuscript is created. The collation is the first formalized meeting between the director and the cast, where the director presents the premise for the ensemble, with explanations of certain elements of the play and their relations to the premise. The director interacts with the actors through the explicit directing during the rehearsals which can reveal flaws in stage directions, characterizations or even the story or plot, which makes it necessary for the director to analyze and redesign the script further. (Abelli and Révay 2004)
- **The actor's process – mediating the information.** The actor reads the manuscript to chisel out the characteristics and traits as described in the script for his own character. At the collation the director presents the premise for the current production, and gives each actor keys to the relations towards the premise and the other characters in the play. The actor deconstructs the character into biological, physiological and psychological traits, i.e. creating a background to discover the motivations for the character's actions and reactions in any situation that can occur. The actor then reconstructs the character into the play, to map out the actual actions and reactions, as well as what emotions and expressions the character should show for each section and scene. In this process the actor's "W" plays an important part in defining the motivations; Where am I?, Who am I?, Why am I here?, Where do I come from?, Where am I going? (Kemecsi 1998) During the rehearsals the actor makes use of the traits, motivations, actions and reactions from previous phases, but also modifies them iteratively. (Abelli and Révay 2004)
- **The audience' process – receiving the information.** The audience experiences the performance as a whole; from the moment they see the advert for the play, buying tickets at the foyer, waiting in the foyer to enter the salon. For maximal effect, the surroundings of the performance can be made to emphasize the audience' likely conception of the play, and in this area not only the sceno-

graphy and the salon plays a part of the conception, but also supporting processes such as marketing and customer services. (Abelli and Révay 2004)

# 3 Case study: a Folk high school

To test how the model of Abelli and Révay (2004) can be suitable for an analysis of the manual information flow within an organization, the study was made in another context than theatre. One of the criteria for the study was to include a context with plenty of human-to-human interaction, and the choice fell on doing it as a case study in a Swedish folk high school. A folk high school is a special type of school that educates adults mainly on a level corresponding to the Swedish upper secondary school. The study included all formal participants in the process, principals, executive board, headmaster, teachers, pupils and administrative staff. It was made with ca 500 hours of observations followed by interviews with the staff of which fifteen are teachers. In addition to the staff, interviews have also been made with the executive board and a sample of the pupils. (Abelli 2006)

In the school environment, it's not a one-to-one mapping of the roles in the school towards the core roles in a theatre production, as their processes rather are shifts between the core processes in theatre productions. Each of the school roles varies between perspectives or rather functions in the explicit situations. In the one and same situation a teacher can change from being the director and actor of the play, to become an audience to the pupils or colleagues' performances. (Abelli 2006)

There are not many situations where there exists a ready manuscript in the theatre sense with dialogue and stage directions, but there are plenty of texts and premises, formulated in school statutes, course books, curricula, etc. These are to be put into performances, such as lectures and other lessons, staff and team meetings, etc, with addition of visual, audial and other elements. This human-to-human interaction corresponds in the model to the meetings between roles in the collation, rehearsals and performances (fig. 1). (Abelli 2006)

The "playwrights" don't have to create characters as they already exist in flesh and blood, as teachers, pupils, principal, etc. As there is no fixed manuscript, the "ensemble" tends to create the script through improvisations over the subject at hand, with specific information in mind, depending on the specific situation, whether it's a lesson or a meeting. The story, plot, dialogue and stage directions are "written" instantaneously in the situation they occur. (Abelli 2006)

A previously published paper based on this case focused on the meetings between teachers and pupils, which showed the usability as well as the generalizability of the model. The lessons were categorized into two types of scenarios; the first dealing with pure lecturing, superficially corresponding to the performance situation in the theatre production, while the other type contained different types of tutoring, corresponding more to the rehearsal situation, where the pupils were directed by the teacher to perform what they learn. Almost none of the teachers in the study used pure uni-directional lectures, but emphasized on dialogue and activity based pedagogy (Lundgren 1996), and the pupils don't just sit and listen, but reacts and acts on the subject at hand, making their own scripts to perform. This developed the lessons into sequences of continuously written, directed, enacted and performed small scenes, creating feedback to the teachers who adapted to the situation, and changed their way of teaching instantaneously. Generalized to a higher level this could be seen as a double-loop learning approach in the small (Argyris and Schön 1978). Each situation is unique, where the personal traits of the teachers as well as the pupils become important parts of the context. A consequence of this is that the context for an organization in certain situations must be narrowed to sub-contexts with separate premises derived from the previous. (Abelli 2006)

## 3.1 The interaction between teachers

The teachers in this study are organized in teams according to which courses they are assigned to, some of them divided into separate classes called "profiles" and "base groups". In practice the teams overlap, as the teachers can be assigned to more than one course at the time.

The team meetings are the teachers' formalized time for planning and evaluating the education in the course they're teaching in. The content of these meetings differ a lot between the teams; the meetings on courses consisting of single classes are more apt to discuss pedagogical issues and overall purposes of the course, where the meetings on courses with several classes tend to discuss only logistics – which pupil to be in which base group, profile, etc.

What premise to mediate varied even within explicit situations, which made the teacher need to become the playwright instantaneously, and as a consequence of this, the teacher can have all of the roles during a specific situation. Collation-like situations occur frequently in the team meetings, e.g. when planning for a new module or a new class. In these situations the teachers with assigned responsibility in this study informs about not only the goals and purposes of the task at hand, but also tries to give a further meaning and context to it, in order to get better arguments to motivate the colleagues. Most of the teacher's playwriting occurred in the direct situation, where he needs to create a new script based on the instant feedback from the colleagues. The premise can then be the same as before, but more often in more detail, or an extracted part of the original premise. The characters of the new script are often based on the colleagues themselves, telling a story to which they more easily can relate. The dialogue and stage directions mostly comes spontaneously from, and in parallel with, the teacher's cognitive processes, i.e. instantaneously. In these situations the teachers tend to increase their use of rhetorical techniques.

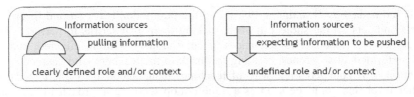

**Fig. 2.** The teacher's inclination to use pull techniques or depend on push

There's a significant difference in how the teacher expects to retrieve information in different situations. In his individual role as director and actor when planning explicit lessons, he's more apt to act autonomously in retrieving information necessary to perform the lessons, e.g. retrieving material on a specific subject (left diagram in fig. 2), but when dealing with information that isn't clearly defined as his responsibility, he's more likely to expect the information to be "given" to him (right diagram in fig. 2). This could be the result of the teaching profession, which in large is considered a clearly defined role, and there's not many questions on how to "act as a teacher", while other situations goes beyond this role.

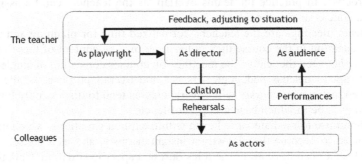

**Fig. 3.** The interaction between the teacher and its colleagues

This also reflects the teacher's situation in the team meetings. In those teams where pedagogic issues are discussed concerning the course as a whole, all of the teachers tend to take on the roles of playwrights and directors, using a pull technique to retrieve information. They appear more comfortable in these situations than in the situations concerning issues not directly connected to their teaching role. In this scenario they iterate between rehearsal and performing states (fig. 3). The roles as playwrights, directors, actors and audience shifts between the teachers during not only the meeting depending upon the item at hand, but also during the items on the agenda. These shifts are not only connected to the assigned responsibilities to the teachers (such as responsible for a base group, a profile or a subject), but even more so connected to their personal traits (extrovert, introvert, informal leaders, etc).

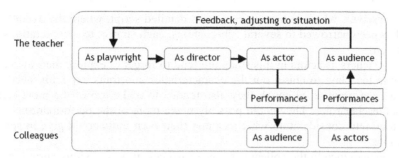

**Fig. 4.** The interaction between the teacher and its colleagues

There are also situations where the teachers direct themselves, which makes its colleagues a mere audience, but in this process the colleagues can also respond with their own scripts (fig. 4). The teacher makes use of all the traits from the playwright, the director and the actor, more in a sequential fashion, when the item at hand of the meeting is more closely connected to a specific responsibility to which the teacher has been assigned.

In both scenarios the teachers will adapt to the situation, using their newfound information and experiences to incorporate it into a new script, which in turn will be used to return feedback, e.g. as suggestions of actions, but also instantaneously through direct feedback with questions to clarify things. Even small details as their body language gives feedback to see if the colleagues have received the intended information or not, which in turn the teacher reacts upon with a new script for the same premise, giving an alternative route for the colleagues to understand the material.

The teachers are keener to adapt themselves to the situation in the first scenario than in the second, but we see that the "plain" sequentiality in the second scenario only is superficial, as the roles of playwrights, directors and actors really are merged into one, where the teacher as playwright has one overall premise, as director searches for alternative interpretations, reconstructs the play, and as actor performs the chosen parts in order to give the colleagues as many angles as possible on the discussion at hand.

Even though the play mostly has these kind of given premises, there's no guarantee that it will be mediated in a manner that it's understood by the audience as the actors wants. The traditional view on the role of a teacher does simplify things, as they have some common basic principles for how to perform their roles as teachers. This includes preparations for lectures, tutoring and other lessons. In this work, the teacher as director looks for alternative ways to mediate the premise for the actual subject, and makes cognitive stage directions for the upcoming performance.

Pure performances are scarce, in benefit of an iterative approach, giving and receiving information during the meetings, where all of the attending teachers have great influence on the script used. The real situation is more recursive, with a starting point in the collation, giving the frames for the items at hand, moving onto a rehearsal, with the teachers improvising on the theme, refining their motivations for themselves, which in turn gives a more detailed script, where the overall context has been narrowed to several sub-contexts, each subject to new iterations and recursions.

The teachers as actors in this study did tend to forget to explore their own characters in the play; to chisel out the characteristics and traits explicitly needed to mediate the premise, although they also tended to make use of the more stereotypical teacher roles. They could possibly make more of the performances if they also took into consideration what meaning their own traits could give in specific situations.

As an audience to the colleagues' performances, it was obvious during the observations that the surroundings of the performance influenced the teacher's conception of what they had to say, which in turn had impact on what the teacher experienced as instant feedback, and consequently also influenced his further playwriting, directing and acting.

## 3.2 Implications for Information System Development

Not everything is suitable for computerization, and even when they seem to be, a more thorough analysis is necessary to make, in order to understand what actually happens in the manual information process. Abelli and Révay (2004) pointed out some areas where theatre productions differs from development processes for explicit computer based systems. This study has shown that those areas are generalizable to other contexts than just theatre productions.

**Specific enhancements to interpret information;** A theatre production includes elements of information that otherwise is not easy to codify; e.g. expressions of emotions and the articulate reasoning in dialogues between the characters, which enhances the experience and makes it easier to interpret (Abelli and Révay 2004). In the school situation expressions of emotions and the articulate reasoning in dialogues between the participants are frequently used both as performance enhancements, but also as feedback responses in the specific situations in order to evaluate whether the intended information has reached the recipients. In these situations all traits of the "performing characters" are needed to be taken into consideration; moods, social situations, background knowledge, etc. As each teacher has an individual set of traits, each situation must be handled differently, i.e. playwritten, directed and enacted instantaneously.

**Continuous deployment and adaptations of the system itself;** The theatre production is an *ongoing* process on more than one level. For the actors *each* performance is a complete deployment of the system. Unlike a finished and deployed computer based system, each theatre performance is different. Since manual routines are performed by humans, who can't replicate the routine exactly each time, there is a possible difference in perception of the information, depending on "which performance" the user consumes (Abelli and Révay 2004). Each team meeting uses a recursive model varying between performances and directing into more detailed sub-contexts. The school context is filled with situations where the system is adapted and re-deployed over and over again, each time depending on the specific situation at hand.

**Artistic engineering;** In the theatre production the main methodology is based on a *narrative* approach, which in traditional system development is only used for parts of the development, not for the whole process. In theatre productions there is an element of individual *artistic* creativity, that can or can not exist in computer based development, but is *essential* in theatre productions, whereas the focus in computer based development lies on the engineering perspective rather than imaginative creativity (Abelli and Révay 2004). Much of the teacher's profession lies in the skill to mediate information in a performative way. Just as in a theatre production, this is based on a narrative approach, and the notion of the "developer as an artist" is very much needed in the situations in this study.

Apart from the findings of Abelli and Révay (2004) on the development process of theatre productions, this study has also shown the special techniques of *using rhetoric* in this case study when transferring information. When there's no consensus in the team, the teachers rely on argumentative communication.

Even if some of the team meetings would be possible to transfer into a computer based information system, there are many contextual elements that would be missed, as the meetings fill more functions in the school environment than just passing of information. It seems more possible to automate those situations in the team meetings where the responsibilities are clearly assigned to individuals, as the responsible teacher's role then becomes more uni-directional to the actual performance, but its uni-directionality is only superficial, as each such item on the agenda contains moments where the teacher reverts to playwriting and directing. The parts least possible to automate of the team meetings are those situations where responsibilities aren't clearly assigned to any individual teacher, but they have to come to common solutions. In these situations they use the whole set of skills they possess, explicit and tacit knowledge as well as their personal traits. Neither of the scenarios can be completely computerized, as it's still not possible to completely mimic the unconsciously used body language and other means of expression, which gives much information in the feedback process in order to adjust and alter the script during the performance.

# 4 Conclusions

The study has shown that the "theatre approach" can add further value to the analysis of a manual information system, especially when dealing with human-to-human interaction. Much as in historical development processes, this approach acknowledge that not everything is possible to transform into its computer based counterpart, but through this type of analysis, it can throw new light on why some things can't or shouldn't be automated.

As each unique situation should be considered sub-systems as well as sub-organizations of the overall system, each of them must be further analyzed in detail. The team meetings show that the human-to-human interaction contains important elements that are incorporated in the context giving enhanced meaning to the information at hand. The personal traits of the teachers become important parts of the context.

Using the model from theatre productions revealed significant details on several levels. In situations where the teachers took a more active role than as a mere audience to their colleagues, they also were more apt to take on the roles of developers of the information system, giving even more feedback. This type of spontaneous development isn't equally possible in fully automated systems, as the responses are created in the specific situations with their specific sub-contexts.

Another example of an explicit finding in this part of the case study was that the teachers in some situations had a lack of characterization. When the purpose or responsibilities for specific information was not clear, the teachers missed some of the actor's "W's". A consequence of this could be to define a new premise for these situations, which would involve all participants and make their responsibility for the outcome clearer. Another option could be to accept this lack of self-characterization, which in turn could mean that these situations very well can be subject for automation with e.g. computer based systems for planning and scheduling classes, lessons and pupils in the courses.

Though the study is done in a specific environment and organization, a conclusion from this study must be that the development model of theatre productions can be generalized to many contexts as the team meetings described in this study easily can be transferred to other types of organizations as well. The described types of contextual elements in human-to-human interaction, such as body language, environment, individual behaviors and traits, etc, aren't exclusive for teachers and pupils.

Any existing manual process dealing with human-to-human-interaction that is subject to be automated into a computer based system, could benefit from an analysis made with the theatre model as base, in order to see which contextual elements that will pose as potentially problematic to exclude. Existing techniques for business analysis should benefit to be complemented with a process as this, to be able to conceptualize behaviors and other individual traits. It can then be a valuable aid to determine whether the process is suitable for transformation into a computer based information system or not, and give clues to what parts of an information process that needs special consideration, or as in this study, discover areas that can be improved within the manual system itself.

At the least it can be used to discover what sacrifices must be made, when replacing manual processes with automated systems. If those processes were to be fully automated, the study shows that under certain circumstances it could drain the organization of tacit knowledge crucial to the information processing. With this type of analysis, a foundation is created for developing better manual routines, whether as a manual system of its own, or as manual processes supporting computer based systems.

# References

Abelli B (2006) Enacting the e-Society. Proceedings of IADIS International Conference e-Society 2006, Dublin, Ireland, 285-298

Abelli B, Révay P (2004) To Be or Not To Be Computer Based. Proceedings of microCAD 2004 International Scientific Conference, Miskolc, Hungary, 1-8

Argyris C, Schön D (1978) Organizational Learning: A Theory of Action Perspective. Addison-Wesley, Reading, Mass

Brocket OG (1987) History of the Theatre, 5th edn. Allyn and Bacon, Boston

DSDM Consortium (2002) Dynamic Systems Development Method, Version 4.1. eWay Limited, Ashford, Kent, UK

Firesmith DG, Henderson-Sellers B (2002) The OPEN Process Framework: An Introduction. Addison-Wesley, Harlow

Hugoson M-Å, Hesselmark O, Grubbström A (1983) MBI-metoden - En metod för verksamhetsanalys. Studentlitteratur, Lund

Jacobson I (1992) Object-Oriented Software Engineering. Addison-Wesley, Reading, MA

Kemecsi F (1998) Skådespelarens skapande process enligt Stanislavskij-metoden. Liber, Stockholm

Lundgren UP (ed)) (1996) Pedagogisk uppslagsbok. Från A till Ö utan pekpinnar. Lärarförbundet/Informationsförlaget., Stockholm

Rational Software Corporation (2003) Rational Unified Process. 2003.06.00.65 edn. Rational Software Corporation, Cupertino, CA

Révay P (1977) RAS - SIS' handbok 113 - i teoretisk och praktisk belysning. Department of Information Processing. The Royal Institute of Technology and The University of Stockholm, Stockholm

Wieringa RJ (1995) Combining Static and Dynamic Modelling Methods: A Comparison of Four Methods. The Computer Journal 38:17-30

Wigander K-O, Svensson Å, Schoug L, Rydin A, Dahlgren C (1979) Strukturerad analys och konstruktion av informationsbehandlingssystem. Studentlitteratur, Lund

Viller S, Sommerville I (2000) Ethnographically informed analysis for software engineers. Int. J. Human-Computer Studies 53:169-196

# Several Outlines of Graph Theory in Framework of MDA

Natalja Pavlova

Riga Technical University, Latvia, natalya.pavlova@inbox.lv

## 1 Introduction

One of the modern research goals in software engineering is to find a software development process, which would provide fast and qualitative software development. Most now proposed methodologies, approaches etc. try to make the development process easier and still more qualitative. In order to achieve the goal in the approaches, a role of explicit models is considerably more important. In last time, the more preferable approach is Model Driven Architecture [1].

The Model Driven Architecture (MDA) is a framework being built under supervision of the Object Modelling Group (OMG) [2]. MDA separates the system business aspects from the aspects of system implementation on a specific technology platform. The MDA defines the approach and tool requirements for specifying systems independently of platforms, specifying platforms by choosing particular platform for the system, and transforming business domain specification into one for a chosen platform. The MDA separates certain key models of systems and brings a consistent structure to these models. Models of different systems are structured explicitly into Computation Independent Model (CIM), Platform Independent Model (PIM) and Platform Specific Model (PSM) [3].

The MDA idea is promising – raising up the level of abstraction, on which systems are developed, we could develop more complex systems more qualitatively. Fig. 1 gives the general idea of separating system aspects according to the levels of abstraction.

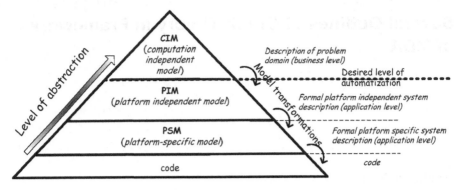

**Fig. 1.** Levels of abstraction in the framework of MDA

The main idea is to achieve formal system representation at the as high as possible level of abstraction. Nowadays in MDA tools, formalization begins somewhere in the middle of the PSM stage, and researchers try to "raise" it up as high as possible to fulfill the main statement of the MDA [1]. Unfortunately, many of important MDA aspects are not clear still. One of the most important and problematic stages in MDA realization is derivation of PIM elements from a problem domain, and PIM construction in the form that is suitable for the PSM. It is necessary to find the way to develop PIM using formal representation, so far keeping the level of abstraction high enough. According to [4] transformations CIM - > PIM and PIM - > PSM are defined within different solutions [3, 5, 6, 7, 8, 9, 10, 11], but there is no any solution, where complete transformation CIM -> PIM -> PSM would be defined, and the weak point is exactly PIM construction.

| | VMT and Larman solutions [9] | RUP and OMT solutions [7] | Solution based on DIM [6] | 2HMD solution [8] | Agile MDA solution [5] | UML and OCL combination [11] |
|---|---|---|---|---|---|---|
| CIM | (only customer requirement's specification) | ~ inclusive model, more formal then in *Agile* MDA solution | UML + OCL, formal requirement specification | BP+conceptual model, formally represents business domain (structure and behavior) | Inclussive model | **?** |
| PIM | UML | UML | UML + OCL | UML | xUML profile+ASL | UML + OCL |
| PSM | **?** | **?** | **?** | **?** | | UML profile for a specific platform |
| code | **?** | **?** | **?** | **?** | | code |

**Fig. 2.** Realization levels of transformations in the framework of MDA in some advanced solutions

Solutions that are focused on CIM -> PIM transformation [6, 7, 8] can't insure that a PIM contains all the necessary information, and that the presentation of the PIM is formal enough to be able to transform it into the correct PSM [4]. Moreover, there is no defined how the PIM must be elaborated to perform PIM->PSM transformations. That is why these solutions doesn't guaranteed that as a result of CIM - > PIM transformations we will get a qualitative PIM. The table with MDA solutions is shown in Fig. 2 [12]. The table indicates that no one methodology presents full formal transformation from the CIM to the PSM through the PIM.

On the other hand, solutions that are focused on PIM ->PSM [5, 11] transformations completely define what every PIM element has to contain in order to get a PSM element from it, but there are not considered aspects, which are related to the correct PIM developing from the view of the business domain [3, 5, 7, 8]. Moreover, these solutions don't implement the complete chain of transformations CIM -> PIM -> PSM -> code also [4].

So far the answer on the question either formal development of PIM in the framework of MDA is a myth or a reality can be that formal development of PIM in the framework of MDA now is much more realistic myth then it looked some years before, but to make it real still needs additional researches [4]. One of them can be to take the existing approach with still high enough level of formalization, and to try to eliminate most weak points in the circuit of MDA realization.

The paper offers to make one of the solutions for MDA realization, exactly the Two-Hemisphere Model Driven (2HMD) [8, 12] approach, more formal for further automation to try to raise up a nowadays possible level of automation in the framework of MDA. Several issues of graph theory, mathematics and a transformation algorithm are discussed in the paper, and are used for formalization needs in the approach offered by the paper. The main statements of the 2HMD and its formalization are described in Section 2. Practical example of applying the formalized 2HMD approach is shown in Section 3.

## 2 Two-Hemisphere Model Driven Approach: Formalization Aspects

The initial version of the Two-Hemisphere Model Driven (2HMD) approach was proposed in [8], where the general framework for object-oriented software development has been discussed, and its application for driving school's software development has been demonstrated. The strategy supports gradual model transformation from problem domain models into program components, where problem domain models reflect two fundamental notions: system functioning (processes) and structure (concepts and their relations).

Conceptual scheme of the 2HMD approach is shown in Fig. 3

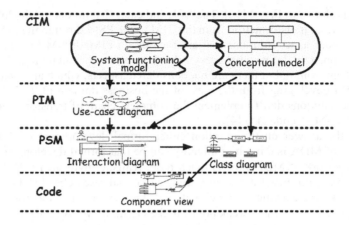

**Fig. 3.** 2HMD approach

Graphical representation of influence of several aspects of formalization on the 2HMD approach is shown in Fig. 4. It is a sketch of tools, which could be useful in formalization of system analysis and design approaches [13]. These tools were used for formalization, and the result is represented in this paper.

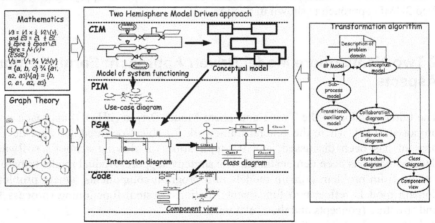

**Fig. 4.** Formalization of the 2HMD approach

The aspects, which impact the 2HMD approach, are the following:

- Transformation algorithm – an algorithm of information transformation during system modeling. Some additional models are included into the original 2HMD method to refine it with some more formalized transformations [12].
- Graph theory – transformations of models are performed according to rules of graph transformations [14];

- Mathematics – using mathematics is explained the application of graph theory, and model transformations.

In the current research, a use-case model is replaced by a sub-process model, and a transitional auxiliary model. And, as it is shown in the transformation algorithm, the approach is enhanced with extra models – a collaboration diagram, and a statechart diagram.

The sub-process model should be constructed for each process from a business process model.

## 2.1 Information Transformation Algorithm

As shown in Fig. 3, the use case diagram is one of the models included into the 2HMD transformation algorithm. During improvement and formalization of this algorithm, the necessity to replace the use case model with sub-process models was determined.

The reason of use case removing is problems, which could be caused by them. These problems are discussed in different publications. The most mentioned problems are the following [15]:

1. A set of Use Cases does not provide a system developer with all of the information about client's requirements necessary for the developed system.
2. It seems that Use Cases are very easy. Unfortunately, there is a reverse side of this simplicity – an analyst does not have to work very hard to understand the basic Use Case concepts, because of this the quality of the developed use case diagram falls.
3. The concrete methods how use cases should be selected from user requirements are missed. And nobody may warranty that the developed use case diagram reflects user requirements in whole.

According to the MDA, the CIM should provide the business system definition, basing on which it would be possible to make many different representations of the application domain (by analogy of the PIM definition – the PIM must provide such definitions of the application domain that could be useful to different programming paradigms and platforms). So far, it is possible to get formal presentation of PIM by formalization of the transition from the CIM to the PIM (e.g. combination of Conceptual model and Model of system functioning in the 2HMD approach), thus to solve the problem of developing the PIM to be suitable for PSM generation.

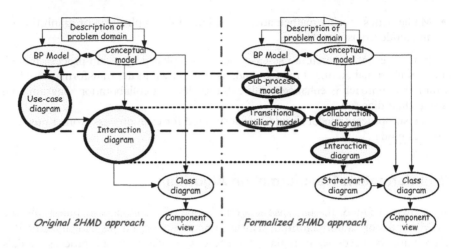

**Fig. 5.** 2HMD transformation algorithms

In the original 2HMD approach, the PIM is presented only as a use case diagram. In Fig. 5 two algorithms are presented – "Original 2HMD approach" and "Formalized 2HMD approach". There are selected changes performed during improvement of the 2HMD approach discussed in the paper. The first change is that in the "Formalized 2HMD approach" the PIM is presented as two models – the sub-process model and the transitional auxiliary model instead of the use-case diagram in the "Original 2HMD". The sub-process model for each process to be automated should be constructed on the base of the Model of system functioning. This is the formal base for further system design. For facilitating of transition from the sub-process model to the interaction model, the transitional auxiliary model is used. The transitional auxiliary model is generated from the sub-process model using an approach of graph transformation.

And the second major change is bipartition of the Interaction diagram with introducing of the collaboration diagram and introducing of the statechart diagram at the PSM level.

The collaboration diagram is added as a more logical sequel of the sub-process model for object interaction representation. The statechart diagram is needed for adjustment of the class diagram – the more specific definition of class operations.

Applying this transformation algorithm the formalized 2HMD approach is received.

## 2.2 Using of Graph Theory in Formalization of 2HMD

The theory of graphs gives us algorithms of graph transformations. For the formalization of the 2HMD method, we need to apply transformation, wherein arcs of the first graph are transformed into nodes of the second graph, and nodes of the first graph are transformed into arcs of the second graph. The scheme of this transformation is shown in Fig.6 [14].

In Fig.5, there are two graphs G1{P', U'}, where P = {P1', P2', P3', P4', P5'}, and U' = {A', B', C', D', E', F'} and G2 {U',..}, where U'= {A', B', C', D', E', F'} are arcs received from nodes of G1 and nodes for G2 could be received from arcs of G1. The receiving of G2 nodes is used and described below.

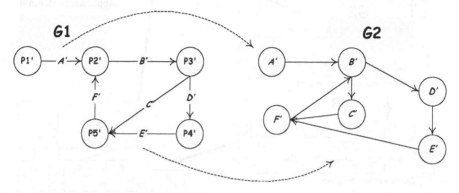

**Fig. 6.** Formal transformation of graphs

It is necessary to investigate a sub-set of models of the 2HMD as graphs in order to be able to apply the graph theory. The first graph in Fig.7 - G1 (P', U') - corresponds to the system functioning model, where P'= {Pe', P1', P2', P3', P4', P5'} is the set of system business functions, and U'= {A', B', C', D', E', F', G'} is the set of information flows among the processes. The process Pe' is an external process. The following graph G2 (U, P) that corresponds to the transitional auxiliary model consists of the same sets, but therein the set of processes is the set of arcs, and the set of information flows is the set of nodes. This transformation was performed to simplify transition from the business process model (the graph G1) to the collaboration diagram (the graph G3). The graph G3 (P, U) contains the set of nodes U= {A, B, C, D, E, F, G}, which are objects received from the set U', and the set of arcs P= {Pe, P1, P2, P3, P4, P5}, which are interactions between objects received from the set P'. During transition from G1 to G3 through G2 each process and each data flow was transferred into the collaboration diagram. Fig. 7 illustrates this process [4].

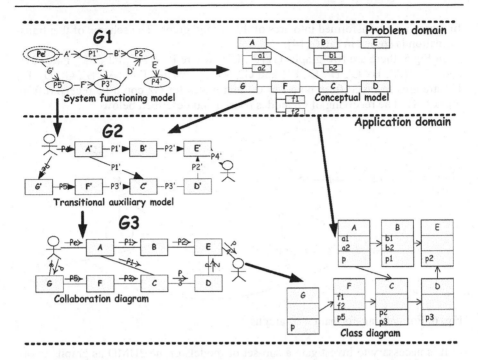

**Fig. 7.** Model transformation in the 2HMD approach [4]

The following stage of transition is the class diagram. This transition could be rated as the most important off all the transitions in the information transformation process. The class diagram is a final state of the analysis process. The quality of the whole system depends on quality and precision of the class diagram. For this transformation, all elements of the set P (which are interactions) should be operations of a class, and all elements of the set U (which are objects) should be classes or instances of classes. In the class diagram, the set of attributes is represented, too. First time the attributes (e.g. the set A={a1,a2}) are shown on the conceptual model as properties of elements of the set U. Here attributes are the same. Associations among classes are defined basing on the graph G3 and using the following dependency: if there is an arc between A and B, than in the class diagram an association between A and B will exist [12].

Performing all the described transformations we could receive a class diagram, which is suitable for code generation.

# 3 Formalized 2HMD Approach: a Case Study

The proposed methodology could be illustrated with a practical example. The problem domain is Hotel room reservation [12]:

A system gives the opportunity to reserve a room in the hotel. Client fills a blank for reservation of the room in the hotel by using hotel's Web-site. Client has to input his name, type of the room to reserve (single or double), and the period for staying in the hotel. The system updates the information about requested room and if a room is available for the defined period the system makes a reservation and sends a confirmation. If there is no available room in the hotel the system displays a message that reservation is impossible.

When client arrive to the hotel, at the reception he has to request the room reserved and the administrator has to check all the information. Administrator input all the information about client's staying in the hotel. Every day 1 p.m. the system checks reservation records to define either reservation is valid (i.e. client is taking the room requested) or invalid (i.e. at the requested date client is not coming to the hotel). In the case reservation is invalid the room defined in the reservation is marked as free for further reservations.

By the proposed algorithm, the first step is to receive the Conceptual model based on the System functioning model. Fig. 8 shows a fragment of information transition from the BP model to the conceptual model with arrows.

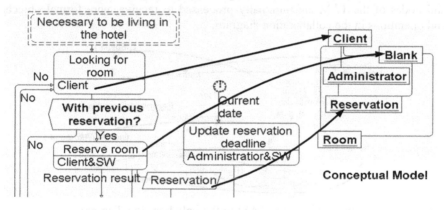

**Fig. 8.** Receiving of the conceptual model from the BP model

Construction of sub-process models is not shown here. These should be constructed for each process from the initial model. By the proposed approach the next major step of model transformation is receiving of the transitional auxiliary model (TAM) from the sub-process model. A fragment of this transformation is shown in Fig.9. It is assumed that both models are graphs. As shown in graph transformation, nodes from the sub-process graph will be transformed into arcs of the TAM, and arcs of the sub-process will be transformed into nodes of the TAM.

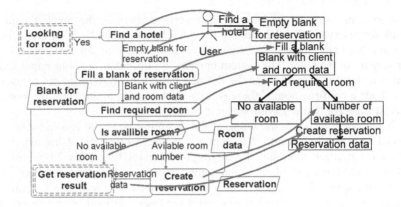

**Fig. 9.** Example of TAM receiving

The TAM without further transformations is a useless model. Fig. 10 presents transformation from the TAM to the collaboration diagram. Information on arcs and nodes of the TAM are minimally processed to receive more formal objects and operations in the collaboration diagram.

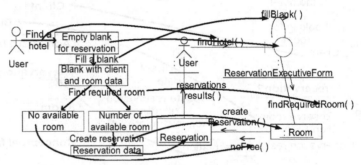

**Fig. 10.** Transformation from the TAM to the collaboration diagram

The transformation from the collaboration to interaction diagram could be processed automatically by different CASE-tools, therefore it is not considered in the research. The following is a final class diagram [12], which could be constructed basing on received information.

A business process model is more formal than use case models or any similar. The business process model serves as a clearly defined problem domain at the level of the CIM [12].

## 4 Conclusions

This paper is based on the previous researches [16, 17] where different software development methods were analyzed. All these methods could provide promising results in the realization of MDA statements, but quantity of the expanded effort is different.

The 2HMD approach was proposed on the previous researches [8, 16, 12], and in the current paper it is improved with introducing of several formalism, and trying to reduce required effort for software development.

The use of graph theory for formalization of the 2HMD gives positive results. When software design models are considered as graphs, it becomes easier to abstract system business details, and to make transformation in order to receive the final class diagram (the object model). The rigor rules of graph theory should be researched in more detail. Only after that, it will be possible to apply them in software design process automation.

Formal transformation used in this research helps in receiving additional models. The approach becomes more formal with them, and makes it possible to raise the level of automation up to the desired level. It is possible to use outlines of graph theory for transformations between MDA models.

One more innovation received during practical experiments is enlargement of the PIM. The interaction models are moved from the PSM to the PIM for system structure representation at this level. Moreover, the practical example discussed in the paper shows that application of the formalized Two-Hemisphere Model Driven approach could make the process of system analysis and design easier. If the further formalization of the 2HMD will be successful it will be possible to automate the system analysis and design in order to reduce required software developers' efforts.

The paper can be of interest for scientists and practitioners involved in the stream of people indented in the MDA realization ideas.

This work has been partly supported by the European Social Fund within the National Programme "Support for the carrying out doctoral study programm's and post-doctoral researches" project "Support for the development of doctoral studies at Riga Technical University"

## References

1.  Sendall Sh, Kozaczynski W (2003) Model Transformation: The Heart and Soul of Model-Driven Development. J IEEE Software 9/10: 42-45
2.  MDA Guide Version 1.0.1, http://www.omg.org/docs/omg/03-05-01.pdf
3.  Kleppe A, Warmer J, Bast W (2003) MDA Explained : The Model Driven Architecture – Practise and Promise. Addison Wesley
4.  Nikiforova O, Kirikova M, Pavlova N (2006) Two Hemisphere Driven Approach: Application for Knowledge Modeling. In: 7th Internation Conference on Data Base and Information Systems, in press.

5. Ambler S W, Approaches To Agile Model Driven Development (AMDD), http://www.agilemodeling.com/essays/amddapproaches.htm #manual
6. Ceponiene L, Nemuraite L (2005) Reconsilation of UML models for development of information systems. In: Scientific Proceeding of RTU, the 5th Series – Computer Science, Applied Computer Systems, pp. 7-19
7. Jacobson I, Booch G, Rumbaugh J (2002) The Unified Software Development Process. Addison-Wesley
8. Nikiforova O, Kirikova M (2004) Two-Hemisphere Model Driven Approach: Engineering Based Software Development. In: Proceeding of the 16th International Conference Advanced Information Systems Engineering Caise'2004, A. Persson and J. Stirna (Eds.), Lncs 3084, Springer – Verlag Berlin Heidelberg, pp. 219 – 233
9. Larman C (2000) Applying UML And Patterns: An Introduction To Object-Oriented Analysis And Design. Prentice Hall, New Jersey
10. Tkach D, Fang W, So A (1996) Visual Modeling Technique: Object Technology Using Visual Programming. Addison Wesley
11. Kleppe A, Warmer J, (2003) The Object Constraint Language: Getting Your Models Ready for MDA, Second Edition. Addison-Wesley
12. Pavlova N, Nikiforova O (2006) Formalization of Two-Hemisphere Model Driven Approach in the Framework of MDA. In: Proceedings of the 9th International Conference "Information System Implementation and Modelling" (ISIM'06), April 25-26, 2006, Přerov, Czech Republic. - Ostrava: Jan Štefan MARQ, pp. 105-112
13. Axelsson J (2002) Model Based Systems Engineering Using a Continuous-Time Extension of the UML. J Systems Engineering, Vol. 5, No. 3, 2002
14. Grundspeniks J (1997) Causal Domain Model Driven Knowledge Acquisition for Expert Diagnosis System Development. Kaunas University of Technology Press
15. Ferg S (2003) What's Wrong with Use Cases? http://www.ferg.org/papers/ferg--whats_wrong_with_use_cases.html
16. Nikiforova O, Kuzmina M, Pavlova N (2006) Formal Development Of PIM In The Framework Of MDA: Myth Or Reality. In: Scientific Proceedings Of Riga Technical University, The 6th Series – Computer Science. Applied Computer Systems
17. Pavlova N, Nikiforova O (2005) An overview of advanced approaches for construction of platform-independent system model. In: Scientific Proceedings of Riga Technical University, The 5th Series – Computer Science. Applied Computer Systems

# Designing Software Components for Database Consistency – An Enterprise Modeling Approach

Lars Jakobsson and Peter Bellström

Department of Information Systems, Karlstad University, SE-651 88 Karlstad, Sweden. Lars.Jakobsson@kau.se, Peter.Bellstrom@kau.se.

## 1 Introduction

The ubiquitous use of databases (DB) in information systems (IS) today is a direct result of complex and enormous amounts of data processing required in modern businesses. The complexity of the data processing requires software to support the organization in being competitive in an increasingly demanding business climate. The software must support the organization in creating business advantages, thus the need for robust, yet flexible software solutions is increasingly important to maintain or gain effectiveness [1]. Building high quality IS in short time demands a high level of re-use. Component based software engineering focuses the design of IS on assembling reusable software components. An IS should be designed to support an enterprise and the activities performed within the enterprise. Therefore, it is essential to match the enterprise architecture with the architecture of the supporting IS. The values of architectural descriptions have been recognized by many organizations, but still most architectures are constructed for separate organizational domains [28]. Architectural approaches for domain dependent modeling languages include Unified Modeling Language (UML) [7] for modeling applications or technical infrastructure and the Business Process Modeling Notation for modeling business processes. However, the Enterprise Modeling (EM) approach focuses on establishing a consistent and coherent view of an enterprise from a holistic perspective [14].

A holistic approach is important, not only for enterprise architecture, but also when dealing with DB consistency, since i.e. a DB transaction may consist of grouped updates. The responsibility for preserving DB consistency is shared between the Database Management System (DBMS) and the application developers

[9]. The DBMS can ensure consistency to some extent, by enforcing all constraints that have been specified on the DB schema. This is not sufficient for a complete DB consistency, since it is impossible to ensure DB consistency falling outside the scope of what the DBMS can control. To ensure consistency in implementation dependent constructs we need to address the consistency at a higher level of abstraction, which can be achieved by applying an EM approach to analysis and design [13].

This paper is organized as follows. Firstly, we describe the semantic dependencies, both static and dynamic, applied in the EM approach. Secondly, we describe and illustrate how to apply these dependencies for conceptual software component modeling and conceptual DB design. In the third section, we focus on how to avoid inconsistency in conceptual descriptions of databases, information systems and software components and then we describe how to design for consistency using the semantic dependencies of the EM approach. Finally, the paper is summarized and conclusions are discussed and described.

## 2 Dependencies in the EM Approach

The ability to describe an IS in a clear and sufficiently rich way, although still comprehensible and easy to use, is acknowledged as crucial in many areas including IS and software engineering. Typically, semantic dependencies are defining semantics in different perspectives such as the "what", "who", "where", "when" and "how" [30]. For instance, in the object-oriented approach [21] the "what" perspective is defined using the class diagram, the "how" perspective can be defined by using the activity diagrams and the "when" perspective in a large part can be described by the state-transition diagrams. The different semantic views are critical for bridging the gap between various kinds of people such as information technology planners, business owners, system designers, builders, users, and programmers.

Understanding the strategic dependencies [29] is essential for reaching a consensus on what the current and future situation looks like. The dependencies between various technical and organizational components involved describe the "who" perspective.

In EM, semantic dependencies are of two kinds: static and dynamic. Dynamic constituents in the extended communication flow and action dependency are represented in Figure 1. State dependencies are represented by solid arrows; defining semantic relationships between states (see states A and B).

The static concept dependencies define the "what" perspective. These dependencies are stemming from various semantic models that are intro-duced in the area of IS analysis and design [21]. The static dependencies adapted from EM are illustrated in Figure 2.

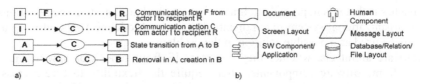

**Fig. 1.** Dynamic dependencies (a) and syntactic elements (b) [17].

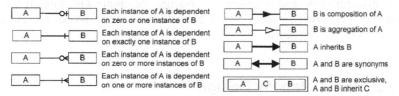

**Fig. 2.** Adapted and modified representation of static dependencies in EM [17].

It should be noted that in the EM approach, alike in object-oriented methods, all kind of the static and dynamic dependency links could be inherited [12].

## 3 Software Component Modeling

Information systems are normally described using views in a high level of abstraction. There are numerous ways of describing the IS graphically. However, most of these use a fragmented view on the IS, with different view (diagram) types for static, dynamic and syntactic properties [16].

The software component paradigm is based on reuse of existing solu-tions. We need methods and techniques for reusable component engineer-ing to achieve a successful engineering of IS, both when designing *for* reuse and when designing *by* reuse [1]. Two principles are essential for a successful reuse approach: the abstraction principle and the variability principle [1]. Both of these principles require the use of a model driven approach [12] since model driven approaches are well suited to express the inter-relations among enterprise elements. Model driven approaches can help in alleviating the language barriers between the different domains of the enterprise [28].

For software specifications, including software components, UML [7, 21] has for some time been viewed as a de facto modeling language. At the same time, this affects research carried out in the software specification area where one large research track lies in checking consistency between two or more schemata or schemata types [19].

Misunderstanding between IS users and designers is a common problem, not only for traditional systems, but also for component based systems. A precondition for a successful concurrent engineering process is a mutual understanding between stakeholders. It cannot be achieved without close cooperation of the actors involved. One of the problems in most conventional system engineering approaches is that it is impossible to bridge from the technical system specifications to the organizational system requirements. Enterprise Modeling [13] and integration can be used as a possible solution to the problem.

Software architects, whether they construct IS from scratch or assembling a system from software components, often require the flexibility to create cross-domain views to ensure inter- as well as intra view consistency. Thus, there is a need for a well-defined meaning of concepts and a possibility to keep consistency between different views and schemata. A modeling technique with support for integrated views covering syntactic, static as well as semantic properties and dependencies is therefore needed.

## 4 Conceptual Database Design

To be able to design a DB that is consistent and fulfills the customer's requirements, a DB design method has to be used. A DB design method has at least three phases: *conceptual database design, logical database design* and *physical database design* [9, 11] and the first phase is the most critical phase [3, 10]. During conceptual DB design, the designer focuses on what information the stakeholder wants and needs to store in the DB. For conceptual DB design, the Entity Relationship (ER) modeling language [8] or some extensions of it [26] has been seen as a de facto standard [25]. In this paper, conceptual DB design is seen as divided into two distinct parts: *view design* and *view integration*. During view design, views for each end user or user group are defined (see Figure 3a and 3b). During view integration the defined views are integrated into one global conceptual DB schema (see Figure 3c).

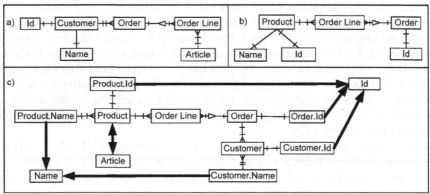

**Fig. 3.** Identification and resolution of inconsistency in view integration.

The primitives used in Figure 3 are illustrated and described in Figure 2. In EM, the static dependencies are used not only to define and illustrate what is stored in the DB but also to illustrate what data that is needed by the IS. This means that the data structure illustrated in Figure 3c is used to store not only the persistent data in the DB but also to store temporal data in the software components.

In [6], a generic and integrated EM approach is described and proposed. One advantage with this approach is that it can be used, not only for databases and software components, but also for static and dynamic dependencies during both view design and view integration.

View integration is a critical [27] and important [18] part of conceptual DB design since inconsistencies and conflicts are identified and resolved in and between views, and finally the views are merged into one conceptual schema (see Figure 3c). Inconsistencies and conflicts arise because there is often semantic heterogeneity between the views [20]. One of the most quoted definitions of schema integration, the origin of view integration, defines schema integration as "[...] the activity of integrating the schemas of existing or proposed databases into a global, unified schema." [3]. In this definition, the concepts, view and schema should be treated as synonyms.

Summing up, to reach a consistent conceptual DB schema we need to define and design views for each end user or user group, identify and resolve inconsistencies in and between these views and finally merge the views into one global and final conceptual schema. Therefore, there is a need for modeling languages that not only bridge the shortcomings of the traditional modeling languages (e.g. ER or UML) but also cope with all the described challenges. A modeling language that that is suitable for this is the EM approach [17].

# 5 Avoiding Inconsistency

To understand and to be able to reach a consistent DB we have to understand and deal with its opposite – *inconsistency*. This section describes and discusses the inconsistency concept in connection with two perspectives. The first perspective concerns DB inconsistency in connection with transactions executed on an implemented DB, the use of the developed and implemented DB and IS. The second perspective concerns inconsistency in the designed conceptual schema including both the static and dynamic dependencies of the chosen modeling language, the design of the DB and IS.

A consistent implemented DB is defined as "[...] a database is consistent if and only if it contains the results of successful transactions." [15]. This definition focuses on the states of consistency such as state Order[Stored] and state Order[Updated] in Figure 4. However, another definition [9] concerns not only the states, but also the transformation between two consistent states (see for instance state transformation (action) Update in Figure 4) as follows: "A transaction must transform the database from one consistent state to another consistent state.". This definition is closer to our perspective on DB consistency.

**Fig. 4.** Illustration of transaction consistency definitions.

As previously mentioned, to reach a consistent DB we also have to reach consistency in the global conceptual schema that on a high level of abstraction represents the DB and IS with its software components. The problem of inconsistent descriptions of databases and IS has been a headache for both DB and IS researchers for many years. For instance, identification and resolution of inconsistent specifications during view integration in conceptual DB design [4, 5, 6] are two research areas. However, in the DB research area, inconsistencies are instead called conflicts [20, 23].

Identification and resolution of inconsistent specifications [19] in software development [22] is another research area that deals with the inconsistency problem.

Nevertheless, starting from the end users perspectives and defining smaller schemata, user views, of a DB and IS is important because these preserve and highlight differences between the end users views of the organization while a global schema may instead mask these [24]. Sometimes it is even desirable or necessary to tolerate inconsistency in and between different descriptions [22]. This may not only prevent premature design decisions but also ensure that all stakeholders (end users) views of the organization are taken into account. Even so, the final result of conceptual DB design and conceptual software component design should be a set of consistent views (diagrams) if UML is the applied modeling language and one final and global consistent schema if EM is the applied modeling language. The EM approach is an appropriate approach to apply when identifying solutions to the inconsistency problem in conceptual DB design and conceptual software component design [13]. Finally, as also argued in [5] using the semantic dependencies of EM simplifies the integration process and reduces the risk of semantic loss occurring.

Summing up, the concept of inconsistency is henceforward used in con-nection with conceptual design of DB, IS and software components and is therefore in this paper defined as: *a state of inconsistency may occur if two or more different descriptions are used for one phenomenon in the system specification views*. For instance, using two or more concept names for the same concept, or using different pre- and post conditions, which are contradicting, for the same action.

# 6 Designing for Consistency

Design of software components and databases, that are supposed to co-exist in the same IS require design principles and tools for analysis that support a holistic and integrated approach to the design process. It has been shown that EM can be used to achieve a generic and integrated approach to designing databases and components [6]. Some consistency issues can be resolved by the DBMS, but far from all. All transactions that may transform the DB from a consistent state to a state of inconsistency must be addressed by the DBMS or the component communicating with the DBMS. Furthermore, a design procedure containing the steps, 1: Customer requirements, 2: Database view modeling, 3: Software component modeling, 4: Conceptual database integration, 5: Conceptual software component integration, 6: Conceptual model integration into global schema containing software components and database, has been defined [6].

Since we need to be able to analyze the DB states and the actions generating the state changes (static and dynamic behavior) we need to use a modeling technique supporting joining the static and dynamic properties into one view. Figure 5 shows the integrated schema on the transaction for storing an order in a DB in a sales system (5a) and a schema describing updating an existing order (5b). The integrated schema is representing the system in a high level of abstraction, showing what should be addressed by the system, but not how. Using this schema as a starting point for defining the interaction between the User – Software Component – DB illustrates some rules on the global level for the system.

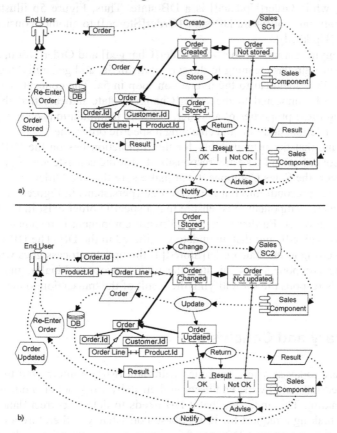

**Fig. 5.** An integrated schema on storing and updating an order in a sales system.

In Figure 5, end user interaction in the system is illustrated in terms of user interface screens (SalesSC1, Order Stored and Re-Enter Order). The pre- and post conditions shown in Figure 5b corresponds to the state transitions shown in Figure 4. This means that we can and should use the state transitions as pre and post conditions for the software components to ensure consistency. The synonym relationship between Order[Created] and Order[Not Stored] in Figure 5a illustrate that the two states are representing the same state from different perspectives, Order[Created] as temporal, and Order[Not Stored] as persistent. In this example the Sales Component attempts to create an entry in the DB, and the result of the transaction (successful or not) is returned from the DBMS to the component.

The static description of the DB, defined during the conceptual DB design, is illustrated in Figure 3c. In Figure 5, we have defined that in order to store an order we need only some of the items from the global DB schema. This is illustrated by the Order concept with its connected properties.

In Figure 5b, the user initiates an update operation on an order stored in the DB using SalesSC2. The DB-state Order[Stored] is used as precondition for changing an order. Order[Changed] is an intermediate non-persistent state in the software component, while Order[Updated] is a DB-state. Thus, Figure 5b illustrates the transition from one consistent DB-state (Order[Stored]) to another consistent DB-state (Order[Updated]).

The synonym relationship between Order[Changed] and Order[Not updated] in Figure 5b has a similar meaning to the synonyms in 5a, and generally, the interaction loop in 5b is identical to the interaction loop in 5a. The concepts Order Line and Product.Id, connected to the Order[Changed] state indicate that the user is manipulating these properties of an order. Possible manipulations on these properties include deletion, addition and changing a specific order line.

This means that the responsibility for the transaction lies on the DBMS – the Sales Component cannot take any responsibility for the consistency of the transaction. However, the Sales Component can make sure that the Order is created as a temporal state (precondition) but not yet stored (persistent) in Figure 5a. In Figure 5b, the software component must ensure that a specific order exist in the DB prior to changing an order. Furthermore, the software component is responsible for the state Order[Changed], and that an update is initiated in the DB. The DB is responsible for reverting to the state Order[Stored] if the update process goes wrong after the software component has initiated the update process. Finally, the software component is responsible for notifying the result of the transaction to the user.

## 7 Summary and Conclusion

Databases are today serving companies with data that are interpreted to information and used not only by the end users in their daily work but also during critical decision-making. This indicates that a DB needs to deliver correct data when an end user is making a request for it. Database consistency is therefore a critical issue because an inconsistent DB may deliver erroneous data to an end user which in the long run may influence how profitable a company is. Therefore, when designing an IS and DB, we first of all need to address consistency on a high level of abstraction using a modeling language and approach that is suitable for this.

In this paper, it is argued that EM is one such modeling approach. By applying EM during conceptual design of both software components and databases, inconsistencies may be identified early in the design process. This is the case since EM allows us to integrate both static and dynamic dependencies into one conceptual schema which at the same time gives us a holistic schema of the future IS and DB. In addition, by applying the EM approach during conceptual DB design the view integration process is simplified because the only primitives that are given names are concepts.

It this paper it has also been illustrated that pre- and post conditions used in the dynamic software component views corresponds to state changes in a DB. Not only can we use the DB states in a dynamic modeling process, but we should do so in order to maintain consistency in and between views.

Using this approach it is possible to clearly identify the responsibilities between software components and DBMS, since this is dictated by the DB-states as well as the pre- and post conditions for the software components. In addition we are able to create consistency between the different views used for the IS design as well as DB design, ensuring a consistent modeling of IS properties and interactions.

Finally, by applying the EM approach for designing software components for DB consistency, as illustrated in this paper, the inconsistency problem is reduced. This is because the designer is able to illustrate both the state changes and the properties that are needed by state changes in one schema. At the same time the EM approach helps the designer to better fulfill that the final conceptual schema is not only consistent but also coherent and complete.

# References

1   Aniorte P (2003) A distributed adaptable software architecture derived from a component model. Computer Standards & Interfaces vol 25 no 3, pp 275-82.

2   Batini C, Lenzerini M, Navathe B L (1986) A comparative analysis of methodologies for database schema integration. ACM Computing Surveys vol 18 no 4, pp 323-363.

3   Batini C, Ceri S, Navathe S B (1992) Conceptual Database Design An Entity-Relationship Approach. The Benjamin/Cummings Publishing Company, Inc., Redwood City, California.

4   Bellström P (2005) Using Enterprise Modeling for identification and resolution of homonym conflicts in view integration. In: Vasilecas O, Caplinskas A, Wojtkowski W, Wojtkowski W G, Zupancic J, Wrycza S (eds) Information Systems Development Advances in Theory, Practice and Education, Springer, pp 265-276.

5    Bellström P (2006) View integration in conceptual database design –
     Problems, approaches and solutions. Licentiate thesis, Karlstad Univer-
     sity Studies, 2006:5.
6    Bellström P, Jakobsson L (2006) Towards a generic and integrated En-
     terprise Modeling approach to designing databases and software compo-
     nents. In: Nilsson A G, Gustas R, Wojtkowski W, Wojtkowski WG,
     Wrysza S, Zupancic J (eds) Advances in Information Systems Develop-
     ment: Bridging the Gap between Academia and Industry, Springer,
     pp. 635-646.
7    Booch G, Rumbaugh J, Jacobsson I (1999) The Unified Modelling Lan-
     guage user guide. Addison Wesley Longman, Inc., Massachusetts.
8    Chen P (1976) The Entity-Relationship model – Toward a unified view
     of data. ACM Transactions on Database Systems vol 1 no 1, pp 9-36.
9    Connolly T, Begg C (2005) Database systems A practical approach to de-
     sign, implementation, and management. Addison Wesley, England.
10   Dey D, Storey V C, Barron T M (1999) Improving database design
     through the analysis of relationships. ACM Transactions on Database
     Systems vol 24 no 4, pp 453-486.
11   Elmasri R, Navathe S B (2004) Fundamentals of database systems. Addi-
     son Wesley, Boston.
12   Gustas R (1998) Integrated approach for modelling of semantic and
     pragmatic dependencies of information systems. In: Ling T W, Ram S,
     Lee M L (eds) Proceedings of ER'98, Springer, pp 121-134.
13   Gustas R, Gustiené P (2004) Towards the enterprise engineering ap-
     proach for information system modelling across organisational and tech-
     nical boundaries. In: Camp O, Filipe J, Hammoudi S, Piattini M (eds)
     Enterprise Information Systems V, Kluwer Academic Publishers,
     Netherlands, pp 204-215.
14   Gustas R, Jakobsson L (2004) Enterprise modelling of component ori-
     ented infor-mation system architectures. In: Fujita H, Gruhn V (eds) Pro-
     ceedings of SoMeT_W04, IOS Press, pp 88-102.
15   Haerder T, Reuter A (1983) Principles of transaction-oriented database
     recovery. Computing Surveys vol 6 no 4, pp 287-317.
16   Jakobsson L (2004) Component based software – Implications on the de-
     velopment process and modeling techniques. Licentiate thesis, Karlstad
     University Studies, 2004:7.
17   Jakobsson L, Gustas R (2004) Towards a systematic modeling of compo-
     nent based software architectures. International SSCCII-2004, Amalfi,
     Italy.
18   Johannesson P (1993) Schema integration, schema translation, and inter-
     operability in federated information systems. PhD thesis, Department of
     Computer & Systems Sciences, Stockholm University, Royal Institute of
     Technology, No. 93-010-DSV, Edsbruk.
19   Kozlenkov A, Zisman A (2004) Discovering, recording, and handling in-
     consistencies in software specifications. International Journal of Com-
     puter & Information Science vol 5 no 2, pp 89-108.

20  Lee M L, Ling T W (2003) A methodology for structural conflict resolution in the integration of Entity-Relationship schemas. Knowledge and Information System vol 5 no 2, pp 225-247.

21  Martin J, Odell J J (1998) Object-oriented methods: A foundation (UML edition). Prentice-Hall, Englewood Cliffs, New Jersey.

22  Nuseibeh B, Easterbrook S, Russo A (2001) Making inconsistency respectable in software development. The Journal of Systems and Software vol 58, pp 171-180.

23  Parent C, Spaccapietra S (1998) Issues and approaches of database integration. Communications of the ACM vol 41 no 5es, pp 166-178.

24  Parsons J (2002) Effects on local versus global schema diagrams on verification and communication in conceptual data modeling. Journal of Management Information Systems vol 19 no 3, pp 155-183.

25  Spaccapietra S, Parent C (1994) View integration: a step forward in solving structural conflicts. IEEE Transactions on Knowledge and Data Engineering vol 6 no 2, pp 258-274.

26  Teorey T J, Tang D, Fry J P (1986) A logical design methodology for relational databases using the extended Entity-Relationship model. Computing Surveys vol 18 no 2, pp 197-222.

27  Teorey T J (1999) Database modeling & design. Morgan Kaufmann Publishers Inc, USA.

28  van Buuren R, Jonkers H, Lacob M-E, Strating P (2004) Composition of relations in enterprise architecture models. In: Ehrig H, Engels G, Parisi-Presicce F, Rozenberg G (eds) Proceedings of ICGT 2004, Springer-Verlag Berlin / Heidelberg.

29  Yu E, Mylopoulos J (1994) From E-R to 'A-R' - Modelling strategic actor relationships for business process reengineering. In: Loucopoulos P (ed) Proceedings of ER'94, pp 548-565.

30  Zachman J A (1996) Enterprise architecture: The issue of the century. Database Programming and Design Magazine.

# Trust-Related Requirements: A Taxonomy

Guttorm Sindre

Dept of Computer and Information Science, NTNU, NO-7491 Trondheim, Norway. Guttorm.Sindre@idi.ntnu.no. (And visiting ISOM dept., U. Auckland, New Zealand while this paper was written)

**Abstract:** With the advent of e- and m-commerce and inter-organizational business processes, the notion of trust is becoming increasingly important. Yet, the trust-related requirements to a system are seldom addressed in early development phases, rather delayed to design and coding. Since general experience shows that it is significantly more expensive to fix requirement defects at later stages than fixing them during analysis, it would be useful to handle trust requirements early. But the notion of trust requirements is so far weakly understood. This paper provides a taxonomy of trust-related requirements and also discusses possible styles for expressing them. Such a taxonomy may be useful for teaching and training requirements engineers, and may be a starting point for developing guidelines and checklists that can be used during requirements analysis of systems where trust is essential.

## 1 Introduction

With the advent of e- and m-commerce, inter-organizational business processes, and novel system architectures consisting of independently operating agents or services, security and privacy is becoming increasingly important even for the ordinary IT user. In the same vein, the notion of trust is also growing in importance (Grandison and Sloman 2000), and has become the focus of a task group within the INTEROP[1] project. Trust is clearly related to security and other dependability

---

[1] INTEROP (IST-508011, 2003-2007, http://www.interop-noe.org/) is an EU Network of Excellence project with 47 partners from 15 countries, coordinated by University Bordeaux 1, France. The main focus of the project is semantic in-

requirements, but whereas security concerns a system's objective capability to withstand malicious attacks, trust concerns the *subjective beliefs* among users or collaborating systems that the system is secure enough to be trusted. Hence, a system may have good security and privacy and yet be distrusted. For instance, a successful and highly publicized criminal attack against an internet banking application would be likely to reduce customer trust not just towards the particular application in question, but also towards other banks running different applications. An application could also be highly insecure, yet receive undeserved trust from its users – bogus applications used for phishing attacks being among the cruelest examples. Such attacks may in turn lead to undeserved distrust of genuine applications in the same business domain.

Customers need to trust applications to be willing to proceed with business transactions, and in e-commerce customer distrust in the applications is seen as a major cause for loss of business (Lowry et al. 2005). On the other hand, applications also need to make trust decisions about customers, or about other applications they are cooperating with. One major motivation for thorough requirements engineering is that it is cheaper to correct defects in early phases of development than if these defects are carried onwards through later phases or into the fielded system (Boehm and Papaccio 1988). Often, reworking in late development phases defects that originated in the requirements phase can consume as much as 40-50% of the project budget (Jones 1996).

Hence, the importance of dealing with requirements early is gradually being recognized, also for issues that have traditionally been dealt with during design or coding, such as security (Firesmith 2003). But the notion of requirements relating to trust is currently poorly understood, for instance there are yet no accepted techniques for specification of trust (Grandison and Sloman 2000). If this situation does not improve, there is a danger that future software development projects will suffer a lot of rework because the delivered systems have shortcomings related to trust.

It will be beyond the scope of this paper to solve the entire problem of trust-related requirements specification, which would include complex issues of formal analysis techniques, supporting tools, trust management, standardization of trust models and protocols. But a valuable initial contribution could be to provide a systematic discussion of *what* can sensibly be required of a software system in relation to trust, and *how* this can be expressed, as a first step, in natural language, and present the outcome of this discussion as a taxonomy of different types of trust-related requirements.

The rest of this paper is structured as follows: Section 2 discusses various related work which form a baseline for our taxonomy. Section 3 then develops the taxonomy itself. Section 4 discusses various usages of the taxonomy, and draws conclusions.

teroperability of information systems, combining expertise in ontologies, software architecture, and enterprise modelling.

# 2 Related Work

The most relevant baseline for making a taxonomy of trust-related requirements can be grouped into two categories of related work: 1) some which present classifications, taxonomies or ontologies of some aspects of trust, but which do not directly deal with requirements related to trust, and 2) some that present taxonomies for other types of requirements (e.g., security, usability) but not for trust-related requirements. In the following two subsections we will review works of both these categories.

## 2.1 Taxonomies and Ontologies of Trust

In general trust can be seen as a relationship between a *trustor* (the party who trusts or needs to decide whether to trust) and a *trustee* (the party being trusted, or for whom trustworthiness is being evaluated), where a party might be an individual human, an organization, or an automated system or component. McKnight and Chervany (1996) make a thorough discussion of the meaning of trust, focussing primarily on human trustors, arriving at a classification in 6 dimensions: 1) *Trusting Intention*: the trustor is willing to depend on the trustee in a certain situation, with a relative feeling of security even if negative consequences are possible. 2) *Trusting Behaviour*: the trustor voluntarily depends on the trustee in a certain situation, again with a relative feeling of security although negative consequences may happen. 3) *Trusting Beliefs*: the extent to which the trustor believes that the trustee is trustworthy (i.e., willing and capable of acting in the best interest of the first party). 4) *System Trust*: whether the trustor believes that there are impersonal/institutional structures in place to ensure the success of a future endeavour, e.g., contracts, guarantees, regulations. 5) *Dispositional Trust*: a trustor has a consistent tendency to trust other parties, across different situations. 6) *Situational Decision to Trust*: an intention to trust in certain situations, more or less independently of who might play the role of trustee.

Grandison and Sloman (2000) make a survey of trust in internet applications, arriving at 5 different types of trust: 1) *Resource access trust*: the trustor allows the trustee to access a resource, feeling confident that the trustee will do this in an appropriate manner. As the authors observe there might be different levels of trust here depending on the nature of the resource, for instance you need higher trust to let someone run code on your workstation than to let someone read a specific file. 2) *Service provision trust*: the trustor trusts the trustee to provide a service which does not imply access to the trustors resources. 3) *Trustee certification*: the trustor trusts the trustee based on certificates presented by the trustee, granted by an appropriate third party. 4) *Trust delegation*: the trustor delegates responsibility to the trustee, i.e., trusts the trustee to act on its behalf. 5) *Infrastructure trust*: the trustor needs to trust his own infrastructure (e.g., PC hardware and operating system, local servers and network).

Zhang et al. (2004) make a classification of trust functions in reputation-based trust management along 4 different dimensions:

1. *Subjective vs. objective*, i.e. based on opinions of previous users or objectively measured from log data.
2. *Transaction-based vs. opinion-based*, i.e., based on information about individual transactions or on stated opinions of previous users.
3. *Complete info vs. localized info:* whether the trustor has the needed information or needs to broadcast requests for it to other nodes in the network.
4. *Rank-based vs. threshold-based:* whether various service providers are ranked, or it is only determined if each is above or below a threshold.

Ruohomaa and Kutvonen (2005) provide a survey of the field of trust management. First they look at *Trust Management Models*, considering certificates, security policy systems and reputation systems. Then they look at *Trust Information Models,* i.e., what information a system needs to make trust decisions. Finally, they discuss the tasks of a *Trust Management System,* which are summarized as 1) *initializing a trust relationship*, i.e., the trustor decides to trust the trustee, after assessing the risk vs. the potential gain, based on policies and available information. 2) *observation* while the trust relationship is ongoing, e.g., controlling whether the trustee behaves in accordance with the trust agreement, and 3) *evolving reputation and trust,* changing the reputation information of various trustees based on the above observations.

Viljanen (2005) defines an ontology of trust. Her first step is to make a taxonomy of existing trust models, finding that they are based on various criteria. For instance, the trustor can trust the *identity* of the trustee, its *actions*, the *business value* of the planned transaction, the *capability* or *competence* of the trustee in performing this transaction. Furthermore, the trustor will have a certain level of *confidence* in the trustee, and this will often be based on the *context,* the trustee's *history*, or on *third party information*. Based on this, the ontology is proposed in the form of a UML class diagram. The top of the diagram shows a Trustor trusting a Trustee, this trust association may then have several aspects: context, confidence, action (risk, benefit, importance -> business value), competence, 3rd party info (reputation, recommendation, or external credentials), history, capability – as elicited from the survey of trust models.

Finally, Jøsang et al. (2005) look at security functions that need to be in place for trust to be justified in web service applications, in particular identity management. They concentrate mostly on solution aspects, not on the formulation of trust-related requirements for new systems. They discuss trust issues for various types of identity management: isolated, federated, and centralized.

## 2.2 Taxonomies of Other Related Types of Requirements

While there are many categories of non-functional requirements that might be relevant to look at for inspiring a taxonomy of trust requirements, it would be too exhaustive for a single paper to look at all of them. Here we concentrate on security and usability requirements, because trust is closely related to security since distrust often comes from fear of lacking security, and usability, while less directly related to trust, has similar aspects of subjectivity as trust, and just as trust emerges as a relationship between the user and the system, rather than just being a property of the system itself.

For security requirements, the most comprehensive taxonomy has been developed by Firesmith (2005). Based on a previous taxonomy of safety-related requirements, his taxonomy of security-related requirements distinguishes between:

- *security requirements*, which are the "pure" security requirements, indicating a wanted level of security without specifying how this should be achieved.
- *security-significant requirements*: these are requirements in other quality categories than security but which are believed to affect security positively.
- *security system requirements* are requirements for certain subsystems to deal with various aspects of security, for instance an antivirus program.
- *security constraints* are requirements that go even more into detail about the solution, for instance demanding the use of passwords of a certain length and containing both upper and lower case letters as well as numbers and special signs, whereas a pure security requirement would only say that users should be authenticated.

As for usability (Lauesen and Younessi 1998) identify six styles of usability requirements. *Performance style* and *defect style* requirements give a quantified measure for how well the user should perform with the system (or opposite: how many defects can be tolerated). *Subjective style* requirements demand that the system should make a certain score when users are asked about their satisfaction with the system. All these three types correspond to pure security requirements above. *Design style* and *guideline style* requirements go into detail about the solution, rather than focussing on pure requirements, e.g., prescribing certain screenshots or the following of certain UI guidelines. These correspond to security constraints above. Finally, Lauesen and Younessi discuss *process style* requirements, such as demanding the use of iterative prototyping during development of the system. This has no obvious counterpart in Firesmith's taxonomy, but prototyping is more relevant for usability than for security.

# 3 The Taxonomy

An initial high level taxonomy is given in figure 1. Since trust-*related* requirements can be almost any kind of requirements, as also observed by (Firesmith 2005) for security-related requirements, one can expect that the normal subtypes of requirements such as quality, function, data, interface, constraints, and process requirements may be of relevance. The five first are also used in the Firesmith-taxonomy for security-related requirements, while the sixth is mentioned by (Lauesen and Younessi 1998) as highly relevant for usability requirements. Apart from this, a first obvious division of trust-related requirements will be between requirements for the new system as trustor, and as trustee. In many respects, these will be quite different: trustor requirements will be concerned with the system's capability to make correct trust decisions, while trustee requirements will be concerned with its capability to achieve trust from its human users or from computerized agents. The distinction between trustor and trustee is orthogonal to the one about quality, functional, data etc. requirements, as both the trustor and trustee may have all kinds of requirements posed towards them.

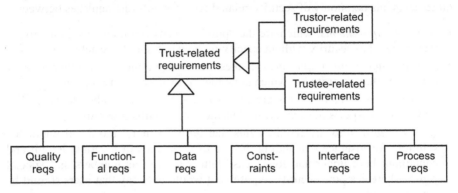

**Fig. 1.** Initial high-level taxonomy

## 3.1 Trustor-related requirements

Trustor-related requirements are about the system's ability to make correct trust decisions. As (Firesmith 2005) does for security requirements, one could talk about

- "pure" *trustor quality requirements*, specifying wanted levels of perfection in the trust decisions made by the system
- *trustor-significant requirements* – which are requirements belonging to other quality types than trust, but which have an impact on trust decision quality. For instance, security may have significance here – with lacking security, it might be possible for malicious attackers to tamper with the system's trust evaluation functions, hence reducing the quality of trust decisions.
- *trustor-subsystem requirements*, e.g., requirements posed towards a trust management subsystem within the system (or possibly even outside the system, as one might envision outsourcing not only certification or reputation management but the entire trust decision process to a third party)
- *constraints*, which are design choices lifted to the requirements level.

In figure 2 the "pure" trustor quality requirements are investigated in further detail. One important observation coming out of the background literature is that trust implies risk, so some trust decisions will turn out to be wrong in the end. Hence, 100% requirements like "The system should always make correct trust decisions" would not be useful. Moreover, different levels of precision will be needed for different kinds of trust decisions that the system is supposed to make, based on factors such as the amount of information available and the difficulty of the decision. Hence, the requirements for quality of trust decisions may have to mention

- various *trust challenges* that the system needs to deal with, in the lower part of the diagram, inspired by (Viljanen 2005; Grandison and Sloman 2000),
- various *types of trust decisions (outcomes)* wanted, shown top and left in the diagram, inspired by (Zhang, Yu et al. 2004).
- various *quality measures* that can be given for the trust decisions of the system (right side of the diagram).

These are orthogonal to each other, e.g., one could make subjective or objective trust decisions, and rankings or threshold-based trust decisions, for any of the given trust challenges. Moreover, all of these are also orthogonal to the quality measures, for which we have identified three different possibilities:

- *Internal validity* presumes the existence of some rules (policies) prescribing what information must be present and how it should be evaluated to decide whether to trust or distrust. The quality measure then becomes the extent to which the trust decisions are correct wrt. the given rules and the information available. Example: "The business value trust decisions made by the system should be consistent with the given policies in 99.9% of the cases".
- *External validity*, on the other hand, would be the much more ambitious concern whether the trust decisions made are *really* correct (e.g., if trusted parties indeed turn out to be trustworthy throughout the trust relationship, and if distrusted parties indeed were not trustworthy). Example: "Objective threshold-based trust decisions on service provision should turn out to be correct (i.e., service is acceptably provided) in at least 90% of the cases."
- *Feasibility* would consider not only the degree of validity of trust decisions, but also the economic effect of the decisions. The rationale for formulating requirements in this way would be that often it is not the number of trust mistakes which is the most important, but the losses associated with the mistakes. Hence, a system could be accepted to make a substantial number of trust mistakes as long as the loss associated with each mistake is minor, whereas on the other hand, one single trust mistake could be disastrous if the loss was huge. Example: "The economic loss resulting from incorrect service provision ranking decisions should be maximum 50% of the gain resulting from correct service provision ranking decisions."

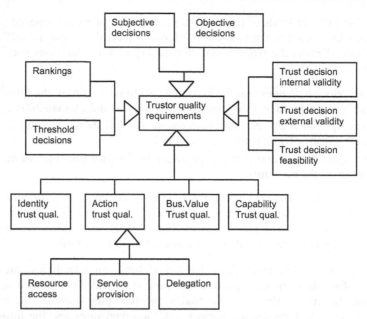

**Fig. 2.** Trustor quality requirements, more detailed taxonomy

For the internal validity of objective decisions, traditional 100% requirements can sometimes make sense, e.g., "The system shall always make correct identity trust decisions according to the policies in situations where all the needed information is available". Still, it is not certain that a 100% requirement would be preferable, as the cost of achieving this might be higher than the losses avoided compared to a less accurate trust decision (for instance because the trust evaluation would need to be based on more information, possibly gathered for a cost, because the calculation would take longer and perhaps lead to unacceptably slow performance of the system, etc.). Hence, even for internal validity one might want to allow defects, and this would be unavoidable when moving to external validity and feasibility requirements. Indeed, requirements related to external validity or feasibility may be very hard to test or evaluate, and in many cases it may be beyond the scope of the system alone to ensure them – hence, ambitious statements regarding the external validity and feasibility of the trust decisions made by the system may in some cases better be considered *goals* than requirements. For a distinction between goals and requirements, see for instance (van Lamsweerde 2004).

In addition to the trustor quality requirements, we will also briefly discuss other kinds of requirements for the trustor:

- *Trustor functional requirements* could have subclasses like 1) trust initiation functionality, 2) trust monitoring functionality (logging what happens during the trust relationship, and potentially for discovering whether the behavior of the trustee is such that trust should be modified), trust evolution functionality (updating information about single trustees) and trust policy evolution functionality, i.e., functionality for changing the encoded policies of the system. The first three are taken from (Ruohomaa and Kutvonen 2005), the fourth added on our own accord.

- *Trustor data requirements* describe what data the trustor needs to store (or access from third parties), e.g., information about the context and history (Viljanen 2005), various kinds of identification data for the potential trustees, as well as reputation data, recommendation data, service quality data.
- *Trustor interface requirements* would, e.g., describe which interfaces the trust management subsystem needs to perform its necessary communication with trustees and third parties.
- *Trustor constraints* would be design choices elevated to the requirements level, such as a requirement to use one particular standard for trust evaluation, one particular trust management system, or particular approaches for trust decisions.

All of these would belong to the category of *trust system requirements* if taking an approach analogous to the one (Firesmith 2005) has used for security requirements. In addition, one might consider *trustor process requirements* such as demanding an iterative development process with early prototyping. As shall be seen later, process requirements may be more interesting for trustees, but if the trustor's ability to deal with trustees is considered one of the most complex and risky parts of the project, one might be interested in clarifying this early to reduce the risk, i.e., prototype the trust decision functionality to be tried out with potential trustees.

## 3.2 Trustee-related requirements

Trustee-related requirements are about the system's ability to *achieve* trust from prospective users and collaborators. Naively, the system owner might want the system to be trusted by every potential user in all possible situations. But this might mean that the system is trusted even in situations when it is not trustworthy (e.g., believed by the user to have capabilities that it does not have). Such a deceptive system (or its developer or owner) could be considered unethical, cf. code of ethics by ACM/IEEE (1999), in particular principles 1.03, 1.04, and 1.06. Moreover, while an over-trusted system could bring initial gain by increased business, it could also easily backfire financially by causing badwill for its owner by dissatisfied users.

Hence, our taxonomy will be based on the more ethical assumption that the objective for the system is to be trusted when it is indeed trustworthy, and to be distrusted when it is not. This makes trustee quality requirements quite symmetrical to trustor quality requirements in that they can be evaluated for their degree of validity, in terms of false positives and false negatives. The same symmetry could apply for types of trust decisions. The trustee wants to be trusted both for identity, actions, business value, and capability, wants to pass threshold-based decisions as well as achieve high placement in trust rankings, whether these are subjective or objective.

Yet there are also important differences. Pure quality requirements relating to validity or feasibility of trust decisions are even harder to state on the trustee side than on the trustor side. First of all, it is the trustor that chooses whether or not to trust, hence the fulfillment of any validity or feasibility requirement would be mostly beyond the trustee's control. With a changing array of potential trustors, and the irrationality of human users, pure quality statements make sense only as higher level goals. Moreover, a trustee necessarily needs to adapt to the preferences of the persons or systems it wants to be trusted by. Some issues that were design-oriented constraints for the trustor, could be pure requirements for the trustee. For instance, if the systems you need to be trusted by demand certificates, you need to provide certificates.

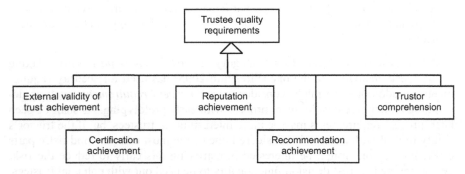

**Fig. 3.** Trustee-quality requirements, partial taxonomy

Figure 3 shows a partial taxonomy for trustee quality requirements, emphasizing the parts that are different from the previous taxonomy for trustor quality requirements. The leftmost "External validity of trust achievement" is symmetrical to the external validity for the trustor – but note that requirements of this style may be hard to state (and even harder for developers to take responsibility for) since trust decisions are made by the trustors and therefore often beyond the control of the trustees. Also note that Internal validity is not relevant on the trustee side since the trust decision is made by the trustor, and feasibility type requirements are also less relevant as it is primarily the trustor who loses money on a bad trust decision. Instead, various new subtypes of quality requirements have been shown for the trustee:

- *Certification achievement.* This would be requirements stating that the system should satisfy criteria to be certified, either by certain named certification agencies, or more generally for instance by certification agents together controlling at least 90% of the market for 3$^{rd}$ party certification in the domain.
- *Reputation achievement.* This is more difficult to specify as a direct requirement than certification achievement, as a new system initially has no reputation. If at all, such requirements must therefore be specified with a time perspective, e.g., that after a certain number of usages of a service offered by a system, it should have achieved a reputation so and so.

- *Recommendation achievement.* This could be specified for instance as a wanted minimum percentage of users (human or computerized agents) who are willing to recommend the system after having used it. Again, however, this is hard to establish during development or even at acceptance testing but needs some time of usage before one can know whether the requirement was met.
- *Trustor comprehension.* To avoid both false positives (system over-trusted) and false negatives (system under-trusted) it is important to communicate the capabilities and limitations of the system to its users. Comprehension requirements would state acceptable levels for the trustors' understanding of the trustee system. Examples: "At the point where credit card number is requested, at least 90% of the users shall have understood that this is transmitted through a secure channel."; "At least 80% of the users shall have understood that the name and address is transmitted through an insecure channel in the web page for requesting more information by ordinary mail."

Some of these subtypes of requirements will be hard to accept by developers except maybe for in-house development. In contract development, it would be unreasonable for a developer to promise that the system should achieve a certain level of reputation or recommendations within a certain time since this is dependent on a lot of factors beyond their control. Hence, other classes of trustee-related requirements would also be important:

**Trustee-significant requirements**, i.e., requirements that belong to other quality types but contribute to trust achievement. Security and privacy would be obvious examples, as would usability and performance. Also, a requirement that company logos be clearly visible on all web pages – while primarily being considered a branding requirement – could also have a positive impact on trust.

**Process requirements** such as prototyping with users to establish that the system is found trustworthy by humans would also be more relevant for trustee requirements than for trustor requirements. But while it is well understood how usability can be tested with a mock-up prototype, it is uncertain whether trust could be addressed in a similar manner. For instance, if users try out a mock-up interface of an internet banking application, they would just be toying with money transfers, not run any risk of losing money or disclosing information about their economy to outsiders. Hence, their answers to questions whether the application seemed trustworthy might be unreliable.

# 4 Discussion and Conclusions

Two main types of usage can be envisioned for a requirement taxonomy: 1) training and 2) development projects. While taxonomies exist for many other types of quality requirements, there are no existing ones that deal with trust-related requirements. In training (for instance in a course in requirements engineering) a taxonomy of trust requirements may give more detailed insight into what trust is (in the IT meaning of the word) and what can possibly be required of a system with respect to trust. Perhaps most importantly, it can help the students distinguish between the requirements level, stating WHAT should be achieved by the system in making trust decisions (system-as-trustor) and achieving trust from others (system-as-trustee), and the design level, concerning various solutions that are known or believed to solve trust problems.

In industry projects, a taxonomy can be used to generate checklists of quality requirements to consider, this can for instance be used to evaluate whether a specification is complete or not. Unlike functional requirements, trust requirements may be unlikely to pop up directly from traditional elicitation techniques such as user interviews or workshops – unless the analysts are conscious to address trust issues.

While the taxonomy presented here is a contribution to a better understanding of the field of trust-related requirements, it must be admitted that this field is still in an early phase, and more work is needed on the taxonomy, both theoretically and gaining practical experience with its use, before it can result in clear guidelines to system developers on how to handle requirements related to trust in industrial projects.

## 5 Acknowledgments

The author would like to thank partners in the INTEROP project, and in particular those involved in TG7 "Interoperability challenges of trust, confidence/security and policies", for inspiration and feedback.

## References

ACM/IEEE-CS (1999) Software Engineering Code of Ethics and Professional Practice. Technical report, ACM/IEEE-CS Joint Task Force on Software Engineering Ethics and Professional Practices. http://www.acm.org/serving/se/code.htm#full. Last accessed: 3.3.2006.

Boehm BW, Papaccio PN (1988) Understanding and Controlling Software Costs. IEEE Transactions on Software Engineering 14(10): 1462-1477.

Firesmith DG (2003) Engineering Security Requirements. Journal of Object Technology 2(1): 53-68.

Firesmith DG (2005) A Taxonomy of Security-Related Requirements. In Proc.: International Workshop on High Assurance Systems (RHAS'05), Paris, France.

Grandison T, Sloman M (2000) A survey of trust in Internet applications. IEEE Communications Surveys and Tutorials 3(4): 2-16.

Jones C (1996) Applied Software Measurement, McGraw-Hill, New York.

Jøsang A, Fabre J, Hay B, Dalziel J, Pope S (2005) Trust requirements in identity management. In: Proc. Australasian Information Security Workshop (AISW'05), Newcastle, Australia.

Lauesen S, Younessi H (1998) Six styles for usability requirements. In: Proc. Fourth International Workshop on Requirements Engineering: Foundations of Software Quality (REFSQ'98), Presses Universitaires de Namur, Belgium.

Lowry PB, Roberts T, Caine B (2005) Familiarity Effects on Trust with Mobile Computing Device Websites. In: Proc. 11th International Conference on Human Computer Interaction (HCI-2005), Las Vegas, NV.

McKnight DH, Chervany NL (1996) The meanings of trust. Technical report, University of Minnesota, MIS Research Center.

Ruohomaa S, Kutvonen L (2005) Trust management survey. In: Proc. iTrust 3rd International Conference on Trust Management, Roquencourt, France.

van Lamsweerde A (2004) Goal-Oriented Requirements Enginering: A Roundtrip from Research to Practice. In: Proc. 12th IEEE Int'l Conference on Requirements Engineering (RE 2004), Kyoto, Japan, IEEE Computer Society.

Viljanen L (2005) Towards an ontology of trust. In: Proc. 2nd Int'l Conf. on Trust, Privacy and Security in Digital Business (TrustBus'05), Springer Verlag.

Zhang Q, Yu T, Irwin K (2004) A classification scheme for trust functions in reputation-based trust management. In: Proc. International Workshop on Trust, Security, and Reputation on the Semantic Web, Hiroshima, Japan.

# Design of a Peer-to-Peer Information Sharing MAS Using MOBMAS (Ontology-Centric Agent Oriented Methodology)

N. Tran[*], G. Beydoun[*,**], G. Low[*]

[*]School of Information Management and Technology Management, University of New South Wales, Australia
[**]School of Economics and Information Systems, University of Wollongong, Australia, emails: {g.beydoun, g.low, numitran@unsw.edu.au}

**Abstract:** Most existing agent-oriented methodologies ignore system extensibility, interoperability and reusability issues. In light of this, we have developed MOBMAS – a "Methodology for Ontology-Based MASs" which makes use of ontologies as a central modeling tool, utilising their roles in facilitating interoperability and reusability. As part of an ongoing validation of MOBMAS, we demonstrate in this paper its use on a peer-to-peer (P2P) community-based information sharing application. MOBMAS is used by an experienced software developer, who is not an author of the methodology, to guide the development of the P2P application.

## 1 Introduction

Ontologies are an explicit formal specification of a shared conceptualization [10][1]. They have been successfully used to enhance extensibility, reusability, interoperability and verify various products of software development e.g. [5, 13, 16]. Few prominent agent-oriented methodologies use ontologies in the design process

---

[1] *Conceptualization* is the way a domain is perceived and this is expressed in a collection of terms and a set of relations between the terms. When formally described they constitute an *ontology*.

[15]. When they do, their use tends to be confined to the early phase of the development (the *analysis* phase). For example, GRAMO [9] specifies how a domain model that includes goal and role analyses is developed from an initial ontology. Another example, MASE [3] uses ontologies to mediate the transition between the goal and the task analyses. Our use of ontologies in developing MAS is perhaps closest to recent work in [1] which recognizes the role of using ontologies for verification of models during the analysis phase. Outside the analysis phase, ontologies currently are mainly used to express a common terminology for agent intertions in an MAS e.g. [4].

Towards enhancing reusability and interoperability of MAS components, our new framework [14] supports the creation of methodologies supporting and making use of ontologies throughout much of the development lifecycle. To illustrate our ideas, we developed an ontology based agent-oriented methodology, MOBMAS – a "*M*ethodology for *O*ntology-*B*ased *MAS*s" that explicitly and extensively investigates the diverse roles of ontology in MAS development and provides support for these roles. It has an ontology-based MAS development process and ontology-based MAS model definitions. MOBMAS provides support for the following key areas of MAS development: analysis, agent internal design, agent interaction design and MAS organizational design. MOBMAS takes advantage of the existing agent-oriented methodologies, by reusing and enhancing their techniques and modeling definitions where appropriate. It endeavors to combine the strengths of the existing methodologies into one methodological framework .

This paper is part of ongoing validation of MOBMAS. Specifically, the test case shown in this paper examines the effectiveness of MOBMAS as a tool to guide a developer in producing an analysis and design of an MAS based on a given set of requirements. The verification of the reusability of the outcome of MOBMAS is the next step of the verification and is not the current focus of the paper.

## 2 MOBMAS Methodology

Using MOBMAS, the MAS development starts with a domain ontology which is initially used to identify goals and roles of the system to index an appropriate set of problem solving capabilities from an appropriate existing library of capabilities. Individual ontologies corresponding to the knowledge requirements of each capability are then extracted from the initial common ontology, to provide knowledge representation and allow reasoning by individual agents. Those ontologies form the basis for an iterative process to develop a common communication ontology between all agents and verify the knowledge requirements of chosen capabilities. Individual localised ontologies may also require incremental refinement during the iterative process. Appropriate ontology mappings are needed between local ontologies and the communication ontology. The development of MAS using MOBMAS has five activities. Each focuses on one of the following key area of MAS development: Analysis, Organization Design, Agent Internal Design, Agent

Interaction Design and Architecture Design. The development process of MOBMAS is highly iterative. MOBMAS activities are detailed as follows:

**Analysis Activity:** This activity aims to form a conception of the target MAS from the domain ontology and the system requirements, giving a first-cut identification of the roles and tasks that compose the MAS. This activity consists of developing the following five models: System Task Model, Organizational Context Model, Role model, Ontology Model and as well as identification of Ontology-Management Role. The Role Model is developed in a highly iterative manner with the System Task Model, given the association between roles, role tasks and system tasks. The Ontology Model is used to refine and validate those models (and vice versa). This activity also specifies the ontological mappings between the MAS Application Ontologies.

**MAS Organization Design:** This activity refines the organizational structure of the target MAS and identifies a set of agent classes composing the system. If the MAS is a heterogeneous system that contains non-agent resources, these are also identified and their applications are conceptualized. This activity consists of the following four steps: Specify the MAS Organizational Structure, Develop the Agent Class Model; Develop the Resource Model; and Refine the Ontology Model of the previous activity. The developer also specifies the mappings between Resource Application Ontologies and relevant MAS Application Ontologies, to enable the integration of these resources into the MAS application and to support the interoperability between heterogeneous resources.

**Agent Internal Design:** For each agent class, this activity specifies belief conceptualization, agent goals, events, plan templates and reactive rules. It consists of the following five steps: Specify Agent Class' Belief Conceptualization identifying which part(s) of the Ontology Model are needed by an agent class to conceptualize its run-time beliefs; Specify Agent Goals identifying the states of the world that an agent class aims to achieve or satisfy using the Role Model; Specify Events in the environment that agents need to respond to at run-time; Develop Agent Behavior Model specifying how each agent class behaves to achieve or satisfy each agent goal as planning behavior or reactive behavior; and Update the Agent Class Diagram with the details identified in the previous three steps and checking Agent Behavior Model for consistency against the Ontology Model and vice versa.

**Agent Interaction Design:** This activity models the interactions between agent instances, by selecting a suitable interaction mechanism for the target MAS and modeling the interactions. It has two steps: Decide upon which interaction mechanism is best suited to the target MAS (direct or indirect); and then Define how agents interact depending on the selected interaction mechanism. The resultant Agent Interaction Model is represented by a set of Interaction Protocol Diagrams. The developer validates the Agent Interaction Model against the Ontology Model. The Agent Class Model is also checked to ensure that all communicating agent classes share the same application ontologies that govern their interactions. Lastly, the Agent Relationship Diagram is updated to show descriptive information about each interaction pathway between agent classes.

**Architecture Design:** This activity deals with various design issues relating to agent architecture and MAS architecture. It has the following five steps: Identify

Agent-Environment interface requirements; Select Agent Architecture for the most appropriate architecture(s) for agents in the MAS; Specify MAS Infrastructure facilities identifying system components that are needed to provide system-specific services; Instantiate agent classes; and Develop MAS deployment plan.

Details of MOBMAS will be illustrated in the next section by applying it to develop a community based search engine.

# 3 Community-based P2P Information Sharing MAS

In this section, we illustrate the use of MOBMAS on a P2P information sharing application by an experienced system developer. The application and its specifications are based on Klampanos and Jose [11] and Mine et al.'s [12] conception of a P2P information sharing architecture.

## 3.1 Application Description

Each human user is represented by an agent in the network to act on his/her behalf. This agent locates files and responds to queries by other similar agents. The collection of all these agents and agents assisting them in their tasks form the P2P community based searching MAS.

An agent representing the human user has access to a knowledge base containing electronic files that the user is willing to share with other users. Each file is identified by its title and type (e.g. HTML, pdf, music or video). The collection of human users form a network of peers. A human user can pose a query to request files. Each query is made up of one or more keywords. The system is responsible for  locating sites  where files matching the queries may reside, based on the behavior of the users at those sites (as represented by their agents). The mediation between the human users is performed by the system and is initiated by the agent representing the human making the request. The agent of the like-minded user responds either by providing details about the files it can supply, or refusing the service. When all responses are received, the agent combines and refines the results to compose a list of files that satisfy the query. The agent initiating the query can then select which file(s) it wants to download to the human it represents and initiates the file transfer process. After a successful transfer, the knowledge base located where the query was made, is updated to contain the received file(s).

For all agents involved in processing the query, their knowledge base is also updated with additional information reflecting the interests of the agent which initiates the query. This information will be used in future queries. At each node in the network, each user-agent thus keeps a record of its history of information sharing. The history contains two records: one of the past queries that it made on behalf of the human user and its respective responders, and one of the past queries received  and their respective agent senders (acting on behalf of other human users). The former needs to be updated every time the user-agent receives a result

list from the system, while the latter requires update every time the user-agent replies to a query sent by the system. The history is used to produce short lists of
candidate nodes for future queries, by calculating the similarity between the current query and a past query . If no nodes can be short-listed, or if all candidate
user-agents do not provide the service required, the agent-user broadcasts the
query to a wider circle of user-agents in the community, to identify new candidate
providers. The new providers are eventually added to the history, thereby expanding the user-agent's contact circle. This strategy of information sharing can be
applied to any domain, but we limit our application to the Movies domain. Accordingly, the information to be shared amongst user-agents is assumed to be movie-
related files, such as movie trailers, movie posters or movie web pages.

The rest of this section describes the sequence of steps in the analysis and design phases of MOBMAS to generate described P2P system. The steps are too involved to be completely shown. Snap shots of each model are instead presented as
an illustration.

## 3.2 P2P Analysis

The first step of the Analysis activity constructed a System Task Model to specify
the required system functionality and its decomposition structure. For the P2P information sharing application, the core system task was "Satisfy file-sharing request", which was composed of two sub-tasks "Process user search query"
and "Carry out file-transfer process". Each of these sub-tasks was further decomposed into smaller-grained sub-tasks. The next step in the Analysis activity
was to investigate the organizational context in which MAS will reside and support, to elicit any existing organizational structure that the MAS may imitate. In
this application, the target MAS does not reside within any human organization,
thus this step was omitted in (Figure 1).

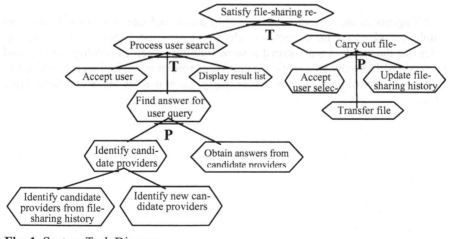

**Fig. 1.** System Task Diagram

The developer identified roles by grouping closely related tasks in the System Task Model. For example, all tasks dealing with user interactions were assigned to a "User Interface" role (Figure 4). Similarly, all tasks related to the file-transfer history were allocated to a "History Manager" role. An "Information Retriever" role was also defined to handle all tasks relating to processing user query and file transfer. Finally, a "Portal" role is identified to act as a broker in the P2P network, by identifying new information providers when required. An Ontology Model was then constructed to define the necessary application ontologies for the target MAS. At this stage, only MAS Application ontologies were examined. Resource Application ontologies were identified later in the Organization Design activity. An information sharing MAS for the Movies domain would require two MAS Applilition ontologies: one for conceptualizing the Movies domain and one for conceptualizing the Information Sharing domain (Figure 2 and Figure 3).

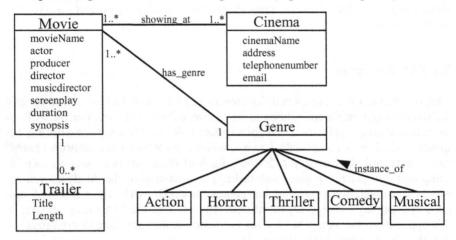

**Fig. 2.** Movie Ontology (based on DAML ontology at  *http://www.cse.dmu.ac.uk/*)

All agents in the system are expected to know and use these two Application ontologies which are not expected to change at run-time, hence the developer decides that the ontologies are stored at some publicly-accessed ontology servers and be accessed freely by all agents. No particular role or agent is therefore needed to manage or control these servers. Accordingly, no new roles are added to the Role Model.

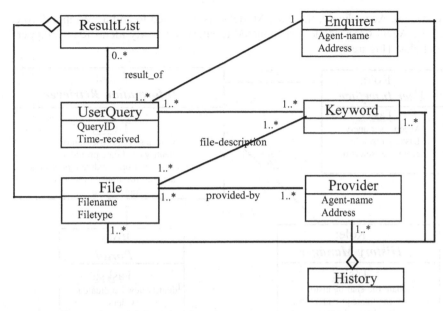

**Fig. 3.** Information Sharing Ontology

## 3.3 P2P MAS Organization Design

The first step in this activity was to refine the initial Role Model developed in Section 3.2 to specify authority relationships between roles. In the P2P application, role "Information Retriever" has a peer-to-peer relationship with role "User Interface" and role "Portal", meaning that they assume an equal authority in their cooperation (Figure 4). However, role "Information Retriever" engages in a superior-subordinate relationship with role "History Manager" (expressed by a "control" association in Figure 4) because role "Information Retriever" has the authority to delegate work to role "History Manager", and the latter is obliged to perform the delegated tasks and should not reject a request from the former.

Agent classes were then identified from roles via one-to-one mappings. As such, there were four agent classes in the P2P MAS, each assuming one role. A preliminary Agent Relationship Diagram was constructed to show the tentative agent classes, their roles and their acquaintances (i.e. interaction pathways) (Figure 5). These acquaintances were derived directly from the acquaintances between roles played by the agent classes (c.f Figure 4). At this stage, the Agent Class Diagram for each agent class was mostly empty, since no internal details were yet apparent.

Non-agent software resources were also identified. In this informationsharing application, non-agent resources included knowledge sources containing movie-related electronic files, e.g. web servers or directories. Each knowledge source needed to be managed and controlled by a specialized wrapper agent. This wrapper agent provides an interface to the resource when requested by other agents in the system. Accordingly, the Role Model was extended to add a "Wrapper" role, and the Agent Class Model was updated to show the newly identified "Wrapper" agent class (Figure 8).

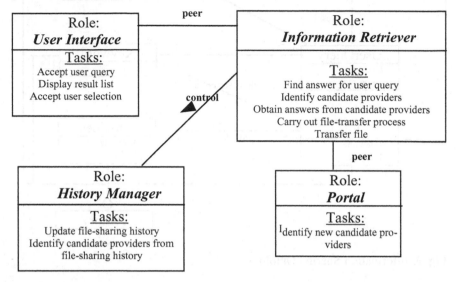

**Fig. 4.** Role Diagram

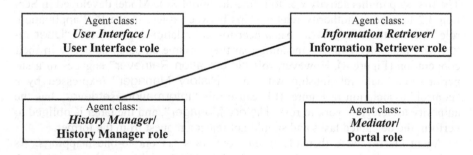

**Fig. 5.** Preliminary Agent Relationship Diagram

The ontology conceptualizing each knowledge source was defined and added to the Ontology Model.

## 3.4 P2P Agent Internal Design

The internal design of each agent class started with the identification of the agent class' belief conceptualization; that is, the identification of ontologies conceptualizing the agent's potential run-time beliefs. For example, the "Information Retriever" agent class in the P2P application needed to commit to two ontologies:

"Movie Ontology" and "Information Sharing Ontology", because the agents of this class would need to hold beliefs about the movie domain and the information sharing domain at run-time. Meanwhile, the "Wrapper" agent class should commit to the "MovieTrailer Resource Ontology" apart from the "Movie Ontology" and "Information Sharing Ontology", because wrapper agents would have to access the MovieTrailer knowledge source at run-time.

Agent goals were identified directly from role tasks. However, while role tasks were specified using imperatives, agent goals were specified in the form of "something is achieved". For instance, role "History Manager" in Figure 4 has a task "Identify candidate providers from file-sharing history". This task indicates a goal "Candidate providers are identified from file-sharing history" for agent class "History Manager".

Events affecting agents' courses of actions were also identified. Example events concerning "Information Retriever" agents are "Reception of user query from User Interface agents" (which activates an agent goal "Answer is found for user query"), "Input of user's file selection" (which activates an agent goal "File is downloaded") and "Input of user's cancellation" (which signals the agent to forfeit its active goal).

The Agent Class Model was updated to show the listing of belief conceptualization, agent goals and events for each agent class. illustrates the Agent Class Diagram for the "Information Retriever" agent class (see Figure 6).

| **agent class** |
| *Information Retriever* / Information Retrieve role |
| **belief conceptualization**<br>Movie Ontology<br>Information Sharing Ontology |
| **agent-goals**<br>Answer is found for user query<br>Candidate providers are identified<br>Answers are obtained from candidate providers<br>File-transfer process is completed<br>File is downloaded |
| **events**<br>Reception of user query from User Interface agents<br>Input of user's file selection<br>Input of user's cancellation |

**Fig. 6.** Class Diagram for "Information Retriever" agent class

Lastly, an Agent Behavior Model was developed to define agent plan templates and reflexive rules for each agent class to achieve its agent goals. Both planning and reactive behavior was considered for each agent class, in respect of each agent goal. For example, the "User Interface" agent class employed reactive behavior to achieve the goal "User query is accepted". Meanwhile, the "History Manager" agent class required planning behavior to fulfill the agent goal "Candidate providers are identified from file-sharing history". The Reflexive Rule Specification is illustrated in Figure 7.

During its construction, the Agent Behavior Model was validated against the Ontology Model, to ensure that the datatypes of all variables in the agent plan templates and reflexive rules were equivalent to the ontological concepts defined in the "Movie Ontology", "Information Sharing Ontology" and "MovieTrailer Resource Ontology". For example, variable "q" in has a datatype "UserQuery", which is a concept in the "Information Sharing Ontology" (Figure 3). The Agent Class Diagram was also checked to ensure that the agent class' belief conceptualization contained the ontology involved (in this case, the "User Interface" agent class should specify the "Information Sharing Ontology" in its belief conceptualization).

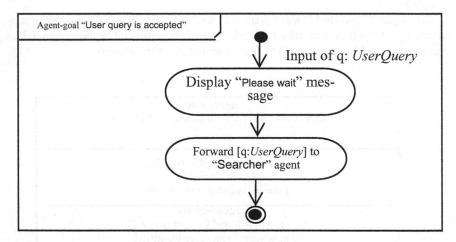

**Fig. 7.** Reflexive Rule Specification for "User Interface" agent class

## 3.5 P2P Agent Interaction Design

The first step in this activity was to select a suitable interaction mechanism for the P2P MAS. The "direct" interaction mechanism (using ACLs) was chosen over the "indirect" mechanism (using tuplespace/tuple-centre), because the speech-act performatives provided by ACLs were expected to support a higher level of communication semantics than Linda-like primitives used by the tuplespace mechanism. The target application can also reuse many interaction protocols provided by the existing catalogues, such as FIPA's Protocal Library.

An Agent Interaction Model was then developed to define interaction protocols between agent instances. Each protocol was depicted by an AUML Interaction Protocol Diagram (not shown here for lack of space). The developer also checked the Agent Interaction Model against the Ontology Model, to make sure that the datatypes of all variables in the interaction protocols were equivalent to the ontological concepts in the "Movie Ontology" or "Information Sharing Ontology" (except for basic datatypes like string and integer). After constructing the Agent Interaction Model, the Agent Relationship Diagram was updated to show various descriptive information about each interaction pathway between agent classes (Figure 8). The descriptive information specified were:
- the name of the Interaction Protocol Diagram depicting the protocol governing the interactions; and
- the name of the ontology used to define the interactions' semantics.

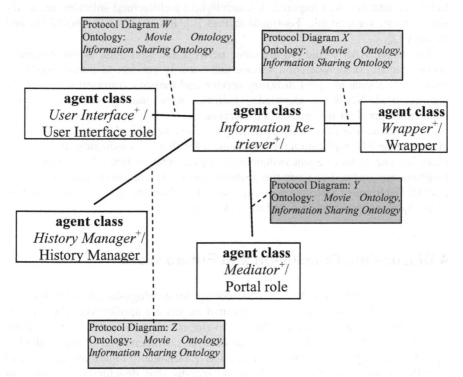

**Fig. 8.** Updated Agent Relationship Diagram

## 3.6 Architecture Design

The characteristics and requirements of agent perception, effect and communication mechanisms were firstly identified. With regard to perception and effect, the environment of the target information sharing MAS did not contain any physical objects. Thus, the agents' sensors and effectors did not need to connect to, or control, any hardware sensing and effecting components. However, the sensor and effector of the "User Interface" agents should be connected to an elaborate user-interface component, since this is the only means of getting inputs and providing outputs to human users in this application. The "Wrapper" agents should also be equipped with an ability to connect physically and virtually to its wrapped knowledge sources. With regard to communication, the implementation platform should be able to support the exchange of binary data such as rich multimedia files. An Agent-Environment Requirement Specification was constructed to document these characteristics and requirements. The developer then decided upon which agent architecture was appropriate to the target MAS. Since agent classes in the system adopted both planning behavior and reflexive behavior for achieving their goals, a hybrid architecture was required. Various hybrid architectural solutions are available for use, for example TouringMachines [6], RAPs [7], ATLANTIS [8] and Prodigy [2].

The target MAS would require basic network facilities such as agent naming service, agent creation/deletion service and security service. Common coordination facilities such as agent directory service and message transport service were also required. Necessary knowledge facilities were ontology servers, protocol servers and problem-solving methods servers.

The instantiation cardinality of each agent class was also determined. All agent classes in the P2P application were instantiated with a "+" cardinality; that is, each class has one or more agent instances at implementation time. The Agent Class Diagram was updated to show this instantiation configuration (Figure 8). Finally, a MAS Deployment Diagram was constructed to show the physical configuration of the system (Diagram is omitted for lack of space).

## 4 Discussion, Conclusion and Future Work

We demonstrated MOBMAS – a methodology for ontology-based MAS development – on a P2P community-based information sharing application. The use was conducted by an experienced software developer, who was not an author of the MOBMAS methodology but was given detailed documentation of the methodology. The developer's responses to a detailed questionnaire regarding the usage of MOBMAS, indicated that he valued the step-by-step development process of MOBMAS and the provision of many heuristics and techniques to support each step. MOBMAS also provided *verification and validation*: The steps of MOBMAS enforce consistency checking amongst the major model kinds. For example, the Ontology Model is used to verify and validate the System Task Model,

Agent Class Model, Agent Behavior Model and Agent Interaction Model. Currently, we do not have a tool to enforce this checking. We are in the process of formalizing the current manual checking. This will be usable as a stepping stone to develop a tool.

This paper confirmed the ease of use of MOBMAS and its support for validation and verification. We still need to confirm that systems developed with MOBMAS are interoperable and extendible. We plan to deploy a completed P2P system in a heterogeneous environment to validate its interoperability. With respect to extensibility, we are intending to develop a webportal using MOBMAS and then vary the initial requirement of the system and assess how easy it is for developers to modify the original portal. We anticipate that because new knowledge sources and agents can be easily added to the MAS shown in this paper, and since in any application core models of MOBMAS are composed of ontologies and ontological concepts (namely, Agent Belief Conceptualization, Agent Behavior Model and Agent Interaction Model), a design can be adapted to a new application by changing the ontologies involved. However, some further details in MOBMAS need to be worked out in order to manipulate ontologies within the development process. For example, in case two ontologies with different conceptualization of the same domain are used during the requirement changes, then ontology mappings would be required.

# References

1.  A.A.F. Brandao, V.T.d. Silva and C.J.P.d. Lucena: Ontologies as Specification for the Verification of Multi-Agent Systems Design, in *Object Oriented Programmings, Systems, Languages and Applications Workshop (2004)*. 2004. California.
2.  J.G. Carbonell, C.A. Knoblock and S. Minton: PRODIGY:An Integrated Architecture for Prodigy, in *Architectures for Intelligence*, K. VanLehn, Editor. 1991, Lawrence Erlbaum Associates: New Jersey. p. 241-278.
3.  J. Dileo, T. Jacobs and S. Deloach: Integrating Ontologies into Multi-Agent Systems Engineering, in *4th International Bi-Conference Workshop on Agent Oriented Information Systems (AOIS2002)*. 2002. Italy.
4.  M. Esteva: Electronic Institutions: From Specification To Development, in *Artificial Intelligence Research Insitute*. 2003, UAB - Universitat Autonòma de Barcelona: Barcelona.
5.  D. Fensel: *Ontologies: A Silver Bullet for Knowledge Management and Electronic Commerce*. 2001, Berlin: Spring-Verlag.
6.  I.A. Ferguson: TouringMachines: An Architecture for Dynamic, Rational, Mobile Agents. 1992, University of Cambridge: Cambridge.
7.  R.J. Firby: Adaptive Execution in Dynamic Domains. 1989, Yale University: Yale.
8.  E. Gat: Integrating Planning and Reacting in a Heterogenous Asynchronous Architecture for Controlling Real-World Mobile Robots, in *10th*

*National Conference on Artificial Intelligence*. 1992. San Jose, California: The MIT Press.

9. R. Girardi, C.G.d. Faria and L. Balby: Ontology-based Domain Modeling of Multi-Agent Systems, in *OOPLSA Workshop*. 2004.

10. T.R. Gruber: Automated Knowledge Acquisition for Strategic Knowledge. *Machine Learning*, 1989. 4: p. 293-336.

11. I.A. Klampanos and J.M. Jose: An Architecture for Peer-to-Peer Information Retrieval, in *SIGIR'03*. 2003.

12. T. Mine, D. Matsuno, A. Kogo and M. Amamiya: Design and Implementation of Agent Community Based Peer-to-Peer Information Retrieval Method, in *Cooperative Information Agents (CIA2004)*. 2004. Germany: Springer-Verlag.

13. M.J.R. Shave: Ontological Structures for Knowledge Sharing. *New Review of Information Networking*, 1997. 3: p. 125-133.

14. N. Tran, G. Low and G. Beydoun: A Methodological Framework for Ontology Centric AOSE. *Computer Science Systems and Engineering*, 2006. March.

15. Q.N. Tran and G. Low: Comparison of Methodologies, in *Agent-Oriented Methodologies*, B. Henderson-Sellers and P. Giorgini, Editors. 2005, Idea Group Publishing: Hershey. p. 341-367.

16. M. Uschold and M. Grueninger: Ontologies: Principles, Methods and Application. *Knowledge Engineering Review*, 1996. 11(2): p. 93-195.

# Recognition and Resolution of Linguistic Conflicts: The Core to a Successful View and Schema Integration

Peter Bellström[*], Jürgen Vöhringer[**] and Alexander Salbrechter[***]

[*]Department of Information Systems, Karlstad University, Sweden.
Peter.Bellstrom@kau.se
[**] Department of Business Informatics and Application Systems, University of Klagenfurt, Austria. Juergen@ifit.uni-klu.ac.at
[***]R&S Software GmbH, Feldkirchen, Austria. Alexander.Salbrechter@rs-software.at

## 1 Introduction

In the field of information system (IS) design and modeling the topic of integrating different views and schemata to a common conceptual schema is a central issue. Integration of two schemata means that they are compared, conflicts between them are identified and resolved, and finally the schemata are merged. Integration is often based on a global ontology that provides the valid concepts and interdependencies of a domain. In this paper we adapt the definition of ontology [8]: "An *ontology* is an explicit specification of a conceptualization.". Traditional integration techniques are often based on concept name comparison which even more motivates the use of an ontology as a domain lexicon.

The goal of any integration process is to create a correct, complete, minimal and understandable unified common schema. Mismatches in schema integration can be ascribed to naming, semantic, structural and data model conflicts. In this paper we propose a number of methods that support the integration of generic modeling approaches through the recognition and resolution of linguistic conflicts. These methods will be discussed on the basis of two exemplary user-near modeling approaches, namely the Klagenfurt Conceptual Predesign Model (KCPM) approach and the Karlstad Enterprise Modeling (EM) approach, that were developed at University of Klagenfurt, Austria, and Karlstad University, Sweden, respectively.

After comparing our modeling-, recognition- and resolution approaches we point out commonalities and possible synergies.

This paper is structured as follows: firstly we present and compare our light-weight modeling approaches, that both work on an end-user-near level. Secondly, we show the principal integration problems, in particular regarding linguistic problems. We propose a selection of integration techniques that suggest being generally applicable for user-near modeling languages like KCPM and EM. The paper is concluded by a preview on future research.

# 2 Two user-friendly Modeling Approaches

## 2.1 KCPM – The Klagenfurt Conceptual Predesign Model

KCPM was developed at the University of Klagenfurt as a part of the NIBA[1] project [5]. It is an acronym for the Klagenfurt Conceptual Predesign Model and refers to a modeling approach that tries to counter the trend of increasingly extensive and complex modeling languages by acting as an interlingua between end users and systems designers. It presents an intermediate schema between natural language texts and common, more complex conceptual schemata like UML. Only the domain relevant concepts are modeled, whereas design decisions and implementation details are left for the succeeding design phase of the conceptual modeling process [9].

KCPM comprises static as well as dynamic schemata. Static schemata (Figure 1) consist of thingtypes, connectiontypes and perspectives. Thingtypes are similar to entities in UML static schemas (though classes and attributes are not distinguished) and connectiontypes represent relationships between thingtypes. For each connectiontype two perspectives exist: one for each involved thingtype.

Dynamic KCPM schemata are defined by operationtypes, cooperationtypes and pre- and postconditions. Operationtypes describe the operations that are possible in the modeled IS and constitute a link between dynamic and static KCPM schemata, since each operation can be assigned an executor and several callers and parameters, which are all modeled as thingtypes from the corresponding static KCPM schema.

---

[1] NIBA is a German acronym for "Natural language requirements analysis". The NIBA project was financed partly by the Klaus-Tschira-Stiftung Heidelberg.

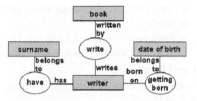

**Fig. 1.** Example of static KCPM schema.

When operationtypes can be executed concurrently and have the same preconditions, they are grouped within cooperationtypes. Conditions are used to structure dynamic KCPM schemata by defining sequential processes. Operations can only be executed if the preconditions of their cooperationtype are true. Postconditions apply after the operations of a cooperationtype have been executed. In this paper we focus on the integration of static KCPM schemata, though subsequent publications will deal with dynamic KCPM integration (see [15]).

Although the NIBA project focuses on the treatment of German texts, KCPM itself is language independent. Thus we prefer integration-techniques that are generic regarding the schemata and the language.

## 2.2 EM - The Karlstad Enterprise Modeling Approach

Karlstad Enterprise Modeling approach (EM) refers to a modeling approach developed to address the *pragmatic, semantic* and *syntactic* aspects of an IS or some part of it. EM focuses on defining and integrating the business processes of the organization in focus [14]. Another way of describing EM is as a generalization and extension of system analysis when modeling the three previously mentioned levels of an IS and database (DB) [6]. This means that EM takes a broader perspective than traditional modeling languages such as the Entity-Relationship (ER) model or some object-oriented method. However unlike schemata defined with traditional modeling languages the EM views are independent of implementation.

The pragmatic part is represented by a set of pragmatic dependencies used to illustrate goals, problems and opportunities. Besides these three both positive and negative influence dependencies can also be defined.

The semantic part is represented by a set of semantic dependencies which includes both a set of static and a set of dynamic dependencies. The static dependencies are used not only to define and illustrate what is stored in the database but also to illustrate the data that is needed by the IS. In EM every concept is illustrated as a box. This means that two concepts that have a dependency are illustrated by means of boxes with a special kind of dependency drawn between them. At the same time this means that while defining the static database views the only primitive that is given a name is a concept. The dynamic dependencies are divided into state and communication dependencies. Communication dependencies are used to illustrate relations between different actors and their actions and communication flows. State dependencies are used to illustrate state changes together with pre- and post-conditions for an action.

The syntactic part is represented by a set of syntactic primitives. It represents an implementation perspective and should be viewed as the CASE tool-dependent part for defining the future DB and IS.

Since this paper focuses on integration on static views the static dependencies used in EM are illustrated in Figure 2.

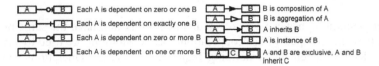

**Fig. 2.** Adapted and modified representation of static dependencies in EM [6].

The main idea behind EM is to define a consistent, coherent and complete specification of the future IS and DB [6] using the same schema type [7]. This is important since recent studies have indicated and proved that it is more confusing to have several schema types and switch between these than keeping them in one schema type [13].

Finally, it has also been argued that the use of the EM semantic dependencies simplifies the integration process and reduces the risk of semantic loss [3].

## 2.3 KCPM and EM – A Comparison

KCPM supports static modeling by providing exactly one relationship-type between two static concepts (the connection-type), while in EM nine (see Figure 2) different types of static relationships exist. The EM-relationship-types are not named, but when mapped to the respective KCPM connection-type they can all be represented by a distinct name. In KCPM entities and attributes are all represented as thingtypes and not distinguished, and in EM all concepts are also treated equally and illustrated as boxes.

Most current conceptual modeling languages allow no explicit modeling of business goals, but the EM-approach provides a set of explicit relationships for representing business goals, problems, influences and opportunities. KCPM on the other hand has currently no specific connectiontypes for this purpose, since it is kept as simple as possible. The representation of business goals may however be possible in future KCPM versions.

Despite the obvious differences KCPM and EM also have similarities. Both KCPM and EM are considered light-weight modeling approaches that abandon the inclusion of more complex design and implementation issues in their static schemata in favor of better end user understandability: they describe only the essential concepts and dependencies of a given domain. A mapping from static EM to KCPM schemata is definitely possible: all EM concepts are mapped to KCPM thingtypes, and all EM dependencies are mapped to KCPM connectiontypes that are given a fitting name. An exception would be the EM-dependency instance-of, since instances are not modeled as connectiontypes in KCPM but as a feature of thingtypes. The inverse mapping from static KCPM to EM schemata is trickier because static KCPM schemata may include connectiontypes described by agentive verbs which would be treated as actions in dynamic EM schemata. In KCPM such connectiontypes usually mean that an additional dynamic KCPM schema exists, that describes the respective operation in detail. Dynamic KCPM and EM schemata have common features: the state changes in EM correspond to operations that have pre- and post-conditions in KCPM. The actor-communication however can only be mapped to KCPM by explicitly defining a corresponding operation where the involved actors are modeled as executors or parameters.

Although having a different focus – EM is tailored for the modeling of enterprises and its processes while the main goal of KCPM consists of modeling requirements of IS – both KCPM and EM deal with similar integration conflicts. In the following chapters we present and compare the abilities of our approaches for linguistic conflict recognition and resolution, which should be generic regarding the modeling language, meaning they should also be adaptive to both modeling approaches.

# 3 Dealing with Linguistic Conflicts in KCPM and EM

## 3.1 The Concept Determination Method (CDM)

Automatic schema integration is still a largely unsolved problem. CDM (Figure 3) supports the partially automatic recognition and resolution of linguistic conflicts based on domain-specific ontologies. It was inspired by similar view integration attempts based on semantic dictionaries [11] and currently focuses on the integration of KCPM schemata.

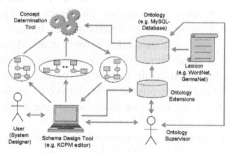

**Fig. 3.** The concept determination method (CDM).

We propose ontologies that contain the concepts of a particular domain, their semantic meaning and the relationships between them. A domain-independent base ontology can be used optionally to identify word similarities when the domain ontology yields no results. While domain ontologies are constructed gradually through projects, the base ontology is automatically extracted from a linguistic lexicon, e.g. WordNet. It therefore contains universal, non-specific word meanings and relationships.

CDM supports both schema generation and integration. Schema integration with CDM has the following steps: *synchronization with the domain ontology, reduction of the source schemata, concept name comparison, concept environment comparison, generation of integration proposals, integration of the source schemata, expansion of the integrated schema.*

In the first step the noun concepts of the source schemata are synchronized with the domain ontology in order to reduce linguistic conflicts by minimizing ambiguity. For all redundant concepts within one source schema, the user is asked to specify the respective meanings. Noun concepts that are hitherto unknown in the domain ontology are proposed for insertion in the ontology. These proposals have to be approved by ontology supervisors, who must possess comprehensive domain knowledge. The ontology quality would rapidly deteriorate if all new data would be incorporated, regardless of being correct and consistent for the domain. If the noun concept is already known in the ontology, a significance score for the noun in the domain ontology is calculated (based inter alia on concept features like being a composite or being a verb nominalization). If the significance score lies above a threshold value, the noun concept is immediately accepted, else the standard domain ontology meaning is proposed and the user is asked whether to accept it or not.

In the second step, the source schemata are reduced, in order to decrease their complexity. This is done by temporarily removing noun-concepts that are no central parts of the schema and therefore not relevant for integration, though they might bring forward naming conflicts if they were left in. In the case of KCPM, attribute candidates can be removed, which are identified based on KCPM-UML-mapping heuristics [9].

In the third step the noun concepts of the source schemata are compared by their names and the results interpreted as the similarity of the noun concepts themselves. Based on the ontology data matches, similarities and mismatches are identified and each concept is assigned similarity scores in regard to concepts of the other schema. Three results are possible, namely equivalence (i.e. the concepts have the same names or are definite synonyms according to the domain ontology), similarity (i.e. any other relationship is defined between the concepts in the domain or base ontologies, e.g. meronymy or hypernymy) or dissimilarity (i.e. there is no relationship defined between the concepts in the domain and base ontologies).

In the fourth step a checkup is performed that determines whether two noun concepts are really equal or similar. Thus their surroundings are compared, i.e. all relationships of the schemata were the controlled noun concepts are involved, plus the involved adjacent noun concepts. This is necessary since noun concepts with equal names might have different environments, which indicates homonyms. On the other hand concepts with different names but similar environments indicate synonyms. The environment comparison results in a reliability score for the similarity scores from step 3. If the compared noun concepts have the same environment, a lower familiarity of the connection verb concept indicates an even higher reliability of the similarity scores.

In the fifth CDM step the possible conflicts, their reliability and the resolution proposals are displayed and in the sixth step the identified linguistic conflicts can be manually resolved or an automatic resolution is attempted by the CDM tool based on the proposals. The following actions are proposed based on the comparison results:

- If the noun concepts are equal or definite synonyms, then they should be merged to one concept in the target schema.
- If a similarity exists between the noun concepts, then both should be transferred to the target schema and they should be connected by the appropriate similarity-relationship from the ontology.
- If the noun concepts are independent and no similarity exists, then they should both be transferred to the target schema but no new relationship is introduced.
- If the noun concepts have the same name but different meanings, then one of the names should be replaced with a synonym from the ontology or the concept should be renamed manually.

In the seventh CDM step, the reduction of the source schemata is reversed and the integrated schema is extended with the previously removed noun concepts. These are usually attached to their original neighbors. If a non-attribute-type noun concept with an equal name already exists in the integrated schema the concepts in its vicinity are inspected in order to decide whether the nouns concepts are equal.

CDM also supports creating new schemata from scratch, with the goal to reduce ambiguity and possible linguistic conflicts already in the schema creation phase, which leads to easier schema integration later on. Any new schema is synchronized with the domain ontology as described above.

Parts of the CDM tool have already been implemented as a prototype. English and German base ontologies were constructed as MySQL databases and automatically populated from the WordNet and GermaNet lexicons respectively. New KCPM schemata can be constructed with a graphical development and visualization tool [10], but no tools exists yet to support schema integration. The CDM prototype currently allows identifying semantic dependencies for nouns. The creation of domain ontologies and the implementation of further functionality of the CDM tool are currently in the works.

Since in requirements analysis based on linguistic techniques the results depend on the quality of the underlying texts, the University of Klagenfurt also researches a form based text processing approach in the context of dynamic KCPM schema creation and integration. The approach was inspired by [12] and demands structured sentences without unnecessary subordinate clauses. This poses an alternative to the non-formalized natural language texts from which KCPM schemata are usually generated, while improving the requirements text quality and allowing machine interpretation of the standardized texts without prohibiting their readability. The occurrence of linguistic conflicts is also reduced, particularly when CDM is used in order to prevent ambiguous concepts in the current domain. This in turn later facilitates partially automatic schema integration.

In the form based approach, only conditional and/or temporal sentences are supported, which follow the structure of IF-THEN clauses. The words "IF" and "THEN" are provided by the requirements-form and the user has to complete the sentences by building correct clauses. These sentences can be seen as procedural rules, where the IF-clause then represents pre-conditions for a succeeding action or activity and the THEN-clause describes the corresponding action. While this allows building chunks of pre-conditions and succeeding actions it doesn't solve the problem of relating these chunks. It must therefore be possible to mark certain actions' preconditions as other actions' post-conditions. The form based approach will be investigated and implemented in further research.

## 3.2 The Dependency Approach (DA)

DA was first developed for manual identification of homonym conflicts in view integration while applying the static dependencies of EM [2]. However, in this paper we extend DA in order to apply it also to manual identification of synonyms, hypernyms and hyponyms.

The first step in DA is the comparison of concept names from two views. If they are equal the connected concepts and dependencies are compared, because a homonym conflict actually hides two distinct concepts with different meanings behind one concept name. For instance two *Name* concepts were identified in figure 4 and DA moves on to study the dependencies between the identified concepts. In EM the homonym conflict is resolved by introducing the dot (".") notation [2]. This means that an additional concept is created and placed between the two original concepts (see *Customer.Name* and *Product.Name* in Figure 4). When introducing the new concept the dependencies between the concepts also change. The dot notation gives the concept a new name that includes its context and at the same time retains the original concept name.

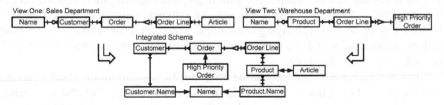

**Fig. 4.** Example of EM views and schema.

A synonym occurs if two or more concept names are used for one concept, a hypernym occurs if one concept name is defined as a generalization of another one and a hyponym occurs if one concept name is defined as a specialization of another concept. Identifying synonyms, hypernyms and hyponyms is a bit trickier than identifying homonyms and therefore external specifications, i.e. more information about the concepts, are needed. One way to gain information regarding a concept is to study their surroundings. This means that not only the concept names but also the dependencies between the concepts are studied in DA. Therefore one way to identify a synonym conflict is to identify a name match where the concepts are equal and then study the concepts' surroundings. In Figure 4 *Order Line* is used in both views and both concepts are equal. The next step is to study the dependencies of the *Order Line* concept. In view one we identify a surjective dependency (1,1; 1,*) between *Product* and *Order Line* and in view two we identify the same dependency between *Article* and *Order Line*. This dependency together with the different concept names (*Product* and *Article*) indicates a synonym conflict. In EM the synonym conflict is resolved by introducing the mutual inheritance dependency ("◄—►") [2][3]. This means that a new dependency is introduced and placed between concepts that are identified as synonyms (see *Product* and *Article* in Figure 4).

Sometimes two concepts from different views seem to be synonyms at first but upon studying them a bit closer differences between them can be identified. These differences can indicate another type of dependency between the concepts such as a hypernym and hyponym dependency. View one in Figure 4 contains the *Order* concept and view two the *High Priority Order* concept. Both concepts are connected to the *Order Line* concept in the views and if they are not analyzed deeply enough they might be marked and treated as synonyms. However, upon deeper analysis of the concept names it can be found that the *Order* concept is a more general concept than the *High Priority Order* concept which is a more specialized concept than *Order*. This also indicates that the *Order* concept should be viewed as a hypernym and the *High Priority Order* concept as a hyponym. Hypernym and hyponym dependencies are not really conflicts; instead they express that two concepts are related to each other by certain constraints. In EM the hypernym and hyponym dependencies are resolved by introducing the inheritance dependency ("◄—") between the two concepts [3]. In Figure 4 this resolution technique is illustrated by introducing the inheritance dependency between the *Order* and the *High Priority Order* concepts and connecting all other concepts to the *Order* concept which is the most general one.

In the integration example in Figure 4 there is no problem regarding the aggregation dependencies between view one and view two. However, it is important to note that this type of inter-schema property might in principle occur in and between other views. In Figure 4 the *Order* concept should be viewed as a holonym and the *Order Line* concept as a meronym. In EM the holonym and meronym dependencies are resolved by introducing the aggregation or composition dependency.

Finally, by applying the recognition and resolution techniques described above all concept names are retained. This is a strength of DA since otherwise the language used in the views or schemata can impoverish when several concept names are compressed into one [1]. Concept name compression has also been defined as "a state which may occur if several concept names are merged (compressed) into one concept name [...]" [3]. However, retaining all concept names at the same time means that an over-specification for the resolved name conflicts may still exist [4].

## 4 Conclusions and Future Work

In conceptual modeling there is a trend to offer increasingly powerful modeling methods. As their complexity increases, it gets harder however to identify inconsistencies and to verify that a schema is complete and coherent. KCPM and EM are two more light-weight modeling methods that both concentrate on describing domain concepts and their relationships rather than implementation and design details.

In this paper we first compared those modeling methods and indicated that view and schema integration is an important research topic for both approaches. When integrating user-near pre-design-schemata like KCPM or EM structural conflicts become less of an issue while linguistic conflicts are prevalent. We gave an overview about various generic methods that can be used to identify and resolve linguistic conflicts in light-weight-models. While CDM was presented for the first time, DA was extended to also be applicable for recognition of synonyms, hypernyms and hyponyms.

This paper has illustrated differences as well as commonalities and possible synergies between the KCPM and the EM integration approaches. Integration of EM models is currently done manually following DA, while CDM is currently researched, which allows automatic schema and view integration, but still includes user feedback in the integration process. Another difference is that CDM aims to provide a preferably general process for doing semi-automatic integration without specifying the source and target schema language and specific integration rules. DA on the other hand contains specific integration rules that describe how to identify and resolve semantic conflicts in EM. It is clear however that the domain-ontology-based semi-automatic integration proposed by CDM could be applied to EM also. For KCPM schema integration CDM could be extended by adapting integration rules of the EM approach. DA is a specific conflict recognition method that could replace steps 3 and 4 in CDM or be performed additionally to them. We plan to analyze these possible synergies in greater detail in future publications.

## References

1. Bellström P, Carlsson S (2004) Towards an understanding of the meaning and the contents of a database through design and reconstruction. In: Vasilecas O et al. (eds) Proceedings of ISD'2004, pp 283-293.
2. Bellström P (2005) Using Enterprise Modeling for identification and resolution of homonym conflicts in view integration. In: Vasilecas O et al.

(eds) Information Systems Development Advances in Theory, Practice and Education, Springer, pp 265-276.

3.  Bellström P (2006) View integration in conceptual database design – Problems, approaches and solutions. Licentiate thesis, Karlstad University Studies, 2006:5.

4.  Bellström P, Jakobsson L (2006) Towards a generic and integrated Enterprise Modeling approach to designing databases and software components. In: Nilsson A G et al. (eds) Advances in Information Systems Development Bridging the Gap between Academia and Industry, Springer, pp 635-646.

5.  Fliedl G, Kop C, Mayr H C, Mayerthaler W, Winkler C (2000) Linguistically based requirements engineering – The NIBA project. Data & Knowledge Engineering vol 35, pp 111-120.

6.  Gustas R, Gustiené P (2004) Towards the enterprise engineering approach for information system modelling across organisational and technical boundaries. In: Camp O et al. (eds) Enterprise Information Systems V, Kluwer Academic Publishers, Netherlands, pp 204-215.

7.  Gustas R, Jakobsson L (2004) Enterprise modelling of component oriented information system architectures. In: Fujita H, Gruhn V (eds) Proceedings of SoMeT_W04, IOS Press, pp 88-102.

8.  Gruber T R (1993) A translation approach to portable ontology specifications. Knowledge Acquisition vol 5, pp 199-220.

9.  Kop C, Mayr H C (1998) Conceptual predesign – Bridging the gap between requirements and conceptual design. In: Proceedings ICRE'98, pp 90-100.

10. Kop C, Vöhringer J, Hölbling M, Horn T, Irrasch C, Mayr H C (2005): Tool Supported Extraction of Behaviour Models. In Kaschek R et al. (eds) ISTA2005, GI Edition Lecture Notes in Informatics, pp 63-73.

11. Métais E, Kedad Z, Comyn-Wattiau I, Bouzeghoub M (1996) Implementation of a third generation view integration tool. In: Proceedings of 2nd International Workshop on Applications of Natural Language to Data Bases.

12. Rupp C (2004) Requirements Engineering und –Management, 3rd edition, Hanser, Vienna, pp 239ff

13. Turetken O at all (2004) Supporting systems analysis and design through Fisheye views. Communications of the ACM vol 47 no 9, pp 72-77.

14. Vernadat F B (1996) Enterprise modeling and integration principles and applications. Chapman & Hall, London.

15. Vöhringer J, Mayr H C (2006) Integration of schemas on the pre-conceptual level using the KCPM-approach. in: Nilsson A G et al. (eds) Advances in Information Systems Development Bridging the Gap between Academia and Industry, Springer, pp 623-634.

# Contextual Method Integration

Mauri Leppänen

Department of Computer Science and Information Systems, P.O. Box 35 (Agora), FI-40014 University of Jyväskylä, Finland, mauri@cs.jyu.fi

**Abstract:** Information systems development (ISD) methods are commonly engineered by integrating method components from existing methods into a new or a current methodical body. Finding suitable components and integrating them into a coherent, consistent and applicable ISD method requires that the purposes and conceptual contents of method components are described in a strict manner, typically through metamodeling. In this paper we present a contextual view of method component which, based on the contextual approach, expresses, more closely than earlier presentations, semantic features of those parts of an ISD context which are involved by method components. We also show, with a large example, how method integration can be carried out based on this contextual information of method components.

**Keywords:** method engineering, method component, method integration, contextual approach

## 1 Introduction

Despite the existence of numerous methods for information systems development (ISD) more methods, generic, organization-specific and project-specific, are continuously engineered. There are three main strategies of method engineering (ME): engineering "from scratch", engineering by adaptation, and engineering by integration. Here, our focus is on the latter. *Method integration* means an ME strategy according to which an ISD method is engineered by assembling components of existing methods.

Method components, or method fragments (e.g. [5]), may be models, such as the ER model, techniques, such as the normalization technique [1] and the use case technique [7], or structured conceptual constructs, such as generalization/ specialization structure [22]. Applying the integration strategy in a practical situation means that suitable and compatible method components are searched for and extracted from a method base, prepared for integration, and then integrated, streamlined and checked for coherence, consistence and applicability. To be successful, the purposes and contents of the method components should be described in a comprehensive and exact manner. Only this way, suitable method components can be identified and the process of integration can lead to the establishment of a coherent, consistent and applicable ISD method.

The ME literature suggests a variety of integration strategies and procedures with different conceptions of method components [24, 6, 25, 9, 23, 5, 21, 26, 13, 29, 8, 20, 27, 19]. Common to them is that the views reflected by method components about ISD are quite narrow-scoped. They only recognize features related to ISD deliverables (i.e. products [25, 5, 4], artifacts [24], data [29]) and ISD actions (i.e. processes [5, 4, 23], actions [24], activities [6, 25]). There are only a few presentations in which method components recognize ISD actors (Who is doing?), ISD purposes (Why is it done?), facilities, locations, etc. in ISD. The limitations in scopes and manners in which the conceptual contents of method components are described make it difficult to identify suitable components and to engineer a desired method by integration.

The purpose of this study is first to present, based on the contextual approach [14], a contextual view of a method component which brings out, in a more comprehensive and accurate manner than the current presentations do, features of those parts of ISD contexts which are to be supported by the method component. Second, our purpose is to describe, with a large example, the process by which the integration of this kind of method components can be carried out. This process of method engineering is called *contextual method integration*.

The rest of the paper is organized as follows. In Section 2 we define the notion of method component, present categories, elaborate the notion of contextual view of a method component, and derive a contextual interface of a method component. In Section 3 we describe three method components in meta models and show how they can integrated based on their contextual interfaces. The paper ends with a summary and conclusions.

# 2 Contextual Method Component

## 2.1 Method Component: Notion and Categories

Reuse is an essential objective towards which software engineering has strived for the last few decades. The most effective means to achieve this objective has been the construction of compatible components or modules that are general enough for reuse. The component-based paradigm has also been deployed as a means to construct ISD methods. A reusable part of a method is called a methodology component [11], a method component (e.g. [24, 4, 29, 27]), a method fragment (e.g. [5]), a method chunk [19], a building block [25], or a task package [6]. We prefer to use the term 'method component' and define it as follows: A *method component* means a well-defined part of a method that can be integrated to other ISD method components to form a meaningful, coherent and consistent ISD method. A method component is reusable if it is specifically developed for reuse (cf. [29]).

Method components can be classified according to several dimensions [14]. First, components may involve different ISD phases and ISD workflows [24, 29]. Second, method components may reside on different meta levels [29]. A code component, for instance, is on the type level, and so is the normalization technique [1]. The ER model specifying the concepts and constructs allowed in ER schemas is on the meta level. Some components may contain parts on more than one level. A data flow diagramming technique, for instance, comprises one part that prescribes ISD actions and ISD deliverables (i.e. the type level) and the other part that specifies the concepts and constructs allowed in the data flow diagrams (i.e. the meta level). Third, method components can be situated on various granularity levels [29, 5, 4, 23], such as the levels of method, stage, model, diagram, and concept [7]. Fourth, method components can be differentiated based on the contextual features they recognize in ISD. Commonly, method components recognize aspects of ISD actions and ISD deliverables, as mentioned in Section 1.

## 2.2 Contextual View of a Method Component

Based on a large literature review about the notion of context in several disciplines, such as knowledge representation and reasoning, pragmatics, computational linguistics, sociolinguistic, organizational theory and information systems, we have selected semantics (e.g. case grammar [3]), pragmatics [18], and activity theory [2] and defined, based on them, seven domains which serve concepts for specifying and interpreting contextual phenomena. These contextual domains are: purpose, actor, action, object, facility, location, and time. To structure the concepts within and between these domains, we have specified the Seven S's Scheme: *For Some* purpose, *Somebody* does *Something* for *Someone,* with *Some* means, *Sometimes* and *Somewhere.* According to the *contextual approach*, individual things in reality are seen to play specific roles in a certain context, and/or to be contexts themselves. The contexts can be decomposed into more elementary ones and related to one another through inter-context relationships.

We have previously applied the contextual approach to enterprises [15], information systems development [17] and method engineering [16]. Here, we apply it to the integration of ISD method components. Based on the contextual approach, we see *information system development* as a context in which ISD actors carry out ISD actions to produce ISD deliverables contributing to a renewed or a new IS, by means of ISD facilities, in a certain organizational and spatio-temporal context, in order to satisfy ISD stakeholders' needs. As seen from above, the notion provides an extensive view on the contextual aspects of ISD.

Implied from the above, we state that in order to be comprehensive an ISD method has to reflect, to a large extent, the contextual features of all the ISD domains. A method component concerns, naturally, only a fragment of the whole ISD context, but in order to ensure that the assembly of method components successfully forms a comprehensive and useful method, it is of high importance that the purpose and contents of the method components are described, in an comprehensive manner, about the fragments of the ISD context they refer to. We argue that applying the contextual approach to describing method components helps satisfy this requirement.

The application of the contextual approach to the method components benefits method integration in many ways. First, the concepts of method components can be classified according to the contextual domains. Second, based on the kinds of concepts included in the method components, we can categorize them into single-domain components and multi-domain components. Examples of the single-domain components are a goal model [12] (ISD purpose domain), a model of organizational structure (ISD actor domain), a normalization procedure [1] (ISD action domain) and a genre-based classification of ISD deliverables [28] (ISD object domain). The classifications of concepts and method components help finding and integrating method components. Third, the contextual domains can be used to define the interfaces of method components. We consider this in the next section.

## 2.3 Contextual Interface of Method Component

In software engineering (SE) a reusable component must have a well-defined interface. The interface shows the services the component provides for the other components and the services it demands from the other components. In the object-oriented paradigm the services are specified through operation signatures with parameters. Converting this directly into the contextual viewpoint it would mean that an interface is specified by concepts of the action domain (cf. operation call) and the object domain (cf. parameters). When the component-based paradigm has been applied in ME, this kind of conception has survived (cf. [9, 20]). Consequently, it is common to think that two method components can be integrated if one component receives a specific piece of data from the other component and conducts the next actions for the data in the pre-defined order (cf. [9]). Although this kind of conception is adequate in SE/ISD, and for technical artifacts, components in ME are much more multifaceted and require a more elaborated notion of interface.

Based on the contextual approach we argue that each of the seven contextual domains may be of importance to revealing the real nature and meaning of the interface of a method component. Therefore, we define the interface of a method component as follows: A *contextual interface* is a white-box like description of those contextual relationships through which a method component can be integrated with other method components. The contextual relationships are inter-domain relationships and/or intra-domain relationships. Figure 1 illustrates the contextual interface of a method component. The component C has the interface that is composed of seven 'threads'. Each of them specifies an important contextual relationship by which concepts of the method component should be connected to concepts of other method components.

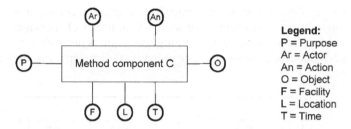

Fig. 1. Contextual interface of a method component

# 3 The Process and an Example of Contextual Method Integration

In this section we illustrate the notions of method component and contextual interface and demonstrate the importance of the contextual approach to the integration of method components. We consider three method components, two of which are modeling techniques (i.e. the use case technique and the sequence diagramming technique [7]), and one that is a description model (cf. the goal model adapted from [12]). These method components are selected because they are commonly known and suitable to the consideration of integration. Next, we first presents models of the method components, then discuss the nature and properties of them, and finally describe the process of integrating the components based on their contextual interfaces.

The *use case technique* is "a systematic and intuitive way to capture the functional requirements with particular focus on the value added to each individual user or to each external system" ([7], p. 131). Requirements capture in the use case technique produces two kinds of ISD deliverables: a glossary and a use case model. A *glossary* defines common terms used to describe a system. A *use case model* is a "model of a system containing actors and use cases and their relationships" ([7], p. 133). The use case model is composed of two parts: a use case diagram and use case descriptions. Because the technique contains the specification of a description model and prescriptions for how to make an instance of that model, the model of the technique consists of models at two levels (see Figure 2). The upper model, presented in a data flow diagram extended with ISD actors, prescribes the context in which an IS model is to be produced. The other models, called the IS meta data models, describe the concepts and constructs with which the use case model can be created. These are presented in UML. In Figure 2 the IS meta data model on the left side specifies the conceptual contents of a use case diagram. The IS meta data model on the right side specifies the conceptual contents of structured descriptions of use cases.

A *sequence diagram* describes interaction between the system and its actors, as well as interaction between the parts of the system [7]. An (human) actor interacts with the system by manipulating and/or reading interface objects. Interaction between the parts of the system occurs through sending and receiving messages. A sequence diagram emphasizes logical or temporal ordering of messages. The IS meta data model of the sequence diagramming technique is presented in the lower part of Figure 3. Sequence diagramming proceeds with the steps seen in the upper part of Figure 3.

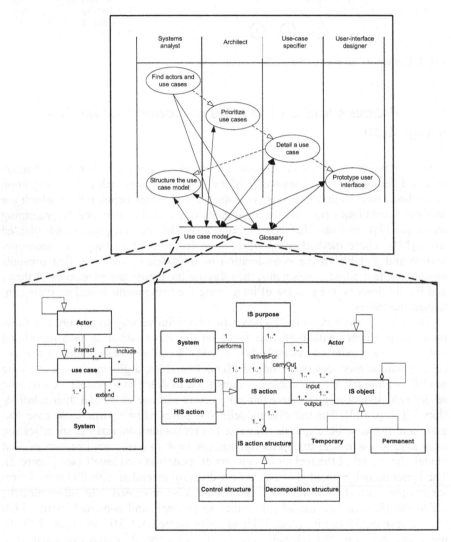

**Fig. 2.** Models of the use case technique

The *goal model* is a description model for conceiving, structuring, classifying and representing goals and relationships between them (cf. [12]) (see Figure 4). A

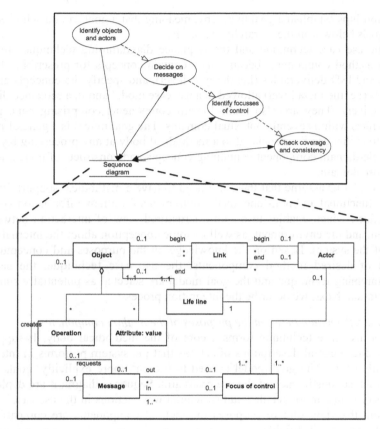

**Fig. 3.** Models of the sequence diagramming technique

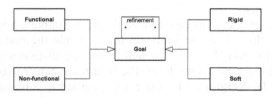

**Fig. 4.** Meta model of the goal model

goal is a required or desired state of affairs [10][1]. The goals are classified into rigid goals and soft goals, as well as into functional goals and non-functional goals [12], and interrelated through the refinement relationships. The refinement

---

[1] A goal is defined as in [10], because Lee et al. do not provide any definition for this notion.

relationships establish a goal hierarchy, meaning that a goal can be achieved when the goals below it in the hierarchy are reached.

The use case technique and the sequence diagramming technique are multi-level method components because they contain concepts for prescribing ISD actions and ISD deliverables (i.e. the type level), and specify the concepts and constructs (i.e. the meta level) allowed in a use case model and in a sequence diagram, respectively. They are also multi-domain components comprising concepts and constructs within several contextual domains. The goal model is a general-purpose construct that can be associated to a methodical body at any processing layer. It is a single-domain component containing concepts and constructs of none but the IS purpose domain.

Now, let us assume that there is a need to have a methodical support for specifying functional and non-functional requirements for a new information system in a manner, which enables to obtain a structured view of interaction between the system and the environment, as well as some conception about the internal behavior of the system. Based on the knowledge on the purposes and conceptual contents of desired method components, the use case technique, the sequence diagramming technique and the goal model are selected as potentially suitable to integration. Next, we describe the integration process:

- *Check the match between the purposes of the method components*
  The use case technique forms a core of the methodical body. It supports to produce general descriptions of actions that the system performs in interaction with actors. The goal model is used to present, more explicitly, goals toward which actions in each of the use cases aim. Sequence diagrams are deployed to specify, in a more detailed and structured way, actions in the use cases. Hence, from the viewpoint of purposes the method components are compatible and integration is justifiable.

- *Check the match between the presentation forms of the ISD deliverables in the method components*
  Use cases are presented in easy-to-read diagrams supported by descriptions in structured English. These presentation forms enable the understanding of the deliverables for non-IT-experts as well. Sequence diagrams and goal models are presented in a semi-formal form. The former are constructed and used by IS analysts and IS designers. The latter are specified to advance the discussion between users and IT-professionals. The variety of presentation forms used in the method components and their match with the skills and profiles of the intended ISD actors strengthen the view that the components are suitable for integration.

- *Relate the contents of the ISD deliverables in the method components*
  Based on the meta data models in Figures 2, 3 and 4, we can find counterparts in several IS domains: (a) an actor in the use case model roughly corresponds to an actor in the sequence diagram; (b) a system in the use case technique is decomposed into objects in the sequence diagram; (c) an IS action, or more specifically a computerized action, in the use case technique is realized by actions requested by messages in the sequence diagrams; (d) a computerized

action is composed of operations of one or more object; (e) a human action in the use case technique can be seen as a pro-action or reaction of a human actor in the sequence diagram; (f) an IS object in the use case technique is embedded into attributes of objects (cf. permanent IS objects) or transmitted via messages (cf. temporary IS objects); (g) purposes of the use cases can be made more explicit by relating the concept of a goal, and its sub-concepts and relationships, to the concepts of a use case. It is also possible to refine the use case diagram by defining one more specialization of goals yielding actor-specific goals and system-specific goals. Actor-specific goals are objectives of IS actors, and system-specific goals are requirements on services the system must provide. Relating the actor-specific goals to the IS actors enables to explicitly specify the goals of the actors of the system. To conclude, the three method components are highly inter-related also through concepts of several IS contextual domains.

- *Relate the ISD actions in the method components*
  There are many ways to structure and associate the actions of constructing use case models, sequence diagrams and goal models. Most commonly the actions are performed partly in parallel. For each use case it is considered whether it is useful to make one or more sequence diagrams. Especially in situations where textual descriptions are written about complex use cases, it may be beneficial to sketch, in parallel, sequence diagrams to find out what kinds of actions and events there actually are and an order in which they occur in the use case. The identification of objects and actors for sequence diagrams is based on the use case descriptions (see Figure 2). Checking the coverage and consistency of sequence diagrams is carried out by comparing them to the corresponding use case description(s). Working with the sequence diagrams increases the understanding of the textual descriptions of the use cases and may, in turn, cause changes in them. Likewise, goals and requirements related to use cases can be elaborated and structured with the concepts and constructs of the goal model.

- *Relate the ISD actors in the method components*
  The ISD actors are clearly defined in the use case technique (see Figure 2). In contrast, the sequence diagramming technique does not provide exact specifications of ISD actors. We can, however, assume that the ISD actors concerned are IS analysts and IS designers. Integration of these techniques for the part of ISD actors can now be done, either (a) by including the responsibility of making sequence diagrams in the role of the use-case specifier, or (b) maintaining the roles of IS analyst and IS designer and including the responsibilities of the use case specifier into the role of IS analyst.

The result of the integration of the three method components is presented in Figure 5. Due to the page limit it only covers the IS meta data models. Lines in bold show the original boundaries between the IS meta data models. Integration has been done through shared concepts (i.e. an actor) and by defining contextual relationships between concepts of the meta data models. The more relationships cross the boundaries, the more complicated is the way in which the interfaces of the method components are utilized in the integration. The use case technique and the sequence diagramming technique are integrated through four relationships: partOf (Object, System), partOf (Computerized action, Operation), isA (Message, Temporary IS object), and isA (Attribute:value, Permanent IS object). The goal model and the use case technique are integrated through four relationships: strivesFor (System, System-specific goal), strivesFor (Use case, Goal), strivesFor (Actor, Actor-specific goal), and partOf (IS purpose, Goal). The inter-related concepts represent five different contextual domains.

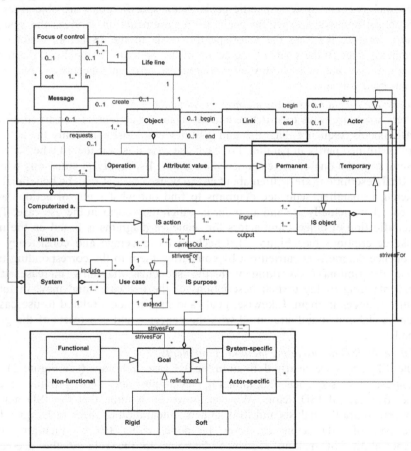

**Fig. 5.** Meta data model of the integrated method components

To conclude from the above: The method components can appear in various types, sizes and forms. Small components, such as the goal model, can be specified through a simple interface. But integration of larger method components must be based on the explicit specification and consideration of the conceptual contents and contextual interfaces. For instance, the ISD techniques considered above extend to two levels (i.e. the type level and the meta level) and to eight contextual domains (i.e. ISD actor domain, ISD action domain, ISD object domain, IS purpose domain, IS action domain, IS actor domain, IS object domain, and IS facility domain). An approach commonly suggested in the ME literature (e.g. [25, 5]) to manage the integration is to attach attributes as some kinds of "contextual properties" to the method components. This approach does not, however, provide specifications that would be detailed and structured enough to be matched with one another in the integration process. Our way of specifying contextual interfaces provides a natural and well-defined means to structure and realize those "attributes" and thus furthers the right interpretation of the nature and contents of the method components and the use of this knowledge in the method integration.

# 4 Summary and Conclusions

In this paper we have applied the contextual approach to define the notion, categories and contextual interface of a method component. According to the contextual approach, ISD is seen as a context in which ISD actors carry out ISD actions to produce ISD deliverables contributing to a renewed or a new IS, by means of ISD facilities, in a certain organizational and spatio-temporal context, in order to satisfy ISD stakeholders' needs. As a method component is a fragment of an ISD method, it should closely reflect features of those parts of the ISD context, which it is intended to support. In order to help finding and integrating method components these contextual features should be clearly expressed in the purposes and contents of the components.

We have also presented the process to carry out contextual method integration by modeling method components with contextual concepts and constructs, by searching for method components that fulfill generic and compatibility requirements, and finally by connecting the components to one another with intra-domain and inter-domain relationships. We have illustrated this process with the large example of three method components.

An ME is commonly experienced as extra work that unnecessarily burdens the budget of the ISD project. For this reason, there is a need to find means to accomplish ME work as systematically and efficiently as possible, preferably with the support of a CAME (Computer-Aided Method Engineering) tool (e.g. [5, 4]). To ensure the efficient use of such a tool it is necessary to describe ISD components in a semantically rich manner and carry out the process of integrating compatible components with steps that are based on these descriptions. We argue that the notion of contextual interface of a method component and the procedure of contextual integration help make the descriptions of method components richer and the process of integration more structured.

Our work differs favorably from the previous works in many ways. In most of the existing presentations views about the method components are narrow-scoped, simply referring to ISD actions and ISD deliverables. In only a few works ISD actors (e.g. through 'discipline' in [6]) and ISD purposes (e.g. through 'rationale' in [27]) are involved. None of the presentations provide a comprehensive view of the contextual features of the ISD context. Due to these limitations in the conceptual basis of method components, integration processes suggested involve only part of those features that affect the compatibility of method components.

In the research to come, we aim to elaborate our contextual concepts and constructs in order to enable semantically richer descriptions of methods, and parts thereof. In addition, we will specify in more detail the process of method integration such that some of the steps could be presented in algorithms for the future use of a CAME tool.

## References

1. Codd, E. 1972. Further normalization of the data base relational model. In R. Rustin (Ed.) Data Base Systems. Englewood Cliffs: Prentice-Hall, 33-64.
2. Engeström, Y. 1987. Learning by expanding: an activity theoretical approach to developmental research. Helsinki: Orienta-Konsultit.
3. Fillmore, C. 1968. The case for case. In E. Bach & R. T. Harms (Eds.) Universals in Linguistic Theory. New York: Holt, Rinehart and Winston, 1-88.
4. Gupta, D. & Prakash, N. 2001. Engineering methods from method requirements specifications. Requirements Engineering 6(3), 135-160.
5. Harmsen, F. 1997. Situational method engineering. University of Twente, Moret Ernst & Young Management Consultants, The Netherlands, Dissertation Thesis.
6. Hidding, G., Freund, G. & Joseph, J. 1993. Modeling large processes with task packages. In Proc. of Workshop on Modeling in the Large, AAAI Conference, Washington, DC.
7. Jacobson, I., Booch, G. & Rumbaugh, J. 1999. The Unified Software Development Process. Reading: Addison-Wesley.
8. Karlsson, F., Ågerfalk, P. & Hjalmarson, A. 2001. Method configuration with development tracks and generic project types. In J. Krogstie, K. Siau & T. Halpin (Eds.) Proc. of the 6th CAiSE/IFIP8.1 International Workshop on Evaluation of Modeling Methods in Systems Analysis and Design (EMMSAD'01).
9. Kinnunen, K. & Leppänen 1996. M., O/A matrix and a technique for methodology engineering. Journal of Systems and Software 33(2), 141-152.
10. Koubarakis, M. & Plexousakis, D. 2000. A formal model for business process modeling and design. In B. Wangler & L. Bergman (Eds.) Proc. of 12th Int. Conf. on Advanced Information Systems Engineering (CAiSE 2000). Berlin: Springer-Verlag, 142-156.
11. Kumar, K. & Welke, R. 1992. Methodology engineering: a proposal for situation specific methodology construction. In W. Kottermann & J. Senn (Eds.) Challenges and Strategies for Research in Systems Development. Chichester: John Wiley & Sons, 257-269.

12. Lee, J., Xue, N.-L. & Kuo, J.-Y. 2001. Structuring requirement specifications with goals. Information and Software Technology 43(2), 121-135.
13. Leppänen, M. 2000. Toward a method engineering (ME) method with an emphasis on the consistency of ISD methods. In K. Siau K. (Ed.) Proc. of the Fifth CAiSE/IFIP8.1 International Workshop on Evaluation of Modeling Methods in Systems Analysis and Design (EMMSAD'00).
14. Leppänen, M. 2005. An ontological framework and a methodical skeleton for method engineering. Ph.D. thesis, Jyväskylä Studies in Computing 52, University of Jyväskylä, Finland.
15. Leppänen, M. 2005. A context-based enterprise ontology. In G. Guizzardi & G. Wagner (Eds.) Proc. of Int. Workshop on Vocabularies, Ontologies, and Rules for the Enterprise (VORTE'05), Enschede, The Netherlands, 17-24.
16. Leppänen, M. 2005. Conceptual analysis of current ME artifacts in terms of coverage: A contextual approach. In J. Ralyté, Per Ågerfalk & N. Kraiem (Eds.) Proc. of the 1st Int. Workshop on Situational Requirements Engineering Processes (SREP'05), Paris, 75-90
17. Leppänen, M. 2006. Towards an Ontology for Information Systems Development. In J. Krogstie, T. Halpin & E. Proper (Eds.) Proc. of the 10th CAiSE/IFIP8.1 Workshop on Exploring Modeling Methods for Systems Analysis and Design (EMMSAD'06), Luxemburg, June 5-6, Presses Universitaires de Namur, 363-374.
18. Levinson, S. 1983. Pragmatics. London: Cambridge University Press.
19. Ralyté, J. 2004. Towards situational methods for information systems development: engineering reusable method chunks. In Proc. of the Int. Conf. on Information Systems Development (ISD'04), Vilnius, Lithuania, September 9-11, 271-282.
20. Ralyté, J., Deneckere, R. & Rolland, C. 2003. Towards a generic model for situational method engineering. In J. Eder & M. Missikoff (Eds.) Proc. of the 15th Int. Conf. on Advanced Information Systems Engineering (CAiSE'03). LNCS 2681, Berlin: Springer-Verlag, 95-110.
21. Saeki, M. 1998. A meta-model for method integration. Information and Software Technology 39(14), 925-932.
22. Smith, J. & Smith, D. 1977. Database abstraction: aggregation and generalization. ACM Trans. on Database Systems 2(2), 105-133.
23. Song, X. 1997. Systematic integration of design methods. IEEE Software 14(2), 107-117.
24. Song, X. & Osterweil, L. 1992. Towards objective, systematic design-method comparison. IEEE Software 9(3), 43-53.
25. Vlasblom, G., Rijsenbrij, D. & Glastra, M. 1995. Flexibilization of the methodology of system development. Information and Software Technology 37(11), 595-607.
26. Wieringa, R. & Dubois, E. 1998. Integrating semi-formal and formal software specification techniques. Information Systems 23(3/4), 159-178.
27. Wistrand, K. & Karlsson, F. 2004. Method components – rationale revealed. In A. Person & J. Stirna (Eds.) Proc. of the 16th Int. Conf. on

Advanced Information Systems Engineering (CAiSE'04). LNCS 3084, Berlin: Springer-Verlag, 189-201.

28. Yates, J. & Orlikowski, W. 1992. Genres of organizational communication: a structurational approach to studying communication and media. Academy of Management Review, Vol. 8, 299-326.

29. Zhang, Z. & Lyytinen, K. 2001. A framework for component reuse in a metamodelling-based software development. Requirements Engineering 6(2), 116-131.

# A Framework for Situational and Evolutionary Language Adaptation in Information Systems Development

Jörg Becker[*], Christian Janiesch[*], Stefan Seidel[*] and Christian Brelage[**]

[*] European Research Center for Information Systems, Leonardo-Campus 3, 48149 Münster, Germany
[**] SAP Research CEC Karlsruhe, Vincenz-Prießnitz-Str. 1, 76131 Karlsruhe, Germany

## 1 Introduction

Information systems (IS) are socio-technical, man-machine systems that are used to provide effective support for the management and coordination of information and communication while maintaining economical efficiency (cf. (Davis and Olsen 1985), similarly (Hirschheim et al. 1995; Checkland and Scholes 1999)). According to Hirschheim et al. (1995) IS development is a change process undertaken in object systems in a number of environments by a development group to achieve objectives. To facilitate the exchange of thoughts, opinions, and beliefs about the IS development process and its objectives, the development group constructs representation forms of the object system. Conceptual modeling is considered to be a suitable means for creating such representation forms (Frank 1999).

The design of these modeling languages has to precede any other phase of the IS development process to form a consistent picture of the subject matter and the objectives. Different domains and different purposes of modeling have to be regarded differently (Luoma et al. 2004; Becker et al. 2006), both on a more general as well as a project or company specific level (Harmsen 1997). The controlled adaptation of a more generic modeling language by the means of meta modeling seems to be a promising approach (Marttiin et al. 1995; Rossi et al. 2004). Hence, the research question is: What is the shape of a framework for situational and evolutionary language adaptation? Addressing our research objective, the research method chosen is that of conceptual and interpretive design research. Hence, we will provide logical arguments rather than empirical ones. However, our arguments will (where applicable) also refer to empirical research results.

The structure of the paper is as follows: In Section 2 we motivate why there is a need for meta modeling tools that facilitate modeling language adaptation. In Section 3 we elaborate on evolutionary language development as a major factor in the sophistication of modeling languages. We present a framework for situational and evolutionary modeling language adaptation as well as a suitable repository with means to define and adapt modeling languages. Accordingly, we present tool support based on the repository. The paper concludes with as summary and the ongoing research agenda for the development of the approach and prototype.

## 2 Meta Modeling in Information Systems Development

Conceptual models are language artifacts that are expressed by using a conceptual modeling language (Wand and Weber 2002). The modeling language itself can be modeled. A model of a language is a so-called language-based meta model (Oei et al. 1992; Strahringer 1996; Tolvanen 1998). It is obvious that language plays a crucial role in the IS development process in a twofold way.

First, a language (natural or artificial) is used by a development group in order to create representation forms of an object system (the system to be implemented or changed). The model is an instantiation of a modeling language. Second, the modeling language itself is an instantiation of a meta model depicted in a meta modeling language (Strahringer 1996; Holten 2003b). If the capabilities of the language are considered to be imprecise or in any other way unsuited, two alternatives are conceivable: the development of a new modeling language or the adaptation of an existing one.

An approach concerned with adaptations is called (situational) method engineering (cf. for instance (Odell 1996; Harmsen 1997; Brinkkemper et al. 1999), for an overview of related approaches cf. (Aydin et al. 2004)). Thus, modeling languages can be characterized to be rather specific (situational methods) or general in nature. There has been a strong tendency of researchers in the past to propose new modeling languages. This proliferation of modeling languages resulted in a bewildering variety of modeling languages which are often lacking a sound justification and scientific background. Oei et al. (1992) characterize this situation by coining the term YAMA syndrome (Yet Another Modeling Approach). Hence, some researchers argued that existing modeling approaches should be evaluated before new ones are proposed (cf. for instance (Wand et al. 1999; Wand and Weber 2002)).

As a consequence of this discussion, we argue that there is a permanent need for developing, adapting and abolishing modeling languages. The environment in which conceptual modeling takes place is in constant flux: Technologies, languages, social factors, and goals are changing permanently. Perception of reality is elusive and subject to the limitations of our languages, whether they are natural or artificial. Like natural languages, modeling languages are changed in an evolutionary process that constantly redefines, revokes, and recreates concepts that represent phenomena. A prominent example of evolutionary language development is the Entity-Relationship Model (ERM) language (Chen 1976) which was extended to the eERM (Smith and Smith 1977; Scheer 1998) and adapted to different applications (e.g. SERM (Sinz 1988) or ME/RM (Sapia et al. 1998)).

Consequently, modeling approaches have to change as well if they are supposed to serve as tools for achieving a mutual understanding. It is neither possible nor desirable to develop the "ultimate" modeling language. If, however, the necessity of developing and adapting modeling approaches is accepted, it becomes necessary to outline means which allow doing so in a sensible and understandable way. Two alternatives of adapting modeling languages can be distinguished. Firstly, the representational aspect of a language can be adapted for instance by using a different graphical representation but the same underlying grammar (Strahringer 1996). This adaptation does not change the linguistic means. Secondly, the grammar itself can be adapted which changes the language's capability to express phenomena, for instance by introducing new concepts.

Depending on the philosophical background, a radical redesign of modeling approaches or a smooth transition to another dialect can be desired (order versus conflict). We propose to change modeling approaches cautiously in order to avoid disorientation and confusion of modelers and model users. An approach to achieve this can be the usage of certain patterns. Patterns describe general structures that are used to model phenomena (e.g. hierarchies, graphs, tables, and sequences). If consistently applied, they can evoke a certain familiarity with a modeling language even if it is adapted.

In the following, we propose a framework for situational and evolutionary modeling language adaptation using meta modeling. Furthermore, we introduce a meta modeling tool that is particularly suited for modeling hierarchies. A general purpose meta case tool such as MetaEdit+ (Kelly et al. 2005) was not found to be suitable for this matter since the modeling of extensive hierarchies requires built-in model navigation and management features to efficiently access the models. A hierarchy is understood as a transitive, irreflexive, and asymmetric relationship of entities. It is represented as a connected directed acyclic graph with a designated initial (root-)node forming a tree structure. Hierarchies represent an inherent concept of abstraction and have been found to be intuitively understandable for users. Gordon (2000) argues that learning processes are dependent on prior knowledge. In a broader sense this means that cognition is hierarchical because the understanding of new knowledge often relies on the prior understanding of existing knowledge, thus, strengthening the statement above.

Common examples for hierarchies can be found among other sciences as e.g. biology, physics, mathematics, linguistics, ethics, and theology and are therefore part of a prospective user's general education. The Linnaean taxonomy, the order of living beings, in biology is a prominent example from other sciences.

The definition of hierarchical modeling languages is tool supported and considered to be a social process which is supposed to achieve a mutual understanding of the linguistic means that are necessary to create appropriate representation forms for the focal domain. Therefore, the primary purpose of the tool and the modeling languages created therein is the support of communication and domain analysis.

# 3 Towards Situational and Evolutionary Modeling Language Adaptation in IS Development

## 3.1 Framework for Situational and Evolutionary Modeling Language Adaptation

As stated above, a framework is needed that facilitates situational and evolutionary modeling language adaptation by using meta modeling. Most generic languages fail to provide sufficient support in a rapid changing environment. They need to undergo an evolutionary development process or fade away (for further justification cf. (Rossi et al. 2004)). Hence, we propose a framework that acknowledges the need for adaptable languages that supports both, the development of new conceptual languages and, more importantly, the adaptation of the existing languages within this evolutionary process.

Since we do not favor a YAMA approach, an existing *general purpose modeling language* is taken as a basis whenever possible. We believe that a certain familiarity with the core of the modeling language fosters the effective and efficient use of any adapted form thereof. This familiarity is achieved more easily with purpose-spanning and/or domain-spanning languages that are generally available. The language is adapted regarding the context and specific case in which it is to be utilized. There are basically two courses of action: Firstly, the representation can be changed. Secondly, the language's grammar can be adapted. Here, we propose to adapt both, representation and grammar. Furthermore, certain *patterns* can be chosen to facilitate the application of the language. The steps I. to V.b depict this process of modeling language adaptation. For an overview of the approach cf. Figure 1.

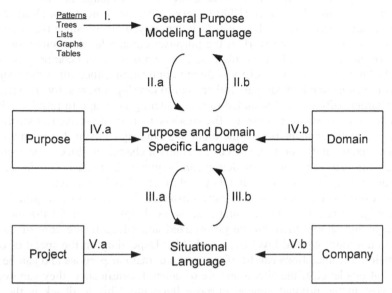

**Fig. 1.** Framework for Situational and Evolutionary Language Adaptation

If no suitable general purpose language is at hand, it has to be explored whether parts of existing modeling languages can be utilized to develop a new conceptual language. The concept of contexts (for the basics on this idea cf. the repository in the subsequent section) is an approach to aggregate and integrate meta model fragments of modeling languages to facilitate this task.

As mentioned before, in the example we focus on hierarchical structures (i.e. trees) as patterns that are found to be intuitively understandable for users (cf. Section 2). Thus, a choice would be to take into consideration only general purpose modeling languages that can be visualized in tree structures (I.). Depending on the situational context, the choice of other patterns might be sensible. The selection is not limited, combinations or no choice of patterns occur.

Following that the language of choice has to be adapted (II.a) regarding a particular purpose such as the development of data warehouse systems or web information systems (IV.a). New or altered language constructs and relationships may be necessary to ensure the proper fit. The requirements of data modeling e.g. are different to those of organizational modeling although both could be performed with the same general purpose modeling technique (Becker et al. 2006). In addition to that, the domain of interest has to be taken into account (IV.b): Users in a banking environment face a different set of issues/ areas of concern in comparison to users in retailing. The enrichment of modeling languages with domain knowledge facilitates a mutual understanding of the problem domain and fosters communication (Holten 2003a). This task in particular serves the socio-technical aspects of IS development. Summarizing, these two steps are necessary to ensure the fit to the requirements of a *purpose and domain specific language*.

For the application in a real world context, the language has to be adapted towards a *situational language* (III.a) to serve a certain project goal (V.a) respectively to suit the company where it is to be employed (V.b). Since the "one-size-fits-all" approach does not work at the purpose/ domain level, it surely does not work for the application in a specific case: Every project, every company is different (Aydin et al. 2004) as is every software application. Since often the project's aim is to set up standard software rather than to develop a new software, specifics of the target software can be added to the modeling language to provide a better basis for the subsequent reuse of the models in a model-driven environment. Moreover, with an adaptation of the modeling language – even if it is only of superficial nature and importance or covers solely a change in object type representation – the acceptance of the modeling can be greatly increased. The demands of the (future) users are picked up and they feel involved in the project.

The experience of how to overcome obstacles that arise only in practice, i.e. knowledge gained from project and case work, helps to improve the modeling language and should therefore be generalized and added to the core of the language on a more general level (III.b and II.b). Depending on the specifics of the adaptation, the alterations can be of use to the domain or purpose and can be integrated at this level. If the alterations are of general significance, they can even be integrated in the original general purpose language. This feedback is the main driver in the continuous and, thus, evolutionary improvement and sophistication of the general purpose modeling language.

Still, this framework can only provide hints to feasible procedures to ensure the proper fit of a modeling language to a specific problem situation. Not all of the steps have to be taken in this particular order. For example, it is possible to work with a domain-independent modeling language as well as to neglect company-specific issues to make the results comparable for other subsidiaries or for further applications like cross-company benchmarking. Besides, it has to be kept in mind is that evolution tends to be an unforeseeable process. Consequently, few to no estimation can be made on the frequency and/ or the quality of the adaptations although proper guidance of the process can prevent the oversight of beneficial change.

## 3.2 Repository of a Meta Modeling Software

To enable tool support for situational and evolutionary language adaptation a repository is needed that contains both language specifications and the actual models to allow for the adaptation of the meta models even during the modeling process (Bernstein 1997). Consequently, the repository consists of two parts. The first part represents a container to create language specifications (meta model) (Strahringer 1996). The second part represents actual models that are instances of a certain language which in turn are the models related to the real world.

A language consists of several elements called *ObjectTypeDefinitions*. These ObjectTypeDefinitions represent real world constructs. Between ObjectTypeDefinitions respectively their instances there are relationships. These are represented by *ContextRules*. Several ContextRules set up a so-called *Context*. A *LanguageDefinition* represents a modeling language and consists of several Contexts. Therefore, this part of the repository's schema can be seen as a language based meta meta model that describes the conceptual part of meta modeling languages used to define models of actual modeling languages. These models of modeling languages are meta models related to the real world.

The instances of ObjectTypeDefinitions are called *ObjectDefinitions*. ObjectDefinitions are part of a model and represent real world objects. Relationships between two ObjectDefinitions are represented by *ObjectOccurrences*. Any ObjectOccurrence is based on a certain ContextRule and is part of a *ContextInstance* (every root element in a Context including the subsequent sub tree make up a ContextInstance). Hence, the same ObjectTypeDefinition can have several relationships. Consequently, on instance level ObjectDefinitions can be part of several ContextInstances. Thus, different views on the same element can be expressed. It is possible to define rules concerning a Context's structure. These rules can either be related to the Context in general or to a *ContextInstanceGroup* that is a set of ContextInstances. ContextInstanceGroups have to be defined during the modeling of the instances. Properties for the groups can be defined.

Figure 2 shows an excerpt from the repository's data model discussed above in ERM notation. *AttributeTypes* and *Attributes* have been omitted for the sake of simplicity. They can be assigned to any shaded entity type or they can be modeled explicitly as an ObjectTypeDefinition. Other entity types that are left out include but are not limited to *HierarchyLevels* to further describe ObjectOccurrences, *EdgeTypes* to type edges (e.g. with cardinalities), *ConfigurationObjects* to create views of models, and *AccessObjects* for user administration.

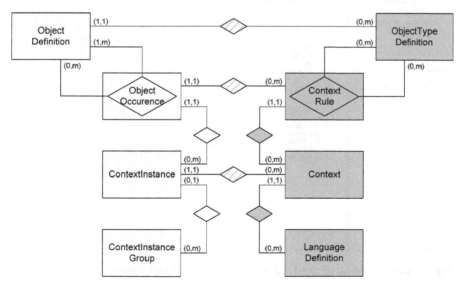

**Fig. 2.** Excerpt from the Repository's Schema

This repository is flexible enough to fulfill the requirements concerning situational and evolutionary language adaptation as stated above. Though the implementation of this repository that is presented in the subsequent section is focused on languages that describe models with hierarchical structures, generally, it can be used for other types of languages as well.

## 3.3 Prototypical Tool Support for Modeling Language Development and Adaptation

In the following, we introduce a prototypical implementation of the repository described above, the H2 Toolset. It allows for the definition of various modeling languages as well as for the actual modeling and management of models. H2 consists of a meta modeling editor, the so-called *language editor* to define modeling languages, an *attribute editor* to define attributes and attribute groups independently of the modeling constructs used, a so-called *hierarchy level editor* to define hierarchy levels that can be used to structure the trees created, and a *model editor* to create actual models in a particular language. The latter will not be covered here in more detail. For a screenshot of the toolset cf. Figure 3.

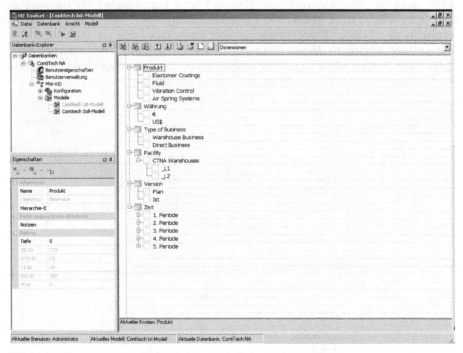

**Fig. 3.** Main Window of the Toolset with Opened Model Editor

The language editor consists of two main components. The *object type editor* allows for the definition of the language's object types. Each element type can be given a name, description, and a graphical representation. Previously defined attributes and attribute groups can be assigned. The *context editor* puts multiple object types into relation with each other and thus constructs different sets of rules that are part of a particular language. One such set of rules is called a context. Within each language multiple contexts can be created. Furthermore, one object type can be used in more than one context. While *CreateDefinition* rules enable the modeler to create new objects, *CreateOccurence* rules enable the modeler to create new occurrences of an existing object. There is a third type that is called *Create DefinitionExplicit*. Context rules of this kind trigger two actions. Not only a new occurrence of an existing object is created but also the relationships of the object's origin, i.e. the corresponding sub-tree, are copied. Attributes and attribute groups can be assigned to object types.

As mentioned above, besides the language editor with its components there is an attribute editor as well as a hierarchy level editor: The attribute editor provides an interface to define attribute names, attribute types and default values independently for object types, contexts, and context rules. Single attributes can be arranged in attribute groups. The hierarchy level editor provides a means to name levels in the hierarchical trees created with the defined languages in the model editor. Hence, hierarchy levels help to structure models and provide a means to facilitate navigation within the trees.

The development of modeling language specific modules, e.g. to transform models into an application specific exchange format that can be used to configure and set up standard software, as well as the integration of configuration mechanisms to create user specific views on models are currently being investigated.

# 4 Conclusion and Further Research

Following an interpretive design research approach we argued that conceptual modeling is an appropriate means in IS development. Any development process has to be preceded by a systematic reconstruction of the linguistic means. Since organizations and requirements vary and/or change over time, different needs for languages to develop IS exist. A smooth transition to another dialect is preferred rather than the invention of YAMA. Thus, we propose to change modeling approaches cautiously in order to avoid disorientation and confusion of modelers and model users alike. This process of adaptation is conducted on two levels: on a domain and purpose level and on a situational level that incorporates specific requests based on project and organizational issues. The process of language evolution proceeds in the reverse direction and enables the experiences made on the situational level to be included for domain languages as well general purpose languages.

The prototypical software is a specialized meta modeling toolset that allows for the definition of languages to construct hierarchical structures of elements. This particular pattern was identified to be easily understood by both, modelers and model users. Consequently, the software does not enable the modeler to create any possible modeling language. On the one hand this limits the scope of the tool to a certain group of languages. On the other hand it aims at supporting this group of languages by a meta modeling language that comprises different constructs such as Contexts and ContextRules. These concepts have been identified to be useful for the construction of these languages. A model editor enables the user to create and browse models consisting of hierarchical structures. Hence, the tool aims at finding a balance between the flexibility of general purpose concepts and specific features that support particular modeling domains.

Further immediate sophistication is necessary in defining a proper theory of contexts as well as the improvement of the general usability of the software. Language specific modules are a promising way to allow prospective users and especially prospective customers to see the benefit of a meta modeling solution that is able to adapt models to the changing needs of any organization as well as (semi-)automatically reuse them for system specification. Their design and implementation will be one of the next steps to follow up in the development of the toolset.

# References

Aydin MN, Harmsen F, Slooten van K, Stegwee R (2004) Appropriate Delivery of Advice and Guidance on Method Adaptation. 10th Americas Conference of Information Systems (AMCIS 2004), New York, pp 1675-1681.

Becker J, Kugeler M, Rosemann M (eds) (2006). Process Management: A Guide for the Design of Business Processes. Springer, Berlin, Heidelberg, New York. To Appear.

Bernstein PA (1997) Repositories and Object Oriented Databases. Datenbanksysteme in Büro, Technik und Wissenschaft (BTW 1997), Ulm, pp 34-46.

Brinkkemper S, Saeki M, Harmsen F (1999) Meta-modelling Based Assembly Techniques for Situational Method Engineering. Information Systems 24:209-228.

Checkland P, Scholes J (1999) Soft Systems Methodology in Action, Chichester.

Chen PP-S (1976) The Entity-Relationship Model. Toward a Unified View of Data. ACM Transactions on Database Systems (TODS) 1:9-36.

Davis GB, Olsen MH (1985) Management Information Systems - Conceptual Foundations, Structure, and Development, New York.

Frank U (1999) Conceptual Modelling as the Core of the Information Systems Discipline - Perspectives and Epistemological Challenges. 5th America's Conference on Information Systems (AMCIS 99), Milwaukee, pp 695-697.

Gordon JL (2000) Creating Knowledge Maps by Exploiting Dependent Relationships. Knowledge Based Systems 13:71-79.

Harmsen AF (1997) Situational Method Engineering. Dissertation, Utrecht.

Hirschheim R, Klein HK, Lyytinen K (1995) Information Systems Development and Data Modeling. Conceptual and Philosophical Foundations. Cambridge University Press, Cambridge.

Holten R (2003a) Integration von Informationssystemen - Theorie und Anwendung im Supply Chain Management. Habilitation, Münster.

Holten R (2003b) Specification of Management Views in Information Warehouse Projects. Information Systems 28:709-751.

Kelly S, Rossi M, Tolvanen J-P (2005) What is Needed in a MetaCASE Environment? Enterprise Modelling and Information Systems Architectures 1:25-35.

Luoma J, Kelly S, Tolvanen J-P (2004) Defining Domain-Specific Modeling Languages: Collected Experiences. 4th OOPSLA Workshop on Domain-Specific Modeling (DSM 2004), Vancouver, pp.

Marttiin P, Lyytinen K, Rossi M, Tahvanainen V-P, Smolander K, Tolvanen J-P (1995) Modeling Requirements for Future CASE: Modeling Issues and Architectural Consideration. Information Resources Management Journal 8:15-25.

Odell JJ (1996) A primer to method engineering. In: Brinkkemper S, Lyytinen K, Welke RJ (eds). Method engineering: Principles of method construction and tool support. London, Chapman & Hall, London, pp 1-7.

Oei JLH, van Hemmen JGT, Falkenberg ED, Brinkkemper S (1992) The Meta Model Hierarchy: A Framework for Information Systems Concepts and Techniques, University of Nijmegen Technical Report 92-17. Nijmegen.

Rossi M, Ramesh B, Lyytinen K, Tolvanen J-P (2004) Managing Evolutionary Method Engineering by Method Rationale. Journal of the Association for Information Systems 5:356-391.

Sapia C, Blaschka M, Höfling G, Dinter B (1998) Extending the E/R Model for the Multidimensional Paradigm. International Workshop on Data Warehouse and Data Mining (DWDM 1998), Singapore, pp 105-116.

Scheer A-W (1998) Wirtschaftsinformatik. Springer, Berlin.

Sinz EJ (1988) Das Strukturierte Entity-Relationship-Modell (SER-Modell). Angewandte Informatik 30:191-202.

Smith JM, Smith DCP (1977) Database Abstractions: Aggregation and Generalization. ACM Transactions on Database Systems (TODS) 2:105-133.

Strahringer S (1996) Metamodellierung als Instrument des Methodenvergleichs - Eine Evaluierung am Beispiel objektorientierter Analysemethoden. Dissertation. Shaker Verlag, Aachen.

Tolvanen J-P (1998) Incremental Method Engineering with Modeling Tools - Theoretical Principles and Empirical Evidence. Dissertation, Jyväskylä.

Wand Y, Storey VC, Weber R (1999) An Ontological Analysis of the Relationship Construct in Conceptual Modeling. ACM Transactions on Database Systems (TODS) 24:494-528.

Wand Y, Weber R (2002) Research Commentary: Information Systems and Conceptual Modeling - A Research Agenda. Information Systems Research 13:363-376.

# Towards Estimating Quality of Experience with Passive Bottleneck Detection Metrics

Pál Varga, Gergely Kún, Gábor Sey

*Department of Telecommunication and Media Informatics
Budapest University of Technology and Economics
Magyar tudósok körútja 2., Budapest, Hungary, H-1117
Tel/Fax: +36-1-463-3424/ +36-1-463-3107
E-mail: kun, pvarga@tmit.bme.hu
**Aitia International Inc., Czetz J. u. 48-50. Budapest, Hungary, H-1037
E-mail: gsey@aitia.ai

## 1 Introduction

Quality of Experience (QoE) metrics describe the service usability from the end-users' point of view. In a networking environment QoE metrics are very close to Quality of Service (QoS) metrics, except the fact that end-user experience is subjective in nature, moreover, it is also influenced by the access capabilities of end users and the used service path. Our ultimate aim is to find methods determining QoE by passive measurements on an aggregated network link. One step towards this is determining the correlation between network overload and QoE. There can be several scenarios where the experienced service quality becomes less than satisfactory.

The roughest QoE degradation is the unavailability of a service. This actually happens more regularly than one might expect. Examples of temporal and/or regular service-unavailability include an unsuccessful paying procedure at a webshop, a broken download, or a "webpage unreachable" message [1]. These cases are very hard to measure from a central site, since continuous application monitoring and data processing is not always feasible.

Another type of QoE violation is tied to network QoS, hence can be correlated with some kind of QoS metrics. Network-related QoE-degradation can manifest itself as extended response time, decreased download speed, less enjoyable audio and video streaming. This is usually caused by one or more network bottlenecks, where packets get congested, queued, then delayed or dropped. In this paper we describe our experimental results on correlating the severity of a network bottleneck and the experienced service quality.

There can be several link properties applied to characterize the presence of bottlenecks in packet data networks [2]. Since we carry out our measurements on aggregated links (rather than at the user's end terminal), we focus on packet level measures utilizing packet interarrival times, packet size information and packet loss information for their calculation.

## 2 Bottleneck metrics

Usually in a networked-service environment the overload of the network immediately causes QoE degradation. Traffic congestions appear at the bottlenecks, where the network is lack of some resources. Bottlenecks could be defined through a number of traffic-properties. Our paper considers a link as "bottleneck" where traversing packets experience continuous, severe queuing and even being dropped due to the finite queue-lengths that as a rule results in user satisfaction degradation.

In order to satisfy network users and achieve a high QoE in a network, all corresponding network parameters, such as loss, throughput limits, high utilization, significant delay, etc. should be interpreted end-to-end [3].

### 2.1 A metric on packet interarrival times

Monitoring passively a network link and capturing the packets with correct timestamps would give the operator plenty of data to analyze. One way to detect bottlenecks is to order the packets by their arriving time, and analyze their interarrival times. Our investigations showed that the $4^{th}$ central moment (kurtosis) of the packet interarrival times (PIT) probability distribution function (PDF) could provide valuable information about existence of bottlenecks and their severity [4].

The theory behind this observation is the following. In case a node aggregates numerous links with various capacities (and there are actually no queuing), the PIT PDF at that node should appear to be flat. This is due to the fact that packets are traveling on network links with absolutely random interrarrival times. Once the link gets busier, the relevant network node must queue some packets, and place them on the line right after the previous packet (back-to-back). The more of this queuing is applied, the less "flat" the PDF becomes: spikes starting to appear at the interarrival times where queued packets has followed each other back-to-back [5].

Generally it can be said, that if there is a narrow aggregated link on a path in front of that some queuing occurs, the shape of the PDF of interrival times of packets will suggest it: the PDF will have spike(s) at typical time values. There are a number of different queuing cases with corresponding PDF patterns are discussed in [5]. As a rule of the thumb we found that the examined link is congested if the first spike of the PDF is the highest, while the other lower spikes indicate queuing somewhere in front of that link. This kind of "spikeness" of the packet interarrival times PDF can be characterized by its 4$^{th}$ central moment (kurtosis). Our studies show that PIT kurtosis value is positive for traffic that crosses bottleneck links, and negative for traffic flowing with its own pace [6].

## 2.2 Delay factor calculus

The end-user often decides a network-service unusable if he/she experiences long delays.

By definition, delay factor (DF) could be calculated as the ratio of the *ideal* and the *measured* sojourn times ("traveling times") of a traffic flow that traversing on a network path. Delay factor, however, can be derived from the interarrival time of flows as well, with the help of M/G/R–PS arrival model. According to the model, the transmissions will be served by a number of servers (R), which could be derived in the following way R = [C/r$_{peak}$], where C is the capacity of the specific aggregated links, and r$_{peak}$ is the maximum transfer rate of the flows, determined by the access rates of the users. According to our assumptions and experiences (detailed in [7]), calculating the delay factor for one server (R=1) still gives satisfactory result. The calculation of the M/G/R-PS-based delay factor then could be simplified the following way:

$$f_R = 1 + \frac{E_2(R, R\rho)}{R(1-\rho)}\bigg|_{R=1} = 1 + \frac{\rho}{1-\rho} = \frac{1}{1-\rho}. \tag{1}$$

In Equation (1), $\rho$ stands for the link utilization of the measured link. This could be specially derived from the flow arrival rate ($\lambda_e$), the average flow size ($x_{mean}$), and the capacity (C) of that link: $\rho = (\lambda_e\, x_{mean})/C$.

According to original definition of delay factor in a non-congested situation the delay factor is around one (the ideal and the measured sojourn time is roughly equal), and reaches higher values if there is some congestion.

Our flows supporting delay factor estimation (DFest) share the following attributes [8]. Flows are identified merely by their source and target IP addresses, have a maximum size limit, furthermore have a limitation on the interarrival times of the packets they contain. Flows can be broken due to finished capture. Some flows started close to the end of the capture are not finished, hence usually undersized.

## 2.3 Loss based metric

Both users and network operators tend to think of packet loss as the ultimate QoS metric. This is not necessarily correct. Since packet loss for streaming services cannot be easily and correctly calculated at the core network, performance management systems usually log packet loss for elastic traffic (where entities are using acknowledgements e.g. with TCP) only. Packet loss in TCP, however, shows little correlation with the service quality, since TCP controls its throughput by minimizing the congestion window – until the packet loss falls into a range that TCP implementation is satisfied with. This means that the actual volume of the lost TCP packets under high congestion is similar to what is observed at normal traffic conditions. In [9] the authors describe various types of retransmissions, making clear that no all retransmissions are really caused by packet loss. They found that there can be applications where some retransmissions is caused by special types of errors (i.e. some radio channel misbehavior of GPRS networks may cause of spurious timeouts). This paper, however, also state that analyzing retransmission-volume can be useful when done in a focused way, but misleading when applied in general. We will demonstrate this effect when evaluating packet loss as a possible QoE metric.

## 2.4 Simple throughput calculation

Throughput of the users's access link may give valuable information about the provided networking service for applications such as ftp or peer-to-peer download. On an aggregated link, however, throughput looses its QoE-like informative nature, since the throughput of such a link is an accumulated value. Various uncontrollable factors – including link capacity, number of users, active service-requests, average packet size, application distribution and many more – influences throughput, which makes it unsuitable for being an absolute metric for QoE. Nevertheless, comparing throughput of various links at different times could provide information of the network status – which can be correlated with user satisfaction.

## 3 Methodology

Our aim is to correlate the end-user experience with measurable properties of the traffic. The metrics that correlate better with the end-user experience will be more effective QoE measures than the ones that do not show direct correlation. To reach this aim we had set up a configurable DSL-like environment in a segment of our university department, where the department staff was the suffering object of our QoE testing.

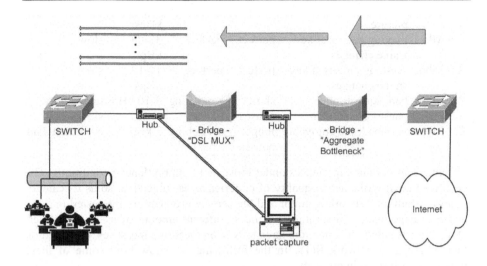

**Fig. 1.** Measurement architecture with marking the formation of download volumes after the two artificial bottlenecks

Altogether about 50 end-user machines were involved in the test. We have degraded the usual 100 Mbps Internet access to 1Mbps DSL-like lines. Moreover, we have introduced an artificial bottleneck for the department segment. Later this bottleneck was changed from 7 Mbps to 2.5 Mbps in six steps. To avoid loosing the users' nerve, the downgrade was not linear; sometimes we have upgraded the service – pretending as if it was going to be normal. We have allowed each of these bottleneck scenarios to last 30 minutes. During the tests we have captured the traffic at two measurement points, and made notes on our experiences as network application users. The measurement scenario is depicted by Figure 1.

## 4 Experiences and measurement results

We have extensively used various networking applications and services during the test. Applications included audio and video streaming, web-browsing, ftp and peer-to-peer downloads, Internet-telephony (Skype), database access and many more. Our experiences – in function of the bottleneck-severity – are as follows.

**Table 1.** Perceived quality of network services at different bottleneck scenarios

|  | Video stream | Audio stream | Skype | P2P traffic | Web browsing |
|---|---|---|---|---|---|
| 7.0 Mbps | perfect | perfect | perfect | 33-95 kBps | good |
| 5.0 Mbps | occasional squares in | perfect | perfect | 33-90 | good |

|  | picture |  |  | kBps |  |
|---|---|---|---|---|---|
| 4.5 Mbps | playing pauses at key-frame changes | perfect | perfect | 33-88 kBps | slow |
| 4.0 Mbps | sec-long pauses at key-frame changes | perfect | perfect | 12-14 kBps | slow |
| 3.5 Mbps | bad; squares and pauses are regular | short pauses | scratching | 3-10 kBps | unbearably slow |
| 2.5 Mbps | very bad; not enjoyable | longer pauses | scratching | 3 kBps | extremely bad |

Table 1 shows our experiences under loose and tight bottleneck conditions. The perceived quality (the actual quality of experience) is subjective, so as its categorization. Both the network operator and the service provider are interested in these end-user experiences. Since interviewing significant amount of users about their QoE is not feasible, the operators have to rely on QoS-like measures, collected on their aggregated network links. In the following we show how some of these measures performed in our tests.

## 4.1 Delay factor – to show how much the user has to be patient

In this section we present the results of two network-performance parameters: the delay factor (DF) and the measured throughput. Delay factor was calculated as we described in Section "Delay factor calculus", while measured throughput was derived by the packet level information. Each, approximately 30 minutes long measurement periods were chopped into 180 seconds long intervals for which the two parameters were calculated for. Figure 2 and Figure 3 depict our results. On the horizontal axes the elapsed time can be seen continuously. Since the changes between different scenarios took a few minutes (during which the packet capture had been stopped), there are some gaps in the processed results – which can clearly be identified in the graphs.

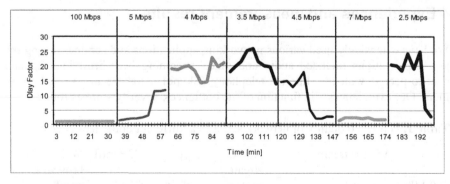

**Fig. 2.** Delay factor values in function of elapsed time

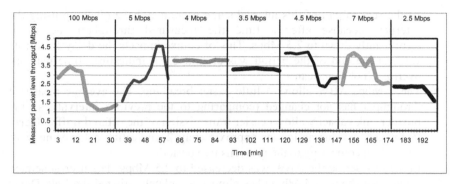

**Fig. 3.** Measured throughput level (in Mbps) in function of elapsed time

In Figure 2, delay factor values are presented at specific bottleneck scenarios in function of elapsed time through the seven scenarios. Figure 3 depicts the measured throughput - generated by users - during the same time intervals as delay factor was calculated for. Considering the results the following deductions can be made:

1. 100 Mbps Available Bandwidth (ABW) – in this scenario there were no bandwidth restrictions. This measure was taken to get to know the properties of traffic under normal conditions. The delay factor was a very little higher than 1 (maximum of 1.04) – indicating no congestions on the examined link. Checking the measured throughput properties at the same interval in Figure 3 shows that the user-generated aggregated traffic volume has not exceeded even the volume of 4 Mbps.
2. Next, the available bandwidth was diminished as far as 5 Mbps. Although it was a huge jump, the delay factor has not changed significantly at the first part of this period (2.2 on average). In the second part of the interval the throughput exceeds 4.5 Mbps, which causes an increased delay factor value up to 11. Although this value generally should be considered as a congested situation, in this case there was very little service quality degradation perceptible from the users' view.
3. At 4 Mbps ABW the network link was working at around its maximum: the packet level throughput was about 3.8 Mbps. At this point the web browsing response time was significantly higher then previously, and also the throughput of P2P traffic had decreased. Delay factor values now fluctuate between 22.6 and 14.3, indicating a severe bottleneck.
4. Decreasing the ABW down to 3.5 Mbps caused transferring errors for all kind of examined applications. Delay factor reflects the congested situation properly: it reaches its highest value at 25.9 during the whole measurement. The user-generated throughput (at packet level!) was 95% of the physical link bandwidth.
5. At this point the ABW increased by 1 Mbps to help the users regenerate their traffic a little. As Figure 3 shows, the user-generated throughput immediately jumped up to 4.2 Mbps, but the DF has decreased down to 14.8.

At the second part of this interval some users may have given up using the Internet, because after a time the measured throughput decreased significantly down to 2.5 Mbps. This of course impacts the delay factor: its value at the end of the period was around 2.5 – indicating some network overload (not significant).

6. The 7 Mbps ABW allows a little easier breathing. The average measured throughput has not changed (comparing to the previous interval), so the broader link capacity allows easier transmission of the offered traffic. Delay factor gets a value as low as approximately 2, indicating a lower network congestion comparing to the previous two periods.

7. In the last period the ABW was decreased to 2.5 Mbps. The user-generated throughput (being 2.4 Mbps) has almost completely utilized the link. Delay factor exceeded values as high as 24.8, again. In this scenario the network was actually halted, all the network applications had stopped. After a while users has stopped trying to reach any network service, thus at the end of the period the measured throughput broke down, causing the delay factor dropping down to 5.5, then 2.8.

We can conclude that DF is significantly higher for cases when the end-user was dissatisfied; hence DF is an informative QoE metric.

## 4.2 Analysis of cumulated traffic properties

This section provides some aggregated measurement results on the same captured traffic that was analyzed in the previous part of the paper. Figure 4 depicts the results, calculated for each of the seven scenarios described previously. The horizontal axes in the graphs show the ABW for the seven scenarios, while the vertical axes are the values of the specific metrics.

Figure 4.a presents the measured throughput in Mbps, calculated as the ratio of the sum of the transferred bits and the length of the whole measurement interval. According to this graph we can assume that in the first two cases the network link was underutilized (below 50%) – of course this average hides the occasional higher throughput values. This metric alone cannot be used for determining end-to-end QoE, however, it is a good complementary metric to make the other suggested metrics more accurate.

The packet loss ratio (PLR) for the whole measurement is shown by Figure 4.b. As in our previous works [2] we have found that the calculation of an average packet loss ratio cannot reflect the severity of the congestions. In the presented real case the relative PLR was the highest when the link was least of all used (100 Mbps ABW). A weak correlation can be noticed between PLR and the degree of congestion at ABW values of 4.5-2.5 Mbps, although the lower value of PLR at 4.5 and 4 compared to PLR value at 5 cannot be explained.

The average delay factor values are presented in Figure 4.c. The metric reflects properly the degree of congestion almost in all cases (100 to 3.5), but at 2.5 Mbps ABW the relatively lower average delay factor values does not show the real situation: actually the network was halted. This forced the users to give up using the Internet – causing the drop of DF. We have already analyzed this metric in the previous section.

Average PIT kurtosis values for specific ABW scenarios are depicted by Figure 4.d. As we described in [4], PIT kurtosis should be below zero in uncongested situations, while positive values suggest certain heavy loads. As one could expect the lower the ABWs are, the higher the kurtosis values become. The metric suggests properly the more and more congested situations, showing positive correlation with the service quality experienced by the users. Nevertheless in the last three scenarios there could be no data presented because the artificial bottleneck realization (CBQ queuing method in a Linux-based bridge) biased the shape of the PIT PDF, which led to false kurtosis values.

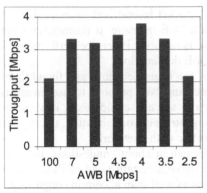

**a.** Measured throughput

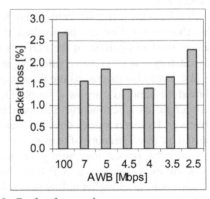

**b.** Packet loss ratio

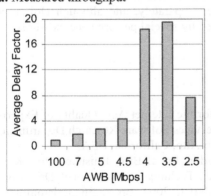

**c.** Average delay factor

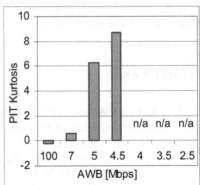

**d.** Average PIT kurtosis

**Fig. 4.** Average of bottleneck metrics for the whole measurement period

## 5 Conclusion

This paper investigated network performance metrics and aimed to correlate these with the end-users perception of network-service quality – the so-called Quality of Experience. Our standpoint is that the metrics used for detecting bottlenecks are able to reflect QoE as well. In order to prove our ideas we presented a number of measurement scenarios in real network with looser and tighter bottleneck conditions.

Delay factor – as a QoE metric – calculates the network utilization from the packet interarrival times and the packet sizes, based on the M/G/R Processor Sharing arrival model. Our method works on packet-level data and provides a delay factor value between one and infinity, suggesting more and more severe network congestion.

PIT kurtosis – the 4th central moment of packet interarrival times probability distribution function can be handled also as a QoE measure. It characterizes certain peakedness-pattern of the PDF; its value is negative if service performance is satisfactory, but its positive values suggest QoE degradation.

We have also discussed the throughput of the examined links and found that it should be handled only as a simple QoS measure. We propose to use measured throughput as a secondary, informative metric, since it could easily mislead the observer. Its lower values does not mean congested network situation, usually it is caused by lower amount of user-generated traffic in the network.

Similarly, packet loss ratio gives no information about congestions. In a network environment active TCP flows always have a certain level of PLR, and its values could even higher at low network loads as well than at certain congestion.

The presented measurement results reflected clearly, that the QoS and QoE network service parameters should handled separately, and although QoE is a genuine subjective metric, it can be estimated by special performance measures.

## References

1.  Aad van Moorsel (2001) Metrics for the Internet Age: Quality of Experience and Quality of Business. E-Services Software Research Department, Hewlett-Packard Laboratories, Palo Alto, California, USA.
2.  Pál Varga, Gergely Kún, Péter Fodor, József Bíró, Daisuke Satoh, Keisuke Ishibashi (2003) An Advanced Technique on Bottleneck Detection. Proc IFIP WG6.3 workshop, EUNICE 2003, pp 52-56, Balatonfüred, Hungary.
3.  Yoshihiro Ito, Shuji Tasaka, Yoshihiko Fukuta (2004) Psychometric Analysis of the Effect of End–to–End Delay on User–Level QoS in Live Audio-Video Transmission. Proc the ACM Workshop on Next-Generation Residential Broadband Challenges (NRBC'04), pp 2-10, New york, NY, USA.

4.  Pál Varga (2005) Analyzing Packet Interarrival Times Distribution to Detect Network Bottlenecks. Proc IFIP WG6.3 workshop, EUNICE 2005, Balatonfüred, Hungary.
5.  Dina Katabi, Charles Blake (2002) Inferring congestion sharing and path characteristics from packet interarrival times. In Technical Report MIT-LCS-TR-828, MIT.
6.  Pál Varga, Gergely Kún (2005) Utilizing Higher Order Statistics of Packet Interarrival Times for Bottleneck Detection. In IFIP/IEEE E2EMON'05, Nice, France.
7.  L. Kleinrock, (1975) Queuing systems, volume 1: Theory. John Wiley and Sons, Inc., ISBN 963 10 2725 2.
8.  Gergely Kún, Pál Varga (2006) Utilizing MGR-PS model properties for bottleneck characterization, Proc WTC2006, Budapest, Hungary.
9.  Francesco Vacirca, Thomas Ziegler, Eduard Hasenleithner (2006) An Algorithm to Detect TCP Spurious Timeouts and its Application to Operational UMTS/GPRS Networks. Journal of Computer Networks, Elsevier.

# Socio-Technical Perspectives on Design Science in IS Research

Jörg Becker, Björn Niehaves, Christian Janiesch

European Research Center for Information Systems, Leonardo-Campus 3, 48149 Münster, Germany

## 1 Introduction

In information systems (IS) research major problems are discussed in literature, often regarded as crucial for the identity and existence of the discipline itself (Benbasat and Zmud 2003). Lee (2000) summarizes and describes major dilemmas that the IS discipline is confronted with:

*Rigor vs. relevance.* The rigor vs. relevance debate had strong impact on the discourse in the discipline and is a long way from being solved (cf. Darke et al. 1998; Applegate and King 1999; Benbasat and Zmud 1999; Lyytinen 1999; Markus and Davenport 1999; Benbasat and Zmud 2003) while the angles of the dilemma can be simplified as: a) 'Rigorous research has not produced relevant outputs' versus b) 'Relevant research has not been carried out in a rigorous way' (Lee 2000). This means that, on the one hand, some researchers claim to conduct relevant research, while others argue that it lacks scientific rigor in terms of, for instance, generalizability or traceability. On the other hand, some researchers claim to conduct rigorous research, while others argue, for instance, that this research would address trivialities and the knowledge gained would be too marginal to have an impact, especially on IS practice.

*Reference discipline vs. independent discipline.* A major issue affecting the field is the discussion whether the IS discipline is an independent discipline or not (cf. Keen 1980; Banville and Landry 1989; Galliers 1997; Benbasat and Zmud 2003). While referring to other disciplines as reference discipline would undercut the IS identity, however, a clear set of expectations and blueprints which would be a prerequisite for being an independent discipline is not available yet (Lee 2000). In consequence, an ongoing effort on defining the core properties of the IS discipline can be observed (Benbasat and Zmud 2003).

*Technology vs. behavior.* The discussion of technology vs. behavior is closely connected to the discussion of IS being an independent discipline. Lee (2000)

argues about the dilemma as follows: If a just technology-oriented approach would be taken, IS would be not different from the engineering or computer science discipline, a solely behavioral approach would make IS not different from other behavioral fields, such as sociology or psychology (Hevner et al. 2004).

These dilemmas have strongly affected the discussion in the IS discipline. In accordance to Lee (2000) we argue that particular concepts which are already known to the IS field can very well address the problems mentioned above. Most importantly these concepts are:

*Systems thinking.* System theory has long been known and applied to IS studies (Churchman 1979; Beer 1985; Checkland and Scholes 1990). It foremost provides the means to identify, to render, to analyze, and (preferably) to change a phenomenon of interest, i.e. a *system*. The system perspective allows to define systems and sub-systems as well as to analyze interrelationships between them. Here, especially the socio-technical approach emphasizes that information systems comprise behavioral sub-systems, for instance people or culture, as well as technological sub-systems, for instance hardware or software (cf. Bostrom and Heinen 1977; Mumford and Weir 1979; Walls et al. 1992; Heller 1997; Markus and Davenport 1999). Thus, focusing on socio-technical systems can very well render the IS discipline independent from related disciplines which focus on either one of the sub-systems (cf. reference vs. independent discipline). Socio-technical system thinking also suggests that a prerequisite for successfully studying IS is to address behavior and technology in unison (cf. technology vs. behavior). While Lee (2000) argues that the systems approach itself is rigorous and relevant, we emphasize that focusing on the relevant system – the social and the technical sub-system – is a necessary precondition for conducting relevant research (cf. rigor vs. relevance). Hence, socio-technical system thinking provides a valuable perception of the phenomenon of interest, information systems, also with regard to the major problems the IS discipline is facing.

*Design science.* Several research endeavors have been undertaken in order to conceptualize design science (Simon 1981) in IS research (cf. Boland 1989; Nunamaker et al. 1991; Walls et al. 1992; March and Smith 1995; Rossi and Sein 2003; Hevner et al. 2004). While a research process can comprise diverse stages (Mingers 2001), understanding and acting being major categories, design science focuses on the latter being a "problem solving paradigm" (Hevner et al. 2004). The complementing "problem understanding paradigm" is often referred to as natural science or behavioral science (Simon 1981; March and Smith 1995; Hevner et al. 2004). Design science focuses on problem solving, which, undoubtedly, is a shared perspective with IS practice (cf. relevance). However, literature provides us with particular guidelines how to conduct and to evaluate design science in IS research (Hevner et al. 2004). While it is argued that behavioral and design science are two complementary views on IS research (March and Smith 1995; Hevner et al. 2004), this interconnection provides a perspective for differentiating the IS discipline from either only behavioral or only design oriented disciplines (cf. reference vs. independent discipline).

It becomes clear that the concepts of system thinking as well as design science are vital to the IS discipline. However, an integrated view, especially from the design science perspective, is not yet to be found to a sufficient extent. Though several efforts were made in order to theorize design science (cf. Nunamaker et al. 1991; Walls et al. 1992; March and Smith 1995; Lee 2000; Hevner et al. 2004) an explicit socio-technical stance has not yet been taken. Here, we can observe a significant shortcoming in understanding the concept of design science with regard to socio-technical concerns. The shortcomings also become obvious regarding the debate on IT artifacts (Weber 1987; Walls et al. 1992; March and Smith 1995; Orlikowski and Iacono 2001; Weber 2003; Hevner et al. 2004). Often the goal of design science is described as "creating new and innovative IT artifacts" (Hevner et al. 2004) which implicitly contrasts to an integrated design of behavioral and technical sub-systems. Therefore, we seek to address the following research question within this paper: *How does the concept of design science in IS research and how does the understanding of IT artifacts alter when taking an explicit socio-technical stance?*

Addressing our research objective, the research method chosen is that of conceptual/philosophical research, in particular that of critique (in the Kantian understanding). This research method is dedicated to identifying, scrutinizing, and questioning the presuppositions of research approaches in order to determine their scope, applicability, possibilities, and limits towards a given research objective (Kant, 1929). We will hence provide philosophical-logical arguments rather than empirical ones. However, our arguments will (where applicable) also refer to empirical research results. Furthermore, we will present additional evidence by giving examples of socio-technical design science.

## 2 Design Science and Information Systems Research

A widely used logic to systematize distinct IS research approaches is the differentiation between behavioral science research (BSR), also referred to as natural science, and design science research (DSR) (March and Smith 1995; Hevner et al. 2004). DSR has its roots in engineering and other applied sciences. An important foundation is *"The Sciences of the Artificial"* (Simon 1981) which has been taken up and further developed (Nunamaker et al. 1991; March and Smith 1995; Rossi and Sein 2003; Hevner et al. 2004). Here, the design science approach has consecutively become more IT-specific, meaning that what is supposed to be the core of the discipline. While it was first associated with, for instance, the schools of engineering, architecture, and medicine (Simon 1981) in the IS field the object of design is argued to be information technology (IT) in terms of IT artifacts (cf. Figure 1).

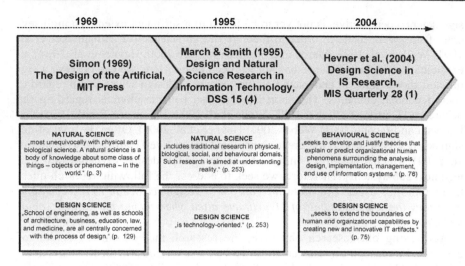

**Fig. 1.** Development of Design Science Thinking in IS

While, following the IS research-specific approach (March and Smith 1995; Hevner et al. 2004), behavioral science is primarily focusing on development and justification of theories on human-computer-interaction, design science seeks to create IT artifacts intended to solve existing problems. The former is called a *problem understanding paradigm*, the latter is titled as *problem solving paradigm* (Hevner et al. 2004). Therefore, the primary aim of behavioral science is to produce 'true knowledge' while design science seeks to take this knowledge into account building IT artifacts.

Moreover, behavioral science and design science are understood as two complementary parts of IS research (March and Smith 1995; Hevner et al. 2004). Acquiring knowledge about IS employed in an organizational context requires the application of both research paradigms: Starting from pre-scientific observation of IS usage in practice, theories about IS-related issues are developed by behavioral researchers (cf. Figure 2).

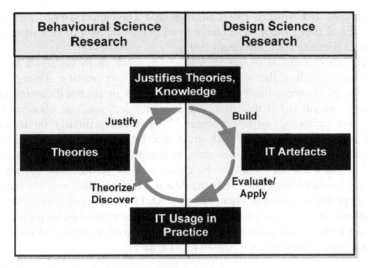

**Fig. 2.** Information Systems Research Cycle

Behavioral science theories are supposed to primarily explain and predict human behavior, information system function, and issues interrelated with both of these aspects. By justification, these theories are considered to be true or valid. Thus, they provide a basic understanding of the (real world) problem situation described as a primer. This understanding then presents the basis for designing one or more IT artifact(s) which address(es) a given problem situation. By actually applying them, IT artifacts are supposed to become useful in terms of problem solving. Thus, they change present IS usage in practice and, for that reason, provide new impulses for theory development. As a consequence, IS research is a process which comprises both behavioral science as well as design science (March and Smith 1995; Hevner et al. 2004). Thus, these two approaches are not only commensurable; they are calling for each other (Niehaves 2005).

# 3 Socio-Technical Reflection of Design Science

System theory is fundamental to the field of information systems (IS), not only reflecting in its name. It has long been known and applied to IS studies (cf. Churchman 1979; Beer 1985; Checkland and Scholes 1990). System theory primarily provides the means to identify, to render, to analyze, and to change a phenomenon of interest, i. e. a *system*. At this juncture, socio-technical approaches emphasize that IS comprise behavioral sub-systems, for instance people or culture, as well as technological sub-systems, for instance hardware or software (Bostrom and Heinen 1977; Mumford and Weir 1979; Heller 1997; Markus and Davenport 1999). Within this socio-technical context, also the political nature of information systems implementation becomes highly important (Hirschheim and Newman

1991; Knights and Murray 1994; Markus and Davenport 1999). Furthermore, socio-technical design approaches have been discussed as a branch of critical research in IS (Brooke 2002; McGrath 2005).

The current discussion of design science research in IS reveals a significant shortcoming regarding the socio-technical design perspective. Though Hevner et al. (2004, p. 77) argue that "technology and behavior are not dichotomous in an information system [, but that] they are inseparable," one can observe a strong emphasis on technology-oriented design. "We focus primarily on technology-based design although we note with great interest the current exploration of organizations, policies, and work practices as design artifacts" (Hevner et al. 2004, pp. 77-78). As a consequence, the perception of an information system design process is a two-step approach: first, one designs an IT artifact and, second, this IT artifact is applied in a certain organization. "An IT artifact [is] implemented in an organizational context" (Hevner et al. 2004). For that reason, behavioral science is understood to take into account organizational as well as technical issues, while design is foremost technology-oriented (cf. Table 1).

**Table 1.** Behavioral vs. Design Science: System in Focus

|  | Information Technology | Organization |
|---|---|---|
| Behavioral Science Research | BSR studies "organizational human phenomena surrounding the analysis, design, implementation, management, and use of information systems" (Hevner et al. 2004) | |
| Design Science Research | "We focus primarily on technology-based design" (Hevner et al. 2004) | --- |

It is legitimate that the authors focus their research approach. However, we argue that, according to the socio-technical approach, the purely technology-oriented perspective on design science only provides an incomplete perspective on the topic (Bostrom and Heinen 1977). Also from a theoretical perspective, a solely technology-oriented understanding of design science is questionable. While BSR analyses organization and technology, design science creates (only) technology. Regarding this presentation of thoughts, the question arises, if designing organizations and especially designing organizations and technology integratedly would or would not be a part of IS research. Consequently, we consider the socio-technical viewpoint on design science research as a further contribution to the stream of thoughts of design science. We understand this as a special focus which, however, is crucial for a successful design of information systems.

# 4 IT Artifacts and Socio-Technical Design

The processes of DSR are inextricably connected to IT artifacts: Both form the noun and verb of design science (Walls et al. 1992). It is therefore necessary to consider both, the research cycle as well as its output.

Theorizing the IT artifact has been a major research effort in recent years. Emphasis has been laid – desperately so to speak – on the conceptualization of the creation itself, its relation to theory and on rigor and relevance in and of the design. IT artifacts are "things that serve human purposes" (March and Smith 1995) or more casually spoken are "those bundles of material and cultural properties packaged in some socially recognizable from such as hardware and/or software" (Orlikowski and Iacono 2001). As mentioned, the process steps of *artifact creation* and *artifact evaluation* are commonly associated with the design of the IT artifact (Hevner et al. 2004). However, further steps have been proposed: *need identification, learning, theorizing* (Walls et al. 1992; Rossi and Sein 2003). This supports the notion of IS research described in the previous section(s).

According to March and Smith (1995) and Hevner et al. (2004), IT artifacts are of four types: constructs, models, methods, and instantiations. Constructs are the vocabulary of a domain, a specialized language and shared knowledge of a discipline or sub-discipline. Models are a set of propositions or statements expressing relationships among constructs. Methods are goal directed plans for manipulating constructs so that the solution statement model is realized. Instantiations (also implementations) operationalize constructs, models, and methods resulting in specific products.

March and Smith (1995) observe that IT artifacts serve human purposes, that they have utility and value, and that they are perishable. Orlikowski and Iacono (2001) extend this list by arguing that artifacts are not natural, neutral, universal or given but shaped by interests, values, and assumptions. They are embedded in time, place, discourse, and community, made up of components which require bridging and integration. They are not fixed or independent but emerge from social and economic practices and are not static or unchanging but dynamic.

Combining and integrating the above, the following can be summarized about IT artifacts: They are not of monolithical design. IT artifacts contain other IT artifacts. They are either loosely coupled or tightly integrated but nevertheless there is more to it than just one element. IT artifacts are commonly divided into aspects of knowledge, i.e. constructs, models, and methods, into instantiations or situated implementations that then are objects of the real world. IT artifacts have certain capabilities which can be divided into managerial, methodological, and technological aspects (Benbasat and Zmud 2003). Similarly the practices in the design process of artifacts can be considered to be of managerial, methodological or operational character (whereas design in this case does include planning, constructing, and implementing the artifact). Furthermore, an IT artifact is always the product of its time. Cf. Figure 3 for an overview of these key facets.

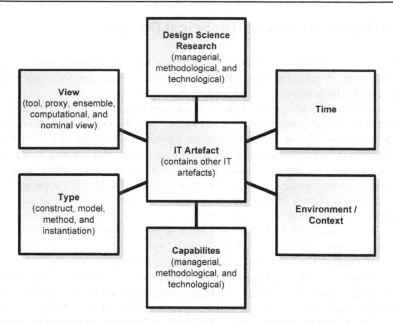

**Fig. 3.** Facets of the IT Artifact

Definitions of the IT artifact's relevant environment or context differ greatly: The context can be as mathematical as the dependent variable and as abstract as simply structures (Orlikowski and Iacono 2001). Hevner et al. (2004) state that the organizational context is of importance only to the behavioral aspect of IS research and thus neglects the necessity of explicitly incorporating the context into design science. Thus, people or parts of organizations are not understood as parts of IT artifacts since the capabilities of any artifact are regarded as the crucial aspect of design science.

IT artifacts, however, are intended to solve organizational problems. Any situated implementation can only function properly when embedded in its social context. Furthermore, a common understanding of the constructs, models, methods and instantiations used has to be reached. As (Fischer et al. 1995) argue different stakeholders perceive objects differently. Thus, a common socio-technical ground has to be found or rather founded. The explicit consideration of this common ground either has to be part of the process of artifact creation or has to be established before the artifact is placed into the application context. Walls et al. (1992) argue that the processes of design are inextricably entwined with the artifact itself supporting the first point. We argue that all (change) processes concerning the IT artifact are part of the matrix concerned with socio-technical IT artifact design and, thus, have to be taken into consideration explicitly.

To operationalize our findings we provide a comprehensive example in the following section. We utilize the Architecture of Integrated Information Systems (ARIS) (Scheer 2000) to support our argumentation.

## 5 Socio-Technical Design and Business Reengineering

As new software is to be introduced, a work group is redesigned. By means of roles, organizational units, and hierarchies (*constructs*) organigrams (*method*) are created. These models depict the to-be state of the work group (*model*). Its implementation is a new structure of work in the work group (*instantiation*).

An early step in the design of this new software is to select a technique for the conceptual specification of the final artifact. Thus, a modeling language – a *method* – has to be chosen. At this point UML is a common choice but to better illustrate our point we select the Event-Driven Process Chain (EPC) of the ARIS framework to focus on the modeling of the processes that are to be carried out by the software. The core *constructs* that are used are functions and events. The result of the modeling is an EPC *model* depicting the control flow of the new software. The final implementation of these control flows is the *instantiation*. Its capabilities may be efficient and effective given the technological perspective but without the integration of the organizational perspective its efficacy is hardly given.

Utilizing an integrated socio-technical perspective it is possible to design organizations and IS concurrently so that both designs are not at cross-purposes. The Architecture of Integrated Information Systems (ARIS) is an example of a framework that offers researchers and practitioners the possibility to model in an integrated socio-technical perspective. All *constructs* mentioned in the above (functions, events, organizational units, roles, and hierarchies) can be combined in an integrated modeling technique (*method*) that is called the Extended Event-driven-Process Chain (eEPC). In this way it is possible to link the organizational as well as the technical *models* so that an integrated understanding and design of a to-be specification of the IS is possible. The final result, i.e. the *instantiation*, is an aligned software and structure of work and/ or organization that incorporates both, organizational as well as technological aspects of IS development and, thus, fosters a more efficacious system application. Cf. Table 2 for an overview of the different IT artifacts created.

**Table 2.** Distinct Perspectives on Design Science

| Design Science Artifact | Technological/ IT Perspective | Organizational Perspective | Integrated Socio-Technical Perspective |
|---|---|---|---|
| Overall Aim | Designing IT/ systems | Designing Organizations | Integrated design of organizations and IS |
| 1. Construct | Functions, events etc. | Org. units and hierarchies etc. | Functions, events, organizational units, and hierarchies etc. |
| 2. Method | EPC | Organigram Modeling | eEPC |
| 3. Model | EPC model (control flow) | Organigram (To-be model) | To-be eEPC model: control flow, business flow, and org. responsibilities |
| 4. Instantiation | Software | (New) structure of work | Aligned software and structure of work |

# 6 Conclusions

The concepts of system thinking as well as design science and natural/ behavioral science are vital to the IS discipline. However, an integrated view, especially from the DSR perspective, is not yet to be found to a sufficient extent. This shortcoming is especially present in the discussion about IT artifacts as their design primarily focuses on technological capabilities.

As a starting point we identified BSR and DSR as two complementary parts of IS research. IS research is a process or rather a cyclic action which comprises both behavioral science as well as design science. Based on this understanding, the analysis of socio-technical design revealed that the organizational perspective in design science is not properly aligned. These findings were underpinned by the analysis of the IT artifact as the central construct in design science: The inclusion of context was not found to be ample to the task. The explicit utilization of an integrated socio-technical design provides a sophisticated means allowing the consideration of further organizational factors to improve to the design and application in research and practice. An example based on the ARIS framework underpins this conclusion.

# References

Applegate LM, King JL (1999) Rigor and relevance: careers on the line. MIS Quarterly 23:17-18.

Banville C, Landry M (1989) Can the Field of MIS Be Disciplined? Communications of the ACM 32:48-60.

Beer S (1985) Diagnosing the System for Organizations. Wiley, Chichester.

Benbasat I, Zmud RW (1999) Empirical Research in Information Systems: The Practice of Relevance. MIS Quarterly 23:3-16.

Benbasat I, Zmud RW (2003) The Identity Crisis Within the IS Discipline: Defining and Communicating the Discipline's Core Properties. MIS Quarterly 27:183-194.

Boland R (1989) The Experience of System Design: A Hermeneutic of Organizational Action. Scandinavian Journal of Management 5:87-104.

Bostrom R, Heinen JS (1977) MIS Problems and Failures: A Socio-Technical Perspective. MIS Quarterly 3.

Brooke C (2002) Critical Perspectives on Information Systems: An Impression of the Research Landscape. Journal of Information Technology 17:271-283.

Checkland P, Scholes J (1990) Soft Systems Methodologies in Action. Wiley, Chichester, U.K.

Churchman CW (1979) The Systems Approach. Dell, New York/NY.

Darke P, Shanks G, Broadbent M (1998) Successfully completing case study research: combining rigour, relevance and pragmatism. Information Systems Journal 8:273-289.

Fischer G, Nakakoji K, Ostwaldl J (1995) Supporting the evolution of design artifacts with representations of context and intent. Symposium on Designing Interactive Systems archive: Conference on Designing Interactive Systems: Processes, Practices, Methods & Techniques (DIS 1995), Ann Arbor, MI, pp 7-15.

Galliers RD (1997) Reflections on Information Systems research: twelve points of debate. In: Mingers J, Stowell F (eds). Information Systems Research: An Emerging Discipline. London, pp 141-157.

Heller F (1997) Sociotechnology and the Environment. Human Relations 50:605-624.

Hevner AR, March TS, Park J, Sudha R (2004) Design Science in Information Systems Research. MIS Quarterly 28:75-105.

Hirschheim R, Newman M (1991) Symbolism and information systems development: Myth, metaphor and magic. Information Systems Research 2:29-62.

Keen PGW (1980) MIS Research: Reference Disciplines and a Cumulative Tradition. Proceedings of the First International Conference on Information Systems. Philadelphia/PA, pp 9-18.

Knights D, Murray F (1994) Managers Divided. Wiley, Chichester.

Lee AS (2000) Systems Thinking, Design Science, and Paradigms. Heeding Three Lessons from the Past to Resolve Three Dilemmas in the Present to Direkt a Trajectory for Future Research in the Information Systems Field (Keynote Speech). 11th International Conference on Information Management, Kaohsiung, Taiwan.

Lyytinen K (1999) Empirical Research in Information Systems: On the Relevance of Practice in Thinking of IS Research. MIS Quarterly 23:25-28.

March TS, Smith G (1995) Design and Natural Science Research on Information Technology. Decision Support Systems 15:251-266.

Markus ML, Davenport TH (1999) Rigor vs. Relevance Revisited: Response to Benbasat and Zmud. MIS Quarterly 23:19-23.

McGrath K (2005) Doing Critical Research in Information Systems: A Case of Theory and Practice Not Informing Each Other. Information Systems Journal 15:85-101.

Mingers J (2001) Combining IS research methods: towards a pluralist methodology. Information Systems Research 12:240-259.

Mumford E, Weir M (1979) Computer Systems in Work Design - The ETHICS Method. Associated Business Press, London, UK.

Niehaves B (2005) Epistemological Perspectives on Pluralist IS Research. 13th European Conference on Information Systems (ECIS 2005), Regensburg, Germany.

Nunamaker JF, Chen M, Purdin TDM (1991) Systems Development in Information Systems Research. Journal of Management Information Systems 7:89-106.

Orlikowski WJ, Iacono CS (2001) Research Commentary: Desperately Seeking the "IT" in IT Research - A Call to Theorizing the IT Artifact. Information Systems Research 12:121-134.

Rossi M, Sein M (2003) Design Research Workshop: A Proactive Research Approach. IRIS 2003, Helsinki, Finland.

Scheer A-W (2000) ARIS - Business Process Modeling Springer-Verlag, Berlin.

Simon H (1981) The Sciences of the Artificial. MIT Press, Cambridge, MA.

Walls J, Widmeyer G, El Sawy O (1992) Building an Information System Design Theory for Vigilant EIS. Information Systems Research 3:36-59.

Weber R (1987) Toward a Theory of Artifacts: A Paradigmatic Basis for Information Systems Research. Journal of Information Systems 1:3-19.

Weber R (2003) Still Desperately Seeking the IT Artifact. MIS Quarterly 27:iii-xi.

# Modeling Objects Dynamics in Conceptual Models

Vaclav Repa

Department of Information Technologies, University of Economics,
W.Churchill sqr. 4, 130 67 Prague 3, Czech Republic,
repa@vse.cz

**Abstract:** The paper discusses the problem of dynamics in conceptual models. The paper argues for the idea that also the conceptual elements of the reality should be viewable dynamically – as a process. Such view is the way to understanding the basic process constrains of the Real World, which is critically important for the correctness of business processes design.Two basic types of dynamics in the Real World are discussed – internal dynamics of objects on one hand (their life-cycles) and their behavior on the other hand (business processes). Possibilities of modeling object life-cycles are analyzed specifically regarding the UML. The rules for mutual consistency of different objects life cycles are defined with the use of the structural coherency rules according to the theory of M.A. Jackson.

## 1 Introduction

This paper discusses the problem of dynamics in conceptual models.

Conceptual model is traditionally regarded as a static image of the reality. In such a view the dynamics of the Real World seems to be an exclusive matter of the process modeling. This paper argues for the idea that also the conceptual elements of the reality should be viewable dynamically – as a process. Such process is really conceptual one, and as such it is substantially different from which ones called "business processes". The paper also argues for the idea that such view is very important for understanding the conceptual substance of the Real World – it is the way to understanding the basic process constrains of the Real World which is critically important for the correctness of business processes design.

The paper is organized, except of this Introduction, into the four main chapters.

In chapter "Conceptual modeling in the OO age" the nature of the conceptual modeling is discussed with specific respect to the object-oriented paradigm.

In chapter "Modeling Object Life Cycles with UML" the possibilities of modeling objects dynamics in the UML are analyzed. As the structural view on the process is very important in this case, together with the absence of this view in the UML, the differences between State Chart versus Structure Diagram are discussed in detail.

Chapter "Mutual consistency of objects life cycles" contains definition of the rules for mutual consistency of different objects life cycles. The basis for these rules are structural coherency rules expressed by M.A. Jackson in [Jackson 1975].

Chapter "Consequences and conclusions" foreshadows some important contextual topics in the area of information systems development as well as in the area of business processes analysis and modeling.

## 2 Conceptual modeling in the OO age

The concept "conceptual" has been first used in the area of data modeling. It expresses the fact that the database should describe the essential characteristics of the Real World: objects and their mutual relationships. This origin is still visible in common understanding of the adjective "conceptual" in the sense of modeling with the UML:

Object-oriented analysis and design materials written by Craig Larman for ObjectSpace describe conceptual modeling such as:

- Classes represent concepts from the real-world domain.
- Binary associations describe relationships between two concepts.
- The concepts can have attributes but no operations.

Cris Kobryn [Kobryn 2000], Co-Chair UML Revision Task Force, takes conceptual model into the account speaking about "Structural Model" as a view of a system that emphasizes the structure of objects, including their classifiers, relationships, attributes and operations. The purpose of such a model is to show the static structure of the system.

- the entities that exist,
- internal structure,
- relationship to other entities.

Roni Weisman [Weisman 1999] from Softera also speaks about the "conceptual system model". He distinguishes three types of objects:

- Entity (object which hold the system's data)
- Boundary Object (interface objects which directly interact with the external world - actors)
- Control Object (objects which manage the system operations)

As visible from previous paragraphs, there are several approaches to the conceptual modeling in the area of object-oriented methods. Each of them reduces the Object Model (represented by the Class Diagram) to the model of objects and relationships between them, represented by their attributes, but not by their methods. This reduction is present also in Roni Weisman's approach (see above) even if he regards besides "Entities" also "Control Object". Just the fact of distinguishing between "static" and "dynamics ensuring" objects is the best demonstration of such a reduction. The common understanding of the term "conceptual" thus tends to the synonym for "static".

However such an approach contrasts with the basic principle, and the main contribution, of the object-oriented paradigm – unity of data and operations. This principle evokes the idea that it is necessary to model not only static aspects of the Real World but also its dynamics. The existence of the object as the collection of data (attributes) and functions (methods) is to be the right reason for data processing operations control (strictly speaking: the object life cycle) - see Figure 6 at the end of this article.

Regarding the conceptual point of view together with principles of object orientation it is impossible to take the object's methods just as a heap of procedures usable for communication with other objects. It is necessary to find the deeper (conceptual) sense of them as a whole (the substance of their synergy). Such a conceptual meaning of the object's methods is represented by the object life cycle.

Figure 6 illustrates the object life cycle as a complement to the Class Diagram. The object life cycle is described in the structural manner by the tool called Structure Diagram, which is explained in more detail in section 2.2 of this paper. It is visible that all methods of the conceptual object should be ordered into one algorithm which describes for each method its place in the overall process of the object's life. This placement of the method defines the conceptual meaning of it. In this sense it is obviously absurd to take into the account such methods as "give_list" or "send_status" as well as it is absurd to speak about "sending messages" between objects (discussion between the Order and the Goods in this example). Such a point of view is suitable for the model of objects in a program system but in case of conceptual objects it is obviously improper.

## 2.1 Dynamics of objects versus Real World behavior

The last paragraph argues for recognizing the dynamics inside the conceptual model. The problem of dynamics in the Real World model is usually closely connected with the phenomenon of business processes. Hence the model of business processes is usually regarded as the only significant description of the Real World dynamics. Consequently the conceptual model is usually regarded as clearly static description of the Real World. Another extreme opinion regards the Class Diagram as the sufficient tool for business process description and reduces the natural need for describing the process dynamics to the description of the business processes global attributes, and relationships among them (the standard UML profile for BP modeling, for example).

Experience shows that above stated opinions inadmissibly reduce the substance of the problem of the Real World dynamics and finally lead to the incorrect conclusions.

Figure 1 describes two main dimensions of the Real World model:

- the <u>structure</u> of the Real World (the view on the Real World as a set of objects and their relationships),
- the <u>behavior</u> of the Real World (the view on the Real World as a set mutually connected business processes).

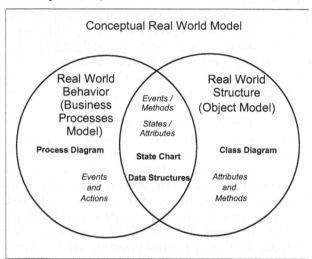

**Fig. 1.** Two Types of Real World Dynamics

At the figure it is clearly visible that the concept of "behavior" cannot be regarded as a synonym to the "dynamics". Both dimensions have common inter-section. Even inside the Real World structure it is thus necessary to regard some dynamics – the intersection contains, besides the static object aspects as attributes and data structures, also typical dynamic aspects as events, methods, and object states. Thus the description of dynamics is not just the matter of the behavioral model. It is the matter of the conceptual model as well.

Obviously there are two types of dynamics in the Real World:

- dynamics of the Real World objects, represented by their life cycles,
- behavior in the Real World, represented by business processes.
  Some argumentation for the above stated ideas follows.

The Real World objects cannot be regarded as business processes because:

- objects are not behaving – their life cycles are rather the description of business rules in a process manner,
- the process of the object life has no goal (except the "death" of the object), nor product, it is rather the expression of the objective necessity,
- although we describe the process of the objects life-cycles, that description still remains the structural one – whole context is described statically (structurally), it is subordinated to the Real World structure,

- objects are typically taking different roles in different processes giving them the context (Real World rules).

From the opposite viewpoint the business process is quite a different kind of process than the life-cycle of the object because:

- business process has the goal, and the product, it is typical expression of the human will,
- business process typically combines different objects giving them the specific meaning (roles of actors, products, etc.).

For detailed discussion of the main differences between object life cycles and business professes see [Repa 1996], [Repa 1999], [Repa 2000] and [Repa 2003].

The above mentioned facts support the need for modeling the dynamics of the conceptual objects as something different from the behavior of the Real World, which is traditionally represented by business processes. Although in both cases we regard the modeling of processes, at the same time we have to take into the account the fact that modeling of the conceptual objects dynamics has its specific logic, different from the logic of the modeling business processes. This logic primarily reflects the specific nature of the object life cycles, discussed above.

## 2.2 Structural coherency - approach of M.A. Jackson

Roots of the idea of structural coherency are in ideas of Michael Jackson, formulated in his method "JSP" [Jackson 2002].

By the words of the author the fundamental idea of JSP was: program structure should be dictated by the structure of its input and output data streams [Jackson 1975]. If one of the sequential files processed by the program consisted of customer groups, each group consisting of a customer record followed by some number of order records, each of which is either a simple order or an urgent order, then the program should have the same structure: it should have a program part that processes the file, with a subpart to process each customer group, and that subpart should itself have one subpart that processes the customer record, and so on.

The execution sequence of the parts should mirror the sequence of records and record groups in the file. Program parts could be very small and were not, in general, separately compiled.

The resulting structure can be represented in a JSP structure diagram, as in Figure 2:

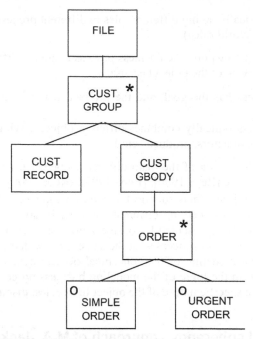

**Fig. 2.** Structure of a File and of a Program [Jackson 2002]

The structure is simultaneously the structure of the file and the structure of a program to process the file. As a data structure it may be verbalised like this:

*"The File consists of zero or more Customer Groups. Each Customer Group consists of a Customer Record followed by a Customer Group Body. Each Customer Group Body consists of zero or more Orders. Each Order is either a Simple Order or an Urgent Order"* [Jackson 2002].

Based on the above stated idea Jackson proposed the process of designing the program which consists of the following steps:

1. Draw data structures for program input(s) and output(s).
2. Form program structure based on the data structures from the previous step.
3. List and allocate operations to the program structure.
4. Create the elaborated program structure with operations and conditions added to the basic program structure
5. Translate the structure diagram into structure text or program code.

The result of applying JSP is a program that reflects problem structure as expressed in a model of its inputs and outputs (see Figure 3). If changes to the program are required that only affect local components, the changes can be easily made to corresponding program components. A program's structural integrity – its correspondence with the problem's structure – is the primary way that we can reduce errors and costs in software maintenance.

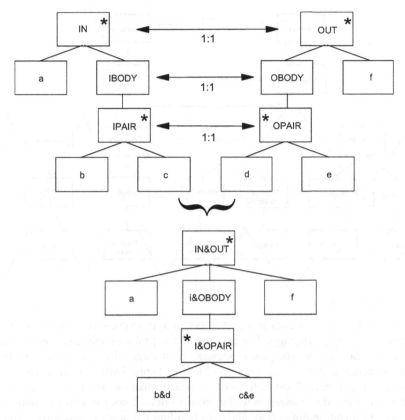

**Fig. 3.** Two File Structures and a Program Structure [Jackson 2002]

The crucial moment of the design process is the first step and the transition from the first to the second step. In fact, the root of the problem is solved by merging data structures together – it requires making the set of crucial decision about the correspondences of particular data structures parts and their merging into the resulting structure (which is, in fact, the structure of transformation process from the input structure(s) to the output one(s)). Therefore Jackson determined the set of rules for merging structures together. In addition to this set of rules he defined the concept of the "structure clash":

*If there are two not corresponding components of the corresponding iterations, and if it is not possible to merge them as a sequence, or as a selection, nor to express the first component as an iteration of the second ones (and vice versa) than there is the structure clash existing between both structures.* (see Figure 4).

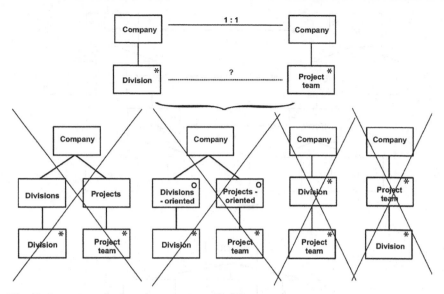

**Fig. 4.** Structure clash

The structure clash means that it is <u>impossible</u> to express the substance of the problem as a <u>simple structure</u>. The process of the problem solution consequently requires several <u>parallel</u> solution processes, each targeted on separate, and relatively independent, part of the whole problem (sub-problem). For instance, in the example at the Figure 4 the solution (i.e. transformation of the company from the division-oriented organization to the project-oriented one) requires breaking the company organization out at first, and then building the new organization which is harmonized with the project management requirements. It is because the division organization and the project organization are mutually independent in so far that it is not possible to make any compromise or to subordinate one structure to the second one.

Thus the <u>structure clash</u> (from the Jackson's theory) is the precise technical <u>definition of the natural parallelism</u> in the process, coming from the nature of the problem itself and therefore present substantially.

## 3 Modeling Object Life Cycles with UML

Unfortunately, the Structure Diagram, used in previous paragraphs, is not the regular diagram of the UML. While using the UML it is necessary to use the State Chart for description of the object life cycles.

State Chart is not primarily intended for the description of life cycle, its roots are in the area of state machines theory, and it is closely connected with the concept of so called "real-time processing". But the concept of the state machine in general is not substantially reducible just to the area of real-time processing. Also in the area of data processing there is the need for recognizing states and transitions among them. The best proof of this idea is the concept of the object life cycle itself – once we think about the objects generally (i.e. in terms of their classes), than we have to strongly distinguish between the class and its instance. In the case of the object life this requires to determine those points in the life of all objects of the same class, which we will be able to identify, and which it is necessary to identify in order to describe the synchronization of the object life with life cycles of other objects. Such points of the object life are its states. So each object instance lives its own life while the lives of all instances of the same class are described by the common life cycle.

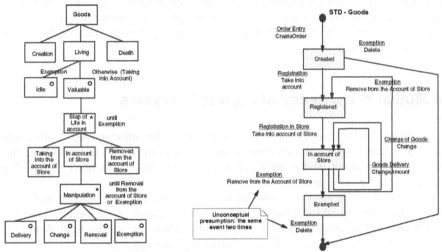

**Fig. 5.** Structure Diagram versus State Chart

It is visible on Figure 5 that the difference between these two styles of describing exactly reflects basic difference between structured and unstructured style of view. In structured view there is the need for creating abstract higher units (as "Living" and "Filling") which serves as the way of understanding the problem. Such a possibility is missing in the case of State Chart. On the other way State Chart allows reverse point of view on the object life cycle – in terms of states and transitions between them. Such a view is very close to the position of a real attendee of the business (i.e. real world behavior) who typically sees the process in detail. The very serious problem is that unstructured description often leads to creating subsidiary abstract concepts which have nothing to do with the real world (i.e. concepts which are not "conceptual"). In our example there is the problem with the presumption that the same event "Exemption" occurs two times what is impossible in the real world. The reason for it is the impossibility to express needed combination of actions connected to this event in given situation (object state).

At the end of this chapter let us resume some limitations of the state-oriented description:

- unstructured view on the process requires the need for the additional reader's abstraction in order to recognize structures,
- for the description of generalized processes it is necessary to use the hierarchy of diagrams (compound states). When we describe the life-cycle of the object class, this necessity is warranted because such process is generalized by definition.

On the other hand the main limitation of the operation-oriented description is the fundamental need for the reader's abstraction – the reader needs to generalize sets of operations in order to recognize basic structure types (iteration, sequence, and selection). Such a need is not present in the state-oriented view on the life-cycle, where the description strictly follows particular state transitions. Nevertheless this abstraction is the necessary way to recognizing deeper – structural – consequences of models.

## 4 Mutual consistency of objects life cycles

Jackson's rules for merging structures, described at the sub-chapter 2.2, allow taking the structure as a common denominator for both the data and the process and use of this structure as the basis for mapping deeper conjunctions among data structures and processes.

Moreover, there are some other general analogies which would be usable for use of Jackson's ideas for reflecting the natural consequences in Real World models, which follow from the nature of the relationships among the Real World objects. In the following text I call them "structural consequences".

The main and the most important general analogies, mentioned above, are:

- The sequence type of structure is an analogy of the aggregation type of hierarchy, while the selection type of structure is an analogy of the generalization type of hierarchy. In connection with this it is necessary to take into the consideration that the iteration type of structure is just the special case of the sequence (where all its parts are of the same structure), hence it is an analogy of the aggregation.
- The cardinality of the relationships among objects is an analogy of the aggregation (as the aggregation reflects the quantity and says nothing about the quality), while the optionality of the relationship is an analogy of the generalization (as the generalization reflects the quality and says nothing about the quantity (including the ordering)).
- Similarly, the generalization (inheritance) type of relationship in the class diagram should be reflected by some kind of selection, while the aggregation (composition) by some kind of sequence/iteration, with all consequences following from it.

Jackson's theory does not describe the rules for merging structures together only. It also leads to the important idea that the structural coherency is the crucial point for modeling basic relationships between the static dimension of the Real World (what it consists of), and its dynamic dimension (how it is doing). Each point of view on the Real World, including the conceptual model, has these two dimensions. In the conceptual model of the Real World the static dimension is modeled by the conceptual object classes and their relationships, while the dynamics of them is modeled by their life cycles.

Concluding from previous paragraphs we can formalize basic rules for the structural consistency of objects in the conceptual model as follows:

1. Each association between two object classes must be reflected by the specific operation in each class life cycle.
2. The cardinality of the association must be reflected by corresponding type of structure in the life cycle of the opposite class: cardinality 1:n by the iteration of parts, cardinality 1:n by the single part of the structure.
3. The optionality of the association must be reflected by corresponding selection structure in the life cycle of the opposite class.
4. Each generalization of the class must be reflected by corresponding selection structure in its life cycle.
5. Each aggregation association between classes must be reflected by corresponding iteration structure in the life cycle of the aggregating class (container/composite class).

Figure 6 illustrates some examples of structural coherences in the conceptual model. Class diagram represents the static contextual view on reality, while the object life cycle describes the "internal dynamics" of the class. The internal dynamics of the class should be subordinated to the context (i.e. substantial relationships to the other classes), therefore each class contains specific operation (method) for each association (it is obvious that some associations to other classes are missing in this example). The life cycle determines the placement of each particular operation in the overall life history of the object - the internal context of the operation. The internal context must be consistent with the external one, which follows from relationships described between classes in the Class Diagram (associations to other classes, generalizations etc.). Dashed arrows indicate basic consequences of described associations and their cardinalities in life cycles of both classes:

- Optionality of the association (goods may not to be ordered at all) is reflected by the existence of the possibility that the whole sub-structure, representing ordering of goods may be idle in the Goods life cycle. Also the fundamental conditionality of the delivery is the reflection of this fact.
- Multiplicity of the association (one Order may contain several items) is reflected by the iteration of the structure "Filling" in the Order life history which expresses the fundamental fact that the order may be created, fulfilled by several supplies, or changed several times, separately for each ordered item.

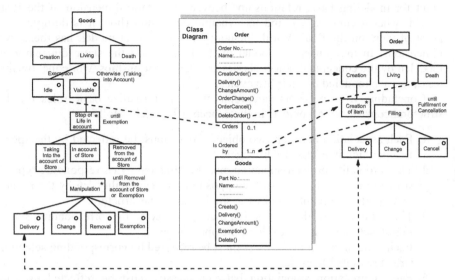

**Fig. 6.** Structural Coherency of Objects and their Life Cycles

The knowledge of structural consequences helps the analyzer to improve the Real World models concerning their mutual consistency as well as their relative completeness (as the completeness is a main part of the problem of consistency).

# 5 Consequences and conclusions

This paper discusses the problem of dynamics in conceptual models. The paper just outlines some basic contingences which follow from the inspiration by the theory of M.A. Jackson in the area of conceptual modeling. It points out the significance of the description of objects internal dynamics, as it is the only way to ensuring the full respect of their structural consistency.

The aim of this paper is not to introduce some new language, nor to add the new diagram into the UML. As stated at the section 3 the Structure Diagram, used in previous paragraphs in order to emphasize the structural consequences of the process and object models, is not the regular diagram of the UML. While using the UML it is necessary to use the State Chart for description of the object life cycles. This fact just means that we are forced, while using the UML, to use the language which do not allow to emphasize the structural consequences. It does not mean that we are not able to respect them. State Chart is the tool strong enough for description of the life cycle of any object. In order to respect the structural consequences we just need to perceive the algorithm of the object life in terms of structures, no matter if the tool helps us or not. This paper argues for such way of thinking at first without discussing the problem of the language.

The paper also outlines several basic rules for the structural consistency of conceptual objects. This enumeration cannot be regarded as complete. More complex and more formal view on this problem offers the "business system meta-model", which is accessible at the web page http://opensoul.panrepa.org. In addition, the detailed elaboration of the rules should be the subject of the further development of the methodology. For instance, the phenomenon of structure clashes together with the general possibilities of their solving, which are excellently elaborated in the JSP [Jackson 1975] and JSD [Jackson 1982] could significantly move forward the theory of conceptual modeling in the future.

# References

[Chen 1976] Chen P.P.S.: The Entity Relationship Model - Towards a Unified View of Data, ACM TODS, Vol 1 No.1, pp. 9-36, 1976.

[Jackson 1975] Jackson, M.A. "Principles of Program Design", Academic Press, London, 1975.

[Jackson 1982] Jackson, M.A.: System Development, Prentice-Hall Inc., Englewood Cliffs, NJ, 1982.

[Jackson 2002] Jackson M.A.: JSP in Perspective; in Software Pioneers: Contributions to Software Engineering; Manfred Broy, Ernst Denert eds; Springer, 2002.

[Kobryn 2000] Kobryn, C "Introduction to UML: Structural Modeling and Use Cases", Object Modeling with OMG - UML Tutorial Series: www.omg.org, 2000.

[Marca 1992] Marca, D., McGowan, C., IDEF0: Business Process and Enterprise Modeling, Eclectic Solutions, 1992.

[Repa 1994] Repa V. "Seeking the Actual Reasons for the "New Paradigm" in the Area of IS Analysis", Proceedings of the ISD 94 International Conference, Bled, 1994.

[Repa 1996] Repa V. "Object Life Cycle Modeling in the Client-Server Applications Development Using Structured Methodology", Proceedings of the ISD 96 International Conference, Sopot, 1996.

[Repa 1999] Repa V. "Information systems development methodology – the BPR challenge", Proceedings of the ISD99 International Conference, Kluwer Academics, Boise, ID, 1999.

[Repa 2000] Repa V. "Process Diagram Technique for Business Processes Modeling", Proceedings of the ISD2000 International Conference, Kluwer Academics, Kristiansand, Norway, 1999.

[Repa 2003] Repa V. "Business System Modeling Specification", Proceedings of the CCCT2003 International Conference, IIIS, Orlando, FL, 2003.

[UML 2003] UML " OMG Unified Modeling Language Specification, v. 1.5. document ad/03-03-01, Object Management Group, March 2003."

[UML 2004] UML Superstructure Specification, v2.0 document 05-07-04, Object Management Group, 2004."

[Weisman 1999] Weisman, R.: Introduction to UML Based SW Development Process: www.softera.com, 1999.
[Yourdon 1989] Yourdon, E.: Modern Structured Analysis, Prentice-Hall Inc., Englewood Cliffs, NJ, 1989

# An Interoperability Classification Framework for Method Chunk Repositories

Per Backlund*, Jolita Ralyté**, Manfred A. Jeusfeld***, Harald Kühn****
Nicolas Arni-Bloch**, Jan B.M. Goossenaerts*****, and Frank Lillehagen******

* University of Skövde, P.O. Box 408, SE 541 28 Skövde, Swe-
den, Per.Backlund@his.se
** CUI, University of Geneva, Rue de Général Dufour, 24, CH-1211
Genève 4, Switzerland, {Jolita.Ralyte, Nicolas.Arni-Bloch}@cui.unige.ch
***Tilburg University, CRISM/Infolab, 5000 LE Tilburg, The Netherlands,
Manfred.Jeusfeld@uvt.nl
**** BOC Information Systems GmbH, Rabensteig 2, A-1010 Vienna, Aus-
tria, Harald.Kuehn@boc-eu.com
***** Eindhoven University of Technology, Den Dolech 2, Paviljoen D 12,
Postbus 513, 5600 MB Eindhoven, The Netherlands,
J.B.M.Goossenaerts@tm.tue.nl
****** TROUX Technologies AS, P.O. Box 482, N-1327 Lysaker, Norwaz,
Frank.Lillehagen@Troux.com

**Abstract:** The competitiveness and efficiency of an enterprise is dependent on its ability to interact with other enterprises and organisations. In this context interoperability is defined as the ability of business processes as well as enterprise software and applications to interact. Interoperability remains a problem and there are numerous issues to be resolved in different situations. We propose method engineering as an approach to organise interoperability knowledge in a method chunk repository. In order to organise the knowledge repository we need an interoperability classification framework associated to it. In this paper we propose a generic architecture for a method chunk repository, elaborate on a classification framework and associate it to some existing bodies of knowledge. We also show how the proposed framework can be applied in a working example.

# 1 Introduction

Interoperability is defined as "the ability of Enterprise Software and Applications to interact" (Interop, 2005). We claim that it is impossible to provide one universal method for interoperability problems solution and we propose to define a knowledge base of reusable method chunks each of them addressing one or more specific interoperability problems. In order to support situation-specific method construction and application, a collaborative tool must be developed supporting method chunks construction and storage as well as their selection and reuse in different projects. The specialisation of such a knowledge management tool for the interoperability domain requires the creation of a mapping from the method chunks to the interoperability problems, i.e. an indexation mechanism associating each method to one or several well-defined interoperability problems. The definition and classification of interoperability problems is necessary for interoperability situation assessment and selection of the method chunks satisfying this situation.

In this paper we view information systems development as knowledge work (Iivari, 2000; Backlund, 2004) with the aim of exploring an interoperability classification framework for a Method Chunk Repository which can be used to solve industry relevant interoperability problems. We propose method engineering as a means for dealing with some aspects of interoperability. However, in order to make an interoperability method chunk repository useful we must supply a classification of interoperability problems which can be used to guide the repository user in composing methods. The proposed repository should deal with interoperability problems within information systems development; hence we will anchor the classification scheme in the information systems body of knowledge (Iivari et al., 2004).

The focus cannot be placed on the applications alone. In order to achieve meaningful interoperability organisations must be interoperable on, at least three levels: a business layer, a knowledge layer and an ICT systems layer (Chen and Doumeingts, 2003). This includes the business environment and business processes on the business layer, the organisational roles, skills and competencies of employees and knowledge assets on the knowledge layer, and applications, data and communication components on the ICT layer. Similarly, but from a more software-architecture oriented view, Schulz et al. (2003) conclude that interoperability is achieved on the following levels: inter-enterprise coordination, business process integration, semantic application integration, syntactical application integration, and physical integration. According to these authors interoperability should be analysed from an enterprise view (i.e. interoperability between two or more organisations), an architecture & platform view (i.e. between two or more applications/systems) and an ontological view (i.e. the semantics of interoperability).

As can be seen from the above descriptions, interoperability is a multifaceted concept. In order to be able to match a specific problem situation of a particular case to method chunks enabling the problem solution, we need a mechanism supporting method chunks indexation on the one hand and situation assessment on the other hand. This mechanism is referred to as a matching/classification framework. It must bring diverse bodies of knowledge together and extend them with interoperability concepts.

The remainder of this paper is organised as follows. In section 2 we introduce a collaborative Method Engineering platform based on a method chunk repository for interoperability. The building blocks of the Method Engineering platform and the roles involved in platform use are presented. In section 3 we briefly analyse interoperability problems in an enterprise context and present a framework to classify interoperability problems and method chunks. Section 4 illustrates how the classification framework is applied to an industrial case. The paper ends with a review of this work, and outlines future research.

## 2 Collaborative Method Engineering Platform for Interoperability

A collaborative platform for situational method engineering must support two main activities: situation-specific method construction and method application in the corresponding system development project. The method construction activity requires capabilities for reusable method chunks definition, storage and classification with respect to the problems they help to solve. It also aims to support the characterisation of each project situation and selection and assembly of method chunks fitting the situation at hand. The method application requires services for the obtained method enactment and evaluation of its applicability in the corresponding situation. The knowledge about positive or negative experience of method application is captured in terms of best practices and/or experience reports. These features are especially important since we know that methods are never used as is in practice (e.g. Fitzgerald and O'Kane, 1999; Fitzgerald et al., 2002). Even though we don't address these issues in particular in this paper we would like to point out that best practices and experience reports may help in method application.

Figure 1 illustrates the architecture of our platform divided into three layers: *usage, service* and *data*.

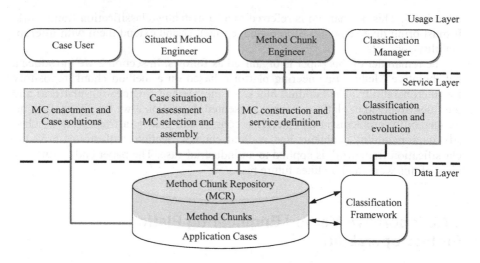

**Fig. 1.** Architecture for a collaborative method engineering platform

The *data layer* concerns the knowledge repository, called the *Method Chunk Repository* (MCR), used by the platform. This repository contains two types of interconnected knowledge: the method knowledge expressed in the form of reusable method chunks and the knowledge related to the experience of method chunks application in specific industrial cases. A *method chunk* is an autonomous, cohesive and coherent part of a method providing guidelines and defining related concepts to support the realisation of some specific information system development activity in a particular context. Within the scope of the Interop NoE (Interop, 2005), our objective is to define and store method chunks providing solutions for various interoperability issues. The metamodel of a method chunk can be found in (Ralyté and Rolland, 2001; Mirbel and Ralyté, 2005). Furthermore, the MCR collects the practice and experience of using the method chunks in terms of *application cases*.

Each case included exhibits a number of interoperability issues that instantiate the interoperability issue types identified in the *classification framework*. In order to match the problem situation of a particular case to method chunks thus enabling a solution, we need a mechanism supporting method chunks indexation on the one hand and situation assessment on the other hand. This mechanism is referred to as a matching/classification framework. In this work we focus our attention to the classification part of this framework. Each method chunk stored in the MCR is explicitly related to one or several interoperability issues defined in the classification framework.

The *service layer* of our platform provides several services supporting method engineering and method usage activities including: construction of method chunks and related services, classification framework management (construction, extension, and adaptation), method chunks selection, adaptation and assembly for specific cases, and case-specific method enactment and validation.

Finally, the *usage layer* defines different categories of platform users including: method chunk engineer, classification manager, situated method engineer and case user. The *method chunk engineer* is an expert in the method engineering domain. His/her role is to populate the MCR with method chunks, which can be extracted from existing traditional methods or defined from scratch on the basis of domain knowledge and experience. The method chunk engineer will also develop services for method chunks application and provide a descriptor (Ralyté and Rolland, 2001; Mirbel and Ralyté, 2005) for each method chunk characterising, with the help of the classification framework, the context of its application and the interoperability issues it helps to solve.

The *classification manager* is responsible for defining and managing the method chunk classification framework. Such a framework should be extensible and evolutionary. Good knowledge about the information systems development domain and some selected application or problem domain, such as interoperability in our case, is required to enact this role.

The *situated method engineer* is in charge of constructing a case-specific method for each case. His/her work consists of three main tasks: characterising the case situation by using the classification framework, selecting method chunks satisfying this situation and assembling retrieved method chunks in order to provide a coherent and complete method for the specific case.

Finally, the *case user* will apply the case-specific method in the development of a corresponding project and will provide an experience report including the evaluation of the applied method chunks and their fitness to this case.

The interoperability classification framework forms an important part of the MCR structure since it is used for method chunk classification as well as for case assessment. Therefore, we focus our attention to a set of interoperability problems in order to illustrate its applicability in an industrial case. However, it may be noted that the framework itself comprises a broader scope.

# 3 Classification of Interoperability Issues

Based on a survey of literature (Rahm and Bernstein, 2001; Xu and Newman, 2006; Botta-Genoulaz et al., 2005; Domínguez and Zapata, 2000) and collective industrial experience in NoE Interop (Interop, 2005) and IP Athena (Athena, 2005) we identify and characterise a set of interoperability issues in enterprise information systems (section 3.1) prior to proposing a classification framework in section 3.2.

## 3.1 Interoperability Classes

Interoperability issues can be summarised to comprise five different classes:

- Business Management,

- Process Management,
- Knowledge Management,
- Software Management, and
- Data Management.

In general, they reside in the various levels of the framework presented in (Schultz et al., 2003) including: communication (interconnection and protocols), data (access to and change of information), service (access to and exchange of services/functions), processes (sequences of activities and rules), knowledge (knowledge assets and organisational roles) and business (method of work, legislation and contracts) level. In the following we briefly illustrate these classes in order to characterise the basic conditions for the classification framework.

The utilisation of repetitive business processes across multiple organisations constitutes a potential area for improvement throughout the entire supply chain. Many aspects are generic and involve repeated periodic processing of similar or identical orders. Business decision-making activities are of paramount importance to enterprises, affecting day-to-day operations as well as medium and long-term planning and execution of activities. Therefore, an integral mechanism is required to support the decision-making process at various levels, by considering results coming out of daily operations. The provision of (near) real-time aggregated views of key business information in relation to the above business decision-making activities can be done by accessing and integrating data in existing legacy systems. Such aggregated views will enable actors to take more accurate and timely decisions, exploiting to the full extend the capabilities of existing ICT systems.

The time from order to delivery could be shortened by better process interoperability. This can be achieved by the ability of a process to make its requested and offered services/interfaces "visible". Shortening the time between different processes, e.g. from raw materials suppliers, has a direct effect on the delivery date. In this context we identify the fact that applications focus on transactions as opposed to processes as an issue to take into account.

The knowledge associated to a product over its entire lifecycle needs to be shared between stakeholders. This entails an adequate and common understanding of product and process information rather than merely transferring information between stakeholders. Knowledge can be organized according to domain standards.

To make knowledge sharing efficient there is a need for support for stakeholders' collaboration. This implies communication/collaboration infrastructure integration by using standard middleware and communication protocols, which allow the seamless communication and interoperability of model-generated workplace applications. We identify two critical issues in this matter: shared data integration and data access synchronization. Shared data integration entails reconciliation of business level information exchanged between the stakeholders that support collaboration and common understanding.

As enterprises are more and more using commercial of the shelves software (COTS), the used solutions are highly generic and require an important parameterisation/customisation and administration to adapt the solution to the business context. This customisation should be as easy as possible by operators, without implying modification of technical interfaces by software engineers. This fact makes easy customisation of software products and automatic reorganisation of the technical interfaces even more important. The need for documented publication of applications and software product services increases.

Data format interoperability is the ability of a process/application to exchange data with one/more partners by means of a common data format or via a mapping between the proprietary format and an intermediate common format. Hence the enterprise architecture has to take the support of the main technical middleware frameworks in a coherent way into account.

## 3.2 Interoperability Classification Framework

Recently there has been an increasing interest in creating a body of knowledge for software engineering (Swebok, 2004) and information systems development (Iivari et al., 2004) respectively. These efforts aim to structure relevant knowledge within the areas that they are to cover. Notably, neither of them explicitly deals with the concept of interoperability.

Iivari et al. (2004) propose five ontological domains (in the terminology of Bunge (1983), each of these domains merges both ontological and epistemological aspects) for information systems experts.

The *organisational domain* refers to the knowledge about social contexts and processes in which the information system is used. The *application domain* refers to the knowledge about the application domain for which the information system is intended. The *development process* knowledge refers to the methods and tools used in systems development. The *IT application* domain refers to the knowledge about typical IT applications and their use in a certain application domain. The *technical domain* refers to the hardware and software of an information system. Fig. 2 indicates relationships between the IS ontological domains (first column) and the classes (third column) of interoperability issues (examples in fourth column) identified in section 3.1. In the technology and IT application domains we find issues of data management and software management, hence relating the IS field closely to the field of software engineering. Application domain knowledge includes issues concerning business management and process management, i.e. how typical applications work in a particular domain. Finally, organisational domain knowledge has to do with knowledge management in a general sense even though certain issues may be refined to specific application domains.

The software engineering body of knowledge (Swebok, 2004) refines the technology and systems development process knowledge domains of the IS body of knowledge (Iivari et al., 2004) by identifying the following knowledge areas: (software) requirements, design, construction, testing, maintenance, configuration management, engineering management, engineering process, tools and methods and quality. Even though we do not use those exact terms in Fig. 2 we note that, in Swebok (2004), interoperability is seen as an emergent property, which is dependent on the system architecture, with the focus set on software interoperability. Apart from that, not much attention is paid to interoperability. Hence we may add an interoperability aspect to all knowledge areas of Swebok (2004) as well as the IS body of knowledge.

The Enterprise Ontology (2003) is a collection of concepts and their definitions from the business domain. It is subdivided into the aspects activities and processes, organisation, strategy, and marketing. The Enterprise Ontology can be used to further characterise the business domain in a similar way as Swebok (2004) can be used to characterise the ICT development domain.

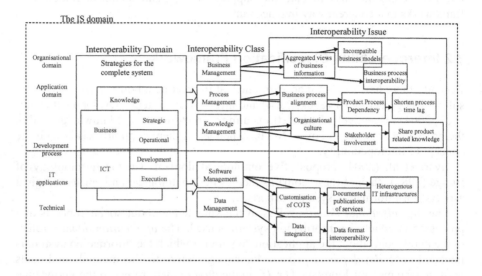

**Fig. 2.** Interoperability Classification Framework

As indicated in Fig. 2 we bring together the IS domain and the interoperability domain to provide a structure for classifying interoperability issues. Interoperability is not only a problem concerning software and technologies. It is also a problem that concerns knowledge and business references that must be shared in order to achieve interoperability (Chen and Doumeingts, 2003). Thus the interoperability domain comprises knowledge about business/organisational as well as technical aspects (Wainwright and Waring, 2004). Development process knowledge, as described by Iivari et al., (2004), resides in both spheres since the total of all aspects has to be taken into account in IS development.

We envisage an approach to understand the technical, strategic and organisational behaviours from a holistic perspective. That is, organisations are complex and any effort has to handle multiple aspects in order to achieve interoperability between systems. Furthermore, interoperability is a strategic issue; hence interoperability has to incorporate strategic planning for the entire system. To conclude, interoperability between two organisations is a multifaceted problem since it concerns both technical and organisational issues, which are intertwined and complex to deal with.

We also make it possible to incorporate the knowledge areas of the software engineering body of knowledge through the software management and data management interoperability classes. Hence, we propose an extensible classification framework, which is anchored in the information systems body of knowledge and the software engineering body of knowledge. Moreover, we cater for the possibility to allocate problems to the epistemological domain that has the proven methods and knowledge available to solve them. This is particularly useful since real world problems typically concern a combination of ontological areas. The method chunks stored in the MCR are indexed by the classification scheme allowing for better support to all roles identified in the usage layer of Fig. 1.

# 4 Applying the Classification

A typical case from the real world contains multiple interoperability issues. We use as an example the experience from the *public utility sector*, here the water sector consisting of organisations that *supply fresh water*, organisations that *process sewage water*, and local municipalities that *raise taxes* on both, in particular wrt. the sewage water. In the Netherlands, fresh water supply and sewage water processing are done by organisations that have no need to exchange data since the cost for fresh water supply is based on consumption whereas the cost for sewage water is based on the number of persons in a household. A European guideline stimulates countries to base the sewage water invoice on consumption as well. Since there are no metering devices installed for sewage water per household, the only way to do so is to rely on the metering for the fresh water consumption of the household. To complicate the situation further, the local municipalities use to include taxes on the sewage water invoice that are currently based on sewage water price. As the computation of the sewage water price changes, the tax calculation has to change as well. In the following, we analyse the interoperability problems occurring in the case and classify them into our framework.

*IP1*: The *business models* of the three organisations are incompatible. The fresh water organisation raises income based on the consumption. The sewage water organisation and the local municipalities use number of persons in a household as basis for their invoice. Moreover, the participating organisations have different concepts for the addressee of the invoice. The fresh water organisation has a concept of a customer linked to a fresh water supply end point. The other two organisations use the concept of a household with a number of citizens associated to it. To integrate the business models of the three organisations, one needs to come up with calculations on a common data basis that fulfils the expectations of the three organisations.

*IP2*: The *business processes* of the three organisations are not aligned. In particular, the invoicing processes are taking place at different points of time. Specifically, the time when a fresh water invoice is printed is completely independent from the time when the sewage water invoice is printed. The processes for maintaining the customer and citizen data sets in the participating organisations need to be aligned since it may well be that a person is still in the customer data set of the fresh water organisation while already being removed from the citizen data set.

*IP3*: The three organisations use completely heterogeneous *IT infrastructures*. The data exchange between the local municipality and the sewage water organisation is done by physically sending spreadsheet files on computer-readable media. The fresh water organisation relies on an ERP system to manage all its data and processes. It is unclear whether to use a common platform to which all three organisations supply data, or to send data directly to each other, or for one of the three organisations to play the role of a data integrator.

*IP4*: The *data structures* are heterogeneous. That holds for all fields relevant for creating the invoices, e.g. the address field, the date field etc. The heterogeneity is resolved by ad hoc procedures to reformat the exchange files. For those parties that do not yet exchange data, the problem of heterogeneity is not yet analysed.

*IP5*: The *cultural background* and habits in the three organisations is different und difficult to harmonise. The non-profit character of the local municipalities may clash with the more commercial attitude found in the fresh water company. The challenge is to make the right people communicate and exchange information about their respective goals and capabilities. A further complication is that the co-operation is forced upon the participating organisations by the European directive.

Table 1 classifies the five identified interoperability problems into the framework represented in Fig. 2. The classification of the case problem is a manual process and is the first step of the MC enactment and cases solutions service of the MCR. The classification limits the scope of applicable solutions as well as the type of change to be expected from the solution. We applied the following approach for the classification of the case problems:

1. Determine the IS domain of the case problem: The IS domain is characterising the type of knowledge that is necessary to understand the case problem. For example, IP4 belongs to the IS domain 'Development process'. Here, the Swebok (2004) knowledge base can be used to characterise the field.
2. Determine the interoperability domain: This classification characterises the type of interaction that causes the case problem. For example, IP2 is about the alignment of business processes of operational users at different enterprises.
3. Determine the interoperability class: This class is specifying which type of management activity is related to the interoperability problem. It also specifies which expert is to be consulted to solve the problem.
4. Determine the interoperability issue: The set of issues is build upon experience, i.e. whenever a case problem occurs one looks up whether there is a similar issue in the method chunk repository. The issues are the most specific abstractions of past case problems. The interoperability issue is the item that is linked to the potential solutions in the method chunk repository.

This stepwise approach focuses the case user (see Fig. 1) towards the most relevant interoperability issue for the case problem to be classified. By linking the case problem to the respective categories, the case user also pre-selects the group of people to be involved in solving the problem at hand. The closer the case user describes the case problem along the 4 categories, the easier is the classification process. We plan to support the classification by a user interface that provides questions for classifying the case into the first 3 categories and then proposes the most applicable interoperability issues. If no issue is found, an update request for the classification manager of the method chunk repository is formulated.

**Table 1.** Case classification

| Case prob-lem | IS Domain | Interoperability Domain | Interoperability Class | Interoperability Issue |
|---|---|---|---|---|
| IP1 | organisational | business/strategic | business management | incompatible business models |
| IP2 | organisational | business/operational | process management | business process alignment, bp interoperability |
| IP3 | IT application | ICT/execution | data management | heterogeneous IT infrastructures |
| IP4 | development process | ICT/development | data management | data integration, data format interoperability |
| IP5 | organisational | business/operational | knowledge management | organisational culture |

Out of the five identified case problems (see Table 1), three originate from the organisational domain, i.e. require a solution that is not just a technical one. Only problem IP4 apparently requires to change the IT systems, namely to provide the required data in the right format at the right time. By this example we show how the outcome of the case classification is used to search for applicable method chunks in the repository.

We note that a case like the one discussed above touches multiple interoperability issues, which need to be tackled in an orchestrated effort. An open problem is still whether the solution to a complete case should be regarded as a whole, because the solutions to the interoperability problems highly depend on each other, or whether the individual solutions to the individual interoperability problems should be regarded as stand-alone.

# 5 Conclusion

In this paper we have outlined a generic architecture for an interoperability method chunk repository. One important aspect of such a repository is a classification framework, which can assist in selecting appropriate method chunks for resolving multifaceted interoperability problems. We note that neither Swebok (2004) nor

Iivari et al. (2004) address interoperability explicitly. Hence, we introduce this as a new aspect to take into account. Our results are summarised as follows:

1. We propose a generic architecture for a method chunk repository.
2. We propose an application of method engineering concepts to organise interoperability knowledge for management and interaction.
3. We define a framework consisting of the IS domain, the interoperability domain, interoperability classes, and interoperability issues.
4. We show how this framework can be applied to a real world case.
5. We propose a stepwise procedure designed to focus the MCR user towards a suitable interoperability issue matching the problem at hand.

The strength of the proposed classification framework is that it incorporates the business/organisational domains as well as the technical domain. Furthermore, the current framework is extendible to comprise more detail.

In order to show the applicability of the framework we have used it to classify a set of interoperability issues in a real world case. In a future application of a similar scheme, we claim that it will be possible to guide a method chunk user in the selection of relevant method chunks. This selection process will be particularly useful in the orchestration of method chunks resolving intra and inter organisational interoperability issues.

Related work concerning tool and platform independence aims to develop a generic platform, which caters for the combination of tools. This is considered an interoperability problem between modelling tools, whereas our work is more focused on domain specific interoperability problems. Hence our work is considered to be a practical utilisation of such a platform. Future work within our project will include the construction of a method chunk repository prototype using the Metis platform (Troux Technologies, 2005). We propose using existing technology to build the repository in order to enhance the utilisation in practice for the proposed approach. To ensure the usability of the proposed approach we include a value and risk analysis in the architecture description of the method repository. Our ongoing work indicates that the utilisation of existing modelling tools is a feasible approach for future work. As a first step, this will lead to a practical application of method chunks within the NoE Interop (2005).

**Acknowledgements.** This research has been carried out within the INTEROP Network of Excellence. Commission of the European Communities under the sixth framework programme (INTEROP Network of Excellence, Contract N° 508011, <http://www.interop-noe.org>). This work was partially supported by the Swiss National Science Foundation; grant N° 200021-103826.

# References

ATHENA (2005) European Integrated Project No. 507849. Available at http://www.athena-ip.org. Accessed 2005-12-09.

Backlund, P (2004) An Analysis of ISD as Knowledge Work – an Analysis of How a Development Method is Used in Practice. In Information Systems Development (ISD 2004): Advances in Theory, Practice and Education, pp. 125-136

Botta-Genoulaz, V., Millet P.-A. and Grabot B. (2005) A survey on the recent research literature on ERP systems. Computers in Industry (56) pp. 510-522

Bunge, M. (1983). Epistemology & Methodology I: Exploring the World, Treatise on Basic Philosophy Vol. 5, Reidel, Boston.

Chen, D. and Doumeingts G. (2003) European initiatives to develop interoperability of enterprise applications — basic concepts, framework and roadmap. Annual Reviews in Control (27) pp. 153-162.

Domínguez, E. and Zapata M.A. (2000) Mappings and Interoperability: A Meta-modelling Approach. ADVIS 2000, Ed. T. Yakhno. LNCS 1909, Springer-Verlag, pp. 352-362.

Enterprise Ontology (2003) Enterprise Ontology Project, http://www.aiai.ed.ac.uk/project/enterprise/enterprise/ontology.html. Accessed 2005-12-14

Fitzgerald, B. and O'Kane, T (1999) A Longitudinal Study of Software Process Improvement. IEEE Software 16, pp. 37-46.

Fitzgerald, B., Russo, N. and O'Kane, T (2992) Software Development Method Tailoring in Motorola. Communications of the ACM 46, pp. 64-70.

INTEROP (2005) Interop Network of Excellence IST – 508011 Presentation of the Project. http://interop-noe.org/INTEROP/presentation . Accessed 2005-12-07

Iivari, J. (2000) Information Systems Development as Knowledge Work: The body of systems development process knowledge. Information Modellinga and Knowledge Bases XI, IOS Press, pp. 41-56.

Iivari, J., Hirschheim, R. and Klein, H.K (2004) Towards a distinctive body of knowledge for Information Systems experts: coding ISD process knowledge in two IS journals. Information Systems Journal (14) pp. 313-342.

Mirbel, I. and Ralyté, J. (2005) Situational Method Engineering: Combining Assembly-based and Roadmap-driven Approaches. To appear in the Requirements Engineering Journal, electronic publication is available at: http://dx.doi.org/10.1007/11568322_14.

Rahm, E. and Bernstein P. A. (2001) A survey of approaches to automatic schema matching. The VLDB Journal, 10, pp. 334-350.

Ralyté, J. and Rolland C. (2001). An Approach for Method Reengineering. Proceedings of the 20th International Conference on Conceptual Modeling (ER2001), LNCS 2224, Springer-Verlag, pp. 471-484.

Schulz, K., et al. (2003) A Gap Analysis; Required Activities in Research, Technology and Standardisation to close the RTS Gap; Roadmaps and Recommendations on RTS activities. Deliverables D 3.4, D 3.5, D 3.6. IDEAS Thematic Network - Contract no.: IST-2001-37368.

SWEBOK (2004) Guide to the Software Engineering Body of Knowledge 2004 Version. Available at http://www.swebok.org/. Accessed 2005-12-08

Troux Technologies (2005) Metis by Troux: Providing the Capabilities for EA Success. http://www.troux.com/ Accessed 2005-12-14

Wainwright, D. and Waring T. (2004) Three domains for implementing integrated information systems: redressing the balance between technology, strategic and organisational analysis. International Journal of Information Management 24 (2004) pp. 329-346

Xu, X.W. and Newman S.T. (2006) Making CNC machine tools more open, interoperable and intelligent—a review of the technologies. Computers in Industry 57, pp. 141-152.

# Configurable Satisfiability Propagation for Goal Models Using Dynamic Compilation Techniques[1]

Elena Navarro[*] Patricio Letelier[**], David Reolid[*] and Isidro Ramos[**]

[*]Computing Systems Department, UCLM, EPSA, Campus Universitario
s/n, Albacete, 02071, Spain, [enavarro|dreolid] @info-ab.uclm.es
[**]Department of Information Systems and Computation, UPV,
Camino de Vera s/n, 46022, Valencia, Spain, [letelier|iramos]@dsic.upv.es

## 1 Introduction

It is frequently the case that at early stages of the requirements engineering process, critical decisions about what the system should provide are taken. Stakeholders and developers must evaluate alternatives and conflicts among the system requirements. In addition, a great deal of work must be done through focused brainstorming, validation, negotiation, and decision-making associated to vague or not completely defined requirements. In this context, Goal-Oriented modeling techniques emerge as a suitable way of defining and analyzing requirements, but also as an effective way to provide the necessary traceability towards other derived software artifacts.

This work aims at introducing a framework for exploiting Goal Models that allows the analyst to customize the analysis mechanisms according to the project needs. Our approach is based on the propagation algorithm proposed by (Giorgini et al. 2003), which establishes the essential computation of propagation. Using metamodeling techniques we provide the analyst with extensibility and customization mechanisms to modify the computation according to particular Goal Model elements, application domain, business rules, etc. These facilities are supplied by MORPHEUS, a tool we have developed for supporting our proposal.

---

[1] This work has been funded by the Spanish CICYT project DYNAMICA TIC2003-07776-C02-02.

The remainder of this work is structured as follows. In section 2 a brief introduction to Goal Models and their analysis capabilities for requirements is presented. Section 3 describes our proposal presenting the integration of metamodel elements in rule description that are used in a propagation algorithm. Section 4 describes MORPHEUS, a tool developed to give support to our framework and especially an add-in incorporated to exploit the Goal Model by means of satisfaction/denegation propagation. Eventually, in section 5 conclusions and future work are presented.

## 2 Background

A Goal Model is built as a directed graph by means of a refinement from the systems *goals* (or concerns). This refinement lasts until goals have enough granularity and detail so as to describe an *operationalization*, i.e., a solution that provides the target system to meet users' needs and expectations. This refinement process is performed by using *AND/OR* refinement relationships. An AND (OR) relationship between a goal $Goal_X$ and a set of sub-goals $G_1 \ldots G_N$ is established if the whole set of (at least one) sub-goals has to be satisfied in order to satisfy $Goal_X$. In addition, operationalizations are associated to the requirements (leaf goals) by means of *contribution* relationships that denote how they collaborate to achieve a goal.

Once a Goal Model is defined mechanisms can be used to analyse its satisfiability. The satisfaction (denegation) of a goal means that it will (will not) be provided by the system-to-be, i.e., user's needs and expectations will (will not) be met. The propagation to carry out this reasoning about goal satisfaction is addressed by means of two approaches:

- *Qualitative approach.* The idea is to establish positive or negative influence (for instance, by means of ++, +, #, -, -- symbols) of contributions from operationalizations to goals in the Goal Model. These operationalizations can be designs, agents, events on the market, etc., depending on the specific Goal Model that is being used. In this sense, the degree of satisfaction does not have a precise interpretation, i.e., it is not based on domain or system properties but on the analyst criteria. (Chung et al. 2000) and (Giorgini et al. 2003) are examples of this approach.

- *Quantitative approach.* In this case, weights are set to contribution relationships describing the satisfaction degrees that goals have among them. The propagation is performed in a similar way to the previous case, but now a specific value of satisfiability is achieved. Those weights can be assigned according to quite different criteria:

  1. *Subjective assignment* where only the analyst criteria is used to decide, as for instance (Giorgini et al. 2003)'s proposal.
  2. *Objective assignment*, which is based on domain properties. Some proposals are that presented by (Letier and Lamsweerde 2004) for reasoning about par-

tial satisfiability of requirement; or (Hansen et al. 1998) to analyze safety constraints of system-to-be with fault-trees.

Figure 1 shows a summary example of a Goal Model which has been defined within the European project Environmental Friendly and cost-effective Technology for Coating Removal (EFTCOR, 2003). Its aim is to design a family of robots capable of performing maintenance operations for ship hulls. On the left of the image, it can be observed how goals are refined from a high level goal (suitability) towards requirements (operationalizable goals) and operationalizations. For instance, it can be observed that to achieve a suitable system-to-be both *"ApproachRobot"* and *"CatchObject"* have to be satisfied; or how *"MoveUsingMUC"* positively contributes to *"MoveStepArms"*. In addition, on the right side of the image the result of the propagation for that selected operationalizations is shown. The explanation of the used rules is presented in the next section.

Currently, there is no standard notation for goal-oriented specification but several proposals have appeared that address different activities and perspectives in the Requirements Engineering Process[2]. In this sense, Goal Models are mainly exploited for evaluating alternative designs such as those described by (Chung et al. 2000) (Letier and Lamsweerde 2004), business goals (Giorgini et al. 2003), etc. However, there is no consensus on which the most appropriate mechanism or proposal should be. For this reason, it is the analyst who finally has to make the final decision about which should be used for a specific project.

Similarly, the propagation of satisfaction/denegation through the Goal Model depends on the application domain and the expressiveness of the Goal Model (provided by its elements such as kinds of refinements, artefacts and associated attributes). Furthermore, the propagation rules could also be specific for the project or could even be modified in the same project in order to reflect some additional consideration during the analysis. This required flexibility is missing in the current

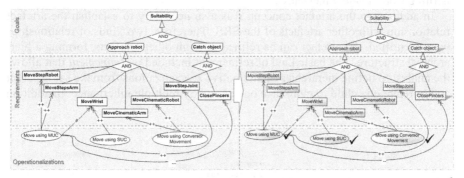

**Fig. 1.** Propagation of Satisfiability/Denegability(Selected Operationalization ✔, Satisfied Goal or Requirement ⬛Satisfied⬛, Denied Goal or Requirement ⬛Denied⬛ )

---

[2] (Kavakli and Loucopoulos 2004) offer a detailed comparative framework about these proposals and their role in Requirements Engineering

proposals and constitutes an important obstacle while applying a specific Goal Model.

## 3 Our proposal

Our proposal took shape in the context of the ATRIUM methodology, presented by (Navarro et al. 2003), that guides the analyst through an iterative process, from a set of user/system needs to the instantiation of a Software Architecture. This proposal employs a Goal Model which is based on the (Dardenne et al. 1993) and (Chung et al. 2000) proposals. This Goal Model was extended by (Navarro et al. 2004) integrating the Aspect-Oriented approach, in order to achieve both the efficient management of crosscutting and the correct organization of the SRS (Software Requirement Specification). A set of techniques have been also incorporated to identify and specify *variability*, from the requirements stage, so that product lines and dynamic architectures can be dealt with. In this context, mechanisms for exploiting the ATRIUM Goal Model had to be defined and developed that do not only deal with specific expressiveness of the model but customize these techniques according to other specific needs.

In order to facilitate this customization a proposal for requirements metamodeling was developed and introduced in (Navarro et al. 2006). In this work, the most widely known notation for requirements specification (use cases, goal models, etc) were studied so as to identify the essential terms and concepts of each of them. Taking into account this study a metamodel for the essential concepts was defined that allows one to deal with generic expressiveness. The core concepts and their relationships are shown in Fig. 2. The first topic to consider was to define the metamodel is the description of artefacts. It allows one to describe any element to be included in the SRS. In this sense, any needed artefact can be described by inheriting from *Artefact* metaclass.

In addition to the artefact concept, it is also necessary to establish the artefact relationship with other artefacts of the SRS. Therefore, two kinds of relationships were identified. An artefact can be refined through other artefacts, forming a hierarchical structure. The basic kind of refinement included is *Refinement* that allows the analyst to define hierarchies of alternative specializations from the same parent and to relate one child to more than one parent by multiple inheritance. In addition

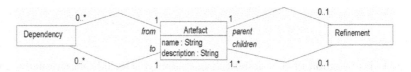

**Fig. 2.** Core Metamodel for Requirements Engineering

the *dependency* relationship has also been included in the metamodel. Perhaps this is the most conflictive relationship for consensus. For this reason, it is represented in its most generic form, i.e., by means of *Dependency* metaclass which is applicable to artefacts in the core. This metamodel has to be tailored according to the specific needs of expressiveness. With this purpose in mind, several steps were suggested to adapt and/or extend the metamodel. They need not be applied sequentially but in accordance with the analyst's preferences to describe new kinds of artefacts, relationships, attributes, constraints, etc, extending that described in the core.

In order to allow the analyst to customize the rules to be used during the propagation process an extension to the algorithm proposed by (Giorgini et al. 2003) has been developed. In this sense, the customization allows the analyst to include any kind of relationship and artefact along with their attributes to describe the propagation rules.

| | $(G_2,G_3)\xrightarrow{and}G_1$ | $G_2\xrightarrow{+S}G_1$ | $G_2\xrightarrow{-S}G_1$ | $G_2\xrightarrow{++S}G_1$ | $G_2\xrightarrow{-S}G_1$ |
|---|---|---|---|---|---|
| $sat(G_1)$ | $\min\left\{\begin{matrix}sat(G_2),\\sat(G_3)\end{matrix}\right\}$ | $\min\left\{\begin{matrix}sat(G_2),\\P\end{matrix}\right\}$ | N | $sat(G_2)$ | N |
| $den(G_1)$ | $\min\left\{\begin{matrix}den(G_2),\\den(G_3)\end{matrix}\right\}$ | N | $\min\left\{\begin{matrix}sat(G_2),\\P\end{matrix}\right\}$ | N | $sat(G_2)$ |

**Fig. 3.** Qualitative Propagation rules described by (Giorgini et al. 2003), where $\xrightarrow{++S}$, $\xrightarrow{-S}$, etc. are describing contribution relationships

(Giorgini et al. 2003) have described a set of rules to specify how the propagation has to be compute that Fig. 3 depicts. Sat($G_i$) and Den($G_i$) specify the satisfiability and deniability, respectively, of the goal $G_i$, whose value is taken from the ordered set {"++","--","+", "-", "#"}. For example, let $G_2$ and $G_3$ subgoals of $G_1$ refined by using an AND relationship, the satisfiability of $G_1$ is set to the minimum of satisfiability of its subgoals. This means that $G_1$ is undefined, partially satisfied or totally satisfied depending on which minimum value between $G_2$ and $G_3$ is. As can be observed in Fig. 1 "*ApproachRobot*" is fully satisfied because each one of its subgoals is satisfied. Regarding contribution relationships, Fig. 3 depicts that an asymmetric propagation is performed. For instance, $G_2\xrightarrow{+S}G_1$ means that if $G_2$ is satisfied, then there is some evidence that $G_1$ is satisfied, but if $G_2$ is denied, then nothing is said about the satisfaction of $G_1$. On the contrary, if the relationship is $G_2\xrightarrow{-S}G_1$ then there is some evidence that $G_1$ is denied whether $G_2$ is satisfied, but if $G_2$ is satisfied, then nothing is said about the satisfaction of $G_1$. But Giorgini et al.'s have also described the rules for symmetric propagation. In that case, these rules consider the propagation of both satisfiability and deniability. An example could be the relationship $G_2\xrightarrow{+}G_1$ that means that if G2 is satisfied (denied), then there is some evidence that G1 is satisfied (denied).

**Table 1.** Propagation algorithm based on (Giorgini et al. 2003)'s proposal

```
label array Label_Graph(graph (G, R); label array Initial)
    Current=Initial;
    do
        Old=Current;
        for each Gᵢ ∈ G do Current[i] = Update_Label(i, (G, R) Old);
    until (Current==Old);
    return Current;

label Update_Label(int i; graph (G, R); label array Old)
    for each Rⱼ ∈ R s.t. target(Rⱼ) == Gᵢ do
        satᵢⱼ = Apply Rules Sat(Gᵢ;Rⱼ ;Old);                      //dropped
        denᵢⱼ = Apply Rules Den(Gᵢ;Rⱼ ;Old);                     //dropped
    return (maxⱼ(maxⱼ(satⱼ);Old[i].sat), max(maxⱼ(denᵢⱼ);Old[i].den))
```

```
        for each Aₖ∈ A AND Aₖ∈ set_valuable_attributes(Gi)        //added
            if applicable (Aₖ, Gᵢ, Rⱼ, Old)                       //added
                valuate (Aₖ, Gᵢ, Rⱼ, Old)                         //added
        return set_valuable_attributes(Gᵢ);                       //added

boolean applicable(Attribute Aₖ;Artifact Gᵢ;Relation Rⱼ;         //added
labelarray Old)
    // depending on the specific rule it will check if            //added
    // the valuation can be performed                             //added

valuate(Attribute Aₖ; Artifact Gᵢ; Relation Rⱼ;                  //added
        label array Old)                                          //added
    // depending on the specific rule it will perform             //added
    // the valuation of the attribute Aₖ                          //added
```

Table 1 shows how Giorgini et al.'s algorithm has been modified for customization purposes, highlighting the added pseudo-code with shadowed text and the dropped pseudo-code with a grey text. Two main functions were initially described by Giorgini et al.'s: *"Label_Graph"* which iterates through the goal model until there is no changes in the satisfibiality and deniability; and *"Update_Label"* which apply the appropriate rule, from those described in Fig. 3 and depending on the kind of relationship, to compute the satisfibiality and deniability of each node of the graph. As can be noticed, the initial proposal only describes the valuation for two attributes (sat and den) with a fixed set of rules (Fig. 3). However, with our proposal this set and attributes can be customized according to the specific needs of the project, as will be described below.

It is shown in Table 1 that whenever a rule has to be applied two steps must be performed. First, *applicable* describes which state or situation has to be satisfied in order to apply a specific rule. Second, *valuate* specifies the propagation computation when a rule is applied. In view of this, the grammar for defining both quantitative and qualitative rules is introduced by using the Backus-Naur Form (BNF). Table 2 and Table 3 show how applicable and valuate can be described, respectively. By using this grammar the rules defined by (Giorgini et al. 2003) can be easily described as shown in formulae (1) and (3).

**Table 2.** BNF for describing condition grammar

```
<condition> ::= `(`<condition>`)'<relational_op>`(`<condition>`)'
                | not `(`<condition> `)' | <node> <logic_op> <node>
<node>    ::= <identifier>|<expression>| <function>`(`<identifier> `)'
<identifier>   ::= <id_kind_artefact>`.'<id_attribute>
              | <id_ kind_relation>`.'<id_attribute>
<function>   ::= max | min | count | avg
<relational_op>::= `&&' | `||' | `%%'
<logic_op>:::= `>' | `>=' | `=' | `!=' | `<=' | `<' | `>'
<expression>   ::= `''<string>`'' | <number>
```

**Table 3.** BNF for describing valuation grammar

```
<valuation>::=id_kind_artefact>`.'<id_kind_enum_attr>`=' <val_enum>
      | <id_kind_artefact>`.'<id_ kind_numb_attr> `=' <val_ numb>
<val_enum>   ::= <id_kind_artefact>`.'<id_ kind_enum_attribute>
   |<expression_enum>
   |<funct_enum>`(`<id_kind_artefact>`.'<id_ kind_enum_attribute> `)'
<funct_enum>   ::= max | min
<val_ numb>::=`(`<val_numb>`)'<op_numb>`(`<val_numb>`)'| <ident_num>
            | <funct_num> `(` <ident_num> `)'| <expression_num>
<funct_num> ::=  max | min | count | avg | sum | prod
<ident_num> ::= <id_kind_numbered_artefact>`.'<id_attribute>
            | <id_ kind_relation>`.'<id_attribute>
<op_numb>   ::= `+' | `-' | `*' | `/'
```

For instance, considering how the *CONTRIBUTION* relationship ( $G_2 \xrightarrow{label} G_1$ ) is evaluated by Giorgini et al. we can appreciate that both the state of this relationship and the Goal source ($G_S$) are used to determine if the rule can be applied or not. In this sense, the condition could be described as: $G_S(satisfied)$ && *label=--S*, i.e., $G_S$ has an attribute that describes if $G_S$ is satisfied. It is similarly applied to *label*, i.e., *CONTRIBUTION* relationship needs an attribute for specifying *--S* as its current state. In these terms, the best alternative is to represent these attributes following a syntax as described in Table 2 for *<identifier>*, i.e., by prefixing the attribute name with the name of the artefact or the relationship (see (1)).

In addition, when refinement relationships are considered, for instance an AND relationship ( $(G_1 K G_n) \xrightarrow{and} G_D$ ), some functions may be needed to determine the condition being applied to the set of artefacts $G_1$ to $G_n$. For this reason, an easy alternative is to use group functions as *<function>* describes in Table 2.

Furthermore, it is worthy of note that conditions can be combined to express other more complex ones. This will be described by using relational operations. This means that it would be possible to describe conditions such as:

$$\text{(Goal}_S\text{.satisfied ='Full') and (CONTRIBUTION.label) = '-S'} \qquad (1)$$

$$\text{(Goal}_i\text{.type ='Peformance') and (Goal}_i\text{.priority ='High') and} \qquad (2)$$
$$\text{min(Goal}_i\text{.satisfied ='Full') = 2}$$

In a similar maner, the syntax for the valuation is described by using the BNF (Table 3). As was stated in section 2, both quantitative and qualitative valuation should be described. For this reason, we have to distinguish between the two in order to make the peculiarities inherent in both kinds of valuations available. While describing qualitative valuations only enumerated attributes are made available to the analyst. This restriction is straightforward so that possible valuations are always constrained to a set of values. For instance, when considering the satisfiability, as described by Giorgini et al., the set *{Full, Partial, None}* is used. It also facilitates the valuation of this kind of attributes by describing functions for enumerations (*<function_enum>*). This requires that the set be defined as an ordered set in order to be able to properly apply these functions (min and max). This means that the valuation for an AND relationship (Fig. 3) could be easily described as appears in (3).

$$\text{Goal}_D\text{.satisfied} = \text{min(Goal}_i\text{.satisfied)} \qquad (3)$$

Related to the artefacts involved in a refinement relationship, aggregated functions (*<function_num>*) can be used for its treatment as described in:

$$\text{Goal}_D\text{.satisfied} = \text{sum(Goal}_i\text{.satisfied) - prod(Goal}_i\text{.satisfied)} \qquad (4)$$

Some specific rules had to be introduced since ATRIUM Goal Model was defined to facilitate the analysis of variability. For instance, it has to be considered that whenever a *variation point* is described, its *multiplicity* must be defined, i.e., how many variants must exist at the same time in a product or architecture when the variability is being removed. Table 4 shows how rule OR relationship has been modified for dealing with variability.

**Table 4.** Defining rules for variability analysis

|  | Relationship | Condition | Valuation |
|---|---|---|---|
| Giorgini et al. | Satisfiability ($G_1...G_n \xrightarrow{OR} G_D$) |  | $\text{Goal}_D\text{.Sat} = \text{max(Goal}_i\text{.Sat)}$ |
| Variability | Satisfiability ($G_1...G_n \xrightarrow{OR} G_D$) | (count(Goal$_i$.Sat=="+S") + count(Goal$_i$.Sat=="++S")) >= OR.multiplicity.min && (count(Goal$_i$.Sat=="+S") + count(Goal$_i$.Sat=="++S")) <= OR.multiplicity.max) | $\text{Goal}_D\text{.Sat} = \text{max(Goal}_i\text{.Sat)}$ |

# 4 Morpheus: Using dynamic compilation techniques

With the aim of supporting this proposal a tool called MORPHEUS has been used. Due to the fact that it has to manage each model defined by ATRIUM (Requirements Model, Scenarios Model and Software Architecture Model) three different environments are provided by MORPHEUS (Fig. 4). Related to the Requirements Model, MORPHEUS is able not only to define both new kinds of artefacts and relationships but also to instantiate and exploit them, in such a way Goal Models with different expressiveness can be defined. For this reason, the Requirements Model environment has been split into two different working contexts. The first one allows analysts to establish the requirements metamodel to be used by means of the Metamodel Editor; and the second provides analysts with facilities for modelling according to the defined metamodel by using the Model Editor.

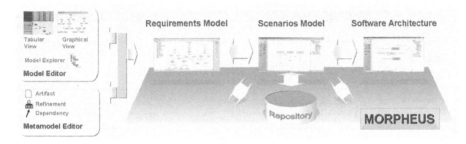

**Fig. 4.** Describing MORPHEUS capabilities MORPHEUS capabilities

In addition, MORPHEUS has been developed with capabilities to extend its functionality with analysis techniques. The main reason is that as new metamodels are defined, their related techniques can also be included and exploited. An example of this capability has been the development and integration of an add-in for Goal Model analysis based on satisfability propagation. Fig. 5 shows how this add-in has been designed. It has been split into three main components: a Rules Editor, a Code Compiler and a Propagation Processor.

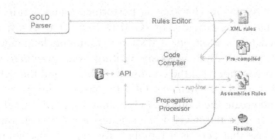

**Fig. 5.** A sketched view of the propagation add-in

Figure 6 shows what MORPHEUS looks like whenever the Rule Editor is loaded. For its development several alternatives were evaluated. However, the usability of the proposal was one of the main characteristics to be achieved. For this reason, a user interface (Rule Editor in Fig. 5) that allows the analyst to introduce the rules in a simple and comprehensible manner was developed. The Rule Editor is split into three main parts: a browser, a rules descriptor and an editor. The browser allows one to navigate through the relationships and the artefacts connected by them. The rules descriptor displays the applicable rules, for a selected relationship and source and destination artefacts. It can be appreciated that the *when* text box describes the condition and next to it appears the valuation. Below the rules descriptor, a visual control permits to edit the condition and the valuation. This provides the analyst with several buttons and capabilities that prevent him from knowing any detail about how his/her metamodel is described in the repository or how rules are internally implemented.

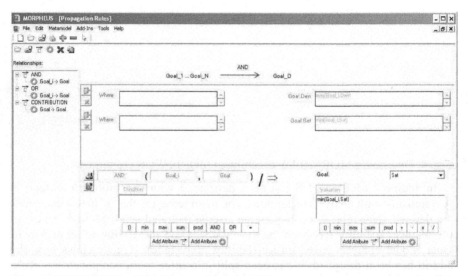

**Fig. 6.** MORPHEUS while loading the Rule Editor

In addition, a syntactic checking is performed when a rule is being defined thanks to the capabilities provided by (GOLD 2005). This is a free parsing system that can be used to develop one's own programming languages, scripting languages and interpreters by previously writing your grammar using BNF. The BNF, which was described for the condition (Table 2) and the valuation (Table 3), was introduced in GOLD. Then, the GOLD Parser Builder was used to analyze this grammar and create the Compiled Grammar Table file (CGT) used by a compilation engine. It uses this CGT file to generate a C# skeleton program with a custom parser class that acts as a template for parsing any source satisfying the BNF grammar. By means of this template, the specific compilation to the objective code can be described. In this case, a translation to C# code was performed to make available artifacts and relationships from the repository, and that computation which was needed for both condition and valuation. So, for each rule its valuation and condition description along with their respective compilation to C# is stored in a XML rules file to be lately used for the Code Compiler. The performance could have been seriously compromised due to the necessity of representing these rules as code for its use in run-time. For this reason, the approach of dynamic compiling, while it is more complex, provides us with a proper solution. Microsoft .NET Code Document Object Model technology, as described by (Harrison 2003), has been used for this purpose for the implementation of the Code Compiler.

By using Code Compiler (Fig. 5) a set of assemblies, containing both the rule code and other functionality, is generated at run time. For each rule, which is saved in a XML rule file, a C# class is generated which inherits from IRule. It is an abstract class with two abstracts methods to override for each inherited class: applicable function, which checks if the rule can be applied; and valuate function, which performs the propagation computation. This class also has a set of functions to perform the minimum, maximum, etc. So, while generating code, each rule C# class is going to override the abstract methods with that code stored in the XML rule file. Other classes are also used for the management of the generated classes which are previously pre-compiled to speed up this process.

Afterwards, these assemblies are accessed by the Propagation Processor to perform the propagation on a specific goal model and generate the results. In terms of integration, Propagation Processor makes use of the MORPHEUS API to access the model and will pass through the relations and artefacts retrieved from the repository.

# 5 Conclusions and further work

Goal Models are a very promising technique to improve requirements elicitation. Thanks to their special capabilities to analyze goals/requirements, they can be used at early stages of requirements engineering process, when alternatives are explored, conflicts are identified and, in general, the project is in the phase of requirement negotiation. However, Goal Model techniques must face a common obstacle in requirements engineering: the diversity of proposals with an evident lack of integration; and the specific needs of the project (or domain), which usually requires a customization of the requirement method and its notation.

We have presented a framework to cope with the integration and customization problem in requirements engineering techniques. In this work, we have used our framework to provide customizable support in Goal Model propagation analysis. We have illustrated how the propagation rules can be defined according to a specific metamodel. In this way, we can not only establish propagation rules for analysis but also redefine the propagation rules whenever it is necessary. This functionality was provided by means of dynamic compilation techniques using CodeDom. MORPHEUS, a tool we have developed to give support to our approach, was extended with an add-in which allows the analyst to define propagation rules associated to the established metamodel and perform their computation.

Following this line of research, our ongoing work covers several issues. First, we intend to go more deeply into the analysis and exploitation of Goal Models using the specification of the goal/requirements itself apart from its attributes and relationships with other goals/requirements. This entails working with formal specifications of requirements (at least at some level of formalization) to perform a deeper verification and provide some automated support for the Goal Model specification. Other interest is to improve the mechanisms for analyzing the propagation, including graphical visualization (apart from tabular representation) and predefined report analysis. Finally, we are working on the establishment of precedence mechanisms for solving conflicts when more than one rule is applicable.

# 6 References

Chung L, Nixon B A, Yu E and Mylopoulos J (2000) Non-Functional Requirements in Software Engineering, Kluwer Academic Publishing.

Dardenne A, Lamsweerde A van, and Fickas S (1993) Goal-directed Requirements Acquisition. Science of Computer Programming, 20, pp 3-50.

Giorgini P, Nicchiarelli E, Mylopoulous J, and Sebastiani R (2003) Formal reasoning techniques for goal models. Journal of Data Semantics, 1: 1-20.

GOLD Parsing System, http://www.devincook.com/GOLParser/ index.htm, 2005.

Hansen K M, Ravn A P, Stavridou V (1998) From Safety analysis to software requirements. IEEE Tran. on Software Engineering, 24(7):573-584.

Harrison N (2003) Using the CodeDOM. O'Reilly Network, http://www.ondotnet.com/pub/a/dotnet/2003/02/03/codedom.html.

Kavakli E and Loucopoulos P (2004) Goal Driven Requirements Engineering: Analysis and Critique of Current Methods. In: Krogstie J, Halpin T and Siau K (eds) Information Modeling Methods and Methodologies, 102-124.

Lamsweerde A van (2000) Goal-Oriented Requirements Engineering: A Roundtrip from Research to Practice. In: Proc 12th IEEE International Requirements Engineering Conference, IEEE Computer Society, Los Alamitos, pp 4-7.

Letier E and Lamsweerde A van (2004) Reasoning about Partial Goal Satisfaction for Requirements and Design Engineering. In: Taylor R N, Dwyer M B (eds) Proc of 12th ACM International Symposium on the Foundations of Software Engineering, ACM Press, New York, pp 53-62.

Navarro E, Letelier P, Mocholí, J.A. Ramos I (2006) A Metamodeling Approach for Requirements Specification. Journal of Computer Information Systems, 46(5): 67-77, Special Issue on Systems Analysis and Design.

Navarro E, Letelier P and Ramos I (2004) Goals and Quality Characteristics: Separating Concerns, Early Aspects 2004: Aspect-Oriented Requirements Engineering and Architecture Design Workshop, collocated to OOPSLA.

Navarro E, Ramos I and Pérez J (2003) Software Requirements for Architectured Systems. In Proc of 11th IEEE International Requirements Engineering Conference, IEEE Computer Society, Los Alamitos, pp 365-366 (position paper).

# Cookie-Chain Based Discovery of Relation between Internet Users and Real Persons

Csaba Legány, Attila Babos, Sándor Juhász

## 1 Introduction

It is very important for Internet content providers to keep track of the amount of visitors of their sites. The content of the pages and advertisements can be improved by knowing statistical properties of the visitors.

The amount of visitors is not easy to be estimated because the human user cannot be identified and distinguished directly on the servers. In order to solve this problem, instead of real persons Internet users are used. An Internet user is essentially a browser related session of a user logged in to a specific computer. These sessions can be identified on server-side by cookies. Unfortunately more Internet users can belong to the same real person (e.g. a businessman uses his home and office computers) or more real persons can belong to the same Internet user (e.g. public access at school).

The number of Internet users can be estimated by providing each client a unique identifier. The most common method for identifying Internet users is based on client-side cookies. There are two different types of cookies used, the $3^{rd}$ and the $1^{st}$ party cookies [1, 2]. The main difference between these cookies is that while $1^{st}$ party cookies are provided by the page browsed currently, $3^{rd}$ party cookies are placed by foreign, third party sites. This third party site in our case belongs to a web-auditing company [3, 4, 5]. Since web pages often contain advertisements from foreign sites, they can also set $3^{rd}$ party cookies on the clients, so client-side security software might remove them periodically. Servers-side web logs are used to track the client activity by recording the pages visited by Internet users. These log records usually contain the user identifier stored in the cookie, the client IP address, the URL of the visited pages and other statistical data.

In this paper we provide a method that helps to estimate the relation of Internet users and real persons. This method requires the efficient management of web log entries, so we developed a new data structure called Linked Reversed Tree (LRT). The LRT has been optimized for both **building** and searching the user data. The rest of the paper is organized as follows. Section 2 introduces our basic notations (cookie-chains and nets), while Section 3 discusses common data structures allowing to handle them. Section 4 contains the description of our new data structure. LRT. In Section 5 we provide measurements to compare the new approach to the other data structures. We conclude by summarizing our results.

## 2 Cookie-Chains and Networks

The web log entries in server side web log files contain detailed information on the whole user activity. As the log is written in chronological order records of several users are interleaving. In order to estimate the number of visitors during a time period the information belonging to a given user must be separated. Let an entry sequence in the web log be called a cookie-chain (noted by CC) if these entries belong to the same Internet user.

A cookie-chain is built based on the user ID-s carried by the $3^{rd}$ party and $1^{st}$ party cookies. If these cookies are removed from a computer, all the cookie-chains on the server side will be closed. If the user continues to browse the web, new cookies will be set, and the new server-side log entries will belong to a new cookie-chain. If a person uses multiple computers for browsing, he/she will have entries in several cookie-chains, because he/she will be identified as a different Internet user. In order to join these cookie-chains (and Internet users) in both cases, a non-cookie based identification method is required. Websites having registration database (e.g. e-mail providers) identify their users with special unique login identifiers (noted as UID-s). These sites can track their users independently from the computer they use. Cookie-chains can be connected with each other by common UID-s to form cookie-networks. There are two cookie-chains visible in Figure 1, having three UID-s each. They can be joined to a cookie-network because they have one UID in common (filled gray on the figure).

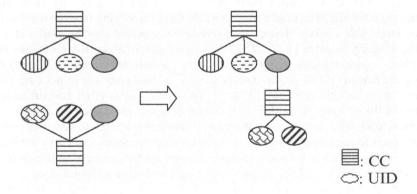

$\boxplus$: CC
$\bigcirc$: UID

**Fig. 1.** Joining cookie-chains

The cookie-networks are disjoint sets of log entries having no connection to the other networks (no common $3^{rd}$ or $1^{st}$ party cookie, or UID). Figure 2 shows typical cookie-networks.

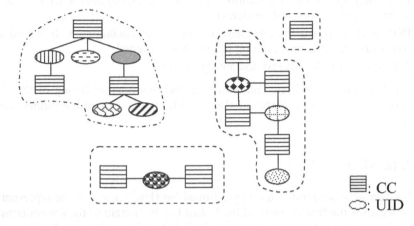

**Fig. 2.** Cookie-networks

The disjoint sets of cookie-networks are the starting point of further processing since the size of them is much smaller than the total size of web log entries, which means that more complex business rules can be run much easier on them. The business rules making possible to find the ID-s belonging to the same visitors and discovering the number of real persons behind the Internet users are out of the scope of this paper, here we only concentrate on the first step, the efficient separation of cookie-networks.

## 3 Theory of Disjoint Sets

Section 2 introduced how web log entries can be joined to form cookie-chains and how they can be connected into disjoint cookie-networks. The algorithm for creating disjoint sets is made up of the following steps [6, 7, 8, 9]:

1. In the beginning we *create* a set separately for each CC and for each UID, containing only the given element.
2. We iterate through all the CC-s. We *find* the set containing the CC and the sets containing the UID-s belonging to this CC, and we *join* the found sets.

Necessary operations highlighted above will be implemented by the following operations: MAKE-SET, FIND-SET and UNION.

Sets should be represented by a data structure, which allows the previous algorithm to run with the smallest possible amount of memory load and execution time. Every set will be accessible through its representative element, which must be the same until the set changes.

Three functions should be supported by the data structure according to the algorithm [7, 8, 12]:

- MAKE-SET(x): creates and returns a new set containing only x which is also chosen to be the representative element.
- FIND-SET(x): returns the representative of the set containing x. It should always return the same result if a set has not been changed.
- UNION(x, y): unifies the sets containing x and y.

As it is obvious, this basic data structure does not support listing of the elements of a set, so this feature should also be added in order to enable further processing.

## 3.1 Linked List

This data structure models a set by a linked list (Fig. 3.), where the representative of the set is the first member of the linked list. Each item of the list contains a Data value, a pointer to the next item of the list (Next), a pointer to the first item (Head). There are two special fields that are only valid in the representative element: a pointer to the last element (Last) and the size of the set.

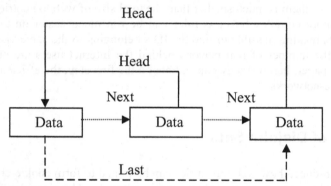

**Fig. 3.** Linked List

Implementation of basic functions:

- MAKE-SET(x): Creates a new list element containing only x, Head points to itself, Next is NULL, and Size is 1. Return value is a pointer to the only member of the list.
- FIND-SET(x): Returns the Head pointer of x.
- UNION(x, y): Finds the Head pointers of x and y. If the pointer are the same, it indicates that x and y belong to the same set, so nothing further is to do. If not, append the shorter list to the end of the longer.

Since we have to change the Head pointer of each element in the appended list, it is worth to join the shorter one to the longer.

It is vital that MAKE-SET and FIND-SET are of O(1) complexity, while UNION takes O(k) time if k is the length of the shorter list. It has been proven that a sequence of m MAKE-SET, UNION, and FIND-SET operations, n of which are MAKE-SET operations, takes

$$O(m + n * \log n) \tag{1}$$

time [8, 11].

## 3.2 Reversed Tree

Compared to the linked list, the representative of each set is the root of the tree. Every node contains a Data value, a pointer to the parent node (Parent). The size of the set should be stored in the root (Fig. 4).

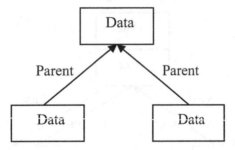

**Fig. 4.** Reversed Tree

Implementation of basic functions:

- MAKE-SET(x): Creates and returns a new node containing only x, whose Parent pointer is NULL, and the size is 1.
- FIND-SET(x): Returns the root of x by moving upward in tree along the Parent pointers. Each node's Parent pointer should be set to the found root (path compression, [9]).
- UNION(x, y): It finds the roots of x and y. If the pointers are the same, x and y belong to the same set, so nothing more is to do. If not, then the smallest tree's root should be added to the other tree as a child (size-based unification).

MAKE-SET is of constant time, but the other two operations depend on the depth of the trees. Without path compression and size-based unification it would be slower than the operations of the linked list. It has been proved that a sequence of *m* MAKE-SET, UNION, and FIND-SET operations, *n* of which are MAKE-SET operations, takes

$$O(m \, \alpha(n)) \tag{2}$$

time where $\alpha(n)$ is the inverse-Ackermann function, which is constant in practice (if $n <= 10^{80}$, $1 <= \alpha(n) <= 4$) [8,9].

## 4 Linked Reversed Tree

Cookie-networks can be found with the reversed tree quite fast, but we cannot list the items of the sets efficiently because we do not have any pointers from the root downwards since the tree is reversed. It is very easy to enumerate the items of a linked list however the unification of sets takes long. We suggest using a new data structure that combines the advantages of the above mentioned ones. The new data structure named Linked Reverse Tree (LRT) contains a Data value, a pointer to the parent node (like the reversed tree), a pointer to the next value (like the linked list), the size of the set and a pointer to the last item (like the linked list). Size and Last pointer are only valid in the representative item. The items should be linked in a way that the root of the tree should be the head of the list, so we will get the same representative handling independent from handling it as a simple reversed tree or a linked list. LRT is displayed on Figure 5.

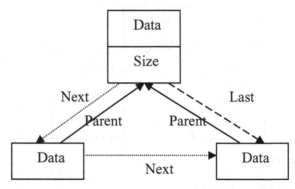

**Fig. 5.** Linked Reversed Tree

Implementation of basic functions:

- MAKE-SET(x): Same as the function of reversed tree
- FIND-SET(x): Same as the function of reversed tree. Note, that path compression does not harm the linkages.
- UNION(x, y): Like the function of the reversed tree, but the Last and Next pointers should be set.

UNION contains only constant time operations but for the two FIND-SET function calls. These increase a bit the creation time, but the members of the sets can be listed quickly from the root along the Next pointers.

The LRT can be used for finding disjoint sets as follows on Figure 6, supposing that the UID-s belonging to each cookie-chain are available directly (these lists can be made during the pre-processing phase, when the cookie-chains are discovered).

```
FOR EACH cc IN CCList
    ccs.Add(cc,MAKE-SET(cc));
```

```
FOR EACH uid IN UIDList
  uids.Add(uid,MAKE-SET(uid));
FOR EACH cc IN CCList
  FOR EACH uid IN cc.UIDList
    UNION(ccs.GetByKey(cc),uids.GetByKey(uid));
```

**Fig. 6.** Use of LRT-s to make disjoint sets

The algorithm creates a new 1-element set separately for each CC and for each UID, containing only the given element. It iterates through all the CC-s. It finds the set containing the selected CC and the sets containing the UID-s belonging to this CC, and joins the found sets. Due to efficiency reasons, the pointers returned by MAKE-SET will be stored in hash tables, separately for CC-s and UID-s (*ccs* and *uids*), because later we need these reference. The *Add* function of ccs and uids adds a new cc-set pair to the hash table, while the *GetByKey* function returns the set for the input key. Note, that if the structure representing a cookie-chain is created by ourselves, then we can reserve a field in it for the reference to an LRT element instead of using hash table. The UID is typically a number, therefore the other hash table is always needed.

Cookie-networks can be listed by finding root elements and listing the nodes of the trees by following the Next pointers. Each CC network will be listed once with this algorithm.

The memory required by the algorithm depends on the size of the data to be stored in the trees. As we mentioned in 3.2 if we have a sequence of $m$ MAKE-SET, UNION, and FIND-SET operations, $n$ of which are MAKE-SET operations, it takes $O(m\ \alpha(n))$ time to build a reversed tree. If Linked Reversed Tree is used and we have n cookie-chains, m UID-s and p CC - UID pairs, creating the disjoint sets requires n + m MAKE-SET and p UNION operations and listing all the cookie-nets is linear. So the whole time complexity is

$$O((n + m + p)\ \alpha(n + m) + n + m) = O((n + m + p)\ \alpha\ (n + m)) \tag{3}$$

# 5 Experimental Results

The building time of CC networks was been measured with different types of synthetic data. There is a measurable difference in the building time for each data structure even when relatively few cookie-chains are used. Single cookie-networks containing 1023...16383 cookie-chains were generated, each of them contained two real persons.

As expected from the theory, the building of the tree took the smallest amount of time, the LRT's building time was only a bit greater, while the building time of the list should be the largest since we had to change the Head pointer frequently because of the high number of UNION calls. Our results are detailed on Figure 7 and it can be stated that the difference in building time between the list and the tree-based data structures increases with the size of the cookie-chains. The building time of the tree is only a bit smaller than the building time of the LRT. However, if there are only a few CC-s in the network, there is no significant difference between the building times of the different data structures.

Figure 8 contains the results of listing the elements of the sets. As expected, the use of tree data structure is the slowest, and there is no significant difference between the results of the list and the LRT.

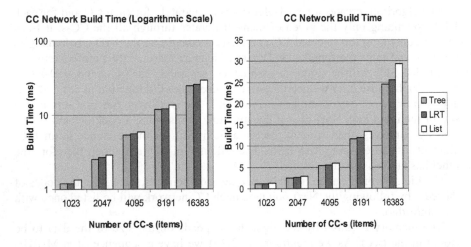

**Fig. 7.** Comparison of creation time of cookie-networks

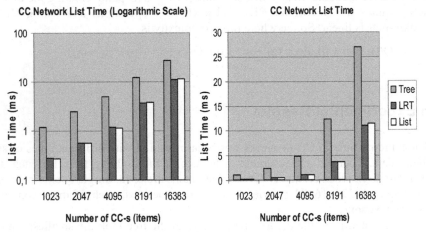

**Fig. 8.** Comparison of listing time of cookie-networks

# 6 Conclusions

This paper presented an optimization method for cookie-based estimation of the relation between the number of Internet users and real persons in a given scenario. Without detailing the actual business rules, we focused on speeding up the preparation step, namely building the disjoint cookie-networks out of cookie-chains belonging to different Internet users. After a short description of these concepts we gave a detailed description of a new data structure, the Linked Reversed Tree (LRT) developed for their efficient management. The new approach combines the advantages of the two well-known data structures (linked list and reversed tree). It has been shown by measurements that with LRT it takes only slightly longer to build the cookie-networks than with the reversed tree however it proved to be as efficient in listing the elements as the list structure was. These experiments showed that in processing large web logs LRT has a considerable advantage. Performance measurements and comparisons on real web logs in the near future is important part of our plans.

# References

1.  Understanding cookies http://www.microsoft.com/resources documentation/windows/xp/all/proddocs/en-us/sec_cook.mspx?mfr=true
2.  AboutCookies.org, a guide to deleting and controlling cookies http://www.aboutcookies.org
3.  Cookies: The Perfect User Identification Snack http://www.clickstream-datawarehousing.com/article06.html
4.  Coremetrics auditing http://www.coremetrics.com/technology/first_party.html
5.  Median webaudit http://www.webaudit.hu/
6.  Dexter C. Kozen. *The Design and Analysis of Algorithms.* Springer-Verlag, 1992.
7.  John E. Hopcroft and Jeffrey D. Ullman. Set merging algorithms. *SIAM Journal on Computing,* 2(4): 294–303, 1973.
8.  Cormen – Leiserson – Rivest – Stein: Új algoritmusok (Section 21.)
9.  Alfred V. Aho, John E. Hopcroft, and Jeffrey D. Ullman. *Data Structures and Algorithms.* Addison-Wesley, 1983.
10. Robert E. Tarjan. Class notes: Disjoint set union. COS 423, Princeton University, 1999.
11. Robert E. Tarjan and Jan van Leeuwen. Worst-case analysis of set union algorithms. *Journal of the ACM,* 31(2): 245–281, 1984.
12. Aho, A. V., J. E. Hopcroft, and J. D. Ullman [1974]." The Design and Analysis of Computer Algorithms," Addison-Wesley, Reading, Mass

## 6 Conclusions

## References

# Requirements Modeling and MDA – Proposal for a Combined Approach

Christian Kop*, Heinrich C. Mayr* and Nataliya Yevdoshenko**

*Alpen-Adria-Universität Klagenfurt, Klagenfurt, Austria
(chris | mayr )@ifit.uni-klu.ac.at
**National Technical University, Kharkiv, Ukraine
yevdoshenko@gmail.com

## 1 Introduction

Conceptual modeling and MDA is becoming more and more important for Information Systems (IS) development. Tools which support code generation are already on the market. However, the problem still remains, that end users who are not familiar with these models do not understand them. As a result, the communication is still on a very concrete level based on the natural language description of requirements with all it's deficiencies (e.g. ambiguity, incompleteness and huge requirements documents).

To overcome this problem a requirements modeling language which is something in between pure natural language specifications and conceptual modeling languages seems to be necessary. Such a language must achieve certain criteria. It must be handled easily. As any other modeling language it must deal with structural, behavioral as well as non functional aspects. Simple basic notions should be used.

Several methodologies have been developed so far which focus on different concepts and techniques to improve the communication (e.g. goal modeling [6], scenario based approaches [12],[13] and story boarding [14]). Furthermore the need for a controlled natural language as a meeting point between natural and formal languages was proposed in [2].

To encourage the communication between end users and designers, KCPM (Klagenfurt Conceptual Predesign Model) focuses on a user centered representation concept and a small set of modeling notions. The representation concept of KCPM is based on a glossary notation which was introduced firstly in [1]. In our opinion, the glossary notation provides the possibility to make checks for blanks.

If there is no entry in a line/column, then it seems that some information is missing. Since end users often work with tables and glossaries (e.g. EXCEL sheets) communication during requirements analysis can be improved. However, also a graphical notation for more visual oriented users was developed.

Concerning the modeling notions, KCPM restricts itself to some basic notions which will be described in detail in section 2.

A requirements modeling language should also provide at least transformation heuristics to models of later IS development phases. KCPM does not provide source code generation but it provides transformation heuristics to generate conceptual models (e.g. UML). To provide a continuous modeling support from requirements to source code, thus it is obvious to combine KCPM with a MDA tool available on the market. The OLIVANOVA[1] modeling toolset with its modeling language (herein after referred to as OLIVANOVA model or target model) was chosen for the conceptual modeling phase and the source code generation. This combination has the following advantage for the communication between end-users and designers: End users can directly check the glossaries and they can see the resulting system sooner. Thus designers/system analysts and end-user can talk with each other using only well known and familiar representations.

In this paper we describe the combined approach by presenting both models and the mapping from KCPM to the target model for the notions thing type, connection type and operation type. Therefore these notions are introduced in section 2. Then the OLIVANOVA modeling paradigm is described (section 3). Whereas in the fourth section similarities and differences of KCPM and OLIVANOVA notions are discussed, in the fifth section the mapping methodology is explained in detail. The paper is concluded with future directions for this approach.

## 2 KCPM

An important aim for the development of KCPM was to provide both developers and end-users with an interface for their mutual understanding. The most important modeling notions of the static part of the approach are: thing-type and connection-type.

**Thing-type** is a generalization of the conceptual notions class and attribute. Thus, typical thing types are e.g. *author, book, contract* as well as descriptive characteristics like *customer name, product number, product description*. It seems to be easy to decide, which of the above examples is a class and which one is an attribute, but what about a notion used in a domain which is not well known by the designer (e.g. the notion *ICD10* in the medical domain). Using KCPM the question whether the notion is a class or an attribute will not be the main question since this will be supported during the mapping process. Instead the system analyst can concentrate on gathering additional information for that notion, which is much more important during requirements analysis. Meta-attributes which name the

---

[1] OLIVANOVA is a registered trademark of CARE Technologies, Spain.

glossary columns (e.g. Examples, Synonyms, etc.) give hints to ask the right questions (see Figure 1).

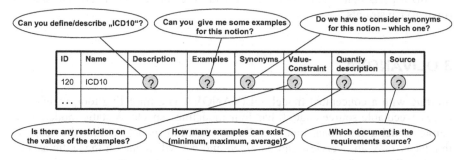

**Fig. 1.** Thing type glossary

This glossary approach works similar for all the other KCPM notions (connection type, operation type etc.) using other specific meta-attributes.

Things are related within the real world. To capture this, the KCPM model introduces the notion of **connection-type**. Two or more thing-types can be involved in a connection-type. This corresponds to the NIAM object/role model [8]. A Sentence (business rule) leading to a connection type could be the following: *Authors write books*.

The model is open for specific semantic connection-types (possession, composition, generalization, identification etc.) e.g. *An ISBN number identifies a book*.

For modeling behavior in the context of requirements analysis of business information systems, it proves to be useful to concentrate on the following principles:

- actors are capable to execute tasks/services,
- the execution of a task depends on some pre-conditions,
- the execution of a task results in some post-conditions,
- objects are related to pre- and post conditions.

Therefore, KCPM is restricted to the following main concepts: operation type, co-operation type and condition.

**Operation types** are used to model services as described in [3]. As such they may be seen as a generalization of the conceptual notions such as use case, activity, action, method, service. Each operation type is characterized by references to so-called thing types, which model the actors (executing actors and calling actors of the resp. operation type) and service parameters. For instance an ATM could be the executing actor which provides a service *give money*. A customer is the calling actor of that service. The thing type *money* could be an outgoing service parameter. Thing type *customer-code* could be the ingoing service parameter.

UoD dynamics emerge from actors (thing types) performing operations under certain circumstances (**pre-conditions**) and thus creating new circumstances (**post-conditions**). This is captured by the KCPM concept of **co-operation type**, a term which was adopted from object oriented business process modeling [4].

UoD aspects that cannot be modeled using the above notions are captured by (textual) constraints.

# 3 OLIVANOVA

Starting with a conceptual model, OLIVANOVA is a modeling tool, which produces executable source code. It has four modeling aspects. A static model, a dynamic model a functional model and a presentation model. Within the scope of this paper only an overview can be given and we will focus on the static aspects which will be needed for the mapping approach described in the next sections. For a more detailed description we refer to [9],[10],[11]. The static model consists of **classes, attributes, associations** and **services**. For each attribute the designer can specify features like the attribute type (constant, variable, derived), the data type it's size and a default value. Associations between classes have multiplicities as well as a static and a dynamic part. The static and the dynamic part of an association express how strong the relationships between objects in this association are. A service can have inbound and outbound parameters. Special classes (agents) can access attributes of other classes either directly or by the use of the services of these classes. A service itself can be categorized either as an **event**, an **operation** or a **transaction**. An event is an atomic service. Operations and transactions are complex services with the following distinction: transactions have a commit/rollback feature whereas operations have not. The OLIVANOVA modeler automatically generates three events for inserting, changing and deleting instances of a class.

In the functional model the designer can specify how attribute values are changed if an event is executed.

The dynamic model describes the behavior of the instances for the classes. Therefore state transition diagram and object interaction diagrams are used. For each class a standard state transition automatically is generated describing the necessary states of each instance of that class.

The presentation model is an abstract definition of how the user interface should look like.

# 4 A Comparison between the two models

Both described models have some similarities. However they have also differences, thus a 1:1 mapping is not always possible. Before the mapping process is described in the next section these differences have to be highlighted and discussed. Since this paper is a first proposal for the mapping, it is restricted to the most important structural aspects of both models.

## 4.1 Classes, attributes vs. thing types

This is the main difference between the two models. The target model uses the classical paradigm that each universe of discourse (UoD) has several objects with properties. Objects with the same properties are modeled as classes. This paradigm is essential for all the later stages of information system development. KCPM follows the principle that during requirements analysis the main task is to find concepts. It is not necessary to find out, which of them are classes or attributes. Therefore each named concept in the UoD has the same valence and hence is categorized as a thing type. Nevertheless, according to the collected information it is possible to map thing types to classes or attributes. Thus the designer can concentrate on collecting concepts and facts without thinking on such details.

## 4.2 Association vs. connection type

A connection type is a more general concept than an association. It will become an association, if both involved thing types are mapped to classes. If a connection type becomes an association we can derive the multiplicities from the cardinalities given in the KCPM schema.

For the static and dynamic part of an association default assumptions must be applied (e.g. each association has only dynamic parts).

There is one remaining problem: KCPM allows more than two involved thing types (e.g. ternary connection types with three involved thing types). If these entire thing types will become classes, there is currently now way, how such a ternary association can be presented in the target model. This problem will be discussed in section 5.2.

## 4.3 Service, event, transaction, operation vs. operation type

The target model provides three kinds of services: Event, Transaction and Operation. KCPM only offers the notion operation-type. The following mapping is possible

*Operation-types are mapped to services.*

Thus it is open which kind of service it will become.

In both models, parameters for services, respectively operation-types exist. Thus a 1:1 mapping can be applied:

*Ingoing and outgoing Parameters of operation types in the source model (KCPM) are mapped to inbound respectively outbound parameters of services in the target model (OLIVANOVA).*

## 4.4 Agent, classes vs. calling actor and executing actor

The target model distinguishes between classes that provide a service and classes (agents) that use a service or can access the attributes of the other kind of classes directly if they have agent-relationships to those classes. In KCPM the concept agent relationship does not exist. However KCPM has the concept of the calling actor and the executing actor. The executing actor is a thing type to which an operation type belongs and the calling actor is a thing type which uses the provided operation type of an executing actor. Agents and agent-relationships can be derived at least by mapping calling actors to agents having an agent relationship to the services which were derived from the called operation type. Thus the following two mapping hints can be applied:

*A calling thing type in the source model (KCPM) is mapped to an agent who calls a service in the target model (OLIVANOVA)*

*An executing thing type in the source model (KCPM) is mapped to a class that provides a service in the target model (OLIVANOVA)*

# 5 The Mapping Process

From the comparison of the two models and the first mapping hints, it should be clear that the main task of the mapping process is the derivation of classes and attributes from thing types. Afterwards a 1:1 mapping is much easier although some remaining concepts must be restructured. As already shown in the previous section, this mapping process is based on the idea to get a valid schema of the target model. Thus the mapping has two steps.

* In the first step the thing types should be detected which can be mapped to classes or attributes.
* In the second step concepts which cannot be mapped directly (e.g. ternary associations) must be restructured manually (restructuring step).

## 5.1 First step – mapping to classes and attributes.

The first step is based on a method which was developed to map KCPM notions to UML class diagrams [7]. This method is based on the idea, that classes and attributes can be derived from thing types, if all the collected information for each thing type in the KCPM schema is analyzed. The rules were divided into laws and proposals. Proposals give a hint that a thing type will become a certain target concept (e.g. a class) because of certain information collected in the KCPM schema. A law forces a certain target concept since otherwise the target schema will not be syntactically correct. Furthermore the rules are divided into direct and indirect rules. In a direct rule a KCPM concept can be mapped to a target concept (class, attribute) only with the given KCPM notions. An indirect rule can be applied to a KCPM concept which is currently not mapped but has some relationships to concepts which were already mapped to a target concept. From the definition of an indirect rule it follows that the first step itself has two sub-steps. Firstly, the mapping process tries to apply all direct rules for each thing type. The results are two sets. A set R of classes and attributes derived from thing types and a set T of thing types that could not be mapped for the moment. Secondly indirect rules are applied to the set T. In particular each element (thing type) t of T is determined if a rule can be applied because t has a specific connection to at least one element of R. This step is done iteratively until no more rules can be applied. The results of the second sub step are two sets: T' and R'. In the optimal case the set T' is empty which means all thing types could be mapped and thus belong to the set R'. For a non empty set T' the elements of T' must be mapped manually by the decision of the designer.

Meta rules are used to handle the priorities between the rules. In particular that means: A law overrules a proposal. If two contradicting laws can be applied for the same thing type t (e.g. one law says that t is a class where as the other says t is an attribute) then this contradiction must be solved manually by the designer.

Below a list of the most obvious rules is given in order to demonstrate the idea. There are also other rules but these rules require more specific knowledge of KCPM than can be presented in this paper.

### Rule 1 (Law/Direct)
*If a thing type is an executing actor in an operation type then it is a class.*

### Rule 2 (Law/Direct)
*If a thing type is a calling actor in an operation type then it is a class.*

### Rule 3 (Law/Direct)
*If a thing type is involved in a generalization as the general or the special thing type, then it is a class.*

### Rule 4 (Law/Direct)
*If a thing type is involved in an aggregation or in a composition as a part or an aggregate then it is a class.*

### Rule 5 (Proposal/Direct)
*If a thing type is involved with minimal cardinality 0 in a connection type then it may be mapped to a class.*

### Rule 6 (Proposal/Direct)
*If the name of a thing type has endings like "...type", "...number", "...date", "title" etc. then it may be mapped to an attribute. (Remark: the given examples ...type, ...number, ...date as well as the others must be stored in a domain specific dictionary)*

**Rule 7 (Law/Indirect)**
*If thing type t is connected to a thing type x (via a connection type) and x was mapped to an attribute in a former mapping iteration then t must be mapped to a class.*

The rules 1 – 4 represent specific situations which appear only with classes in the target model. Only classes can provide and use services (rule 1 and 2 since operation types will be mapped to services). Only classes can be involved in aggregation and generalization relationships in the target model. Therefore, thing-types involved in KCPM notions equivalent to generalization and aggregations must also be classes. Rule 5 is a proposal which means that the designer may overrule it. This proposal considers the minimal cardinality of a perspective as an existence dependence indicator: if the minimal cardinality is 0 then an instance of a thing-type may exist without a connection to the instance of another thing-type. Such a situation in our opinion is a hint that the thing-type might be mapped to a class. If the name of a thing type ends with the examples given in rule 6 then in a specific domain this thing type could be a candidate for an attribute. Rule 7 is an example of an indirect rule expressing that no two attributes should be connected directly. In other words the target schema must always consist of connections between a class and an attribute but not of connections between attributes only.

At the end of this step, all connection types where at least two classes have been derived from the involved thing types will become associations.

## 5.2 Restructuring

Although the mapping has produced associations, attributes, classes, services, agent and agent relation ships so far, there is still the following problem. What happens with **n-ary associations**, **attributes in associations** and **association classes**. These possibilities can be derived also from the KCPM schema but they are not legal in the target model. For all these three cases the same solution is proposed. The association itself is mapped to a class with connecting binary association to the classes which where involved in that association.

## 5.3 Tool support

To demonstrate the feasibility of the rules and the mapping process described in the previous sections, a mapping prototype was developed (see Figure 2). A specific project (diagram) can be selected and with the "Start mapping" button rules mentioned in section 5.1 are applied to each thing type of that project. The mapping result can be saved, imported and presented in the OLIVANOVA tool set. In order to import the mapping result into the OIVANOVA tool, the prototype transforms it to a XML representation of the OLIVANOVA model.

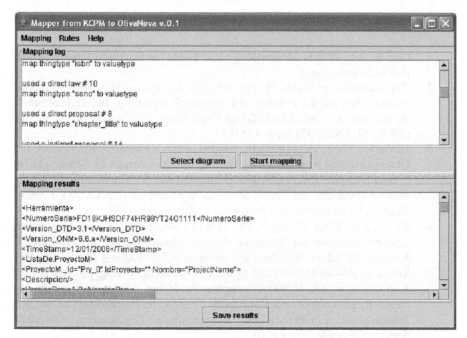

**Fig. 2.** Prototype which supports a first mapping from KCPM to OLIVANOVA

## 6 Conclusion

In this paper a combined modeling approach with KCPM and OLIVANOVA has been proposed. Functional requirements are collected and categorized first with KCPM. They will become thing types, connection types, operation types etc. The concepts can be presented in glossaries or graphically for validation. Then a mapping process transforms the KCPM schema to a first cut schema readable for the OLIVANOVA tool.

A prototype was developed for a feasibility study of the mapping approach. One future research task will be the definition of mapping rules to generate behavior models from the dynamic aspects of the KCPM model.

## 7 Acknowledgement

The authors would also like to thank the team of CARE Technologies, especially Harald Kirschner, for their substantial support.

# References

1. Ceri S (ed.) (1983) Methodology and Tools for Database Design, North Holland Publ. Comp.
2. Hoppenbrouwers SJBA, Proper HA, van der Weide TP (2005) A fundamental View on the Process of Conceptual Modeling. In.: Delcambre L et. al.: (eds.), 24th International Conference on Conceptual Modeling (ER2005), LNCS 3716, pp. 128-143
3. Hesse W, Mayr, HC (1998) Highlights of the SAMMOA Framework for Object Oriented Application Modelling. In: Quirchmayr G, Schweighofer E Bench-Capon JM. (eds.): Proceedings of the 9th International Conference of Database and Expert Systems Applications (DEXA'98), Lecture Notes in Computer Sience, Springer Verlag, pp 353-373
4. Kaschek R, Kohl, C, Mayr, HC (1995) Cooperations – An Abstraction Concept Suitable for Business Process Reengineering In: Györkös J, Krisper, M, Mayr HC. (eds.): Conference Proceedings ReTIS'95, Re-Technologies for Information Systems. Oldenburg Verlag, pp. 161 -172
5. Kop Ch, Mayr HC (1998) Conceptual Predesign – Bridging the Gap between Requirements and Conceptual Design. In Proceedings of the 3rd International Conference on Requirements Engineering. Colorado Springs Colorado, April 6-10
6. Mylopoulos J, Chung L, Yu, E (1999) From object oriented to goal oriented Requirements Analysis. In: Communications of the ACM, Vol. 42, No. 1, pp. 31-37
7. Mayr HC, Kop Ch (2002) A User Centered Approach to Requirements Modeling, Proc. Modellierung 2002, Lecture Notes in Informatics LNI p-12, GI-Edition, 2002, pp. 75-86
8. Nijssen GM, Halpin,TA (1989) Conceptual Schema and Relational Database Design – A fact oriented approach. Prentice Hall Publ. Comp.
9. Pastor O, Gomez J, Insfran E, Pelechano V (2001) The OO-method approach for information systems modeling: from object-oriented conceptual modeling to automated programming. Information Systems 26 (7), pp. 507-534
10. Pastor O, Molina JC, Iborra E (2004) Automated Production of Fully Functional Applications with OlivaNova Model Execution. In: ERCIM News, No. 57, April 2004, pp. 62-64
11. Pelechano V, Pastor O, Insfran E (2002) Automated code generation of dynamic specializations: an approach based on design patterns and formal techniques. In Data and Knowledge Engineering, 40 (3), pp. 315-353
12. Rolland C, Souveyet, C, Ben Achour C (1998) Guiding Goal Modeling Using Scenarios. In: IEEE Transaction on Software Engineering, Vol. 24, No. 12, 1998, pp. 1055-1071
13. Sutcliffe A, Maiden NA, Minocha S, Manuel D (1998) Supporting Scenario-Based Requirements Engineering In IEEE Transactions on Software Engineering, Vol 24, No. 12, pp. 1072-1088

14. Schewe KD, Thalheim B, Zlatkin S (2004) Modelling Actors and Stories in Web Information Systems. 3rd International Conference on Information Systems Technology and its Applications, LNI p-48, pp. 13-23

# Moral Problems in Industry-Academia Partnership – The Viewpoint of Clients on a Project Course

Tero Vartiainen

Turku School of Economics, Pori Unit, P.O. Box 170, FIN-28101 PORI, Finland

**Abstract:** Industry-academia partnerships are common in the IT field because they benefit both parties. Research on moral issues in these relations is scarce, and this case study is aimed at increasing knowledge in this area by investigating moral problems in a form of partnership, a collaborative IT project with a university. Twenty-one client representatives from IT firms or organisations were interviewed during a project course in information systems. The analysis was inspired by phenomenography. The results show that concern for the beneficial objectives of the client organisations typically conflicts with concern for students and their learning objectives. A two-dimensional structure constituting six types of moral problems was determined. The results are compared with the existing literature, and recommendations for practice and research are presented.

## 1 Introduction

Industry-academia partnership benefits both parties, and there are several forms of co-operation. These include training programmes, research centres, and industry advisory boards (Watson and Huber 2000; Keithley and Redman 1997). The main-tenance of inter-organisational collaboration is based on two fundamentals: for the industry it provides opportunities to acquire human resources, and for academia it ensures that research and teaching activities are relevant. Collaborative student projects are a common feature in the IT field (e.g., Bergeron 1996). They benefit industry by providing it with project results and contacts with students –possible future employees - and the students reap benefits by learning communication (Fritz 1987), team-building, and interpersonal skills (Roberts 2000), for example. Indeed, project work is recognised by computing disciplines (information systems, software engineering, computer science) as an essential component in the educa-tion of future computer professionals (Gorgone et al. 2002). Although academia-industry relationships are common in the IT field, research on the underlying ethical issues is still an untouched area. Scott et al. (1994) and Fielden (1999) reported ethical dilemmas from the viewpoint of academia, but studies from the perspective of industry are lacking. The aim of this study[1] is to fill this gap by investigating morally relevant decision-making situations, i.e. moral problems, perceived by client representatives involved in a project course, and formulating the means to tackle these problems. Although there are various definitions of a moral problem (e.g., moral conflict/dilemma; Gowans 1987), for reasons of simplicity the term moral problem is used here to mean any morally relevant issue (cf. the definitions of a moral dilemma in Audi 1995).

Information about moral problems was collected through interviews, the analysis of which was inspired by phenomenography. As the study focuses on investigating individuals' subjective interpretations, and on how they interact with the world around them, it is interpretative in nature (Trauth 2001). The results show that the beneficial objectives of the clients (the results and the employment of students) and concern about the effects of the project on the students were the most significant determinants of moral problems.

The article is organised as follows. After the introduction, the research design and results are presented, the results are discussed and evaluated, and finally, recommendations for both academia and industry are offered.

## 2 Research Design

Twenty-one client representatives involved in a project course were interviewed, and the analysis followed the ideas of phenomenography to some extent. The aim of the phenomenographical method is to identify and describe qualitative variation in individuals' experiences of their reality (Marton 1986). What is characteristic of it is the endeavour to capture conceptualisations that are faithful to individuals' experience of a selected phenomenon. These conceptions, which are typically gathered through interviews, are then categorised, and relations between the categories are further explored (Francis 1993). A phenomenographic researcher seeks qualitatively different ways of experiencing the phenomena regardless of whether the differences are between or within individuals.

The selection of the course was based on my presence at the Department of Computer Science and Information Systems at the University of Jyväskylä, Finland, which arranges a project course entitled Development Project (DP). During the course, groups consisting of five students implement a project task defined by a client, typically an IT firm such as a software house or the IT department of an organisation such as an industrial plant. Each student is expected to use 275 hours in implementing the project task, and 125 hours to demonstrate project-work

---

[1] This article is a partial report of a study investigating moral conflicts perceived by clients, students, and instructors involved in a project course (Vartiainen 2005).

skills in areas such as project leading, group work, and communications. In total, a five-student group uses 1,375 hours planning and implementing a client project. Each student is expected to practice the role of project manager for about one month during the project, which spans from five to six months. The project tasks range from extreme coding to developmental work and research. Client organisations pay the university €8500 (ca. FIM 50 000) for the co-operation.

Client representatives were interviewed during 2000-2001 and 2001-2002. The interviewees were presented with the following task: "*Describe the moral problems and issues worth noticing from the moral viewpoint that are related to the fact that you act as a client in the Development Project.*"

In the analysis I coded the main issues that emerged from the interview extracts in order to acquire understanding of the matters that were raised by the subjects. Then I started to group similar problems shared among them, that is to say I produced "pools" of moral conflicts. This coding phase was repetitive in nature, and I studied the extracts numerous times. I used flap boards and the network views supplied in Atlas.ti software (Muhr 1997) to visualise the categorisation procedure. It is worth noting that the phenomenographic researcher does not question the validity of the subjects' perceptions, but faithfully produces categorisations incorporating them all. In sum, I found two dimensions of moral conflict: the external and the internal. These dimensions were based on my interpretation of the source material – except that I applied moral-psychology theory in defining the latter. The results are presented in the following section.

# 3 The Classification of Moral Problems

Six categories of moral problems perceived by the client representatives were identified (Table 1). They are presented next in the order of the external dimension (see Vartiainen 2005 for full descriptions with the interview extracts). As far as the internal dimension was concerned, the analysis was inspired by Piaget's (1977) finding on children's development from egocentrism to perspective taking, i.e., to the ability to take others into account.

**Category 1: "How do we avoid aiding our competitors?"** A client representative confronts a moral problem in which her concern and care are targeted and restricted to the utility of her organisation, and which relates to external parties. The possibility for the client's competitors to benefit from the particular co-operation with the student group is a moral problem for clients. They face this problem when making decisions about providing students with something that could benefit competitors in cases in which they are hired by them. The client faces a risk in disclosing confidential corporate information to students, and in putting resources into their education because this could also benefit competitors. For example, one client representative said that in order to get the maximal utility from the project clients should be aware of the students' plans, and should refrain from educating them if they did not want a job in the client organisation. The fact

**Table 1.** Moral problems perceived by client representatives involved in a project course.

|  |  | Self-centred | Other-directed |
|---|---|---|---|
| The internal dimension |  | Motivation and concern are based on the utility of a moral agent's organisation. | Motivation is based on caring and concern for other parties. |
| The external dimension |  | The moral agent's deliberation and concern are restricted to her organisation. | A moral agent's deliberation and concern extend to other parties. |
| External relations | Relations with parties outside the project collaboration (educational institutes, vendors, society) | Category 1: "How do we avoid aiding our competitors?" | Category 2: "How should we fulfil our social responsibilities?" |
| Project task | Attaining the objectives of the parties in the project co-operation and implementing the tasks when attaining the objectives. | Category 3: "What do we get from collaboration with universities?" | Category 4: "How should we take into account the objectives of our partners?" |
| Interpersonal | Treatment of the individuals who are participating in the project. | Category 5: "How do we benefit from the students' efforts?" | Category 6: "How should we take into account the effects of the project on students?" |

that educated students may be employed by other (possibly competing) IT firms affects future-oriented decision-making.

**Category 2: "How should we fulfil our social responsibilities?"** A client representative confronts a moral problem in which her concern and care are extended to others, and which relates to external parties. External parties include educational institutes and other actors in the business field. As far as educational institutes and society in general are concerned, client representatives deliberate on whether there are social responsibilities towards them, and if so, whether the clients should fulfill them. This moral problem emerges in the two following cases: the selection of an educational institute, and contributing to the development of an educational institute. Selecting an educational institute incorporates a moral problem related to contributing to the local community surrounding it. When the firm selects the institute, it contributes to the community in which it is located. As far as other actors in the business field are concerned, clients deliberate about the effects of exercising power over outside parties: by exercising power one is able to cause detrimental consequences.

**Category 3: "What do we get from collaboration with the university?"** A client representative confronts a moral problem in which her concern and care are targeted and restricted to the utility of the organisation, and which relates to the objectives of the project. The results of the project, together with the employment of students, are the main motives and objectives driving the clients in the collaboration. There is the possibility that potential clients will provide the university with false information beforehand in order to be accepted as a collaborating partner. Prioritising between student-project and other business-project-related work tasks is also considered a moral problem. During the project the client representatives confront decision-making situations in which they produce cost-benefit analyses. A client may observe that the co-operation may be a failure if they do not reach the objectives. The reasons for failure may lie in the overall co-operation and in the functioning of the student group, for example. Presenting arguments for quitting the project, and also the timing of quitting, were considered moral problems.

**Category 4: "How should we take into account the objectives of our partners?"** A client representative confronts moral problems in which her concern and care are extended to others, and which relate to the objectives of the project. Respecting the objectives of the university and the students is such a moral problem: clients adhere to their own objectives but they also show respect for those of the university and the students. They also see a moral problem in the possibility that they might not respect the learning aspects of the project co-operation. However, they are ready to give up some of their utility-based demands because of the students' status as students. Client representatives confront prioritisation decision-making situations in which the decisions may harm students or the employees of the client organization.

**Category 5: "How do we benefit from the students' efforts?"** A client representative confronts a moral problem in which her concern and care are targeted on and restricted to the utility of the organisation, and which relates to individuals in the project. Client representatives believe that their utility-based objectives could be safeguarded by not being open, by refraining from telling the truth, or by being dishonest about various issues to do with the project task or their attitude towards the functioning of the student group. Getting a good team for the project, keeping up the spirits of the student group, and employing students are the benefits the clients are aiming for by refraining from telling the truth or by lying. Client representatives also make decisions in which the students are the objects, and which are made to safeguard results. According to the clients, making demands on students, giving them feedback, and employing them during the co-operation process constitute moral problems.

**Category 6: "How should we take into account the effects of the project on the students?"** A client representative confronts a moral problem in which her concern and care are extended to others, and which relates to individuals in the project. Client representatives consider it a moral problem if some of their acts harm the students: proper feedback, offering employment, and excessive guidance are considered in some cases to have harmful effects. They deliberate about carrying out their duties towards the students, and about safeguarding their rights and treating them in an impartial and equal way. These issues relate to keeping promises, ensuring that students get real-life experience in the project, giving them feedback about their abilities, and teaching them to respect other individuals and parties.

# 4 Discussion

This study revealed that client representatives involved in a project course confront moral problems and, according to the interpretation taken in the analysis, the problems are divided along two dimensions (external and internal). Clients enter the collaboration in order to benefit from the results and to find potential employees. However, the results of a student project may be at stake when the representatives are forced to find a balance between their regular business-critical and student-project-related work tasks. The more the client invests in guiding the student project the better the results, but other critical work tasks may suffer. It is common for the student project to be overridden in such a situation. Some client representatives were confused about their role as clients. On the one hand, they perceived that they had a significant role in making demands on the students, but on the other hand they felt that they did not know how they should relate to the students, who are not professionals and are not paid for the work, and who cannot be expected to engage in professional practice.

There are counterparts of the three major themes along the external dimension in different studies on IS and management (e.g., Brittain and Leifer 1986; Culnan 1987). For example, Semprevivo (1980, 114) states that project managers engaged in information-systems development need skills in external relations and task/project management, along with considerate leadership. Starting with external relations, Boddy (2002, 31) defines the context of a project as including the contemporary setting within and beyond the organisation. In this study, social responsibilities towards educational institutes and the local community around them became visible, as did the effects of the collaboration on vendors and of taking competitors into account. Project-task and interpersonal problems find counterparts in the management (concern for production) and leadership (concern for leadership) orientations in the classical managerial grid produced by Blake and Mouton (1978).

The internal dimension describes the mental intention in the descriptions of moral problems, and it finds its counterparts in the literature on management and social psychology. Krebs and Denton (1997) reported that when people engage in moral decision-making they anticipate the consequences for themselves and others. Greenberg and Baron (1995) state that organisational conflicts have been recognised to include two key dimensions: integration (concern for one's own outcomes) and distribution (concern for others' outcomes). Self-centredness is visible in Category 1: "How do we avoid aiding our competitors?", Category 3: "What do we get from collaboration with the university?", and Category 5: "How do we benefit from the students' efforts?" In these categories the client representatives emphasise the interests of their firms, and indeed, profitability, and the production of goods and services at a profit (Buchholz and Rosenthal 1999, 303) is a fundamental motive in these deliberations. The results of student projects are typically preliminary inputs for business projects, or they otherwise support the attaining of the objectives of the client organisation. The traditional interest of industry in academia is based on the supply of an educated workforce (Louis and Anderson 1998, 87). During the research period, this interest was a significant determinant for clients to start their collaboration.

The decision taken in this study to interpret both self-centred and other-directed deliberations as moral problems may face two objections. First, it runs contrary to the strictest philosophical definitions of a moral problem, such as that found in Audi (1995, 508): "A situation where an agent morally ought to do each of two acts but cannot do both". Choosing between an egoistical impulse and moral value is not a moral problem in this sense. However, egoistical impulses are recognised in moral psychology as possible factors in moral conflicts (Packer 1985; Hoffman 1982). An egoist impulse may override a moral value, and as the findings of this study show, the flouting of the moral value of honesty emerged when client representatives negotiated with the university on potential collaboration, or when clients marketed their project tasks to student groups (categories 3 and 5). As far as honesty is concerned, Vitell et al. (2000) reported similar results as they found that professionals in small businesses confronted honesty-related ethical problems such as honesty in contracts and agreements, and in their external and internal communications. According to my interpretation, withholding self-centred deliberations from the resulting framework would only partially represent the moral problematic faced by client representatives. Secondly, given that client representatives are bound to the interests of their employers, in other words private firms, self-centred moral problems are closely tied to the fact that it is the client representatives' loyalty as employees that makes them adhere to the objectives of their employers (Johnson 1995, 565): describing their deliberation as egoistic would therefore be misleading and wrong. As there is a point to this objection, as I see it, the dependency and loyalty relation between the client representative and her employer means that they both have similar interests in benefiting from project co-operation. Thus, the self-centred moral problems reported in this study are self-centred in nature, although they arise from the self-centred interests of the employer (firm).

Other-directedness is visible in Category 2: "How should we fulfil our social responsibilities?", Category 4: "How should we take into account the objectives of our partners?", and Category 6: "How should we take into account the effects of the project on the students?" Here concern is extended to societal actors, partners and students. Social responsibilities in business, summarised by Carroll (1999,

142)[2], include engaging in ethical practices and philanthropy, which are visible in these other-directed categories. As far as concern for others is concerned, it is noteworthy that even though the client representatives confronted pressures in terms of gaining benefits from the co-operation, they were genuinely concerned about how it affects the parties involved. As it takes place in close contact with the students, the client representatives were concerned about how the project and the attainment of beneficial objectives would affect them. Employing students may prolong their studies, giving harsh feedback may discourage them, and the collaboration may provide them with a false image of working life. The consequences of projects on employees in the organisation and on vendors were also found to be of concern.

## 4.1 Recommendations for Practice and Research

First, for academia, it is recommended that the objectives of collaboration are clearly articulated, and that the position of the students and their treatment are discussed. The co-existence of the two objectives, the beneficial objectives of clients and the learning aspect upheld by the university, should be included in critical discussion among all parties. Guidelines for the collaborative project should be published. The external dimension of moral problems may be used as a sense-making tool to introduce clients involved in a project course to the moral problematic of this co-operation. Secondly, for industry it is recommended that collaboration with educational institutes is planned for, and that adequate resources are allocated in order to prevent prioritising problems. Thirdly, as this study is a case study, the results cannot be generalised to other courses, and conducting comparative studies in other environments, such as in other countries or other disciplines, might reveal differences. Fourthly, the results suggest that participants in other forms of industry-academia co-operation may be prone to moral problems. Fifthly, as business IT projects are known for their turbulence, it is assumed that participants in IT projects will confront moral problems. More in-depth studies in this area are needed. Finally, in Rest's (1994) terms, moral behaviour can be studied from the perspectives of "knowing" (moral sensitivity and judgment) and "implementation" (moral motivation and character). This study concentrated on the moral-sensitivity component by identifying moral problems as perceived by the subjects. Accordingly, future research should focus on the moral judgments produced in these decision-making situations, and on how individuals implement the decisions.

## 4.2 Evaluation of the Study

I evaluated the study according to the principles put forward by Klein and Myers (1999). Some critical points are presented here, while the full evaluation is to be

---

[2] Carroll (1999, 142) states that the four social responsibilities in business are profitability, legal obedience, engaging in ethical practices, and philanthropy.

found in Vartiainen (2005). As far as the interviews were concerned, the dangers concerning rationalisation, lack of awareness, and the fear of being shown up (Fielding 1993) are significant. Interviewees might consider interview situations stressful or shameful, because they might disclose thoughts that may not be creditable or honourable. It could be argued that the client representatives agreed to the interviews because of the stated and beneficial objectives to maintain good relations with the university. Because I was not just a researcher, but also a staff member of the project course, client representatives' participation in the interviews might have been interpreted as a goodwill gesture towards collaboration and the university. It is impossible to know why the subjects agreed to take part, but it is noteworthy that the moral problems they described included non-honourable issues such as the possibility of lying.

# References

Audi, R. (Ed.) 1995. The Cambridge Dictionary of Philosophy. Cambridge: Cambridge University Press.

Bergeron, B.P. 1996. Academia, Privacy and Modern Information Technology: Partnering With Industry in the Modern Economy. SIGDOC'96. 243-245.

Blake, R.R., Mouton, J.S. 1978. The New Managerial Grid. Houston: Gulf Publishing Company. Rererenced in F.E. Kast, J.E., Rosenzweig 1985. Organization & Management, A Systems and Contingency Approach. New York: McGraw-Hill.

Boddy, D. 2002. Managing Projects: Building and Leading the Team. Harlow, Essex: Prentice Hall.

Brittain, K., Leifer, R. 1986. Information Systems Development Success: Perspectives from Project Team Participants. MIS Quarterly 10 (3), 215-223.

Buchholz, R.A., Rosenthal, S.B. 1999 Social responsibility and business ethics. In Frederick, R.E. (ed.) A Companion to Business Ethics. Oxford, UK: Blackwell Publishers. 303-321.

Carroll, A.B. 1999. Ethics in Management. In R.E. Frederick (Ed.) A Companion to Business Ethics. Oxford, UK: Blackwell. 141-152.

Culnan, M.J. 1987. Mapping the Intellectual Structure of MIS, 1980-1985: A Co-Citation Analysis. MIS Quarterly 11 (3), 341-353.

Fielden, K. 1999. Starting Right: Ethical Education for Information Systems Developers. In C.R. Simpson (Ed.) AICEC99 Conference Proceedings, 14-16 July 1999. Melbourne. Brunswick East, Victoria: Australian Institute of Computer Ethics. 147-156.

Fielding, N. 1993. Qualitative Interviewing. In N. Gilbert (Ed.) Researching Social Life. London: SAGE Publications. 135-153.

Francis, H. 1993. Advancing Phenomenography. Nordisk Pedagogik 13 (2), 68-75.

Fritz, J.M. 1987. A pragmatic approach to systems analysis and design. In A.K. Rigler, D.C. St. Clair (Eds.) Technical Symposium on Computer Science

Education. Proceedings of the eighteenth SIGCSE technical symposium on Computer science education, St. Louis, Missouri, United States. New York: ACM Press. 127-131.

Gorgone, J.T., Davis G.B., Valacich, J.S., Topi, H., Feinstein, D.L. Longenecker, H.E.Jr. 2002. IS 2002. Model Curriculum and Guidelines for Undergraduate Degree Programs in Information Systems. Association for Computing Machinery (ACM), Association for Information Systems (AIS), Association of Information Technology Professionals (AITP). Communications of AIS 11, Article 1.

Gowans, C.W. 1987. The Debate on Moral Dilemmas In C.W. Gowans (Ed.) Moral Dilemmas. New York: Oxford University Press. 3-33.

Greenberg, J., Baron, R.A. 1995. Behavior in Organizations. Prectice Hall.

Hoffman, M. 1982. Affect and moral development. In H. Cicchetti (Ed.) New directions for child development. San Francisco: Jossey-Bass. Referenced in Packer, M.J. 1985. The Structure of Moral Action: A Hermeneutic Study of Moral Conflict. Basel: Karger.

Johnson, D.G. 1995. Professional ethics. In D.G. Johnson, H. Nissenbaum (Eds.) Computers, Ethics, and Social Values. New Jersey: Prentice Hall. 559-572.

Järvinen, P. 2001. On Research Methods. Tampere, Finland: Opinpaja Oy.

Keithley, D., Redman, T. 1997. University-industry partnerships in management development. A case study of a "world-class" company. Journal of Management Development 16 (3). 154-166.

Klein, H.K., Myers, M.D. 1999. A Set of Principles for Conducting and Evaluating Interpretive Field Studies in Information Systems. MIS Q. 23 (1), 67-94.

Krebs, D.L., Denton, K. 1997. The forms and functions of real-life moral decision-making. Journal of Moral Education 26 (2).

Louis, K.S., Anderson M.S. 1998. The Changing Context of Science and University-Industry Relations. In (eds.) Etzkowitz, H., Webster, A., Healey, P. 1998. Capitalizing Knowledge. Albany: State University of New York.

Marton, F. 1986. Phenomenography – a research approach to investigating different understandings of reality. Journal of Thought. 21 (3), 28-49.

Muhr, T. 1997. Atlas.ti. A software programme. Berlin: Science Software Development.

Packer, M.J. 1985. The Structure of Moral Action: A Hermeneutic Study of Moral Conflict. Basel: Karger.

Piaget, J. 1977. The Moral Judgement of the Child. Harmonsdsworth: Penguin.

Rest, J.R. 1994. Background: Theory and Research. In J.R. Rest, D. Narvaez (Eds.) Moral Development in the Professions: Psychology and Applied Ethics. Mahwah: Lawrence Erlbaum Associates. 1-26.

Roberts, E. 2000. Computing Education and the Information Technology Workforce. SIGCSE Bulletin 32 (2), 83-90.

Scott, T.J., Tichenor, L.H., Bisland, R.B.Jr., Cross J.H. 1994. Team dynamics in student programing projects. SIGSCE 26 (1), 111-115.

Semprevivo, P.C. 1980. Teams in Information Systems Development. New York: Yourdon Press.

Trauth, E.M. 2001. Qualitative Research in IS: Issues and Trends. Hershey: Idea Group.

Vartiainen, T. 2005. Moral Conflicts in a Project Course in Information Systems Education. Jyväskylä: University of Jyväskylä. Jyväskylä Studies in Computing, 49. Dissertation thesis.

Vitell, S.J., Dickerson, E.B., Festervand, T.A. (2000) Ethical Problems, Conflicts and Beliefs of Small Business Professionals. Journal of Business Ethics. 28, 15-24.

Watson, H.J., Huber, M.W. 2000. Innovative ways to connect information systems programs to the business community. Communications of the AIS 3, Art. 11.

# Outlining "Data Track": Privacy-friendly Data Maintenance for End-users

John Sören Pettersson[*], Simone Fischer-Hübner[*], Mike Bergmann[**]

[*] Karlstad University, Sweden. john_soren.pettersson@kau.se
[**] Technical University Dresden, Germany. mb41@inf.tu-dresden.de

## 1 Introduction

We present a complex function that we argue enhances the usefulness of so-called Privacy-Enhancing Technologies (PETs [4]). The background for this conceptual development is PRIME, Privacy and Identity Management for Europe – an integrated EU project within the Information Society Technology track of the 6th Framework Program [12]. The project is directed towards a holistic architecture and framework for identity management where data processors and citizens alike will be able to engage in secure and privacy-friendly communication over the Internet and mobile phone networks.

Fundamental in the architecture being elaborated is the use of network pseudonyms to allow users to be anonymous and digital credentials to allow users to prove their identity or parts thereof, such as being 18 years old or older. Other features involve aid to the users to gauge the privacy policies of service providers and to negotiate about policies. All such functions are important parts of a privacy-friendly Internet and Mobile Phone data communications, and, indeed, there are already products that, to various extents, incorporate such functions.

To further improve users/citizens privacy rights, we argue that users should have a method to keep track of their releases of personal data. We call this method and all the concomitant functions "Data Track". The Data Track has already been partially implemented in some prototypes within the project. In our presentation we go beyond these implementations and discuss the wider conceptual framework for Data Track.

The Data Track should serve as the base for several functions which users so far have been in complete lack of. It stores transaction records comprising personal data sent, date of transmission, purpose of data collection, recipient, and recipient's privacy policy. We furthermore see the Data Track as a base for users to exercise their legal rights and to get information on how to go about if something seems to be wrong with how their personal data have been treated. It should contain help on how to rectify and revoke data sent. It can also help to maintain anonymity: by helping the user to reuse pseudonyms the user can identify himself as a previous contact but still be anonymous.

It is not only user side application developers that need to take this into consideration. Information system developers working for service providers must know of privacy-friendly identity management architectures to build systems meeting the requirements of data processing laws and their client organisations' commitments to customers, business partners, and employees. Furthermore, service developers, including 'back-end' developers, must realise that such tools will in the near future also be available to customers of their client organisations.

## 1.1 Outline of the presentation

To provide the background for the ideas we present, we briefly bring up some directives from the European Union concerning privacy requirements on data processing, and after that we give a snapshot overview of the PRIME system architecture. The emphasis of this presentation is on how such an architecture can affect ordinary people, especially how the history function that such an architecture supports can be employed by ordinary citizens to manage their privacy rights in the networked society. We expound on functions of the Data Track (we concentrate on computer usage, not mobile phones); especially important is to assist people who have low trust in or are unfamiliar with the technology. Finally, we acknowledge that handling the transaction records constitutes a problem in itself – people are in general unfamiliar working with huge data pools – and give a glimps of our work in progress on this matter. We conclude by pointing to the uniqueness of the broad technological scope of the PRIME identity management system but emphasise the utility of the history function it provides for privacy-enhancing end-user data maintenance.

## 2 Legal requirements on data processing

A fundamental privacy principle is transparency: a user must be able to see who is processing his personal data and for what purpose. The EU Data Protection Directive 95/46/EC aims to guarantee transparency by providing a set of rights to individuals, such as Art. 12 (a): *information about recipients* or categories of recipients to whom the data are disclosed; *communications* in an intelligible form to the individual about the data undergoing processing. In addition, the EU Directive enhances user control by, for instance, Art. 12 (b): the right of individuals to obtain from the controller the *rectification, erasure, or blocking* of data concerning them each time the processing does not comply with the requirements of the Directive; Art. 14: the *right to object* to the data processing (especially for direct marketing).

## 3 Architectural PET requirements

Privacy-enhancing identity management technologies are built on architectures satisfying at least the following requirements. They should support anonymity/pseudo-anonymity, unlinkability and provable linkage, tools and protocols for data request/disclosure and last but not least privacy policy driven data storage. Beside these major requirements we may find various other important topics. A description of the details can be found in publicly available PRIME documents (e.g. [12] [6]).

### 3.1 PRIME architecture

The PRIME architecture is based on a symmetric interceptor approach, intercepting the existing applications to add the privacy supporting functionality as shown in Figure 1.

This approach enhances existing solutions. The PRIME architecture is based on an anonymising communication layer to fulfil the anonymity requirement. Without this basic element no valuable privacy and identity management is possible because of the IP address capabilities (similar for mobile phones and WAP). On top of this layer the supplementary elements of the system including interceptor, data bases, etc. are placed. The interceptor is an optional component to address the need of adopting legacy applications to PRIME solutions. If applications become PRIME-enabled, the application communicates directly through the PRIME system and the interceptor is not longer necessary.

The PRIME middleware receives the application requests and responses, tracks and verifies the privacy implications and communicates with the whole PRIME system to effect the storage and delivers requests for entities' personal data. It is possible to let the application-to-application

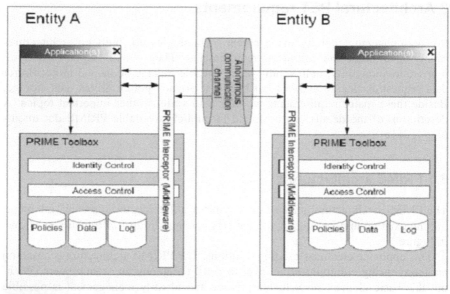

**Fig. 1.** Architecture Overview

communication bypass the middleware and the communication may still be ano-nymised, but privacy-aware communication cannot be guaranteed.

The PRIME system adds properties like anonymity and pseudonymity, linkabil-ity evaluation functionality, digital evidence by usage of digital signatures for all transactions and the possibility to track/trace the transactions. This approach al-lows keeping the data history. The architecture is beneficial to business-to-business communication in that data handling policies are interchanged as swiftly as data is interchanged. Moreover, in the PRIME architecture, one of the entities in Figure 1 could equally well be an end-user, i.e. a citizen with ownership rights to personal data processed by other entities. What is called "Logs" in Figure 1 can be (the base for) "Data Track" on user side (and "Policies" would more likely be called "Preferences" in user interfaces for end-users).

## 4 Related work

Borking and Raab [5] argue that feedback and control is a good way to safeguard the rights of the parties involved when personal data is processed. To compare, ex-isting technologies are somewhat incomplete. Web browsers can keep trace of contacts made and the browsers provide user interfaces for history functions, but they are far from the kind of record keepers needed for users to exercise their legal rights. E-mail applications are interesting in that they naturally provide history re-trieval by allowing users to do different kinds of sorting and searching, but they are far from an aide in legal matters, except merely as writing tools.

The PISA project [4] continued the ideas expressed by Borking and Raab and addressed how legal privacy principles derived from the EU Data Protection Directive can be mapped to HCI requirements and further to possible UI design solutions. The Art. 29 Working Party has discussed guidelines for how legal requirements for providing information to a person when requesting personal data from him can be satisfied by a layered UI design [2] but not explored how users would keep record of their data releases. The recent InfoCard initiative from Microsoft strives to present an architecture-independent protocol to serve the user with a coherent user interface [7]. PRIME functions may well appear in the InfoCard dress in the future, but the Microsoft initiative does not go far in addressing the tasks we assign to Data Track.

To set also the PRIME architecture in perspective, we note that the W3C Platform for Privacy Preferences project, P3P [10], is in its current form 'passive' as it only checks if people's preferences are matched against promises made by the enterprise; it is not about letting users edit policy rules or providing feedback to users on the on-going execution of policy rules. The Enterprise Privacy Authorization Language, EPAL [17], triggers rule executions by authorization rules while the PRIME solution relies on an event-driven model for rule representation (including time events, system and trust-based events, contextual events etc. [8]).

## 5 Data track functions for privacy protection

Inspecting one's own data transactions is a basic function of the Data Track and, as we argue, it is sensible to group other functions under the same umbrella, because the transaction records will constitute the basis for actions performed by other functions. We present here four functions starting with the logging function and then connect to the legal requirements with functions for exercising legal rights and assisting the worried user. We finally mention a function for raising the user's privacy awareness.

### 5.1 Logging function

As mentioned before, our point is that users should have a method to keep track of their releases of personal data. It is not enough to have privacy-friendly technology for gauging privacy policies and minimizing data releases. In many situations, personal data have to be released. Therefore, the user side PET system should collect the data releases and allow the users to inspect their own transactions.

The legal requirements for requesting data from a data subject is, as noted above, that information about the request is available to the data subject before data disclosure. With an active PET system mediating data releases, no data should be released if such information cannot be obtained. This makes it also possible to record this information at the user side. We also make the point that it is not only the 'basic' information – personal data, recipient, and purpose – that should be recorded but also the **privacy policy** issued by the collecting party. This policy should contain the premises for how the collected data is used and stored. For this reason, it would constitute a valuable document in case a user feels that something is wrong with how his data has been used. Presently, people may inspect privacy policies published on web sites but if they later on come back to these web pages, they cannot be sure that the same version is still available. This severely restricts transparency.

For the project in which we develop the concept for the Data Track, it is also considered how specific obligations within a privacy policy can be negotiated. If the purpose for a data collection is to send marketing information, the person subscribing to this might not only give away his e-mail or physical address, but might like to set certain conditions, such as "delete my address after six month" or "notify me whenever my address is sold to another organisation" and "let any third part organisation use my address only once". Such negotiated obligations should be added to the stored privacy policy. It might be questioned if people would like to and be able to set such conditions. However, for the few obligations that could be of interest in any specific situations, our (as yet unpublished) pilot tests show that most first-timers are able to set obligations and furthermore like the sense of control this obligation management gives them.

In additions to these items that have to do with the involved parties as legal entities, it should be recognised that in order to make the log files useful for a user, some other information should also be added. First, as our project elaborates on anonymous communication and therefore the use of **communication pseudonyms**, it will be convenient in some situations for the user to refer to the pseudonyms used by his system during the transactions. By referring to pseudonyms a user can in principle identify himself as a previous contact but still be anonymous, or if he was not anonymous at the previous contact, he can at least use the pseudonym employed at that time to demonstrate that it was he who previously released personal information.

This authorisation can also be achieved through the use of **digitally signed credentials** disclosed during the previous contact. These credentials may be general, perhaps issued by the government, and used many times, or they may have been given by the company at the previous data exchange as a password. In any case, the credentials disclosed or received are as important to store in the transaction record as other types of personal information. They will, at a later time, facilitate the re-identification of the user, and as such belongs to a well-functioning identity management system even without a history function such as the Data Track. But for exercising legal rights using the Data Track, users need to have records where individual items are stored in relation to the conditions of each transaction.

There should also be a possibility for users to **label transmission records** in order to group them in a meaningful way ("Holiday 2006" includes both travel and hotel bookings) and add comments ("I phoned them to make clear that all our children are under 12"). This is not necessarily performed at transaction time, and thereby not purely a logging function, but from the user's perspective it makes sense to see this information as part of the transaction records.

## 5.2 Rectifying data and changing obligations

The PRIME architecture, with nearly identical user side and services side systems, will make it possible for users to authorise themselves versus the service side systems and then to directly exercise their rights to inspect, correct, block their data, and change the conditions for data use; cf. [13] where the rights vs. architecture topics are also discussed. (The right to change conditions derives from their right to withdraw consent for data processing – if a company would not agree to the altered condition, the user would anyhow have his right to block any further use of his data.) A full-blown obligation management component should give access to metadata about when different obligations have been employed for each individual data item, and when and why certain obligations have not been followed. (Within the PRIME project, a demonstrator for service side is under development; PRIME partner HP Labs has furthermore implemented a prototype in HP Select Identity [9].) A full-blown Data Track function should be able to access services side's obligation management systems, and also to compare their data with the locally stored data track, for the user to be assured that obligations displayed by services side are the ones he put there in the first place. Naturally, this could be automated, so that the user would only have to react on alerts from Data Track when it has spotted fulfilment failures.

Of course, there may be many cases when there is no PRIME system on the service side. Contacting organisations that have collected information about oneself might be done by other means than by directly connecting to a service side PRIME system. If the user's Data Track contains information about the data releases and recipients, it can also help users to contact the recipients and provide standard messages for users' request for inspection, correction, etc.

## 5.3 Taking care of worried users

Many user surveys show that people are not trusting networked data processing to preserve privacy (for an overview, see [14]). Therefore the question of potential users' trust in a PET system such as the PRIME system is important.

Given a systems such as the PRIME user side system, users may think that "Internet is insecure anyway because people must get information even if it is not [traceable by the PET application]", to partly quote one test participant in an early PRIME usability test [16]. Of course, information about this person might be released by someone else, but if his Data Track has not recorded any agreement from his side to the data processing, this should encourage him to claim that a specific occurrence of his personal data has not been granted by him.

To continue with user data and the trust problem, the above citation demonstrates that even if users understand that they have special software on 'their' side, they will not necessarily believe that it will be able to help them. The test subject just quoted continued by saying about the Data Track function, "And even if it is good to see what information has been sent it is too late anyway because you cannot undo it." This is only partly true. Possibly, one cannot always directly from the user-side system withdraw information sent to a data processor, even if 'PRIME-enabled' service providers are capable to allow such actions, as outlined above; tax / bookkeeping regulations for instance may prevent deletion. But a function such as the Data Track should inform users about rights to actions such as rectification and erasure (or blocking) of their data. The Data Track should furthermore help the user to, e.g., immediately write an e-mail letter to the data processor about this request, as also outlined above. We have in various usability tests on prototypes seen that ordinary Internet users may not be aware of their rights, as exemplified by the citation, but in later pilot experiments when seeing links or buttons to such function, test subjects have appreciated the possibility to be helped with such tasks.

In another test, one participant commented that it is very fine to see what information has been released but remarked that: "On the other hand, I don't know what I would have done if I had seen a list of strange places that had received my data…" Hopefully, the PRIME technology should prevent users from releasing data to 'strange places'. Nevertheless, a prospective user is obviously able to conceive such a situation and to doubt that the system would help in such a case. Thus, there must be conspicuously placed information ensuring worried users that they will find helpful instructions within the system. We have exposed test users in pilot studies to a simple design with only a few entry points for the most needed assistance situations, and such a design seems promising, but several further steps might be needed in some cases.

Help functions could also inform about external help to enhance people's trust in PRIME – compare the user request that e-commerce companies provide "Access to helpful people" found in a study by Nielsen and co-workers [15]. For a user-side PRIME system there could be updated information on consumers' organizations, data protection authorities, police, and possible helpdesks if it is made clear that they help with legal issues and not only with software support. No-one who sees a demonstration of the program should think that they are left alone with the PRIME software system if they start to rely on it. They may doubt that the system per se can help them all the way through all conceivable situations but the within-system help functions should also refer external help systems. ([1] discuss 'trust' both from a socio-psychological perspective and from the perspective of user interface design.) In the section "How the user meets the Data Track" we outline a user interface start page for an active user guide.

## 5.4 Linkability computation function

The Data Track can also serve as a basis for finding out possible connections between different releases of data sets: "If company A buys company B, what does the joint company knows about me?" From the recorded obligations the user should also have the possibility to find out if the joint company really has the right to have this more complete view. However, this legal aspect of linkability computation will be harder to automate depending on how much privacy policy information is in plain text and how much has been subordinated to an automated obligation management system. The user might have to read, and understand, two long policy texts to derive the constraints for the data processing at the joint company AB.

Nevertheless, such computations may be illustrative and promote users' interest in privacy management and in particular the Data Track.

## 6 How the user meets the data track

While the previous sections have dealt with requirement areas for a user-side privacy-friendly data tracking function, we finally outline how a user interface can be designed for such a complex function (used in probing usability tests, but not tested on a large scale yet).

For the Data Track, where the basic function is record keeping, it could be natural to leave the window area for search facilities and put help functions in the menu bar, but indicate already in the main window that Data Track provides more than merely a database search function (Figure 2).

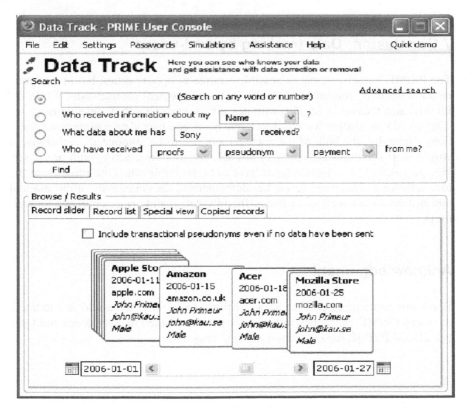

**Fig. 2.** Template sentences and a scrollable track

The *Help* menu is a traditional Help function to help the user with how to use the program, while *Assistance* is to help the user to deal with real world issues. *Simulations* have been envisaged in early PRIME work to make users understand better what has been sent (compare the data transaction animations in the Town-Map [3]) and what could be privacy threats (compare the previous section). PRIME's special activity on education might further develop the conceptual basis; c.f. the simulations in [11].

While the functions for exercising rights is a major step in enabling people to take control over their personal data, there are other issues involved when users meet the Data Track. Searching databases is not easy for many people. In PRIME several ways are presently being pilot tested, such as, a simple search box, template sentences, and a scrollable transaction track (Figure 2). For the beginner, the amount of transaction records may not be very large. For the more advanced user, the scrollable transaction track can be used in combination with other search methods.

However, the users may be so familiar with web search engine results, that an approach like a web search engine in a browser window might be desirable. Experiments should evaluate the usefulness of such an approach.

## 7 Conclusion: Data tracking by end-users

The PRIME framework makes possible a range of opportunities, but in this presentation we have concentrated on data self-management on user-side. While the PRIME architecture in itself constitutes advancement in PET development, we want to add an outline for the development of end-user data maintenance functions. Naturally, the bulk of the management has to be automated – otherwise it will in most situations appear as an obstacle for users interacting with or via service providers. But reliable records have to be available when the situation or the user calls for it. This presentation has demonstrated the complexity of the task and outlined the components of a privacy-friendly data maintenance approach for end-users.

## Acknowledgement

While this paper represents the views of the authors only, we would like to thank the many PRIME colleagues and students that have aided in discussions and tests. For official PRIME reports see www.prime-project.eu.

# References

1. Andersson Ch, Camenisch J, Crane S, Simone Fischer-Hübner S, Leenes R, Pearson S, Pettersson JS, Sommer D (2005) Trust in PRIME. In Proceedings of the 5th IEEE Int. Symposium on Signal Processing and IT, December 18-21, Athens, Greece, 2005.
2. Article 29 Data Protection Working Party. Opinion on More Harmonised Information provisions. 11987/04/EN WP 100, November 25, 2004. http://ec.europa.eu/justice_home/fsj/privacy/workinggroup/wpdocs/2004 _en.htm.
3. Bergmann M, Rost M, Pettersson JS (2005/6) Exploring the Feasibility of a Spatial User Interface Paradigm for Privacy-Enhancing Technology. In Nilsson et al. (eds.) Advances in Information Systems Development, Vol. 1, (proc. ISD 2005) Springer-Verlag, pages 437-448.
4. Blarkom GW van, Borking JJ, Olk JGE (eds) (2003) Handbook of Privacy and Privacy-Enhancing Technologies. College bescherming persoonsgegevens, The Hague. http://www.andrewpatrick.ca/pisa/handbook/handbook.html
5. Borking, J, Raab, C, 2001. Law, PETs and Other Technologies for Privacy Protection, Journal of Information, Law and Technology, Vol. 1.
6. Camenisch J, Shelat A (2006) PRIME Deliverable D16.1.e Second Annual Research Report. https://www.primeproject.eu/prime_products/reports/res/
7. Cameron K, Jones MB (2006) Design Rationale behind the Identity Metasystem Architecture. http://research.microsoft.com/~mbj/papers/Identity_Metasystem_Design_Rationale.pdf
8. Casassa Mont M, Pearson S, Crane S, 2005. Handling Privacy Obligations and Constraints to Underpin Trust and Assurance, HP External Technical Report, HPL-2005-54, http://www.hpl.hp.com/techreports/2005/HPL-2005-54.html.
9. Casassa Mont M, Pearson S, Thyne R (2006) A Systematic Approach to Privacy Enforcement and Policy Compliance Checking in Enterprises, 3rd International Conference on Trust, Privacy & Security in Digital Business, TrustBus 2006, 4-8 Sep., Krakow, http://www.icsd.aegean.gr/trustbus06/
10. Cranor L, Langheinrich M, Marchiori M, Presler-Marshall M, Reagle J (2002) The Platform for Privacy Preferences 1.0 (P3P1.0) Specification. W3C Recommendation 16 April 2002. W3C, http://www.w3.org/TR/P3P/.
11. Donker H, Liesebach K, Borcea-Pfitzmann K (2006) PRIME Deliverable D13.1.c General Public Tutorial. https://www.prime-project.eu/ prime_products/reports/tuto/

12. Fischer-Huebner S, Andersson Ch, Holleboom T (eds) (2005) PRIME Deliverable D14.1.a Framework V1. https://www.prime-project.eu/prime_products/reports/fmwk/

13. Korba L, Kenny S (2002) Towards Meeting the Privacy Challenge: Adapting DRM. Inst. for Information Technology, National Research Council of Canada. http://iit-iti.nrc-cnrc.gc.ca/iit-publications-iti/docs/NRC-44956.pdf

14. Leenes R, Lips M (2004) Social Evaluation of Early Prototypes, chapter 3 in PRIME Deliverable D6.1.b Evaluation of Early Prototypes. See [16] below.

15. Nielsen J, Molich R, Snyder C, Farell S (2000) E-commerce user experience: Trust. Nielsen Norman Group.

16. Pettersson JS, Fischer-Hübner S (eds) (2004) PRIME Deliverable D6.1.b Evaluation of Early Prototypes. https://www.prime-project.eu/prime_products/reports/eval/

17. Schunter M, Powers C (2003) The Enterprise Privacy Authorization Language, EPAL 1.1 specification, http://www.zurich.ibm.com/security/enterprise-privacy/epal/

# Improving Trust in E-Government Through Paralingual Web Design

Roy Segovia and Murray E. Jennex

San Diego State University

## 1 Introduction

Can web design improve electronic government (e-government)? This paper proposes that the use of paralingual web design can overcome the largest issue in e-government, that of trust, when used with bilingual populations. An experiment was conducted where e-government web pages were converted to paralingual format with site visitors surveyed on their resulting trust in the content and readability. Readability was surveyed to ensure that paralingual format did not reduce site usability (in this case usability can only be viewed as readability as no other functions are possible using the web sites.) The results of the experiment show that trust was improved for the minority language speakers with the majority language speakers remaining neutral. This is important for societies with large bilingual populations with issues of trust between them and the majority speakers.

## 2 Background

The impetus to implement e-government can be attributed to government's growing awareness of the need to attain more democratic governance (Coleman and Gotze 2001: OECD 2001), coupled with a widespread public interest in the potential of ICT to empower citizens and to increase government accountability (Hart-Teeter, 2003). Cost control and improved service to citizens is another driver. The United States E-Government initiative targets use of improved web technology to make it easy for citizens and businesses to interact with the government, save taxpayer dollars, and streamline citizen-to-government communications (USOMB, 2005).

Trust in government has historically been problematic; constituent citizens are known to have a high level of distrust in their governing bodies. Trust in government has been declining for more than three decades now, and has been the topic of a substantial amount of research in political science (Levi and Stoker, 2000 and Hibbing and Theiss-Morse, 2002). In the state of California, a recent study exposed an unexpectedly high level of distrust in government by California citizens. During 2004, a series of dialog-oriented seminars were held by Viewpoint Learning in various locations in California. One of the seven major findings of the study was that "profound mistrust of government and elected officials emerged as a central underlying issue..." Furthermore, "this mistrust was both more intense and more persistent than expected, outstripping the levels that have been measured by polls and focus groups" (Rosell, Gantwerk, and Furth, 2005).

There are also known issues with trust in e-government websites. This is clearly the effect of the general mistrust by citizens in their government bodies, as mentioned previously. The main reason given for mistrust of the Web is an artifact of the internet itself. Namely, the internet is now perceived to be beyond the control of the hosts and providers in terms of security and trust. Despite the use of lock icons, digital signatures, passwords, privacy policy statements, and other security techniques, internet users feel that "hosts and providers have lost control of the digital data transport medium as well as the software infrastructure that supports it." This has impeded the growth of e-government (Mercuri, 2005).

Improvement of trust in government is a critical issue. In the study by Viewpoint Learning, citizens voiced a strong desire to find constructive solutions to problems facing the state (Rosell, Gantwerk, and Furth, 2005). In a geographical area with a high proportion of bilingual speakers, usage of e-government websites may be improved in the same way as has been shown effective in electronic commerce (ecommerce). That is, with regard to language issues, researchers have found that customers are far more likely to buy products and services from Web sites in their own language, even if they can read English well. Furthermore, attention to site visitors' needs should be an important consideration in Web design, because such attention can help a site build trust with customers (Schneider, 2003).

Countries with multilingual populations expect that trust will be less than single language countries. This makes the challenge of providing e-government resources as twofold. First, how to provide website resources that adequately addresses the language issues of the multilingual citizens; second, how to improve trust in the governing body from those citizens; and both must be done without lowering usability. We propose that parallingual design will improve trust in multilingual nations, without impacting usability. Paralingual design involves placing content in both languages side by side. This allows readers who are bilingual to easily see both versions and readily determine if the same information is being provided, allowing for trust to increase through this citizen validation process.

## 3 Research Question

This research seeks to determine if paralingual website design will improve trust in E-government websites without lowering usability. One hypothesis was tested:

Use of paralingual web pages will increase trust in the page content and government sponsor.

## 4 Research Methodology

This research utilizes an experiment to test the hypothesis that paralingual website design for E-government will increase trust in the users. To conduct this experiment several web pages of a municipality were converted to the paralingual format. The municipality was located approximately 10 miles from the US border with Mexico. This municipality was known to have a 60% Hispanic population and a high proportion of English-Spanish bilingual residents.

The original English content on three pages of the municipality website was supplemented with the equivalent translation in Spanish. Municipality officials encouraged constituents and residents in the vicinity through a series of public announcements to visit the modified web pages and to complete a brief survey documenting their opinions on the website. The respondents to the survey had the choice of filling out the survey in English or Spanish. The survey consisted of eight questions. Four dealt with respondent demographics. Two dealt specifically with trust. The last two dealt with language awareness and how usable the web site was with respect to reading and comprehending the web page material. Responses to the trust and usability questions were based on a Likert scale and were analyzed statistically for significance of differences between groups.

Translation of the English content in the original selected web pages was performed taking into account the following:

- Variations in the style and vocabulary of Spanish. A style to reflect the local style was chosen. This style is mostly Mexican in its structure and vocabulary, so these were kept in perspective at all times.
- The level of writing was kept at approximately a high school level of comprehension (the same as the English version).
- The Spanish translation was written to conform strictly to correct language structure, syntax, and spelling. This is demonstrated by the correct application of diacritical marks, such as accents, tildes, and umlauts.

The translation task was performed by a native Spanish speaker with professional training and experience as a translator. The translated content was then evaluated and modified by a Spanish language professor with a specialization in translation studies.

## 5 Analysis Methods

The significant point in selecting and using these methods is that the survey data being analyzed is ordinal level data requiring the use of nonparametric statistics tests. Three nonparametric statistical tests are applied to the survey data. Spearman's rho is applied to data from Questions 5 and 6 within each language group to measure the correlation of the answers to those questions. Spearman's rho is the nonparametric equivalent of the typical Pearson correlation coefficient r.   The Mann-Whitney U test, for comparing central tendencies (means) between two sets of data is used to compare responses to Question 5 and 6 between the two language groups.   The Wilcoxon T test for matched pairs is applied to the same sets of data as with the Spearman's rho, and it will compare central tendencies between the two sets of responses in each language group.

All collected surveys were used for the analysis. Data was grouped based on the respondent's answer to survey question 3. This question asked the respondent's primary language for communication. The range of response choices was from "English only" to "Spanish only"; an additional choice was "some other combination of languages." In order to generate analysis results that are more representative of the language component of the sample data, the English sample data included only those who indicated English only or mostly English; the Spanish data included those that indicated Spanish only, mostly Spanish, or half English and half Spanish. This resulted in 97 English responses and 36 Spanish.

# 6 Results

## 6.1 Mann-Whitney U on Grouping by Language Choice

The Mann-Whitney U test was performed first on English Question 5 and Spanish Question 5. This question measures the respondent's improvement of trust in their understanding of the information on the paralingual page. The test determines if there is no statistical difference in the distribution of the answers between the English and Spanish respondents. The calculated z value is $z = -1.907$. Figure 1 shows the output from SPSS.

➡NPar Tests

**Descriptive Statistics**

| | | | | | | | Percentiles | |
|---|---|---|---|---|---|---|---|---|
| | N | Mean | Std. Deviation | Minimum | Maximum | 25th | 50th (Median) | 75th |
| English and Spanish Q5 | 119 | 4.39 | 1.678 | 1 | 7 | 4.00 | 4.00 | 5.00 |
| English/Spanish | 133 | 1.27 | .446 | 1 | 2 | 1.00 | 1.00 | 2.00 |

**Mann–Whitney Test**

**Ranks**

| | English/Spanish | N | Mean Rank | Sum of Ranks |
|---|---|---|---|---|
| English and Spanish Q5 | 1 | 86 | 56.38 | 4849.00 |
| | 2 | 33 | 69.42 | 2291.00 |
| | Total | 119 | | |

**Test Statistics[a]**

| | English and Spanish Q5 |
|---|---|
| Mann-Whitney U | 1108.000 |
| Wilcoxon W | 4849.000 |
| Z | -1.907 |
| Asymp. Sig. (2-tailed) | .057 |

a. Grouping Variable: English/Spanish

**Fig. 1.** SPSS Output Mann-Whitney U test English-Spanish Item 5.

The second Mann-Whitney U test was performed on English Question 6 and Spanish Question 6. This question measures the respondent's improvement of trust in the information on the paralingual page, based on having the information in the two languages on the same page. This test determines if there is no statistical difference in the distribution of the answers between the English and Spanish respondents. The calculated z value is z = -4.046. Figure 2 shows the output from SPSS.

➡NPar Tests

Descriptive Statistics

| | N | Mean | Std. Deviation | Minimum | Maximum | Percentiles | | |
|---|---|---|---|---|---|---|---|---|
| | | | | | | 25th | 50th (Median) | 75th |
| English and Spanish Q6 | 119 | 4.00 | 1.855 | 1 | 7 | 3.00 | 4.00 | 5.00 |
| English/Spanish | 133 | 1.27 | .446 | 1 | 2 | 1.00 | 1.00 | 2.00 |

**Mann-Whitney Test**

Ranks

| | English/Spanish | N | Mean Rank | Sum of Ranks |
|---|---|---|---|---|
| English and Spanish Q6 | 1 | 86 | 52.23 | 4492.00 |
| | 2 | 33 | 80.24 | 2648.00 |
| | Total | 119 | | |

Test Statistics[a]

| | English and Spanish Q6 |
|---|---|
| Mann-Whitney U | 751.000 |
| Wilcoxon W | 4492.000 |
| Z | -4.046 |
| Asymp. Sig. (2-tailed) | .000 |

a. Grouping Variable: English/Spanish

**Fig. 2.** SPSS Output Mann-Whitney U test English-Spanish Item 6.

## 6.2 Spearman's rho on Grouping by Language Choice

Spearman's rho was performed on English Questions 5 and 6. The correlation, 0.504, is significant for a 2-tailed test. Figure 3 is the SPSS output.

➡**Nonparametric Correlations**

Correlations

| | | | English Q 5 | English Q 6 |
|---|---|---|---|---|
| Spearman's rho | English Q 5 | Correlation Coefficient | 1.000 | .504** |
| | | Sig. (2-tailed) | . | .000 |
| | | N | 86 | 86 |
| | English Q 6 | Correlation Coefficient | .504** | 1.000 |
| | | Sig. (2-tailed) | .000 | . |
| | | N | 86 | 86 |

**. Correlation is significant at the .01 level (2-tailed).

**Fig. 3.** SPSS Output Spearman's rho of English Questions 5.

Spearman's rho was also calculated for Spanish Questions 5 and 6. The calculated correlation, 0.563, is significant for a 2-tailed test (Figure 4).

**➡Nonparametric Correlations**

Correlations

| | | | Spanish Q 5 | Spanish Q 6 |
|---|---|---|---|---|
| Spearman's rho | Spanish Q 5 | Correlation Coefficient | 1.000 | .563** |
| | | Sig. (2-tailed) | . | .001 |
| | | N | 33 | 33 |
| | Spanish Q 6 | Correlation Coefficient | .563** | 1.000 |
| | | Sig. (2-tailed) | .001 | . |
| | | N | 33 | 33 |

**. Correlation is significant at the .01 level (2-tailed).

**Fig. 4.** SPSS Output Spearman's rho of Spanish Questions 5 and 6.

## 6.3 Wilcoxon T Test on Grouping by Language Choice

The Wilcoxon T test was performed on data sets similar to those tested with the Mann-Whitney U test. In the first test with English Questions 5 and 6, the calculated z value is $z = -3.188$. Figure 5 is the SPSS output.

⇒**NPar Tests**

**Descriptive Statistics**

|  | N | Mean | Std. Deviation | Minimum | Maximum |
|---|---|---|---|---|---|
| English Q 5 | 86 | 4.2209 | 1.78491 | 1.00 | 7.00 |
| English Q 6 | 86 | 3.5930 | 1.81093 | 1.00 | 7.00 |

## Wilcoxon Signed Ranks Test

**Ranks**

|  |  | N | Mean Rank | Sum of Ranks |
|---|---|---|---|---|
| English Q 6 – English Q 5 | Negative Ranks | 23[a] | 19.89 | 457.50 |
|  | Positive Ranks | 10[b] | 10.35 | 103.50 |
|  | Ties | 53[c] |  |  |
|  | Total | 86 |  |  |

a. English Q 6 < English Q 5
b. English Q 6 > English Q 5
c. English Q 5 = English Q 6

**Test Statistics[b]**

|  | English Q 6 – English Q 5 |
|---|---|
| Z | -3.188[a] |
| Asymp. Sig. (2-tailed) | .001 |

a. Based on positive ranks.
b. Wilcoxon Signed Ranks Test

**Fig. 5.** SPSS Output Wilcoxon T test of English Questions 5 and 6.

In the next test with the Wilcoxon T test on Spanish Questions 5 and 6, the calculated z value is $z = -1.034$. Output from SPSS is shown in Figure 6.

➡**NPar Tests**

**Descriptive Statistics**

|  | N | Mean | Std. Deviation | Minimum | Maximum |
|---|---|---|---|---|---|
| Spanish Q 5 | 33 | 4.8182 | 1.28585 | 2.00 | 7.00 |
| Spanish Q 6 | 33 | 5.0606 | 1.53987 | 1.00 | 7.00 |

## Wilcoxon Signed Ranks Test

**Ranks**

|  |  | N | Mean Rank | Sum of Ranks |
|---|---|---|---|---|
| Spanish Q 6 – Spanish Q 5 | Negative Ranks | 5[a] | 6.20 | 31.00 |
|  | Positive Ranks | 8[b] | 7.50 | 60.00 |
|  | Ties | 20[c] |  |  |
|  | Total | 33 |  |  |

a. Spanish Q 6 < Spanish Q 5
b. Spanish Q 6 > Spanish Q 5
c. Spanish Q 5 = Spanish Q 6

**Test Statistics[b]**

|  | Spanish Q 6 – Spanish Q 5 |
|---|---|
| Z | -1.034[a] |
| Asymp. Sig. (2-tailed) | .301 |

a. Based on negative ranks.
b. Wilcoxon Signed Ranks Test

**Fig. 6.** SPSS Output Wilcoxon T test of Spanish Questions 5 and 6.

## 6.4 Analysis of Question 8

Question 8 of the survey is a measure of usability of the paralingual pages. The choices for responses had a range of five from "it was very difficult" to "it was very easy." The percentages of the English respondents who answered "it was somewhat easy" or "it was very easy" is 61.3 % and the percentage of Spanish respondents answering similarly is 85.7%.

## 6.5 Alternative Analytical Calculations

Performing nonparametric tests is the appropriate method for analysis of ordinal data. These results have been shown in the previous section. However, means and standard deviations are more commonly understood and therefore used more commonly to describe data. Below (Table 1) is a summary of the means and standard deviations for questions, 5, 6, and 8.

Table 1. Means and standard deviations of survey data

| Item | Value Range | English: Mean/StdDev | Spanish: Mean/StdDev |
|------|-------------|----------------------|----------------------|
| 5 | 1 - 7 | 4.2209/1.785 | 4.8182/1.286 |
| 6 | 1 - 7 | 3.5930/1.811 | 5.0606/1.540 |
| 8 | 1 - 5 | 3.88/1.259 | 4.366/0.994 |

# 7. Discussion

For all tests, the alpha value was chosen to be $\alpha = 0.05$. For ease and uniformity of comparison between all tests, the z value will be used. For the chosen $\alpha = 0.05$ and 2-tailed tests, the critical z value is $z = \pm 1.96$.

## 7.1 Mann-Whitney U tests on Questions 5 and 6

The z value from Question 5 is $z = -1.907$. This is in the region of failing to reject the null hypothesis, so we conclude there is no statistical difference between the two groups' answers about trust.

The result from the Mann-Whitney U test on English and Spanish Question 6 is to reject the null hypothesis based on the calculated z value $z = -4.046$. This indicates that the reported levels of trust are different in the two groups when the information on the web pages contains both languages adjacent to each other.

These results partially support the hypothesis H2 that use of paralingual web pages will increase trust in the page content and government sponsor. Since trust levels are different only when the paralingual information is considered, and the Spanish respondents showed higher medians than the English respondents in both Questions 5 and 6, the Spanish respondents show an increased level of trust based on the paralingual content.

## 7.2 Spearman's rho

Spearman's rho was performed to see the degree of correlation of answeres to Questions 5 and 6 in each group. The rho value for English Questions 5 and 6 is 0.504, so the correlation is "significant". For Spanish Questions 5 and 6 the rho value is 0.563. Thus each of the two groups answered consistently in the trust questions.

## 7.3 Wilcoxon T Test

The Wilcoxon T test was performed to measure the central tendency, the mean, of the answers that respondents in each group provided on Questions 5 and 6. The calculated z value for English Questions 5 and 6 is $z = -3.188$. This indicates that there is a statistical difference in the means of the answers to each question. For Spanish Questions 5 and 6, the calculated z value is $z = -1.034$ and we fail to reject the null hypothesis, therefore we conclude that there is no statistical difference in the means of the answers to each question.

## 7.4 Question 8: Readability of the Paralingual Web Pages

Question 8 is a measure of usability of the paralingual pages as reported by how how easy it was to read the paralingual content. Since 61.3 % of the English respondents and 85.7% of the Spanish respondents answered "it was somewhat easy" or "it was very easy", this supports the hypothesis H1 that use of paralingual web pages will not decrease usability.

## 8 Conclusion

This paper is primarily intended to provide guidance to government decision makers, e-government researchers, and e-government web designers for applying paralingual web page design for improving trust in government in regions where there is a high proportion of bilingual residents. An experiment was performed to test the hypothesis that paralingual web design will improve trust in the content of the e-government web page. This hypothesis was confirmed, but not quite as expected. It was found that the paralingual format improved trust for the minority speaker but not the majority speaker. Upon reflection this is an expected finding.

Additionally, we attempted to show that usability, in this case readability as the paralingual pages only dispensed information and did not perform any function, was not changed. It was found that in general respondents did not find the paralingual format hard to read, however, it was noted that the majority speakers were less enthusiastic than the minority speakers.

The conclusion is that paralingual web design is useful for e-government in areas with significant bilingual populations. There are limitations to this use as it appears that there is a risk of backlash from the majority speaking population. This suggests that paralingual web design should be used when there are known trust issues between majority and minority speakers.

## References

Coleman, S., and Gøtze, J, (2001). Bowling Together: Online Public Engagement in Policy Deliberation. Hansard Society, London. Retrieved October 4, 2005 from http://bowlingtogether.net.

Grönlund, A. and Horan, T. A. (2004). Introducing E-Gov: History, Definitions, and Issues. Communications of the Association for Information Systems, 15: 713-729.

Hart-Teeter. "The New E-government Equation: Ease, Engagement, Privacy and Protection," A report prepared for the Council for Excellence in Government, 2003. Retrieved November 27, 2005 from http://www.excelgov.org/usermedia/images/uploads/PDFs/egovpoll2003.pdf..

Hibbing, J.R. and Theiss-Morse, E. (2002). Stealth Democracy: Americans' Beliefs About How Government Should Work. Cambridge University Press, Cambridge.

Levi, M. and Stoker, L., (2000). Political trust and trustworthiness. Annual Review of Political Science 3: 475-507.

Mercuri, R.T. (May 2005). Trusting in Transparency. Association for Computing Machinery. Communications of the ACM, 48(5): 15.

Organization for Economic Co-operation and Development (OECD), (2001). Citizens as Partners, Information, Consultation and Public Participation in Policy-Making.

Rosell, S., Gantwerk, H., and Furth, I., (2005). Listening To Californians: Bridging The Disconnect. Viewpoint Learning, Inc. Retrieved January 15, 2006 from http://www.viewpointlearning.com/pdf/HI_Report_FINAL.pdf.

Schneider, Gary P. (2003). Electronic Commerce, Fourth Annual Edition. Thomson Course Technology, Boston.

United States Office of Management and Budget (USOMB), (2005), E-Gov: Powering America's Future With Technology. Retrieved October 5, 2005 from http://www.whitehouse.gov/omb/egov/index.html.

# A Study of E-mail Marketing: Why Do People Read and Forward E-mail?

Hsi-Pen Lu, Hsin-Chiau Fu, Chia-Hui Yen

chyen@mail.wfc.edu.tw

**Abstract:** Nowadays, e-mail is one of the most popular Internet applications and has become a useful marketing tool. However, e-mail marketing should be thought ineffectiveness due to the rampancy of spams. In order to explore the underlying phenomenon of e-mail marketing strategy, this study based on Theory of Reasoned Action (TRA) and TRA Chain to investigate what factors affect people who read and forward e-mail. Specifically, perception of receivers and e-mail subjects are hypothesized to have positive effect on attitude to read, which in turn have a significant influence on intention to read. Moreover, intention to read, e-mail content, and motivation of sharing all have positive effect on intention to forward. Web-based survey was conducted and 309 questionnaires were collected. The results reveal the good predictors to influence people who read and forward e-mail. Finally, gender influences one's attitude and intention toward forwarding e-mail. Further, this study provides e-mail marketing strategies and offers suggestions focused on different gender for marketing managers.

## 1 Introduction

A survey indicates that global Internet users have reached to 920 million by 2004, which also demonstrates a rapid development of e-mail. Because email has the advantages of fast, cheap, able to forward to numerous people at a time, and simultaneously transmit voice and image, sending email has become the main activity of using Internet (Chittenden and Rettie 2003). Recently, there is an increasing number of marketing executives who contact consumers by e-mail and send e-mail arbitrarily, arising spam problem. It not only wastes internet resources but also brings trouble to users. As to enterprises, spam affects productivity and increases the cost. Otherwise, it creates people's negative impression on email. Therefore, how to establish a correct email marketing strategy needs to pay special attention.

For the purpose of e-mail marketing successes, intention to read is of great importance. However, prior research failed to examine that why were people willing to read and to share e-mail with others? Most researches discussed read and forward separately (Liao 2004). To make sure that every email is meaningful to receivers, and is transmitted by viral marketing, the study focuses on email itself, understanding what meaningful email to users is, being willing to read, and exploring the factors of forwarding email as well. Only by understanding what people think, will businesses achieve marketing goals. This study is based on Theory of Rational Action (TRA) investigating the purposes of reading and forwarding to improve the marketing performance by email. In sum, the purposes of this paper are to investigate receivers' determinant of reading email and to explore the factors that affect receivers to read email and forward after reading.

## 1.1 Literature review

E-mail may be the most important innovation since the development of the printing technology (Hoffman 2000) and it immediately becomes the popular mode of communication (Chittenden and Rettie 2003). As e-mail marketing is growing rapidly, it turns out to be another way for marketing executives to communicate and establish proper relationships with customers and enable prompt interaction. Chittenden and Rettie (2003) pointed out three effective marketing methods of email, including enticing receivers to read email, retaining their consumer satisfaction, and persuading them to respond.

Godin (2001) proposed the term "ideavirus marketing". He mentioned that traditional marketer sell products to consumers directly and without any means of media. Ideavirus marketing creates innovative virus and establishes the environment for virus to reproduce and transmit. It is the virus itself which full fill the marketing task rather than the marketer. Godin's approach seeks to maximize the spread of information from customer to customer. Kaikati and Kaikati (2004) posited that implementing ideavirus marketing needs to ensure the delivery is of an appropriate nature at first. Further, the description of information should be clear and specific because it represents the value of products. Marketers should pay special attention to subject because a proper subject can give receivers a sense of friendliness. Last, but not least, forwarding must be made simple to receivers so the activities may be continued. The above factors make ideavirus marketing successful.

According to Chittenden and Rettie (2003), the main question regarding email marketing is how to encourage receivers to read email? As shown in Chang's research (2002), the higher correlation between email subject and content, the higher the possibility of the email being read. Also topics, which are highly related to the receiver's interest and have personal title, effectively increase the possibility of reading. In addition, the receiver who forwards a letter plays a critical role in viral marketing. Lee (2001) stated some characteristics of forwarding email, which are listed as follows: in marketing reason, interaction between forwarding email dramatically helps companies communicate with clients. As for retain human relationship, simply click the forward button, and quickly transmit message to our close friends and relatives, further, it does not cost much. For share message or knowledge, a user who forwards email to friends and relatives creates a joint sharing experience. In addition, Liao (2004) argued that people are more willing to forward email which has plentiful content and results in a better mood after reading it. Because the forwarded email circulates among acquaintances, they are more willing to trust and respond to the message.

Due to the rampancy of email marketing, mailboxes flood with spam. Hence, enterprises need to adjust their strategies of email marketing rather than sending it blindly. They should stand from receiver's point to understand the reasons why people are willing to read and forward. However, previous studies do not have in-depth exploration on reading and forwarding email, thus this study is to find the factors regarding reading and forwarding email.

## 2 Research model and method

Theory of reasoned action (TRA) is a wildly accepted model to validate individual behavior in numerous contexts. The research model is based on the TRA proposed by Fishbein and Ajzen's (1975), which relies on one's attitude and intention to predict actual behavior. TRA presents that individual actual behavior is directly or indirectly influenced by ones belief, attitude toward behavior, subjective norm and behavioral intention. This study proposes a chain relationship between intention to read and intention to forward. That e-mail is read or forwarded can be affected by different beliefs. The concept of expended TRA and development of the TRA Chain is shown in Figure 1.

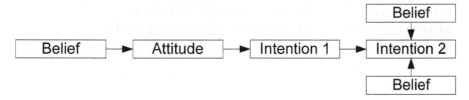

**Fig. 1.** Concept of TRA Chain

In our research model, the email receivers' personal cognition and the mail subject affect their attitude toward email. Further, the receivers' attitudes toward email affect the willingness of reading mail. Otherwise, the users' cognition about email content and their motivation of forwarding affect the possibility of forwarding email. Table 1 gives definitions on different variables and Figure 2 shows the research model.

**Table 1.** Definition of the variables

| Construct | Definition |
|---|---|
| Sender's relationship | The extent of acquaintance between the receiver and the sender. |
| Perceived risk | After clicking email, the receiver anticipates and perceives disadvantage and harmful result. |
| Permission | The receiver recognizes the extent to which receiving the email will not be annoying. |
| Attraction of subject | The receiver recognizes the extent of attraction from email subject. |
| Entertainment of subject | The receiver recognizes the extent of interest from email subject. |
| Informativeness of subject | The receiver recognizes the extent of increasing new knowledge from the email subject. |
| Attraction of content | The forwarder recognizes the extent of attraction from email content. |
| Entertainment of content | The forwarder recognizes the extent of interest from email content. |
| Informativeness of content | The forwarder recognizes the extent of increasing new knowledge from the email content. |
| Mutual benefit | The forwarder recognizes the extent of mutual benefit by forwarding email. |
| Individualism | The forwarder recognizes the extent of his benefit by forwarding email. |
| Altruism | The forwarder recognizes the extent of others' benefit by forwarding email. |
| Reading attitude | The fondness of reading email |
| Intention to read | The willingness of reading email |
| Intention to forward | The willingness of forwarding email |

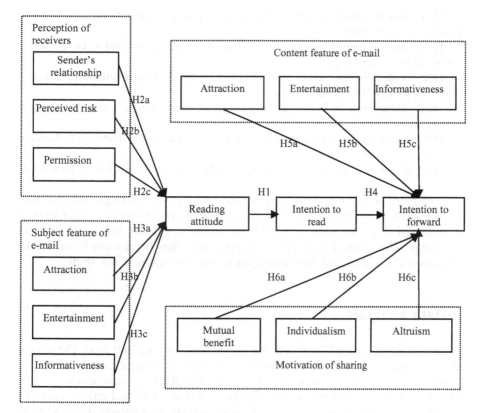

**Fig. 2.** research model

According to other related literature, the addressed research hypotheses are stated as follows:

H1: One's attitude in reading e-mail is positively associated with his reading intention.

H2a: Relationship with E-mail sender is positively associated with receiver's attitude in reading e-mail.

H2b: Receiver's perceived risk of e-mail is negatively associated with his reading attitude in reading e-mail.

H2c: Receiver's permission of e-mail is positively associated with his attitude in reading e-mail.

H3a: Subject attraction of e-mail is positively associated with receiver's attitude in reading e-mail.

H3b: Subject entertainment of e-mail is positively associated with receiver's attitude in reading e-mail.

H3c: Subject informativeness of e-mail is positively associated with receiver's attitude in reading e-mail.

H4: One's intention to read e-mail is positively associated with his intention to forward e-mail.

H5a: Content attraction of e-mail is positively associated with receiver's intention to forward e-mail.

H5b: Content entertainment of e-mail is positively associated with receiver's intention to forward e-mail.

H5c: Content informativeness of e-mail is positively associated with receiver's intention to forward e-mail.

H6a: Mutual benefit is positively associated with receiver's intention to forward e-mail.

H6b: Individualism is positively associated with receiver's intention to forward e-mail.

H6c: Altruism is positively associated with receiver's intention to forward e-mail.

Web-based survey was conducted by this study because the target subjects were e-mail users. The survey questionnaire was posted onto the most popular BBS in Taiwan and all e-mail users were cordially invited to support this survey. Most of the items were adapted from prior research, and other items were based on the definition of variables and then developed by the researchers of this study.

# 3 Data analysis

By the time this survey was closed, 309 questionnaires were collected. The data of the valid samples reveal that male outnumbers female at the percentage of 68.6%. More than half of people are in the age group 21 to 30, which accounts for 58.9%. Of all work status, students account for most of them at 62%. Further, regarding education background, 47.2% of people have university or college degrees. As to the frequency of accessing the Internet, surfing one to two hours a day is the most frequent at 25.9% and second is three to four hours a day at 24.9%. Moreover, a majority of people spend half to one hour on receiving, reading, forwarding and sending email, which is at the proportion of 40.8%. Most people who have three email accounts in average are at 32%. 28.8% of people whose email address books consist of 21 to 40 data and 25.2% of people receive email more than three times a day.

The internal consistency was assessed by verifying Cronbach's α. The values range from 0.88 to 0.95. All were greater than the benchmark at 0.80. The result showed that all measures have adequate reliability. To evaluate the adequacy of the measurement items, factor analysis was performed by SPSS. Otherwise, Exploratory Factor Analysis (EFA) is used to test construct validity. The result conformed to the construct validity of this study and proposed 15 factors. Factor loadings were shown in Table 2, and those were smaller than 0.5 has not been shown in this table.

**Table 2.** Construct validity (N=309)

| Scale | Factor |
| --- | --- |

| Items | 1 | 2 | 3 | 4 | 5 | 6 | 7 | 8 | 9 | 10 | 11 | 12 | 13 | 14 | 15 |
|---|---|---|---|---|---|---|---|---|---|---|---|---|---|---|---|
| SR1 | | | | | | | | | | | | .778 | | | |
| SR2 | | | | | | | | | | | | .812 | | | |
| SR3 | | | | | | | | | | | | .826 | | | |
| PR1 | .901 | | | | | | | | | | | | | | |
| PR2 | .935 | | | | | | | | | | | | | | |
| PR3 | .919 | | | | | | | | | | | | | | |
| P1 | | | | .865 | | | | | | | | | | | |
| P2 | | | | .875 | | | | | | | | | | | |
| P3 | | | | .846 | | | | | | | | | | | |
| AS1 | | | | | | | | | .864 | | | | | | |
| AS2 | | | | | | | | | .872 | | | | | | |
| AS3 | | | | | | | | | .792 | | | | | | |
| ES1 | | | | | | | | | | | .816 | | | | |
| ES 2 | | | | | | | | | | | .810 | | | | |
| ES3 | | | | | | | | | | | .814 | | | | |
| IS1 | | | | | | | | .834 | | | | | | | |
| IS2 | | | | | | | | .857 | | | | | | | |
| IS3 | | | | | | | | .853 | | | | | | | |
| AC1 | | | | | | | | | | | | | .763 | | |
| AC2 | | | | | | | | | | | | | .793 | | |
| AC3 | | | | | | | | | | | | | .755 | | |
| EC1 | | | | | .836 | | | | | | | | | | |
| EC2 | | | | | .856 | | | | | | | | | | |
| EC3 | | | | | .892 | | | | | | | | | | |
| IC1 | | | | | | | | | | .810 | | | | | |
| IC2 | | | | | | | | | | .824 | | | | | |
| IC3 | | | | | | | | | | .809 | | | | | |
| RA1 | | | | | | | | | | | | | | .735 | |
| RA2 | | | | | | | | | | | | | | .741 | |
| RA3 | | | | | | | | | | | | | | .761 | |
| IR1 | | | | | | | | | | | | | | | .747 |
| IR2 | | | | | | | | | | | | | | | .737 |
| IR3 | | | | | | | | | | | | | | | .759 |
| MB1 | | | .879 | | | | | | | | | | | | |
| MB2 | | | .872 | | | | | | | | | | | | |
| MB3 | | | .873 | | | | | | | | | | | | |
| I1 | | .884 | | | | | | | | | | | | | |
| I2 | | .930 | | | | | | | | | | | | | |
| I3 | | .920 | | | | | | | | | | | | | |
| A1 | | | | | | .827 | | | | | | | | | |
| A2 | | | | | | .879 | | | | | | | | | |
| A3 | | | | | | .858 | | | | | | | | | |
| IF1 | | | | | | | .851 | | | | | | | | |
| IF2 | | | | | | | .832 | | | | | | | | |
| IF3 | | | | | | | .837 | | | | | | | | |
| Eigen-values | 2.86 | 2.84 | 2.80 | 2.80 | 2.74 | 2.74 | 2.74 | 2.65 | 2.63 | 2.57 | 2.51 | 2.49 | 2.36 | 2.32 | 2.32 |

| Cumulative Percentage | 6.37 | 12.69 | 18.94 | 25.16 | 31.27 | 37.37 | 43.46 | 49.37 | 55.21 | 60.92 | 66.51 | 72.05 | 77.32 | 82.48 | 87.65 |

The research is adopted Pearson Product Moment Coefficient to analyze coefficient and verify positive and negative coefficient hypothesis of research model. Table 3 presents the correlation coefficients among the constructs. The bi-variate relationships indicated that all the constructs were significantly correlated with each other. Therefore, all hypotheses were supported. In order to avoid collinearity that might influence result, coefficient between two variables should be less than 0.8 or more than -0.8. As can be seen from the table 3, all correlation coefficient are less than 0.8 and collinearity is not existed.

**Table 3.** Correlation analysis

|     | SR | PR | P | AS | ES | IS | AC | EC | IC | RA | IR | I | A | MB |
|-----|-----|-----|-----|-----|-----|-----|-----|-----|-----|-----|-----|-----|-----|-----|
| PR | -.262 ** | | | | | | | | | | | | | |
| P | .438 ** | -.309 ** | | | | | | | | | | | | |
| AS | .346 ** | -.215 ** | .324 ** | | | | | | | | | | | |
| ES | .360 ** | -.111 * | .360 ** | .486 ** | | | | | | | | | | |
| IS | .379 ** | -.229 ** | .409 ** | .284 ** | .328 ** | | | | | | | | | |
| AC | .436 ** | -.224 ** | .444 ** | .415 ** | .405 ** | .269 ** | | | | | | | | |
| EC | .317 ** | -.084 ** | .234 ** | .260 ** | .452 ** | .159 ** | .513 ** | | | | | | | |
| IC | .422 ** | -.228 ** | .332 ** | .342 ** | .312 ** | .481 ** | .453 ** | .338 ** | | | | | | |
| RA | .480 ** | -.302 ** | .453 ** | .418 ** | .418 ** | .389 ** | .488 ** | .344 ** | .549 ** | | | | | |
| IR | .488 ** | -.311 ** | .495 ** | .392 ** | .383 ** | .392 ** | .536 ** | .315 ** | .508 ** | .709 ** | | | | |
| I | .126 * | .107 * | .101 * | .209 ** | .121 * | .171 ** | .228 ** | .115 * | .217 ** | .198 ** | .176 ** | | | |
| A | .286 ** | -.238 ** | .230 ** | .178 ** | .094 * | .236 ** | .342 ** | .143 ** | .360 ** | .335 ** | .409 ** | .268 ** | | |
| MB | .099 * | .045 * | .120 * | .159 ** | .103 ** | .129 ** | .291 ** | .137 ** | .247 ** | .214 ** | .298 ** | .458 ** | .530 ** | |
| IF | .399 ** | -.106 * | .242 ** | .276 ** | .194 ** | .192 ** | .460 ** | .328 ** | .428 ** | .463 ** | .482 ** | .300 ** | .494 ** | .419 ** |

The path significance in the research model and the variance explained ($R^2$) by each construct were examined. Figure 3 presents the standardized path coefficients of constructs. Most were strongly supported, except individualism, which did not have positive effect on intention to forward e-mail. The perception of receivers and subject feature of e-mail had influences on reading attitude ($R^2=0.39$), in turn, one's reading attitude had a positive effect on intention to read e-mail ($R^2=0.50$). Intention to read e-mail, content feature of e-mail, and motivation of sharing all influenced the intention to forward e-mail ($R^2$=0.40). With the exception of individual benefit, all of the other motivation of sharing affected the intention to forward e-mail.

This study also examined the path analysis of different gender. From the male aspect, the path from permission to reading attitude was not significant, and attraction of content was not a significant effect on intention to forward. From the female facet, the path from perceived risk to reading attitude was not significant, and informativeness of content was not a significant effect on intention to forward. Whether male or female, the result also showed that e-mail subject significantly and directly influenced reading attitude, and individualism is not significant.

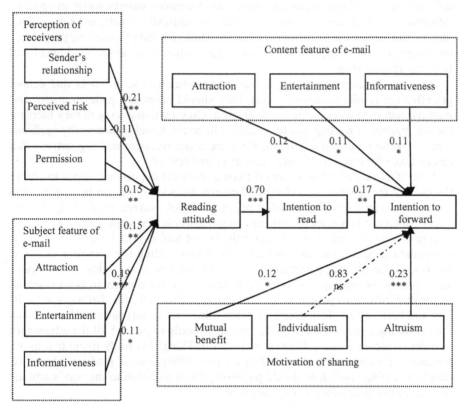

**Fig. 3.** Path analysis of this study N=309        *p<0.05, **p<0.01,
***p<0.001

## 4 Conclusions and implication of research results

The results indicated that the email user's attitude is the main factor which affects the willingness of reading email, and it conformed to TRA theory as well. According to path analysis, the email users' attitude had positive and significant influence on "reading intention". In other words, the more positive attitude toward email, the higher the willingness of reading will be. Hence, factors that affect the attitude of users are of great importance. The research found that increasing the sender's relationship, permission, attraction of subject, entertainment of subject, informativeness of subject, and decreasing perceived risk could promote the user's attitude. The result demonstrates the first purpose of this paper that investigates receivers' determinant of reading email.

The users' intentions to read have positive and significant influence on intentions to forward. The greater intention to read the greater intention to forward because reading intention depends on one's attitude. When the users are willing to read the email, it represents that they accept the email to a certain extent and raise the willingness to forward. Moreover, attraction of content, entertainment of content, informativeness of content, mutual benefit and altruistic benefit are some of the factors that contribute to forward intention. These indicate the second purpose of this paper, that is to explore the factors which affect receivers to read email and forward after reading.

As spam is rampant nowadays, marketing specialists send letters that cannot get effective results invariably. Thus, they should adopt adequate strategies and mail the letters to meet people's satisfaction. Only by doing so, will they increase the willingness of reading and forwarding afterward, which substantially performs viral marketing and reduces spam. Here are some management suggestions that can be taken for email marketing executives' references:

First, if users are willing to read the email, the next importance step is to design the content that people are willing to forward. Email content can be displayed in various ways unlike subject which is restrained by characters. When designing the email content, it is not appropriate to contain a whole text with written words, inserting pictures or animation will make the layout looks vivid. Otherwise, interesting written language encourages readers to finish reading the complete message. Further, if the content is related to the reader's interests or rights, it will foster substantially the willingness to forward. Second, Altruistic benefit is an essential factor that influences people to forward letter. It also indicates that users are selfless and believe that the message benefits others when forwarding. Hence, when the marketing executives design the layout, it needs to present all the advantages in order to increase the willingness to forward. Third, this study found that user's fondness of email had a direct effect on the willingness of reading. Therefore, email-marketing specialists should pay exceptional attention to the user's attitude to achieve maximum marketing efficiency.

Fourth, people are more likely to read the email sent from acquaintances. Before starting marketing, marketers need to develop good relationship with customers to gain their trust. Once you are a friend of the receiver, it will forge success. However, sending too much email might result in inconvenience to others though they are friends. It is better to get permission before sending. This not only shows respect, but also reduces negative effect. Because viruses come along with spam, some people do not even read the email at all. Hence, marketers must assure their computers do not have viruses before sending to avoid damaging customers' computers and lost reliability. Fifth, whether the subject is attractive or not affects one's fondness toward email. An eye-catching subject and interesting written words attract readers' attention immediately. In addition, the subject can be informative, providing knowledge to readers. Finally, if the email marketing is focused on males, it needs to pay special attention that the email is virus free and that the message is relevant and helpful. If the email marketing is designed for females, obtaining permission before sending is an appropriate measure to avoid giving a negative impression. Further, attractive content draws female users' attention easily.

# References

Chang CJ (2003) The study on increasing the click-through rate of commercial E-mail (in Chinese). Master degree thesis, National Yunlin University of Science and Technology.

Chittenden L and Rettie R (2003) An evaluation of e-mail marketing and factors affecting response. Journal of Targeting, Measurement and Analysis for Marketing 11:203-217.

Fishbein M and Ajzen I (1975) Belief, attitude, intention and behavior: an introduction to theory and research. Reading (MA), Addision-Wesley.

Godin S (2001) Unleashing the Ideavirus. Do you zoom, New York.

Hoffman DL (2000) The revolution will not be televised: Introduction to the special issue on marketing science and the Internet, Marketing Science 19(1): 1-3.

Kaikati A and Kaikati J (2004) Stealth marketing: How to reach consumers surreptitiously, California Management Review 46(4): 6-22.

Lee HC (2001) A study on forwarding behaviors among e-mail users (in Chinese). Master degree thesis, Tamkang University.

Liao CW (2004) The research on relationship between contents perception, forms and forwarded intention, retained intention of email (in Chinese). Master degree thesis, National Taiwan University of Science and Technology.

# Key Issues in Information Systems Management in Companies in Slovenia

Stanislav Sotlar[*], Jože Zupančič[**]

[*]RTH d.o.o., Trg revolucije 12, 1420 Trbovlje, stane.sotlar@rth.si
[**]University of Maribor, School of Organizational Science, Kidričeva 55a, 4000 Kranj joze.zupancic@fov.uni-mb.si

**Abstract:** The goal of this paper is to identify the issues in information systems (IS) management expected to be the most important over the next three to five years, to assess the importance of these issues, and compare the results of our study to the findings of similar investigations, with emphasis on the study done in Slovenia in 1992. The two-round Delphi method was used to collect the opinions of IS managers in Slovenian companies. The Q-method and Q-sort ranking were used for data analysis. The study showed that views and opinions of IS department managers in Slovenia are becoming more similar to the views of their counterparts from other countries, revealed by other comparable investigations. This indicates that the economic and cultural environment in Slovenia that was specific after the economic and political transition in the nineties does not deviate considerably from the environment in other countries. Compared to the earlier study, technology-related issues became less important, and business-related issues appear to be more important.

## 1 Introduction

Major issues in IS management have been investigated in the USA since the beginning of the eighties (for example Ball and Harris 1982; Dickson et al. 1994). Similar investigations have been carried out in several other countries: for example, in Australia (Watson 1989), Poland (Wrycza and Plata-Przechlewski 1994), Estonia (Dexter et al. 1993), Indonesia (Samik-Ibrahim, 2002, Norway (Gottschalk 2001), South Africa (Berkowitz et al. 2001), Kuwait (Alshawaf and DeLone (2002), Thailand (Pimchangthong et al. 2003), Slovenia (Dekleva and Zupančič 1996). The primary purpose of these studies was to determine the IS management issues expected to be the most important in the next three to five years and thus deserving the most time and attention by the managers.

A comparison of the results of the early studies (for example Watson and Brancheau 1991; Watson et al. 1997; Gottschalk 2001) showed that the important IS management issues depend on the level of economic development and the cultural environment. They also evolve over time, due to external factors such as rapid IT innovations and their implications on business, globalization, and changes in economic and legal systems. Some of the issues resolve over time, others remain current for a longer period of time, while new issues emerge.

The goals of our investigation are the following: (1) to identify key issues in IS management, which will require significant attention in the next 3 – 5 years, and to rank them by importance, and (2) to compare the results of our survey with the outcome of other investigations, in particular with the results of the study (Dekleva and Zupančič 1996) which was carried out in 1992.

## 2 Research approach

Most of the studies used the methodological framework of the American Society for Information Management (SIM), and applied the Delphi technique, a methodology for organizing and prioritizing collective judgment of a group that involves iterative surveying of the same group (Linstone and Turoff. 2002). The initial procedure of the Delphi technique is to prepare, distribute, and synthesize a series of problem statements for evaluation. Communication among participants in the next rounds (phases, steps, …) of the investigation is based on questionnaires. Frequently, opinions of the participants are collected using a first open ended questionnaire. Participants receive feedback in the form of their own previous responses and statistical or any other data describing the reflections of entire group with each succeeding round. It is believed that this technique leads to consensus on major points, but also uncovers minority opinions.

The target group of respondents in our investigation were IS department managers in companies (but not public institutions) in Slovenia. When selecting the sample of companies to be surveyed, consideration was given to the following:

1. The sample had to be large enough to be able to collect a sufficient number of relevant responses; previous studies showed that the response rate in this type of investigations is relatively low (Berkowitz et al. 2001).
2. We had to survey companies with an organized IS function; one study (Vehovar et al. 2003) showed that most large companies have a formal IS department: only 4% of Slovenian companies with 500 or more total employees had no IS department.

Therefore, we asked the IS department managers in the 400 largest companies in Slovenia to participate in our research. We applied a modified version of the model for key issues selection procedure suggested by (Gottschalk 2000) that was used in the investigation of key IS management issues in Norway (Gottschalk et al. 2001), and - in an adapted form - in South Africa (Berkowitz et al. 2001).

To compare the results of our investigation with results of the earlier study in Slovenia (Dekleva and Zupančič 1996), we used the lists of key issues from other investigations only indirectly, as an aid in shaping the descriptions the key issues identified in our study. The entire list of issues was generated from the opinions of

IS managers in companies, collected in the first round of the Delphi survey. Then, we followed the model described in Gottschalk (2000) which suggests that Q-method (Brown 1996) should be used for ranking instead of rating the key issues using the Delphi technique. The advantage of the Q-sort over Delphi is that Q-sort requires simultaneous consideration of the issues and utilizes the same scale for all the issues (Pimchangthong et al. 2003).

To assure the participation of the respondents who dislike internet-based surveying, we also sent a paper questionnaire in the phase of collecting suggestions for key issues, together with an e-mailed invitation. Ranking of the key issues according to the Q-methodology was done only by a web application.

Q sort, the ranking technique in implementation of Q-methodology, enables that issues are rated in relation one to another, unlike most other techniques where issues are rated independently. It consists of the following steps:

(1) The issues or statements to be evaluated by the respondents are identified and formulated. One of the main assumptions in the Q-methodology is that taken together, all of the issues used in Q-sort represent the possible domain of opinions on topic under consideration.

(2) Depending on the number of issues, an adequate format of the Q-sort is developed: it must always be symmetrical and shaped in the form of normal distribution. For example, if 24 issues to be ranked are identified, the form of Q-sort shown in Figure 1 can be used.

| -4 | -3 | -2 | -1 | 0 | +1 | +2 | +3 | +4 |
|----|----|----|----|----|----|----|----|----|
| X | X | X | X | X | X | X | X | X |
| X | X | X | X | X | X | X | X | X |
|   |   | X | X | X | X | X |   |   |
|   |   |   |   | X |   |   |   |   |

**Fig. 1.** An example of Q-sort

This shape of Q-sort forces all respondents to allocate the 24 issues to all available spaces and utilize the complete scale from -4 to +4. Only two issues can be placed in the most important (+4) and least important (-4) positions while four issues can be placed in the middle (neutral) position. The ranking is completed when the respondent positions all the issues in the available spaces.

For the needs our investigation, we implemented a web application using Typo3 (http://www.typo3.com/ and http://www.typo3.org/ - web page for developers), a Web Content management System, based on open source technologies (MySQL and PHP4). For the ranking of key issues, we adapted the Web application WebQ described in Schmolck (2002). WebQ is based on code written by Rick Watson (Terry College University of Georgia) and is available from the web page http://www.rz.unibw-muenchen.de/~p41bsmk/qmethod/webq/. This application enables easy and clear ranking of issues according to the rules of Q-sort. It includes online help and makes possible to carry out the sorting in one step: the respondent can modify and correct his or her input, but can not submit an incomplete or invalid response. When a respondent logs on, a list of key issues in random order is displayed. The respondent can do the ranking by a click of the mouse on the selected rating.

## 3 The research

The target organizations for our study were companies with 200 or more employees. Forty companies (with less than 200 employees) with the highest income and/or assets in recent years were added. Next, all banks and insurance companies in Slovenia were added. This resulted in a list of 404 companies. Due to the size and industry of these organizations, it was expected that most of them had an IS or IT department. The addresses of the companies were collected from two business directories (PIRS® 2004 and: IPIS® December 2003), using the total number of employees as the main criterion for selection.

In summer 2004, the questionnaire with an accompanying letter explaining the goals and the procedures of the investigation was sent to the 404 IS or IT Department managers. We asked the respondents to define three to five IS management issues expected to be the most important in the next three to five years, and provide short descriptions and their rationales. They were also asked to provide their own and their organization's demographic data. As an alternative, we offered the possibility of entering the same information using a web site. Basic instructions on how to access the web site were given in the accompanying letter. A more detailed description of the investigation was published on the Web. Each accompanying letter included a username and password to access the application.

In the first step of the investigation, 73 respondents provided a total of 260 suggestions for key issues in IS management that were used for the development of a consolidated list of key issues used in the second step of the investigation. Only a minor number of respondents (22) used the paper questionnaire.

Consolidating the suggested key issues into a list to be rated in the second step proved to be difficult and time consuming. It was difficult to shape the issues and their descriptions from respondents' suggestions which were written as free text. In the literature, we found no detailed recommendation on how to generate a uniform list of issues. We used the recommendations by Linstone and Turoff (2002) which were included into the description of the Delphi method. First, we classified all the 260 suggestions into relatively general groups. Then we examined each of the groups separately and classified the suggestions according to the content of their descriptions. This procedure was repeated several times.

Initially, we got 19 groups-issues with five or more suggestions. We consolidated their names and descriptions. Because the number of issues was too small for the applied theoretical framework, we decided to formulate additional issues based on the remaining unused suggestions. The criteria for these issues were: (1) at least two suggestions for issues were provided by the respondents, (2) suggestions didn't refer to a specific narrow area, and (3) the issue was not a consequence of recent events popularized in the media. Using this approach, we defined eight more issues.

In the final selection and formulation of key issues, we used the key issues identified in other investigation as examples; we didn't directly include them in the final list. To generate the consolidated list of 27 key issues we used 229 suggestions, and 31 suggestions remained unused.

The second step of the investigation was carried out in September 2004. We invited all the target group of 404 IS department managers to participate in the second step of the investigation. In the invitation, we briefly described the ranking procedure and the access to the Web application. Each of the participants also received a uniform username and password to log on the web application.

Only 76 (18,8%) invited managers participated in the investigation. Only 29 (39,7%) respondents who provided at least one valid suggestion for key issues in the first step of the investigation participated in the second step. This response rate was expected and comparable to the response rate in similar investigations; it was sufficient for the purpose of our investigation; Q-methodology is a subjective method and does not require a high response rate (Brown, 1993).

# 4 The results

Based on the Q-sorts that reflected the responding managers' views about the importance of key issues in IS management, we first calculated basic statistical measures ( Table 1).

Out of the 26 issues that were identified as the most important in 1992 (Dekleva and Zupančič 1996), 12 also emerged in our study (Table 2). Comparison among the issues was done based on the rationales. All the issues that were ranked as the most important in the study in 1992 also emerged in our investigation. In 1992, most of them (11 out of 12) were ranked on the first 12 places; only one of the issues that emerged in the both investigations (*Ensuring adequate financial resources*) was below the rank 12. In our investigation, most of the issues from 1992 were ranked relatively low.

Key issues that had not emerged in the 1992 study are those which are a consequence of changes in the IS and ICT field. Changes related to the implementation of new technologies (software and infrastructure), are generally rated as less important. Newly emerged key issues indicate the direction of profound change in the perception of the IS mission in the last ten years. They indicate the increasing level of integration of IS into the business system. We can identify two groups of issues as an illustration of two different aspects of the change:

- The first group indicates the need for a stronger influence of IS on the development and implementation of the business system (*Incorporation of IS in the corporate strategic planning, Support of IS to the optimization of business processes, ...*).
- The second group expresses the response of IS on the pressure of the business system, which is a consequence if its dependence on IS and IT (*Ensuring*

*uninterrupted functioning of the IS, Protection of the IS against intrusions, viruses, spam,* etc.)

**Table 1.** Key issues in IS management ordered by the rated importance

| Rank | Issue description | Average | Standard deviation | Median |
|------|-------------------|---------|--------------------|--------|
| 1 | Ensuring uninterrupted functioning of the IS | 1,841 | 1,903 | 2 |
| 2 | Incorporation IS in the corporate strategic planning | 1,333 | 1,840 | 1 |
| 3 | Strategic planning of IS | 1,111 | 1,788 | 1 |
| 4 | Protection against intrusions, viruses, spam, ... | 1,048 | 1,708 | 1 |
| 5 | Support of IS to the optimization of business processes | 0,968 | 1,732 | 1 |
| 6 | Integration of information subsystems into an comprehensive information architecture | 0,905 | 1,757 | 1 |
| 7 | Implementation of a comprehensive safety policy in accordance with standards | 0,857 | 1,625 | 1 |
| 8 | Development and implementation of decision support systems for senior management | 0,619 | 1,879 | 1 |
| 8 | Users' and senior mgts' appreciation of IS | 0,619 | 1,853 | 1 |
| 10 | Ensuring adequate financial resources | 0,492 | 1,848 | 0 |
| 11 | Education of IT users | 0,444 | 1,423 | 0 |
| 12 | Position of IS dept. in the corporate hierarchy | 0,333 | 2,048 | 0 |
| 13 | Ensuring the users prompt (quick) access to data and information | 0,286 | 1,708 | 0 |
| 14 | Implementation of new ITs | 0,190 | 1,625 | 0 |
| 15 | Recruiting and development of IS human resources | 0,143 | 1,712 | 0 |
| 16 | Efficient telecommunications (infrastructure) | -0,016 | 1,591 | 0 |
| 17 | Use of methodologies and project approach in system development | -0,032 | 1,481 | 0 |
| 18 | Consolidation and optimization of corporate ICT infrastructure | -0,254 | 1,685 | 0 |
| 19 | Implementation and management of electronic business – b2b | -0,365 | 1,954 | -1 |
| 20 | Management of ever increasing amount of data | -0,667 | 1,796 | 0 |
| 21 | Implementation of the data DW concept | -0,857 | 1,703 | -1 |
| 22 | Implementation group work support systems | -1,016 | 1,661 | -1 |
| 23 | Electronic documentation systems | -1,063 | 1,564 | -1 |
| 24 | Ensuring mobile access to information | -1,444 | 1,673 | -2 |
| 25 | Implementation of open source systems | -1,746 | 2,071 | -2 |

| 26 | Implementation of ERP, CRM, SCM | -1,857 | 1,654 | -2 |
| 27 | Outsourcing IS services | -1,873 | 1,661 | -2 |

**Table 2.** Comparison of the results from 1992 and 2004

| Issue description | Rank 2004 | Rank 1992 |
|---|---|---|
| Ensuring uninterrupted functioning of the IS | 1 | |
| Incorporation (inclusion) IS in the corporate strategic planning | 2 | |
| Strategic planning of IS | 3 | 3 |
| Protection of the IS against intrusions, viruses, spam, etc. | 4 | |
| Support of IS to the optimization of business processes | 5 | |
| Integration of information subsystems into an comprehensive information architecture | 6 | 7 |
| Implementation of a comprehensive safety policy in accordance with standards | 7 | |
| Development and implementation of DSS for senior management | 8 | 9 |
| Users' and senior managements' appreciation of IS | 8 | 1 |
| Ensuring adequate financial resources | 10 | 21 |
| Education of IT users | 11 | 6 |
| Position of IS department in the corporate hierarchy | 12 | 5 |
| Ensuring the users prompt (quick) access to data and information | 13 | |
| Implementation of new information technologies | 14 | |
| Recruiting and development of IS human resources | 15 | 2 |
| Efficient telecommunication connections (infrastructure) | 16 | 8 |
| Use of methodologies and project approach in system development* | 17 | 4,12 |
| Consolidation and optimization of corporate ICT infrastructure | 18 | |
| Implementation a and management of electronic business – b2b | 19 | 11 |
| Management and control of ever increasing amount of data | 20 | |
| Implementation of the data warehousing  (DW) concept | 21 | |
| Implementation of system that support group work | 22 | |
| Electronic documentation systems | 23 | |
| Ensuring mobile access to information | 24 | |
| Implementation of open source systems | 25 | |
| Implementation of  worldwide used ERP, CRM, SCM systems | 26 | |
| Outsourcing  IS services | 27 | |

\* This issue covers two of the key issues from 1992

The issue *Implementation of a comprehensive safety policy in accordance with standards* integrates the two groups and highlights the interdependence of the business system and IS.

However, most of the issues ranked (see Table 3) at place 10 and below in 1992 study and didn't surface in our investigation, are no longer current. This could be explained by the development of IT and IS: these issues (technologies) are under control and are commonly used now; therefore they are not considered as key issues any more. Also, the economic and regulative environment in Slovenia is not specific any more, as it was when the earlier investigation was carried out. The conditions in the country stabilized and the country was integrated into the international stream of events, so IS department managers are not limited by relations which were a consequence of the circumstances of the time. The question if IS if useful and needed is not asked any more. The responding IS managers did not indicate that they were limited by strict IS cost controls as they were in the past. Most likely, they adapted to them and are able to control them more easily.

**Table 3.** Key issues from the 1992 study that did not surface in our investigation

| Issue description | Rang 1992 |
|---|---|
| National IS/IT standards | 10 |
| Use of modern tools for IS development | 12 |
| Selection of information technology and equipment | 14 |
| Stability of national regulations | 15 |
| Implementation of relational DBMS | 16 |
| Use of external data bases | 16 |
| Improving IS development productivity | 18 |
| Legal protection | 19 |
| Evaluation and enhancement of existing IS | 20 |
| Substitution of mainframes with PCs an LANs | 22 |
| Limited supply of quality IS products and services | 23 |
| IS contribution measurement | 24 |
| IS cost control | 25 |
| Establishment of a national professional association for IS | 26 |

Table 4 presents a summary of the results of some recent investigations of key issues in IS management carried out in other countries. We included all the key issues identified in the investigations in Table 4, except from (Pimchangthong et al. 2003) where the descriptions of only the 10 highest ranked issues were available. In all the investigations used for comparison, researchers started from a list of issues defined in other studies and summarized from different sources. Some of these lists were supplemented with issues generated in the course of the investigations. In our study, we generated all the key issues only from suggestions provided by the respondents, collected in the first step of the investigation. Therefore, some of the descriptions and rationales of the issues do not match completely with the issues used for the comparison. Some issues in our investigation were defined more broadly and can be compared to several issues identified in other studies, for example: *Recruiting and development of IS human resources, Implementation of worldwide uses ERP, CRM and SCM systems* and *Use of methodologies and project approach in system development.*

The comparison presented in Table 4 indicates that issues related to certain technological solutions or specific for a relatively narrow segment of IS activities did not emerge as important in our investigation; for example: *Electronic business (business to consumer), Development and management of distributed systems, Implementation and management of end-user computing, Improving IS infrastructure planning,* and *Implementation of object oriented technology.* Interestingly, *IS contribution and effectiveness measurement* was identified as key issue in three out of the four investigations used in our comparison, but IS managers from Slovenian companies did not consider it as important. This may indicate that Slovenian IS managers are still not as much under pressure to justify the cost of IS as their counterparts in other countries.

No corresponding issues could be fund in the studies used for the comparison for only three issues identified in our study: *Implementation of data warehousing concept* is a merely a technological solution, therefore it might not have appeared important enough to the investigators to include it in the list of key issues. However, the issues *Implementation of a comprehensive safety policy in accordance with standards (Comprehensive safety policy)* and *Consolidation and optimization of corporate ICT infrastructure* are much broader. A possible reason that they were not identified in other investigations might be the way the lists were developed. Other researchers put together their lists on the basis of issues identified in earlier investigations. Therefore, it might have occurred that that these issues which have already become outdated, were included in the list for rating. Conversely, some current (up-to date) issues might have been omitted. Undoubtedly, the two issues stated above are topical now.

The order of the key issues in our study in most cases does not deviate from that in others. Considering the issues that were rated in at least three out of four investigations used in the comparison, it is evident that in our study the following issues were ranked considerably lower: *Ensuring the users prompt (quick) access to data and information, Implementation of new information technologies, Efficient telecommunications, Management and control of ever increasing amount of data,* and *Implementation of system that support group work.*

IS outsourcing was – against our expectations – rated as the least important of the key issues, and it was rated low in importance also in other studies. This may be surprising since commercial literature and presentations by vendors of information technology and services strongly emphasize the usefulness and advantages of IS outsourcing. This indicates that external services – although they are used – have no major influence on IS management. Another possible explanation is that IS managers do not recognize that the increasing adoption of outsourcing is changing their work.

**Table 4.** Key IS management issues from other studies compared to the our results

| Issue description | Our study | Gott schalk, 2001 | Alshawaf et. al., 2002 | Berkowitz et. al., 2001 | Samik-Ibrahim, 2002 | Pimchan-gthong 2003 |
|---|---|---|---|---|---|---|
| Uninterrupted functioning of the IS | 1 | 14 | 1 | 3 | | 8 |
| Incorporation (inclusion) IS in the corporate strategic planning | 2 | 1 | | | | |
| Strategic planning of IS | 3 | 3 | 6 | 7 | 12 | 2 |
| Protection of the IS against intrusions, viruses, spam, etc. | 4 | 14 | 1 | 4 | | |
| Support of IS to the optimization of business processes | 5 | | 12 | | 11 | |
| Integration of subsystems into an comprehensive IS architecture | 6 | 4 | 15 | 11 | 18 | 10 |
| Comprehensive safety policy | 7 | | | | | |
| Development and impl. of DSS | 8 | | 9 | 17 | 9 | |
| Users' and mgts' appreciation of IS | 8 | | 19 | 1 | | |
| Ensuring financial resources | 10 | | 21 | | | |
| Education of IT users | 11 | | 5 | | | |
| Position IS dept's in the corp. hier. | 12 | | 15 | 5 | 15 | 6 |
| Ensuring quick access to information | 13 | 5 | 4 | 2 | 2 | 1 |
| Implementation of new ITs | 14 | 2 | 13 | 6 | | |
| Human resources | 15 | 6 | 8 | 13,15 | 1 | 3 |
| Efficient telecommunications | 16 | 10 | 7 | 14 | 5 | 9 |
| Use of methodologies and project approach in system development | 17 | 7,9 | 18 | 20 | 7 | 4 |
| Consolidation and optimization of corporate ICT infrastructure | 18 | | | | | |
| Implementation and management of electronic business – b2b | 19 | 20 | | 18 | 20 | 5 |
| Management and control of ever increasing amount of data | 20 | 10 | 3 | 8 | 13 | 7 |
| Implementation of the DW concept | 21 | | | | | |
| Impl. group work support systems | 22 | | 13 | 19 | 8 | |
| Electronic documentation systems | 23 | | 13 | | | |
| Ensuring mobile access to infor. | 24 | | | 23 | | |
| Implementing open source systems | 25 | | | | 4 | |
| Implementation of worldwide used ERP, CRM, SCM systems | 26 | | | 10,22 | | |
| Outsourcing IS services | 27 | | 23 | 24 | 16 | |

## 5 Conclusion and recommendations

Analysis of the individual issues highlights the importance of security and uninterrupted operation of the IS. Individual technologies and technological solutions were ranked on the bottom of the list of key issues. From this, we can conclude that the information and communication technology offers considerable more possibilities and opportunities that we are currently able to exploit.

In an earlier research, Brancheau et al. (1996) expressed the expectation that shift from the phase of installing and planning the IS activity towards a phase of implementation and use will occur. Contrary to these expectations, our study indicates that integration of IS activities into the business system is perceived as important yet still insufficient by IS department managers in Slovenia. From the highest ranked issues in our study, we can conclude that – in the opinion of IS managers in Slovenia – the IS function can still essentially contribute to the increased competitiveness and business success of their companies. At the same time, they are aware that the increasing dependence of the business system on IS demands a different approach to the management of IS area.

If we examine the results of our investigation as a whole, we can conclude that views and opinions of IS department managers in Slovenia are approaching the views of their counterparts revealed by other comparable investigations. This indicates that the economic and cultural environment in Slovenia is not very different from the environment in other countries as it was when the earlier study was done (Dekleva and Zupančič 1996). A comparison with this study also indicates that technology-related issues became less important, and business- related issues appear to be more important. Key issues arising from the specifics of the Slovenian environment in 1992 didn't emerge in our investigation.

Results of our investigation provide us with an insight into the current way of thinking of IS managers. Therefore, we recommend repeating such an investigation periodically. The investigations should be upgraded by identifying groups of managers with similar views on the topics under consideration, and common characteristics of the groups.

## References

Alshawaf A, DeLone WH (2002) IS Management issues in Kuwait: Dimensions and implications. Journal of Global Information Management 10(3): 72–80

Ball L, Harris R (1982) SMIS members; a membership analysis. MIS Quarterly 6(1): 19–38

Berkowitz S, Ryan J, Waspe K, Hart M (2001) Key IS Management Issues. http://www.commerce.uct.ac.za/informationsystems/Research%26Publications/2001.asp

Brancheau JC, Janz BD, Wetherbe JC (1996) Key Issues in Information Systems Management: 1994 – 95, SIM Delphi Results. MIS Quarterly, 20(2): 225–242

Brown SR (1999)  Q-Methodology and qualitative research. Qualitative Health Research 6(4): 561–567

Dekleva S, Zupančič J (1996)  Key issues in information systems management: a Delphi study in Slovenia. Information & Management, 31: 1–11

Dickson GW, Leitheiser R, Wetherbe JC, Nechis M (1984)  Key information systems issues for the 1980's. MIS Quarterly 8(3):135–148

Dexter AS, Janson MA, Kiudorf E, Laast-Laas J (1993)  Key information technology issues in Estonia. Journal of Strategic Information Systems, 2(2): 139–148

Gottschalk P (2000)  Studies of key issues in IS management around the world. International Journal of Information Management 20: 169–180

Gottschalk P (2001) Key issues in IS management in Norway: An empirical study based on Q methodology. Information Resources Management Journal 14(2): 37–45

IPIS® Poslovni register Slovenije (Business Directory), December 2004, Noviforum

Linstone HA, Turoff M (2002)  The Delphi Method: Techniques and Applications. http://www.is.njit.edu/pubs/delphibook/

Pimchangthon D, Plaisent M, Bernard P (2003) Key issues in information systems management: A comparative study of academics and practitioners in Thailand, Journal of Global Information Technology Management 6(4): 27–44.

PIRS® Poslovni informator Republike Slovenije (Business Directory), 2004, Slovenska knjiga (in Slovenian)

Samik-Ibrahim RM (2002)  Key issues in information systems management: Indonesia 2001. http://rms46.vlsm.org/1/22.html

Schmolck    P    (2002)    PQMethod    Manual.    http://www.rz.unibw-muenchen.de/~p41bsmk/qmethod/pqmanual.htm

Vehovar V, Lavtar D, Pfajfar A (2003) RIS 2002 – Podjetja: Internet in informacijske tehnologije (in Slovenian). http://www.ris.org

Watson RT, Brancheau JC (1991) Key issues in information system management: an international perspective. Information & Management, 20(3): 213–223

Watson RT (1989) Key issues in information system management: an Australian perspective. Australian Computer Journal 21(3): 118–129

Watson RT, Kelly GG, Galliers RD, Brancheau JC (1997) Key issues in information systems management: an international perspective. Journal of Management Information Systems, 13(4): 91–115

Wrycza S, Plata-Przechlewski T (1994) Key issues in information system development. The case of Poland. In: Zupančič J and Wrycza S (eds) The Fourth International Conference on Information Systems Development ISD'94. Moderna organizacija, Kranj 1994, pp 289–296

# Enterprise Information Systems – Eight Significant Conditions

Anders G. Nilsson

Department of Information Systems, Karlstad University, Sweden,
Anders.Nilsson@kau.se

## 1 Enterprise Information Systems – Introduction

Companies are investing in new information systems in order to achieve higher efficiency in their business operations. But innovations in information technology (IT) in the form of increased productivity have still been modest. This is a well known phenomenon, usually called the "productivity paradox" for investments in IT systems within enterprises (Brynjolfsson 1993). Even if the IT investments made during the last ten years have successively provided improved operational effects, they do not fully come up to the expectations of the top managements. Investments in large enterprise systems will not automatically generate improved efficiency in the organisation (Davenport 2000). The implementation in modern IT systems needs to be supplemented by new innovative business processes and solid investments in competence development to have full potential effects!

The key issue on the top management agenda is to find out solutions for creating business value out of the portfolio of information systems used in the organisation (cf. Keen 1997; Lucas Jr. 1999). We will adopt the concept "enterprise information systems" (EIS) to stand for all kind of systems applied for supporting business processes in enterprises. EIS represents a wide range of systems that support processes within different business functions (such as DSS systems) or between different business functions (such as ERP systems) as well as inter-organisational collaboration over company functions (such as CRM systems). A challenge for future research in the area of "Management and IT" is to investigate the business effects of enterprise information systems in private firms as well as public authorities. Our main research question for this paper will therefore be:

*"What are significant conditions influencing the investment of enterprise information systems within and between organisations"?*

## 2 Enterprise Information Systems – The IS Field

By an "information system" (or nowadays "IT system") we traditionally mean a system for the collection, processing, storage, retrieval, distribution, presentation and use of information (Langefors 1973). An information system is part of the business operations that it is supposed to serve (so called "embedded system"). It is not an end in itself, but intentionally arranged for organising the message exchange or communication between people for supporting their work tasks in organisations (Langefors 1995). Information systems could also have a more offensive or aggressive target for enabling or creating new business opportunities in companies, e.g. Internet Banking and Electronic Commerce (Earl and Khan 2001). In the new service economy information systems play an essential role for promoting a more proactive service management (Edvardsson et al. 2000).

Historically it has been a complex task to design usable information systems in organisations. In fact, this was the real background for building a new academic discipline or subject labelled "Information Systems (IS)" in mid 60's (Davis 1991). Scandinavian researchers have had a great influence on the evolution of Information Systems as a scientific discipline (see Iivari and Lyytinen 1998). The IS subject has a tradition to be multidisciplinary in character trying to study the phenomenon of "information systems" from e.g. technical, economical and pedagogical aspects. Therefore it is a need to integrate knowledge from different disciplines, such as computer science, business administration and behavioural science (Davis 1991) when studying the phenomenon of enterprise information systems.

A *significant condition* is that organisations live with enterprise information systems in an increasingly changing world. There are a number of trends or driving forces in the society around us that will have a growing impact on investments in IT systems (cf. Nilsson 2004), for example:

- The structure of companies is becoming more virtual, horizontal and network-based.
- Information systems are to a greater extent used as inter-organisational or business-to-business (B2B) solutions between companies.
- Actors are increasingly operating on electronic or digitised markets using the modern Internet technology and E-business framework.

In this light, the IS field will play an increasingly important part in the future. We need to invest in enterprise information systems for the professional organisations of tomorrow!

## 3 Enterprise Information Systems – ERP Systems

Enterprise information systems are based on useful IT artifacts to support some kind of business in organisations (Orlikowski and Iacono 2001). By IT artifacts we mean the use of hardware and software solutions to improve the business processes within and between organisations. The IT artifacts can be of a varied character – for example we can create information systems in companies by using tailor-made (bespoke) software, standard application packages or component oriented architectures. Information systems often consist of a mixture of human information processing and computer-based solutions.

Enterprise information systems are used as advanced tools to increase the business capacity in companies and organisations (Themistocleous and Watson 2005). The current trend is that a growing number of IT systems are classified as "ERP-systems" purchased from external IT vendors (Summer 2005). By ERP systems or "Enterprise Resource Planning" systems we refer to large integrated mega-packages or standard application packages that fully cover the provision of information required in a company. ERP systems are made up of extensive administrative solutions comprising management accounting, human resource management, material and service logistics, production and sales control. An essential criterion is that the included parts are closely integrated with each other through a central data base (Davenport 1998). An advantage of ERP systems is that the vendor guarantees that different functions in the package are connected, with thoroughly tested interfaces. A disadvantage is that the different parts in the vendor's ERP system are often of varying quality.

A *significant condition* would be to combine an ERP system with several niche packages and/or migrated parts or components of in-house made IT systems. Systems integration within and between organisations is therefore a key issue on the top management agenda for many companies. The adoption and implementation of ERP systems in organisations should be adapted to the concrete situation and specific business conditions (Markus and Tanis 2000).

# 4 Enterprise Information Systems – Business Reshaping

From earlier experience in the IS field we have noticed that enterprise information systems are going through different stages or phases in reshaping the business operations in companies and organisations (Ploom 1988; Mathiassen 1998):

1. Automation and Efficiency
2. Integration and Cooperation
3. Transformation and Networking

In the *first stage* the focus is on *automating* certain business operations; to do things right, faster and cheaper with IT systems. The primary use of information systems has been to increase the *efficiency* of different functions or activities in organisations, e.g. by automating jobs that earlier were carried out manually. This approach could lead to "information islands" in organisations more or less isolated from each others.

In the *second stage* the focus is on *cooperation* between business operations inside companies – from this viewpoint efficient functions or activities are important but not sufficient. Business people often think more in terms of work flows or processes for achieving expected results. *Integration* of information systems becomes a key issue on the top management agenda. This approach promotes that bridges are being built between "information islands" in the organisation.

In the *third stage* the focus is on *transforming* business operations in the market place for creating competitive power of the IT systems. The value constellation or *networks* of business actors comprise our focal company, customers, clients, suppliers and partners. Information systems from different business actors are linked to each others and shared databases or e-portals are used. This approach supports inter-organisational solutions and connect "information islands" over company boundaries.

A *significant condition* is that all three stages: automation, integration and transformation, are interdependent, which means that we must work with them simultaneously. The "field of play" is to go through the three stages of business reshaping over and over again to make an improved use of enterprise information systems in our organisations!

## 5 Enterprise Information Systems – Levels of Change

Enterprise information systems should be viewed in a wider organisational context. Business performance generally consists of different tasks which can be collected into some appropriate levels. We can recognise three levels of change for work practices in companies with a distinct scope and focus (cf. Österle 1995; Nilsson et al. 1999):

- *Market level;* focusing on corporate strategies for improving the business relationships between our company and the cooperating actors in the market environment.
- *Operational level;* focusing on business strategies for making operations more efficient within our company; the workflow or business processes are improved.
- *Systems level;* focusing on IT strategies for how information systems can be more useful resources for running the business operations more professionally and competitive.

In today's business world, information support has become a more integrated part of business operations and, in many cases, a vital part of the business mission itself. In fact, the information systems could also create new business opportunities for companies to reinforce their competitive edge in the market place. In many cases development of corporate strategies, business operations and information support are often carried out as separate change measures and as independent projects in organisations.

The *significant condition* or challenge is to have a proper organisational coordination and timing between the three levels of work practices in companies. Strategic congruence and integrated control between organisational levels are essential issues on the top management agenda in companies (Nilsson and Rapp

2005). Therefore investments in enterprise information systems should be in harmony with the efforts taken on market and operational levels in organisations.

## 6 Enterprise Information Systems – Distinct Competence

New investments in enterprise information systems such as ERP systems like SAP R/3 and Itentia Movex are made in a changing world, where the progress of society moves towards horizontal organisations, virtual companies and electronic markets. In this connection the purchasing of ERP systems is no longer just a matter for the IT department in a company. The use of these standardised packages is instead becoming a strategic investment for the company, and therefore an issue of growing importance on the top management agenda. The users in the organisation also need to take a more active initiative and assume responsibility for the ERP system to work appropriately in the various processes of the business operation.

When making operational changes, we need to work concurrently with the strategies, processes and systems of the company. Even if we are focusing on a specific area, we still need to make a successive adaptation to achieve a good overall result. According to the organisation theory, a successful company acquires distinct or distinctive competence by creating a good balance between these three areas, thereby achieving harmony in the organisation (Nilsson 2001) (see Figure 1). The basic theory of distinctive competence is explained by the originator Rhenman (1973) and summarised by Stymne (1993).

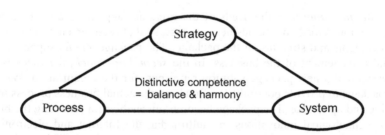

**Fig. 1.** Distinctive competence achieved by a balance between three areas

In change work, we need to combine specialist competence for strategy formation, business processes and IT support, for example in the form of ERP systems. A successful organisation focuses continually on improving the interaction between the three areas, to establish a bond between them, whereby the enterprise acquires distinctive or unique competence on the market.

A *significant condition* is to make sure that the use of ERP systems is in keeping with the management strategy and the business processes, with the aim to create balance and harmony in the organisation. To create the capacity for distinctive competence in the company, the enterprise information system must match the needs that can be understood from formulated business strategies as well as working procedures used in the business processes. Organisations can use the potential of enterprise coordination of "strategy, process and system" to outperform their competitors!

## 7 Enterprise Information Systems – Business Philosophy

How do innovations come into existence in change work? There are two different driving forces to create innovations in development work in organisations. We use the term driving forces, as the ERP system or the package either provides existing business support or works as an enabler to run the business in a new way. See Figure 2, which is based on a previously introduced frame of reference, in Tolis and Nilsson (1998).

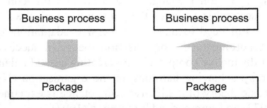

**Fig. 2.** The package as a business support (left) and as an business enabler (right)

In the *first approach* the needs of the users are applied as a starting point. A specification is made of the business process, so that requirements can be made on both contents and structure of the package. The package should support a professional management of the business. In the *second approach*, the focus is on the potential that a new package solution represents for the organisation. We look to the package to provide possibilities of making the actual business process more effective and up to date. The package becomes an enabler for renewing the business. New technological innovations in multimedia, the Internet and electronic commerce can become new value-adding factors to the business. This leads to three different business philosophies or approaches to manage investments made in packages for specific business operations:

- *Vision-driven approach*. The design of new and changed business processes takes place before selection of a package or ERP system is made.
- *Package-driven approach*. The package or the ERP system controls the design of the different business processes in the company.
- *Mix-driven approach*. The design of some business processes is almost a matter of course; run the package-driven approach! Some business processes are of a more strategic nature; use the vision-driven approach!

This practical attitude is often advocated by management consultants (such as KPMG) at the implementation of packages in organisations. When introducing all-inclusive ERP systems, some form of a mix-driven approach is preferable.

A *significant condition* to make good use of an ERP system in organisations is to be able to base the purchase on a clear and deliberate business philosophy. The requirements specification needs to be focused on what should be vision-driven and what should be package-driven for the business. To what extent should the ERP system (package) be a professional support for the operations, and how far should we let the ERP system (package) steers towards new possibilities?

## 8 Enterprise Information Systems – Process Management

An attractive way to develop organisations is to use a process-oriented approach (Becker et al. 2003). Change work in companies by such a process management approach indicates that the requirements specification is important in describing the business situation, both for the present time (the "As Is"-process) and for the future state (the "To Be"-process). In this respect we consider the organisation as made up of a number of important business processes for ongoing change that need strengthening by enterprise information systems (Davenport et al. 2004). To-day we have a trend towards development of process standards for different industries, e.g. the Supply-Chain Operations Reference-model (SCOR 2005) and the MIT Process Handbook Project (Malone et al. 2003). The key issue is how we should structure enterprise information systems so that they could fit into the business processes (Nilsson 2001). See figure 3 below:

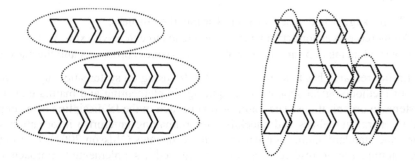

**Fig. 3.** A strongly coupled structure (left) versus a loosely coupled structure (right)

Traditionally, the ERP systems on the market have had a functional systems structure with a set of program modules. An ERP system may be more or less firmly connected to the business processes of the company. In a *strongly coupled structure*, the package will follow the complete work flow in a given business process, from start to finish. This may be realised in techniques for workflow systems, for example. In a *loosely coupled structure*, the package instead supports a set of activities that appear in several business processes. The package becomes an infrastructure for the business processes. In more all-inclusive ERP systems we often find combined solutions, with the options of strongly or loosely coupled structures for the various parts of the package. Nowadays vendors connect a professional method support for process mapping to their ERP systems. The translation between the needs of a working routine in the process and the functionality of the package goes via so called "lowest common" activities. A recent trend among IT vendors is to apply smart use of technologies for "interoperability" of ERP systems such as Web services, Enterprise Application Integration (EAI) and Service Oriented Architecture (SOA) for making companies more dynamic and agile.

A *significant condition* is to make correctly designed requirements specifications as a basis for the investment in an ERP system for the organisation. When a process management approach is used in the organisation, the requirements specification needs to illuminate choices of structuring for the interconnection of the business processes with the package modules.

## 9 Enterprise Information Systems – Systematic Ways

Reliable experience shows that issues concerning the design and use of enterprise information systems in organisations need to be addressed systematically (Avison and Fitzgerald 2006). Nevertheless, quite often the investments in ERP systems are performed following ad hoc strategies. Packages are implemented into more or less chaotic company environments, where too much happens at once. Business people tend to select ERP systems by instinct behaviour (using their "heart") rather than by rational thinking (using their "brain"). Some of the effects of this could be:

- The package is underused, or even disrupts the business.
- An increased vendor dependency, which leads to extensive extra work.
- Constant adaptations are made, both in the business processes and the package.

Earlier research has to some degree been focusing on systematic ways of working or methodological support for acquiring, implementing and maintaining ERP systems in organisations. The traditional approach in the IS discipline is to support with general guidelines and checklists for managing enterprise information systems and standard application packages in companies (Nilsson 2001). From business administration research we have recognised a supplemented approach with specific application templates for package procurement, such as the "Linköping" model for material and production control (MPC) systems (Olhager and Rapp 1985) and the "RP" model for accounting information systems (Samuelson 1980).

A *significant condition* is to be able to combine systematics with inspiration in a sensible manner, when implementing ERP systems in our organisations. We need appropriate "doses" of both methodology and creativity to achieve successful results.

## 10 Enterprise Information Systems – Summing Up

In this paper we have identified and described eight significant conditions influencing the investment of enterprise information systems within and between organisations. We now sum up these significant conditions:

- The phenomenon enterprise information systems connected to *the IS field* and the driving forces we face in our IT society of today.
- The concept of enterprise information systems related to how investment of *ERP systems* could be achieved in a proper way in companies.
- Investments in enterprise information systems and the role of the three stages of *business reshaping* – automation, integration, transformation.
- Investments in enterprise information systems and the need for a harmony with different *levels of change* (market, operation, system).
- Creating a *distinct competence* out of investments in enterprise information systems in balance with business strategies and business processes.
- The requirements specification for investments in enterprise information systems with focus on its *business philosophy* (support, enabler or mix).
- *Process management* as a start up for the change work with enterprise information systems studying interconnections between process/system.
- A *systematic way* of working will guide investments in enterprise information systems – systematics and creativity should go hand in hand!

These significant conditions are grounded from a series of theoretical and empirical studies since the beginning of the 1980's based on a scientific design approach called "consumable research" (Robey and Markus 1998). Besides the eight penetrated conditions, for example user acceptance of enterprise information systems is also an important condition for system success. Even though the eight significance conditions are satisfied users may reject the system for many reasons (e.g. by affective motives). To strengthen this argument Nilsson (2005) has explained that the degree of information systems development success is a function of the system quality, user acceptance and the business value of the system. Moreover Hwang (2005) advocate that the motivation of end-users play an important role in the success of ERP systems.

The concept "significant conditions" is sometimes more drastically labelled as "critical success factors" (or CSFs) as described by Rockart (1979). As a final point we would like to give companies a real challenge:

*"Be open to the new and interesting possibilities that modern enterprise information systems offer. Winners are those who make the best use of the ERP systems in their business operations!"*

# References

Avison DE, Fitzgerald G (2006) Information Systems Development: Methodologies, Techniques and Tools. 4$^{th}$ edn, McGraw-Hill, London

Becker J, Kugeler M, Rosemann, M (2003) Process Management: A Guide for Design of Business Processes. Springer, Berlin Heidelberg New York

Brynjolfsson E (1993) The Productivity Paradox of Information Technology. Communications of the ACM, vol 36, no 12, pp 67-77

Davenport TH (1998) Putting the Enterprise into the Enterprise System. Harvard Business Review, July-August, vol 76, no 4, pp 121-131

Davenport TH (2000) Mission Critical: Realizing the Promise of Enterprise Systems. Harvard Business School Press, Boston, Massachusetts

Davenport TH, Harris JE, Cantrell S (2004) Enterprise Systems and Ongoing Process Change. Business Process Management Journal, vol 10, no 1, pp 16-26

Davis GB (1991) The Emergence of Information Systems as a Business Function and Academic Discipline. Research Report MISCR-WP-92-01, Management Information Systems Research Center, University of Minnesota, USA

Earl M, Khan B (2001) E-Commerce Is Changing the Face of IT. MIT Sloan Management Review, Fall 2001, pp 64-72

Edvardsson B, Gustafsson A, Johnson MD, Sandén B (2000) New Service Development and Innovation in the New Economy. Studentlitteratur, Lund, Sweden

Hwang Y (2005) Investigating Enterprise Systems Adoption: Uncertainty Avoidance, Intrinsic Motivation, and the Technology Acceptance Model. European Journal of Information Systems, vol 14, no 2, pp 150-161

Iivari J, Lyytinen K (1998) Research on Information Systems Development in Scandinavia: Unity in Plurality. Scandinavian Journal of Information Systems, vol 10, no 1&2, pp 135-186

Keen PGW (1997) The Process Edge: Creating Value Where It Counts. Harvard Business School Press, Boston, Massachusetts

Langefors B (1973) Theoretical Analysis of Information Systems (THAIS). Auerbach, Philadelphia and Studentlitteratur, Lund, Sweden

Langefors B (1995) Essays on Infology: Summing Up and Planning for the Future, Studentlitteratur. Lund, Sweden

Lucas Jr. HC (1999) Information Technology and the Productivity Paradox: Assessing the Value of Investing in IT. Oxford University Press, New York

Malone TW, Crowston K, Herman GA (eds) (2003) Organizing Business Knowledge: The MIT Process Handbook. MIT Press, Cambridge, Massachusetts

Markus ML, Tanis C (2000) The Enterprise System Experience: From Adoption to Success. In: Zmud, R.W. (ed) (2000) Framing the Domains of IT Management – Projecting the Future … … Through the Past. Pinnaflex Education Resources, Cincinnati, Ohio, chap 10, pp 173-207

Mathiassen L (1998) Reflective Systems Development. Scandinavian Journal of Information Systems, vol 10, no 1&2, pp 67-118

Nilsson AG (2001) Using Standard Application Packages in Organisations: Critical Success Factors. In: Nilsson AG, Pettersson JS (2001) (eds) On Methods for Systems Development in Professional Organisations: The Karlstad University Approach to Information Systems and its Role in Society. Studentlitteratur, Lund, Sweden, pp 208-230

Nilsson AG (2004) Information Systems Development (ISD): Past, Present, Future Trends. In: Vasilecas O, Caplinskas A, Wojtkowski W, Wojtkowski WG, Zupancic, J, Wrycza S (eds) (eds) (2005) Information Systems Development: Advances in Theory, Practice, and Education. Proceedings of the Thirteenth International Conference on Information Systems Development: ISD'2004, Vilnius, Lithuania, Springer, New York, pp 29-40

Nilsson AG, Tolis C, Nellborn C (eds) (1999) Perspectives on Business Modelling: Understanding and Changing Organisations. Springer, Berlin Heidelberg

Nilsson F, Rapp B (2005) Understanding Competitive Advantage: The Importance of Strategic Congruence and Integrated Control, Springer, Berlin Heidelberg

Olhager J, Rapp B (1985) Effektiv MPS: Referenssystem för Datorbaserad Material- och Produktionsstyrning. Studentlitteratur, Lund, Sweden [Effective MPC: Reference Model for Computer-based Material- and Production Control]

Orlikowski WJ, Iacono, CS (2001) Research Commentary: Desperately Seeking the 'IT' in IT Research: A Call to Theorizing the IT Artifact. Information Systems Research, vol 10, no 2, pp 121-134

Ploom A (1988) Information Technology and the Manufacturing Enterprise. NordDATA 88, Helsinki, Finland, vol 2, pp 275-281

Rhenman E (1973) Organization Theory for Lange Range Planning. Wiley, London

Robey D, Markus ML (1998) Beyond Rigor and Relevance: Producing Consumable Research about Information Systems. Information Resources Management Journal, vol 11, no 1, pp 7-15

Rockart JF (1979) Chief Executives Define Their Own Data Needs. Harvard Business Review, March-April, vol 57, no 2, pp 81-93

Samuelson LA (1980) Models on Accounting Information Systems: The Swedish Case. Studentlitteratur, Lund, Sweden

SCOR (2005) Supply-Chain Operations Reference-model, SCOR Version 7.0 Overview. Supply-Chain Council (SCC), Washington, DC USA

Stymne B (1993) A Note on Distinctive Competence. Research paper no 1993:56, Institute for Management of Innovation and Technology (IMIT), Stockholm School of Economics & Chalmers University of Technology, Sweden

Summer M (2005) Enterprise Resource Planning. Pearson-Prentice Hall, Upper Saddle River, New Jersey

Themistocleous M, Watson E (2005) EJIS Special Issue on Making Enterprise Systems Work. European Journal of Information Systems (EJIS), June 2005, vol 14, no 2, pp 107-109

Tolis C, Nilsson AG (1998) Business Models and IS/IT in Process Orientation. In: Fariselli P (ed) Innovating SME Business Practices: The Compete Methodology and Tools. Nomisma/edizioni Pendragon, Bologna, Italy, pp 27-48

Österle H (1995) Business in the Information Age: Heading for New Processes. Springer, Berlin Heidelberg New York

# Success Factors Across ERP Implementation Phases: Learning from Practice

Piotr Soja

Cracow University of Economics, eisoja@cyf-kr.edu.pl

**Abstract:** This paper analyses how the importance of ERP (Enterprise Resource Planning) implementation success factors changes across project phases. The study is performed on the basis of research conducted among experts working in ERP systems suppliers and dealing with many implementation projects. The findings extract the most important factors and suggest that their significance changes as the project goes through its lifecycle. However, there are factors, such as balanced team composition, with noticeable importance lasting through all project phases. On the basis of the research, conclusions were drawn for the practitioners dealing with ERP implementation projects.

## 1 Introduction

The implementation of an Enterprise Resource Planning (ERP) system is a process of great complexity strongly involving the whole company which has decided to introduce such a system into its organisation. The observation of ERP market, where there are many projects that did not bring about expected benefits, and, moreover, some projects were abandoned, allows us to state that the achievement of success of an ERP implementation is very difficult (e.g. Holland et al. 1999; McNurlin and Sprague 2002). The implementation projects' duration time and budget significantly exceed estimated amounts and the planned scope of the implementation is limited (e.g. Parr et al. 1999). Hence, it is crucial to determine the factors which are necessary for a successful implementation of an ERP system.

The number of research projects regarding ERP implementations keeps growing; nevertheless, it is still not extensive. There are several works dealing with success factors in ERP implementations (e.g. Brown and Vessey 2003; Holland et al. 1999; Parr et al. 1999; Stefanou 1999); however, the issue of changing factor relevance across ERP implementation phases is very rarely discussed. Meanwhile, an ERP implementation project is a multi stage process which can last for a long time. Naturally, the situation and conditions of such a complicated process change over time and various issues could be of critical importance within different phases of the project (e.g. Markus et al. 2000a). Therefore, it is valuable to verify how success factors' importance looks like in successive stages of an ERP implementation project. Among the few research works available, there are theoretical frameworks (e.g. Esteves and Pastor 2004) that need empirical verification, as well as studies based on an empirical survey (Somers and Nelson 2001). The latter is based on an empirical study among American enterprises introducing the ERP system into their organisations and provides valuable findings.

However, an ERP implementation project usually involves two parties – a company introducing the ERP system into its organisation, and a supplier of the ERP package. Both parties have their own perception of an implementation project and also have different experiences. The goal of this paper is to investigate the problem of the success factors relevance through the ERP implementation phases from the point of view of experts, who are people involved in many ERP projects from a system supplier site. Hence, they gained an insight into the conditions of various ERP projects in different organisations. This paper employs success factors model defined in (Soja 2004, 2006) and attempts to analyse how the factors importance changes over the ERP implementation phases.

## 2 ERP Implementation Success Factors

ERP system implementation is a process of great importance for an organisation, with a great many conditions and factors potentially influencing the implementation project. The success factors proposed by the researchers, covering a wide range of aspects, represent various levels of generalization; there are models with only 5 factors (Brown and Vessey 2003), as well as those containing more than 20 elements (Somers and Nelson 2001). Furthermore, the success factors models employ a variety of categorisations without any generally accepted method of factor grouping.

Therefore, since there does not appear to be any single commonly recognised success factors model, this study uses an ERP implementation success factors model described in Table 1 (Soja 2004, 2006). The purpose of this model is to cover the broad range of mechanisms influencing an ERP implementation project. The model was inductively created taking into account the results of previous research and the author's own experience in the business environment. The resulting success factors were validated by several IS researchers and professionals. The factors are divided into groups regarding their broader aspect. The separated groups consist of factors related to implementation participants, top management involvement, project definition and organisation, project status, and information systems (Soja 2004, 2006).

**Table 1.** The general model of ERP implementation success factors

| Factor | Factor description |
| --- | --- |
| | Related to the implementation participants |
| A project manager | The project manager is the person from the enterprise who sacrifices most of his working time to implementation duties |
| B team composition | The implementation team consists of various people having high qualifications and knowledge about the enterprise |
| C team involvement | The project manager and members of the implementation team are strongly involved in the implementation duties |
| D motivation system | There is a motivation system rewarding participation in implementation and on-time task delivery |
| E co-operation with supplier | Good co-operation with the system supplier who is competent and offers a high level of services |
| | Related to the top management involvement |
| F top management support | The top management support for the project and the management members involvement in implementation duties |
| G top management awareness | Top management awareness regarding the project goals and complexity, demanded labour, existing limitations, required capital investment and project inevitability |
| H top management participation | Top management participation in the project schedule and goals definition |
| | Related to the project definition and organisation |
| I linking with strategy | The implementation project linking with enterprise strategy (implementation as a method of the enterprise strategic goals achievement) |
| J implementation goals | The definition of implementation goals – defined in the economic terms at the whole enterprise level |
| K detailed schedule | The definition of detailed implementation scope, plan and schedule with responsibility allocation |
| L pre-implementation analysis | The enterprise analysis and diagnosis prior to the start of implementation, and the creation of the enterprise functioning model with the integrated system support |
| M organisation change | The change in the enterprise organisation and its business processes |
| N monitoring and feedback | The implementation monitoring and feedback – information exchange between the project team and end users |
| O implementation promotion | The implementation promotion – the information broadcasting about the project by the implementation team members to other enterprise employees |
| P fast effects | The visible fast partial positive results of the implementation |
| Q appropriate training | The adequate training program suitable to the enterprise needs |

**Table 1.** continued

| Factor | Factor description |
|---|---|
| | Related to the project status |
| R  investment plan | The formal introduction of the implementation project in the enterprise investment plan |
| S  project team empowerment | The project team members empowerment to decision making and their high position in the enterprise hierarchy |
| T  financial budget | The financial resources assured for during the implementation |
| U  work time schedule | The work time assured for the implementation team members (work time schedule) |
| V  IT infrastructure | The appropriate IT infrastructure assured for the implementation project |
| | Related to information systems |
| W  system reliability | The ERP system reliability, its user friendliness and fit to the enterprise needs |
| X  minimal customisation | The system minimal customisation – the use of defined patterns and solutions embedded in the system |
| Y  legacy systems | The legacy systems adaptation for the operation in the ERP integrated system environment |
| Z  implementation experience | The project team members experience gained during former information systems implementation |

## 3 ERP Implementation Phases

ERP implementation, as a very complex endeavour, can take various shapes depending on particular enterprise and project conditions. ERP implementation projects range from a simple introduction of an ERP system in a single plant to complex multi-national implementation projects covering many branches and requiring many changes in organisation structure (Parr and Shanks 2000b). Furthermore, there is a variety of ERP lifecycle models having various numbers of phases. The proposed models include three (e.g. Parr and Shanks 2000a), four (e.g. Markus and Tanis 2000), five (e.g. Ross and Vitale 2000) up to six (e.g. Somers and Nelson 2001) project stages.

Despite many differences among ERP projects and various terminology used by ERP researchers and system suppliers, the general framework of a model ERP project can be drawn. Below, the main phases of an ERP implementation project are described. Each phase was given a number (in parentheses) in order to ease further references. Some of the stages below may not be present in particular methodologies; other phases may be joined or mixed. Nonetheless, the given framework captures the main steps involved in ERP implementation project.

*Project organisation* (P1) – at this stage, a Steering Committee and Implementation Team are constituted and implementation works are started. The general plan describing implementation tasks is prepared.

*Training how to manage a company with the use of ERP system* (P2) – members of the Steering Committee and Implementation Team are training participants. The goal of the training is to prepare management personnel and ERP system key users to manage a company with the use of the ERP system.

*Enterprise analysis* (P3) – the goal of the analysis is to assess the enterprise condition and the possibilities of its improvement with the help of the ERP system. The particular subjects of analysis are corporate strategy, company organisational structure, economic indicators illustrating business condition, user needs etc.

*Implementation design* (P4) – this phase comprises the project definition and elaboration of the project schedule with the concrete steps of the implementation project with the people responsible. The implementation strategy and project goals with appropriate measures are defined.

*Training on ERP system use* (P5) – this stage is often called "conference room pilot". The implementation team is trained on the use of the ERP package. The training covers the whole ERP functionality being introduced. At this stage, the ERP package parameterisation and customisation are completed.

*Detailed project planning* (P6) – the project schedule receives details respecting the ERP package specificity and actual company condition. The details comprise project stages, dates and duration times, definition of any additional subprojects, etc.

*Pilot implementation* (P7) – at this stage, often called "live pilot", the ERP package is being operated with the use of actual data, together with legacy systems. The goal of this stage is to prove that the ERP package is working correctly and is accepted by users.

*System start* (P8) – in this phase, the ERP package replaces legacy systems and becomes the only system used within the whole company. There are several possible ways to run the system and corresponding names of approaches, e.g. parallel, phased, "big bang", "cold turkey", pilot approach etc. (e.g. Markus et al. 2000b; Parr and Shanks 2000b). Nevertheless, the ultimate goal of this phase is to start the operation of the ERP package on a daily basis.

*Post implementation review* (P9) – the chosen solutions are being verified as regards their usefulness for the company. The project run is subject to assessment and the completion of implementation goals is estimated. If necessary, some changes in solution and complementary training are completed.

# 4 Research Data Characteristics

The research of the ERP system implementation projects was conducted from the perspective of ERP systems and services suppliers. The research sample was comprised of the consultants and experts representing various suppliers of ERP systems.

In order to examine the experts' opinions, the research questionnaire was directed to specialists with experience in implementing various ERP systems—those who were leading implementation projects from the supplier perspective and taking part in many implementations. Therefore, they provide a broad view of the projects' conditions. The experts were presented with the collection of success factors together with the list of project stages. For each implementation phase, they were asked to list the most important success factors at any given stage of a project.

**Table 2.** Respondents and their ERP experience

| Position | Work experience | ERP experience | Number of projects | ERP packages |
|---|---|---|---|---|
| Implementation Department Manager | 8 | 6 | 12 | Platinum for Windows |
| Project Leader | 3 | 2 | 5 | Platinum for Windows, e by Epicor |
| Business Development Manager | 14 | 7 | 5 | MAX ICL, SAP R/3 |
| Project Leader | 6 | 6 | 15 | Digitland Enterprise |
| Consultant | 7 | 6 | 10 | MAX for Windows (Kewill), IFS Applications |
| Senior Consultant, Training Department Manager | 40 | 9 | 15 | MAX ICL, Oracle Process Manufacturing |
| Financial Consulting Manager | 7 | 3 | 9 | SAP R/3 |
| Senior Manager | 16 | 8 | 3 | BPCS, SAP R/3 |

During the research, 8 experts' opinions were gathered. The experts represented 7 firms supplying ERP systems and implementation services. They were involved in a total of 74 ERP implementation projects in Poland which gives an average value equal to 9.3. The ERP systems included internationally known packages such as SAP or IFS, as well as systems developed and known in Poland like Digitland Enterprise. The respondent's experience in dealing with ERP projects ranges from 2 to 9 years with 5.9 average value. The information about the participants and their experience at the time of conducting the research is provided in Table 2.

## 5 Success Factors Relevance

Table 3 contains the numbers of respondent answers as regards their opinion about the subsequent factors importance in the stages of ERP implementation. The stages are denoted by the numbers from 1 to 9. For each factor, the sum of all its indications through all phases was calculated and placed in column *Total*. Additionally, column *Rank* contains the ranks of factors calculated on the basis of the decreasing number of figures in column *Total*. Similarly, for each project phase, the answers as regards all indicated factors by respondents within a particular phase were summarised and placed in a row *Total* in Table 3. The success factors' relevance phase by phase is described in the following.

*Project organisation* (P1) – this is the most demanding phase of an implementation project with the most answers among all phases. At this stage of project run, the most important factors are the project manager (A) and top management awareness (G) – both received 5 answers from 8 experts. Other important factors during the first implementation phase are top management support (F), balanced team composition (B) and their involvement in implementation duties (C). Each of these 3 factors received 4 answers.

*Training how to manage a company with the use of ERP system* (P2) – at this stage, only two factors are of great importance: balanced team composition (B) and appropriate training (Q), each receiving 5 answers. Apart from them, only 4 other factors received single answers from the respondents.

*Enterprise analysis* (P3) – in this phase, respondents perceive balanced team composition (B) as an important factor (4 answers). They also recognise the importance of top management awareness (G) and, naturally, appropriate enterprise analysis prior to the start of an implementation (L). Each of these last two factors received 3 answers.

*Implementation design* (P4) – this stage is very demanding and has many respondent answers. The experts perceive balanced team composition (B) as a very important factor (5 answers) at this stage. In addition, they consider the definition of a detailed schedule (K) as an important factor (4 answers). The respondents notice the importance of the project manager (A), implementation team involvement (C), co-operation with the supplier (E), top management participation (H) and the definition of implementation goals (J) during the process of implementation design (each factor received 3 answers).

**Table 3.** Success factors importance across ERP implementation phases

| Factor | | P1 | P2 | P3 | P4 | P5 | P6 | P7 | P8 | P9 | Total | Rank |
|---|---|---|---|---|---|---|---|---|---|---|---|---|
| A | project manager | 5 | | 1 | 3 | | 3 | 1 | 1 | | 14 | 4 |
| B | team composition | 4 | 5 | 4 | 5 | 2 | 4 | 4 | 3 | 1 | 32 | 1 |
| C | team involvement | 4 | | | 3 | 2 | | 1 | 1 | | 11 | 6 |
| D | motivation system | | | | | | | 1 | | | 1 | 22 |
| E | co-operation with supplier | 2 | 2 | | 3 | 2 | 2 | 3 | 3 | 1 | 18 | 2 |
| F | top management support | 4 | | | 1 | 1 | 1 | | 1 | 1 | 9 | 9 |
| G | top management awareness | 5 | | 3 | 2 | | 3 | 1 | 1 | 1 | 16 | 3 |
| H | top management participation | | | 2 | 3 | | 1 | 1 | 1 | | 8 | 11 |
| I | linking with strategy | | | 1 | 1 | 1 | | | | | 3 | 18 |
| J | implementation goals | 2 | 1 | | 3 | | 1 | 2 | 1 | | 10 | 7 |
| K | detailed schedule | 1 | | 1 | 4 | | 4 | 3 | 1 | | 14 | 5 |
| L | pre-implementation analysis | 1 | 1 | 3 | 1 | 1 | 1 | | 1 | 1 | 10 | 8 |
| M | organisation change | | | | | | | | | | 0 | 25 |
| N | monitoring and feedback | | | | | | | 1 | 1 | 2 | 4 | 17 |
| O | implementation promotion | 1 | | | | | | | | | 1 | 23 |
| P | fast effects | | | | 1 | | 1 | 2 | 1 | 1 | 6 | 14 |
| Q | appropriate training | | 5 | | | 3 | | | | | 8 | 12 |
| R | investment plan | | | | 1 | | | | | | 1 | 24 |
| S | project team empowerment | 2 | | | | | 1 | 1 | 1 | | 5 | 15 |
| T | financial budget | 1 | | | | | | 1 | 1 | | 3 | 19 |
| U | work time schedule | 1 | 1 | 1 | | 2 | | 2 | 2 | | 9 | 10 |
| V | IT infrastructure | 1 | | | | | | 3 | 1 | | 5 | 16 |
| W | system reliability | | | | | | | | 2 | | 2 | 21 |
| X | minimal customisation | | | | | | | | | | 0 | 26 |
| Y | legacy systems | | | | | 1 | | | 2 | | 3 | 20 |
| Z | implementation experience | 1 | | 1 | 1 | 1 | 1 | | 1 | 2 | 8 | 13 |
| | Total | 35 | 15 | 17 | 32 | 16 | 23 | 27 | 26 | 10 | | |

*Training on ERP system use* (P5) – during this phase, respondents notice only the importance of an adequate training program (Q), which received 3 answers.

*Detailed project planning* (P6) – at this stage, respondents consider balanced team composition (B) and definition of a detailed schedule (K) as important factors (4 answers each). They notice the importance of project manager (A) and top management awareness (G) in this phase of the project (3 answers each).

*Pilot implementation* (P7) – in this phase, balanced team composition (B) is considered to be important (4 answers). Respondents recognise the significance of co-operation with the supplier (E), definition of a detailed schedule (K) and appropriate IT infrastructure (V), giving each factor 3 answers.

*System start* (P8) – at this stage, respondents indicate many factors to be important, however, most factors received only single answers. Only two factors: balanced team composition (B) and co-operation with the supplier (E) are perceived as quite important (3 answers each) in this phase of the project.

*Post implementation review* (P9) – in this phase respondents do not distinguish the clear importance of any factors, they indicate only single factors as being important at this stage.

The number of indications of factors within individual phases can be perceived as a measure of particular phase importance. These numbers are present in the row *Total* in Table 3. Thus, taking into consideration the above-mentioned numbers, we can say that the first phase – project organisation – is the most important stage of an implementation project. The second most important phase is implementation design and, what is worth noting, it is also connected with the organisational activities. The next phases in order of importance are: pilot implementation and system start, followed by detailed project planning which is somewhat connected with project definition activities.

Therefore, judging by expert opinions, we can say that the most important stages of an implementation project are those related to project definition and, in the next position, activities connected with the ERP system start. It is worth noting that the planning phase of the project is also considered the most critical by ERP adopters, as Parr and Shanks (2000a) concluded and what could be drawn from Somers and Nelson's (2001) results.

# 6 The Most Important Success Factors

Similarly to the project phases, the number of indications of a particular factor within all implementation stages can be perceived as a measure of the factor importance through the whole project. These numbers are present in column *Total* in Table 3. Additionally, the ranks were calculated on the basis of decreasing numbers of factor indications and were placed in the column *Rank*. According to the order described above, the most important factors are discussed in the following.

1. *Balanced team composition (B)*. It is considered as very important or important for almost all phases of the implementation project, except for stages related to training on ERP system use and post implementation review. Correspondingly, respondents recognise only moderate importance of this factor during the system run.

2. *Co-operation with supplier (E)*. Having importance to a large extent lower than the first one, this factor is of moderate importance through the majority of project stages. There is no separate phase of special importance of this factor. Respondents perceive it as totally unimportant during enterprise analysis and post implementation review.

3. *Top management awareness (G)*. The respondents perceive its special importance in the first phase of a project, i.e. project organisation. They also notice the moderate importance of this factor within the remaining organisational

phases of the project—enterprise analysis, implementation design and detailed project planning.

4. *Project manager (A)*. It has, similar to factor (G), exceptional importance during the organisational phases of a project. Respondents remark on its special importance in the first stage of a project and also consider it important during implementation design and detailed project planning.

5. *Definition of detailed schedule (K)*. It is important, not surprisingly, during 'planning' phases of the project, i.e. implementation design and detailed project planning. This factor is also perceived as quite important at the pilot implementation stage of a project.

# 7 Implications and Conclusions

Taking into consideration the results of the research, several conclusions can be drawn regarding success factors relevance through the ERP implementation project run and resulting consequences for the project organisation and management. The findings suggest that practitioners dealing with ERP implementations should pay special attention to particular phases of a project. They should especially consider the organisational and planning stages of an implementation project, when it comes to the creation of a project team and the definition of implementation tasks. In the next order, they should take special care of the stage connected with system rollout and its preparation activities.

On the basis of expert opinions, definitely the most important factor is balanced team composition (B) with high importance through almost all phases of a project. The second most important factor – good co-operation with the supplier (E) – is also significant in almost all phases of a project, but its importance is considerably lower. On the other hand, the third most important factor – top management awareness (G) – is especially significant in the first phase and has also some meaning in other phases connected with project definition.

It is worth noting that the above-mentioned three most important factors are exactly the same as the ones in the ranking made on the basis of opinions of respondents from enterprises introducing the ERP system into their organisations (Soja 2004). Moreover, in the research conducted by Somers and Nelson (2001), the respondents from enterprises considered top management support as the most important factor, and project team competence, which can be treated as an equivalent of balanced team composition, as the second important factor. On the other hand, the Somers and Nelson's factors describing good co-operation with the supplier, i.e. vendor support and partnership with vendor, received generally low ranks in overall ranking of factors importance (9 and 20 among the total of 22 factors).

Therefore, practitioners should particularly assure top management support for the project and their awareness about the importance of the whole endeavour. They should also guarantee the proper composition of the implementation team, which should contain competent people from various departments. The supporting argument is that, on the basis of the research described, both parties involved in an implementation project agree about the topmost importance of the above-mentioned issues.

People involved in ERP implementations should also be aware of the changing importance of most factors through the implementation project run. They should bear in mind the existence of the most important factors within phases; however, they must not completely overlook other less important factors according to the research described. The practitioners may take into consideration the above mentioned conclusions in planning the implementation tasks, allocating and shifting resources according to particular project stage requirements.

The result of this study should also benefit the academic community, as it shows the need of researching ERP projects taking into account the project lifecycle, in order to fully understand the ERP system implementation. It suggests that the mechanisms governing the ERP implementation tend to change across the project phases. The main limitation of this study is that it is based on the opinions of only 8 ERP suppliers' representatives. However, the experts involved in this research comment on 74 implementations of various ERP systems, which adds credibility to the results.

# References

Brown CV, Vessey I (2003) Managing the Next Wave of Enterprise Systems: Leveraging Lessons from ERP. MIS Quarterly Executive, 2(1):65-77

Esteves J, Pastor J (2004) Organizational and Technological Critical Success Factors Behavior along the ERP Implementation Phases. Proceedings of the 6th International Conference on Enterprise Information Systems, 1:45-53

Holland C, Light B, Gibson N (1999) A Critical Success Factors Model for Enterprise Resource Planning Implementation. Proceedings of the 7th European Conference on Information Systems, Copenhagen, Denmark, 273-287

Markus ML, Axline S, Petrie D, Tanis SC (2000a) Learning from Adopters' Experiences with ERP: Problems Encountered and Success Achieved. Journal of Information Technology, 15(4):245-265

Markus ML, Tanis C (2000) The enterprise system experience - from adoption to success. In: Framing the Domains of IT Management: Projecting the Future Through the Past, Pinnaflex Educational Resources, Cincinnatti, pp 173-207

Markus ML, Tanis C, van Fenema PC (2000b) Multisite ERP Implementations. Communication of the ACM, 43(4):42-46

McNurlin BC, Sprague RH Jr. (2002) Information Systems Management in Practice. 5th edn, Upper Saddle River

Parr A, Shanks G (2000a) A model of ERP project implementation. Journal of Information Technology, 1:289-303

Parr A, Shanks G (2000b) A Taxonomy of ERP Implementation Approaches. Proceedings of the 33rd Hawaii International Conference on System Sciences, Maui, Hawaii, USA

Parr A, Shanks G, Darke P (1999) Identification of Necessary Factors for Successful Implementation of ERP Systems. In: New Information Technologies in Organizational Processes – Field Studies and Theoretical Reflections on the Future of Work, Kluwer Academic Publishers, pp 99-119

Ross JW, Vitale MR (2000) The ERP Revolution: Surviving vs. Thriving. Information Systems Frontiers, 2(2):233-241

Soja P (2004) Important Factors in ERP Systems Implementations: Result of the research in Polish enterprises. Proceedings of the 6th International Conference on Enterprise Information Systems, Porto, Portugal, 1:84-90

Soja P (2006) Success factors in ERP systems implementations: lessons from practice. Journal of Enterprise Information Management, 19(4):418-433

Somers T, Nelson K (2001) The Impact of Critical Success Factors across the Stages of Enterprise Resource Planning Implementations. Proceedings of the 34th Hawaii International Conference on System Sciences

Stefanou C (1999) Supply Chain Management (SCM) and Organizational Key Factors for Successful Implementation of Enterprise Resource Planning (ERP) Systems. Proceedings of the Americas Conference on Information Systems, Milwaukee, USA

# Building the Enterprise Architecture: A Bottom-Up Evolution?

Hakan P. Sundberg

Department of Information Technology and Media, Mid Sweden University, Sweden. hakan.sundberg@miun.se

## 1 Introduction

Organisations today have information systems that support many tasks, such as decision-making, co-ordination, control, analysis and development (Pereira and Sousa, 2004). However, most enterprises are burdened with a vast array of computers and applications that are linked together through a variety of ad-hoc mechanisms.

One major challenge is to understand the overwhelming array of products, technologies, and services, all promising easy solutions to new business challenges (Cummins, 2002). Architecture is referred to as one of the most important issues for control of the interfaces and the integration of all the individual components into one system (Pereira and Sousa, 2004), being a link between business problems and IT solutions (Britton and Bye, 2004). Without an appropriate architecture it would be hard to integrate stovepiped applications, electronic commerce solutions and commercial off-the-shelf solutions, in order to provide solutions that are optimised for just that enterprise (Cummins, 2002).

### 1.1 Enterprise architecture

Architecture has evolved through the years, from the standalone applications of the 1970s and 1980s, to today, where information is seen as a corporate resource with supporting tools and techniques (Evernden and Evernden, 2003). Kaisler et al. (2005) see enterprise architecture as "the set of processes, tools, and structures necessary to implement an enterprise-wide coherent and consistent IT architecture for supporting the enterprise's business operations". An enterprise architecture identifies the information systems and the main components of the organisation, including business processes, staff, technology, information, financial, and other resources, and the way in which these components function together. There are many models, methods, frameworks and architectures on the market (see e.g. Whitman et al. 2001).

Many definitions of enterprise architecture identify separate architectural disciplines, with the enterprise architecture acting as the glue that integrates each of these disciplines into a cohesive framework (Pereira and Sousa, 2004): First, the *business* architecture is the result of defining the business strategies, processes and requirements. The *application* architecture is a portfolio of the applications and services needed to support the business processes and functions of the enterprise. The *information* architecture is a result of modelling information and describes data concepts and the logical aspects of data as well as their physical aspects. Lastly, the *technical* architecture defines the computing services and platforms that form the technical infrastructure, e.g. standards, configurations, integration and security.

The most common reasons for developing an enterprise architecture are to define the organisations' guiding principles and standards, to develop blueprints for describing the business and technology at an appropriate abstraction level, to build common services and to create a roadmap to an IT future state (Erder and Pureur, 2003). Enterprise architecture can also provide a good prerequisite for capturing requirements (Erder and Pureur, 2004). An early understanding and construction of architecture provides a basis for discovering further requirements and constraints, and determining solutions (Nuseibeh, 2001).

## 1.2 Critical problems in enterprise architecture

Investments in organisation, culture and infrastructure are required to support the architecture process. Kaisler et al. (2005) have identified the challenges that architects and organisations are likely to face, classified into three areas, wherein critical problems arise in the process of enterprise architecture, see table 1. Modelling is used to visualise the enterprise architecture and the control and data flow through the architecture to the stakeholders, see table 1. Management requires program, project and portfolio management, which is essential when developing and deploying the enterprise architecture. The architects face multiple challenges when co-ordinating interdependencies, constraints, and interoperability at interactions. Maintenance addresses tensions between the continuing operations and the introduction of changes or new systems. This requires careful scheduling and integration of changes to the architecture.

**Table 1.** Critical problems in enterprise architecture (Kaisler et al., 2005)

| Modelling | Management | Maintenance |
|---|---|---|
| Business view representation and alignment | Managing the integrated enterprise life cycle | Continuing technical innovation |

| Limited modelling tools | Assessing technical architecture maturity | Evolving business models |
| Stakeholder's perspectives | | Mobility |
| Representing dynamics | Assessing infrastructure stress | Integrity |
| | The system architect's value proposition | Security |
| | Virtual enterprises | |
| | Evaluating enterprise architecture maturity | |
| | Assessing the enterprise architecture | |
| | Scalability | |
| | Enterprise architecture metrics | |
| | Best practices | |

# 2 Purpose and research method

The purpose of the present paper is to identify current issues in the architecture process and in the vast range of problems, i.e. what factors are most important in the enterprise architecture process?

The present study is based on a series of interviews with eight enterprise architects, IT-architects or business developers, possessing an enterprise-wide overview, from seven Swedish private and public organisations. A qualitative research method has been employed (Hartman, 1998) with a total of seven semi-structured interviews carried out between December 2005 and January 2006. The organisations were selected as follows: Three private organisations, including two international corporations of Swedish origin (31700 to 64000 employees) and one small consultancy company working with enterprise architecture for its clients, and four Swedish public organisations (ranging from 345 to 22000 employees).

Personal interviews were carried out with individuals. Pre-interview preparation involved sending out a document describing the background to the interview. During each interview the background to the study was presented, and the critical problems from table 1 were used as a starting point and basis for questions in all interviews. The total length of each interview was between 1 and 1.5 hours with one interviewer and one interviewee (in one of the interviews there were two interviewees). The interviews were recorded on paper and tape. The results have been analysed in relation to the critical factors from table 1 and in relation to the challenge outlined above.

# 3 Analysis of empirical data

## 3.1 The value of the enterprise architecture

The most frequently discussed issue from the interviews is the enterprise architecture's value, i.e. that the architecture activities must reflect themselves in improved productivity, end-to-end performance, better IT investment, portfolio management, etc. Since the implementation of enterprise architecture is considered immature in most of the interviewed organisations, enterprise architecture value becomes an important issue when convincing resisting stakeholders. This issue was frequently discussed at all interviews and, in most, it was put top of the list.

The major problems highlighted lie in the business organisations' lack of understanding for the need for investment in enterprise architecture. The architecture covers a wide perspective across applications and often leads to infrastructure investment decisions. While this is apparent from the IT organisations' views, the business organisations are considered more unwilling. Kaisler et al. (2005) see the architect's value proposition as one of the critical problems, with apparent challenges being the architect's contribution to the bottom line and how the architect's activity reflects in e.g. improved productivity.

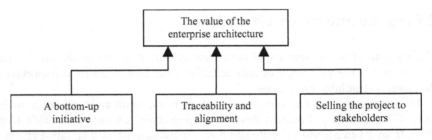

**Fig. 1.** The most frequently discussed issues from the series of interviews

Three issues were identified in the interviews as affecting, directly or indirectly, the enterprise architecture value and the enterprise architecture implementation process, see figure 1. In the following, these issues will be further explored and analysed.

## 3.2 A bottom-up initiative

It was stated in all interviews that, while enterprise architecture is, or should be, an interest for the enterprise, it is, however, in most cases, an issue that has originated and is pushed hard for by the IT organisations. But there is a difference in viewpoint. The starting point for the IT organisations is the planning and use of the information system (IS) assets for support of IS responses to business strategies. An overall goal, however, should be to plan enterprise assets for support of enterprise transformation.

This difference is illustrated in figure 2, originating from one of the interviewed organisations (which still has not reached the enterprise viewpoint). Figure 2 suggests that, while the enterprise architecture evolves, it will, given time, evolve into something of interest from the enterprise viewpoint. Thus, it will, more or less, propose its own value and will eventually move out from the IS box and turn into a responsibility for the business organisation. This particular organisation predicted that this could take another five to seven years. Altogether, the perspective evolves from the IS viewpoint and the implementation process is pushed "bottom-up" by the IT organisation. Other change initiatives, however, often originate in top management decisions and the management of implementing change is a "top-down" process.

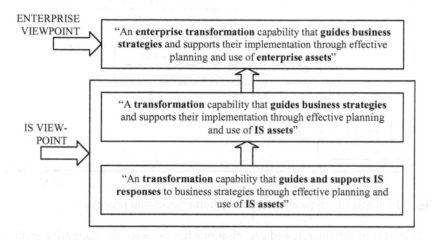

**Fig. 2.** The enterprise architecture focus starting with the IS viewpoint and evolving into the enterprise viewpoint

This leads to an explanation of enterprise architecture maturity. First, an example from one of the other interviewed organisations illustrates the evolution of frameworks and processes, see figure 3. The time scale is not particularly relevant; in fact it may be rather un-typical. Rather, it shows an evolutionary path and that the emergence of frameworks, processes and models, which, all except for process orientation, have had their origins in the IT organisation.

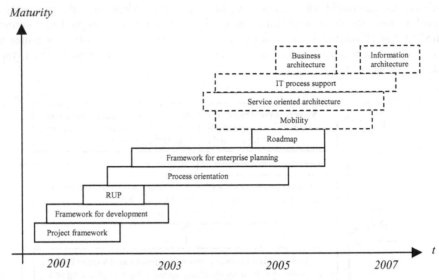

**Fig. 3.** Example of a typical evolution of frameworks and processes

Only one of the interviewed organisations has assessed the enterprise architecture maturity and is considered to have come only 20-60% (depending on category/factor) of the way. A rough estimate shows this also to be the case in the other interviewed organisation. In the U.S., a framework for assessing enterprise architectures, briefly presented in Kaisler et al. (2005), has been released by the Government Accounting Office. On the basis of that framework, the interviewed organisations have passed the initial level of creating enterprise architecture awareness and are struggling with building a management foundation and developing enterprise architecture products. The organisations were on their way to building enterprise architecture organisations; in most cases, architecture boards managing the enterprise life cycles. This is in accordance with the discussion of governance in Kaisler et al. (2005). Higher levels, like completing enterprise architecture products and leveraging the enterprise architecture to manage change, however, still lie in the future.

There seems to be no difference between the private and the public organisations. The information architecture, as seen in figure 3, is pointed out as an important and difficult task, and is yet to be fully implemented. The interviewed public organisations struggle with the integration of information and systems for interagency co-operation. They confessed that even what are considered to be simple tasks, e.g. specifying basic information such as citizens names and addresses, prove to be complex and time-consuming. Layne and Lee (2001) foresee that the full potential of IT can only be achieved by integrating government services across walls between organisations. Evernden and Evernden (2003) point out that the typical corporate budget for technology is still much greater than the budget for information structure and design and that the organisations need an information architecture and complementary technology that work together.

## 3.3 Traceability and alignment

Another factor, contributing to the value and the business perspective of the enterprise architecture, is the traceability and alignment between different parts of the architecture, e.g. a certain business process defined in the business architecture is supported by a system or systems in the application portfolio, requiring certain information, and is realised in the data tier of the technical architecture. This is a cornerstone and is realised in many of the modelling tools available on the market. Actually, as discussed above, the idea of an enterprise architecture is to act as the glue integrating each of the disciplines (Pereira and Sousa, 2004).

The interviews, however, point out that there are different levels of abstractions. Business requirements and customer strategy give the direction for information and application support, which, in turn, provides needs and priorities for the IT strategy. This abstraction and order of dependencies is not only described in e.g. Knox et al. (2003) but also in the popular Balanced Scorecard (Kaplan and Norton, 2001). The technical architecture is, in many cases, after suggestions from enterprise architecture vendors, the first to be developed by the organisation embarking on an enterprise architecture project. Interviewees could foresee an unwanted situation where the IT organisations also become business modellers, with the implication that business models and IT descriptions are on the same level. In fact, in many of the organisations, this was already the case.

A framework and tools for modelling is considered necessary for ensuring traceability and alignment. The interviewees disagree with the view, presented in Kaisler et al. (2005), that current modelling tools are limited. It was, in general, considered that many vendors provide reasonably well-integrated solutions. Rather, the need is for an easily understood business model, transferable to IT concepts. The tools for business modelling need not be advanced; rather they should be something that the business organisations feel comfortable using. Most businesses are used to traditional business process modelling (e.g. Rentzhog, 1998) and should not be forced into (by what is perceived in the business organisations as) "complicated" tools. UML, Unified Modelling Language (Rumbaugh et al., 2005), was not considered appropriate in this case; although one of the interviewees showed how higher levels of conceptual modelling could be achieved with UML.

## 3.4 Selling the project to stakeholders

This framework for assessing enterprise architectures is not the only central government initiative. In the U.S., the Federal Government has mandated the need for enterprise architectures and, furthermore, the Clinger-Cohen act has mandated a Chief Information Officer (Kaisler et al., 2005). Such central government initiatives are missing in the Swedish perspective.

With no outside pressure, the change has to come from inside, selling the idea of an enterprise architecture to different stakeholders in the organisation. Different stakeholders in the business organisations, system owners and purchasers of services from the IT organisations, need to be convinced of the benefits of enterprise architecture, as is top management. In general, the message in the interviewed organisations had begun to reach to the management level, directly under the CEO, but it still has a long way to go.

The key benefits of enterprise architecture, as pointed out by one of the interviewed organisations, are:

- To improve current business by enabling business initiatives, by efficient use of IS assets, and by improved standards' adherence and exploitation giving reduced cost.
- To provide new business models by enabling the unification of the corporation, by a clear and visible link between strategy and IS implementation, and by improved decision support and dialogue.

Another of the interviewed organisations saw the enterprise architecture as the most important "mechanism" for improvement of the co-operation between the business and IT organisations. The enterprise architecture creates a process for continuous adaptation between the business and IT organisations. This view is shared by several of the interviewed organisations. Relations between the business and IT organisations are also put under stress in the popular purchaser-contractor arrangements. Studies show that enterprise architecture is needed for improving co-operation across borders and stovepiped departments (Sundberg and Wallin, 2005).

**Table 2.** Relevant questions gathered after a workshop with stakeholders

| Planning | Organisation and competencies | Processes | Information technology |
|---|---|---|---|
| Can we see patterns controlling the future? | How do we increase cost efficiency? Are we organised for cost efficiency? | Which principles guide process development? | Which principles guide the architecture? |
| Which investment in architecture is needed? | How do we develop the customer perspective and an innovative culture? | Which general concepts and jargon are used? Are they traceable throughout the architecture? | Which resources are available and which must be acquired? |
| Which processes should be prioritised? | Which processes need modelling and development? | Which information is available? | Which general concepts and standards should be used? |
| Where are the costs in the processes ? | Which competencies are needed? | Which products are affected by which processes? | How are rules documented? |
| Which professions exist and which are needed? | How will competencies be developed? | Which rules control which processes? | Who is the purchaser? |
| Which new IT products do we have? | Can development of competencies and training be more effective? | Which professions are available? Where is actual work performed? | Who owns which system? |
| Which goals do we have for information technology support? | Which platform is used for training and | Which external actors and processes | Do we have a sufficiently known development process? |
| Will there be large consequences for in- | | | |

| formation technol-<br>ogy support?<br>How are costs<br>spread? | competence? | are interdependent?<br>Which resources<br>must be in place?<br>Which model for<br>process development<br>is in use? | How can functions<br>be mapped to IT<br>products?<br>Which dependen-<br>cies exist between<br>applications?<br>Which applica-<br>tions support<br>which processes? |
|---|---|---|---|

Still, stakeholders need to be convinced, which implies a bottom-up process for "change management". When asked about how the organisations manage these processes, replies from merely "hard work" to more elaborated processes for stakeholder conviction were forthcoming. One organisation had very actively involved stakeholders in a process of workshops, where questions concerning the enterprise architecture were gathered. An example of this is shown in table 2.

Altogether, it takes planning, motivation and agreement on how to implement an enterprise architecture. Boster et al. (2000) take the top-down perspective, with business owners initiating and taking decisions about enterprise architecture, but conclude that the business owners have only a vague idea of why an enterprise architecture should be built. Organisations assume that an enterprise architecture automatically adds business and technical value.

**Table 3.** Business perspectives of the initial steps of the enterprise architecture process (Boster et al., 2000)

| Business activities | Business skills | Business products |
|---|---|---|
| Create readiness for architecture | Ability to articulate and | Business drivers |
| Overcome resistance to change | sell a vision | Performance measures |
| Identify stakeholders | Team building | Current business models |
| Encourage open participation and | Insightful | |
| involvement | Investigative | |
| Reveal discrepancies between | High tolerance for ambi- | |
| current and desired states | guity | |
| Make it clear to everyone why | | |
| change is needed | | |
| Convey credible expectations | | |
| Communicate valued outcomes | | |

When discussing the value, three contexts contribute: The architects, the process and the final product (the architecture itself, drawings and models). Boster et al. (2000) see the process as the primary factor. Both the selection of architects and the outcomes; the products, depend on the process. Most organisations, however, lack a defined process balancing technical and business concerns. It is common to see the architecture process from a technical view only, or even, many organisations don't see that the architecture process has a business part at all. This discussion of process importance and stakeholder (business) view corresponds well to the findings from the interviews. Table 3 summarises the business view of the initial steps in an enterprise architecture process. Motivation is a big part of these efforts, as is the assessment and characterisation of the current environment.

# 4 Conclusion

In conclusion, the findings from the study will be summarised in relation to Kaisler et al. and the critical problems and factors in table 1. Permeating the findings is the need for, or lack of, a business view.

*The value of the enterprise architecture* relates to the discussion about the system architect's value and that activities must reflect themselves in improved productivity, end-to-end performance, better IT investment, portfolio management, etc. What is pointed out, in the present study, is that the business view seems to be lacking in the organisations' enterprise architecture efforts, or, if present, the IS viewpoint dominates and IT organisations act on behalf of the business organisations.

The *bottom-up perspective* relates to both evaluating enterprise architecture maturity and managing the integrated enterprise life cycle. What is pointed out, in the present study, is the apparent proactivity of the IT organisations and the enterprise architecture focus evolving from the IS viewpoint to the enterprise viewpoint. The question of maturity can provide an explanation. The business view is pointed out as an important part of the initial efforts, and the interviewed organisations are early in the architecture processes with enthusiasts advocating future needs, creating readiness and overcoming resistance. The U.S. central government initiatives mandating enterprise architectures can affect readiness, resistance and, gradually, maturity. This is different to the Swedish perspective and can explain the focus on business value and other stakeholder propositions.

*Traceability and alignment* relates to the discussion about business view representation and alignment, and modelling tools. The alignment between business processes, functions, data and information systems is considered a must for encompassing the organisation's mission and strategic business, and for mapping IT development to stakeholder needs. What is pointed out, in the present study, is that disregarding the different levels of abstractions can lead to unwanted clashes and a predominant IT perspective. Modelling should be oriented towards the business organisations, and be something that the business organisations feel comfortable using.

*Selling the project to stakeholders* relates to the stakeholders' perspectives in table 1. What is pointed out, in the present study, is that taking stakeholders' perspectives, encouraging participation and involvement can improve the enterprise architecture's technical and business value. Workshops with stakeholders seem to be a good solution for enabling involvement and understanding. The business view is also important in the architecture *process*, which is implied but not apparent in table 1. There are business activities, business skills and business products that need to be cultivated, especially in the initial phases of the process.

The most distinct findings from the present study are the IS perspective on enterprise architectures and the focus on the enterprise architecture's value. While maturity still needs development and while perspectives are evolving, it is expected that these perspectives and focuses will prevail for some time.

# References

Boster M, Liu S, Thomas R (2000) Getting the Most from Your Enterprise Architecture. IT Pro, IEEE Computer Society, July-August 2000, pp 43-50

Britton C, Bye P (2004) IT Architectures and Middleware Strategies for Building Large Integrated Systems, Second edition. Addison-Wesley, Boston

Cummins FA (2002) Enterprise Integration – An Architecture for Enterprise Application and Systems Integration. Wiley Computer Publishing, New York Chichester Weinheim Brisbane Singapore Toronto

Erder M, Pureur P (2003) QFD in the Architecture Development Process. IT Pro, IEEE Computer Society, November-December 2003, pp 44-52

Erder M, Pureur P (2004) Defining Business Requirements Quickly and Accurately. IT Pro, IEEE Computer Society, July-August 2004, pp 51-56

Evernden R, Evernden E (2003) Third-Generation Information Architecture. Communications of the ACM, vol 46, no 3, pp 95-98

Kaisler H, Armour F, Valivullah M (2005) Enterprise Architecting: Critical Problems. In Proceedings of the 38th Hawaiian International Conference on System Sciences, pp 1-10

Kaplan RS, Norton DP (2001) The Strategy-Focused Organization – How balanced scorecard companies thrive in the new business environment. Harvard Business School Press

Knox S, Maklan S, Payne A, Peppard J and Ryals L (2003) Customer Relationship Management – Perspectives from the marketplace. Butterworth-Heinemann, Oxford

Layne K, Lee J (2001) Developing fully functional E-government: A four stage model. Government Information Quarterly, no 18, pp 122-136

Hartman J, (1998) Vetenskapligt tänkande: Från kunskapsteori till metodteori. Studentlitteratur, Lund

Nuseibeh B (2001) Weaving Together Requirements and Architectures. In IT Pro, IEEE Computer Society, March 2001, pp 115-117

Pereira CM, Sousa P (2004) A Method to Define an Enterprise Architecture using the Zachman Framework. Proceedings of the 2004 ACM Symposium on Applied Computing, pp 1366-1371

Rentzhog O (1998) Processorientering: En grund för morgondagens organisationer. Studentlitteratur, Lund

Rumbaugh J, Jacobson I, Booch G (2005) The Unified Modelling Language, Second Edition, Addison-Wesley, Boston

Sundberg HP, Wallin P (2005) Co-ordination of Business and IT Development Processes – Managing Stovepiped Organisations. International Journal of Public Information Systems, vol 2005:1, pp 53-69

Whitman L, Ramachandran K, Ketkar V (2001) A Taxonomy of a Living Model of the Enterprise. Proceedings of the 2001 Winter Simulation Conference, pp 848-855

# Contract Type and Pricing Structure and the Practice of Information Systems Development – An Economical Perspective

Karlheinz Kautz, Bjarke Nielsen

Department of Informatics, Copenhagen Business School, Howitzvej 60, DK-2000 Frederiksberg, Denmark, Karl.Kautz@cbs.dk, Bjarke.Nielsen@tiscale.dk

## 1 Introduction

Information systems development takes place within an economical context. Cost overruns are frequently reported and the delivery of information systems within appropriate time and cost limits has even been given as one justification for the utilization of information systems development methodologies [2]. However, the economical conditions, which shape systems development practice, are hardly ever researched and while outsourcing of IT services has been studied for quite a while (see f. ex. [6], [12]), an economical perspective on systems development is rarely applied by the information systems community.

A number of IS-related studies (see f. ex. [1], [3], [5], [17], [20], [21]) describe features of contracts, contract types and pricing structures and investigate their economical role, but only relate them to a limited extent to systems development practice.

Exceptions are [13], [14]. Considering software development as outsourcing and based on an economical perspective there a number of hypotheses are formulated about the relationship between frequency of milestones, project risk, uncertainty and price structure as determined in systems development contracts, but no clear results are found.

Bjerknes & Mathiassen [4] discuss the balance between trust and control with regard to contracts and client-contractor relationships. In line with [18] they argue, while trust promotes creativity and mutual learning, necessary elements of systems development, a contract promotes decisions and monitoring of progress according to the agreement. They conclude that it is impossible to improve systems development practice without changing the current form of contracts. A case study by [15] supports this argument and indicates that iterative development and the explicit focus on systems development as a learning process cause difficulties, when systems development is performed according to a fixed price contract.

This is the background for our research question how a given price structure influences the way systems development projects are performed in practice. As our study is a first attempt to get an understanding of the relationship between pricing structure and systems development in practice it is exploratory and we have limited it to the development of new information systems for a particular customer.

The remainder of the paper is structured as follows: Section 2 describes our research method and setting. Subsequently, section 3 presents and discusses the research findings and section 4 contains the resulting model for the impact of pricing structure on systems development practice. We finish with some conclusions in section 5.

## 2 Research Method and Setting

Our research question implies that we are investigating how practice behaves instead of investigating if practice behaves in a specific way. Thus, our study is not experimental in nature and can not be made in a laboratory, because of its explorative nature. Its open and emergent strategy leaves us with no specific hypothesis and advocates an open method. Thus, we adopted an approach with many explanatory variables. Without hypotheses to be verified or invalidated, the data collection had to be more extensive than a search for the impact of already known factors and implied that our study would be narrower without a number of observation units. We therefore opted for a multiple case study. Based on our experience from earlier studies [9] [11] we chose an analysis, which utilizes an approach inspired by the Grounded Theory methodology [8] [19]. As there exists no specific theory on contract types, pricing structure and systems development in practice Grounded Theory is particularly appropriate as it does not require an existing theory, on the contrary it grounds an emerging theory on the collected data.

The data collection is based on twelve semi-structured qualitative interviews with representatives from 7 companies. To avoid any sector or product specific bias we chose organizations, which covered as diverse sectors as aerospace, banking & finance, media & advertisement, health and public administration and which provide content management, document handling, e-business, process management and many other kinds of information systems. The sample includes companies with as few as 10 employees as well as 40 000 employees. The companies were between 6 and 40 years old. As the project aimed at understanding the impact of a chosen price structure on systems development projects we were interested in data from those stakeholders involved in the tasks spanning from the actual sales to the delivery of the final product. Thus, we interviewed 2 sales personnel, 4 project managers and 6 developers across the different companies with 3 to 25 years of experience in the field. The questions in the individual interviews were based on existing literature within the subject, and for this purpose we worked out interview guides for the individual interviews. As we worked with semi-structured interviews, the interview guide was used as a checklist for issues that had to be covered during the interview and not as an actual outline for the interviews. The nature of the interviews had been open, and when the conversation moved towards new and interesting areas relevant to the subject, we pursued and probed the new directions. All interviews lasted between 60 and 75 minutes and were tape recorded and transcribed. The interviewees had the opportunity to see and approve the transcripts.

With the collected data from the interviews we performed as mentioned above an analysis based on Grounded Theory. The Grounded Theory framework describes a way to search relevant topics and relations through three sequential steps: the purpose of open coding is to open the data material. This is done by looking for different meanings in the statements and classifying part-statements with labels to explain the meanings of the different parts. The result is a range of different codes and concepts comprising the thoughts, ideas and meanings of the text. The purpose of axial coding is to find the categories into which the discovered codes/concepts can be classified. The meanings behind the concepts are compared and categorized in main and subcategories or concepts, which together present patterns or a set of axes to explain the data material and relationships between the concepts. Thus, the located axes reflect the parameters that are important for the study's subject. Based on the axes categories, the purpose of selective coding is to explain relationships and contexts to refine the overall explanation into a coherent picture of the observations. The overall picture is based on central categories and represents a complete framework of explanations for the field in focus.

However, although no specific theory relating pricing structure and systems development in practice exists, by taking an economic perspective, our study is of course informed by the existing literature and in particular by economic writings concerning pricing structures and theories of supplier-customer relationships. As such Ciborra's [5] work on transaction cost theory with its possible implications for systems development builds the general background for our study. With regard to pricing the literature distinguishes between fixed price and time and material approaches and variations of these such as fixed price with payment for extra efforts or time and material with an upper limit (see f. ex. [16]). With regard to the relationship between suppliers and customers principal-agent theory provided a suitable background for our study. It describes how a principal, a customer, should build up an incentive structure, a pricing structure or scheme, to achieve a desired behaviour from an agent, a supplier. Principal-agent theory is based on the assumption that people not always keep the contracts and the agreements they have made. Such behaviour, which might lead to advantages at the expense of others, is called opportunistic behaviour [7]. Characteristic for opportunistic behaviour is that only some people, and they also only some times, exhibit it. It is difficult, if not impossible to distinguish honest from dishonest people before they actually show opportunistic behaviour. Principal-agent theory deals with the avoidance of opportunistic behaviour. In this context two concepts are important, namely risk, in particular the possibility of loss, and here especially the suppliers relationship to risk, and observability, in particular the customers' possibility to observe a supplier.

# 3 Findings and Discussion

As a background for our further investigation we asked our respondents about the pricing structures they are using during the contract negotiations for new systems development projects with customers. In line with the literature we identified the above mentioned pricing structures and found a 5th one called framework agreements. A fixed price comprises all costs of a development project and the suppliers' profit depends on their ability to provide the desired system within time and budget. With its origin in a given task with fixed scope, a fixed deadline and a fixed price, fixed price with payment for extra effort contains an explicit mechanism for dealing with changed or additional requirements. Time and material bills the actual effort, while time and material with an upper limit sets a threshold for the maximum expenses. Finally, framework agreements comprise a maximum number of hours, which a customer can book a supplier within a given time frame. This might give a customer a lower price per hour and gives both parties the liberty to negotiate the actual use of the hours according to all available pricing structures.

## 3.1 Choice of Pricing Structure impacts Risk Distribution and Price Level

We found that pricing structures have an embedded distribution of risk between both the supplier and the customer. Using fixed price as the pricing structure it is solemnly the supplier who carries and manages the risk. The pricing scheme fixed price with payment for extra efforts moves the part of the risk, which deals with changes of the project scope towards the customer, because these are described and billed for separately. The supplier carries the risk for the original project, while the customer carries the risk for the changes. The customer assumes the whole risk when a project is paid according to time and material. Every hour suppliers disburse contributes to secure their earnings from a project. This means that the risk for delays, changes and unexpected costs is carried by the customer. When time and material with an upper limit is applied a part of the risk is pushed back to the supplier as costs which are above the determined limit are defrayed by the supplier. The supplier has guaranteed the customer a maximum expense, but is willing to let the customer get the savings in case the project is finished before the maximum budget has been exceeded. Both time and material with a limit and fixed price with payment for extra efforts are hybrids of fixed price and time and material. For them the exact distribution of risk between supplier and customer is hard to determine. However, the tendency is clear. The more a pricing structure resembles a fixed price, the more risk has to be carried by the supplier, and the more the structure resembles time and material the more risk has to be carried by the customer. A project manager and a salesman expressed this clearly *"Time and material ... the customer's risk. Fixed price ... my risk. It's just that simple."*

Framework agreements differ from the others as the contract does not specify any task and any kind of billing. The risk is on the customers' side as they have paid for some work before it is delivered. However, when a concrete project is performed under a framework agreement the risk can be pushed towards the supplier again depending on the actual pricing structure used.

Our investigation has also shown that the price for a project is influenced by the distribution of risk between the supplier and the customer. When suppliers work under a pricing model which induces an element of risk on them they compute a risk premium, which they add to the project's price. The same project leader said *"When we give a fixed price we always add another 10-15% as contingency to cover unexpected costs, and then the customer gets the account as fixed price. That's how we do it. If there is a high uncertainty we even put in a higher contingency for that respective task, which can be up to 25%."* The risk supplement rises corresponding with the risk. Another project manager stated that there is a natural limit for how big a risk suppliers are willing to take. If a project is too risky, they reject fixed price as an acceptable model.

## 3.2 Distribution of Risk and Price Level impact Behaviour

As with the distribution of risk opportunistic behaviour can be found both with the supplier and the customer. The behaviour is however different depending on who is carrying the risk.

When the suppliers carry the risk time pressure is often a consequence, as one developer put it *"I'll say time, whether you're able to stay within the time, that's the biggest challenge."* and as a result the suppliers might not be able to deliver the desired functionality. They then just try to satisfy the minimum requirements and sometimes they choose to change the scope without the acceptance of the customer. A developer admitted: *"When you suddenly see that you have problems to deliver within the determined time frame you have two possibilities, you can change the scope or you can change the time frame."* Suppliers also choose to deny customers the possibility to change the requirements during the project or by applying requirements management try to minimise their amount and extent. A project manager reported *"One can very well keep oneself off the change of requirements and say, this does not concern us: we do what the requirements specification says. As one can say, that's what you described and that's what you get."*

As a consequence the customers might not get the systems they want and they might choose another supplier in the future.

When suppliers do not longer have the risk, they also no longer have an incentive to steer a project strictly towards a deadline. According to a project manager project management and project work become different, more relaxed tasks *"The customer needs to put more effort in, it's them who need to follow up every week.*

*They have to allocate time to keep track of the project. With time and material, we have all the time the customer wants.*

Even when the suppliers are in situations where they need personnel, material or knowledge from the customer to solve a problem, their effort to get these resources is not that big *"With time and material we clearly give the customer a longer leash as compared to fixed price. After all it's them who pay when we are busy waiting"* as one project manager put it. He also experienced more flexibility and fewer problems to change deadlines, if the change is caused by circumstances, which the customers are responsible for.

When the customer carries the risk, projects have a tendency to slide away from their original scope, which sometimes leads to an extension of the scope. One project manager reported that he has difficulties to steer projects under these conditions. One developer confirmed this view. He expressed that his efforts are not specified and controlled in the same way as they are in projects where the supplier has the risk. As a reason for the lesser control he provided that a potentially inadequate effort does have no direct economical consequences for the supplier company: *"I have much freer hands from my company when it's not a fixed price as we can't sit with any extra bills afterwards. We might get a problem, but we do not sit with any extra unpaid bills."* Another developer stated that he to a larger extent tries new things in projects where the customer carries the risk and he reported a concrete case where he actually together with the customer experimented with new things that expanded the project's scope: *"Some of the customer's folks could very well see that this was exciting and asked whether we just could try this and that … Yes, you can well say that there is a risk that one runs a little bit too fast and little bit off the track to see the exciting things."*

When the customer carries the risk, developers have a larger tendency to not just be content with satisfying the customer's requirements, but to further develop a system single-handedly without their management's or the customer's acceptance. This phenomenon is called gold plating and all the interviewed developers justified their motivation with professional pride: *"It should be as good as possible and there should not be any errors. And it should also be able to do this and that. And it would be smart if it even could do this and that. Sometimes it's the technology which is interesting. One can also just do this, or just try that … ."* However beyond professional pride, extra payment for overtime work in the evening has also been mentioned as a reason for gold plating by one developer: *"Yeah, well then you might not be so effective during the day, because you know if you stay longer, your hours will count more and give you more money"*

Our respondents expressed that customers too show opportunistic behaviour. When the supplier carries the risk some customers might not see any incentive to support them. Still, the suppliers' earnings depend on the customers' efforts in a number of areas. One of these is the provision of material and devices. One developer described his experience as follows: *"I am supposed to be out at a customer's and there should be a computer for me so that I can carry out the project. When it's a fixed price project, it might very well be that the customer does not see the incentive to provide the device … if you are at a customer, who has got a bill be-*

*fore and the project is run with time and material, they'll take utter care of that you get your screen to work at ... ."*

Another challenge is to get access to the right personnel. Developers experienced that often those staff members they need are also those the organisation is most dependant on and are not made available. As a result suppliers insist on specifying the customers' efforts in the contract and - according to one developer *"that the customers provide competent people, because when they then don't do that, one can go in and say, that's what we have a contract about."*

The limited access to competent personnel has to be seen in a wider context. Often customers consider the requirements specification as a complete description of the desired system and are not willing to provide further more business knowledge. One developer summarised his experience as *"Requirement specifications can be a help, so that we understand each other right, but when you put them instead of communication, so that's what will go wrong. They'll say' haven't we written down what we want to have, read it and do it'... "* and concluded that this attitude and the limited contact to the customer is one reason why information systems do not live up to the customers' expectations.

When the risk for a project lies with the supplier, suppliers also experience that customers do not put in an effort that is oriented towards meeting a deadline, even if from a business perspective this would be sensible. The contributions and the productivity of the customers' employees do not live up to the agreements made between the two parties. The respondents think that this might be related to the lack of a direct incentive for the employees or for the customers in general with regard to the particular projects where this occurs. To counteract this effect some suppliers specify the required customer effort even more detailed in their contracts.

On the other hand - beyond the accepted general phenomenon that both suppliers and customers learn more about a system's potential during the course of a development project - when they are not carrying the risk, customers have a tendency to late in a project press extra requirements into the scope of the project that might lead to rework and extra resources. The dilemma for the project managers and developers is that, denying the changes might have consequences for the future co-operation with the customer, accepting them leads to extra workload, time pressure and shifting of deadlines. The respondents think that the customer behaviour is not necessarily based on a malicious exploitation of the situation. According to one project manager it might be the missing experience that results in customers not being able to accept the relationship between the amount of requirement changes and the run time of a project.

When carrying the risk themselves, customers pay strong attention to how and for what a supplier uses the hours and the suppliers need to put in extra time to provide the demanded evidence. As a developer put it *"The customer has a larger focus on what you are doing and they like to have an account of what you are using your time for. They make much bigger fuzz out of this in a time and material project than they do in a fixed price project."*

Customers are also less willing to accept a price for a provided effort when billing is done according to time and material especially without an agreed estimate.

In such a situation it can be hard to collect the charges for some provided development work. A project leader reported *"When they pay for time and material it is their right to ask for changes. But as with all customers it is much easier for them to ask for something than to look at the bill afterwards. So there easily can crop up a conflict if one does not steer a project sharply with estimates, but even then it happens."*

## 3.3 Behaviour impacts Distribution of Risk and Price Level

The suppliers' and customers' behaviour in return has an impact on the distribution of the risk between the two parties and on the price for a project.

The respondents have described a number of situations, which increase the risk for the supplier. Lacking access to customer personnel and knowledge and lacking customer efforts increase the workload of the supplier. This comes in form of a larger expenditure of hours to compensate for the customers' missing dedication. The extra hours that become necessary are often not included in the official project plan and the developers are forced to work overtime to be able to finish their tasks on time. A developer described the situation: *"Well, the less time you have, the more you have to work everyday so that you can reach the goals which have been set, isn't it like that. So this means automatically longer working hours."* Another developer had similar experiences from a project where a customer late in the project came up with new requirements. In this case the customer had provided the agreed effort, but the new requirements had not been taken into account in the original planning of the project. This increased the developers' workload as they were bound to a fixed deadline and *"Yeah well, so we simply worked more. So we put in these 45-55-60 hours per week, where we work until 10 or 11 pm in the night."* This has consequences for the supplier, especially when it is not possible to demand a payment for the extra effort, as it usually necessitates payment of the overtime to the company's developers. As one developer said *"We are so fortunate here that we get fixed wages and a payment for overtime, which we so really get paid. So it costs the company, when we work extra."*

On the other hand gold plating is an example for a behaviour exhibited by suppliers, which has an impact on the customer's risk and on the price for a project. It is often connected to projects where the customer from the outset carries the risk. Although the developers do not keep to the requirements as described by the customer and develop extra functionality, suppliers still try to get a payment for that work by selling it as utility value. A developer said *"Because when you've got 20 hours for doing something and then the whole thing starts to slip, because you have been sitting and done some gold plating, it then gets hard to explain to the customer why the task took double the time."*

To prevent such situations attuning expectations in the beginning of a project is important, especially with regard to the effort both parties expect from each other to put into the project and these expectations can then be part of the contract. One project leader shared his experiences in this respect: *"So, there are some things that one should agree to settle in the start. If one gets a good balancing, one gets a good project ... customers like it when one agrees on things up front, they hate it when one comes sweeping afterwards ... so in the plan, there are the things they should do and when I expect them ready, specified down to the week ... and that is what they have to live up to, otherwise I can't hold my fixed price."*

## 3.4 Distribution of Risk and Price Level impacts Choice of Pricing Structure

According to the suppliers the customers' perception of the distribution of risk and of the costs has an influence on their demands for the price structure of future projects with a given supplier. In the beginning of a co-operation between a supplier and a customer both parties are uncertain about each others capabilities to render an effort, which lives up to the mutual expectations of a good co-operation. There is also uncertainty whether the other party's intentions are honest and trustworthy. New customers are quite reluctant with regard to take on risk and in general prefer a fixed price contract. One developer said *"As a rule there is not really a choice between the two pricing structures, because the customer typically demands a fixed price project"* and another confirmed *"It's nearly always the customer who demands a fixed price."* One project leader provided as an explanation that the customers are uncertain whether they can rely on the suppliers' estimates and that there is no basis for trust in these earlier stages of the first contract negotiations due to a lack of familiarity of each other. The customers might be afraid of being burdened with further costs after the end of the negotiations. He described the situation: *"When we come to a new customer, the question always is 'will this run away?' So, what shall we answer: 'Listen I am a quite honest person, it will cost this and this, as this is what is written there."* All respondents confirmed this initial mistrust and some gave examples of customers' earlier experiences where their trust was abused.

It however is possible to sell time and material projects, especially when the supplier and the customer know each other and by virtue of their co-operation have built up trust to each other. This trust is built up through continuous co-operation over a longer period of time or through many projects. One salesman put it that way *"We have also time and material projects; it really depends on the customer. But typically these are customers we know."* and another added: *"The more projects we have performed, the better we know each other, the better we can also work in a less restricted setting."* With trust building up between the parties, it becomes possible for the supplier to convince the customer to take larger parts of the risk, which allows them to cut down the risk supplement of the fixed price offers. This enables the supplier to deliver a system for a lower price and thus gives them a competitive advantage. As one salesman concluded *"Ultimately, it is about getting the price down so that we have a bigger chance to get the assignment."* Experience from previous co-operation can also lead to a situation, where the customers dare to take the larger part of the risk in future projects, however as stated above earlier experience can also result in the opposite reaction, namely that a customer only wants to work under conditions, where the supplier carries the full risk.

The same salesman summarised this as *"If one once has been offered to do something on a time and material basis and has abused it, you'll not get this kind of contract another time."*

## 4 A Model for the Impact of Pricing Structure on Information Systems Development Practice

Our study made use of the principal-agent theory, recognizing customers as principals and suppliers as agents, and of its significant concepts opportunistic behaviour, risk and to a lesser extent observability. By identifying fixed price, time and material, fixed price with payment for extra efforts, time and material with an upper limit and framework agreements it validates and extends the literature on pricing structures for the field of information systems development. On this background we provide a model for the impact of pricing structure on systems development practice. Its main elements are choice of pricing structure, risk distribution and price level, and opportunistic behaviour (see figure 1).

Choice of pricing structure impacts risk distribution and price level. In step with incorporating fixed prices in contracts the risk is allocated to the supplier. If, in contrast a time and material pricing structure is chosen, the risk moves over to the customer. The suppliers are rather risk averse, thus the price level raises in accord with the risk supplements, which correspond to the supplier perception of risk's dimension.

Distribution of risk and price level have an impact on behaviour. Both suppliers and customers show opportunistic behaviour. When suppliers carry the risk their opportunistic behaviour is derived from the time pressure to reach the deadline. The supplier might comprise the functionality of the product to be delivered as well as the customer expectations and as such the system's quality. When the customer carries the risk, the suppliers' behaviour might be based on the fact that their earnings will be higher the longer time they use for a project. Again, the customers might not get the systems they want and they might choose another supplier in the future. The customers' opportunistic behaviour differs depending on which party is carrying the risk. When the suppliers hold the risk, their earnings depend on the customers' efforts, which these not always provide. Customers also try to press new requirements into the projects. This is a problem for the suppliers as denying these demands might have an impact on future business with the customer, while accepting them results in extra hours, time pressure and changes of deadlines. When the customers themselves carry the risk they demand more documentation with regard to the hours the suppliers use in the project, which leads to larger administrative expenses for those. Customers also show less accept for the suppliers' use of time which sometimes results in a reluctance to pay for the suppliers' efforts. In that situation it can be hard to collect the charges for some provided development work.

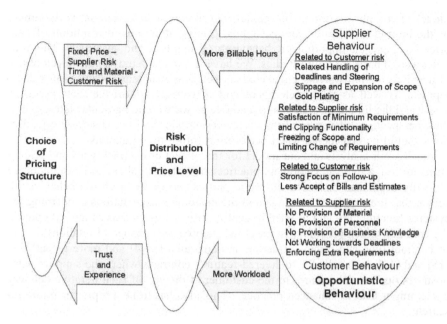

**Fig. 1.** The Impact of Pricing Structure on System Development Practice

The suppliers' and customers' behaviour in return has an impact on the distribution of the risk between the two parties and on the price for a project. As described above lacking customer efforts might lead to increased workload and economical strain for the suppliers and relaxed project steering and handling of deadlines might cause more billable hours and thus higher costs for the customer. The same is true for slippage and expansion of scope as well as for gold plating.

The customers' experiences from previous projects with regard to distribution of risk and price level have an impact on the choice of pricing structure for future projects. The basis for trust is created when suppliers live up to the customers' expectations, which means that the customers will be more willing to choose a pricing structure where they carry more of the risk. However, when suppliers abuse this trust either by decreasing functionality or raising prices, mistrust develops and customers will not accept the same degree of risk in future projects.

## 5 Conclusions

Our study demonstrates the merits of principal-agent theory for information systems development research and confirms the literature on pricing structures, but goes beyond reporting the mere distribution of the different contract types and pricing structures as well as abstract economic reflections.

The investigation into contract types' and pricing structures' influence on systems development in practice has provided new insights resulting in an explanatory model of the phenomenon. The model contributes with a cumulative treatment of the interrelationship of contract types, pricing structures, distribution of risk, price level and the opportunistic behaviour of suppliers and customers. This provides a solid basis for future studies. We have limited our study to the development of new information systems and excluded operation, maintenance and further development as well as the development and adjustment of off-the-shelf products. These and the limitation - though defendable as we were in particular interested in their perspective - that we only interviewed supplier and not customer organisations should be considered when performing future investigations.

Finally, our analysis and our model for the impact of contract types and pricing structures on systems development practice show that suppliers and customers are mutually dependant on that none of the parties shows opportunistic behaviour to secure that the suppliers' earnings and the customers expectations concerning the systems functionality and ultimately quality turn into what was as agreed upon in the contract. Given the role trust plays in this process a change of relationship and of contract type and pricing structure as demanded by [4] and more recently by [15] and [10], who calls for 'delivered-feature' contracts where the supplier demonstrates operational features to the customer at the end of each iterative delivery cycle, might lead to enhanced practice. This also has to be a topic for future research.

## References

1. Ang, S., Beath, C. M.: Hierarchical Elements in Software Contracts. Journal of Organisational Computing, 3(3) (1993) 329-361.
2. Avison, D.E., Fitzgerald, G.: Information Systems Development: Methodologies, Techniques and Tools, McGraw-Hill, Maidenhead, UK (1995).
3. Banerjee, A., Duflo, E.: Reputation Effects and the Limits of Contracting: A Study of the Indian Software Industry. Quarterly Journal of Economics, 115(3) (2000), 989-1017.
4. Bjerknes G., Mathiassen L.: Improving the Customer-Supplier Relation in IT Development, In Proceedings of the 33rd Hawaii International Conference on Systems Sciences (HICSS) (2000).
5. Ciborra, C.: Teams, Markets and Systems. Cambridge University Press, Cambridge, UK (1996).
6. Dibbern, J., Goles, T., Hirschheim, R., Jayatilka, B.: Information systems outsourcing: a survey and analysis of the literature. ACM SIGMIS Database, 35(4) (2004) 6-102.
7. Douma, S., Schreuder, H.: Economic Approaches to Organizations. Third edition. Prentice Hall (2002).
8. Glaser, B. G., Strauss, A. L.: The Discovery of Grounded Theory - Strategies for Qualitative Research. Aldine De Gruyter, New York, USA (1967).

9.  Hansen, B., Kautz, K.: Grounded Theory Applied –Studying Information Systems Development Methodologies in Practice. In Proceedings of the Hawaii International Conference on System Sciences (HICSS-38) (2005).
10. Highsmith, J.: Agile Software Development Ecosystems. Addison-Wesley, Pearson Education, Boston, USA (2002).
11. Kautz, K., Hansen, B., Jacobsen, D.: The Utilization of Information Systems Development Methodologies in Practice. Journal of Information Technology Cases and Applications, 6 (4) (2004).
12. Lacity, M.C., Hirschheim, R.: The Information Systems Outsourcing Bandwagon. Sloan Management Review, Fall, (1993) 73-86.
13. Lichtenstein, Y. & McDonnell, A.: Pricing Software Development Services. In Proceedings of the European Conference on Information Systems, Naples, Italy, June 16-21, (2003).
14. Lichtenstein, Y.: Puzzles in Software Development Contracting. Communication of the ACM, 47(2) (2004) 61-65.
15. Madsen, S., Kautz, K.: Applying system development methods in practice - the RUP example. In Proceedings of 11th International Conference on Information Systems Developments, Methods & Tools - Theory & Practice, Riga, Latvia, September, 12-14, (2002).
16. Overby, M. L., Vang, J., Mahnke, V.: Strategic IT outsourcing (In Danish), Thomsen, Copenhagen, DK (2003).
17. Richmond, W., Seidmann, A.: Software Development Outsourcing Contract: Structure and Business Value. Journal of Management Information Systems, 10(1) (1993) 57-72.
18. Sabherwal, R.: The Role of Trust in Outsourced IS Development Projects. Communications of the ACM, 42 (2) (1999) 80-86.
19. Strauss, A. and Corbin, J.: Basics of Qualitative Research. SAGE Publications, London, UK (1998).
20. Wang, E. T. G., Baron, T., Seidmann, A.: Contracting Structures for Custom Software Development: The Impacts of Informational Rents and Uncertainty on Internal Development and Outsourcing. Management Science, 43(12) (1997) 1726-1744.
21. Whang, S.: Contracting For Software Development. Management Science, 38(3) (1992) 307-324.

# An Approach of the Knowledge Management for the Development of the Organisational Commitment

Adriana Schiopoiu Burlea

University of Craiova, 13, Street A. I. Cuza, 200585, Dolj, Craiova, Romania, aburlea2000@yahoo.it

**Abstract:** This paper focuses on the relationship between Knowledge Management and Human Resources Management that will change the system of values in the 21$^{st}$ century. Today, the modern organisations have intelligent systems covering the technical necessities. With the help of these intelligent systems various areas of the organisation can be tracked: *sourcing, production, quality, stocks, and human resources management.* The methodology used in this article involved theoretical development and empirical research. The main idea stated that the research must identify some situations in which all research strategies might be relevant (Mellander, 2001, Yin, 1994).

The research reported in this paper focused on a study of the organisational commitment of the employees using data from two Romanian organisations. In this context, knowledge management and human resources management will interweave in the analysis of organisational commitment and will contribute to the establishment of strategic priorities of the organisations. In a modern organisation, the good flexibility of informational systems offers the opportunity of adjustment to a more and more competitive environment based on knowledge.

Taking into consideration the knowledge management – the detection and development of strategic human capital are made on three levels: *individual* – knowledge and expression; *collective* – interaction and *organisational* – competition. Those organisations that will strategically administrate their human resources will successfully pass through the strategic process. This implies a flexible model of knowledge management, model that takes into consideration the employees commitment and their loyalty to the organisation.

Consequently, at the human resources level, bad knowledge management can generate hard feelings, lack of motivation, and even confusion, in the moments in which the organisation would need creativity and total commitment from their employees.

# 1 Introduction

The external environment complexity is a disadvantage for the organisations, which sometimes cannot adjust to the changes and cannot motivate the employees; therefore, it needs means and instruments to rapidly control economic, social and political flotation.

The economic and cultural stakes are emphasised through the acquisition and sharing of knowledge in due time. Consequently, the surviving organisation of the 21st century will be a network organisation. The manager of an intelligent organisation must have a strategic vision and knowledge of capturing and using explicit and tacit knowledge of his organisation.

The advanced technology, incorporating various data, generates:

- changes in the traditional organisation structure;
- downsize of the firm;
- increase of the responsibilities and personal competence;
- increase of dynamics of internal communication.

Channelling the variety of connections among the members of an organisation toward a common entity is a strong point for the organisation, leading to the development of knowledge management.

# 2 The relationship between knowledge management and organisational commitment

Knowledge management is the premise of new strategic and managerial approaches, ensuring the success of initiative employees within the organisation.

Knowledge management and organisational commitment can:

- become effective mechanisms to help avoid the disturbances that generate internal disequilibrium within the organisation.
- remediate the negative effects of the instability of environment.

The information and knowledge become "raw materials" for intelligent organisations; their management requires simple solutions.

The centralised administration and the hierarchic structure are no longer compatible with the vision and strategy of the organisation. The flexibility of intelligent information systems offers new possibilities to face an increasing competition.

The efficiency of the organisation depends on:

- the degree in which important information and knowledge management are disseminated and utilised;
- the way in which knowledge passes from the employees who possess it to the employees that need that knowledge;
- the degree of analysing the knowledge;

- the solidity of the relation between employees/organisation, and between organisation/clients.

Therefore, we need to examine employees' commitment as we have done in this article, in order to come to a better understanding of the impact that knowledge management has on the organization.

## 2.1 Knowledge management in organisation

Knowledge Management is based on an inexhaustible capital: the employees' knowledge and competence. Within the organisation framework, this capital is quite primitive and should be identified and channelled towards the final product or services to be offered to the clients (Styhre 2004).

Knowledge exploitation is even more difficult within an IT organisation. This difficulty originates in the wide range of knowledge and in the complexity of the organisational commitment.

IT organisations are not rare and the consequences are to be seen especially within the other organisations. This management faces specific problems whose resolution depends on the informal leader's support (Stacey 2001).

Knowledge management is a process of efficient administration and handling of knowledge within an organisation. It is important for a person to make a connection between a new phenomenon and the phenomena he already knows (this depends on his intelligence).

IT organisations based on knowledge management have the following objectives:

- identification and protection of knowledge;
- development of knowledge and organisational commitment;
- improvement of the access to the existing knowledge.

The efficient use of knowledge management requires an intellectual co-operation among the team members, and the development of an external co-operation with the clients and suppliers as well.

The intellectual co-operation can be interpersonal co-operation (more persons work together) and/or inter-organisational co-operation (more teams or organisations work together).

The elaboration of a co-operation social contract, supported by the ethics of co-operation must state the rights and individual responsibilities based on co-operation behaviour.

The knowledge management must be sustained by co-operation and by a collective strategy of the organisation.

The existing intelligent information systems in the field of human resources management are complex and offer users a new perspective. Taking into account their complexity some information is useless (Brennan and Connell 2000). The developers of solutions for human resources management seek to adapt to the particularities of the field and to identify the necessary information in order to take an efficient decision.

## 2.2 Organisational commitment and it role in the management of organisation

The complexity of the environment often makes the organisation unable to adapt to changes and to stimulate employees. Therefore, it is necessary to use instruments allowing a fast approach toward the economic, social and political fluctuations.

Over time many specialists paid a special attention to the study of employees' commitment, which is considered either a complex issue that cannot be represented by a mono-factor model, (Bennet and Durkin 2000), either a force that boosts the performance of an organization (Sulliman and Iles 2000, p. 408).

Organisational commitment falls into three categories according to the position within the organisation. Allen and Meyer (1990) stated that are three types of commitment: affective, continuance and normative.

- Affective commitment reflects an employee's emotional attachment to, identification with, and involvement in an organization (Buchanan, 1974; Porter et al. 1974; Mowday et al. 1982; Legge, 1995b). Employees have a *desire* to do so.
- Continuance commitment is related to the costs and benefits associated with staying or leaving an organization (Wiener and Vardi 1980, Allen and Meyer 1990).
- Normative commitment reflects the view that an employee has a duty or an obligation to stay with an organisation.

According to Skyrme (2003, p.157) "commitment grows through high levels of communication and interchange ideas".

His observation coincides with our approach, in that commitment can by better managed by making knowledge disponible in organisation.

The commitment is part of the values of the employees, so that it is necessary for the organisation to adapt the strategy to the cultural values in order to avoid false commitment.

The identification of organisational commitment can be centralised in a dynamic database that gathers all the information and knowledge from the organisation. Within intelligent organisations, the development of centres for competence management using IT has a key role.

## 2.3 The levels of the quality in the organisation depending on knowledge management

Besides the relationship between knowledge and performance, some attention has been paid to the relationship among knowledge and quality and cost dimensions (Ofek and Sarvary, 2001 Skyrme and Amidon, 1997).

The knowledge management dimensions at the IT organisational level are reflected in quality as follows:

**A. Management quality:** the way in which organisation goals and values are harmonised. Knowledge Management within individual commitment becomes the strongest support for key competence. Knowledge management aims to assess the knowledge type necessary to ensure Total Quality Management.

**B. Work environment quality** – work environment can become tensed with a series of conflicts. Every organisation has at its disposal general and technical knowledge, which cannot be quantified and managed as employees have different perspectives to it. This personal perspective is not identifiable with the overall perspective. Therefore, to reach a consensus, the work environment should be a top priority. The motivation system should be both, flexible and complex, able to satisfy the various knowledge demands. The quality of work environment is also influenced by the institutional, national and international legal system, which can enhance or prevent the sharing of knowledge within the organisation framework.

**C. The quality of products and services** – this reflects in the image of the organisation, leading to small market shares. The strong bond between the quality of products and services and the quality of the clients is sustained by the quality of incorporated knowledge and is considered a determinant of the organisation efficiency.

Knowledge management can lead to a new strategic and managerial approach, ensuring the success of employee's initiatives within the organisation (Burlea Şchiopoiu 2002).

# 3 The model of Human Resources Management

The literature developed many approaches of human resources management and commitment (Beardwell and Holden, 1996; Armstrong 1997; Pfeffer 1998, Torrington and Hall 1998, Burlea Schiopoiu 2004).

These models analyzed the relationship between the proactive behaviour and the commitment of employees in social, cultural and technical context.

In our model, knowledge management emphasizes the role of satellite of each type of commitment (Fig. 1.).

Based on literature, past findings and model of Human Resources Management, we considered states that:

- commitment (affective and normative) is a significant predictor of success in creation-development-transfer of knowledge in organizations,

- perceived continuance commitment will have a negative effect on the intention to share knowledge,
- the employees with a continuance commitment do not want to share their knowledge due to the feeling of minimizing the chances of success in organization.

According to Bock and Kim (2002), the individual's behaviour or commitment into organisation is influenced by expected rewards that discourage the formation of a positive attitude toward knowledge sharing.

The commitment plays an important role in promoting the knowledge management, because if the employees accept to share the explicit and tacit knowledge, they could also share their responsibilities.

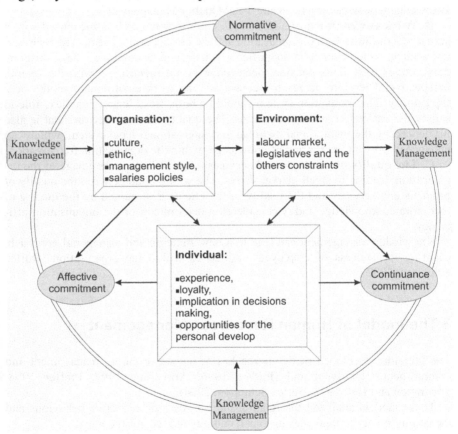

**Fig. 1.** The model of Human Resources Management

# 4 Methodology

The methodology consists in semi-structured interviews. We began by asking participants to explain how they thought career was perceived in general and how they saw their knowledge operating both now and in the future.

We used an interview framework adapted from Meyer and Allen (1990):

**Affective Commitment**

1. Would you be happy to spend the rest of your career in this organisation?
2. Do you enjoy sharing the knowledge with yours colleagues?
3. Do you feel emotionally attached and a strong sense of belonging to the organisation?
4. Do you feel like the organisation's knowledge is your own?

**Continuance Commitment**

1. Are you staying with the organisation because of necessity or desire?
2. Would it be costly to leave the organisation in the near future?
3. How many options do you have if you decide to leave?
4. Your knowledge is important for the organisation?
5. What is the labour market like for jobs in your area?

**Normative Commitment**

1. Do you believe that loyalty to an organisation is important?
2. Do you believe that ethic and duty to an organisation are important?
3. Do you think that an efficient knowledge management is important for you and for the organisation?

Each interview lasted for 20 to 35 minutes and led to questions concerning the relationship between knowledge management and commitment.

# 5 Case study

The case study performs an empirical evaluation of the relationship between the knowledge management and organizational commitment from two Romanian companies belonging to the IT sector and to construction material sector.

In each of the two case study organisations, evidence was sought through the interview process and existing procedures about:

- the present approach to knowledge management;
- the relationship between the style of management and the organizational commitment;
- the way these changes were perceived (positive and negative).

For the evaluation of the interdependence between the knowledge management and organizational commitment we studied the following variables: age groups, qualification level and sector of activity.

**Organisation A – IT sector -** offers many possibilities to its employees in what concerns the knowledge management. This company has 16 employees, all men, average age 33.6 years. The youngest has 26 years old and is computer specialist, the oldest, 42 years old, is the owner of the company. All the employees have higher education in IT or economics.

**Organisation B – construction materials –** has 845 employees – 660 men (78.1%) and 185 women (21.9%). Structure by age is presented in Table no. 1.

**Table 1.** The structure of employees of organisation B, based on age groups

| Age group (years) | Number of employees | Share (%) | Sample | |
|---|---|---|---|---|
| | | | Number of employees | Share (%) |
| < 30 | 87 | 10.3 | 9 | 10.30% |
| 31-40 | 290 | 34.3 | 29 | 10.00% |
| 41-50 | 331 | 39.2 | 35 | 10.60% |
| >50 | 137 | 16.2 | 14 | 10.40% |
| *Total* | 845 | - | 87 | 10.30% |

The organization A has a homogenous structure (average 33.6 years) while in the organisation B more than 50% of the employees are over 41 years old.

The structure of employees of organisation B, based on study levels is presented in table no. 2

**Table 2.** The structure of employees of organisation B, based on study levels

| Study level | Number of employees | Share (%) | Sample | |
|---|---|---|---|---|
| | | | Number of employees | Share (%) |
| Unqualified workers (S1) | 150 | 17.8 | 15 | 10.00% |
| Qualified workers (S2) | 83 | 9.8 | 9 | 10.80% |
| Employees with high school (MS) | 532 | 62.9 | 55 | 10.30% |
| Higher education employees (SE) | 80 | 9.5 | 8 | 10.00% |
| *Total* | 845 | - | 87 | 10.30% |

We interviewed all the employees of the organisation A and for the employees of the organisation B we established a representative sample of 87 employees.

The analysis of the interviews showed that:

- 56.3% of the employees of the organisation A and 34.5% of the employees of the organisation B consider that they wish to work in their respective organisation (affective commitment) and want to used several types of tool that improve creativity in organisation (they consider knowledge is one of the most important factor to ensure high business performance in their organisation);

- 12.5% of the employees of the organisation A and 49.1% of the employees of the organisation B consider that they must work in their respective organisation due to objective reasons (continuance commitment) and they are indifferent relating to identifying new patterns and knowledge;

- 31.2% of the employees of the organisation A and 16.4% of the employees of the organisation B considers that they must remain in their respective organisation from ethical reasons (normative commitment) and they consider that is their duty to make tacit and explicit knowledge more efficient.

The paradox is that the affective commitment has not been established between the employee and organisation, but between employee and the nature of his activity.

The employees of the organisation A are involved in decision-making process and in creation-dissemination of knowledge, because they try to promote the values of the organisation and the development of economic performance.

The employees of the organisation B consider that the creation and dissemination of knowledge is reserved only to persons with managerial tasks or with higher education.

Regardless the activity field (at organisational level), the relationship between knowledge management and the three types of commitment are the same, the difference appearing at individual level – depending on studies and age.

The employees with IT knowledge have a strong affective and normative commitment, while the employees that do not have these skills have a commitment imposed by the limited possibility to find another working place.

The development of the competences of employees in IT field and the promotion of knowledge management at organisational level will lead to an increase in organisational efficiency and to the development of affective commitment.

# 6 Concluding remarks

This research breaks new grounds in the area of human resources management and its relationship with knowledge management.

From the theory and practice, although employees hold positive attitude toward the tacit knowledge and explicit knowledge, they are not likely to form a strong intention to perform a certain type of commitment if they believe that they do not have any motivational factors to do so.

If the process of globalisation continues to require the combination of both human resources management and knowledge management, then the organisation will have to successful combine knowledge with commitment of employees. In the case if this won't happen or be possible, organisations will be both less effective and less efficient.

# References

Allen N, Meyer J (1990) The measurement of antecedents of affective, continuance and normative commitment to the organisation, Journal of Occupational Psychology 63:1-18

Armstrong M (1997) A Handbook of Human Resource Management, Kogan Page, London

Beardwell I, Holden L (1996) Human Resource Management, 2nd ed., Pitman, London

Bennett H, Durkin M (2000) The effects of organizational change on employee psychological attachment. An exploratory study, Journal of Managerial Psychology 15:126-47

Brennan N, Connell B (2000) Intellectual capital: current issues and policy implications, Journal of Intellectual Capital, 3:206-40

Buchanan B (1975) To walk an extra mile, Organisation Dynamics, 3:67-80

Burlea Șchiopoiu A (2002) Knowledge Management in Multicultural Organisations, Economy Informatics, pp. 20-25

Burlea Schiopoiu A. (2004) Human Resource management. Theory and Practice, UNIVERSITARIA Publishing House, Craiova.

Legge K (1995) Human Resource Management, Rhetoric's and Realities, Macmillan, Basingstoke

Mellander K (2001) Engaging the human spirit: a knowledge evolution demands the right conditions for learning, Journal of Intellectual Capital 2:165-71

Mowday R, Steers R, Porter L (1982) Employee-organisation Linkages: The Psychology of Commitment, Absenteeism and Turnover, Academic Press, London

Pfeffer J (1998) The Human Equation, Harvard Business School Press, New York, NY

Porter L, Steers R, Mowday R, Boulian P (1974) Organisational commitment, job satisfaction and turnover among psychiatric technicians, Journal of Applied Psychology 59:603-609

Skyrme J. D. (2003), Knowledge Networking. Creating the Collaborative Enterprise. Elsevier, Butterrworth-Heinemann

Stacey R (2001) Complex Responsive Processes in Organizations: Learning and Knowledge Creation, Routledge, London

Styhre A (2004) Rethinking knowledge: a Bergsonian critique of the notion of tacit knowledge, British Journal of Management 15:177-188.

Suliman A, Iles P (2000) Is continuance commitment beneficial to organizations? Commitment-performance relationships: a new look, Journal of Managerial Psychology 15:407-426

Torrington D, Hall L (1998) Human Resource Management, 4th ed., Prentice-Hall, Hemel Hempstead

Wiener Y, Vardi Y (1980) Relationships between job organisation and career commitments and work outcomes - an integrative approach, Organisational Behaviour and Human Performance 26:81-96

Yin R (1994) Case Study Research, Sage, London

# Educational Management Information Systems: An Example for Developing Countries

John Traxler

University of Wolverhampton, Wolverhampton WV1 1SB UK
john.traxler@wlv.ac.uk

**Abstract:** In developing countries, mobile, nomadic and handheld technologies have the capacity to gather, store, deliver and enhance information in ways that are completely different from countries where mains electricity, computer hardware and internet connectivity are stable, reliable, cheap and abundant. They also have the capacity to subvert the received wisdom on IS development. This paper describes work currently under way in Kenya to support education nationally with a project specifically developed to meet the infrastructural and organisational requirements of an environment dramatically different that of most IS projects.

The work discussed in this paper is part of a project called SEMA! that was originally designed to support national in-service training. The University of Wolverhampton developed SMS messaging alongside audio and video cassettes developed with BBC support and print material developed with CEL support. The University of Wolverhampton has been working to bring together Kenya policy-makers, technologists and educationalists to develop a messaging targeted bulk SMS system for the 200,000 in-service teacher participants. This SMS system will help structure the study programme, address the isolation of distance learners and deliver learning simply, sustainably and cost-effectively. The technologies chosen are the most robust, appropriate and socially inclusive and the development process has been designed to promote dialogue and capacity across the various local communities of practice and expertise.

The project has revealed the sophistication and agility of the mobile phone networks in Kenya and of the developers of their 'value-added' services, and subsequent work, described in this paper, has been exploring the possibility of running much of the country's schools' statistical returns off SMS. Currently it seems that schools provide regular statistical returns to District and Provincial education offices and that these returns place a vital role in national planning and in the allocation of resources to individual schools. These returns are currently transmitted by letter-post, courier or by phone conversation. These are potentially slow, expensive and error-prone. Many or most of them are however never used, only stored. Further research has been undertaken to document the exact nature of the returns, the use to which they are put and the various ways in which they are submitted. The notion of using SMS as the main input medium and also the medium for exception-reporting is still very novel but a trial system has been specified, developed and trialled.

Trials are now underway to explore both aspects of large-scale SMS use. The project is supported by DfID, because of its relevance to models of appropriate mobile learning for the countries of sub-Saharan Africa, and is intended to explore regionally relevant solutions. More importantly, the project is intended to help build capacity locally and challenge models of ICT and IS rooted in Europe, the Far East and America. This account looks at developing IS capacity and is based on ongoing research and consultancy taking place in the UK and Kenya starting in 2004

**Keywords:** SMS, EMIS, sub Saharan Africa, appropriate technology, in-service teacher training, messaging, mobile phones

# 1 Introduction

Recent publications (Kukulska-Hulme & Traxler 2005), (JISC 2005) and recent conference proceedings (for example Attewell & Savill-Smith 2004) have put a large number of case studies documenting the use of mobile and wireless devices in education into the public domain. In looking at these, we can see in a forthcoming account (Kukulska-Hulme & Traxler 2006) some broad categories emerging:

- Technology-driven mobile learning
- Miniature but portable e-learning
- Connected classroom learning
- Informal, personalised, situated mobile learning
- Mobile training/performance support
- Remote/rural/development mobile learning.

The use of mobile and wireless devices to support the administration of education rather the delivery of education is however at an interface between mobile education as categorised above and conventional IS development. This paper looks at an ongoing project in Kenya where mobile devices will support educational administration and so takes place at an interface between development studies, conventional IS development and mobile education. This is not a well documented field because it falls between three rather different communities of practice.

# 2 Background

Most people including administrators, educators and their students are unaware of the fact that SMS text messages can be bought in bulk at a considerable discount. They are also unaware of the fact that SMS text messages can be written and sent from a conventional computer, for example a networked desktop PC or wireless-enabled laptop PC, using an interface no more complex than that of a standard office email client such as Eudora or Outlook. They can also be sent from web-enabled PCs in Internet cafes or business centres. This opens up enormous possibilities for using mobile phones, as cell phones are known in the UK, to enhance, supplement and support student administration and learning. It is also possible to write and send targeted bulk SMS text from a mobile phone itself and this means that learning can be delivered, supported and enhanced using mobile phones to generate bulk SMS text as well as receive it.

The underlying platform and technology for any sophisticated SMS text system is obviously built around phone networks and computer systems. The dominant model for delivering computer-based and network-based IS shares much of this technology and there is thus the possibility of IS that is based around the mobile phone blended with IS that is based around the computer.

# 3 Kenya and Sub Saharan Africa

In common with much of sub Saharan Africa, Kenyan physical infrastructure is characterised by:

- Poor roads and postal services
- Poor landline phone networks
- Poor mains electricity
- Little or no Internet bandwidth outside one or two major cities
    - Often just internet cafes or hotels in a few large cities
- Very few modern PCs or peripherals in the any of the public sector
    - And little or no user expertise, especially in smaller towns and rural areas.

These characteristics are often balanced by

- Lively and energetic mobile phone networks
- The potential for solar power
- A regulatory and licensing system in a state of flux
- High levels of mobile phone ownership, acceptance and usage

The two mobile networks in Kenya operate contrasting business models in their tariffs and coverage, and this is significant in terms of access and equity. Safaricom take the view that the base of the socio-economic pyramid, including obviously the less affluent rural areas, represent a massive business opportunity and price network access on a 'per second' basis to attract less affluent and more cost-conscious customers. Their competitors Celtel apparently take a different view and use a 'per minute' tariff that seems less economically effective in gaining market share. Both networks are extending their network coverage into rural areas and the limiting factor currently appears to be the rollout of mains electricity by the 'parastatal' producer and distributor.

Safaricom currently cover 70% of the country's population in 30% of the country's area. At a local level, coverage is still incomplete and unreliable and rural users often charge their phones and receive SMS text on their weekly trips to the local market town, often going first to a generator for electricity then to a hillock for coverage. There is a 'lively' market in imported 'grey' handsets exerting downward pressure on the cost of ownership and networks attempt to ensure subscribers can replace lost SIM cards quickly to keep business and maintain stability in the subscriber-base. Tariff structures mean many Kenyans use two phones (or SIM cards) to exploit intra-network calls and minimise inter-network ones.

As a prelude to the project with schools and in-service teachers, Digital Links International undertook a scoping study in the autumn of 2004 looking at aspects of ICT attitudes, access and usage amongst teachers in eight case study areas. This showed teachers to be likely early adopters of SMS technologies as soon as they received network coverage and generally an interest and acceptance of using SMS in learning (but that teachers would be understandably unhappy with SMS schemes that displaced messaging costs onto them). The study also considered the professional, institutional, logistical, and cultural and equity issues of access to information and communications technologies. In particular, it examined the likely feasibility and effectiveness of using multi-media to deliver the in-service training programme. The conclusion was that this approach would be successful, but would need careful organisation at district level to take into account the challenges posed by constraints in equipment and infrastructure.

There was almost universal interest among teachers in becoming computer literate and having access to computers. The potential of a laptop with Internet access as a resource for teacher advisory centre (TAC) tutors was widely recognised though the significance of the ongoing GPRS roll out went un-remarked. At this stage, there was no plan to support administration and information management using SMS and so sadly these issues were not raised with the Digital Links respondents.

## 4 Free Primary Education in Kenya

In January 2003, the new democratically elected Government of Kenya placed the highest priority on education, announcing the introduction of Free Primary Education (FPE) from January 2003. This led to an increase in primary enrolment of nearly one million, with the number of pupils increasing in individual schools between 10% and 25% and placing great demands upon the Ministry of Education (MoEST) at all levels. The subsequent fall of the school population pointed to a retention problem aggravated by over-crowding. A major challenge was the need to rapidly increase the numbers of trained teachers whilst at the same time improving the quality of the school system and using it as a vehicle for radical social and cultural transformation across issues including child-marriage and other tribal practices, endemic corruption, poor communications, an over-centralised education system and widespread adult illiteracy (and general poverty and disease). Underpinning much of this agenda was the need to monitor and manage school enrolment numbers at a local and national level.

In the course of 2003, the World Bank offered a grant of $55m to assist the implementation of Free Primary Education in Kenya. The World Bank's Free Primary Education Support Programme (FPESP) has four sub-components:

- school based teacher development
- school accounting system
- education management system (now called EMIS)
- system design and programme preparation

The School-based Teacher Development Program (SbTD) used distance learning, with face-to-face support to train the following groups:

- 35,000 additional Key Resource Teachers (KRTs) in Kiswahili and in Guidance and Counselling
- 54,000 already trained Key Resource Teachers
- 7,500 Head Teachers (HTs)
- 1,500 Teacher Advisory Centre (TAC) Tutors and Zonal Inspectors

Imfundo, a unit within DfID set up to use education and ICT to address extreme deprivation in sub Saharan Africa, supported the implementation of Free Primary Education (FPE) by the Ministry of Education Science and Technology (MoEST) in Kenya since September 2003. This support built on earlier engagement with the MoEST in the shape of the PRISM project dating back to 2002.

For the purposes of educational administration, the country is divided into Provinces. These are in turn divided into Districts and then Zones. A further subdivision into Clusters is now formalised.

## 5 The School Empowerment Programme

Imfundo helped the Ministry of Education, Science and Technology (MoEST) build capacity, specifically in the development of the School Empowerment Programme (SEP) as well as its predecessor the SbTD. Both were in-service distance learning programmes with content and delivery specifically intended to meet Kenyan needs. The BBC WIL supported Kenyan video, radio and sound studios produce video cassettes, audio cassettes and radio broadcasts, whilst the Centre for Educational Leadership (CEL) at Manchester University worked with local writers on print material. Imfundo's other priority, alongside in-service teacher training, was educational information management systems.

In discussion with the MoEST INSET team in 2003, the need for Imfundo support in developing the School Based Development Program was identified and endorsed. MoEST established a team of stakeholders. This team worked with Imfundo on the design and development of the School Based Development Program in Imfundo-facilitated workshops in September, October and December 2003 and in May and August 2004. With the support of Imfundo, the School Empowerment Programme was conceptualised. This directly targeted the 17,500 Head Teachers and the 54,000 Key Resource Teachers (KRTs) - that is the Head teacher and three KRTs from every school in the country.

The School Empowerment Programme, now being delivered, is a distance-learning course designed to develop the capacity of the whole school by training Head Teachers and Key Resource Teachers to deal with the challenges of Free Primary Education in Kenya. The programme will be mainly delivered through print-based material and supported by multi-media (audio, video and radio). The material is designed to meet the needs of two key groups:

- The Head Teacher materials will reflect the areas relevant to them in bringing about change in the school, working with the community, management, leadership etc.
- The Key Resource Teacher material will support classroom practice and delivering this training on to the rest of the teachers.

Imfundo is continuing its support to MoEST by assisting them to prepare to deliver high quality teacher training through new emerging ICT platforms and this now includes SMS mobile technologies in collaboration with the University of Wolverhampton. The attractions of an SMS component within SEP identified by the University of Wolverhampton consultancy included the fact that the costs of SMS included either

- Capital: negligible, unlike other ICT interventions, teachers buy or already own the necessary hardware or
- Running: minimal, basically discounted bulk SMS messages

The University was instrumental in drawing up the specification and requirements documents for the SMS component of SEP and for commissioning Cellulant, a Nairobi VAS company, to develop and deliver it. This SMS component was to be called SEMA!

## 6 Educational Management Information Systems

It became apparent during this requirements phase of SEMA! that there was also considerable potential for addressing problems associated with the statistical educational data needed to manage and finance the school system. Accurate and up-to-date statistical returns are needed from every school in order to allocate per-capita funding for the schools, to monitor schools for local and national attendance and enrolment problems and to provide central government with appropriate management information to support planning. At present, these returns reach the district and provincial offices by courier, by phone call and by post. This is often slow, error-prone and costly. Currently data analysis is often non-existent because of the central data entry overhead involved in transferring un-standardised paper-based returns to a computer system. The state of the computer infrastructure would mean large-scale analysis would still be vastly problematic even if data were entered.

Early proposals for implementing an improved educational management information system (EMIS) for Kenya's schools were based on annual, termly and monthly returns from each head teacher using 'instruments', that is questionnaires, that were paper-based, large and complex, and in parts seemed repetitive and ambiguous. They would feed into national statistics on a Provincial basis but this process in early trials was taking three months owing to data entry overheads. The slow return of these instruments from remote areas was further delaying the process by perhaps nine months. This makes intervention to prevent fraud very difficult and obstructs the accurate implementation of the orphan feeding programme (one in sixth children in Kenya's primary schools are orphans, depending on targeted government food aid.)

The precise nature of EMIS was still being defined and implemented but in broad terms, there were plans to capture enrolment, the most critical figure (or rather, the most critical set of figures), and a handful of other headline figures on a monthly basis for transmission to District and national HQ. The enrolment in fact unpacks to a set of figures giving enrolment by year and gender and perhaps by class or stream. There were proposals already being implemented to capture drop out, number of teachers on a quarterly basis and to capture physical infrastructure along with financial status and physical amenities on an annual basis. This information would be 'cleaned', processed and analysed using MS Access, but there are proposals to move to a more powerful database system running SQL.

It was agreed that SMS could provide solutions to this data gathering because mobile phones in each school could be used. Head teachers would merely send a standard format message each week or month, perhaps giving pupil numbers by age and gender, to a specified phone number. The system would automatically validate this incoming data (that is, check for any that were obviously defective) and message the sender in the event of any queries or anomalies. It could easily remind head teachers of late returns and could automatically message schools inspectors and ministry officials in the event of any pre-determined situations that might require personal intervention, such as a sudden decline in girl-child attendance in a particular school. This functionality would be supported by conventional data processing technologies hosted either in the networks' massive and secure servers or in the ministry itself and able to deliver routine management reports as emails to officials or as presentations available via secure access at Internet cafes or business centres.

Discussion of SMS proposals with EMIS representatives suggested that the monthly returns, which had yet to be implemented,  were clear candidates for SMS messaging, providing "snapshots for policy planners" (for grants, school feeding programmes, bursaries). There was considerable discussion of the message format for these monthly census returns from head teachers. One possibility was a terse, coded format compressing a week's data into one message; the other possibility was a verbose natural language dialogue. Major issues in choosing between these were cost, accuracy and user acceptance. A vital contribution that any computer-based system, including one based on SMS messaging, would make is data validation. Fortunately, it would be possible to validate the schools since each one has a unique MoEST ID: The composition of this is all numeric,

| Province | 1 digit | [1 ...... 8] |
| District | 2 digits | [01 ...99] |
| Division | 2 digits | [01 ....99] |
| Zone | 2 digits | [01 ... 99] |

followed by an individual school code, namely

| ECDE | 3 digits | [001 ....199] or |
| Primary | " | [200 ... 299] or |
| Secondary | " | [300 ... 399] or |

One major practical overhead with any large-scale or distributed SMS system such as SEMA! would be setting up the system, particularly capturing and entering all the head teachers' phone numbers and details. The details needed are the details that categorise the teachers and define the different potential targets groups for targeted bulk SMS. These details might include their districts, their names and their status. As a manual data entry problem, capturing and maintaining this volume of data would be prohibitively expensive and other solutions are needed. Fortunately the technology and the 'value-added services' (VAS) organisations had a solution: if the teacher can all receive one extra sheet of paper in their initial mailing the problem is solved. This piece of paper would ask them to send an SMS text to a specified number in a specified format, giving for example, their name, school, district, subject and role. These details would be transferred automatically to a database (effectively a searchable address-book) that would then underpin subsequent targeted SMS broadcasts and enable messages to be sent by district, by role etc. Extra check and perhaps manual authorisation based on a cascade system (i.e. each applicant would be authorised by the user immediately above them in the regional hierarchy) could be built into the system.

Recent changes in emphasis in the development community have moved away from un-coordinated and ad hoc projects, however worthwhile, towards embedding innovation within sector-wide planning. This is especially sensible in the case of large-scale IS projects where a system-wide perspective is paramount. The case for small-scale projects is not so much that they might scale up to larger projects or become incorporated into other parallel initiatives (they won't - it won't work!) but that they will serve to inform policy-makers and catalyse collaboration and discussion with educationalists and technologists. Small-scale IT projects in this context must be viewed as potentially 'throw-away prototypes'.

## 7 The Project So Far

Key findings from the first phase of consultancy undertaken by the University (February 2005) were:

- SMS texting is potentially an imaginative component of School Empowerment Programme delivery and support and, in the longer term, a viable and innovative technology for improving EMIS operations.
- The resources, expertise, systems and technology to develop this potential all exist locally and cheaply.
- There are simple arguments in favour of SMS in terms of its cost, speed and accuracy, and in terms of its educational power and flexibility and some reservations about current network coverage and reliability.
- Implementation of a large-scale SMS system to support and deliver education and administration would represent a considerable national asset in terms of know-how, reputation and profile.
- There is however insufficient awareness of the exact nature of these opportunities and challenges amongst the various different groups of potential stakeholders.
- There is therefore a strong case for further discussion and interaction between policy makers, budget holders, technical experts and teaching professionals to create and sustain the necessary synergy. In the coming months, the work of connecting the potential stakeholders must continue.

In the second phase of the consultancy started in September 2005, trials across about 170 schools in contrasting rural and urban areas are starting in two phases, the first in two of the Digital Links districts, Kajiado and Nairobi in May 2006, the second in the remaining districts later in the year. They will inform this process and move it forward. The procurement, training and set-up stages are currently underway (January 2006); messaging formats have now been agreed.

## 8 The Wider Picture

We conclude by exploring the wider significance of the project for IS in sub Saharan Africa and some of the wider but unanswered policy issues raised by IS in developing countries. The project raised a variety of questions and possibilities, for example:

- Inclusion
    - Will SMS and other mobile technologies within management enhance inclusivity
        - What about rural areas, different tribes and cultures
        - …. and what about female staff?
    - Should GPRS and other higher-specification less ubiquitous technologies be used to support exemplars of good IS practice at the expense of equitable low-specification GSM?

- Development
    - o    Do SMS and other mobile technologies have the potential to create a new paradigm for development
    - o    Must we re-enact Developed Countries' evolution of IS?
    - o    Does SEMA! point to the possibility of IS not building from static large-scale resources
    - o    How will wider social, economic and cultural problems interact with the development and delivery of IS?
    - o    Does capacity building fit comfortably alongside technical development and delivery
    - o    Do mobile and handheld technologies enable an alternative to the centralised, massive, static and expensive technologies and infrastructures of IS in the Developed World?
- Evaluation
    - o    What is the most efficient, appropriate, authentic, effective format for evaluating innovative IS in Developing Countries? (see Wagner et al 2005)
    - o    What forms of evaluation will provide evidence suitable for informing the donor community, and national policy-makers (see Crossley 2005)?

The next phase of the project will illuminate some of these issues.

# References

Attewell, J. & Savill-Smith, C. (2004). Proceedings of MLEARN2004, Lake Bracciano, Italy, London: LSDA

Crossley. M., Herriott, A., Waudo, J., Mwirotsi, M., Holmes, K. & Juma, M. (2005). Research and Evaluation for Educational Development – Learning from the PRISM experience in Kenya; Oxford: Symposium Books

JISC (2005), Guide to Innovative Practice in e-Learning, Joint Information Services Committee, London

Kukulska-Hulme, A. & Traxler, J. (2005) Mobile Learning: A Handbook for Educators and Trainers; Routledge: London,

Kukulska-Hulme, A. & Traxler, J. (2006) In H. Beetham & R. Sharpe (Eds) (2006). Rethinking Pedagogy for the Digital Age London: Routledge

Wagner, D.A., Day, B., James, T., Kozma, R.B., Miller, J., & Unwin, T. (2005) The Impact of ICTs in Education for Development: a Monitoring and Evaluation Handbook, Washington DC: infoDev

# Management Support Systems Design: A Competing Values Approach

Sven A. Carlsson and Jonas Hedman

Informatics, School of Economics and Management, Lund University
School of Business and Informatics, University College of Borås

## 1 Introduction

Management Support Systems (MSS) are computer-based systems that are supposed to be used by, or at least to support, managers. A major problem in MSS development is requirements specification. There exist a large number of systems development methods (SDM) (Avison & Fitzgerald 1999; Jayaratna 1994). Watson et al. (1997) point out that there are differences between traditional SDM and MSS development methods and that the former are not very useful in MSS development. In a study focusing on the MSS development methods used by organizations in the US, Watson et al. (1997) found that only two formal methods were used, namely: the critical success factors (CSF) method (Rockart 1979) and the strategic business objectives (SBO) method (Volonino & Watson 1990-91). They, as well as other less used methods, focus primarily on specifying managers' information needs and how an MSS can fulfill information needs. Although, they can be useful, they have one major limitation. Since they primarily focus on information needs they are not complete in generating MSS requirements. More complete needs requirements specification can be generated by focusing on managerial roles and how an MSS can support a manager's different organizational roles. We present an MSS design approach based on a current management theory and model. In doing so, we build on three postulates.

First, MSS is not a particular technology in a restricted sense, but primarily a perspective (vision) on managers and managing, the role of MSS and how to realize this vision in practice. Our approach is based on a well-established theory and model: the competing values model (Quinn et al. 2004). Second, it is a misconception to think of MSS as systems that just provide managers with information. MSS are systems that should support managerial cognition and behavior. Third, effectiveness is a critical construct in Information Systems (IS) research and practice.

Our approach is based on the competing values model (CVM) which has an effectiveness perspective.

The remainder of the paper is organized as follows. The next section presents CVM and MSS design. This is followed by a presentation of our CVM-based MSS design approach. The final section presents conclusions and suggests further research.

## 2 The Competing Values Model and MSS Design

The approach we took in developing our MSS design approach was to review some of the management literature. The assumption was that the review should point to areas in which MSS can logically aid managers. The theory/framework/model we will use build on the work of Robert Quinn and associates. The main reasons for using their work are:

- They present a comprehensive framework of management work and there is a strong link between their theory/framework and empirical studies.
- They address the link between how managers perform their managerial roles and performance (effectiveness).
- Their framework can be used to understand how MSS can support managers.

Organizational effectiveness is one of the foundations of management and organization theory, research, and practice (Lewin & Minton 1986). CVM was, in part, developed to clarify the effectiveness construct (Quinn & Rohrbaugh 1983). The CVM perceives organizations as paradoxical (Cameron 1986). It suggests that to achieve high performance requires an organization and its managers to simultaneously perform paradoxical and contradictory roles (Hart & Quinn 1993). The CVM incorporates three fundamental paradoxes acknowledged in the organizational effectiveness literature: flexibility and spontaneity vs. stability and predictability (related to organizational structure); internal vs. external (related to organizational focus); and means vs. ends (Quinn & Rohrbaugh 1983).

Quinn and Rohrbaugh (1983) found that most effectiveness measures reflect one of four organizational models: internal process (IP) model, rational goal (RG) model, open systems (OS) model, or human relations (HR) model. The four models provide competing views on organizational effectiveness. The *HR model* focuses on internal flexibility to develop employee cohesion and morale. It stresses human resource development, participation, and empowerment. The *IP model* focuses on internal control and uses information management, information processing, and communication to develop stability and control. The *RG model* focuses on external control and relies on planning and goal setting to gain productivity and accomplishment. The *OS model* focuses on external flexibility and relies on readiness and flexibility to gain growth, resource acquisition, and external support. An organization does not pursue a single set of criteria. Instead an organization pursues competing, or paradoxical, criteria simultaneously. Organizations are more or less good in pursuing the criteria, and, according to the CVM, organizations differ in their effectiveness (Denison et al. 1995).

Quinn (1988, Quinn et al. 2004) translated the construct of effectiveness into managerial roles—two for each of the four organizational models. In the *monitor role* (IP) a manager collects and distributes information (mainly internal and quantitative information), checks performance using traditional measures, and provides a sense of stability and continuity. In the *coordinator role* (IP) a manager maintains structure and flow of the systems, schedules, organizes and coordinates activities (logistic issues), solve house keeping issues, and sees that standards, goals and objectives, and rules are met.

In the *director role* (RG) a manager clarifies expectations, goals and purposes through planning and goal setting, defines problems, establishes goals, generates and evaluates alternatives, generates rules and policies, and evaluates performance. In the *producer role* (RG) a manager emphasizes performance, motivates members to accomplish stated goals, gives feedback to members, and is engaged in and supports the action phase of decision making.

In the *innovator role* (OS) a manager interacts with the environment, monitors the external environment (environmental scanning), identifies important trends, is engaged in business and competitive intelligence, develops mental models, convinces others about what is necessary and desirable, facilitates change, and shares "image and mental models." In the *broker role* (OS) a manager obtains external resources, is engaged in external communication, tries to influence the environment, and maintains the unit's external legitimacy through the development, scanning, and maintenance of a network of external contacts.

In the *facilitator role* (HR) a manager fosters collective efforts, tries to build cohesion and teamwork, facilitates participation and group problem solving and decision making, pursues "moral" commitment, and is engaged in conflict management. In the *mentor role* (HR) a manager is engaged in the development of employees by listening and being supportive, is engaged in the development of individual plans, and gives feedback for individual and team development.

After Quinn and Rohrbaugh's initial work, research on CVM has proceeded. For example, Denison et al. (1995), in a contingency-based study, empirically tested the CVM and the associated roles. They found support for the model and the roles, especially for managers that were considered high performing. Denison et al.'s study led them to define effective leadership as "...the ability to perform the multiple roles and behaviors that circumscribe the requisite variety implied by an organizational or environmental context."(ibid.). Based on the CVM and Denison et al.'s definition of effective leadership, we define an *MSS to be effective to the extent that it is used by a manager in such a way as to support the manager in his different managerial roles, and support managerial cognition and behaviors that circumscribe the requisite variety implied by the organizational and environmental context.* Hence, the goal of our approach is to be a guide in MSS design and should lead to the development of MSS which when used will lead to increased effectiveness.

## 3 A CVM-based MSS Design Approach

Figure 1 depicts our MSS design approach.

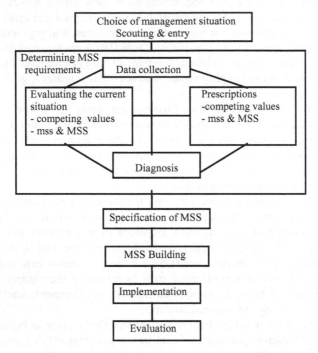

**Fig. 1.** MSS design approach

The approach starts with the choice of management situation, scouting and entry phase. It includes how to set up the MSS design project and finding sponsors and champions. The importance of this phase is stressed in the MSS literature and since a good body of knowledge on these issues exists we will not address the phase here (see, Watson et al. 1997).

Determining MSS requirements consists of data collection, evaluation of the current situation, diagnosis, and prescriptions. The third phase includes the technical specification of the MSS, which is followed by the building phase. We, as well as other MSS writers, have found it useful to use prototypes and to develop MSS iteratively. Implementation includes implementing the MSS, i.e. putting the MSS in the hands of the managers. It also includes education/training and especially for new users a hot-line (in some cases available on a 24 hours basis). The final phase is evaluation. Although, the figure shows a straightforward process, there are in most cases iterations between the different phases.

In the next sections we focus on the second and third phase, since these are the strengths of our approach and the most critical phases in MSS design.

## 3.1 Determining MSS requirements

This phase consists of four activities: the *collection of data* in order to *evaluate the current situation*, to be able to *diagnose*, and to *prescribe desired changes*.

*Evaluating the current situation*
Evaluating the current situation includes: 1) evaluating the competing values and what managerial roles are performed, and 2) evaluate the ess (non-computer based systems) used, and if an MSS is used, evaluate the use of it. To evaluate the current situation, different instruments developed and tested by Quinn and associates can be used (Cameron & Quinn 1998, Quinn 1988, Quinn et al. 2004). By using the instrument it is possible to evaluate what different managers perceive as the effectiveness constructs, which roles they perceive as critical, and how much effort they are putting into the different roles. In using our approach, we have, for example, used the "competing values leadership instrument: self-assessment" (Quinn 1988). This instrument captures a manager's perception of what roles he is playing and to what degree. We have also used the "competing values leadership instrument: extended version" (Quinn 1988). This instrument consists of 32 questions (behaviors) and a person completing the instrument has to, on a 7-point scale, respond to how frequently the person performs a specific behavior today and how often the behavior should be performed. The "competing values organizational effectiveness instrument" (Quinn 1988) has also been used—this instrument measures perceptions of organizational performance. The results can be presented for individual managers or as a summary of individual managers' perceptions.

In part, due to the problem of involving users (managers) in the design process, we have developed a supplementary way to identify the requirements for managerial behavior and cognition. Following the definitions of effective management and effective MSS, requirements for managerial behavior and cognition can be "derived" from an organization's external and organizational context. Three contextual characteristics can be used to identify requirements for managerial behavior and cognition: organizational environment, organizational strategy, and organizational structure. The following characteristics has been used: 1) for the external environment: turbulence, competitiveness, and complexity (Huber et al. 1993), 2) for the strategy: prospectors, defenders, analyzers, and reactors strategy (Miles & Snow 1978), and 3) for the organizational context: centralization of decision making, standardization of procedures, specialization of functions, and interdependence of organizational units and processes (Huber et al. 1993).

The purpose of evaluating ess and MSS use is to evaluate how ess (non-computer-based systems) and MSS are used by the managers. Using the CVM we can identify four ideal ess/MSS subtypes: MSS-IP, MSS-RG, MSS-OS, and MSS-HR (Figure 2). A specific MSS is a combination of the four subtypes. Here it is crucial to get perceived use and usefulness in relation to effectiveness constructs and managerial roles—this can be supplemented by logging actual use of the MSS.

The first subtype (MSS-IP) has an internal and control emphasis. The ends for MSS-IP are stability and control. Most functional and cross-functional quantitative

CBIS can be used as MSS-IP. Traditional accounting information systems and production systems are good examples of systems used for supporting the IP-model. In most cases the MSS-IP can be built "on top of" transaction-based IS (operational systems). From a manager's point of view the performance objective of MSS-IP is to provide user-friendly support for control and monitoring processes.

The second subtype (MSS-RG) has an external and control emphasis. MSS-RG should support a manager in handling semi-structured problems. Examples of MSS-RG capabilities and features are what can be found in "traditional" Decision Support Systems (DSS), i.e. support for goal setting, forecasting, simulations, and sensitivity analyses. Although many DSS have an individual focus, DSS can also be group-oriented (GDSS) and support management teams in e.g. strategic planning processes.

| **Human Relations Model** | | **Open Systems Model** | |
|---|---|---|---|
| | **Structure** | | |
| | | *Flexibility* | |
| Ends: Value of human resources | | Ends: Resources acquisition, External support | |
| Means: Cohesion, Moral | | Means: Flexibility, Readiness | |
| Systems characteristics and capabilities: Communication & conferences (CSCW & groupware) | | Systems characteristics and capabilities: Environmental scanning & filtering (vigilantly) Interorganizational linkages | |
| *Internal* | | *External* | **Focus** |
| Ends: Stability, Control Means: Information management, Communication | | Ends: Productivity, Efficiency Means: Planning, Goal setting, Evaluation | |
| Systems characteristics and capabilities: Monitoring & Controlling, Record keeping, Optimizing | | Systems characteristics and capabilities: Modeling, Simulation, Forecasting | |
| | | *Control* | |
| **Internal Process Model** | | **Rational Goal Model** | |

**Fig. 2.** Competing values model and systems characteristics and capabilities

The third subtype (MSS-OS) has an external focus and an emphasis on structural flexibility. MSS-OS supports a manager in identifying problems and possibilities by support for environmental scanning, issue tracking, and issue probing. Environmental scanning can be quantitative or qualitative oriented and can include: industry and economic trends, legislative issues, competitor activities, new product and process development, patents, mergers and acquisitions, alliances, national and international events.

The MSS-HR subsystem helps an organization and its managers in the development of the human capital of the organization. MSS-HR capabilities and features of importance are similar to what can be found in Computer Supported Cooperative Work (CSCW) systems and groupware. ICT, like e-mail, voice mail, and videoconferencing (increasingly IP-based) can be used in MSS-HR to overcome distance and time.

The above has been used in developing a number of instruments that can be used to evaluate ess and MSS use—the instruments are ideal instruments that have to be adapted to a specific context. The instruments—16-32 questions and 5/7-point scales—are used to have individuals to evaluate how frequently they use ess/MSS for performing specific behaviors (managerial roles) and the person's perceived value of the support (the ess/MSS). We have also in some cases asked the respondents to answer questions about an ideal situation.

Using the instruments and other informal methods and techniques it is possible to evaluate the current use of ess and MSS and the perceived usefulness.

*Diagnosis and desired changes (prescriptions)*

A good fit between the current situation and the desired situation (i.e. the managers see no need for a change and the support they receive is perceived to be good) means that there is no need for a new MSS. But, it is still possible to discuss the design of an MSS, but the primary purpose of the MSS would be to improve the efficiency—the MSS will primarily reinforce and improve the current state (MSS as a personal tool).

If there is a misfit between the current situation and the desired situation or there is a misfit between current support and desired support, then there is a possibility to develop an MSS. In this case the MSS will be used as a means (tool) for focusing organizational attention and learning as well as a means for organizational change (Watson et al. 1997, Vandenbosch 1999).

The result of the diagnosis phase will be recommendations concerning how the competing values should be changed and how an MSS should support the different managerial roles in the future. The result will be used in the next phase.

*Specification of MSS*

In the Specification of MSS phase desired changes will be transformed into MSS specifications; taking the requirements and specify MSS characteristics and capabilities. We now discuss how MSS can support the different managerial roles by looking at MSS capabilities and MSS information content. To discuss the usefulness of ICT for MSS we adapt a classification presented by George et al. (1992). They describe seven different ICT-based building components: 1) communication technologies are used to foster and support intra- and inter-organizational communication, 2) coordination technologies are used to coordinate resources, projects, people, and facilities, 3) filtering technologies are used to filter and summarize information, 4) decision making technologies and techniques are used to improve the effectiveness and efficiency of decision making processes, 5) monitoring technologies are used to monitor the status of organizational activities and processes, industry trends, etc., 6) data/knowledge representation technologies are used to represent and store data, text, images, animations, sound, and video, and 7) processing and presentation technologies are used to process data and present information. Figure 3 suggests the extent to which each of the seven ICT can be useful in building the different MSS subsystems. A specific MSS will be built using several building components.

| MSS subsystem Model: Building components / MSS Type: | Internal process MSS-IP | Rational Goal MSS-RG | Open Systems MSS-OS | Human Relations MSS-HR |
|---|---|---|---|---|
| Communication | ** | ** | ** | *** |
| Coordination | *** | ** | * | *** |
| Filtering | *** | ** | *** | * |
| Decision making | ** | *** | * | ** |
| Monitoring | *** | ** | *** | ** |
| Data/knowledge representation | ** | *** | ** | * |
| Processing & presentation | ** | *** | ** | ** |

Key requirement: ***
Somewhat useful: **
Little use: *

**Fig. 3.** ICT technologies for the four MSS subsystems

For MSS-IP the key capabilities are: 1) monitoring the status of organizational activities and processes, 2) filtering and summarizing critical information, and 3) support for coordination of resources, projects, people, and facilities. *Monitoring* support can be provided by using "standard" MSS software to build MSS for status access and exception reporting and enhanced with drill down capabilities. MSS can also include the use of data warehouses, multidimensional databases, and OLAP (On Line Analytical Processing) which, for example, can give a manager the ability to slice and dice a multidimensional database (datacube). Portals are becoming an almost universal MSS interface (Carlsson & Hedman 2004). A portal can be used to integrate an MSS with the organization's IS. In general, new capabilities make it possible to use traditional internal control systems more actively and in an ad hoc manner. *Filtering* support can be provided by using technologies for filtering and summarizing information from internal information sources. If an organization uses a data warehouse or data marts filtering can be done in the "extract, transfer, load" process and in the "analysis and presentation" process. In order to enhance this, software agents and push technology can be used. *Coordination* support can be provided by project management tools, electronic calendars, and workflow management systems. It is possible to use information generated in a workflow management systems to monitor workflows.

Managers in organizations acting in increasingly turbulent environment are likely to increase their use of internal real-time information (Bourgeois & Eisen-hardt 1988). Traditional MSS are often based on financial data, but many organizations are rethinking their performance measures. There is a shift from treating financial figures as the foundation for performance measurement to treating them as one among a broader set of measures (Kaplan & Norton 1996). Performance measures related to quality, customers, learning and growing, and even intellectual capital are increasingly used by organizations. Balanced Scorecard (BSC) software has been launched by a number of companies and BSC will probably be a standard feature of MSS software and Enterprise Systems (ES). ES can in part fulfill new information requirements. Alternatively, ES make it possible to in a simple way pipeline data from the enterprise system to, for example, a data warehouse that are used by an MSS.

For the MSS-RG three capabilities are key: 1) support for improving the effectiveness and efficiency of decision making processes, 2) data/knowledge representation, and 3) processing and presenting numerical data, text, images, animation, sound, and video. Capabilities found in traditional DSS and GDSS can be used for generating and evaluating more alternatives, do simulations and quantitative analyses. Many of a manager's decisions are single shot decisions where, for example, decision analysis tools can be used to get consistent decisions. Decision making technologies could also be used to support team meetings. GDSS can have tools for: electronic brainstorming, idea organization, voting, stakeholder identification and analyses.

For the MSS-OS two capabilities are key: 1) filtering, and 2) monitoring. Filtering techniques can be used to facilitate electronic communication applying artificial intelligence techniques to sort, distribute, prioritize, and automatically respond to electronic messages (Sprague & Watson 1996). There is also monitoring and filtering techniques to be used for environmental scanning. These techniques include, for example, the use of intelligent agents and push technology for scanning the internet. An example of this is robot-based detect and alert systems that monitor internal and external data sources and deliver alerts to the desktops of managers in the form of personalized electronic newspapers.

For the MSS-HR two capabilities are key: 1) communication for fostering and supporting individuals and teams, and 2) coordination. Coordination technologies, like project management tools and calendars, can be used to manage and organize the execution of decisions and processes. A major purpose of MSS-HR is to help a manager communicate information that will motivate and allow organizational members to be creative within defined limits of freedom (Simons 1995). Communication technologies can be used to communicate: 1) basic values, purposes, and direction for organizational members, and 2) codes of business conduct and operational guidelines. For these purposes ICT like e-mail, videoconferencing, electronic documents, and multimedia can be useful.

The output of this phase will be a specification of what should be built.

## 4 Conclusion and Further Research

We presented a new MSS design approach. The content of the approach builds on Quinn and associates' competing values model. The process of the approach builds on prescriptions found in most MSS writings, for example, the importance of having sponsors and champions, the iterative process, and the use of prototypes and exemplars. The approach has been used successfully in practice.

Future research on our approach will include the development of better instruments and better support for the second and third phase. Future research will also include empirical studies addressing the relationship between MSS use and support for managerial cognition and behavior and how this is linked to individual and organizational performance.

## References

Avison D, Fitzgerald G (1999) Information Systems Development. In WL Currie and B Galliers (eds.) Rethinking Management Information Systems, Oxford University Press, Oxford, pp. 250-278.

Bourgeois LJ, Eisenhardt KM (1988) Strategic Decision Processes in High Velocity Environments: Four Cases in the Microcomputer Industry. Management Science, Vol. 34, pp. 816-835.

Cameron KS (1986) Effectiveness as Paradox: Consensus and Conflict in Conceptions of Organizational Effectiveness. Management Science, Vol. 32, pp. 539-553.

Cameron KS, Quinn RE (1998) Diagnosing and Changing Organizational Culture. Addison-Wesley Longman, Reading, MA.

Carlsson SA, Hedman J (2004) From ERP Systems to Enterprise Portals. In F Adam and D Sammon (eds.), The Enterprise Resource Planning Decade: Lessons Learned and Issues for the Future, Idea Publishing, Hershey, PA, pp. 263-287.

Denison DR, Hooijberg R, Quinn RE (1995) Paradox and Performance: Toward a Theory of Behavioral Complexity in Managerial Leadership. Organization Science, Vol. 6, pp. 524-540.

George JF, Nunamaker JF, Valacich JS (1992) ODSS: Information Technology for Organizational Change. Decision Support Systems, Vol. 8, pp. 307-315.

Hart SL, Quinn RE (1993) Roles Executives Play: CEOs, Behavioral Complexity, and Firm Performance. Human Relations, Vol. 46, pp. 543-574.

Huber GP, Sutcliffe KM, Miller CC, Glick WH (1993) Understanding and Predicting Organizational Change. In GP Huber and WH Glick (eds.), Organizational Change and Redesign, Oxford University Press, New York, pp. 215-265.

Jayaratna N (1994) Understanding and Evaluating Methodologies. McGraw-Hill. London.

Kaplan RS, Norton DP (1996) The Balanced Scorecard. Harvard Business School Press, Boston, MA.

Lewin AY, Minton JW (1986) Determining Organizational Effectiveness: Another Look, and an Agenda for Research. Management Science, Vol. 32, pp. 514-538.

Miles RE, Snow CC (1978) Organizational Strategy, Structure, and Process. McGraw-Hill, New York.

Quinn, R.E. (1988) Beyond Rational Management: Mastering the Paradoxes and Competing Demands of High Performance. San Francisco, CA: Jossey-Bass.

Quinn RE, Cameron KS (eds.)(1988) Paradox and Transformation: Toward a Theory of Change in Organization and Management. Ballinger, Cambridge, UK.

Quinn RE, Rohrbaugh J (1983) A Spatial Model of Effectiveness Criteria: Towards a Competing Values Approach to Organizational Analysis. Management Science, Vol. 29, pp. 363-377.

Quinn RE, Faerman SR, Thompson MP, McGrath MR (2004) Becoming a Master Manager, Third edition. John Wiley & Sons, New York.

Rockart JF (1979) Chief Executives Define Their Own Data Needs. Harvard Business Review, Vol. 57, No. 2, pp. 81-93.

Simons R (1995) Levers of Control. Harvard Business School Press, Boston, MA.

Sprague RH, Watson HJ (1996) Decision Support for Management. Prentice-Hall, Upper Saddle River, NJ.

Vandenbosch B (1999) An Empirical Analysis of the Association Between the Use of Executive Support Systems and Perceived Organizational Competiveness. Accounting, Organizations and Society, Vol. 24, pp. 77-92.

Volonino L, Watson HJ (1990-91) The Strategic Business Objectives Method for Guiding Executive Information Systems Development. Journal of Management Information Systems, Vol. 7, No. 3, pp. 27-39.

Watson HJ, Houdeshel G, Rainer, RK (1997) Building Executive Information Systems and Other Decision Support Applications. Wiley, New York.

# Activity Based Costing System for a Medium-sized Trade Company

Arkadiusz Januszewski

Department of Management Information Systems,
University of Technology and Agriculture in Bydgoszcz, Poland
arekj@mail.atr.bydgoszcz.pl

## 1 Introduction – Assessment of Profitability in Trading Enterprises

Market competition drives companies at searching for new clients. Small and medium-sized entities often accept any client that would be willing to acquire their products, commodities and articles. However, there are numerous examples when not all customers render benefits, but some of them causing losses as well (Kaplan 2000), (Zielinski 2005). This seems to be a challenge for those companies that produce differentiated products or deal with customers who demand sophisticated packaging or special terms and distance deliveries (Cokins 1996), (Cokins 2001).

In trade companies there is no need to account for production costs because all activities are preformed to ensure the exact running of purchasing and selling processes. This is why proper accounting for costs of dealing with clients is of highest importance for those entities.

Small and medium-sized trade companies practically analyse only their gross margin, i.e. the difference between revenue from sale and the cost of goods sold. This kind of margin takes into account neither costs of dealing with customers nor costs of cooperation with suppliers. As a result, it does not allow them to assess if a customer or supplier is ultimately profitable or not.

The proper measurement of profitability of customers is achievable with application of activity-based costing (ABC) that was first elaborated by the end of 80-ies of the last century (Johnson 1987), (Cooper 1988), (Kaplan 1988). This method logically accounts for costs of resources (i.e. vehicles, premises, employees, etc.) with straight connection to its true usage in different processes and activities. Costs of products are differentiated due to various use of manufacturing activities by products, whereas costs of dealing with clients are shaped by a wide range of activities that are necessary to satisfy clients.

## 2 The Reason for Applying and General Architecture of an ABC System For a Medium-sized Trading Company

There are two main reasons why implementation of activity-based costing in small and medium-sized trade companies is recommended.

First, simplified ways of recording only cost by nature do not support any deeper analyses of clients profitability than up to gross margin. Hence, there is no way to know whether clients are really profitable or not. As a result, customers who contribute much to the welfare of the company (but of that we really do not know) might be handled with non-sufficient care and those that yield less or nothing could be given exaggerated concern. That was exactly the case of many enterprises before they applied ABC.

Second, due to less complexity of the model the implementation of ABC into small and medium-sized trading companies can potentially be easier than that into big production firms. The final shape of ABC model for a small (medium) enterprise is relatively simple and thus doable in principle by one or two consultants in several weeks. Not excessively complex scope of data required for necessary computations can be obtained with relative simplicity as well.

The implementation procedure in an IT environment can be relatively easy and time-reduced. An IT system that supports ABC in a small or medium-sized trade company is of less compound architecture and needs less input data than it is in the case of a producer (figure 1). The latter requires complex data not only from the area of purchasing and selling but first of all from that of production. It is not easy to obtain data necessary for ABC purposes even from production modules of systems of an MRP II class. Another difficult task for production companies is to develop a proper way of accounting for costs of running and maintaining the machinery and equipment (Januszewski 2006). In a trade company the above mentioned problems do not exist at all.

The aims of this paper are to: present the model of ABC for a medium-sized trade company, describe its implementation in an IT environment and discuss the outcomes returned. The model is designed to assess profitability of clients and suppliers. The returned outcomes fully justify the theses put forward at the beginning of the paper.

Examples of other models of ABC that have been proposed by the author for other food processing companies are described in: (Januszewski 2003), (Januszewski 2004) and (Januszewski 2005).

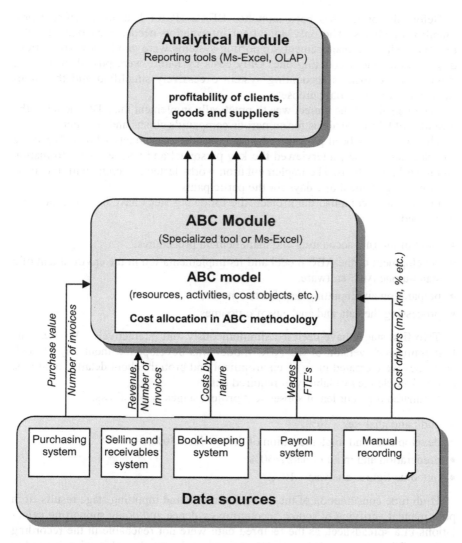

**Fig. 1.** Data Flow and Architecture in an ABC System For a Medium-sized Trading Company

## 3 Steps of the Project

The researched company, named BERG HURT, employs 50 people. Its core business focuses on trade in sweets and snacks all over Poland. The company has round 400 retail chain markets and wholesale clients as well as 6 own retail outlets seated in supermarkets. Deliveries are secured by over 100 contractors – established brand producers of sweets and snacks.

Before the project has been launched BERG HURT had not calculated profitability of clients. The only analytical information needed was that on sales revenues. The sole management supporting systems were goods flow (reception-dispatch) one and accounting one. Only costs by nature were posted in the GL, making the company's accounting system excessively simplified and thus non-sufficient for managerial purposes.

The main aim of the project was to practically implement the ABC model in the area of profitability analysis for numerous company's clients and suppliers.

The project has been performer by two outsider consultants who analyzed the company's processes, interviewed the key personnel and verified the information and recording systems. The implementation works lasted 3 months with the average week engagement of 2 days for the participants.

In order to accomplish the project, the following steps have been planned and performed:

- audit of internal accounting and management procedures,
- development of the ABC model and its implementation in the environment of a stand-alone ABC software,
- preparation and inputting data for the model,
- processing the data and analysis of outcomes.

Two first stages have been led simultaneously and interactively. Whereas the first framework version of the ABC model was developed without any IT tool, next ones were created in an IT environment and brought about detailed analyses, as for example the availability of required data.

Estimated time burden of subsequent project stages is as follows:

- audit and analyses – 30%,
- development and implementation of the model – 30%,
- preparation and input of data – 30%,
- outcome figures analysis – 10%.

High time consumption of the data preparation and inputting stage results from pure manual verifying of source accounting evidence and doing supporting calculations in a spreadsheet, as the required data were not reachable in the recording system of the company. For example, reports on the number of invoices issued to every client or the number of invoices received form every supplier were not produced in the company's systems, and additional calculations were needed in order to establish the purchase cost of goods sold to each client as well. The author's experience acquired at previous projects shows that IT tools being in application in small and medium-sized companies very often do not support even basic managerial reporting.

## 4 The Development and the Implementation of the Model in the Environment of a Stand-alone ABC Software

In order to build the ABC model, the project team had to:

- identify the objects for costing and profitability measurement purposes,
- analyze processes and activities in the domains of purchases, sales and distribution, transport, commerce, administration and management,
- categorize company's resources and costs thereof,
- define activities that are required by particular cost objects,
- define resources that are used up by particular activities,
- decide on how to allocate costs of resources to activities and costs of activities to costs objects.

The critical analysis of trial balances of cost and revenue accounts from the book-keeping system, revision of purchases and sales reports as well as personal interviews have been applied as distinguished methods in managing the project.

In the course of defining the ABC model the essential difficulty was to match costs recorded in the general ledger to the respective resources. In order to do this, 30 types of resources categorized into 7 groups had been identified. Next, costs by nature have been matched to particular resources. Additionally, 5 main business processes and 22 activities in total have been defined and matched to resources that are used up and consumed by particular activities. Cost objects are the last unit in the ABC model. The project team isolated over 500 of cost objects categorized in 4 groups. Almost 10 000 relationships between the elements of the model have been identified. They depict flows of costs by nature to respective resources and further through activities to suppliers and customers. The overall structure of the model is shown in the figure 2.

The OROS Modeler was the IT environment the model has been based upon. OROS is a part of SAS ABM software package developed by SAS Institute and is said to be one of most popular tools of the *stand-alone* type for ABC modelling (Miller 2000). OROS Modeler has been taken as an example tool, and the beneath description is to illustrate the way the ABC model has been implemented which is quite similar in any other *stand-alone* environment.

The structure of the ABC model is as follows:

- Costs of resources – unit: "Resources",
- Costs of activities – unit: "Activities",
- Costs of cost objects – unit: "Cost Objects".

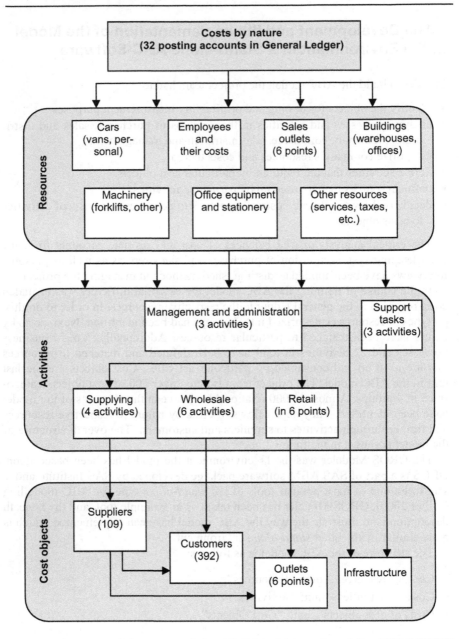

**Fig. 2.** The General Structure of the ABC Model Developed for BERG-HURT Company

In any unit of the package cost centers together with cost accounts nested therein can be defined. Amounts of costs come out as totals of costs by nature.

In the next step, cost allocation paths have been defined. A cost allocation path is a procedure that links aggregated costs by nature to target accounts. Examples of cost allocation paths are depicted on Figure 3.

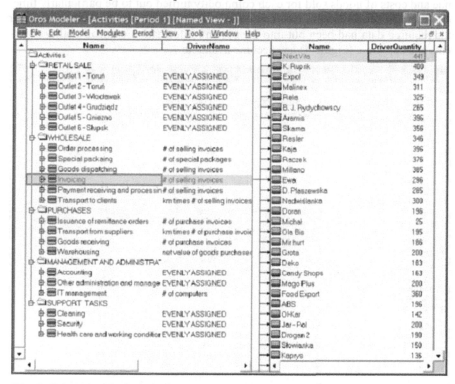

**Fig. 3.** Example of Allocation from "Activities" to "Cost Objects"

After the costs allocation paths had been defined, cost drivers have been established and matched thereto.

In the last step, views of profit and profitability have been designed by including additional columns into the "Cost Objects" view:

- Costs of Goods Sold (CoGS),
- Net Sales Revenues (NSR),
- Contribution Margin I (NSR – CoGS),
- CM I ratio (CM I / NSR * 100%),
- Contribution Margin II (NSR – CoGS – Client-related Costs),
- CM II ratio (CM II / NSR * 100%).

For its proper running the model has to be provided with the following data:

- costs by nature,
- cost drivers of resources and activities,

- net sales revenues and costs of goods sold.

The identification of cost drivers figures together with recording of sales revenue and costs of goods sold for each commodity turned out to be particularly time-consuming and challenging processes in the course of applying the model. After the required data had been put into the system, information on profitability of clients and suppliers (Figure 4) has become available.

| Name | Net sales revenue | Costs of goods sold | CM I | CM I ratio | Client-related Costs | CM II | CM II ratio |
|---|---|---|---|---|---|---|---|
| Cost objects | | | | | 1 546 722 | | |
| RETAIL CLIENTS | 538 378 | 249 432 | 288 946 | 53.7% | 168 258 | 120 688 | 22.4% |
| Outlet 1 - Toruń | 53 279 | 26 194 | 27 085 | 50.8% | 30 291 | -3 206 | -6.0% |
| Outlet 2 - Toruń | 108 135 | 49 491 | 58 644 | 54.2% | 18 917 | 39 727 | 36.7% |
| Outlet 3 - Włocławek | 125 108 | 53 518 | 71 590 | 57.2% | 36 600 | 34 990 | 28.0% |
| Outlet 4 - Grudziądz | 119 889 | 55 640 | 64 249 | 53.6% | 34 820 | 29 429 | 24.5% |
| Outlet 5 - Gniezno | 51 738 | 24 165 | 27 573 | 53.3% | 15 022 | 12 551 | 24.3% |
| Outlet 6 - Słupsk | 80 229 | 40 424 | 39 805 | 49.6% | 32 608 | 7 197 | 9.0% |
| WHOLESALE CLIENTS | 14 462 717 | 12 483 270 | 1 979 447 | 13.7% | 1 073 844 | 905 603 | 6.3% |
| Next Vita | 601 527 | 499 267 | 102 260 | 17.0% | 30 955 | 71 305 | 11.9% |
| K. Rupnik | 574 092 | 476 496 | 97 596 | 17.0% | 18 692 | 78 904 | 13.7% |
| Expol | 551 009 | 468 357 | 82 652 | 15.0% | 23 963 | 58 689 | 10.7% |
| Malinex | 555 675 | 472 324 | 83 351 | 15.0% | 26 604 | 56 747 | 10.2% |
| Rela | 377 446 | 313 280 | 64 166 | 17.0% | 22 017 | 42 149 | 11.2% |
| B. J. Rydychowscy | 318 684 | 270 882 | 47 802 | 15.0% | 18 476 | 29 326 | 9.2% |
| Aramis | 311 351 | 258 421 | 52 930 | 17.0% | 22 505 | 30 425 | 9.8% |
| Skarma | 289 033 | 251 459 | 37 574 | 13.0% | 16 412 | 21 162 | 7.3% |
| Resler | 279 794 | 237 825 | 41 969 | 15.0% | 17 544 | 24 425 | 8.7% |
| Kaja | 275 289 | 233 995 | 41 294 | 15.0% | 19 465 | 21 829 | 7.9% |
| Raczek | 243 020 | 206 567 | 36 453 | 15.0% | 16 355 | 20 098 | 8.3% |
| Millano | 226 363 | 194 672 | 31 691 | 14.0% | 23 545 | 8 146 | 3.6% |
| Ewa | 204 357 | 173 704 | 30 653 | 15.0% | 13 953 | 16 700 | 8.2% |
| D. Płaszewska | 205 995 | 175 096 | 30 899 | 15.0% | 10 584 | 20 315 | 9.9% |
| Nadwiślanka | 198 833 | 169 078 | 29 755 | 15.0% | 12 306 | 17 449 | 8.8% |
| Doran | 192 768 | 163 853 | 28 915 | 15.0% | 6 956 | 21 959 | 11.4% |
| Michał | 181 196 | 157 641 | 23 555 | 13.0% | 11 828 | 11 727 | 6.5% |
| Ola Bis | 183 306 | 155 810 | 27 496 | 15.0% | 13 534 | 13 962 | 7.6% |
| Mir hurt | 165 679 | 142 484 | 23 195 | 14.0% | 12 045 | 11 150 | 6.7% |
| Grota | 166 565 | 141 580 | 24 985 | 15.0% | 6 559 | 18 426 | 11.1% |
| Deko | 173 664 | 152 824 | 20 840 | 12.0% | 17 623 | 3 217 | 1.9% |
| Candy Shops | 151 874 | 132 131 | 19 743 | 13.0% | 16 290 | 3 453 | 2.3% |

**Fig. 4.** "Contribution Margin and Contribution Margin ratios" view

# 5 Analysis of Profitability of Clients and Suppliers

During the researched year 2004 the company generated contribution margin I (or gross margin) at the amount of 2,230 KPLN, i.e. an average of 15.1% of sales (see table 1). This margin is the difference between sales revenue and costs of goods sold. It does not consider any operational costs and can be calculated without ABC on the base of the goods flow system. For retail the CM I/S ratio was significantly higher (53.7%) than that for wholesale (only 13.7%). Those dissimilarities in margins have to some extent been erased by taking into account operational costs of dealing with clients (and cooperation with suppliers – see table 1) at the amount of round 1,250 KPLN. The average CM II was at 6.8% of sales, whereas the retail channel returned 22.4% of sales against 6.3% in the case of wholesale.

**Table 1.** Profitability on Clients

| Item | Wholesale | Retail | Total |
|---|---|---|---|
| Net sales revenue | 14 462 717 | 538 378 | 15 001 095 |
| Costs of goods sold | 12 483 270 | 249 432 | 12 732 702 |
| Contribution Margin I (CM I) | 1 979 447 | 288 946 | 2 268 393 |
| CM I/S ratio (%) | 13,7% | 53,7% | 15,1% |
| Client-related costs | 1 073 844 | 168 258 | 1 242 102 |
| CM II | 905 603 | 120 688 | 1 026 291 |
| CM II/S ratio (%) | 6,3% | 22,4% | 6,8% |

Source: own research.

Additional analyses revealed that only one retail outlet (a newly-opened) operated a negative margin (-6%) and another one generated an impressive margin of 36%, whereas last 4 outlets scored from 22% to 28% of CM II.

Analysis of margin for 392 wholesalers delivered extremely interesting outcomes (see figure 5).

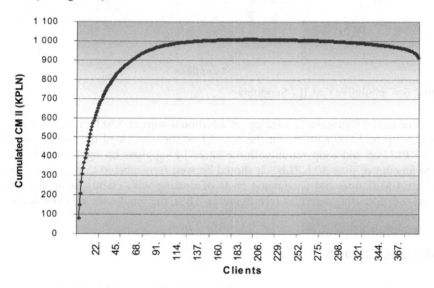

**Fig. 5.** Cumulative CM II – wholesale clients

Round 20 of them (5% of total wholesale clients) generated CM II in the joint amount of 500 KPLN. Next 100 of them (25% of the total number) yielded next 500 KPLN. It additionally turned out that when costs of dealing with clients are taken into account, near to 66% of wholesalers (249) do not return any profit and one eighth of them (12.5%) cause losses. As a result, the total CM II generated by first 120 wholesale clients has been lowered from above 1,073 KPLN to slightly above 900 KPLN.

Similar analysis can be performed for suppliers. It revealed that benefits from purchasing at different sources can be very dubious. The graph depicting cumulative contribution margin II for suppliers (figure 6) shows that not more than 6 best suppliers (out of 109) boosted the CM II to as much as 950 KPLN which is slightly over a half of the total.

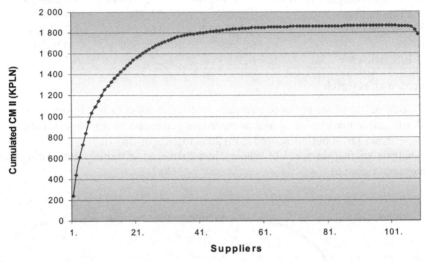

**Fig. 6.** Cumulative CM II - Suppliers

The next 35 suppliers added up an additional sum of 850 KPLN, building the CM II up to 1,800 KPLN. But the next 54 of them elevated the margin only by 62 KPLN up and cooperation with the latter 14 suppliers brought about losses at the amount of over 80 KPLN. It should be well remembered that in case of suppliers CM II does not encompass costs of dealing with clients or other indirect costs of supporting activities (see figure 2). Thus, the real losses are even deeper.

# 6 Conclusions

One of important parts of company information system is the sub-system of cost accounting. Information received from that sub-system is a base for profitability assessment and decision-making in the portfolio of products and cooperation with clients. When modelling a company's information system great emphasis should be put on the choice of proper costing method aimed at returning true figures. Neither advanced technologies, nor well-projected information flows, nor sub-systems integration could be a sole factor ensuring obtaining true information aimed at answering the basic questions about whether articles are profitable or clients yield profits or not.

For trading companies the recommended method of accounting for client-related costs is ABC. As the paper shows, benefits of its application can be traced both in big enterprises with complex distribution chains and in small ones as well.

The following conclusions can be drawn from the realization of the project:

- The cost recording system in small and medium-sized firms is of little use for management purposes. The provided information can be significantly distorted and hence the assessment of profitability of activities can be mistaken or impossible.

- Advantages of the project are irresistible – now the company has real knowledge about the efficiency of its suppliers and clients. ABC yields different profitability figures for various clients and suppliers and thus creates the base for decision-making in the field of cooperating with them.

- Similarly to author's other ABC implementation projects for SMEs, in this case the most complicated stage was again that of getting required data for proper costing procedures but not that of designing the model, the main reason for that being the lack of satisfactory reports in the company's recording systems. So again it is a very true opinion that simplified accounting recording systems used by SMEs are major obstacles for quick ABC implementation.

- For ABC modeling a specialized tool is worth applying. Even in small- or medium sized trade companies there are a lot of elements and relationships between them in an ABC model. So in the author's opinion a spreadsheet would not be a sufficient tool to succeed.

# References

Cokins G (1996) Activity-Based Cost Management. Making It Work, McGraw Hill, pp. 20-22

Cokins G (2001) Activity-Based Cost Management. An Executive's Guide, John Wiley & Sons, Inc., New York 2001, p.100

Cooper R, Kaplan RS (1988) Measure Costs Right: Make the Right Decisions, Harvard Business Review, September-October, pp. 96-103

Januszewski A (2006) Rozliczenie kosztów produkcji z wykorzystaniem pakietu OROS Analytics. In: Komputerowo zintegrowane zarządzanie, Vol. I, Oficyna Wydawnicza Polskiego Towarzystwa Zarządzania Produkcją. Opole, pp.521-529

Januszewski A (2003) Zastosowanie oprogramowania OROS Modeler do modelowania rachunku kosztów działań w przedsiębiorstwie przetwórstwa mięsnego. In: Nowoczesne technologie informacyjne w zarządzaniu, Prace Naukowe AE we Wrocławiu nr 986, Wrocław, pp.471-488

Januszewski A (2004) Komputerowo wspomagany model rachunku kosztów działań dla firmy garmażeryjnej, In: Acta Universitatis Lodziensis, Folia Oeconomica 183, Łódź, pp.59-68

Januszewski A, Kujawski J (2005) Using SAS ABM Package for ABC Modelling – a Case Study. In: Proceedings of the 2005 International Conference on E-Business, Enterprise Information Systems, E-Government, and Outsourcing, EEE'05, Ed. H.R. Arabnia, CSREA Press, Las Vegas, Nevada, USA, June 20-23, pp.45-50

Johnson HT, Kaplan RS (1987) Relevance Lost: The Rise and Fall of Management Accounting, Harvard Business School Press, Boston

Kaplan RS (1988) One Cost System Isn't Enough. Harvard Business Review, January-February, pp.61-66.

Kaplan RS, Cooper R (2000) Zarządzanie kosztami i efektywnością, Dom Wydawniczy ABC, Kraków, pp.245-246

Miller JA (2000) Zarządzanie kosztami działań, WIG-Press, Warszawa, p.172-175.

Zieliński T (2005) Wieloryby w dystrybucji – wykorzystanie systemów ABC/M. Controlling i rachunkowość zarządcza, No. 11, pp.45-49

# Managing a Software Development Organization with a TQM Approach for Balance in a Period of Rapid Growth

Mirja Pulkkinen* and Marko Forsell**

*University of Jyväskylä, Information Technology Research Institute, P.O. Box35, FIN-40014 University of Jyväskylä, Finland, pulkkinen@titu.jyu.fi
**SESCA Innovations Ltd. iPark Vaasantie 6, FIN-67100 Kokkola, Finland, marko.forsell@sesca.com

**Abstract:** Software organizations rely on quality models designed for their specific purposes, the Capability Maturity Model Integration (CMMI) being the most prominent model to follow. However, in striving for both product and process quality in their activities, small and medium sized enterprises with a limited legacy of organizational culture and tradition in quality work, may profit from quality frameworks following the Total Quality Management (TQM) principles. The ISO quality standards (the 9000 series) provide such principles. A further framework suggested by the European Forum for Quality Management (EFQM) also gives a set of principles to follow. In a case study, we investigate how the principles of the EFQM model can be translated into practical use in a relatively young but rapidly growing software company. We suggest a "double bladed" quality tool to be used by small and medium sized software organizations: supporting the managerial work with TQM principles derived from the EFQM, together with process improvement efforts following the CMMI model.

**Keywords:** Software Organization, Management, Total Quality Management, Quality Standards, EFQM, CMMI

## 1 Introduction

An expanding organization faces many challenges. The efforts towards better performance and capability improvement up to the standards of a quality model are hampered by the complexities of the organizational change process necessarily following the growth. In this study we investigate the quality management efforts at SESCA Innovations, an SME class company finding itself in an organizational change period including acquisitions and organic growth. The company philosophy is characterized by a determination to follow the principles of quality management. We suggest points to consider that would promise a smoother and better managed change promoting growth and high quality processes and products.

In the software business, several stories are told of quick rises and unfortunately, as quick falls of small software companies. For a company wanting to pursue sustainable growth and capability development instead of cashing in on quick revenues in a time of a sudden market expansion, careful management considerations are needed. For companies in the software business, field specific quality models like the CMMI® model [2] provide guidance for the improvement of process and product quality. However, it seems that these models are at their best in organizations that have passed the earliest phases of organizational growth and established their structures of management and organization of activities [6], or are finding themselves in an evolutionary rather than a revolutionary change [8]. In the process of establishing a new organization, and also in the later phases of organizational growth and development, quality management principles provide reliable guidelines for overcoming the growth crises.

This case study analyses the situation at SESCA Innovations as it is in the beginning of the year 2006. SESCA Innovations is facing a situation where there are new customers and new business models and there are different kinds of quality requirements from customers. These situations are not handled well by the current processes that were created with ISO 9001 guidance. In a series of interviews and using a survey of employee satisfaction, points to consider were distilled. By synthesizing management literature and TQM principles suggestions are made how to find a balance and stabilize the overall efforts towards a better managed software organization with high quality processes and products.

From the inquiry and employee satisfaction survey, some areas for investigation emerged as research questions for the study.

- How to organize and manage work during and for the purpose of change without losing quality focus?
- How to enable quality thinking and quality work at the daily work level of individual developers?

Behind these questions were several observations. Firstly, there was a huge need for the developers to actively inquire for the information they need for their work in order to keep their development updated and to follow the best practices of software development. Also, they needed initiative and to organize their work themselves. All this was perceived as a challenge to the management.

To the managers, on the other hand, the new situation presented challenges of time management, a re-distribution of work and responsibilities causing the need for active inquiry and learning of the new responsibilities, and last but not least, communication.

These were particularly emphasized since the software development organization is now partly distributed over several sites. This issue became a research area in its own right, with an emphasis on communication and collaboration in distributed software development environment [1].

The paper is structured as follows: In section 2, background information on SESCA is summarized. In section 3, the research method and the European Foundation for Quality Management (EFQM) is presented. In section 4, the results are presented and analysed from the quality management point of view with the EFQM criteria. In section 5, the study is summarized. Further, concluding thoughts and directions for further inquiry are presented.

The current research undertaking is part of a collaborative research project called MODPA (Mobile Design Patterns) that deals with software and process patterns in software development organizations. This study was conducted during the second project year concentrating on software processes and their improvement.

# 2 SESCA Innovations' background

## 2.1 History

The history of SESCA Innovations starts in the year 1998 when SESCA Technologies was established. SESCA Technologies aimed right from the beginning for rapid growth, and expansion has always been one of the guiding principles of the organisation. SESCA Technologies has been the fastest growing IT and software company in Finland three years in a row (2002, 2003 and 2004) according to the Finnish business magazine Talouselämä. SESCA Technologies employed 130 people at the end of 2005.

The growth, however, was based on one industry sector only, namely telecommunications and this was seen as a risk. This issue was addressed in 2004 by buying 39% of the engineering company AVECON which had customers in the process industry. A year later the stock-owners of SESCA Technologies and AVECON established SEVECON Group which owned both SESCA Technologies and AVECON.

SEVECON Group has continued its growth strategy and has bought and established five more companies. SEVECON's strategy is to combine skills in IT and automation so that it can produce services for telecommunication, process and energy sectors. With these acquisitions, spin-offs and organic growth SEVECON employed more than 300 people at the beginning of 2006 and is still committed to growth.

Over the period of three years SESCA Technologies has grown from 30 employees to be a part of a group with more than 300 people. To maintain growth two spin-offs were created from SESCA Technologies at the beginning of 2006. SESCA Innovations focuses on operators and SESCA Solutions on industrial software production.

Together these three companies are called SESCA companies. They still share many of their administrative activities and all of them share together ISO 9001:2000 quality certification.

## 2.1 Quality Work

At SESCA, a high level of quality in products and processes is seen as a key success factor. Quality has been articulated for organizational internal interpretation at SESCA as follows: "To fulfill the customers' needs in the agreed time, and with the available resources. This includes the price the customer is willing to pay, the time frame given for the task, and the capabilities and skills the company has to offer."

The main concern in SESCA's case is to enhance the quality of the software engineering process

- To make the processes more repeatable, stable, smoother and faster.
- Quality assurance is sought for solving new problems, which are unique at the time.
- These new problems need to be solved effectively and efficiently according to the customer's expectations
- The individual solutions must be of good quality to enable the produced module to have high quality as well.

To achieve these goals, there is a need for self-directed inquiry and learning, in which the employees need to be guided.

SESCA has been certified according to ISO 9001:2000 –certificate and a current goal is CMMI certification. This means that quality is measured and indicated by the practices of CMMI. The target is to implement quality practices from bottom-up rather than top-down. This means, that individuals and teams are at the centre of the quality practices, in contrast to the processes at organisational level.

Product quality is achieved through efficient process performance. Component and pattern based development is believed to contribute to the product quality and is strongly encouraged.

Although customers are important for the company, the employees are the prerequisite of the company success. Individuals and teams are seen as key factors for process performance, thus the well-being of individuals is emphasized in the internal values of the company.

## 3 Research Method

The material for the study was collected in October 2005 – February 2006 in interviews (telephone and face-to-face) with a top manager of the company. The semi-structured interviews [5] covered the topics of:

- The quality policies and standards in use
- Software development methods in use
- Process improvement efforts and their state
- Perceived problems in the processes

- Perceived problems in the development projects
- Development target refining for the current research effort.

The interviews were conducted by two researchers. Notes were taken and later discussed with the interviewee to ensure a common understanding. This means following the principle of negotiated text [5]: the researcher and the subject co-structuring the interpretation.

At the same time, a survey of employee satisfaction was conducted in the company internally. The survey of employee satisfaction summarized issues that are considered to be in good shape and issues that need improvement. The following issues were considered to be in good shape:

- There is no harassment
- Physical environment is excellent
- Employees feel that they are trusted, they want to develop themselves and their skills in SESCA, SESCA is continuously improving its operations and that SESCA emphasizes customer service
- Employees trust that SESCA will excel in the future
- Employees know what their project team is trying to achieve
  On the other hand, following issues need to be improved in the future:
- Internal communication
- Collaboration between different locations
- Education and familiarization with work and training opportunities
- Work's contribution to the company's vision and ability to achieve goals with current work

The results were discussed with the employees and during those discussions it became evident that SESCA is a company that employees feel proud of working for and they want to continue working for it. On the other hand, the main improvements that need to be made are in delegation, empowerment and communication. Employees feel that they can take more responsibility and they want to know more about what is happening in the other SEVECON Group's organizations.

The interviews and employee satisfaction survey results are analysed through The European Foundation for Quality Management (EFQM) criteria and the points to consider or issues to improve are given.

EFQM is an independent association that supports European organisations in striving for better quality in their activities and within society as members of it. This model was chosen for this study because it provides a European approach, being to an extent more easily adaptable to small and medium sized companies than other models. It is understood that all organizations, and their stakeholders, despite the size of the organization, profit from a quality approach.

The EFQM quality model consists of eight "excellence" areas that represent different, interrelated aspects of activities and management. These eight quality criteria help the companies to focus their efforts to achieve a better overall quality and to improve their performance. The areas are highly interdependent. As the

Total Quality Management concept suggests, it is not possible to achieve a high overall performance by improving only one of the areas but finding a balance is essential. In Table 1 (below), the EFQM criteria are presented.

**Table 1.** The EFQM quality criteria and the related concepts

| THE CRITERION | THE CONCEPT |
| --- | --- |
| 1. Results orientation | Excellence is achieving results that delight all the organisation's stakeholders. |
| 2. Customer focus | Excellence is creating sustainable value for customers. |
| 3. Leadership and constancy of purpose | Excellence is visionary and inspirational leadership, coupled with constancy of purpose. |
| 4. Management by processes and facts | Excellence is managing the organisation through a set of interdependent and interrelated systems, processes and facts. |
| 5. People Development and Involvement | Excellence is maximising the contribution of employees through their development and involvement. |
| 6. Continuous Learning, Innovation and Improvement | Excellence is challenging the status quo and effecting change by utilising learning to create innovation and improvement opportunities |
| 7. Partnership Development | Excellence is developing and maintaining value adding partnerships. |
| 8. Corporate Social Responsibility | Excellence is exceeding the minimum regulatory framework in which the organisation operates and to strive to understand and respond to the expectations of their stakeholders in society. |

The EFQM excellence criteria highlight the issues that are important in striving for a balance between different stakeholder interests: the customers, shareholders, employees at all levels as well as other stakeholder groups found in the immediate community and wider society. In the following, the problem areas recognized at SESCA are discussed in the light of the criteria that were found relevant with the current challenges.

## 4 The Results and Implications in the Case of SESCA Innovations

In this section, we compare the findings in the company with the EFQM criteria presented above. Practical suggestions are made to overcome and avoid problems of a growing organization. It is evident that the problems map to only part of the criteria, this is why not all of the criteria are discussed thoroughly.

## 4.1 Results Orientation

SESCA is conscious of the interests of its stake-holders, and is willing to move forward in all aspects.

- The current organizational development stage is favourable for this, and taking advantage of this fact can be recommended.
- It seems to be well understood that quality improvement means primarily seeking a balance between different interests. In further development efforts seeking a balance is essential.

## 4.2 Customer Focus

The SESCA quality definition (see above) is in accordance with this criterion. In this study, we focus more on the internal factors of the software organization.

# 5 Leadership and Constancy of Purpose

Good leadership principles are shown in the values of the company. It also demonstrates good leadership to search for process improvement possibilities and individual and organizational learning possibilities. Consistency of purpose is confirmed over time. Leadership and the managers' role is found to be crucial in any quality effort and organizational development. With the given problem statement, the following suggestions are made:

- For good leadership, the persons in leading positions need to focus on their own time management as a priority. Drucker [4] has stated that a manager needs to first take care of himself and his own time management before he can take care of his/her subordinates. Also, Drucker [3] states that in order to manage others one has to first manage him or herself.
- Managers who only recently took their position and prior to that had a lower position and possibly (more) involvement in production tasks may lack the trust and skills to delegate. However, efficient management means task division and taking time for the management itself, even though the manager would still be partly involved in production related tasks.
- With changes in the organization, a transparent division (re-allocation) of roles and responsibilities helps, and it is advisable to be kept transparent. Follow up to find shortcomings in the task division is essential.
- A new task causes time pressure both for those leaving a task and those taking up a new task. Not everyone learns as quickly – and not in the same way. A knowledge of learning styles would help to avoid frustrations; e.g. some people prefer learning alone, others prefer learning in a group, or with a supervisor.

Leadership is essential in providing an environment where everyone can and will perform at their best. This reflects on all other areas, but very significantly on Criterion 5, People Development and Involvement as well as Criterion 6. Continuous Learning, Innovation and Improvement. Leading people to enable them to develop to the best of their potential is the challenge. The importance of leadership is also confirmed in further criteria.

## 5.1 Management by Processes and Facts

### Processes

The OTSA process (SESCA's software development process) was found to be in need of updating. Negotiating the process and going into the procedure of updating it to the common framework of reference of the new organization would be a good opportunity now that the company has been upgraded (mergers and spin-offs have taken place) and organizational changes have been made. It could help in unifying different parts of the organization and in bridging the distances within a distributed development environment.

Comparing the company SE practices to the SE best practices currently available, is a possible way to improvement. The development of a common method or a commonly defined software engineering process can be undertaken incrementally with the help of a chosen quality model and by working in steps towards a common software engineering framework, process and deliverables at the conceptual level.

It is a challenging task to genuinely raise the organizational maturity level since true organizational change takes place in a time frame of 3-5 years. However, starting right away with small steps takes you there sooner than ignoring the need for changes.

### Facts

Measurement has been introduced – it is advisable to consider well what and how to measure. It has been observed that measuring has a wash-back effect on the activities measured, so it is a powerful tool in guiding the work. Standardized tools (e.g. the Goal Question Metrics, GQM) can be of help. Having defined processes will give a basis for the process metrics.

## 5.2 People Development and Involvement

The values reflect a very positive atmosphere, so SESCA is likely to be strong in this area of quality. The company is committed to its employees. The value the company produces is understood to be created by the people. The current research effort can be seen as an attempt to bring the reflection of work to the personal level. The challenge is to bring the quality thinking to the grassroots, the daily work of individuals. This can be achieved by paying attention to the following Senge [7]:

- Recognition of people in ways suitable to the company culture.
- Sharing the visions and (to an extent) the concerns of the manager both in informal communication and formally on a regular basis.
- Draw people to decision making. Empowerment and responsibility for arranging their own work also motivates people and allows "inner entrepreneurship".
- Encouraging the organization of self-directed teams for learning.
- Dedicate time to training where necessary and follow up the results.

## 5.3 Continuous Learning, Innovation and Improvement

In the values the search for innovation and a willingness to learn to support both individual and organizational learning is stated. Also, SESCA has proved to have organizational capabilities by obtaining the ISO 9001 quality certificate. This study was a further practical attempt to challenge the current situation and seek for ways to learn and improve the organization.

Organizing support for both teams and the whole organization in the form of shared work spaces and communication over various text based channels, like emails, Messenger and chat is a start in collecting an organizational memory. Along the way it can be considered how to organize the memory, and how to create defined bases of information, so that when substantial collections are available they can be stored in an organized way.

## 5.4 Partnership Development

As a growing company, SESCA is becoming more attractive to its business partners. Current relations will be extended to further collaboration if the company continues in a well managed way. Partnership development is likely to be one of the future focus areas in quality efforts.

## 5.5 Corporate Social Responsibility

SESCA is taking its responsibility as an employer and pursuing ethical values. The company is making an impact through the expansion of its activities.

## 6 Conclusions

This study set out with the target of investigating a balanced approach to the software process improvement in organizational change caused by rapid growth. The case organization already had previous experience in quality work and had taken on SPI effort following the CMMI model. However, some development targets remain unattained with the process based approach of the software industry quality model. Although the current version of the model also covers managerial and administrative practices, the model is essentially created for measuring achievement, not for finding ways to improve.

Total quality management models by definition cover managerial perspectives. The European Quality Forum Model (EFQM) was taken as a starting point and problematic areas were reflected against this framework. This brought to light some general managerial concerns, the consideration of which helps in finding a balance between different stake-holders' interests. Management literature provides more profound insights for these considerations. Together with managerial principles and quality efforts, organizational learning issues are found essential on the way towards maturing capabilities.

The main finding of our study is that a software organization is well advised to support their managers in revising their own work and mindset. It seems that clear vision and multiple communication channels and situations can overcome some of the problems created by rapid growth. Management literature provides good insights into time management, people management, leadership, change management and other challenges presented by a rapidly growing organization in a period of change.

Maybe the most important factor in a successful company both in quality management terms and in terms of organizational learning is the commitment of the management to continuous improvement and also the commitment of the management to both its own learning, and to creating an organizational culture that encourages and enhances individual learning. It is important that the management also shows learning capabilities. This can be shown very well in taking immediate actions regarding employee feedback or in giving more responsibilities and empowering to employees.

The principles of the EFQM give directions for improvement in the respective fields of management. The emphasis in this is on the quality of processes, whereby the quality of the products and services is improved; Firstly, indirectly through the enhanced processes, but also directly through active inquiry by the developers. An organizational environment that supports learning enables this. Also, the employees are actively involved in improving the organizational activities when empowered to do so. An exchange for the sharing of information is actively supported with communication and collaboration tools. The employees are trusted to be responsible for their immediate work organization and the personal software process. All these factors enhance the work climate and can create a relaxed atmosphere that in turn enables individuals to perform at their best.

# References

1   Ahlgren, Pulkkinen, Berki and Forsell (2006). Using Groupware Technologies to Facilitate Organisational Learning and Software Process Improvement – A Case Study. EuroSPI 2006. forthcoming

2   Chrissis, M.B., Konrad, M., & Shrum, S. (2003). CMMI Guidelines for Process integration and Product Improvement. Boston: Addison-Wesley.

3   Drucker, P. (2001) The Essential Drucker. HarperBusiness.

4   Drucker, P. (2006) What Executives Should Remember. Peter F. Drucker, 1909–2005 Harvard Business Review, Vol. 84 Issue 2, p 144-152.

5   Fontana, A., & Frey, J.H. (2000). The Interview: From Structured Questions to Negotiated Text. In N. K. Denzin & D. Linthicum (Eds.), Handbook of Quali-tative Research (pp. 645-672). London: Sage.

6   Greiner, L.E. 1972. Evolution and revolutions as organizations grow. Harward Business Review, July-August.

7   Senge, P., (1992) Building Learning Organizations. In: Journal For Quality and Participation, March 1992, pp. 57-71.

8   Pettigrew, A.M., (1990) Longitudinal Field Research on Change: Theory and Practice. Organization Science, Vol. 1, No. 3, 267-292.

9   The European Foundation for Quality Management EFQM (2003): EFQM Excellence Model © 1999 – 2003, EFQM.

# Knowledge Management in Higher Education: A Case Study in a Large Modern UK University

Anne Slater and Robert Moreton

University of Wolverhampton, UK

## 1 Introduction

This paper considers knowledge management concepts as applied in UK higher education. The IT Services Department at the University of Wolverhampton is then analysed in terms of current structure and practises with a view to identifying a knowledge management strategy. The analysis of the case study was undertaken using interviews of key staff, papers relating to a recent re-organisation and current strategic priorities.

A set of guidelines for developing knowledge management in IT Services which have been accepted by the Director of IT Services are then presented. The guidelines are a product of the current strategic priorities of the department and indicate how knowledge management practices could improve current performance and inform future initiatives and ideas.

## 2 Knowledge Management Issues in Higher Education

In 1998, the UK Government published a White Paper (DTI, 1998) which spelt out proposals for encouraging UK competitiveness in the global market. The Government identified the role of Universities as crucial to fostering collaboration and innovation. A further White Paper in 2000 (OST, 2000) indicated that advances and investments in science and technology needed to take place, with Universities at the hub of these developments. Clearly, Universities are considered centres of knowledge (and teaching) and, as Rowley (2000) points out, they inevitably display a "significant level of knowledge management activities". However, the 'cult of the individual' is still very strong in academia and universities do not provide seamless access to all the resources available within the institutions. Much of the vast wealth of knowledge and power remains with individual academics or groups. Therefore, although universities possess the elements of successful knowledge-led organizations, the current situation does not necessarily provide a cohesive and integrated model. A significant shift in approach and thinking is required to develop appropriate collaborative and team-based working. As Rowley (2000) states "Although knowledge based organizations might seem to have the most to gain through knowledge management, effective knowledge management may require significant change in culture and values, organizational structures and reward systems."

## 3 Knowledge Management in IT Services at the University of Wolverhampton

An analysis of current beliefs and priorities within IT Services was undertaken by interviewing a select number of staff in the department (Slater, 2002) and by reviewing published strategic priorities, in conjunction with a survey of the literature concerning knowledge management theory and practices. A set of guidelines for developing knowledge management in IT Services was submitted to the Departmental Director and was formally accepted (in March 2002). To place the guidelines in their context, it was necessary to identify current practices in the department that could provide a solid basis for a strategy in knowledge management.

### 3.1 Knowledge Management Practices in IT Services

In February 2002, the department introduced a long-term framework of strategic and operational priorities for IT Services, which acknowledges that University priorities are changing over time. The University has recently, for instance, introduced Business Process Modernisation (BPM) to review and improve processes across the institution, with student records as the first priority. Using a generic approach, it was possible to identify the practises and beliefs that prevailed in the department which could contribute to developing a cohesive and effective knowledge management strategy.

#### *Identify the Business Goal or Objective*

An analysis of IT Services with respect to knowledge management revealed several practices that were consistent with an underlying knowledge management approach although without reference to a specific strategy. An awareness of knowledge management principles influenced some of the initiatives that had been implemented in the department. Previous experience indicated that such approaches are most successful when they are aimed at improving a specific process, which can be terminated when that project has met the stated objectives, to enable a flexible approach to successful service management.

### Identify Existing Knowledge

Following the re-organisation of IT Services, a number of projects were initiated to develop the quality of the skills and services within the department. These projects were based on the proposals for skill development and balancing made by the team responsible for re-organising the department and were represented by a Knowledge Cube (Figure 1).

One such project resulted in an initial Training Needs Analysis for every member of staff, designed to develop a training plan for the department. Another project, Agenda for Change: Critical Actions, specifically aimed to develop a framework within which knowledge management takes place, including skills matrices, technical standards, problem solving, training and development and skill sharing.

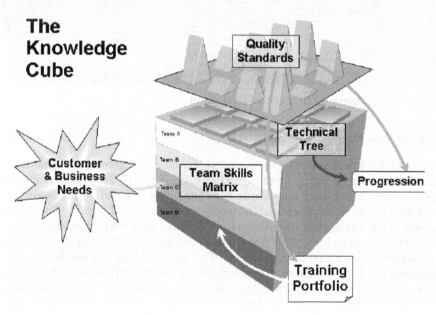

**Fig. 1.** The Knowledge Cube

One outcome of the project resulted in skills matrices (Figure 2) designed to represent skills levels within each team in the department, to highlight areas that required further training and as a visible indication of existing expertise in the department. The skills matrices have never been fully embraced by all staff in the department, however, and some view them with suspicion in the belief that identifying a lack of skills could have a negative impact on their position.

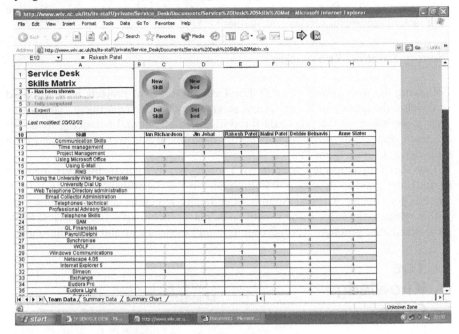

**Fig. 2.** Skills Matrix for the Service Desk team

## Create New Knowledge

A central theme in knowledge management literature is to nominate a specific role to manage the information in an organisation. In 2001, IT Services appointed an Information Co-ordinator whose role is to anticipate information needs and present the current, accurate and useful results in an accessible format. Through the efforts of the Information Co-ordinator, IT Services staff were encouraged to provide information and resources that could be published on the staff intranet to develop knowledge within the department. This was achieved in a number of ways, including the development of a technical library and the introduction of short current awareness seminars. Gradually, staff were encouraged to contribute to the body of knowledge within the department so that this has become an accepted practise without the need for direct intervention by the Information Co-ordinator and senior management.

## Share Knowledge

In June 2000, another project was submitted to the department (Slater, 2000), designed to identify lines of communication within IT Services by mapping out existing links between teams and to highlight areas where communications failed in some measure or simply did not exist. Several problematic areas were identified and the report proposed a number of recommendations for improvements. Examples would include issuing mobile phones to each technical support team to enable contact in an emergency and the development of the Project Register for IT Services (Figure 3) a public, web-based project register to identify the status of all projects undertaken by the department.

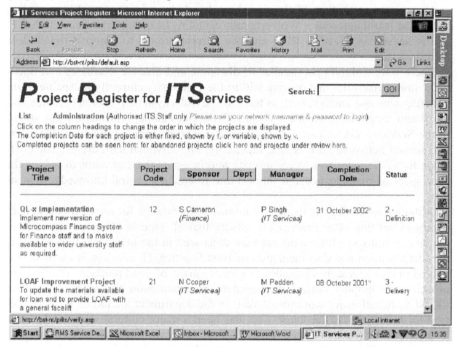

**Fig. 3.** Project Register for IT Services (PRITS)

The report also recorded positive feedback from IT Services staff in support of the information provided on the IT Services intranet, the monthly meeting for managerial staff within the department and shared diary facilities. Several of the respondents also referred positively to the introduction and impact of the call logging and tracking function provided by the IT Service Desk and associated software.

Increasingly, IT Services staff were encouraged to collaborate and share knowledge and experience to provide a seamless and effective service. There are several procedures in place that are intended to document and recognise this contribution. During the re-organisation process, the Progression scheme, again based on the Knowledge Cube (Figure 1), was developed to identify and document capabilities across a number of categories including technical competence, team working ability and customer service skills. Staff are rewarded for their achievements by progression through certain pay scales.

## Utilise and Retain Knowledge

Technology is essential to a successful knowledge management strategy in terms of storage, distribution and access. As the technology providers for the University, IT Services has the capability to provide innovative and appropriate technological solutions for the advancement of knowledge services both within the department and across the institution. IT Services has already been instrumental in providing the online learning resource Wolverhampton Online Learning Framework (WOLF) and is heavily involved in BPM and the current project to improve the student records system.

There were a significant number of disparate and discrete databases and document storage facilities that operate within the University currently incapable of interacting with one another, such as the staff payrolls system, personnel records and email and telephone directories. Within IT Services alone, information was stored in the Service Desk software, the online commercial training resource, the intranet, several networked drives and, inevitably, on individual hard drives. The challenge for IT Services was to co-ordinate and integrate these systems to reduce the time spent on maintenance and support and to create a central knowledge repository.

Although technology is the key to retaining knowledge for reuse, it is also necessary to develop other practices to ensure that all aspects of knowledge are retained and utilised. One useful exercise discussed in the literature (BSI, 2000) is the identification and documentation of Best Practice. IT Services is currently involved in two approaches intended to identify areas of good practice. The first approach is to employ project management documentation techniques, based on PRINCE, for all major work undertaken in the department, including a review period for reflection and feedback. This has been a major cultural shift for the staff in the department and is sometimes difficult to maintain when working in conjunction with staff from other departments. Another important factor to the project management approach is that each individual can potentially contribute knowledge or expertise to a project without reference to their position in the hierarchy. Therefore, the project team can be drawn from any group in the department that has the appropriate skills and knowledge.

Another method of identifying best practice and reusing knowledge employed within the department is the series of Guidance Notes (Figure 4) which document common tasks produced by individual members of staff with acknowledged expertise in the area. The Guidance Notes present a series of step-by-step instructions enabling less knowledgeable members of staff to undertake a task without significant supervision.

## Measure Knowledge

At the outset of this project, IT Services did not explicitly engage in measuring knowledge-based activities in the department, although the RMS Inventory Project was subsequently initiated to improve the reporting functions in the Service Desk software. One of the objectives of the improvements was to enable IT Services to identify trends and requirements in order to establish a flexible and proactive service. This was complemented by a project to identify levels of customer satisfaction with the service they receive and provide a vehicle for feedback to enable IT Services to make adjustments where necessary.

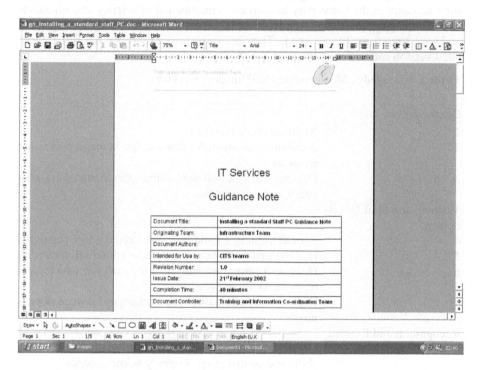

**Fig. 4.** Example of a Guidance Note

# 4 Pursuing a Knowledge Management Strategy

At the time of the study IT Services did not subscribe to a formal knowledge management strategy and the practises that have been identified were as a result of a common sense approach to departmental management with an appreciation of the significance of training, collaboration and team working. The preceding literature review and examination of the case study provided the context for the guidelines and evaluation of knowledge management analysis models.

## 4.1 Guidelines for Developing Knowledge Management in IT Services

The guidelines are intended to suggest strategies and techniques that could be adopted to improve the management of knowledge both within the department and for customers in the University to increase departmental efficiency and effectiveness. These guidelines were submitted to IT Services and University management and have been formally accepted. They are summarised in Table 1, a fuller annotated version can be found in Slater, 2002.

**Table 1.** Knowledge Management Guidelines - Overview

| Organisational Issues | |
| --- | --- |
| 1 | Audit current capabilities |
| 2 | A mission statement for Knowledge Management is not essential |
| 3 | Develop an organisational culture that sustains collaboration and participation |
| Training and Staff Development | |
| 4 | Formal training should be considered for key personnel |
| 5 | Use external collaboration to boost internal capability |
| 6 | Develop a formal training plan for each job which identifies the skills required |
| 7 | Explore the potential for job exchanges between departments |
| Recognition and Reward | |
| 8 | Create a trusting and open environment in which staff skills and contribution is openly acknowledged |
| 9 | Reward need not be in the form of financial remuneration |
| 10 | Publicly recognise who is considered an authority on a subject and who has contributed their knowledge to the department |
| Staff Profiling | |
| 11 | Expand staff information to identify interests and expertise |
| Staff Participation | |
| 12 | Encourage staff to participate in organisational activities |
| 13 | Organise role swapping within the department to increase understanding |
| Knowledge Interviews | |
| 14 | Conduct a formal interview before an employee leaves the department |

| | |
|---|---|
| 15 | Conduct a formal interview to identify new skills |
| 16 | Use a mixture of expertise to gain information at the interview |
| **Project Management** | |
| 17 | Store and organise project documentation centrally |
| 18 | Appoint an official recorder to document all project meetings and feedback |
| **Customer Profiling** | |
| 19 | Develop profiles of customers in the University referring to the specific support requirements |
| 20 | Develop access to details of external suppliers and contacts |
| 21 | Monitor customer satisfaction |
| 22 | Become involved in the recruitment and training of staff in other departments supporting standard University sity hardware and software |
| 23 | Produce a regular report of activities to promote public relations |
| **Measurement** | |
| 24 | Benchmarking should not be adopted immediately |
| 25 | Create a repository for recorded best practice |
| **Tools and Resources** | |
| 26 | Research existing and emerging technology to develop the IT Services web site |
| 27 | Increase awareness of knowledge management solutions |
| 28 | Use data mining to identify useful information that already exists |
| **Current Awareness** | |
| 29 | Document all technological activities |
| 30 | Use a technical library to improve access to information |
| 31 | Promote current awareness using lunchtime seminars |
| 32 | Use interest groups to encourage and develop awareness of new and emerging technology |

It was clear that IT Services engages in a number of practices that encourage the creation, sharing and utilisation of knowledge in the department. These initiatives all enjoy the encouragement and support of not only senior management within the department but also, in some cases, support at the level of University Executive. IT Services is in the fortunate position of being able to demonstrate innovation and good practice in terms of knowledge management to the institution, supported by a cohesive and stable IT environment.

## 4.2 Implementation Issues

During the eighteen months constituting the research period for this project, IT Services demonstrated substantial developments in knowledge management. For example, an Information Co-ordinator was appointed with subsequent improvements in departmental documentation and information resources. Although this initially seemed to invalidate much of the preparation for the guidelines, it actually enabled a much wider and more comprehensive set of recommendations than would have been possible twelve months previously. Given the nature and pace of changes in the University and within the department, there is also only a brief period when the guidelines are fully relevant. As new initiatives are introduced, some guidelines will become more pertinent than others.

Since the guidelines have been submitted, there have been a number of occasions where their influence has been noticeable. A programme of current awareness seminars has been established covering a number of IT related topics, including one on knowledge management. Another telling example is a poster advertising IT training courses organised by IT Services recently displayed around the University with the comment "Knowledge is Power". As the guidelines are more fully assimilated within the department, further and more far-reaching initiatives are expected.

The first guideline recommends that IT Services should include an audit of its KM capabilities. To facilitate this, three KM analysis modules were evaluated (Slater, 2002). Although the evaluation focused on just three of the many knowledge management analysis models available, the issues addressed provide a useful focus should IT Services undertake a knowledge management audit. There were few methods in knowledge management described in the literature to facilitate such an evaluation, unlike other computing methodologies. Coupled with the lack of formal guidelines or standards, this situation compeled an organisation wishing to pursue a knowledge management strategy to undertake a significant amount of research or employ consultancy services. Both options can be expensive in terms of resources and can lead to the ultimate failure for implementing successful and practical knowledge management solutions.

The IT Services Director committed to pursuing the recommendations in the guidelines, in conjunction with Training and Information Co-ordination team, to formally. The guidelines have been considered in their entirety as a means of improving knowledge management within the department. This proposal has enabled IT Services to embrace a holistic and cohesive approach to a successful knowledge management strategy, incorporating the appropriate technological solutions, that will improve internal performance and serve as an example to the wider University community.

# 5 Conclusion

The aims of the research project were to evaluate knowledge management concepts and to produce a set of guidelines and recommendations to introduce or improve knowledge management within the department.

## 5.1 Knowledge Management: Key Success Factors

The discipline of knowledge management is concerned with storing, distributing, identifying, using, creating and measuring knowledge within an organisation. As the literature indicates (Slater and Moreton, 2002), simply building data repositories such as databases and intranets does not constitute a cohesive and successful strategy and this approach is ultimately doomed to failure. An organisation wishing to pursue knowledge management must create a trusting and open environment that encourages and supports the sharing of knowledge with appropriate rewards and recognition. In addition, for a knowledge management approach to be successful, an organisation must endeavour to realise the potential of the knowledge and expertise that already resides with their employees and implement methods of retaining that knowledge for the benefit of the organisation. Technology plays a critical role in facilitating solutions to the knowledge requirements of an organisation, enabling employees to gain access to the required information quickly and efficiently and submit their own contributions in return.

## 5.2 Knowledge Management in IT Services

The analysis of IT Services in the context of knowledge management concepts discussed in the literature identified a number of practices that provided a firm foundation for pursuing a knowledge management strategy. The guidelines proposing a series of recommendations for improving knowledge management within the department received a positive reception from all concerned, both formally and informally. The evaluation of the knowledge management models provided further context for the issues that must be addressed to implement a successful strategy. As the information technology provider for the University of Wolverhampton, IT Services is ideally placed to investigate implementing a knowledge management strategy with appropriate and innovative technological solutions, to provide an example of a successful strategy to the wider University community.

## 5.3 Knowledge Management: no quick fix

As several authors have pointed out (Davenport, 2000; Slater and Moreton, 2002), organisations must recognise that a successful and cohesive knowledge management strategy requires a significant period of time to implement and it may be a number of years before the full impact of the strategy can be measured. Knowledge management is not a 'fad' offering a quick solution to the 21$^{st}$ century problems of information overload but is rather a deliberate and rational approach to identifying the knowledge required for an organisation to flourish both in terms of performance and revenue. Knowledge management requires understanding of a number of related disciplines, such as human psychology, human resources issues and management science coupled with an innovative approach to identifying appropriate technological solutions. The steady growth in literature, consultancy options and academic courses all related to understanding and implementing knowledge management indicate that the discipline is gaining credence in the global management arena as a means of encouraging collaboration and sharing that is consistent with the overall objectives, priorities and environment of an organisation.

# References

British Standards Institution (2001) *Knowledge management: a guide to good practice.* PAS 2001, London: British Standards Institution.

Davenport, T.H. and Prusack, L. (2000) *Working Knowledge: How organizations manage what they know.* Harvard Business School Press.

Department Of Trade And Industry (1998) *Our competitive future: building the knowledge driven economy.* White Paper Cm4176, London: Department of Trade and Industry http://www.dti.gov.uk/comp/an_report.htm (Accessed 6$^{th}$ April 2000).

Office Of Science And Technology (2000) *Excellence and opportunity a science and innovation policy for the 21$^{st}$ century.* White Paper Cm4814, London: Department of Trade and Industry http://www.dti.gov.uk/ost/aboutost/dtiwhite/test/index.html (Accessed 15$^{th}$ January 2002).

Rowley, J. (2000) Is higher education ready for knowledge management? *The international journal of educational management,* 14(7), pp. 325-333.

Slater, A. (2000) *Communication.* Wolverhampton: IT Services, University of Wolverhampton. (Unpublished internal report).

Slater, A. (2002) MSc Dissertation, University of Wolverhampton, UK.S

Slater, A. and Moreton, R. (2002), "An Evaluation of Knowledge Management Concepts and Methodologies". Transactions in International Information Systems, ISSN: 1507-8647.

# Creating Value-Adding IT Solutions for SMEs. A Field Study from Poland

Przemysław Lech

University of Gdańsk, Faculty of Business Administration, 81-824 Sopot, ul. Armii Krajowej 101, Poland, e-mail: Przemyslaw.Lech@lst.com.pl

## 1 Introduction

The aim of this paper is to show the way Management Information Systems can help small and medium-sized enterprises to increase their productivity and gain or sustain a competitive advantage.

This paper is intended to be practice relevant, by presenting implementable indications for the MIS solution development. Although field study documenting this research is based in Poland, general conclusions about MIS value-adding implementations seem to be transferable to other countries, both from emerging economies and the developed ones. The paper includes guidelines for creating value-adding MIS solutions and illustrates practical use of these guidelines in three Polish SME sector enterprises.

## 2 Principles for creating value-adding IT solutions

So called 'productivity paradox' (Brynjolfsson 1993, Loveman 1994) has put into question the role of IT in creating productivity improvements. This resulted in the negation of IT as a strategic resource from one side (Carr 2003) as well as in the intensified research on the factors that distinguish successful IT implementers from the loosing ones. Most of the researchers agree that if IT is supposed to cause productivity growth, it must be used to innovate core business processes (Davenport 1993; Marchand 2000, Remenyi and Sherwood-Smith M. 1997) and support organization's strategic goals (Aitken 2003, Benson et al. 2004, Kaplan and Norton 2004). It remains an open issue, how to put these high level guidelines into life. This problem is crucial for small and medium sized enterprises even more than for the big ones as the former usually would not have resources for hiring external consultants and applying sophisticated methodologies. In spite of this, apart from the few exceptions (Dans 1999, Love and Irani 2004, Street and Meister 2004) the issue of value creation with IT within SMEs is not present in the literature. Thus a set of easy to use 'rules of thumb' coming from the experience of the companies of the same size could be of great benefit to the small and medium sized enterprises looking for benefits from IT.

A field study performed among Polish enterprises, mostly from the SMEs sector, has led me towards general conclusions about implementation conditions that should be fulfilled to generate value-adding IT solutions.

As Polish SMEs use standard EAS packages rather than try to develop home-made IT solutions, the following conclusions concern EAS implementation. The key principles that significantly increase the possibility for high implementation return on investment are:

1. Effort should be put into supporting innovations in the key processes. Key processes are those processes that contribute to the value delivered to the customer. The most important of the key processes are those that create a competitive advantage – processes that differentiate an organization from its competitors and make customers choose its products.

2. In the areas that do not contribute to the value delivered to the customer, standard functionality should be used. If standard functionality does not suit existing processes, those processes should be changed rather than an attempt be made to adjust software. If the above mentioned is not possible these processes should be left out of the project scope and performed manually.

The above mentioned general rules should be expanded into a more detailed set of principles to be practically applicable. This set of principles, based on management information systems development theory, as well as on the author's original concepts, is presented in this section. Although developed independently (Lech 2004), these principles comply with postulates presented in (Benson 2004) of IT link to strategy, focusing on process change and reducing unproductive IT spending.

In order to obtain maximum value from EAS implementation, the project should be divided into separate value areas for which benefits and costs can be evaluated individually. This division should be done according to the enterprise's main processes or functions. The solution should be developed for the areas where benefits exceed costs. Optimal cost/benefit ratio can be achieved either by maximizing benefits for a given cost level or by minimizing the costs of obtaining specified benefits.

The most crucial issue is to determine possible benefits from IT implementation. Two approaches can be applied to do this:

• 'from business concept to technology',
• 'from technology to business concept'.

The first approach assumes creation of an ideal business model first and the identification of IT elements supporting this model afterwards. The second is based on active IT usage to determine possible value creating changes (Lech 2004).

The result of the both approaches is the same: a business model supported by suitable IT elements.

Project implementation strategy

After determining project value areas and assigning possible benefits to each of these it is necessary to define implementation strategy:

- For those areas where possible benefits are high, it is reasonable to adjust the IT solution to the business needs,
- For low benefit areas the goal should be to minimize costs. This can be achieved by using standard functionality even if it does not exactly suit the business needs,
- In those areas where achievement of positive ROI is doubtful it should be considered if any IT support is justified. If exclusion of these areas does not have a negative affect on the solution integration it might be reasonable to keep them out of the project scope.

It is essential to employ rational procedures of determining the project scope and strategy of implementation in each of the value areas. It is quite often that employees of the enterprise try to force the extension of the project scope in the areas of their own interest. It is the project leader's role to look at each of such "temptation processes" from the perspective of the enterprise as a whole. The "temptation process" should only be considered for implementation if including it in the project scope generates positive value for the enterprise as a whole. Areas in which implementation would facilitate work for a group of people without generating value should be abandoned.

In the following section three examples of applying these rules in practice will be presented.

# 3 Case studies

All the three enterprises presented in this section are Polish managed SMEs. Enterprise one and two are branches of international holdings whilst the third one is a fully local enterprise. The EAS implementations in the enterprises one and two were conducted without the significant influence from the international headquarters on the solution architecture. Moreover, solutions developed in Poland were recognized as exemplary within the holdings, and knowledge coming out of these implementations was then disseminated to the other branches in the countries such as France and Germany. The first two companies have implemented a medium-sized ERP suite offering the functionality both in the 'standard' areas such as financials, purchases, sales, stock management as well as more sophisticated ones, including CRM, service management and project management. The suite allows to parameterize the existing functionality and also offers the development workbench which makes it possible to expand it according to the company's specific needs. The third company has implemented a small off-the-shelf, easy to implement solution, offering the standard functionality in the financials, sales, purchases, stock management and CRM areas with little parameterization and no development possible.

All the data about the cases presented below was collected by personal active participation, as I was a project leader from the side of the consulting company supporting the implementation. The cases are presented in the chronological order.

## 3.1 TAC Polska - Front to back - office link

TAC Polska is a Polish branch of TAC, one of the world leading producers of 'intelligent buildings' infrastructure. TAC Polska's core business is developing integrated building management infrastructure such as climate control, fire systems, elevator control systems etc. The value for the customer is defined as making a building 'intelligent' and thus easier to manage.

In 2000 a decision was made to replace the existing DOS-based system with an integrated Enterprise Application Suite. Soon after, an analysis was performed to establish the implementation scope and main requirements for the system. Operating in the low margin market, TAC faced problems with project cost and revenues control. Quite often cost estimations for the new projects were inaccurate and the planned margin was not realized. The main reason for that problem was not lack of necessary information to prepare cost estimations correctly, but rather a lack of understanding of financial issues amongst engineers performing the projects. So the main task to be solved was in the back-office, as the value for customer features (price, performance and service, time and quality) were at a good level. The issue was to develop a solution both for engineers performing projects and for the financial department that would fulfill the following requirements:

- let the engineers prepare  a project budget and post actual usage of equipment, materials and workforce in natural units,
- automatically assign values to the resources used and update costs,
- post revenues from the project,
- allow financial department to control planned and actual costs and settle project phases to G/L accounts.

A simple solution based on standard functionality of the EAS to be implemented was proposed. It fulfilled all the requirements stated above but it soon became clear that the engineers would not be satisfied with it as the system created more work for them rather than simplifying it. They found the solution to be a tool designed to control them, not to help them, and this proved to be the case. The group of engineers taking part in the project came up with a set of additional requirements that would make the solution useful for their work. The additional functionality they required concerned project scheduling, project management and project cost/benefit simulations. As the EAS platform on which the solution was based included a  development workbench it was possible to fulfill their additional requirements. Value analysis from the enterprise's perspective as a whole resulted in the conclusion that the main benefit from additional functionality would be making the engineers happy. Additional benefit would be work reduction as engineers would use one solution instead of two separate ones and would maintain only one materials and resources database. The costs of making additional project life exceeded those benefits and so it was rejected.

The initially proposed solution resulted in less projects with a zero or negative margin and better control by the financial department over realized projects.
Other value areas that were considered were:

- logistics with headquarters,
- sales,
- asset management,
- accounting,
- HR and payroll.

Logistics with the headquarters was the only area influenced by the international holding company. To be able to supply projects with specified equipment imported from abroad EDI interfaces between TAC Polska and TAC Sweden were established. This resulted in shorter delivery times.

Sales, asset management and accounting were supported with standard EAS functionality. The value obtained in these areas was not substantial and the main benefit was the reduction of redundancy in sales and asset accounting postings. Sales and accounting were included in the solution because the architecture of the integrated EAS solution forced it. The main reasons for the inclusion of asset accounting were that it was not properly supported by the existing system and the cost of including it was not high. These value areas were identified as of neutral value.

The last area analyzed was human resources and payroll. According to complicated and ever changing legal regulations this area is very difficult to implement. The Application Suite supplied a Polish specific solution in this area but it was excluded from the implementation scope. The reasons for this were as follows:

- Payroll delivers no benefits from on-line integration with the other functional areas. One way interface of payroll postings to accounting is a satisfactory solution.
- The existing DOS system works well and after many corrections fits organizational specificity.

Because of the above reasons, the existing system was interfaced to the new application at almost no additional cost.

This way the optimal solution was designed and implemented according to the principles listed in the previous section:

- key processes of project financial control and logistics with headquarters were supported with customized application,
- 'temptation process' of project management was rationally assessed and rejected from implementation,

- neutral value areas like accounting, sales and asset management were supported with standard functionality,
- the negative value area of HR & payroll was left outside the project scope.

## 3.2 J. J. Darboven Poland - Developing key functionality

J.J. Darboven has been on the coffee market since 1866. It offers high quality products to upper market segment customers. Its best known products are Alfredo Espresso, Idee Kaffee, Mövenpick and Eilles. In Poland J.J. Darboven focuses on delivering complex solutions for the preparation of hot beverages for the catering business. The offer includes coffee-machine supply and service, coffee making know-how and coffee supply to the customers' location.

During the IT based business solution development the approach *from business concept to technology* was used.

Problems that J.J. Darboven faced concerned excessive delivery time, difficulties in fast purchase order placing, incomplete product and stock information during order placing and lack of cross-selling. The other kind of problems concerned insufficient information about receivables and payments, sales people activity as well as about coffee-machine service and costs. J.J. Darboven Poland CEO found out that most of the problems were tightly connected to the customer care and sales and delivery processes. A concept to radically reengineer these processes was developed as a response. In the opinion of the J.J. Darboven CEO the solution would need to be based on central customer, sales order and stock management. A key element of the reengineering plan was the creation of a teleservice unit responsible for the sales order and customer info acquisition, as well as coordination of the local delivery units' activity. The obstacle in putting the reengineering plan into action was the lack of a suitable IT solution. In 2001 J.J. Darboven Holding AG made the decision to implement EAS in its Polish subsidiary. The implementation plan followed the rules presented in the previous section:

- the key business process was centralized customer care, sales and delivery so an attempt was made to develop dedicated functionality supporting it. This resulted in the creation of a "teleservice pulpit" gathering information about previous customer orders, payment history, payment conditions and allowing the creation of new purchase orders, invoices and delivery notes. Sales documents are then sent by e-mail to the salesman, who delivers them to the customer together with the purchased items.
- neutral areas such as purchase and accounting were supported with standard system functionality. Some requirements regarding these areas where thus ignored and either are performed out of the system or changes were made to adjust the organization to the system's requirements.
- as in the first case-study – the HR and payroll area was considered to be of negative value and thus was not included into the implementation scope.

J.J. Darboven reports the following benefits from the described implementation:

- stock level decrease by 15%,
- average receivables overdue decrease by 10 days,
- employment in sales department decrease by 6 persons,
- project payback period of 24 months.

The other area where IT could add value to the business was machine supply and service. J.J. Darboven Poland has two ways of supplying customers with coffee machines: one can buy the machine, or borrow it and pay a higher price for the coffee. The price is then related to the volume of purchase per month. Before system implementation the following problems were identified in this area:

- there was no easy way of checking if the amount of coffee declared by the customer was really purchased each month,
- there was no clear evidence which machines each customer had,
- service costs were not known.

An additional functionality showing machines lent, service costs and a coffee purchase summary was developed and added to the "teleservice pulpit".
Focusing on critical value adding processes has led to a low cost, high benefit implementation which was considered by the J.J. Darboven Holding AG as exemplary for the whole group.

The main "temptation process" that occurred during implementation, was developing full CRM functionality and sales representative tool integrated with the back-office system. CRM area was not supported by the standard EAS functionality and J.J. Darboven was thinking of developing it as a part of system extensions. The benefit of including a CRM and sales representative tool would be on-line integration with the rest of the system functionality one customer and items database and an on-line sales order information in the back-office. Pre-implementation analysis was performed but it did not show enough benefits to justify additional costs. A decision was made to use off-the-shelf software for supporting these activities.

J.J. Darboven Poland has seen its competitive advantage in dramatically changing customer care, sales and distribution processes. IT was the necessary component of the new business concept and so efforts were made to develop a solution  the new business processes. It required additional work to adjust the standard EAS to new business needs, but it was justified both from strategic and operational perspectives. The rules mentioned in this paper were fulfilled in the following way:

- customer value-adding processes were identified and supported by the dedicated solution within the standard EAS,
- neutral value areas were supported with the standard functionality,
- "temptation processes" of CRM and sales representative tool were abandoned and are now supported by the of-the-shelf solution.
- negative value area (HR & payroll) was left out of the project scope.

## 3.3 Corex – Lean implementation

Corex is one of the biggest 100% Polish capital distributors of office materials. It sells both imported and home-produced pens, pencils, markers, paper materials etc. to big retail nets, wholesalers  and office depots. The enterprise's Board is searching for organizational and technical possibilities to effectively deal with the constantly growing organization and accompanying changes. The owners have hired an external consulting company to help them formulate strategic goals and develop an information system based on Balanced Scorecard.

Value for customer analysis has led to the conclusion that the key factors appreciated by the main customers, concerned service and delivery. What these customers valued most were:

- on-line availability of products,
- short delivery time,
- quick claim processing.

The main strategic goals that were formulated after this analysis were:

- to implement a mechanism for increasing the availability of the products in stock without increasing stock capacity,
- to assure 24 hours delivery time with 100% order-delivery match,
- to shorten special order delivery time.

The Board started to search for an IT solution that would support these strategic initiatives. The first step performed was a one month analysis to determine the optimal solution scope. The IT solution blueprint resulting from it included  a list of requirements for the target system. It consisted of 56 requirements covering all Corex activities and it was followed by a feasibility study for the three Enterprise Application Suites of different size:

- medium sized EAS designed as the standard solution for small and medium sized enterprises,
- open platform system for medium sized enterprises allowing the development of customer specific solutions,
- big EAS for mid sized and large enterprises.

The percentage of requirements possible to realize in each of the analyzed systems without considerable programming work was 40, 50 and 70 respectively.

The second and third solution had the possibility to expand standard functionality with additional programming work and fulfill up to 95 of the requirements.

The biggest EAS  also had some potential for further growth, supplying an option for additional investment in the future and to fulfill requirements regarded as optional.

The Board examined three proposals regarding actual and future benefits and compared them to implementation costs. The conclusion was that the solution fulfilling a critical 40 % of requirements at a considerably low cost was the optimal one in the 3 years time perspective, and so the first system was chosen for  implementation.

The implemented solution supplied functionality, supporting key processes in the simplest possible way. It integrated sales and warehouse management giving information about actual stock level, estimated delivery time and necessity of stock replenishment. It allowed EDI with key customers, basic CRM information and supplied standard purchase and financial functionality. It did not support more sophisticated requirements identified during the analysis stage, like advanced warehouse management, advanced stock planning and optimization and call center functionality.

The Board judged these requirements as "nice to have" rather than essential, and reduced the initial expectations.

This case illustrates the business-IT solution development approach following the optimization rule of achieving a certain level of benefits at minimal cost. The must-have benefits were identified in the analysis document and the IT solution that supported them in the least sophisticated way possible was chosen. All supporting processes were left out of the MIS scope.

## 3.4 Summary of the field study

All the three enterprises performed MIS implementation according to the rules stated in this paper. Enterprise One supported its key processes with few modifications to the standard functionality supplied by the medium-sized Enterprise Application Suite. Enterprise Two made efforts to develop a dedicated solution supporting radical process redesign and Enterprise Three used a small standard package to supply core functionality to support key processes at a minimal cost. The presented field study shows different ways of applying the same rules in practice. All enterprises avoided the temptation to cover all activities with the IT solution and this way they obtained optimal benefit to cost ratio.

The summarized information about the three field study cases is shown in tables 1, and 2:

**Table 1.** Positive value areas

| | Key processes | Key processes support | Key benefits |
|---|---|---|---|
| TAC | project budget control | solution developed on the basis of standard functionality | control over project costs, less zero and negative margin projects |
| | project accounting | automatic postings schemes from standard functionality not used in other branches | no redundancy in project costs and revenues postings |
| | purchase from headquarters | standard functionality and interfaces | shorter delivery process |
| J.J. Darboven | customer care | dedicated solution developed on the EAS platform – 'teleservice pulpit', supplying information about customer purchases and payments and allowing on-line sales | better customer service, faster delivery, fewer delivery mistakes, better control of salespeople work, smaller stock level, faster payment collection, less bad debts |
| | sales and distribution | | |
| | coffee-machine service | dedicated solution added to the 'teleservice pulpit' supplying information about machines at the customer site, service visits, spare parts used etc. | better machine management, less machines 'lost', lower service costs, less spare parts used |
| Corex | sales and stock management | standard EAS functionality, EDI interface | increased stock availability control, sales order – goods issue – invoice integration |

**Table 2.** Neutral value areas

|  | Processes | Processes support | Benefits |
|---|---|---|---|
| TAC | accounting fixed assets management sales | standard functionality | integrated process flow, no redundancy in sales and fixed assets accounting, real-time financial information |
| J.J. Dar-boven | accounting fixed assets management purchase | standard functionality | integrated process flow, no redundancy in purchase and fixed assets accounting, real-time financial information |
| Corex | accounting, purchase | standard functionality | integrated process flow, no redundancy in purchase and fixed assets accounting, real-time financial information |

**Table 3.** Negative value areas

|  | "Temptation processes" | Way of managing temptation processes | Processes excluded from the standard project | Reason for excluding / Way of managing |
|---|---|---|---|---|
| TAC | project management tool for engineers | not included in the project, engineers use standalone software | HR & payroll | no necessity for on-line integration interface posting of wages once a month |
| J.J. Dar-boven | full CRM solution sales representative tool | not included in the project, standalone software is used | HR & payroll | no necessity for on-line integration interface posting of wages once a month |
| Corex | advanced stock management and planning functions call center | not included in the system, not performed | fixed assets HR & payroll | no necessity for on-line integration interface posting of wages and depreciation once a month |

## 4 Summary

Value creation with IT is not an automatic process. It is well known that IT must be used to achieve company strategic goals or to improve operational processes, otherwise the investment will be lost. The issue that most practitioners will encounter is how to apply these rules in their practice. This problem concerns both big enterprises and SMEs but for the latter coming to a solution might be more difficult due to the shortage of resources for hiring external consultants and using sophisticated methodologies proposed by them. This paper proposed a set of indications facilitating the implementation of a value-adding IT solution based on the standard EAS package. As they are derived from the field studies performed within the medium-sized enterprises, they are practically relevant and applicable for the SMEs. The main thesis on which these indications are built on, is that an extra effort should be put into supporting only those processes that contribute to the value delivered to the customer. All the other processes should be supported with the standard functionality of the EAS or, if they cannot be successfully adopted to the standard delivered with the system, excluded from the implementation. The practical way of putting these rules into life is to divide the implementation scope into separate value areas according to the enterprise's main processes or functions and to evaluate benefits and costs of each area separately. The solution should then be developed only for those areas, in which benefits exceed costs. The usage of the described method was illustrated by the case studies of the three Polish SMEs, each of them having different business needs and different purposes for the EAS implementation. Despite for the differences in the business models and implementation aims, all those enterprises have complied with the rules synthesized in this paper, concentrating the implementation effort on the positive value areas, supporting the neutral value areas with the standard functionality delivered with the system and excluding the negative value areas from the implementation scope. The main contribution of this paper seems to be the practical illustration of how to manage the EAS implementation project in such a way that it complies with the theoretical assumption of the IT strategy focus present in the literature.

## References

Aitken I (2003) Value-Driven IT Management, Butterworth – Heinemann, Oxford
Benson R, Bugnitz T, Walton W (2004) From Business Strategy to IT Action, Right Decisions for a Better Bottom Line, John Wiley & Sons, Hoboken
Brynjolfsson E. (1993) The Productivity Paradox of Information Technology, Communications of the ACM, 35, pp. 66-77
Carr N (2003) IT Doesn't Matter, Harvard Business Review, May, s. 41-49
Dans E (1999) IT Investment in SME's: Paradoxically productive?, [online], EJISE 1999, vol. 2/2, http://www.ejise.com/volume-4/volume4-issue1/issue1-art7.htm

Davenport T (1993) Process Innovation. Reengineering Work through Information Technology, Harvard Business School Press, Boston

Kaplan R, Norton D (2004) Measuring the Strategic Readiness of Intangible Assets, HBR, February, pp. 53-63

Lech P (2004) 80/20 Rule in ERP System Implementation – A Case Study on Maximizing ROI, Proceedings of the 11th European Conference on Information Technology Evaluation, Royal Netherlands Academy of Arts and Sciences, Amsterdam, pp. 221-225

Loveman G (1994) An Assessment of the Productivity Impact in Information Technologies. In: Allen T, Scott Morton M (eds) Information Technology and the Corporation of the 1990s: Research Studies, MIT Press, Cambridge

Love P, Irani Z (2004) An exploratory study on information technology evaluation and benefits management practices of SMEs in the construction industry, Information & Management, vol. 42:1, pp. 227- 241

Marchand D. (ed.) (2000) Competing with Information, A Manager's Guide to Creating Business Value with Information Content, John Wiley & Sons, Chichester

Remenyi D, Sherwood-Smith M (1997) Achieving Maximum Value from Information Systems, John Wiley & Sons, Chichester

Street C, Meister D (2004) Small Business Growth and Internal Transparency: The Role of Information Systems, MIS Quarterly vol. 28:3, pp. 473-506

# How is Project Success Affected by Replacing the Project Manager?

Tero Vartiainen, Maritta Pirhonen

Turku School of Economics, Pori Unit, P.O. Box 170, FIN-28101 PORI, FINLAND.
University of Jyväskylä, Department of Computer Science and Information Systems, P.O. Box 35, FIN-40014 JYVÄSKYLÄN YLIOPISTO, FINLAND

**Abstract:** Although replacing the project manager in an on-going project is not uncommon in the IT field, studies on the topic are scarce. In order to increase understanding in this area, we investigated the perceptions of ten experienced project managers on replacement from the perspective of project success. We focused on the critical success factors in the projects, on how the interviewees perceived the replacement of the manager, and on the effects it had. We found that replacing the manager was perceived as an attempt to rescue a troubled project, and as a pertinent part of it, especially in cases in which it strengthened the project process. Replacement was found to affect critical factors such as management and human-relations issues. The results are reflected through the literature, and implications for research and practice are presented.
**Keywords:** project management, information systems development

## 1 Introduction

The project is a typical work form in information systems development (ISD), and project-based organizations exist in the IT field. The project manager is a key person as he or she manages all the critical functions, including planning, organizing, staffing, directing, and controlling (Thayer 1987). Project managers face a multitude of challenges (Boddy 2002; Maylor 2003) in hypercompetitive and chaotic business environments (Kloppenborg and Petrick 1999; Yeo 2002), including risks (Wallace and Keil 2004) and quality issues, as well as leadership issues (Smith 1999). According to Jurison (1999), the project manager's broad experience and managerial and interpersonal skills form the basis for a successful project, and in practice, it is very difficult to find an experienced and available manager with the right qualifications. The reasons why projects fail may be traced back to managerial rather than technical problems (Hartman and Ashrafi 2002). If managing a project is a great challenge, what effect does it have if the manager is replaced? The plurality of competencies and the managerial complexity (Blackburn 2002; Aladwani 2002) suggest that if the manager is to be replaced – for whatever reason – if the replacement is poorly handled it may have detrimental effects on the success of the project. Although the role of the manager and his or her leadership style and competence are very seldom identified as critical success factors (Turner and Muller 2005), we suggest that knowledge transfer from the preceding manager to the successor is a complex task. It is therefore worthwhile investigating the phenomenon of replacing the project manager in an ongoing project. Turner and Muller (2005) claim that the impact of the project manager on project success is ignored in the literature, and it is therefore not surprising that we did not find studies on replacing IT project managers in the literature on information systems. We aim to increase understanding in this area by investigating project managers' perceptions on replacement from the perspective of project success. We interviewed ten experienced project managers about this issue, and analyzed the data by taking an interpretive approach. The results show that replacement is mostly related to attempts to rescue a troubled project. Well-planned, it was perceived to strengthen the project process. It appears that replacing the project manager affects critical project-related issues.

Following this introduction, the literature on project management is briefly described, and the research design is presented. Then, the results are given and discussed in the light of the existing literature.

## 1.1 Projects and success factors

Scholars have taken different approaches in investigating success in projects. Research has concentrated on the overall objectives, and research on project-management success typically concerns cost, time and quality (Cooke-Davies 2002). Shenhar and Levy (1997) conducted a study on project success by surveying managers in product-development projects, and identified the following dimensions:

- Project efficiency (Was the project completed on time and within budget?)
- Impact on the customer (Does the project meet performance and functional specifications? Is the customer satisfied?)
- Business and direct success (Is the project providing the sales, income, profits and other benefits?)
- Preparing for the future (Is the firm more prepared for the future?).

Lyytinen and Hirschheim (1987) took a similar approach, albeit from a failure perspective, in defining the following four major categories of information systems (IS) failure:

1. correspondence failure (systems design objectives are not met),

2. process failure (the IS cannot be developed within the allocated budget and/or time schedule),
3. interaction failure (the level of end-user usage),
4. expectation failure (the system does not correspond with its stakeholders' requirements, expectations or values).

The studies mentioned above emphasize project success from the customer viewpoint, whereas research on success factors from the project-management perspective emphasizes the trinity of time, cost and quality, which has been found lacking. Turner (1999) therefore added two other dimensions to be managed: project definition and scope, and organization. He argues that the scope of the project delimits its boundary and is managed through the product and its breakdown, which are derived from a hierarchy of objectives ("vision, mission, facility, and team and individual objectives"). According to Lee-Kelley et al. (2003), Turner's (1999) model does not easily discern people-related issues such as leadership. Human factors were recognized as success factors by Pinto and Slevin (1988), for example, who included the personnel in the context of information systems projects. According to Turner and Muller (2005), the current literature on project success largely ignores the project manager's role. They predict that this will change in the future as more studies are undertaken. Inspired by Turner and Muller, we set out to increase knowledge in this area in this exploratory study concerning the phenomenon of replacing the project manager in a project-in-progress. The research design is described in the next section.

## 2 Research design

In order to obtain a tentative view on the issue of replacing the manager during an on-going project, we interviewed ten experienced project managers on the subject from the perspective of project success. We contacted project managers in software houses in the towns of Jyväskylä, Pori and Tampere in Finland. We used open-ended interview questions in order to encourage the subjects to describe all of the meaningful issues related to the research topic. We then formed categories based on our interpretations of the subjects' perceptions. First, in order to acquire an understanding of their perceptions of project success factors, we asked the following question: *"What issues are critical factors in relation to project success?"* We then asked them to openly describe what came to mind about replacing the project manager: *"Describe what comes to your mind on the subject of replacing the manager of a project-in-progress."* Finally, we asked the interviewees to describe the issues that were affected by the replacement of the project manager, and to say which of these were critical in relation to the project success: *"What issues are affected by the replacement of the project manager? Which of these are critical in relation to the project success?"* To prevent the interviews from becoming intrusive we refrained from directly asking the subjects if they had personal experience of replacement. They all had considerable working experience in software projects, at least five to ten years, and their age and gender profile was as follows (age/Male or Female): 41/M, 42/M, 42/F, 59/M, 46/F, 57/F, 33/M, 50/M, 38/M, and 35/M. The first author of this article interviewed the first five subjects and the second author the others. When the interviewee described his or her ideas, he or she was prompted to describe in more detail what he or she meant. The following prompting questions were used: *"Would you please describe in more detail what you said?"* and *"What else comes to mind"*? We analyzed the interview transcripts separately and produced tentative categories. We then compared our results and produced the final categorizations, which are reported in the following sections.

## 3 IT project managers' perceptions of critical success factors

Three broad categories of critical success factors were identified from the project managers' perceptions: "The management perspective", "The human-issues perspective", and "The context perspective." In our formulation we used concern for the task and human issues as set out in Blake and Mouton's (1978) managerial grid, and the idea that projects are surrounded by context (Boddy 2002). The categories were as follows.

**The management perspective**   Perceptions related to the management perspective concerned the project objectives and their attainment. The following issues emerged:

- shared objectives,
- the management of resources,
- change management,
- the commitment of the client and the project team, and
- communication and interaction between the parties.

The parties involved in the project should have a similar view of the objectives, and the project manager should be capable of determining them. As one interviewee said: *"...the project has to have shared objectives..."* (PM8[1])

The efficient management of resources (human and financial), of the tasks and the schedule, and of any changes is critical to project success. The following extracts exemplify these issues: *"The schedule and money and the business goals are the things that must be achieved with the new application."* (PM4). *"The schedule must be such that it is realizable."* (PM6)

The commitment of the client and of the project team members came up in the subjects' perceptions. The following extract refers to problems when client expectations are unrealistic, or when the client does not invest as much in the way of resources as expected: *"Yes, the client is committed to the outcome of the project and is part of it and of the decision-making."* (PM3). Another point about a good

---

[1] PM stands for the subjects, project managers, interviewed in this study.

team was raised by PM9, who stated that an incompetent project manager with a good team could not make the project fail. Adequate and successful communication and interaction between the parties were critical success factors: *"Well, the first thing that came to my mind, one single thing that covers most of it...it is communication and this kind of successful interaction."* (PM8)

**The human perspective** Human issues that are manifested in relations between people, their mental states and capabilities arose as critical factors in this category. The following issues emerged:

* relationships between people,
* motivation and attitude,
* competence, and
* trust.

Relationships between people participating in the project were perceived as critical. This means that it is not only team spirit and chemistry that affect the results, and that relations with client representatives and the project work culture are also critical. Project participants work in close contact with each other, and any deficiency in relations may put a damper on the whole thing. Openness and truthfulness were also considered important factors, as the following examples show: *"Chemistry and social skills: communicative skills and the ability to co-operate are quite important, and this reflects the organizational culture."* (PM2) *"... And mutual openness, truthfulness and trust."* (PM6)

Motivation and attitude were also mentioned as significant success factors, and in particular common enthusiasm and interest in carrying out the project – on the part of both the customer and the supplier : *"... and then, the customer is interested in the project... it has a big influence on the motivation of the team..."* (PM9)

Adequate competence in the participants (project manager, team members) was identified as critical: *"The project manager has to be mature, he or she must have experience and a view"* (PM1), and *"...skilful people who are able to use the tools... "* (PM6)

Trust between supplier and client was also perceived as critical: co-operation will suffer if there is a loss of trust. In the following extract, the project manager emphasizes the need for trust between the key players: *"The one thing that always matters. You have to gain the trust of the client and especially the trust of the key persons. If it is not gained, things will be relatively difficult. "* (PM4)

**The context perspective** Context is defined as the contemporary setting within and beyond the organization (Boddy 2002, 31; see also Kast and Rosenzweig 1985, 136). Perceptions related to the context refer to how actors affect or are affected by the project. The project receives resources from the surrounding organization, and the results (e.g., a new or modified IS) will be implemented in the environment of the client. The interviewees mentioned that it was essential to understand the business operations of the client and the context of the system use: *"...there the critical factor was that you really understood the environment in which the outcome of the project will be used. "* (PM10). PM9 said that the project had to get support from the organization: *"The project must have the support of* *the organization; the resources, telecommunications, and the infrastructure in general, that are needed in the project, must be available..."*

## 4 Perceptions on the replacement of the project manager

In response to the free-form question about replacing the project manager, the subjects typically described the reasons behind and the situations that led to such an event. These deliberations were divided into two categories: "Replacing the project manager to rescue a troubled project," and "Replacing the project manager as part of the process". Some interviewees also deliberated on how the replacement should be carried out, thereby forming the third category: "Carrying out the replacement." These categories are described below.

**Replacing the project manager to rescue a troubled project.** Most of the subjects referred to replacing the project manager in negative terms: replacement was needed if the project was not going as planned, or was facing dilemmas (for example, the objectives would not be met in accordance with the schedule), and trust in the manager had been lost. When the trust is lost, the client may demand replacement. Similar demands may emerge from inside the project manager's organization, or even from inside the team. Trust in the manager may be lost if his or her capabilities and competence do not meet the requirements of the project, or if his or her way of working and communicating are perceived as deficient. Problems in the personal chemistry between the project manager and the client representatives also emerged as a reason for replacement. The following extracts give examples of the interviewee responses:

> PM3: *"Mainly a situation where the project manager does not enjoy the trust of the client, the steering group or the client's staff. They do not trust his or her competence or way of acting as a project manager, or perhaps he or she is too inexperienced, or then a more experienced manager might be wanted. The situation has changed or has somehow gotten out of hand."*

> PM2: *"Well, it can be a consequence of the fact that the outcomes do not correspond to the requirements or the project does not run on time and these things cause these chemistry concerns. For example, the client and the project manager might not get along with each other and then it is time to replace the project manager."*

**Replacing the project manager as part of the process.** In this case the replacement is described as a pertinent part of the project. The project manager may have special experience and know-how related to the tasks of certain phases. A manager with marketing or testing experience, for example, should be in charge during the related phases. This being the case, replacement between phases was perceived as strength. Secondly, if the project manager is replaced because he or she gets a new job or takes maternity leave for example, or if there is some other justified reason, the replacement is considered a pertinent part of project. In this case it may be easier for the team members to adapt to the new situation than in the cases belonging to the previous category. This kind of deliberation is visible in the next extract:

> PM3: *In a case like this it is easier to familiarize [the new project manager] or transferring the tasks is easier, because there is a mutually accepted reason for this. ... I don't know how to say it, but in a case like that it's somehow part of the project. ... Normally the commitment of the whole group is different in this kind of situation and the solution is sought together.*

**How the replacement should be carried out.** On a few occasions the interviewee perceptions also referred to how the replacement should be carried out. In the worst cases the successor and the replaced manager do not meet at all (if the latter left immediately) and there are no introductory discussions. At best, the new manager comes from the project and has introductory discussions with both the client and the project team. This makes it easier for the new manager to take charge of the project.

# 5 IT project managers' perceptions of the impact of replacement

According to the interviewees, replacing the project manager may or may not have a significant effect on the project and its different aspects. The following two categories emerged: "The issues affected by the replacement", and "No effects if conducted professionally". They are described below.

**The issues affected by the replacement.** Many subjects expressed the view that the replacement affected *"everything"* in the project, including the project team, the client, and the task, and that it brought temporary *"chaos"*. When questioned further, they raised the following issues:

- the schedule and cost,
- team spirit and personal chemistry, and
- communications.

Replacing the project manager affects the project schedule and costs because the process may be temporarily slowed down when the new manager introduces him or herself to the project, the team, and the client:

> PM1: *"... and, of course, these kinds of cost effects may occur. Of course, the project always has a defined budget, within which it operates. The way this shows is that resources for transferring competence to the new project manager are needed, so that he or she understands every single detail. Somehow it delays every function."*

Replacing the project manager affects the personal relations among all parties. When a well-welded team gets a new manager it has to adapt to that person's characteristics and ways of working. Each team member has to build up his or her relationship with the newcomer. Given the pivotal role of the leader in terms of communications in the project, anyone new to the role has to build the communication channels with all relevant parties (team members, clients, for example). Furthermore, information about the replacement should be communicated to all parties. Replacement even affects meeting practices, as managers have different ways of discussing and holding meetings, and it has a great influence on communication with the client: "...*communication with the client. It is, after all, the primary contact party in many cases.* "(PM9)

**No effects if implemented professionally.** Some subjects did not consider replacing the project manager problematic if it was done professionally. As PM8 said, "... *if the project manager leaves within a week, nothing extraordinary follows. Then you just must make sure the replacement is being planned and transfer as much knowledge as you can.*"

# 6 Discussion and implications

We considered the perceptions of ten Finnish project managers about project-manager replacement in terms of the project success. In our analysis of perceptions of success factors, we combined the ideas of Blake and Mouton (1978) about two major management concerns - for the task and for human issues - together with the idea that projects occur in context (Boddy 2002). As a result, we ended up with three perspectives on success factors: management (e.g., cost, schedule, quality), human issues (e.g., relations, motivation), and context (e.g., understanding the context of the client organization). Although different from Shenhar and Levy's (1997) and Lyytinen and Hirschheim's (1987) definitions, we find this interpretation useful as it simplifies the three important aspects of project management into the upper-level themes of the task (management), human issues (leadership), and the context. Our interpretation is based on the qualitative approach, according to which we did not prioritize the subjects' expressions. In their quantitative study, Belout and Gauvreau (2004) conducted a correlation analysis and found a link between project success and the personnel factor, although it was not as significant as other factors such as the project schedule. Nevertheless, many scholars do find human-related issues critical (e.g., Smith 1999; Turner and Muller 2005).

We also analyzed the project managers' free-form perceptions about replacement. On the one hand, replacement of the project manager was perceived as an attempt to rescue a troubled project, but on the other hand it was seen as a pertinent part of the project: a person with special know-how may serve as manager during a particular phase. The interviewees also expressed ideas on how the replacement should be carried out. Discussions between the former and the current manager were considered indispensable. Our interpretation of these perceptions is that, in the case of a troubled project, replacing the manager without having adequate plans concerning replacement may cause significant damage to the whole project. The subjects mentioned the schedule, costs, the team spirit, personal chemistry and communications as being particularly affected.

**Implications for research and practice**  Developing the means of preventing problems from emerging in projects has been an objective of scholars engaged in research on project management and IS. Given the fact that replacing the manager has been and will continue to be used as a means of rescuing projects, the act of replacement should be studied further, and best practices for carrying it out should be collected. The risk of replacement should be taken into consideration in the project-planning phase, and plans made for that eventuality. It is worth noting that replacement could be used as a means of strengthening the project process, and that research on the effects and processes of deliberate and well-planned replacement should be conducted.

**Evaluation of the study**  As Klein and Myers (1999, 74) state: "...the participants, just as much as the researcher, can be seen as interpreters and analysts", and accordingly in this study, the subjects were asked to produce interpretations of project success factors and of the replacement of project managers. The strength of the interviewing method is that it focuses directly on the study topic (Yin 1994). On the other hand, its weaknesses include the risk of bias due to poorly constructed questions, response bias, inaccuracies due to poor recall, and reflexivity, which means that the interviewee says what the interviewer wants to hear (Yin 1994). According to Fielding (1993), the problems with interviewing as a research method include interviewee attempts at rationalization, and the fact that the interviewees may fear being exposed. The implication is that people tend to avoid describing aspects of behavior or attitudes that are inconsistent with their preferred self-image. As far as this study is concerned, we recognize the fact that two researchers with different backgrounds and of different personality types conducted the interviews, and this may have caused response bias. Ten interviewees represent a small population, and more data is needed to produce a richer variety of perceptions. Furthermore, the theme investigated may have been emotionally difficult for the interviewees, and we therefore refrained from asking them if they had experienced being removed from a project. Finally, in our view one of the strengths of the study is that by using subjects who were experienced project managers we drew out the major viewpoints on the issues in question.

# 7 Acknowledgements

We wish to thank the anonymous referees, Professor Kalle Lyytinen, Professor Ronald Rice, Professor Airi Salminen, and lecturer Anne Honkaranta for their insightful feedback in the development of this study.

# References

Aladwani, A.M. 2002. IT project uncertainty, planning and success – An empirical investigation from Kuwait. Information Technology & People, 15, 210-226.

Belout, A. and Gauvreau, C. 2004. Factors influencing project success: the impact of human resource management. International Journal of Project Management, 22(1), 1-11.

Blackburn, S. 2002. The project manager and the project-network. International Journal of Project Management, 20(3), 199-204.

Blake, R.R. and Mouton, J.S. 1978. The New Managerial Grid. Houston: Gulf Publishing Company. Rererenced in F.E. Kast, J.E., Rosenzweig 1985. Organization & Management, A Systems and Contingency Approach. New York: McGraw-Hill.

Boddy, D. 2002. Managing Projects: Building and Leading the Team. Harlow, Essex: Prentice Hall.

Cooke-Davies, T. 2002. The "real" success factors on projects. International Journal of Project Management, 20(3), 185-190.

Fielding, N. 1993. Qualitative Interviewing. In N. Gilbert (Ed.) Researching Social Life. London: SAGE Publications. 135-153.

Hartman, F. and Ashrafi R.A. 2002. Project Management in the Information Systems and Information Technologies Industries. Project Management Journal, 33(3), 5-15.

Jurison, J. 1999. Software Project Management: the Manager's View. Communications of Association for Information Systems. Vol 2, Article 17.

Kast, F.E. and Rosenzweig, J.E. 1985. Organization & Management, A Systems and Contingency Approach. New York: McGraw-Hill.

Klein, H.K. and Myers, M.D. 1999. A Set of Principles for Conducting and Evaluating Interpretive Field Studies in Information Systems. MIS Quarterly, 23(1), 67-94.

Kloppenborg, J. and Petrick, T. 1999. Leadership in Project Life Cycle and Team Character Development. Project Management Journal, 30(2), 8-14.

Lee-Kelley, L. and Loong, K.L. 2003. Turner's Five Functions of Project-Based Management and Situational Leadership in IT Services Projects. International Journal of Project Management, 21(8), 583-591.

Lyytinen, K. and Hirschheim, R. 1987. Information Systems Failures - A Survey and Classification of the Empirical Literature. Oxford Surveys in Information Technology, vol 4, 257-309.

Maylor, H. 2003. Project Management. Harlow, Essex: Prentice Hall.

Pinto, J. K. and Slevin, D.P. 1988. Project success: Definitions and measurement techniques. Project Management Journal, 19(3), 67-73.

Shenhar, A.J. and Levy, O. 1997. Mapping the Dimensions of Project Success. Project Management Journal, 28 (2), 5-13.

Smith, G.R. 1999. Project Leadership: Why Project Management Alone Doesn't Work. Hospital Materiel Management Quarterly, Aug1999, 21, 88-92.

Thayer, R. 1987. Software engineering project management: A top-down view. In Tutorial: Software Engineering Project Management, pp. 15-53. IEEE Computer Science Press., Los Alamitos, California.

Turner, R. and Müller, R. 2005. The Project Manager's Leadership Style as a Success Factor on Projects: a Literature Review. Project Management Journal, 36(2), 49-61.

Turner, J.R. 1999. The handbook of project-based management. 2nd ed. England: McGraw-Hill Publishing.

Wallace L. and Keil, M. 2004. Software Project Risks and Their Effect on Outcomes. Communications of the ACM, 47(4), 68-73.

Yeo, K.T. 2002. Critical failure factors in information systems projects. International Journal of Project Management, 20(3), 241-246.

Yin, K. 1994. Case Study Research, Design and Methods. London: Sage.

# Virtual Organisation Governance by Example of Virtual University

Malgorzata Pankowska

Information Systems Department, University of Economics, Katowice, Poland. pank@ae.katowice.pl.

## 1 Introduction

The paper covers different interpretations of virtual organization and explanation of current managerial theories that have impact on its development. Next, author presents business institution governance issues, particularly focusing on IT governance problems. Last part of the paper contains consideration of virtual university and virtual university governance components. Author argues that virtual university governance requires strategy management, value creation, IT architecture development, resource management by contracts, standardization for controllability, compatibility and interoperability, strategy performance measures and accreditation in education. Experiences gathered during participation in project named Virtual Space of Collaboration of Universities of Economics allowed to formulate theses presented in the paper.

## 2 Virtual Organization Management Theories

A virtual organization is a set of individuals and institutions, with some common purposes or interests, that need to share their resources to pursue their objectives. Virtual organizations are developed to enable a knowledge-based enterprise to exist in a wide area network i.e. Internet.

According to Burn and Ash (2002) a virtual organization is recognized as a dynamic form of interorganisational systems and hence one where traditional hierarchical forms of management and control may not apply. Franke (2002) suggests that the organizational concept of virtual Web organizations encompasses three organizational elements. The first element is a relatively stable virtual Web platform from which dynamic virtual corporations are derived. Secondly, virtual corporations are interorganisational adhocracies that consist temporarily of independent companies in order to serve a particular purpose, such as joint R&D, product development and production. The third element of the organizational construct is the management organization that initiates and maintains the virtual Web platform and facilitates the operation of dynamic virtual corporations.

Byrne (1993) defines the virtual corporation as a temporary network of independent companies – suppliers, customers and even rivals – linked by information technology to share skills, costs, and access to one another's market. This corporate model is fluid and flexible – a group of collaborators quickly unites to exploit a specific opportunity. Once the opportunity is seized, the venture will disband. The group of partners within virtual organization cooperates to utilize opportunities, to overcome barriers, to reduce threats and to achieve strategic objectives. Basically, virtual corporations form value-added partnerships of units, which are autonomous, but depend on their purposes and given circumstances. Lewis and Weigert (1985) say that the pillars of virtual organizations comprise: 1) standardizing interactions, 2) standardizing metadata 3) treating knowledge separately from the individual 4) abstracting information from operations. Virtual corporations are the ideal form for optimal knowledge sharing and innovation. According to Dirksen and Smit (2002), Prusak (1997) and Kisielnicki (2002) the real value of the virtual organization is in the spontaneous gathering of people with shared interests and aims emerging during the development process. They know their mission and vision and they follow them to achieve their strategic goals.

## 3 Corporate Governance versus IT Governance

Governance is defined as a set of responsibilities and practices exercised by the board and executive management with the goal of providing strategic direction, ensuring that objectives are achieved, ascertaining that risks are managed appropriately and verifying that the enterprise's resources are used responsibly (Board Briefing…, 2003). The overwhelming emphasis in governance research has been on the efficacy of the various mechanisms available to protect shareholders from the self-interested whims of executives. Internal mechanisms include an effectively structured board, compensation contracts that encourage a shareholder orientation and concentrated ownership holdings that lead to active monitoring of executives. The role of monitoring (i.e. board oversight of executives) is a central element of agency theory and fully consistent with the view that the separation of ownership from control creates a situation conducive to managerial opportunism. Shareholder activism has emerged as an important factor in corporate governance. Shareholders with significant ownership positions have both the incentive to monitor executives and the influence to bring about changes they feel will be beneficial.

The definition of the word governance implies the action or manner of governing; IT governance according to Weill and Ross is a decision and accountability framework to encourage desirable behaviour in IT field (Mitra, 2005). Participants of the governance body lay down policies around different categories of decisions that need to be made. The body also decides upon the people in the enterprise who are empowered to make those decisions. An effective IT governance council must consider three questions: What decisions must be made to ensure the effective management and use of IT? Who should make the decisions? How will the decisions be made and monitored?

According to Van Grembergen (2004) IT governance is the organizational capacity exercised by the board, executive management and IT management to control the formulation and implementation of IT strategy and in this way to ensure the fusion of business and IT. IT management is focused on the internal effective supply of IT services and products and the management of present operations. IT governance is much broader and concentrates on performing and transforming IT to meet present and future demands of the business (internal focus) and the business' customers (external focus). IT governance is an integral part of corporate governance. There are two important components of IT governance: strategic alignment and the achievement of business value of IT.

Peterson argues that IT governance is the system by which the organization's IT portfolio is directed and controlled (Van Grembergen 2004). IT governance describes the distribution of decision-making rights and responsibilities among different stakeholders in the organization and the rules and procedures for making and monitoring decisions on strategic IT concerns. IT governance thus specifies the structure and processes through which the organization's IT objectives are set, and the means of attaining the objectives and monitoring performance.

The IT Governance Institute established by the Information Systems Audit and Control Association (ISACA) in 1998 was the first organization to use the IT governance term. The Institute continues to develop the ideas included in Sarbanes-Oxley Act of 2002 by introducing a COSO-based framework - the Control Objectives for Information and Related Technology (COBIT). COBIT is an internationally accepted IT control framework that provides organizations with good practices that help in implementing an IT governance structure throughout the enterprise. It aims to bridge the gaps between business risks, control needs and technical issues. The basic premise of COBIT is that in order to provide the information that the organization needs to achieve its objectives. IT resources need to be managed by a set of naturally grouped processes.

The core of the COBIT framework is the control objectives and management guidelines for 34 identified IT processes, which are grouped into four domains: planning and organisation, acquisition and implementation, delivery and support, and monitoring. Here, the control is defined by COBIT as the policies, procedures, practices and organizational structures designed to provide reasonable assurance that business objective will be achieved and that undesired events will be prevented or detected and corrected. Information Services Procurement Library (ISPL), Information Technology Infrastructure Library (ITIL) cover the supplement framework and tools for IT governance. IT Governance Institute recognizes the following works as essential for the governance model in virtual organization:

1. Balanced Scorecard as the help to transform vision and strategy into a coherent set of performance measures.
2. Board Briefing on IT Governance as a document covering high-level guidance to boards of directors.
3. Capability Maturity Model (CMM) as the model providing the principles and practices to ensure IT project maturity.
4. Committee of Sponsoring Organisations of the Treadway Commission (COSO) Enterprise Risk Management Framework  as the conceptual framework for benchmarking enterprise risk management processes.
5. European Framework for Quality Management (EFQM).
6. Enterprise Architecture as the roadmap to optimal performance of business processes.
7. Malcolm Baldridge National Quality Criteria Framework.
8. OECD Principles of Corporate Governance.
9. Technical Reference Model as a common vocabulary of IT terms.

## 4 Virtual University Governance

Nowadays institutions try to virtualize part or the whole of their operations opting for the ad hoc implementation of ICT solutions. Virtual universities as a distinct organizational form can be viewed as loosely coupled systems tied together by a combination of joint aspirations, conversational interactions, collaborating and occasionally competing communities of practice (Prasopoulou et al., 2006). The virtual university is an institution free from the geographical confines of the campus, using the new communication technologies to connect learners, potential learners, teachers, researchers, alumni, employers, research founders and administrators in a flexible ever-changing network organization. Some virtual universities are created within existing universities while a wide range of new institutions and collaborative ventures are being set up independently.

New trends emerging in the university education domain are significantly influencing e-learning:

- The shift from graduating-oriented  studying to learning-oriented studying.
- The shift from student to learner, so the learning process is more cooperative than competitive.
-  The shifts from expertise in a domain to teaching beliefs. One teacher may have diverse beliefs from another and the different actors (students, peers, and teachers) may have diverse beliefs about the domain and teaching methods.
- The shift from the four-year graduate program to lifelong learning.
- The shift from the dominance of the teachers' roles to student-centred pedagogical thinking.
- Decrease in the cost of technologies and services.
- Rapid growth and advancement of Internet technologies.

- Growing political commitment at European Union level to promote the widespread use of educational technologies through partnerships between institutions and businesses.

According to the Bologna Declaration, the key factors to greater consistency and compatibility between courses in different education systems comprise the adoption of a system of easily readable and comparable degrees, adoption of a system essentially based on two main educational cycles, establishment of a system of credits (European Credit Transfer and Accumulation System - ECTS system) as a proper means of promoting the most widespread student mobility, promotion of European cooperation in quality assurance with a view to developing comparable criteria and methodologies, promotion of students and staff mobility and emphasizing European dimension in higher education. Bologna Declaration aims to promote the convergence of different systems to improve the transparency and compatibility of different courses, degrees and diplomas. The resulting project - Tuning Educational Structures in Europe is at the heart of the Bologna-Prague-Berlin-Bergen process. The project focuses not on educational systems, but on educational structures and content of studies (Wagenaar & Gonzalez, 2003). Whereas educational systems are primarily the responsibility of governments, educational structures and content are that of higher educational institutions.

Nowadays in Europe the educational system reforms encourage further discussion i.e. the comparability of curricula in terms of structures, programmes and actual teaching as well as inseparable linking credits and learning outcomes, expressed in terms of comptences. In the reform process the required academic and professional profiles and needs of society should also play an important role.

Step by step, universities have been re-engineered towards virtual organisations. As a less risky approach they apply blended methodology in education and develop university services online. They include e-libraries, instructional networking and computing, media services, the campus course catalogue and schedule, multimedia courseware production. *econet* project – Virtual Educational Space of Collaboration of Universities of Economics in Poland (www.econet.pl) aims to propagate the positive ideas of virtual education among students. The project is to develop additional supplement courses supporting basic offline teaching activities. It is to encourage students to learn online and to persuade teachers that the new educational forms are valuable and effective. Within the project, teachers from some universities prepare course materials. Students are selected in a contest and sign the contract at their own offline universities. Generally this virtual education project is based on agreements among involved universities; however the central service centre is established to ensure educational platform maintainability. This virtual university is a closed organization in which identity–based access control is implemented.

The experiences received during the work within the *econet* project encouraged formulating theses that virtual university governance demands focus on virtual university strategy management, contract management, and information systems architecture development supported by standardization.

## 4.1 Virtual University Strategy Management

Strategy of virtual university focuses on establishing defensible strategic positions by setting organizational scopes, acquiring or building assets and establishing a balanced and authorised set of priorities. Strategies are presented as emerging from the individual university perspective. The following are key points for inclusion in setting strategy for the virtual university environment:

- Being aware of new university risk structures, including the new legal international regulations.
- Developing strategy with a continual focus on creating value through innovation and software tools (i.e. innovative student–oriented learning methods enabling their creativity development).
- Making the strategy a continual process – evolving, linking new initiatives to achieve holistic results.
- Sharing the knowledge required to govern the university effectively through use of a knowledge portal.

Anyway, the strategy of virtual university must be driven by innovativeness. It must develop cognitive abilities of learners and encourage them to creativity and cognition. The value of innovation is the essence of strategy in virtual university's knowledge economy.

At a virtual university managed as the extended institution four perspectives are needed for the strategy roadmap:

- Didactic processes improvement to ensure value creation.
- Customer (i.e. learner) satisfaction increase.
- Financial perspective – costs evaluation and budgeting.
- Growth of network effects.

Virtual university as a collection of autonomous teaching agencies constitutes a heterachic organization. As in traditional educational systems, virtual universities have the dilemma to preserve autonomy or reject it under the pressure of institutionalism. Institutional economics forses them to look at the interaction of law, economics and politics. It requires defining property rights and establishing governance arrangements.

Internet's origins in informal, non-commercial and relatively non-political research and education organizations however place the valuable resources outside the control of existing institutions. The governance problems could only be solved through the development of new institutional arrangements (i.e. service agreements). At virtual university governance structures are needed to deal with the complexity of the network relations and to ensure the implementation strategies. They have to combine flexible institutional arrangements, limited power and commitment of the participants. Having network policies, managers have to consider in what way values can be communicated to all network participants and how to ensure the internalization of the values. At virtual universities product (i.e. courseware) must pass a minimum threshold of adoption to survive in the market and ensure return of investment. Virtual university must resemble a network of distributed intelligence. However, not only disseminated knowledge is important, but also relations among the students, tutors and administration staff. Within virtual university some organizational paradoxes are observed such as coexistence of authority and democracy, efficiency and creativity, and discipline and empowerment which stem from perceptions of opposing and interwoven elements. Cognitive conflicts facilitate cooperation by aiming criticism at tasks. Moreover, the board (i.e. university rectors) and executive committees can play a vital role in maintaining diversity by providing periodical assessments of teaching staff and educational needs.

## 4.2 Virtual University Architecture

Architecture is progressively seen not just as a tactical instrument for designing an organization's systems and processes but as a strategic tool for enterprise governance. Virtual university architecture is expressed in the following four subsidiary architectures:

- Institutional Architecture. Involves the virtual university mission, strategy, courseware components, organizational structure, educational process models, business functions (e.g. payments transactions).
- Information Architecture (also called Data Architecture). Reveals who requires what information to achieve their mission and how this information is made available.
- Application Architecture (also called Functional Architecture). Involves the applications that are necessary for the virtual university mission and the information needs. It also gives insight into the virtual university departments, divisions or teams differently responsible for the courses.
- IT Architecture. Shows which IT services are necessary for the applications; also documents the software, hardware and network products.

Virtual university architecture identifies the organization of data, applications and infrastructure and how they are interrelated both statically as well as during run-time execution within Learning Management System (LMS).

## 4.3 Contract Management

At virtual university the dissemination of knowledge, the distribution of services and the provision of access to different resources are based on contracts and agreements. In IT domain Service Level Agreements (SLAs) are clear description of activities, as performed by a supplier under orders of a recipient. To some degree of detail, an SLA describes when, how and where the activities are executed (Thiadens, 2005). SLAs are aimed at creating certain level of expectation. They record the intention of organizations for cooperating in the long-run. The SLAs are just applied to include agreements on the quality, the quantity and the costs of the IT facilities. But generally agreements between recipients and suppliers are laid down in contracts. In virtual organizations, the contents of the sourcing contracts may include the elements of various contracts provided for in law. It may contain elements of a sales contract, an agreement for provision of services and a data processing agreement. In the part of the contract dealing with purchase and sale, it is indicated which objects are handed over. A second part of the sourcing contract deals with the services to be delivered. This part describes the services, deals with the scope of the provision of services and the way in which one deals with work. Virtual university partners for their own interests' protection should sign the contract for cooperation, usually for the period longer than two years. ECTS Student Application Form and ECTS Learning Agreement have been developed for mobile students, who will spend a limited study period at a university in a foreign country. The Learning Agreement contains the list of course units or modules which the student plans to take. For each course unit the title, the code number and the ECTS credit are indicated. This agreement does not exclude courses delivered online. It guarantees the transfer of credit for courses passed successfully by the student.

## 4.4 Standardization for Virtual Education

Standards play a prominent role in many systems that are characterized by interaction and interrelatedness. In information systems, standards provide compatibility and are a prerequisite for collaboration benefits (Weitzel, 2004). Weitzel (2004) uses the term standard to refer to any technology or product (software, hardware) incorporating technological specification that provide compatibility. Products are said to be compatible when their design is coordinated in a way that enables them to work together. Compatibility standards enable users to participate in networks that allow them to share databases, have access to large selection of compatible software, exchange documents and communicate directly. The network effects in virtual education markets mainly originate from two different areas: the need for compatibility to exchange information and the need for complementary products and services.

Standardization activities extend over a wide variety of areas. The activities of standardization organizations such as ISO, ANSI or DIN can confirm this. Standards set by these types of organizations are often referred to as norms.

Standardized approach to educational process enables mixing and matching content from multiple sources. It enables the development of interchangeable content that can be reused, assembled and disassembled quickly and easily. It makes it possible to verify the view that the learning technology investments are wise and risk adverse.

Whether it is the creation of content libraries, or learning management systems, accredited standards will reduce the risk of making large investments on learning technologies. Accredited standards assure that the investment in time and intellectual capital can move from one system to the next. Such standards are generic for distance learning education not only on academic university level, but also for postgraduate students, advanced professional training, high schools, so they can be applied as supplement to university education systems. Organizations responsible for the development of computer-based training standards are as follows:

- The ARIADNE Foundation [http://www.ariadne-eu.org/].
- The Advanced Distributed Learning (ADL) Initiative [http://www.adlnet.org/]. The ADL Initiative developed the concept and implementation of ADL specifications and guidelines such as the Shareable Content Object Reference Model (SCORM) to define relations of course components, data models and protocols so that learning content objects are shareable across systems that conform to the same model.
- The Aviation Industry  CBT (Computer Based Training) Committee (AICC) [http://www.aicc.org/ ].
- The Australian Consortium EdNA (Education Network Australia) [http://www.edna.edu.au/].
- BAOL Quality Mark http://www.baol.co.uk/qmwhat.htm .
- CEN (Comité Européen de Normalisation)/ The ISSS division (Information Society Standardization System) Workshop on Learning Technology [http://www.cenorm.be/].
- CUBER project  http://www.cuber.net
- DESIRE – Development of a European Service for Information on Research and Education http://www.ukoln.ac.uk/metadata/desire/quality.
- Dublin Core Metadata Initiative. The Dublin Core is a metadata element set intended to facilitate discovery of networked electronic resources http://dublincore.org.
- ETB quality research  project http://www.en.eun.org.
- The IEEE Learning Technology Standards Committee (LTSC) http://ieeeltsc.org
- The IMS (Instructional Management System) project http://www.imsglobal.org
- The ISO and International Engineering Consortium Joint Technology Commitee (ISO/IEC JTC1) [http://jtc1sc36.org].
- Gateway to Educational Materials (GEM) http://www.scitechresources.gov/Results/show_result.php?rec=2538
- Promoting Multimedia access to Education and Training in European Society (PROMETEUS) [http://eml-sig.eulearn.net/].
- Reusable Learning Objects (RLOs) UCeL (Universities' Collaboration in eLearning UCEL) http:// www.ucel.ac.uk.

There is a difference in the European and American way of standardization. Europeans tend to find solutions on a governmental basis and so several governmental institutions and organizations are founded to work in the area. In opposite to that, the Americans often work out of market-driven situations and are pluralistic. Different societies have contradictory educational systems (different school/university models) and therefore a divergent understanding what specifications should handle, what is essential and what is unimportant. The development of a standard for metadata suited for school as the specification is partly based on learning objects, but adds several other school-specific elements.

## 5 Summary

Virtual universities as new organizational forms are to supplement or even substitute traditional education. Standardization of educational processes, clarification strategy and architecture are necessary to create virtual universities as reliable institutions, which work to educate adults and to enable educational activities verifiability. Standardization enables transparency of educational activities, their compatibility and controllability. Contract management for IT services as well for students' mobility is to be the essential way of governance of educational resources within such universities.

## References

Board Briefing on IT Governance (2003), 2$^{nd}$ edition, IT Governance Institute October, Rolling Meadows IL, http://www.itgi.org

Burn JM, Ash C (2002) Knowledge Management Strategies for Virtual Organizations, In: Kisielnicki J (ed) Modern Organizations in Virtual Communities. IRM Press Hershey, pp 1-18

Byrne JA (1993) The virtual corporation, Business Week, February 8, pp 98-102

Dirksen V, Smit B (2002) Exploring the Common Ground of Virtual Communities: Working Towards a "Workable Definition" In: Kisielnicki J (ed) Modern Organizations in Virtual Communities. IRM Press Hershey, pp 67-76

Franke UJ (2002) The Competence-based View on the Management of Virtual Web Organizations, In: Kisielnicki J (ed) Modern Organizations in Virtual Communities. IRM Press Hershey, pp 19-48

Kisielnicki J (2002) Virtual Organization as a Chance for Enterprise Development In: Kisielnicki J (ed) Modern Organizations in Virtual Communities. IRM Press Hershey, pp 100-115

Lewis JD, Weigert A (1985) Trust as a Social Reality, Social Forces, (63)4: pp 967-985.

Mitra T (2005) A case for SOA governance, http://www-128.ibm.com/developerworks/webservices/library/ws-soa-govern/?ca

Prasopoulou E, Poulymenakou A, Pouloudi N (2006) Unraveling the Virtual University In: Klein S, Poulymenakou A Managing Dynamic Networks. Springer Berlin, pp 259-283

Prusak L (1997) Knowledge in Organizations, Butterworth-Heinemann, Boston MA

Thiadens T (2005) Manage IT! Springer Dordrecht

Van Grembergen W (2004) Strategies for Information Technology Governance. IGP Hershey

Wagenaar R, Gonzalez J (2003) UK Bologna Seminar, Tuning Educational Structures in Europe, The Tuning Approach A Case Study, http://europa.eu.int/comm/education/socrates/

Walters D (2002) Operations Strategy. Palgrave Macmillan, NY

Weitzel T (2004) Economics of Standards in Information Networks, Information Age Economy. Springer Berlin.

# Practical Experiences in Web Engineering

M.J. Escalona[*], J.J. Gutierrez[*], D. Villadiego[*], A. León[**], J. Torres[***]

[*] University of Seville, Spain,{escalona,javierj,villadiego}@lsi.us.es
[**] DMR-Consulting, Seville, Spain,'alvaro.leon.camacho@dmr-consulting.com
[***] State University of Campinas, SP – Brazil,
arturo.zenteno@ic.unicamp.br

**Abstract:** Web Engineering is defined like a new area to propose models, techniques, processes, architectures, etc. in order to deal correctly with the special characteristics of the web environment. In the last years, new methodological approaches appeared in this environment. However, Web Engineering is not often applied in industries and real projects. This paper presents a general vision of a web approach, named NDT (Navigational Development Techniques) and it is focused on the study of its practical applications.

## 1 Introduction

Since the Net of Nets was born in the 70's, as a net to spread research material, an amazing change in the use of Internet has taken place. In the last years, Internet has become a popular tool and the number of users who work every day with it has grown crazily.

Companies and organizations find in Internet a suitable way to present their businesses, and also, a powerful way to contact with their clients and employees all over the world [14]. This evolution, the high advance of communications and the increase in the benefits of the equipment, networks and routes of transmission have fomented to the fact that most of the actual systems are developed or adapted to internet. Since the development of software systems in Internet appeared, the research community has detected the necessity of proposing new methodologies, techniques and models to offer a suitable reference environment for the new and special characteristics of internet. For this aim, a new research line in the Software Engineering has been developed in the last years: Web Engineering [5]. Web Engineering is the systematic, structured and quantifiable application of methodological approaches to the development, evaluation and maintenance of web applications [5]. At first, the development of web systems was an ad-hoc process. Applications were developed without following any structured process that guarantees the quality of the results. When the Web Engineering appeared as a new research line, several new methodological approaches were proposed and some surveys and comparative studies agreed that it was necessary to offer new methodological environments to deal with the special characteristics of the web [2][3][12][13][24]. Nowadays, the research community accepts all over the world the idea that web projects have special characteristics (critical navigation, hypermedia, customization, etc) that must be treated carefully in the life cycle. Thus, web projects and that need their own models and techniques [18].

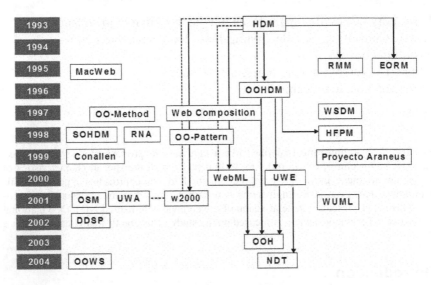

**Fig. 1.** A global vision of the web approaches and its relations

After different comparative studies, we can conclude that a big number of web approaches were proposed in the last years. In figure 1, a chronogram with the most famous approaches is presented. Some of these approaches are an evolution of a previous one and some of them are related between them. A continuous arrow between two methodologies expresses that the destination approach is based on the origin one and a dotted line expresses that the younger approach is an evolution of the oldest one. Most of them are focused on the object oriented paradigm, only the shadow ones are structured. It is out of the scope of this paper to present approaches presented in figure 1. They can be depth studied in [12].

However, recent comparative studies [2][3][12][17][18][24] show that Web Engineering has not been enough applied in the enterprise environment. Very few real applications can be found. This is an important gap for the Web Engineering research.

In this paper, we present a global vision of NDT[9][11][12]. A web proposal to deal with requirements capture and analysis in web systems in section 2. This proposal has been widely applied in real companies and projects. In section 3, these experiences are presented. In section 4, these experiences are presented analyzing the results and the evolution of the proposal. In the last section, final conclusions and future works are presented.

## 2 NDT (Navigational Development Techniques)

NDT is a methodological process focused on the requirements and the analysis phases. NDT offers a systematic way to deal with the special characteristic of the web environment. NDT is based on the definition of formal metamodels, presented in [14], that allow to create derivation relations between models. NDT takes this theoretic base and enriches it with the necessary elements to define a methodology: techniques, models, methodological process, etc. in order to offer a suitable context to be applied in real projects.

In this sense, NDT starts with the theoretic definition of the requirements engineering metamodels and it proposes a methodological environment to drive the team in the capture, definition and validation of requirements following the next ideas:

1. In the elicitation of requirements NDT assumes its own techniques inherited from the requirements engineering environment like interviews, brainstorming or the study of the previous systems [7][21].
2. In order to describe requirements, NDT uses some standard models, like the use cases, and patterns. A pattern is a special template with predefined fields that the development team must develop with the final user [7].
3. In the validation of requirements, NDT also proposes a group of techniques like the traceability matrix [7] or the fuzzy thesaurus [19] adapted to NDT patterns in order to propose a more agile requirements validation.

In this sense, NDT can be considered like a model driven methodology. NDT also normalizes the structure of the results that must be developed during the requirements engineering. It offers a complete definition of the structure.

With the theoretic base of metamodels and relations, the next phase is the analysis phase. In the analysis phase three models are generated:

1. The conceptual model, that defines the static structure of the information and its relations.
2. The navigational model, that defines how users can navigate through the information.
3. The abstract interface model is composed by a group of HTML and XML prototypes that lets validate the conceptual and navigational models [20].

However, the generation of these three models is made in two phases. In the first one, analysis models are generated systematically from the requirements using the theoretic relations defined between models. In this sense, NDT can be defined as a model driven approach. These models are named basic analysis models.

In these basic models, the analyst can make some changes in order to make these models more suitable, getting the final analysis models. The construction of these final models is not systematic and they depend on the experience of the analyst. NDT offers some guides and processes in order to make easier the analyst's revision [12].

Besides, NDT controls that the changes proposed by the analyst are agree with the definition of requirements. In this sense, NDT manages that the final analyst models and the requirements definition are consistence. In figure 2, the NDT life cycle is presented with an activity diagram.

Final models generated in NDT are compatible with other approaches like UWE or OOHDM. For this reason, from them, the development team can continue the life cycle with other approaches that have been widely accepted by the research community.

In conclusion, NDT can be defined as a methodology to the requirements and analysis phases, the rest of the life cycle is dealt with other important approaches. NDT is offered to cover a gap in the treatment of the first phases of the life cycle in the Web Engineering.

Finally, it is important to stick out that NDT has an associated tool, named NDT-Tool [9] that supports all the life cycle of NDT. This tool lets automate all the systematic processes of NDT, applies all its techniques and gets the results automatically.

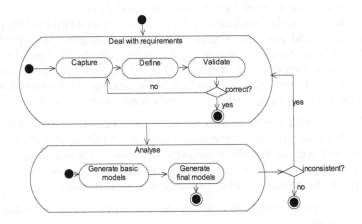

**Fig. 2.** NDT development process

## 3 Practical applications of NDT

With this basic introduction to NDT, which can be extended with its reference manual available in [9], in this section an historical evolution of NDT is going to be presented. NDT was born from some comparatives and analytic studies of the Web Engineering. From them, we concluded that the Web Engineering was a very young area that was the research environment of several important groups, but there were some gaps stuck out even by these research groups [12]:

1. There are not standard notations. In the first years, each approach offered its own models and they were incompatible with other models in other approaches. Everyday, research groups are looking for standard notations, like extensions of UML, in order to offer compatible models.
2. Classically, the most treated phases in the Web Engineering were the design and the implementation ones. In the last years, the research community has stuck out that it is important to offer suitable ways to go from the user's requirements the design models.
3. There is not enough CASE support. Although, nowadays some methodologies like WSDM[6] are working in this line, there are very few approaches, like WebML [4], UWE [17] or OOH[3], that cover completely their life cycle with a tool.
4. The Web Engineering has not been enough applied in the enterprise environment.

For these reasons, NDT is presented like a solution to cover these gaps in the Web Engineering. NDT has evolved to the use of standards and it offers a open way to work with other approaches. For that, the use of metamodels and UML is fundamental. Besides, NDT works in the first phases of the life cycle that are the less treated in Web Engineering, using the suitable results of other approaches in the next phases.

**Table 1.** The analysed project

| Name of the project | Date of starting | Company |
|---|---|---|
| **Systems to manage information about public grants** | | |
| The system to manage information about cultural grants | 2000-2001 | Andalusian Government |
| The system to manage information about international help | 2001-2002 | |
| **Systems to manage information about historical heritage** | | |
| The system of Movable Heritage in Andalusia | 1997-1999 | Historical Heritage Andalusian Institute |
| The Thesaurus of Historical Heritage | 2003-2004 | |
| The system of Historical Heritage Authors | 2005-.. | |
| **System to measure the grade of handicap** | | |
| The system to measure the grade of handicap | 2004-2005 | Alcer Foundation |

But, NDT also has worked in points 3 and 4. With NDT-Tool, NDT offers a suitable CASE support in its application. And with its several practical experiences, NDT has shown how the Web Engineering can be applied in real projects.

In this section, we are going to present these practical experiences. Projects are presented in three subsections depending on its subject: projects to manage information about public grants, projects to manage information about historical heritage, the system to measure the grade of handicap. For each of one, a global vision of the project objects and the development environment is offered and after the conclusions getting in them are analyzed.

Although projects are presented grouped by its thematic, it is important to analyze when they were developed in order to see the evolution of NDT. In the table 1, we presented an abstract with the name of each project, the date of development and the company where they were developed. In the next section, this short schema will be the base to analyze the conclusions in a general way.

## 3.1. Grants management projects

When NDT started to be applied, in 2000, only the requirements metamodels were defined. Patterns and models in the requirements phase were applied in a system to manage the information about grants given by the Andalusia Government for cultural activities. NDT patterns were changed, corrected and modified during this first collaboration. NDT divides requirements into five groups: storage information, actors', functional, interaction and non-functional requirements. The system developed was critical because it had to manage a high amount of information that depended on a complex administrative process where there was a high number of different roles with different necessities. For that, we detected that it was necessary to offer a way to define new data structures. However, the idea of data structure was not oriented to a programming idea.

The data structures that had to be included in NDT must be oriented to the user. They must offer a suitable way to define a set of structured data according to the user's view. For instance, in the system appeared several times the necessity of storing the identification data of different people: users, managers, etc. These data always include the same information: name, address, etc. Despite of defining these data every time, we worked on the idea of offering a way to define this structure in the requirements phase.

With this idea, in NDT the concept of new natures was introduced. A nature is a new special kind of requirement, with its own pattern, that allows to define these data structure requirements.

Other important idea that was added in NDT in this project was the use of graphics. At the beginning, the requirements phase of NDT was only based on patterns. However, we detected that, at the beginning of the project, was more interesting make meetings based on graphical notations. We decided to enrich the basic definition of NDT with the use cases of UML[25]. Use cases model is a standard notation widely known and very easy to be understood by non-expert people. In any way, the textual description of patterns was kept in NDT. After the first meetings, use cases are very ambiguous to capture all the necessary information [15][26].

This modifications in NDT provoked an additional cost in the project that was several months delayed. However, the final results were quite goods and, some months later, a new similar collaboration was born.

Again, the project was a system to manage information about grants in the Andalusian Government. However, in this case, grants were oriented to the international help. Users were not the same and the new ones did not know NDT or the patterns. But, with this new experience, we could test that the introduced changes were very suitable.

The double way to work: patterns and diagrams, offered a more agile way to work with users. However, we found in this collaboration an important barrier in the application of NDT. To keep patterns updated was a very difficult task. Patterns are interrelated and a change or a modification in one of them can produce changes in several ones. For this reason, in this point, we detected that it was completely necessary to develop a tool to support NDT.

## 3.2. Heritage management projects

The oldest project where NDT was applied were the system of Movable Heritage in Andalusia (1997-1999). This system lets manage and spread out information about the movable heritage in Andalusia. The initial patterns in NDT were completed and first tested in it. However, the essential contribution of this project to NDT was the special treatment of the different roles.

This system had different roles of users and the system changed completely depending of each role. The shown information was different depending on the user was an archeologist, an artist, a tourist or others. But, besides, in this system a same user could navigate in the system playing several roles at the same time. Thus, if a user was an archeologist, an artist or an archeologist-artist, the navigation, functionality or the interface were completely different.

The complexity of this role motivated us to find simple but powerful ways to study roles and their relations. From this idea, new models based on heritance and traceability matrixes were added to NDT during this project.

These new ideas was again testing in a similar project with the same group of users in 2003. In this case, we applied NDT to develop a Thesaurus of Historical Heritage [10] obtaining very good results.

This project demonstrated also the advantages of working with users that knew the NDT patterns. Patterns are very intuitive for users and non-expert people in software engineering. When a user works with them, it is very easy for him/her to use it again.

The evolution of NDT and its improvements with the practice were recently value in a project that, nowadays, has just being developed with the same group of users. This new project consists in the development of a system to manage and spread through Internet the information about authors that worked in the Andalusian Historical Heritage. In this project, the development time and also its cost have being lower than in the other projects for several reasons.

The first one is because users and the development team know very well the development environment. Users know NDT very well and it was quite easy to apply patterns and requirements techniques. But, also NDT-Tool is completely developed. It is available via web and it make easier the management of the information and the attainment of the results.

### 3.3. The system to manage the grade of handicap

This system is one of the youngest where NDT was applied[27]. In this case, NDT was a consolidated methodology. For this reason, in the application of NDT to this system, patterns, models, techniques and NDT-Tool could be applied without any changes getting very good results. However, the project was essential for another aspect that was forgotten in the research environment but that was essential in some enterprise environment.

The system to manage the grade of handicap is a system developed with the Alcer Fundation [1]. This system lets apply the Royal Decree 1971/1999 (23/12) of the Spanish Government and drives how the grade of handicap of an patient must be measured by a medical tribunal.

This project offered two important challenges to NDT. The first one was that the environment, the group of users and the terminology was completely new for NDT and the development team and, even, for the group of users because in Spain there is not a similar system. In this sense, the application of NDT was very successfully because it made easier the communication with users.

However, the results in the other line wake the restlessness about a very few treated aspect. In other projects, the validation of requirements was made with techniques like reviews, the following of requirements with traceability matrix and the study of the terminology with glossaries.

Nevertheless, this system worked in a very specific environment with a very complex argot. The ambiguity of the terminology in this kind of projects could provoke serious disasters.

We started to work in more powerful techniques to validate requirements. We made a comparative study and work with the university of Nice in this aspect. This university developed a tool, named fuzzy thesaurus [19], that allows the development team to test ambiguities in software analysis models. After a work together, this tool was adapted to NDT and, nowadays, it is being included in NDT-Tool. The application of the fuzzy thesaurus allows to find errors in the requirements definition provoked by terminology ambiguities in a systematic way. The use of this tool is not always forced in NDT but it is a good technique to validate requirements in complex project with complex environments.

## 4. Global evaluation

During the realization of the projects and with the gotten results, we can present some empirical results. In table 2, we have enumerated each project and we have measured some aspects for each one.

We are going to analyze each of these measures and their justification. However, we are going to start for the last ones. The grade of development of NDT and the availability of NDT-Tool are essential in the results of the other aspects. The oldest project was the system to manage the Movable Andalusian Heritage, in this case, NDT was just at the beginning and several changes were made during the life cycle. In the first two projects, NDT was more developed but, also, some changes had to be made. Besides, in these three projects NDT-Tool was not available. These aspects added a new complexity to the project and provoked some delays.

The first idea presented on the table is the grade of complexity of the system. We measured this aspect with the number of detected requirements during the requirements phase with the next ranges:

- Low complexity: less than 30 requirements
- Medium complexity: between 30 to 50 requirements
- High complexity: more than 50 requirements

The grade of knowledge of users is a more subjective measure. We have divided projects into two groups. In the first group, with grade low, users did not know anything about NDT before the project. In the second one, users (o more than the 50 per cent) worked with NDT before.

The grade of complexity of the environment for the development team expresses if the group of analysts knew the terminology, the company and the group of users before the project. All analyst were expert using NDT, so this knowledge was not included in the table. The two next ones are only quantitative measures to present a deeper vision of the group of work.

But, perhaps, the most interesting rows are the next two. We have presented the estimated time and the real time of the project.The estimation of the project at the beginning was made using the initial method proposed by Gustav Karner [16] and revised in [22] adapted to NDT and its patterns.

**Table 2.** Empirical measures

| | cultural grants | T inter-nat. help subven. | Mov-able Heritage | The Thesaurus | Authors | the grade of handicap |
|---|---|---|---|---|---|---|
| Grade of complexity of the system | Medium | Medium | High | Low | Low | High |
| Grade of knowledge of the users | Low | Low | Low | High | High | Low |
| Grade of complexity of the environment for the development team | High | Medium | High | Low | Low | High |
| Number of users in the requirements phase | 3 | 2 | 5 | 2 | 2 | 2 |
| Number of ana- | 2 | 2 | 2 | 1 | 1 | 2 |

| | | | | | | |
|---|---|---|---|---|---|---|
| lysist in the re-quirements phase | | | | | | |
| Estimated time (months) | 12 | 12 | 20 | 6 | 6 | 8 |
| Real time (months) | 15 | 13 | 25 | 6,5 | 4 | 8,5 |
| Grade of de-velopment of NDT | Medium | Me-dium/High | Low | High | High | High |
| Availability of NDT-Tool | NO | NO | NO | YES | YES | YES |

According to these measures, if we analyze the two first projects we can conclude that these projects, although in fact were very similar in complexity and size, were not similar in the development. The first one was delayer. The reason was the grade of complexity for development team. Analysts were the same in both projects, so, in the second one, they know very well how grants were dealt. Besides, in the first project, as it was presented in the previous section, some changes were introduced in NDT. The incorporation of these changes were a very positive aspect for the system to manage international help grants.

More interesting is the analysis of the projects in the Andalusian Heritage Institute, in the third, fourth and fifth columns. The first project was a very difficult one and it had very bad conditions. The grade of complexity for the development team was very high. They had never worked in this environment and they know nothing about heritage. By other way, the group of users did not work with NDT or any similar methodology before. Besides, NDT was just at the beginning and, as we said, several changes were made in the patterns. Finally, the maintenance of the patterns, the application of algorithms and the results must be developed by hand, because NDT-Tool was not available.

For these reasons, the project was quite delay. Its estimated time was 20 months, but, at the end, it was 25. However, the final results were very good, although the project was delay. Nowadays, the system is running and the number of changes in the initial requirements definition was really low. Users were very agreed with the application of NDT and they wanted to use it for other projects. It is very interesting analyzed the other two projects in the same environment. In this case, NDT was completely defined. Users and developers knew the environment and NDT. In this case, as can be deduced from the table, the delay was lower. In the project of the Thesaurus, the system only was delay for fifteen days. That was because NDT-Tool was developed but it was very young and we have to correct some things during the project. However, in the last project the time of development was lower than the estimated one. In this case, the project had very good conditions and it influenced in a very positive way in the project.

Finally, in the last project, we can observe that there was again a delay. This delay was provoked for the validation of requirements. As it was introduced in the previous section, we noticed that in this project the validation of requirements was a very critical phase and we noticed that it was necessary to develop more powerful techniques. The fuzzy thesaurus was not applied in this project, although its necessity was stuck out during its development. The delay of the project was provoked for that.

In general, we can observe that the successful in the application of NDT depends of several factors. Obviously, NDT and NDT-Tool are now completely developed. Thus, they are not important aspects in our actual and future projects. However, other elements like the user's experience in NDT or the grade of complexity of the environment for the development team are, nowadays, the main factors in the results when we applied NDT.

We noticed that when users work for the first time with patterns, they understand very well because they use the user's vocabulary. Obviously, when users work with patterns for the second time they work better because they know them. Even, in the project of Authors (column five), users used it directly NDT-Tool. They completed the patterns by themselves and, later, these patterns were revised by the rest of users and the development team.

## 5 Conclusions

After this paper, we can conclude that NDT is a methodology that was developed not only with research results. It also has a very deep influence from the enterprise environment.

Frequently, the research line and companies or practical applications are completely separated. In several research forums we can find references about this gap in Web Engineering. This paper presents a global vision about practical experiences in Web Engineering and according to the results we can observe that the practical experience can add important and useful ideas to the research results. Presented projects are not the single ones where NDT was applied. For several years, the Madeira group, where NDT was developed, has applied it in several real projects. The result is a methodology that has grown at the same time in the research and practical environment. For us, the practical experience with NDT is a very interesting work that gives us a more real vision of the software engineering. In order to conclude and related with that, we want to outline that for us, another kind of practical experience was a very important source of interesting. NDT was applied in several final project in our university. When a computer science student finishes his/her grade, he/she has to develop a final software project. Nowadays, NDT was applied like requirements and analysis technique in twenty final projects in the last years. We observed that NDT is also very simple to be applied by people who are not too expert in computer science, like our students, and they are very agree with the use of NDT-Tool because the work is easier. As a future work, we have to indicate that NDT is completed but it is not a closed methodology. The double work in NDT (enterprise/university) offers continuous references to adapt the methodology, to include new algorithms, techniques or models.

We want to foment the open character of NDT with other approaches. Nowadays, we have important collaborations with other research groups, like the UWE one, in order to integrate both methodologies and make compatible NDT-Tool and ArgoUWE. Finally, our interest for continuing with the collaboration with companies is bigger every day. We are starting a very big one in collaboration with the Andalusian Government. The duration of this new project is about two years and the number of analysts and users in the requirements phase is the biggest one where NDT was applied. We hope to continue with these practical applications because we thought that they are essential in Web Engineering.

# References

Federación Federación Andaluza Alcer. www.alcer.info

Barry, C., Lang, M. A Survey of Multimedia and Web Development Techniques and Methodology Usage. IEEE Multimedia. pp. 52-56. Abril-Junio 2001.

Cachero, C. Una extensión a los métodos OO para el modelado y generación automática de interfaces hipermediales. PhD Thesis. Alicante, España. Enero 2003.

Ceri, S., Fraternali, P., Bongio. Web Modelling Language (WebML): A Modelling Language for Designing Web Sites. Conference WWW9/Computer Networks 33 (1-6) pp. 137-157. Mayo 2000.

Deshpande, Y., Marugesan, S., Ginige,A., Hanse,S., Schawabe,D., Gaedke, M, B. White. Web Engineering. Journal of Web Engineering. Vol. 1 N° 1. pp. 3-17.2002. Rinton Press. 2002.

De Troyer, O., Leune, C. WSDM: A User-Centered Design Method for Web Sites. Computer Networks and ISDN systems. 7th International World Wide Web Conference. Elsevier. pp. 85- 94.1998.

Durán A., Bernárdez, B., Ruiz, A., Toro M. A Requirements Elicitation Approach Based in Templates and Patterns. Workshop de Engenharia de Reqisitos. pp.17-29 . Buenos Aires, Argentina. 1999

Dustin, E., Rashka, J., McDiarmid, D. Quality Web Systems. Performance, Security, and Usability. Addison Wesley 2002

Escalona M.J, Mejías M, Torres J, Reina A.M. NDT-Tool: A tool case to deal with requirements in web information systems. Proceedings of IV International Conferences on Web Engineering. ICWE 2003. LNCS 2722. pp. 212-213. 2003

Escalona M.J, León, A., Martín, A., Mejías M, Torres J,. El Tesauro de Patrimonio Histórico de Andalucía. IV Jornadas de Bibliotecas Digitales. pp. 105-114. Alicante, España. Noviembre 2003

M.J. Escalona, M. Mejías, J. Torres. Developing systems with NDT & NDT-Tool. 13th International Conference on Information Systems Development: Methods and Tools, Theory and Practice. pp. 149-159. Vilna, Lituania. Septiembre 2004.

Escalona, M.J. Modelos y técnicas para la especificación y el análisis de la Navegación en sistemas software. Ph. European Thesis. Department of Computer Languages and Systems. University of Seville. Seville, Spain. October 2004.

Escalona, M.J., Koch, N. Requirements Engineering for Web Applications: A Comparative Study. Journal on Web Engineering, Vol.2 No 3, pp. 193-212. Febrero 2004. Rinton Press

Gu, A. Extending Object-Oriented Modelling Languages for Web Applications. M.S.C. Thesis. Univesity of Technology, Sydney, 2001

Insfrán, E., Pastor, O., Wieringa, R. Requirements Engineering-Based Conceptual Modelling. Requirements Engineering Journal, Vol 7 (1). 2002.

Karner, G. Metrics for Objectory. Diploma Thesis. University of Linköping. Sweden NO. LiTHIDA-Ex-9344:21. 1993.

Koch, N. Software Engineering for Adaptative Hypermedia Applications. Ph. Thesis, FAST Reihe Softwaretechnik Vol(12), Uni-Druck Publishing Company, Munich. Germany. 2001.

Lang, M. Hypermedia System Development. Do we really need new Methods?. Site-Where Parallels Intersect. Informing Science. pp. 883-891. June 2002.

Mirbel, I. Un mécanisme d'intégration de schemas de conception orientée object. PhD. Thesis. Laboratory IS3. University of Nice. December, 1996

Olsina, L., Rossi, G. Measuring Web Application Quality with WebQEM. IEEE Multimedia. pp. 20-45. Octubre-Diciembre 2002.

Pan, D., Zhu, D., Johnson, K. Requirements Engineering Techniques. Internal Report. Department of Computer Science. University of Calgary. Canada. 2001.

Peralta, M. Estimación del Esfuerzo Basada en Casos de Uso. Centro de Ingeniería del Software e Ingeniería del Conocimiento (CAPIS).

Pressman, R.S. Ingeniería del Software. Un enfoque práctico. Mc Graw Hill, 2002

Retschitzegger, W. & Schwinger, W. Towards Modeling of Data Web Applications - A Requirements Perspective. AMCIS 2000, Vol 1, pp. 149-155. USA 2000.

The Unified Modeling Language V.2.0. Object Management Group. OMG. 2003.

Vilain, P., Schwabe, D., Sieckenius, C. A diagrammatic Tool for Representing User Interaction in UML. Lecture Notes in Computer Science. UML'2000. England 2002.

Villadiego, D., Escalona, M.J., Torres, J., Mejías, M. Aplicación de NDT al sistema para el reconocimiento, declaración y calificación del grado de minusvalía. Report interno LSI-2004-02. Universidad de Sevilla. Junio 2004.

# Derivation of Test Objectives Automatically

J. J. Gutiérrez, M. J. Escalona, M. Mejías, J. Torres

Department of Computer Languages and Systems.
University of Seville.,{javierj, escalona, risoto, jtorres}@lsi.us.es

**Abstract:** A vital task of software development is to test the correct implementation of functional requirements. Use cases are widely used artefacts that define the functionality of a software system in early stages of the development process. This paper exposes the lack of automatism in existing approaches that deal with the derivation of test cases, and introduces a new approach and tool to derive systematically test objectives from the use cases of the system under test.

**Keywords:** System testing, test objectives, generation of test cases, open-source tools.

## 1 Introduction

The growing complexity of software systems increases the need to assure their quality. The system testing is a technique that helps to ensure the quality of software systems. It is defined as a black-box procedure to verify the satisfaction of the requirements of the system under test (SUT). Several kinds of tests might be performed during the system testing phase. Some of them are: navigational testing, reliability testing, usability testing, etc. This paper is focused on the functional testing from the point of view of external actors and, specifically, from a human user point of view through a graphical interface. Thus, a test case substitutes an actor of the system and simulates the interactions with the actor to check that this system does what it is expected to do. For this reason, the main artefact to obtain system test cases is its functional requirements since they describe all the expected behaviours that have to be tested by the system test cases.

Functional requirements are often defined as use cases. Use cases offer a general vision of the system. They are easier to study and validate for non-technical users. In early development phases, when requirements are being discovered, defined and negotiated, it is quite easier to modify use cases defined as prose or structured natural language, than to make changes in formal requirements.

Most of software testing in industry is conducted at the system level. However, the most formal research has been focused on the unit level [12]. Thus, most system-level techniques are only informally described. The system testing requires a formal process to identify the most important test cases and to measure the grade of efficiency. Another important problem is that the system testing is performed at the end of the development process, when the system is codified. Due to a tight schedule time, the design and execution of system testing are frequently only superficially performed or not at all. This paper tries to resolve one of these lacks. It proposes a systematic process to derive test objectives from use cases, in order to verify the successful implementation of these use cases in the final software system.

A test objective is a named element that describes what should be tested [1]. The test objectives derived from use cases define what we have to test to ensure the right implementation of the use case and the complete implementation of the use cases. Designing good objectives is a vital task for the testing as well as for the software development. However, the UML Testing Profile [1] does not define any notation to represent test objectives. We have resolved this gap using activity diagrams and sequences of activities.

An activity diagram has several advantages over other UML diagrams. UML sequence diagrams need information about the components of the systems and the signatures and parameters of the calls among the components. Moreover, sequence diagrams do not allow to represent alternative or erroneous scenarios. UML state diagrams are focused on the states and transitions of the system, but they do not clearly show the interactions between the actors and the system.

This paper is organized as followed: section 2 briefly describes several surveys about approaches that deal with the derivation of test objectives. Then, section 3 proposes a model and template to define use cases. Section 4 introduces a real application using a case study. Then, section 5 describes the process to derive test objectives from use cases using the template of section 3, and illustrates the process with the system described in section 4. Section 6 describes other related approaches. Finally, section 7 lists the conclusions and future works.

## 2 State of the art

While writing this paper, we have identified several approaches to generate test objectives. Two surveys that analyse and compare 21 different approaches (in total) may be found in [5] and [10]. Next paragraphs reference some of these approaches. A complete list of references may be found in both surveys.

The existing approaches might be divided into three groups depending on the artefacts used for the generation of test cases. The first group includes approaches that generate test objectives directly from use cases, like [2] and [11]. The second group includes approaches that generate a behavioural model from the use cases and derive test objectives from them, like [3], [13] or [4]. Some of the notations used in this group are: activity diagrams, state-machines diagrams, use case transitions systems or scenario trees. The third group describes approaches focused on variables and test values. These approaches identify variables in use cases and perform partition of the domains, like [2] and [7].

The approaches might also be divided into two groups depending on the scope of the generated test objectives. In the first group, we find approaches that generate test objectives from isolated use cases, like [2], [11] or [4]. The second group includes approaches that generate test objectives from sequences of use cases, like [3] or [13]. However, none of the approaches of the first group might automatically derive behavioural models and test objectives from use cases. We can also point out a lack of supporting tools. In the second group, the reference [13] generates test objectives in an automatic way for sequences of use cases, not for isolated use cases. These facts justified a new approach to generate a behavioural model and to derive test objectives in an automatic way. Next section describes the model and template used to define use cases.

## 3 A use case model and template for testing

The systematic generation of test objectives implies some drawbacks. One of them is the need for defining a concrete model for the use cases that may be manipulated in a systematic and automatic way, without loosing the advantages of using prose text. A widely used solution is to structure the use cases in templates that combine prose texts with a concrete structure and fields.

We use the requirement model proposed by the Navigational Development Technique (NDT) [6]. Although NDT is focused on the navigational aspect of web and hypermedia systems, it offers a complete, formal and flexible requirement model. This model may be used with all kind of information systems, as demonstrated [8]. The requirement model of NDT also proposes a template to define functional requirements like use cases. This template is quite similar to the ones proposed by other authors. We have chosen the NDT requirement model and template for three main reasons. First, this model is based on a formal UML meta-model [6], [14]. Second, the templates proposed in NDT only contain the more relevant elements for the use case definition and test objectives derivation, and might be easily extended. Finally, the NDT requirement model has been applied in many real and complex projects like [8]. NDT has also a supporting tool called NDT-Tool.

We have performed a minimal extension to the NDT templates to improve it testability and to allow a systematic and automatic process to derive test objectives. An example of the NDT extended template model is shown in table 1. A real use case defined by this template may be found in table 2.

**Table 1.** Use case template

| Precondition | ... |
|---|---|
| Main sequence | 1. The actor..... |
|  | 2. The system ... |

| | ... |
|---|---|
| Errors / alternatives | 1.1.i. If the system ... then ... and the result is .... |
| | 2.1.p. If the actor ... then ... and the result is .... |
| | 3.1.i. At any time, the [system/actor] may .... then .... and the result is ... |
| Results | 1. System ... |
| | ... |
| Post condition | ... |
| Reliability | ... |
| Priority | ... |

Several fields in the template, like precondition, post-condition, etc., are common to other templates approaches and are widely known and described in other papers and books. Next paragraphs describe special fields and particular characteristics of the extension. The ideas exposed in next paragraphs may be easily adapted to other requirement techniques and models.

*Name*: Te name describes the goal of the use case. Every use case has a unique identifier that starts with "UC" letters following one number.

*Main sequence*: The main sequence is composed of the steps of the use cases execution to allow the actor to obtain his objective. Every step of the main sequence is composed of an identifier (the steps are numerated consecutively starting from number one), who performs the step (an actor or the system) and the performed action.

*Errors / alternatives*: These steps describe the behaviour of the system when an error is found or some alternative flow may be executed. An error or alternative step has got the same elements as the main sequence and some additional elements.

The identification of an error or an alternative step is composed of two numbers. The first number must be an existing step of the main sequence. The second number allows to distinguish among different alternatives or errors of the same step. Every step in an error/alternative section must have an evaluated condition to decide if the error or alternative step might be executed, and also to decide the executed action when the condition is true, and the result, for example the end of the use case or the repetition of a set of steps. Sometimes the action might be the same as the result and the result might be omitted.

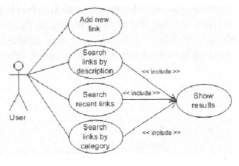

**Fig. 1.** A use case model

The conditions of an error or alternative are classified in preconditions or invariants. A precondition is evaluated before the step starts its execution. An invariant is evaluated during the execution of the step.

*Result*: It indicates which steps (in main sequence and in alternative or erroneous sequences) end with the use case and which is the obtained result to the main actor. Some use cases have not a visible result, or their definition is out of the scope of the use case. This fact is pointed out showing that the result is not a visible result.

Next section describes the system used to apply the approach presented in this paper and it exposes some examples of use cases defined with the template of table 1.

# 4 Case study

The system under test is a web application that allows to manage an on-line link catalogue (found in www.codecharge.com). The system includes two actors: the user and the administrator. However, in this case study, we will only consider the user actor. The UML Use Case diagram of the user is shown in figure 1.

The use cases of the case study are the following ones: "Search link by description" and "Show results". Due to their inclusion relation, both use cases are defined using one instance of the template of section 3 (table 2).

**Table 2.** The use case: "Search link by description"

| Name | UC-02. Search link by description |
|---|---|
| Precondition | No. |
| Main sequence | 1. The user asks the system for searching links by description. |
| | 2. The system asks for the description. |
| | 3. The user introduces the description. |
| | 4. The system searches for the links which matches up with the description introduced by the user. |
| | 5. The system shows the results. |
| Errors / alternatives | 3.1.i. At any time, the user may cancel the search, then the use case ends. |
| | 4.1.p. If the actor introduces an empty description, then the system searches for all stored links and the result is to continue the execution of this use case. |
| | 4.2.i. If the system finds any error performing the search, then an error message is shown and this use case ends. |
| | 5.1.i. If the result is empty, then the system shows a message and this use case ends. |
| Results | 5. The system shows the results of UC-05. |
| | 3.1.i. Out of the limits of this use case. |
| | 4.2.i. Error message. |

| | 5.1.p.  Message of no found results. |
| --- | --- |
| Post condition | No |

The alternative steps are annotated with 'p' if they are preconditions and 'i' if they are invariants. Next section describes how to obtain test objectives from use cases and how to apply the process over this use case.

# 5 Test objectives from use cases

To derive test objectives, first, a behavioural model from a use case is built. Then, the behavioural model is rounded trip to identify the test objectives. Point 5.1 describes the generation of the behavioural model. Then, point 5.2 describes how to derive test objectives, and point 5.3 describes how to manage the coverage of the use case by the test objectives.

## 5.1 Building of a behavioural model

The first task is to build a behavioural model from the use case. As mentioned in section 1, a behavioural model is a UML activity diagram. This model represents the different scenarios or instances of a use case. Next paragraphs describe the steps to build a behavioural model from the use case which is defined with the template of table 1.

In the main sequences, each step is an activity of the behavioural model. A transition is added through two consecutive steps. A behavioural model has got, at least, one ending point. Figure 2 shows an example of a behavioural model from the main sequences of the use case of table 2.

Each alternative or error step is a decision node. If the alternative or error step is a precondition, it is added before the related action. If the step is invariant, it is added after the related action. If the alternative or error step performs an action, the latest will be a new activity. If the result of the use case is to repeat a previous step, a transition to the activity representing the step is added. The condition evaluated in the alternative is attached to a decision node. Alternative and erroneous steps are also classified into three categories. First one, called end, indicates that the alternative ends the use case. An example is shown in figure 3 (alternative 1). Second one, called goto, indicates that the alternative repeat a previous activity. Third one, called action, indicates that he alternative performs a new activity. An example is shown in figure 3 (alternatives 2, 3). Every category is processed in a different way, as can be seen in algorithm "BuildBehaviourModel".

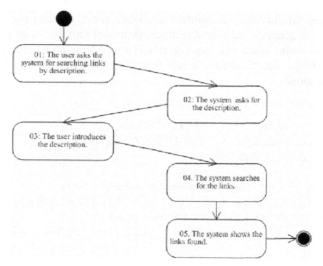

**Fig. 2.** Activity model from the main sequence of use case

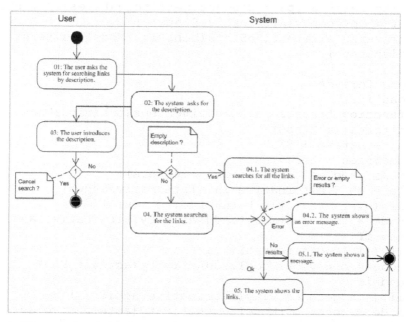

**Fig. 3.** The complete behavioural model

If there is a sequence of decisions nodes, all of them belong to the same actor (including system). They should be merged into one decision node. Finally, the activities are classified by classifiers. The behavioural model will have a classifier for each actor and one more for the system. Each classifier will contain the activities performed by the actor or by the system. Figure 3 shows the final result.

Algorithm "BuildBehaviourModel" describes the algorithm used in the supporting tool to generate the test objectives. A model variable is an activity graph as defined in UML, whereas a step variable is a step from a use case, as defined in section 4. Helper functions have a self descriptive name and their definition has not been included.

```
algorithm BuildBehaviourModel:

var        model : ACTIVITYGRAPH
alternativeSteps : LIST[USECASESTEP]
step : USECASESTEP
init
foreach (step in useMase.mainSequence)
alternativeSteps = useCase.getAlternatives(pre, step)
if ( not_empty(alternativeSteps) )
traverse_alternativeSteps(behaviourModel, alterna-
tiveSteps)
end if
behaviourModel.addActivity(step)
alternativeSteps = useCase.getAlternatives(inv, step)
if ( not_empty(alternativeSteps) )
traverse_alternativeSteps(behaviourModel, alterna-
tiveSteps)
end if
end foreach
end init
function traverse_alternativeSteps(behaviourModel,
alternativeSteps)
alternative : STEP
decision = behaviour-
Model.addDesicion(alternativeSteps))
foreach ( alternative in alsternativeSteps)
if ( is_activity(alternative.action) )
node = behaviourModel.addActivity(alternative.action)
end if
if ( is_end(alternative.action) )
node = behaviourModel.addActivity(activityEnd)
end if
if ( is_gotoActivity(alternative.action) )
node = behaviourModel.getActivity(alternative.action)
end if
behaviouralModel.addTransition(decision, node)
end foreach
end function
```

If each step of the use case defines only one activity, then the maximum number of nodes (activities and decisions; start and end nodes are not included) of a test objective model is: the number of steps in main sequences plus (number of alternative and error steps x 2). From the use case of table 2, we can see that the maximum number of nodes is 5 + (4 x 2) = 13 nodes. The behavioural model of figure 3 shows only 11 nodes, because step 3.1.i does not generate any activity and steps 4.2.i and 5.1.p have been combined in the same decision (decision 3 in figure 3). Next point describes how to identify loops in the behavioural model.

## 5.2 Derivation of test objectives

After the building of a behavioural model, the test objectives are systematically derived from them. The test objectives are defined as paths over the behavioural model. These paths might also be expressed like activity diagrams or text. An example of test objectives is shown in table 3 and figure 4.

However, a test objective is not a test case because it cannot be executed over the system under test. The test objectives have to be completed with test values and expected results, and should be executed in a test director tool or translate into test scripts. An example of how to implement test objectives may be found in [13] and [9].

Several coverage criteria might be chosen to generate sequences from a graph. For example, two classic criteria are all-nodes and all-edges criteria. However, the coverage criterion selected for this approach is the all scenarios criterion (AS). A set of test objectives satisfies the whole scenarios criterion for a behavioural model if each scenario involved in the use case is exercised by one and only one test objective. A scenario is an instance, or a concrete execution, of a use case.

The AS coverage criterion assure that all the obtained objectives are reachable and none of the objectives is repeated. Two test objectives are the same when they have the same number of activities appearing in the same order.

Algorithm "BuildTestObjectives" describes the algorithm used in the supporting tool to generate test objectives. Helper functions have a self descriptive name and their definition has not been included.

```
algorithm BuildTestObjectives
var            objective : PATH
objectives : LIST(PATH)
init
objective = < empty >
objectives = < empty >
traverse(initialNode, path)
end init

function traverse(in node, inout objective)
if ( is_desicion(node) )
traverse_desicion(node, objective)
exit function
end if
objective.add(node)
if ( isEnd(node) )
objectives.add(objective)
exit function
```

```
end if
nextNode = next_node(node)
traverse(nextNode, objective)
end function

function traverse_desicion(in node, inout objective)
foreach (alternative in node.alternatives)
path.add(alternative)
nextNode = next_node(alternative)
traverse(nextNode, objective)
end foreach
end function
```

A set of test objectives are obtained after the application of algorithm 2 on the behavioural model. The test objectives with a AS coverage are listed in the following table 3. The id 1 path is the test objective of the main sequence of the use case.

**Table 3.** Derived test objectives

| Id | Path |
|----|------|
| 1 | 01 -> 02 -> 03 -> D1(No) -> D2(No)-> 04 -> D3(No error & Results) -> 05 |
| 2 | 01 -> 02 -> 03 -> D1(No) -> D2(No)-> 04 -> D3(No error & No Results) -> 05.1 |
| 3 | 01 -> 02 -> 03 -> D1(No) -> D2(No)-> 04 -> D3(Error) -> 04.2 |
| 4 | 01 -> 02 -> 03 -> D1(No) -> D2(Yes)-> 04.1 -> D3(No error & Results) -> 05 |
| 5 | 01 -> 02 -> 03 -> D1(No) -> D2(Yes)-> 04.1 -> D3(No error & No Results) -> 05.1 |
| 6 | 01 -> 02 -> 03 -> D1(No) -> D2(Yes)-> 04.1 -> D3(Error) -> 04.2 |
| 7 | 01 -> 02 -> 03 -> D1(Yes) |

The test objectives might also be represented by activity graphs. Figure 4 shows the activity diagrams that match paths 1 (4(a) ) and 7 (4(b)). As mentioned below, the objectives of table 7 cover 100% of scenarios of the use case. The next section describes a criterion to select the desired coverage.

## 5.3 Coverage of use cases.

The coverage of test objectives measures the number of scenarios from a use case with an attached test objective. The coverage of test objectives might be calculated with the formula of figure 5.

A higher coverage implies more test objectives and more test cases. A coverage of 1, means that every possible scenario has one test objective and will have, at least, one test case (as seen in the section below).

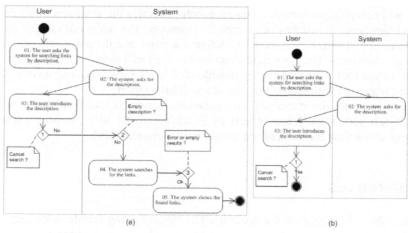

**Fig. 4.** Test objectives as activity graphs

$$\frac{\text{Number of test objectives}}{\text{Number of scenarios}} = \text{Test coverage}$$

**Fig. 5.** Measure of the test objective coverage

The coverage, and the number of test objectives, might be determined by the relevance or frequency of the use case. Both elements are included in the template model proposed in section 3. A coverage criterion is shown in table 4.

**Table 4.** Coverage criterion

| Priority | Coverage |
|----------|----------|
| 0 | No test objectives are generated from the use case. |
| 1 | Only one test objective is generated from the main sequences. |
| 2 | Main sequence and all decisions nodes in actor classifiers. |
| 3 | All the test objectives are generated. |

Next section exposes conclusions and ongoing works.

# 6 Conclusions

Test objectives are basic for a successful testing. They indicate which test cases have to be built to test the implementation of a use case. This paper has presented and has justified a new approach of the systematic derivation of test objectives for use cases. A previous work described how to generate test cases from use cases for web application using existing approaches [9]. However, this approach is highly based on manual work and the decisions of test engineers. The automatic generation of test objectives presented in this paper continues this research and is also the first step to obtain a complete process for the generation of test cases, as we will see in ongoing works. Our approach generates the same test objectives as the referenced approaches of section 2. However, the main advantages are the definition of a semiformal model to define use cases and the automatic generation of test objectives. The algorithms described in section 4 have been implemented in a prototype tool. This tool may be downloaded from www.lsi.us.es/~javierj/ and is being improved with loop management and XMI support.

Future works aim at extending the presented approach. Our final goal is to generate test scripts from test objectives in an automatic way. Some preliminary works about the generation of test scripts may be found in [9].

# References

1. Object Management Group. 2003. The UML Testing Profile. www.omg.org
2. Binder, R.V. 1999. Testing Object-Oriented Systems. Addison Wesley.
3. Labiche, Y., Briand, L.C. 2002. A UML-Based Approach to System Testing, Journal of Software and Systems Modelling (SoSyM) Vol. 1 No.1 pp. 10-42.
4. Ruder, A. 2004. UML-based Test Generation and Execution. Rückblick Meeting. Berlin.
5. Denger, C. Medina, M. 2003. Test Case Derived from Requirement Specifications. Fraunhofer IESE Report.
6. Escalona, M.J. 2004. Models and Techniques for the Specification and Analysis of Navigation in Software Systems. Ph. European Thesis. Department of Computer Language and Systems. University of Seville. Seville, Spain.
7. Ostrand, T.J., Balcer, M.J. 1988. Category-Partition Method. Communications of the ACM. 676-686.
8. Gutierrez, J.J. Escalona, M.J. Mejías, M. Torres, J. 2004. Aplicando técnicas de testing en sistemas para la difusión Patrimonial. V TURITEC. pp. 237-252. Málaga, Spain.
9. Gutiérrez, J.J., Escalona, M.J., Mejías, M., Torres, J. 2005. A practical approach of Web System Testing. Advances in Information Systems Development. pp. 659-680. Ed. Springer Verlag Karlstad, Sweden.
10. Gutiérrez, J.J., Escalona M.J., Mejías M., Torres, J. 2006. Generation of test cases from functional requirements. A survey. 4º Workshop on System Testing and Validation. Potsdam. Germany.
11. Heumann, J. 2002. Generating Test Cases from Use Cases. Journal of Software Testing Professionals.
12. Offutt, J. et-al. 2003. Generating Test Data from Sate-based Specifications. Software Testing, Verification and Reliability. 13, 25-53. USA.
13. Nebut, C., Fleury, F., Le Traon, Y., Jézéquel, J.M., 2006. Automatic Test Generation: A Use Case Driven Approach. IEEE Transactions on Software Engineering Vol. 32. 3. March.
14. Koch, N., Zhang, G., Escalona, M.J., 2006. Model Transformations from Requirements to Web System Design. Webist 06. Portugal.

# Examining OSS Success: Information Technology Acceptance by FireFox Users

Andrzej Słomka[1], Tomasz Przechlewski[1], and Stanisław Wrycza[1]

Gdańsk University, Department of Information Systems
81-824 Sopot, ul. Armii Krajowej 119/121, Poland
ekotp@univ.gda.pl, ekosw@univ.gda.pl

## 1 Introduction

Open source software (OSS) is currently one of the most debated phenomena in both academia and the software industry. Several OSS systems have achieved significant market success but they are rather server-side applications, such as the Apache web server, mail transport agent Sendmail, or other components of IT infrastructure. On the other hand penetration of OSS systems on the market of desktop applications is rather limited and it is virtually dominated by products of one software vendor, i.e. Microsoft. Recently one exception to the rule of non-existence of OSS at the desktop was observed however. Mozilla FireFox, an Open Source web browser achieved 10 million downloads in one single month of December 2004, demonstrating success in the market totally dominated by Microsoft's Internet Explorer. The aim of the paper is to find out factors, which encourage users to adopt FireFox by applying the well-known framework of Technology Acceptance Model.

The paper is organized as follows. A brief overview of OSS is presented in the subsequent section. Conceptual models of users' acceptance of IT including Technology Acceptance Model (TAM) is shortly discussed next. Then the research method and survey design are described, followed by results of the data analysis. Discussion of the findings concludes the paper.

## 2 Open Source Software

At the most basic level, the term open source software simply means software for which the source code is publicly available and which can be distributed freely without any restrictions [1, 2]. Open source software is currently one of the most debated phenomena in both academia and the software industry [3]. However most of the research have been devoted to explain what are the incentives driving individuals and/or organizations to develop software without any obvious economic compensation (cf. [4]). Significantly smaller attention is paid to explain the reasons why OS software is accepted or rejected by the users.

Currently open source software usage ratios are much higher in server applications, such as networking or DBMS applications than at the desktop [5]. For example, the open source Apache is constantly reported to be the most popular web server in use with market share exceeding 70% of the total [6]. Many more examples of fine OS server software exist, such as the popular scripting languages PHP and Python, database systems PostgreSQL and MYSQL, content management systems like Plone or PHPNuke, etc. [7, 5]. Numerous desktop applications were developed too, such as the KDE/Gnome desktop managers, the office suite OpenOffice.org or communication applications such as e-mail clients or web browsers. Although functionally compatible (or even technically superior) to the proprietary counterparts, their usage is much less common. FireFox is the only exception to this rule.

Mozilla FireFox is an Open Source web browser supported by the Mozilla Foundation. FireFox was released in December 2004 and achieved 10 million downloads in one single month [8]. What is extremely unusual in case of OS projects is that its launch was supported with a "traditional" marketing campaign.[1] A survey released by [9] reports that MS Internet Explorer's share in US was down to 88.9% in May 2005. Moreover the survey shows that the FireFox usage tends to vary significantly by country. For example it has more than 22% market share in Germany, almost 7% in the US while less than 3% in Japan.

FireFox is claimed to be superior to MS Internet Explorer with several features: security, compliance to new Web standards and functionality. It is reported to work faster, particularly with older hardware. And of course it is working on a wide range of software platforms, not only the Wintel one.

## 3 Conceptual Models of Users' Acceptance of IT

Several models of adoption and acceptance of IT were developed, including models build on economics of standards theories and diffusion of innovation ones [10]. The former tries to explain the adoption of IT using such economic categories as positive network externalities, switching costs and lock-in [11] while the latter consider various characteristics of innovation, that influence individual adoption decisions. Rogers [10] suggests the following 5 innovation features that influence the adoption process: *relative advantage, compatibility, complexity, trialability,* and *observability*. Prior studies show that compatibil-

---

[1] The Mozilla Foundation raised over $250,000 for a full-page New York Times advertisement through user donations. A similar advertisement was featured in the German newspaper Frankfurter Allgemeine Zeitung. The success resulted soon in full column articles published in Businesswek and Newsweek magazines featuring FireFox.

ity with existing technologies and relative advantage were positively related to adoption[2] while technological complexity was related negatively.

Technology adoption not necessarily is followed by sustained usage, so a different important aspect of IT implementation concerns *acceptance*[3] and effective utilization of IT systems. Several models were proposed to explain IT acceptance, including: Technology Acceptance Model (TAM), Theory of Reasoned Action (TRA), Theory of Planned Behaviour (TPB), and Task Technology Fit (TTF, cf. [12]) ones[4]. All of them originate in social sciences research. A widely used theory explaining the acceptance of IT is the Technology Acceptance Model [15]. The TAM model was derived from Ajzen and Fishbein's TRA and TPB which have evolved from TRA [15, 16]. It is meant to explain the determinants of computer acceptance that is general, capable of explaining user behaviour across a broad range of end-user computing technologies and user populations, while at the same time being both parsimonious and theoretically justified [15]. The original model consists of just a few factors, namely: *perceived usefulness* (PU), *perceived ease of use* (PEOU), *attitude toward using* (ATT), *behavioural intention to use* (BI), and system usage. TAM is depicted in Fig. 1. White boxes and solid line arrows represents the core model; dotted lines and gray boxes depicts extensions.

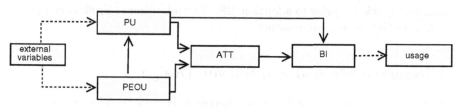

**Fig. 1.** Technology Acceptance Model (TAM), cf. [15]

Perceived usefulness is defined as the user's subjective probability that using a specific application will increase his/her job performance within an organizational context. Perceived ease of use is defined as the degree to which a person believes that using a particular system would be free of effort.[5] The remaining factors are directly adopted from TRA/TPB.[6] TAM postulates that

----

[2] It should be noted however that these innovation features are contradictory: to achieve a greater advantage the innovation is expected to be more incompatible.

[3] Acceptance can be formally defined as "the demonstrable willingness within a user group to employ information technology for the tasks it is designed to support".

[4] More complex models are proposed as extensions or combinations of the classical ones, cf. [13, 14].

[5] One should note that PEOU is very similar to self-efficacy, and thus TAM has much in common with models based on Bandura's self-efficacy theory [17].

[6] Behavioural intention is a measure of the strength of user's intention to perform a specific behaviour while attitude are user's positive or negative feelings about performing target behaviour.

usage is determined by behavioral intention, which is jointly determined by attitude and perceived usefulness. Attitude in turn is jointly determined by perceived usefulness and perceived ease of use. Moreover it is assumed that PU is determined by PEOU (cf. Fig. 1). External variables (such as system characteristics, external/internal support etc.) are fully mediated by PU and PEOU which are fundamental in explaining the user's behaviour.

Many prior studies have extended the above described "classical model" with various external variables, including user characteristics, organizational support, and subjective norms (cf. [18, 16, 19]). Primarily designed for explaining fairy simple IT systems in a business environment, TAM has been successfully tested in various applications areas: on-line shopping [20], Internet banking [21], mobile commerce [22], web site usage [23, 24], search engine adoption [25], etc. A review of TAM-related studies can be found in [26, 27].

On the other side TAM parsimony implies that the model has serious limitations and should not be applied unconditionally. It is pointed out that TAM performs poorly when explaining organizational adoption (mandated use), adoption of complex technologies, or those requiring prior extensive training and/or coordination. TAM demonstrates good explanatory power in case of adoption of innovation by individuals making autonomous choices about whether to adopt personal use innovations that do not require extensive specialized knowledge prior to adoption [28]. The adoption of FireFox is a perfect match to the above requirements.

## 4 Research Method and Survey Design

Facing such a spectacular business success it is very interesting to find out what factors encourage users to adopt FireFox. Such findings will have both theoretical and practical implications as many vendors are nowadays considering to support Open Source Software as well as many organizations—both government institutions and commercial enterprises—are considering to adopt it. Thus the following research question is posed in this paper: Does TAM hold for FireFox users? The question implies the following standard set of hypotheses: *perceived usefulness has a direct effect on intention to use FireFox (H1)*, *perceived usefulness and perceived ease of use have a direct effect on attitude towards using FireFox (H2)*, *perceived ease of use has a direct effect on perceived usefulness (H3)*, and *attitude towards using FireFox has a direct effect on intention to use it (H4)*. To verify them a statistical survey was performed.

Original instruments for TAM as developed by Davis consists of 6-item scales for PU and PEOU [29]. While items for PU focus on features such as productivity, effectiveness and performance, PEOU related questions concentrate on easy to learn and flexibility. In various studies applying TAM, the factors were operationalized with different scales and/or number of items.[7]

---

[7] For example Igbaria et al. [18] use 4 items both for PU and PEOU while Burton-Jones and Hubona [30] extend both scales to 10 items.

Both scales attained high reliability and demonstrate convergent and discriminant validity. To conduct the study the original instruments were adapted and translated into Polish.[8] A pretest questionnaire was conducted resulting in minor changes for improved readability and clarity.[9]

In order to target potential FireFox users, a Web-based survey was employed. An e-mail letter explaining shortly the objectives of the research and containing a link to a questionnaire form was send to the members of a few Polish news groups, known to be visited by experienced IT systems users. The groups selected were: Linux, MS Windows, and OpenOffice users newsgroups as well as two groups related to Web site design/development and browser plugins development. Within a week 247 questionnaires were gathered. Most responses were received within the first two days (170 questionnaires). A few replies contained missing data, so they were excluded from the sample. Also, 4 respondents identified themselves as younger than 14 and further 2 as older than 55. These respondent were excluded from the sample. Finally respondents reporting to work more than 18 hours per day with IT systems were excluded as well[10]. The resulted sample contains 229 usable responses (133 respondents identified themselves as employees, the remaining 96 were students). Reported mean age was 25.9 years (median 23.5, standard deviation 7.4). The respondents appeared to be rather heavy users of IT as they declared to work on the average 8.7 hours per day with IT systems (median 8.2, standard deviation 3.5 hours).

# 5 Data Analysis and Results

Partial Least Squares (PLS), as implemented in PLS-Graph version 3.0 [32], was used to evaluate the model of FireFox acceptance. PLS is a structural equation modelling technique similar to more popular, covariance-based SEM models (Lisrel, Amos) [33, 34]. PLS allows for small sample sizes and makes less strict assumptions about the distribution of the data [35]. The measurement model in PLS is assessed in terms of item loadings and reliability coefficients, as well as the convergent and discriminant validity. The relevant statistics for the measurement model are presented in Table 1.

Convergent validity can be assessed by inspecting factor loadings and the average variance extracted (AVE). Item loadings greater than 0.7 are considered significant [34]. All items load highly on respective constructs except PU1, which have demonstrated exceptionally low loading (0.27). In result this item

---

[8] The authors are unaware of any IT usage survey in Poland based on TAM.

[9] Our instrument consists of 16 items in total, including 5-items, 4-items, and 3-items for PEOU, PU/ATT, and ITO respectively. See [31] and App. A for the details.

[10] The survey was aimed at those respondents who use FireFox in his/her work and not for fun, hobby or personal use. That is why the survey was announced at professional newsgroups and additionally young or elder respondents were removed from the sample.

**Table 1.** Summary of the measurement model

| Construct | Loadings range | $t$-range | CR | AVE |
|---|---|---|---|---|
| Usefulness | 0.886–0.902 | 55.01–103.83 | 0.909 | 0.689 |
| Ease of Use | 0.723–0.886 | 10.94–21.33 | 0.890 | 0.621 |
| Attitude | 0.741–0.931 | 15.16–106.14 | 0.912 | 0.723 |
| Intention | 0.911–0.954 | 49.51–86.99 | 0.953 | 0.872 |

**Table 2.** Discriminant validity of the measurement model

| Construct | PU | PEOU | ATT | BI |
|---|---|---|---|---|
| Usefulness (PU) | 0.912 | – | – | – |
| Ease of Use (PEOU) | 0.646 | 0.872 | – | – |
| Attitude (ATT) | 0.824 | 0.625 | 0.850 | – |
| Intention (BI) | 0.832 | 0.667 | 0.803 | 0.934 |

was dropped from the subsequent analysis, so PU was operationalized with a 4-item scale. Table 1 shows that all loadings surpass the required minimum and the respective $t$-values are highly significant. AVE measures the variance captured by the construct relative to the variance due to measurement error and to be acceptable it should be greater than 0.5 [36]. For all constructs AVE exceed the required minimum value.

Construct reliability was assessed using composite reliability coefficient (CR), the interpretation of which is similar to that of Cronbach's alpha. Value of CR greater than 0.7 is considered acceptable. As shown in Table 1 all reliability coefficient surpass the required minimum.

The discriminant validity of the measures was assessed by comparing the interconstruct correlations with the square root of AVE on the individual construct [36]. For discriminant validity to be demonstrated square root of AVEs of all constructs (diagonal elements in Table 2) should be greater than the interconstruct correlations (off-diagonal elements in appropriate column, cf. Table 2). As shown in Table 2 all constructs were more strongly correlated with their own measures than with any of the other constructs (one should note however that the cross-correlation is rather high). Thus discriminant validity was demonstrated.

The structural model in PLS is assessed by examining the path coefficients and its significance with $t$-statistics. Standard $R^2$ coefficient is used as an indicator of the overall goodness-of-fit measure of the model. The path coefficients (shown alongside the single-headed arrows) and $t$-values (in the parenthesis below the coefficient values) for our model are shown in Figure 2.

As all coefficient values were significant all hypotheses were supported. The model shows very good fit as 84% of variance in BI and 74% in attitude were explained by the model (cf. Figure 2).

The results are consistent with most of TAM studies [16]: perceived usefulness appeared to be the strongest determinant of attitude towards usage and usage intentions, with standardized regression coefficient equals 0.651 and

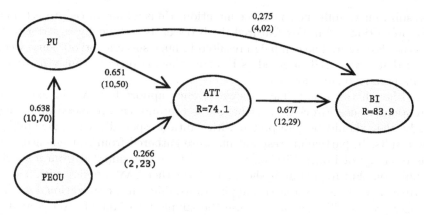

**Fig. 2.** Estimated structural model of FireFox acceptance

0.275 respectively. PEOU, the other key determinant of intention, again consistent with prior studies, exhibits a less significant effect. The above suggests that FireFox usage seems to be motivated by perceived superiority of the browser over MS Internet Explorer. FireFox is claimed to be less likely to be targeted by crackers, so it is more secure and more resistant to spyware and other programs of this sort. Moreover, its interface is more comfortable, with tabs able to display multiple web pages and offers better support for new standards such as CSS.[11] The users believe that FireFox is safer and less vulnerable to security hazard, has a better compliance to standards and functionality.

Prior studies suggest a different explanation of the above phenomenon, namely the effect of ease of use on system usage found significant for inexperienced users becomes insignificant when users get acquainted with the system [16]. Web browsers are one of the most frequently used applications today, so it seems to be reasonable to assume high level of proficiency of an average user. To investigate the effect of user's experience we have extended our model adding user's experience to it (measured as daily average time of work with IT systems) but found it insignificant.

# 6 Summary

Perceived usefulness was identified as the principal determinant of intention to use FireFox while perceived ease of use was found to be a significant but

---

[11] Microsoft strategic decision to integrate its browser into the Windows operating system has helped to defeat Netscape but at the same time has caused that newer versions of IE would only be available with newer versions of Windows (every 3 years or more). In a fast evolving Internet environment it means that IE has become a "sort-of" unsupported product, as no important functional improvements have been added to it for years.

less substantive influence on usage intention. Unusual for an OS project, massive promotion of FireFox featured the browser as technically superior to MS Internet Explorer. The campaign resulted in huge success and our survey confirms that it was well targeted as FireFox usage is predominantly motivated by its perceived superiority.

Although the results have shown strong support for TAM in explaining intentions to use FireFox, nevertheless, as the findings are based on a single study, they should be interpreted with caution especially when generalizing the results. In particular, respondents were gathered from convenience, web-based survey of Polish FireFox users, and were not sampled from a specific population. Future research should test whether TAM applies within other settings as well, i.e. various OSS applications, different organizational settings or user groups. The decision to use the simplest variant of TAM is another limitation of the study and future research should verify more complex models. In the context of OSS adoption it would be interesting to find out the impact on acceptance of such important factors, as: perceived available user resources [19], perceived risk, management support [18], or peer influence.

# References

1. Weber, S.: The Success of Open Source. Harvard University Press (2004)
2. Free Software Foundation: Philosophy of the GNU project (2004) http://www.gnu.org/philosophy/
3. AlMarzouq, M.: Open source: Concepts, benefits, and challenges. Commun. AIS **16** (2005) 1–49
4. Gök, A.: Open source versus proprietary software: An economic perspective (2003) http://abgok.odtum.net
5. Berlecon Research: Free/libre and open source software: Survey and study (2002) http://www.infonomics.nl/FLOSS
6. Netcraft Ltd: December 2005 web server survey (2005) http://news.netcraft.com/archives/web_server_survey.html
7. Wheeler, D.: Why open source? look at the numbers! (2005) http://www.dwheeler.com/oss_fs_why.html
8. Wang, T., Wu, L., Lin, Z.: The revival of Mozilla in the browser war against Internet Explorer. In: ICEC '05: Proceedings of the 7th international conference on Electronic commerce, New York, NY, USA, ACM Press (2005) 159–166
9. WebSideStory, Inc.: Firefox's market share nears 7 percent (2005) http://www.websidestory.com/products/web-analytics/datainsights/spotlight/05-10-2005.html
10. Rogers, E.M.: Diffusion of Innovations. 5th edn. Free Press (2003)
11. Shy, O.: The Economics of Network Industries. Cambridge University Press (2001)
12. Goodhue, D.L., Thompson, R.L.: Task-technology fit and individual performance. MIS Quarterly (1995) 213–236
13. Taylor, S., Todd, P.A.: Understanding information technology usage: a test of competing models. Information Systems Research **6** (1995) 144–176

14. Venkatesh, V., Morris, M.G., Davis, G.B., Davis, F.D.: User acceptance of information technology: Toward a unified view. MIS Quarterly **27** (2003) 425–478

15. Davis, F.D., Bagozzi, R.P., Warshaw, P.R.: User acceptance of computer technology: a comparison of two theoretical models. Decision Science **35** (1989) 982–1003

16. Venkatesh, V., Davis, F.D.: A theoretical extension of the technology acceptance model: Four longitudinal field studies. Management Science **46** (2000) 186–204

17. Campeau, D.R., Higgins, C.A.: Computer self-efficacy: Development of a measure and initial test. MIS Quarterly **19** (1995) 189–211

18. Igbaria, M., Zinatelli, N., Cragg, P., Cavaye, A.L.M.: Personal computing acceptance factors in small firms: A structural equation model. MIS Quarterly **21** (1997) 279–305

19. Mathieson, K., Peacock, E., Chin, W.W.: Extending the technology acceptance model: the influence of perceived user resources. SIGMIS Database **32** (2001) 86–112

20. Shang, R.A., Chen, Y.C., Shen, L.: Extrinsic versus intrinsic motivations for consumers to shop on-line. Information and Management **42** (2005) 401–413

21. Chau, P.Y., Lai, V.S.: An empirical investigation of the determinants of user acceptance of internet banking. Journal of Organizational Computing and Electronic Commerce **13** (2003) 123–145

22. Wu, J.H., Wang, S.C.: What drives mobile commerce? an empirical evaluation of the revised technology acceptance model. Information and Management **42** (2005) 719–429

23. Lederer, A.L., Maupin, D.J., Sena, M.P., Zhuang, Y.: The technology acceptance model and the world wide web. Decis. Support Syst. **29** (2000) 269–282

24. Lederer, A.L., Maupin, D.J., Sena, M.P., Zhuang, Y.: The role of ease of use, usefulness and attitude in the prediction of world wide web usage. In: SIGCPR '98: Proceedings of the 1998 ACM SIGCPR conference on Computer personnel research, New York, NY, USA, ACM Press (1998) 195–204

25. Sun, H., Zhang, P.: An empirical study on the roles of affective variables in user adoption of search engines. In: Proceedings of the Third Annual Workshop on HCI Research in MIS. (2004) http://melody.syr.edu/pzhang/publications/

26. Legris, P., Collerette, P.: Why do people use information technology? a critical review of the technology acceptance model. Information and Management **40** (2003) 191–204

27. Han, S.: Individual adoption of information systems in organizations: A literature review of technology acceptance model. Technical Report 540, Turku Center for Computer Science (2003) http://www.tucs.fi/research/publications/insight.php?id=tHan03b&table=techreport

28. Gallivan, M.J.: Organizational adoption and assimilation of complex technological innovations: Development and application of a framework. Data Base **32** (2001) 51–85

29. Davis, F.D.: Perceived usefulness, perceived easy of use, and user acceptance of information technology. MIS Quarterly **13** (1989) 319–340

30. Burton-Jones, A., Hubona, G.S.: Individual differences and usage behaviour: Revisiting a technology acceptance model assumption. Data Base **36** (2005) 58–77

31. Słomka, A.: Zastosowanie modelu TAM w badaniu akceptacji technologii open-source na przykładzie przegladarki FireFox (2005) Msc thesis (in Polish). Gdańsk Univ., Department of Management
32. Chin, W.W.: PLSGraph User's Guide, version 3.0. University of Houston. (2001)
33. Bollen, K.A.: Structural Equations with Latent Variables. John Wiley and Sons, New York (1989)
34. Hair, J.F., Black, B., Babin, B., Anderson, R.E., Tatham, R.L.: Multivariate Data Analysis. Prentice Hall (1998)
35. Chin, W.W., Marcolin, B.L., Newsted, P.R.: A partial least squares latent variable modeling approach for measuring interaction effects: Results from a monte carlo simulation study and an electronic-mail emotion/adoption study. Information Systems Research **14** (2003) 189–217
36. Fornell, C., Larcker, D.F.: Evaluating structural equation models with unobservable variables and measurement error. Journal of Marketing Research **18** (1981) 39–50

## A Measurement items

The following items were used in survey instrument (all measured using seven-point Likert scale):

**Perceived Usefulness, PU**: Using FF make it easier to do my job (PU1, dropped), Using FF increase my job performance (PU2), Using FF allow to accomplish my tasks more quickly (PU3), Using FF enhance my effectiveness in my job (PU4), I find FF useful in my job (PU5).

**Perceived ease of use, PEOU**: It is difficult to use FF (PEOU1), Learning to use FF is ease for me (PEOU2), Customizing FF is frustrating (PEOU3), Navigating FF menus is ease (PEOU4), I find FF ease to use (PEOU5).

**Attitude, ATT**: The idea of using FF is a mistake (ATT1), I am glad I have found FF (ATT2), I would like to use FF regularly (ATT3), I would not switch from FF to other browser (ATT4).

**Intention, BI**: I will use FF on a regular basis in my job (BI2), I will use FF frequently in my job (BI2), I will recommend FF to others (BI3).

# Ontology-based User Modeling for Web-based Information Systems

Anton Andrejko, Michal Barla and Mária Bieliková

Institute of Informatics and Software Engineering,
Faculty of Informatics and Information Technologies,
Slovak university of Technology in Bratislava, Slovakia
{andrejko,barla,bielik}@fiit.stuba.sk

The Web represents an information space where the amount of information grows exponentially. This calls for personalized interaction between users and web-based information systems providing information. Current systems provide a certain level of personalization, which allows the user to set up her preferences manually. Improved efficiency of information acquisition can be achieved by personalization based on a user's particularities used for the adaptation of content or navigation in the information space. A user model that reflects a real user, who requires information provided by an information system, is required for successful personalization. We present an ontology-based approach to user modeling and describe the user model that we designed for a web-based information system aimed at job acquisition. We point out several advantages of the ontology-based approach, namely the sharing of the ontology with other applications and reusability.

## 1 Introduction

People are often overloaded by information while finding relevant information can be nearly impossible. This problem is yet more exposed in information systems that cover a large information space (e.g., the Web) where we suppose that individual users have different knowledge and information needs. The system's general interface and behavior designed as "one size fits all" is obviously not effective for all categories of users, thus adaptation is desirable.

One approach to solve this problem lies in increasing the efficiency of the user's interaction with the information system by focusing on individual user needs thus introducing personalization as an additional feature of web-based information systems. A user model that reflects the real user who requires information provided by an information system is required for the successful personalization. The aim of this paper is to analyze and discuss possible user model representations in order to show advantages and disadvantages resulting from an ontology-based approach to user modeling in web-based information systems. We discuss an approach to user modeling where the model is expressed by an ontology and present the approach on an example of the user model being developed in the course of the research project Tools for acquisition, organization and maintenance of knowledge in an environment of heterogeneous information resources [15]. In this project the Web is considered to be a heterogeneous information source and software tools are developed for a web-based information system aimed at job offer acquisition. Since we model a user who is looking for a job, we will use the labor market as the application domain throughout the paper.

## 2 User characteristics

A user model represents various user characteristics, which can be used to adapt the content, presentation or navigation. The user model is defined as beliefs about the user that include preferences, knowledge and attributes for a particular domain [14] or as an explicit representation of properties of individual users or user classes [4].

Designers describe user models with terms like attributes, features, characteristics or properties. For the purpose of this paper we use the term *characteristic*. Based on the differences that do not lie only in the terminology, it is obvious that the user modeling area needs to be standardized with the first attempt being the User Modeling Meta-Ontology [21].

As an example of using user characteristics in the process of adaptation, let us assume that a characteristic in the user model describes the minimum acceptable salary per month for a specific user. If the system knows that the user is not interested in job offers where the offered salary is lower (or much lower considering the fuzzy nature of the characteristic) than her expected salary, it will not present offers that do not fulfill this condition. The system adapts information in behalf of the user with the help of the user model.

Other occasions where the user model content can be used, is the interpretation of the user's input [12] (which can be ambiguous, incomplete, with errors, etc.) and the personalization of the system's output (sorting of the results, number of results per page, font, colors, etc.). The more relevant characteristics describing the user are included in the user model the more accurate the adaptation provided by the information system can be. Designers exploit invaluable knowledge of specialists who work in the application domain for which the user model is designed to. Their experiences might help to construct the user model reflecting the real user as accurately as possible.

## 3 User model representations

There are several approaches to representing and storing a user model in a web-based information system. For user modeling it is important to analyze to what extent is a particular representation flexible for different kinds of user characteristics in a uniform manner together with the possibility of reasoning directed to decisions on information content presented to the user. We do not discuss representations that use proprietary formats as this would almost totally prevent the sharing and reuse of the user model.

### 3.1 Non-ontological representations

Markedly the most obvious is the use of a relational database to store data about the user since most information systems already use this kind of application data storage. In this case, the user model is represented as a set of database tables and user characteristics are mapped to attributes in the relational data model and store values assigned to individual user characteristics.

Using a relational database is quite straightforward, offers good performance and several other advantages such as security, data recovery etc. that result from good theoretical background of relational calculus and the maturity of its realization by database management systems. However, user models of web-based information systems often contain semi-structured data as they use an *overlay model*, which follows the representation of the information space with various characteristics defined for concepts from the domain model. Relational databases are not primarily designed to express semi-structured data. Moreover, relational databases are not well suited when frequent changes in data structure need to be performed, which is often the case in user modeling.

Another frequently used approach in current web-based adaptive systems is the representation of the user model by an XML based language using the file system, what results in powerful enough expressiveness. An example is the open source general-purpose adaptive web-based system AHA! [7]. The part of the user model which stores information about the user's name is defined in the AHA! as follows:

```
<record>
  <key>personal.name</key>
  <value>John Smith</value>
  <firsttimeupdated>false</firsttimeupdated>
</record>
```

The performance of this solution is limited by the performance of the used file system (it is effective for user models with few instances and rich structure of user characteristics). Reusability and sharing is better than with the database approach, thanks to the platform independence of XML, while using XML has the advantage that it can be used directly in the Web environment. However, XML as a meta-language defines only the general syntax without formally defined semantics, which leads to difficulties when reasoning. Moreover, everyone can invent his own names for tags; somebody stores attributes as tags; somebody uses the attributes of tags defined by XML syntax.

Both of the above mentioned approaches offer only a way of describing user characteristics and do not offer any added value from the user modeling perspective. An ontology-based approach to user modeling offers a way of moving user modeling from the low-level describing of user characteristics to a higher-level with additional possibilities.

## 3.2 Representing user model by ontology

According to the most cited definition of ontology in the Semantic Web community, an ontology is an explicit specification of the conceptualization of a domain [8]. The term ontology includes a whole range of various models with various semantic richness. In this paper we consider representing the ontology by RDF[1]/OWL[2] formalisms. An approach based on RDF and its extension OWL takes the previously mentioned XML representation (syntax) and eliminates its disadvantage by defining a vocabulary for describing properties and classes. OWL serves as a common language for automated reasoning about the content for the vision of the Semantic Web.

For illustration, bellow is a fragment representing a user's name and working experience that is a part of the ontology-based user model for the job offer acquisition web-based information system:

```
<rdf:Description rdf:about="#name">
  <rdfs:label xml:lang="en">name</rdfs:label>
  <rdf:type rdf:resource= "http://www.w3.org/2002/07/
                                    owl#DatatypeProperty"/>
  <rdfs:domain rdf:resource="#User"/>
  <rdfs:range rdf:resource=
                  "http://www.w3.org/2001/XMLSchema#string"/>
</rdf:Description>
<rdf:Description rdf:about="#hasExperience">
  <rdfs:label xml:lang="en">has working experience</rdfs:label>
  <rdfs:domain rdf:resource="#User"/>
  <rdfs:range rdf:resource="http://www.fiit.sk/
                  classification#ExperienceClassification"/>
  <rdf:type rdf:resource="http://www.w3.org/2002/07/
                                    owl#ObjectProperty"/>
</rdf:Description>
```

The advantages leading to using ontologies for user modeling come from the fundamentals of this formalism. Ontologies provide a common understanding of the domain to facilitate reuse and harmonization of different terminologies [14]. They support reasoning, which is considered as an important contribution of the ontology-based models. Once user characteristics are in ontological representation, the ontology and its relations, conditions and restrictions provide the basis for inferring additional user characteristics. For

---

[1] Resource Description Framework, http://www.w3.org/RDF/
[2] Web Ontology Language, http://www.w3.org/2004/OWL/

example, considering a user who is a programmer and works for a company that develops web-based applications using Java technologies we can infer that she is skillful in Java technologies.

By creating an ontology-based user model and deriving it from the domain ontology, we increase the probability that user characteristics will be shared among a range of systems of the same domain (especially on the Web, where most ontologies are currently represented in OWL). We consider the sharing of user models as one of main advantages of using ontologies for user modeling. One of the most obvious advantages of a shared model is that one system can use the initialized data for personalization from other systems preventing the user from entering the same information into every system (e.g., name, locale settings). However, the key advantage of the shared user model is the availability of user characteristics discovered by other systems since user characteristics acquisition is considered to be the bottleneck of personalization.

As an example consider the web-based information system for the job offer acquisition discovering that the user's education is in the domain of information technologies with deep knowledge of the object-oriented paradigm of programming. As the user searches for a job, she visits another adaptive job offer portal. Because it uses the same user modeling server it has access to information about her education and automatically displays offers seeking specialists on object-oriented design at the top of the results list.

Some authors believe that the solution to syntactical and structural differences between user models which interfere with sharing is in a commonly accepted user model ontology [10]. Since we agree that building common vocabularies is important and useful (we remark the role of standards), considering a large distributed information space (e.g., the Web) we need to make a compromise between enabling diversity and looking for mappings between various models. The idea of a single commonly accepted user ontology is simply impossible to reach in such diverse and distributed environment.

Certainly, a unified representation by ontologies can move the personalization on the Web further and give new possibilities of using user characteristics derived by other applications. Considering structural unification a problem arises when applications using the shared user model evaluate some user characteristic differently. This characteristic would constantly change as the user uses various applications, which can lead to unsuitable personalization in all applications using the respective characteristic. One solution to this problem is to keep track of model changes [19]. This would allow each application to use this tracking as an additional information for personalization.

# 4 User model for the job offer acquisition domain

We developed the user model and software tools for its employing for personalization in the context of research project aimed at the support of acquisition, organization and presentation of information on the Web [15, 16].

The result of the project is a web-based information system in domain of the labor market (both for people who are looking for a job and companies which are looking for employees). The system itself is being developed by means of several cooperating software tools, which support various stages of the data-information-knowledge transformation from raw unknown data from the Web to the information and knowledge related to specific interests of particular users. The interests are stored and maintained in a user model.

The data and knowledge repository is designed as a heterogeneous space [6] where several formalisms are used. Raw data from the Web are stored as files, data extracted from the Web source files are stored in a relational database, the domain model together with the user model both used for personalized presentation of acquired job offers are represented by ontologies.

## 4.1 User model ontology

We have designed the user model in several iterations according to a user dependency criterion, which divides user characteristics into domain-independent and dependent groups. When shared, the user model consists of one domain-independent part and more domain-dependent parts.

*Domain-independent part*

The domain-independent part includes user characteristics that describe a user as a person. This part consists of datatype and object properties (see Figure 1) and is linked with all domain-dependent parts (`includes`). Datatype properties are `hasBirthday` and `hasName`. Object properties represent user characteristics (`GenericUserCharacteristic`). Each such characteristic is assigned a level of *confidence* that represents how reliable the characteristic is and *relevance*, which represents the importance of characteristic to the user when reaching a `Goal`. Generic characteristics are mapped only to the domain ontology parts that are independent from our labor market domain. That way a user's gender, education, various skills etc can be expressed.

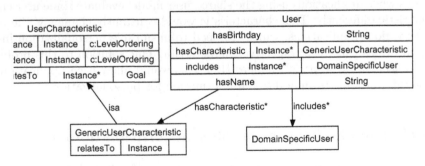

**Fig. 1.** Domain-independent part of the user model.

One possible scenario is that the user will exploit services provided by some user modeling server (e.g. UMoWS [3]) to store her user model. The user will then populate the domain-independent part of the model and let other applications fill-in appropriate domain-dependent parts.

*Domain-dependent part*

The vocabulary of the domain-dependent part of the user model is based on the domain model ontology developed for the project, which represents an explicit conceptualization of job offers. It profits from the advantage of ontology reuse and also uses other ontologies (whose domain is independent from labor market domain) to achieve the desired conceptualization.

The domain model consists of the following ontologies:

- ontology *classification* (prefix "c") – hierarchies for industrial sectors, professions, educational levels, qualifications and various organizations;
- ontology *region* (prefix "r") – domain of regions, countries, languages and currencies that are used in these regions;
- ontology *offer* (prefix "ofr") – general offer domain, which is represented by the ofr:Offer class; any offer has a source and a validity interval.

The JobOffer class is the key class of the ontology and represents a stand-alone job offer. JobOffer has several object and datatype properties. Some selected object properties of the JobOffer class are shown in the Figure 2.

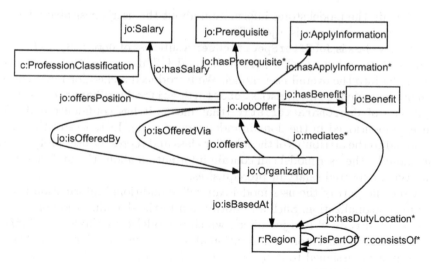

**Fig. 2.** Selected object properties of the JobOffer class.

The aforementioned ontologies provide the base for the user model and a mapping between the domain and user models. Figure 3 depicts the part of the user model created for the domain of labor market. In the case of the job

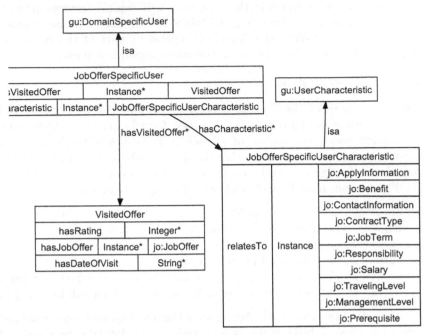

**Fig. 3.** Domain-dependent part of the user model.

offer domain the model stores information about the user's desirable job offer – user preferences towards a job offer.

The key class is `JobOfferSpecificUser` a subclass of `DomainSpecificUser` from the domain-independent part of the model. This enables the inclusion of this model into the overall user model. We introduced a class for representing domain-dependent characteristics `JobOfferSpecificUserCharacteristic` as a subclass of `UserCharacteristic` (that means it has confidence and relevance as mentioned in the domain-independent part). Instances of this class are bound to the attributes of the job offer class and represent user preferences. For example, the user model can contain information about the preferred contract type, expected salary or prerequisites.

A specific part of the user model can define additional information necessary for personalization. Such an information in the domain of job offers can be a list of already visited job offers, which is modeled by the `VisitedOffer` class. The user model stores information about the offer itself (`hasJobOffer`), the evaluation assigned to it by the user (`hasRating`) as well as the date of the visit (`hasDateOfVisit`).

### 4.2 Tools for user modeling support

We employ the described user model to provide personalization [1]. To fill the user model with data we observe user actions within a web-based system combined with explicit input from the user. However, we focus on automated acquisition of the user characteristics. We collect as much data as possible about the user's actions by employing standard server side logging mechanisms as well as a special client side JavaScript logging tool called *Click*. Click records actions, which are not visible on the server (e.g., reload of a page stored in browser's cache, hover on page elements or using the back button, which is important for discovering user interests on the portal).

Afterwards, the collected data are analyzed to estimate selected user characteristics. We analyze user navigation and implicit user feedback derived from the time the user spent by viewing job offers [2]. The estimation uses heuristics and predefined patterns of navigation on the site. Some of these heuristics need to compare two domain concepts to find out their common and different aspects. Once an instance of the model exists in a system, it can be used by other components of the system to perform the adaptation itself, which can be of various types – annotation of displayed content, its sorting etc. Therefore, the comparison between the user ontology and the domain ontology instances is necessary albeit not straightforward.

In contrast to the common attribute-value models, the ontology provides structured data and a one-on-one comparison does not provide satisfactory results because two individuals usually may provide semantically similar information even though they are not on the same level in the hierarchical structure of the ontology. Since a part of the structure of the ontology is known (property subClassOf) we use a recursive algorithm to traverse the hierarchy. Because we consider attributes that have identical parent nodes to be closer, we take into account both a straight path between attributes in the hierarchy and also what branch of the hierarchy tree they belong to.

The user characteristics are used by several software tools aimed at further refinement of user interests. The *Top-k aggregator* tool retrieves the most relevant job offers with respect to user preferences (e.g., salary, education requirements, place) based on ordered lists of user preferences [9]. The *Aspect* tool searches for similar documents (job offers) based on a probabilistic model for soft clustering [17]. Using the described approach for the comparison of domain and user ontology instances the devised clusters are presented the user according to her characteristics.

# 5 Related works

Although several possible user model representations are currently used, the user modeling community has changed focus recently to ontology based approaches, which bring several advantages as discussed above. Several projects, which either concentrate on building reusable user model ontologies or employ the user model ontology as a part of an adaptive web-based system exist.

UserML – the RDF-based user model exchange language [11] extends the XML structure to be able represent graph structure by means of two cooperative levels. The first one defines a simple XML structure for the user model entries and the second one are categories defined in the ontology. The advantage of this approach is that different ontologies can be used with the same UserML tools. UserML served as a base for the reusable user model ontology GUMO – General User Model Ontology [10] represented in OWL. GUMO provides a collection of the user's dimensions (e.g., user's heart beat, age, position, etc.) that might be helpful for several information systems intending to provide personalization based on the user model. These characteristics can be shared also with our user ontology when the web-based information system realizes adaptation according such personal characteristics.

OntobUM (Ontology based User Model) is a generic ontology-based user modeling architecture developed for a knowledge management system [18]. The user model consists of an implicit and an explicit part. While the explicit part contains characteristics such as identity, preferences, the implicit part is related to experiences related to system usage. Our approach of considering domain dependence of user model ontology extends this classification.

Among the projects, which use an ontology based user model representation we mention ADAPT[2] – Advanced Distributed Architecture for Personalized Teaching & Training [5]. It stands for a general framework for distributed education that employs an Ontology Server to user model exchange.

The idea of a shared user model is also elaborated in [13]. Here, the Personis server that uses a proprietary representation of a model based on triplets *component–evidence–source* is described. There is no explicit definition of the triplets' semantics and each application can define its own triplets not regarding the others, which limits its reusability. Another project, UMoWS [3] uses OWL representation of a model. Because the same knowledge can be represented by different ontologies on different levels of abstraction UMoWS supports the representation in multiple ontologies and can provide the mapping between them to applications, so they can share a common model.

# 6 Conclusions

The main contribution of this paper lies in describing advantages of an ontology-based representation of user models aimed at providing personalization in web-based information systems. We concentrated on comparison with other currently used approaches for user model representation. We consider the simplification of exchanging user model data between different applications as the major advantage of using ontologies. The presented ontology developed in the course of a research project aimed at the job offer acquisition application domain contributes to the state of the art by separation of domain-independent and domain-dependent parts of the user model. Separating the domain-independent part of user characteristics allows us to build a general user model. This kind of the user model can be used in a wide-range of applications while only adding parts, which differ from one application to another. We also use the presented ontology as the user model in a research project aimed at developing a recommendation layer for digital libraries that serves for personalization of its services.

An ontology is not the only representation that is advantageous for user modeling in web-information systems. Systems that build user models based on user monitoring represent logs that are also considered to be parts of the user model using simpler data structures as ontologies (often XML files are sufficient). Another example of non-ontological parts of the user model are statistics related to user behavior. Ontological representation is advantageous for those parts of the user model that are related to user characteristics where some reasoning is useful, i.e. checking the consistency of values.

Developed software tools mentioned in the paper can also be used for other domains as that of labor market. The tools are designed to be domain independent realizing their methods with an optional domain-dependent layer. Navigation in the domain is done through a faceted semantic browser [20], which is designed for the use in various application domains.

**Acknowledgement.** This work was partially supported by the Slovak Research and Development Agency under the contract No. APVT-20-007104 and the State programme of research and development "Establishing of Information Society" under the contract No. 1025/04.

# References

1. A. Andrejko, M. Barla, M. Bieliková, and M. Tvarožek. Tools for user characteristics acquisition. In *Datakon'06*, 2006. Accepted.
2. M. Barla. Interception of user's interests on the web. In V. et al. Wade, editor, *4th Int. Conf. on Adaptive Hypermedia and Adaptive Web-Based Systems, AH'06*, pages 435–439, Dublin, Ireland, 2006. Springer, LNCS 4018.
3. M. Bieliková and J. Kuruc. Sharing user models for adaptive hypermedia applications. In *5th Int. Conf. on Intelligent Systems Design and Applications, ISDA'05*, pages 506–511, Wroclaw, Poland, 2005. ACM Press.
4. P. Brusilovsky, A. Corbett, and F. de Rosis. User modeling 2003: Preface. In *9th Int. Conf. on User Modelling*, Johnstown, USA, 2003. Springer, LNCS 2702.
5. P. Brusilovsky, S. Sosnovsky, and M. Yudelson. Ontology-based framework for user model interoperability in distributed learning environments. In G. Richards, editor, *E-Learn 2005*, pages 2851–2855, Vancouver, Canada, 2005. AACE.
6. M. Ciglan, M. Babik, M. Laclavik, I. Budinska, and L. Hluchy. Corporate memory: A framework for supporting tools for acquisition, organization and maintenance of information and knowledge. In *9th Int. Conf. on Inf. Systems Implementation and Modelling, ISIM'06*, Prerov, Czech Republic, 2006.
7. P. de Bra, A. Aerts, B. de Lange, B. Rousseau, T. Santic, D. Smith, and N. Stash. AHA! the adaptive hypermedia architecture. In *ACM Conf. on Hypertext and Hypermedia*, pages 81–84, Nottingham, UK, 2003.

8. T.R. Gruber. Towards principles for the design of ontologies used for knowledge sharing. In N. Guarino and R. Poli, editors, *Formal Ontology in Conceptual Analysis and Knowledge Representation*, Deventer, The Netherlands, 1993. Kluwer Academic Publishers.

9. P. Gurský, R. Lencses, and P. Vojtáš. Algorithms for user dependent integration of ranked distributed information. In M. Böhlen et al., editor, *TCGOV 2005 Poster Proceedings*, Bozen-Bolzano, Italy, 2005.

10. D. Heckmann, T. Schwartz, B. Brandherm, M. Schmitz, and M. von Wilamowitz-Moellendorff. Gumo – the general user model ontology. In L. et al. Ardissono, editor, *10th Int. Conf. on User Modeling, UM'05*, pages 428–432, Edinburgh, Scotland, UK, 2005. Springer, LNCS 3538.

11. Dominik Heckmann and Antonio Krueger. A user modeling markup language (UserML) for ubiquitous computing. In P. et al. Brusilovsky, editor, *9th Int. Conf. on User Modelling, UM'03*, pages 393–397, Johnstown, USA, 2003. Springer, LNCS 2702.

12. J. Kay. User modeling for adaptation. In C. Stephanidis, editor, *User Interfaces for All*, Human Factors Series, pages 271–294, Florence, Italy, 2000.

13. J. Kay, B. Kummerfeld, and P. Lauder. Personis: A server for user models. In P. et al. de Bra, editor, *2nd Int. Conf. on Adaptive Hypermedia and Adaptive Web-Based Systems, AH'02*, pages 29–31, Malaga, Spain, 2002. Springer, LNCS 2347.

14. J. Kay and A. Lum. Ontology-based user modeling for the semantic web. In *10th Int. Conf. on User Modeling, UM'05, Workshop 8*, pages 11–19, Edinburgh, Scotland, UK, 2005.

15. P. Návrat, M. Bieliková, and V. Rozinajová. Methods and tools for acquiring and presenting information and knowledge in the web. In *Int. Conf. on Computer Systems and Technologies, CompSysTech 2005*, Varna, Bulgaria, 2005.

16. G. Nguyen, M. Laclavik, Z. Balogh, E. Gatial, M. Ciglan, M. Babik, I. Budinska, and L. Hluchy. Data and knowledge acquisition with ontology background. In W. Abramowicz, editor, *Business Information Systems, BIS'06*, Poznan, Poland, 2006.

17. G. Polčicová and P. Tiňo. Making sense of sparse rating data in collaborative filtering via topographic organisation of user preference patterns. *Neural Networks*, 17:1183–1199, 2004.

18. L. Razmerita, A. Angehrn, and A. Maedche. Ontology-based user modeling for knowledge management systems. In *9th Int. Conf. on User Modeling, UM'03*, pages 213–217, Johnstown, PA, USA, 2003. Springer, LNCS 2702.

19. M. Tury and M. Bieliková. An approach to detection ontology changes. In *1st Int. Workshop on Adaptation and Evolution in Web Systems Engineering (AEWSE 06) at ICWE 2006*, Palo Alto, California, 2006. ACM Press. Accepted.

20. M. Tvarožek. Personalized navigation in the semantic web. In V. et al. Wade, editor, *4th Int. Conf. on Adaptive Hypermedia and Adaptive Web-Based Systems, AH'06*, pages 467–471, Dublin, Ireland, 2006. Springer, LNCS 4018.

21. M. Yudelson, T. Gavrilova, and P. Brusilovsky. Towards user modeling meta-ontology. In L. et al. Ardissono, editor, *10th Int. Conf. on User Modeling, UM'05*, pages 448–452, Edinburgh, Scotland, UK, 2005. Springer, LNCS 3538.

# IT-Supported Inter-Organizational Services – The Case of a Swedish E-business Portal for Electronic Invoicing for Regional SMEs

Odd Fredriksson

Information Systems Department, Karlstad University, Sweden
Odd.Fredriksson@kau.se

## 1 IT-supported Inter-organizational Services – Business-to-business E-Commerce

In the service marketing management literature, the service provider's perspective is still the dominant paradigm of thinking. Gustafsson and Johnson (2003:1-2) posit that:

> "The business logic of competing through services is simple: solving customer problems with cost-effective service solutions is the best way to keep your customers from doing business with somebody else."

As regards business-to-business (B2B) services, it is however obvious that service solutions ideally should benefit *all* business, or trading, *partners involved*. Ideally, win-win-win solutions should be created for all partners, which in turn, drive further usage of the service solutions in question and thereby keep competitors away.

Business-to-business E-Commerce (EC) is one such significant form of IT-supported inter-organizational service. However, EC is still not a significant global force. Less than 5 per cent of all transactions are exchanged electronically (Turban et al. 2006:6).

### Business-to-business E-Commerce

From a commercial or trading perspective, electronic commerce (EC) provides the capability of buying and selling products, services and information over electronic networks (Kalakota & Whinston 1997).

This paper is focused on *business-to-business* (B2B) EC, that is private, or public, organizations selling goods or services to private, or public, organizations as buyers. It refers to transactions between firms and municipalities conducted electronically over the Internet, extranets, intranets, or private networks (Mahadevan 2003). The major characteristic of B2B EC is that organizations attempt to electronically automate trading or communication processes in order to improve them. Key business drivers for B2B EC is the emergence of effective technologies for intra- and inter-organizational integration, the need for improved collaboration between suppliers and buyers, the ability to save time, reduce delays and increase quality and control (see Warkentin 2002).

In this paper, EC via an e-business portal will be explored. A portal is designed to be a single entry point to internal and external applications, information, and services necessary for completing specific tasks and activities (Carlsson & Hedman 2001).

## Understanding Requires a Relationship Perspective

Increasingly, traditional adversarial, arm's length (i.e. market exchange), relationships are being substituted for closer and more collaborative relationship exchanges. A relationship exchange is less price-driven than a market exchange and is based on a greater recognition of mutual commitment between the trading partners. Managing collaboration involves several complex strategic, economic, social and conflict management issues (Kumar & van Dissel 1996). Often collaboration between organizations require the establishment of information and communication systems between the organizations in the supply/distribution chain (Konsynski & Mc-Farlan 1990).

Given the dyadic relationship nature of EC, the relationship unit of analysis is the natural perspective to apply when trying to understand EC adoption and use processes. Oddly enough, the relationship unit of analysis has been sparsely applied for the empirical data collection in previous B2B EC research. This neglect of the relationship level of analysis has been acknowledged by, e.g., Iacovou et al. (1985), Premkumar et al. (1997), and Kuan and Chau (2001). For EDI, the most highly automated form of EC, solely a relationship perspective is not enough to understand its adoption and diffusion processes. Whether inter-organizational business processes can be simplified and be more efficient by the use of B2B EC or not, heavily depends also on contextual-specific conditions (Sanchez 2004).

## 2 Small and Medium-Sized Enterprises

Despite the exponential growth of EC, it is mostly larger firms that have reaped the benefits from EC use (Riquelme 2002).

Small and medium-sized enterprises (SMEs) have some unique features that distinguish them from larger enterprises. They often have a centralised management strategy, relatively poor management and business skills and a strong desire for independence. They are also often faced with 'resource poverty' (Welsh & White 1981) in terms of being financially ill-equipped, and lacking specialized knowledge and technical expertise (DeLone 1988). SMEs further tend to be subject to higher failure rates (Cochran 1981), which implies a higher degree of caution when it comes to making investment decisions. Costs of EC implementation is often high (Quayle 2002). Therefore, SMEs tend to apply a "wait-and-see approach" as regards EC. Accordingly, the rate of EC adoption in the SME sector has remained relatively low.

## 3 Barriers to EC Adoption among SMEs

The assumption made concerning the value associated with identifying barriers to innovation is that when actions consequently then are taken to eliminate these, the implementation of the innovation process will be successful. However, successful innovation processes are not automatic processes. They require motivation, extra-ordinary efforts and acceptance of risk (Tidd et al. 1997).

The sluggish pace of e-commerce implementation has been attributed to various barriers to implementation. Many small and medium-sized enterprises (SMEs) have found it difficult to implement an e-commerce strategy because of low usage of e-commerce and IT by customers and suppliers, lack of knowledge or IT expertise in the SME, and limited awareness of the opportunities. Another prominent impeding condition has been the lack of e-commerce standardization across different IT vendors (cf. Tuunainen 1998).

MacGregor et al. (2005) conducted a questionnaire survey study on barriers to adoption on regional SMEs in Sweden, Australia and US. The results showed that these barriers could be grouped under two factors: "too difficult" and "unsuitable". The *"too difficult"*-factor in their study was formed by barriers related to the complexity of implementation techniques, range of e-commerce options, high investments/costs and the lack of technical knowledge and time. The *"unsuitable"* factor was formed by barriers related to the suitability of e-commerce to the respondent's business, including the extent to which e-commerce matched the business' products/ services, the organization's way of doing business, their client's way of doing business and the lack of advantages offered by EC implementation. These two factors accounted for 60% of the variance within the Swedish sample and 78% of the variance within the Australian sample. For the US sample, also a third factor was extracted: *"investment & security"*. The three factors accounted for 71% of the variance within the US sample. Thus, there were distinct differences between the EC adoption barriers perceived by the regional SMEs in these three locations (MacGregor et al. 2005). One of their conclusions from this result is that the SME sector should not be regarded as homogeneous.

## 4 E-Business Portal Studied – Portal Meetingpoint Wermland

The present empirical study was conducted in Sweden, which is a country with a relatively advanced e-readiness. In the latest ranking performed by The Economist Intelligence Unit (2006), Sweden ranked as the number four e-readiness country, after Denmark, US and Switzerland.

More specifically, the present empirical study was conducted within the county of Värmland, a county situated in the west of Sweden. There are about 10,000 SMEs in the county of Värmland. This county is far from the large city areas of Sweden. Thus, regional SMEs are studied. The Swedish random selection in the survey study of MacGregor et al. (2005), commented upon above, was drawn from Värmland's population of SMEs.

In the beginning of the current decade, the Wermland Chamber of Commerce realized that the degree of e-commerce adoption and usage within the region of Värmland and in southern Dalecarlia was very low. In 2003, the Wermland Chamber of Commerce therefore decided to launch a "regional hub" marketplace, called the Portal Meetingpoint Wermland (PMW), aiming at providing simple and inexpensive alternative e-commerce solutions to alleviate the concerns of the regional SMEs and municipalities.

After pilot studies had been conducted in 2004, e-invoicing applications were chosen by the municipalities of Värmland to be the first application type for the e-business portal since these turned out to be relatively easier to implement than, e.g., e-purchasing applications. The e-business portal therefore chose to promote the usage of e-invoices among SMEs, municipalities and even some larger firms (Handelskammaren Värmland 2006).

On March 10th 2004, the first e-invoice was sent and received via the e-business portal. To date, the main thrust of its activities, financed by governmental and EU funds, has been directed towards the municipality of Torsby and some 30 of its suppliers. Torsby is a small municipality with a weak economy in the northern part of Värmland. In early 2006, there were five municipalities in the region which were receiving e-invoices to varying degrees: Torsby, Sunne, Vansbro, Arvika and Kristinehamn.

The objectives with the Portal Meetingpoint Wermland are to (Obstfelder Peterson 2006):

- increase IT skills among SMEs and get e-business strategies higher up on the SMEs' agendas.
- make SMEs understand the advantages of e-business, help them identify their e-business opportunities and present existing e-business solutions.
- assist SMEs in implementing their transformation towards e-business and provide specific advice tailored to the needs of the individual SME in order to ensure the most efficient use of the means and technologies available.
- be the link between the local authority/the firm and its suppliers.
- provide a regional resource for businesses and municipalities to generate e-invoices in a format that the recipient's system can process.

In other words, the PMW strives to provide value to its linked user organizations, that are suppliers and buyers, by providing IT-supported services to be used to increase inter-organizational integration in their dyadic trading relationships. One ingredient for PMW to accomplish this is by a continuous process of offering a series of packaged solutions.

A central consequence from this e-business portal initiative is that the costs of applications and equipment are shared among the linked user organizations. In other words, this e-business portal constitutes a network resource for SMEs and other organizations.

In early 2006, this e-commerce initiative was chosen by eBSN (the European e-Business Support Network for SMEs) to be the best practice e-commerce case among European SMEs. One of the project leaders of PMW comments on the perceived success in the following way:

"One unique characteristic of our model, explaining our success, is that we deliberately have chosen to focus relatively sparsely on the technology and instead focus our efforts on solid and well-laid implementation support, for both the receiver and the sender of e-invoices."

Given this background, the main research question chosen for this paper is:

*What are the main driving and impeding conditions influencing on the usage of IT-supported inter-organizational services as applied within the network of SMEs linked to the e-business Portal Meetingpoint Wermland?*

A secondary, and related, research question briefly discussed in this paper is:

*What are the stakeholders' perceptions of the effects from the usage of these IT-supported inter-organizational services?*

## 5 Focused EC-application: Electronic Invoicing

Every organization issues and receives invoices on a regular basis. That process is currently undergoing a number of changes aimed at saving time and money for both parties. An electronic invoice goes directly into the recipient's enterprise system. Online communication between the two parties is a precondition for that to happen. The sender must subscribe to an electronic service suitable for its particular enterprise system, while the recipient must adapt its system to an electronic mailbox. The PMW provides a regional resource for businesses and municipalities to generate e-invoices in a format that the recipient's enterprise system can process. This e-business portal currently supports e-invoicing in accordance with the Single Face to Industry (SFTI) standard.

The recipient obtains a mailbox from which it can retrieve the invoices of participating suppliers. The sender subscribes to a service and transmits a file in a specified format that the e-business portal subsequently converts to match the recipient's requirements. These e-invoices are treated as EDI messages.

Suppliers which lack an enterprise system of their own or that issue relatively few invoices can fill out an online form. The e-business portal makes sure that the e-invoice goes to the recipient's digital mailbox. This procedure is called Web EDI.

Organizations which issue more than 10 invoices per month but do not have the financial or technological resources to generate an EDI message can take advantage of a solution which serves as a virtual printer. The sender downloads the software from the e-business portal and sets the printer to the recipient's address. After writing the invoice, the invoice issuer prints it out to the e-business portal's mailbox.

PMW has designed a number of formats suitable for some of the most common enterprise systems. Thus, the e-business portal provides support and benefits regardless of how a particular business is set up.

The e-business portal is a cost-effective concept, independent of enterprise system or an organization's current ability to send and receive e-invoices. Each of the various approaches allows the sender to simply, efficiently and inexpensively transmit an e-invoice in the desired format without costly expenditures along the way.

## 6 Methodology

The present explorative study was conducted during 2005 and early 2006. Given the novelty of the e-invoicing services provided via the focused e-business portal, the design of the study was chosen to be qualitative. This enabled us to gain a better understanding of the key issues during its initial phase of the diffusion process. The author has since 2001 been a member of the reference group for this EC initiative of Wermland Chamber of Commerce, which in 2003 turned out to become the focal e-business Portal Meetingpoint Wermland. Therefore, the author had a solid pre-understanding of the matters at hand at the outset of the present explorative study. In addition, the author also during the 2003-2005 period had tutored 11 project work reports by students on the undergraduate level.

The buyer–supplier relationship was chosen as the unit of analysis for the empirical data collection. The author therefore conducted personal semi-structured interviews with both users, that are orderers and invoice receivers, and managers/owners/local government officials. The respondents were representing the municipality of Torsby, and four of its regional SME suppliers. The three project leaders of the PMW were each of them interviewed a number of times. In total, there were 13 interviewees.

## 7 Results – Main Driving and Impeding Conditions

The nature of the dyadic business relationship was found to be perceived as a superior, or governing, driving and impeding condition for the actual adoption and use of EC between two trading partners. This finding justifies the choice of applying relationships as the basic unit of analysis.

The problem of lacking integration between the accounting system and the enterprise system, which typically are separated from each other, is seldom acknowledged in the EC research literature. This explorative study shows that these different system types are often supplied by different IT vendors, which want to promote their own systems and do not have enough incentives to integrate the variety of different combinations of systems. As a consequence, despite their use of EC, the trading partners are faced with non-efficient double workload.

Despite the extensive project support from the project leaders of PMW, there have been technical problems, such as for example server problems, encountered which have been disturbing the EC implementation processes.

Increased EC maturity is perceived to influence positively on EC implementation: After the first trading partner 'has been wired', the second one is then perceived to be easier to link with.

A negative experience for both buyer and supplier organizations have been the extensive amount of 'nitty and gritty' work required in order to have the required disciplined and exact business processes to work. As a result, implementation typically takes more time than what is expected in advance.

One of the project leaders of PMW perceives that the change work required is the toughest impeding condition to overcome. This explains why simpler EC applications which do not require so much change work, such as the 'receiving e-invoice' application, seem to be more popular to start with: "the important thing is to get organizations started". The project leaders use the concept 'ripple effect' as a metaphor for their implementation strategy (Obstfelder Peterson 2006):

Our approach was to start on a small scale and wait for a ripple effect to develop. That way we established a solid foundation from which we could move on to a practical, concrete effort. Step by step, we were able to demonstrate results and positive effects. And once you've done that, you can attract and involve even more businesses.

A 'small win/small step' EC implementation strategy, following a 'psychology of a small wins' path, seems to be more popular among the smaller organizations. Obviously, this is less risky while it correspondingly provides only minor net value effects. To realize major net value effects from EC implementation, substantial business process redesign is required.

According to one of the project leaders of PMW, lack of knowledge is a major impediment for the use of e-invoicing. Since there are different 'islands of internal stakeholders', within an organization such as a municipality, there is also a need to ensure that there is sufficient commitment and coordination of the internal workforces. One of the project leaders of PMW has devoted much time on the process of securing that four stakeholder actors on each side of the business relationship are sufficiently committed for change to e-invoicing, i.e. the CEO, the financial manager, the IT manager and a representative for the enterprise system vendor. Across these four stakeholders there are varying knowledge levels, perceptions about the choice of appropriate e-invoice type, and varying degrees of conviction as to whether there is good value from e-invoicing or not. The effort required to gain the necessary commitment from these stakeholders has during this e-invoicing project often turned out to be a very communication and time demanding activity (cf. Benjamin & Levinson 1993, who point out the critical importance of managing stakeholder commitment).

In the municipality of Torsby, a decentralized e-invoice reception capability ongoingly is implemented, meaning that the e-invoices are approved by each individual orderer. This, in turn, requires relatively more preparatory 'commitment work' on the municipality side of the relationship.

In essence, to allocate resources for champions is perceived by many of the respondents to be one critical success condition in order to attain the necessary implementation momentum.

## 8 Results – Perceived Effects

The lion's share of the benefits across an individual business relationship is attained by the buyer, since it is the receiver of the e-invoice. For the buyer organizations in this study, the 'receiving e-invoice' application is popular as the first EC application because it provides them with time-saving administrative effects within relatively short time. The average invoice-handling time was found to decrease with about 60 per cent (from 28 to 11 minutes) for the e-invoice receiver. After digitization, only the invoice authorization activities remain from the traditional receiving-invoice process. However, implementation processes are often slower than expected, or hoped for. During 2005, not more than 6 per cent of all incoming invoices to the municipality of Torsby were received as e-invoices (Persson 2006).

One of the 'receiving e-invoice' buyer organizations linked to PMW reports that it has significantly increased the degree of purchase loyalty towards its suborder suppliers, which has had a positive effect on its purchase costs. This is obviously also positive for the selected suppliers. Some of the regional SME suppliers perceive that they have not gained anything from starting to send e-invoices, except that they hope for a stronger relationship with its larger customer.

In a longer perspective, the e-invoice sending capability enabled by the e-business portal implies that these regional SMEs are enabled to remain as suppliers to the municipalities in the future. To date however, the municipalities in their buyer roles have not yet demanded mandatory e-invoicing from their suppliers.

According to one of the project leaders of PMW, the prime benefit for the regional SME suppliers is the knowledge accessed and acquired as regards how to send e-invoices and what this implies for the own organization. An important constituent of the tutoring attained from PMW has been the assistance in choosing the e-invoice type best fitting the individual SME's situation. The financial support which some of the SME suppliers have received has only been of secondary importance. PMW has carried the required technical investments, which has decreased the individual cost for all the linked SMEs.

According to another of the three project leaders of PMW, the noticeable prime benefit for the regional SME supplier is the emotional, rather than the economical, effect: a simpler invoicing administration effect is attained. As all administration concerning the e-invoice is performed at one and the same occasion, a more structured work procedure is attained and thereby is time spent on administration saved. This contributes to long-term development for the organization.

For buyer firms, also significant reliability effects have been attained from the usage of incoming invoices: elimination of misinterpretations, full communication security and traceability.

Valuable competence has been built among the project leaders of this 'regional hub', which has been inexpensively shared to the new adopters and will continuously be shared to the coming adopters of EC applications in the targeted market area. Thus, the focal e-business portal actor − so far − has functioned as a dynamo, or catalyst, for EC implementation among particularly smaller organizations in the targetted region.

Importantly, the e-business portal represents a regional, impartial effort to strengthen Värmland's private sector and open up avenues that are beyond the financial means of individual firms. As Wermland Chamber of Commerce is a neutral party − in relation to the IT vendors, the buyers and the suppliers − it attains a relatively high trust from the regional trading partner community, which in turn is positive for the probability of reaching a critical mass of use.

By the end of 2007, Swedish national project funds financing PMW will cease. Given the perceived success so far, there is good reason to predict that a critical mass of stakeholders, interested in that PMW successfully turns into a viable business operation, will be reached.

## References

Benjamin RI, Levinson, E (1993) A Framework for Managing IT-Enabled Change. Sloan Management Review, vol 34, no 4, pp 23-33

Carlsson SA, Hedman J (2001) An Assessment of a Role-Based Information Portal. In: Proceedings of the Eight European Conference on Information Technology Evaluation, Oriel College Oxford, UK, 17-18 September, pp 509-517

Cochran AB (1981) Small Business Mortality Rates. A Review of the Literature. Journal of Small Business Management, vol 19, no 4, pp 50-59

Cunningham MT, Culligan KL (1989) Relationships, Networks and Competitiveness: a Study of the Impact of Electronic Data Interchange Industry. In: Proceedings from the 5th IMP Conference. Pennsylvania State University, PA

DeLone WH (1988) Determinants of Success for Computer Usage in Small Business. MIS Quarterly, vol 12, no 1, pp 51-61

European Commission (2006) Conference Summary Report. Conference on the European Charter for Small Enterprises, Vienna, 13-14 June. http://www.ec. europa.eu/enterprise/enterprise_policy/charter/conf2006/index_en.htm (read 2006-06-22)

Gustafsson A, Johnson MD (2003) Competing in a Service Economy. Jossey-Bass, San Francisco, CA

Handelskammaren Värmland (2006) Portalen Handelsplats Wermland: Om projektet (in Swedish)

Iacovou CL, Benbasat I, Dexter AS (1995) Electronic Data Interchange and Small Organizations: Adoption and Impact of Technology. MIS Quarterly, vol 19, no 4, pp 465-485

Johnston R, Gregor S (2000) A Theory of Industry-Level Activity for Understanding the Adoption of Interorganizational Systems. European Journal of Information Systems, vol 9, pp 243-251

Kalakota R, Whinston AB (1997) Electronic Commerce. A Manager's Guide. Addison-Wesley, Reading, MA

Konsynski BR, McFarlan FW (1990) Information Partnerships – Shared Data, Shared Scale. Harvard Business Review, vol 68, no 5, 114-120

Kuan KKY, Chau PYK (2001) A Perception-Based Model for EDI Adoption in Small Businesses Using a Technology–Organization–Environment Framework. Information & Management, vol 38, no 8, pp 507-521

Kumar K, van Dissel HG (1996) Sustainable Collaboration: Managing Conflict and Cooperation in Interorganizational Systems. MIS Quarterly, vol 20, no 3, pp 279-300

MacGregor R, Vrazalic L, Carlsson S, Pratt J, Harris M (2005) How Standard are the Standard Barriers to E-commerce Adoption? – Empirical Evidence from Australia, Sweden and the USA", paper presented at: Fourteenth International Conference on Information Systems Development Conference (ISD 2005), 14-17 August, Karlstad University, Karlstad. In: Nilsson AG, Gustas R, Wojtkowski W, Wojtkowski G, Wrycza S, Zupančič J (eds) Advances in Information Systems Development: Bridging the Gap between Academia and Industry, vol 1. Springer, New York, pp 483-494

Mahadevan B (2003) Making Sense of the Emerging Market Structure in B2B E-Commerce. California Management Review, vol 46, no 1, pp 86-100

Markus ML (1987) Toward a Critical Mass Theory of Interactive Media: Universal Access, Interdependence and Diffusion. Communication Research, vol 14, no 5, pp 491-511

Mattsson L-G (1997) Relationship Marketing" and the "Markets-as-networks Approach" – A Comparative Analysis of Two Evolving Streams of Research. Journal of Marketing Management, vol 13, no 5, pp 447-461

Obstfelder Peterson U (2006) Meetingpoint Wermland – Practical E-Commerce for Värmland's Businesses and Municipalities. Presentation at the Conference on the European Charter for Small Enterprises, Vienna, 13-14 June

Persson A-S (2006) Personal interview including extracting internal municipality statistics about received e-invoices, January 24th, Torsby, Sweden

Porter, ME (1998) Clusters and the New Economics of Competition. Harvard Business Review, vol 76, no 6, 77-90

Premkumar G, Ramamurthy K, Crum MR (1997) Determinants of EDI Adoption in the Transportation Industry. European Journal of Information Systems, vol 6, no 2, pp 107-121

Quayle M (2002) E-Commerce: the Challenge for UK SMEs in the Twenty-First Century. International Journal of Operations and Production Management, vol 22, no 10, pp 1148-1161

Reekers N, Smithson S (1995) The Impact of Electronic Data Interchange on Interor-ganizational Relationships: Integrating Theoretical Perspectives. In: Proceedings of the 28th Annual Hawaii International Conference on System Sciences, pp 757-766

Riquelme H (2002) Commercial Internet Adoption in China: Comparing the Experience of Small, Medium and Large Businesses. Internet Research: Electronic Networking Applications and Policy, vol 12, no 3, pp 276-286

Sanchez R (2004) Understanding Competence-based Management: Identifying and Managing Five Models of Competence. Journal of Business Research, vol 57, no 5, pp 518-532

Schelling TC (1978) Micromotives and Macrobehavior. W.W. Norton & Company, New York

The Economist Intelligence Unit (2006) E-readiness divide narrows. http://www.ebusinessforum.com (read 2006-05-01)

Tidd J, Bessant J, Pavitt, K (1997) Managing Innovation. Wiley, Chichester

Turban E, King D, Viehland D, Lee, J (2006) Electronic Commerce 2006 – A Managerial Perspective. Prentice Hall, Upper Saddle River, NJ

Tuunainen VK (1998) Opportunities of Effective Integration of EDI for Small Businesses in the Automotive Industry. Information & Management, vol 36, no 6, pp 361-375

Warkentin M (2002, ed) Business to Business Electronic Commerce: Challenges and Solutions. Idea Group Publishing, Hershey, PA

Welsh JA, White, JF (1981) A Small Business is not a Little Big Business. Harvard Business Review, vol 59, no 4, pp 46-58

# What Makes a Good Diagram? Improving the Cognitive Effectiveness of Diagrams in IS Development

Daniel Moody

Department of Information Systems and Change Management
University of Twente, Enschede, Netherlands
*E-mail: d.l.moody@bbt.utwente.nl*

**Abstract.** Diagrams play a critical role in IS development. Despite this, ISD practitioners receive little or no instruction on how to produce "good" diagrams. In the absence of this, they are forced to rely on their intuition and experience, and make layout decisions that distort information or convey unintended meanings. The design of ISD graphical notations is *ad hoc* and unscientific: choice of conventions is based on personal taste rather than scientific evidence. Also, existing notations use a very limited graphic vocabulary and thus fail to exploit the potential communication power of diagrams. This paper describes a set of principles for producing "good" diagrams, which are defined as diagrams that communicate effectively. These provide practical guidance for both designers and users of ISD diagramming notations and are soundly based on theoretical and empirical evidence from a wide range of disciplines. We conclude that radical change is required to ISD diagramming practices to achieve effective user-developer communication.

## 1. INTRODUCTION

Diagrams form a critical part of the "language" of IS development: most ISD techniques rely heavily on graphical representations. For example, UML 2.0 consists of 13 types of models, all of which are represented in graphical form [29]. The primary reason for using diagrams in IS development is to facilitate communication. In particular, diagrams are believed to be more effective than text for communicating with end users. Effective user-developer communication is critical for successful development of information systems.

### 1.1 Cognitive Effectiveness: What is a "Good" Diagram?

A diagram is a sentence in a graphical language [24]. The primary purpose of any language is to communicate. Therefore a "good" diagram is one which communicates effectively. *Communication* (or *cognitive*) *effectiveness* is measured by the speed, ease and accuracy with which the information content can be understood. The cognitive effectiveness of diagrams is one of the most widely held assumptions in the ISD field. However cognitive effectiveness is not an intrinsic property of diagrams but something that must be designed into them [19].

### 1.2 Current State of Practice

Despite the importance of diagrams in IS development, practitioners typically receive little or no instruction in how to produce effective diagrams. As a result, they are forced to rely on their intuition and experience (which is often wrong), and make layout decisions that distorts information or conveys unintended messages. Decisions about presentation of diagrams tend to be driven by subjective judgements about "aesthetics" (what looks good), which they are not qualified to make as they typically lack expertise in graphic design. Also, what looks good is not always what communicates most effectively. Current ISD diagramming practices are based on erroneous assumptions about what makes diagrams effective and flawed heuristics about how best to construct them. Examples of commonly-used heuristics include avoiding line crossings, using zigzag lines and expanding symbols to fit labels. While these are designed to improve readability of diagrams, in most cases they have the opposite effect. Despite this, such practices have been perpetuated over time and have become so entrenched that they are often documented as "best practices" [e.g. 1].

The design of ISD diagramming notations is also largely *ad hoc* and unscientific. Decisions about how to graphically represent constructs are based on personal taste, intuition or consensus rather than on scientific evidence. There is usually no theoretical or empirical justification for conventions used, perhaps reflecting a belief that it does not really matter which conventions are chosen. ISD diagramming notations also use a perceptually limited repertoire of graphical techniques and thus fail to exploit the potential power of diagrams [33]. The same graphical symbols (variants of boxes and arrows) are used over and over again while some of the most effective graphical techniques such as colour, spatial layout, size and value are not used at all or used informally [33]. Finally, most ISD diagramming notations are inconsistent with principles of graphic design. This is not surprising as designers of ISD notations typically lack training or expertise in graphic design. However while it is common in other areas of ISD practice (e.g. user interface design, web development) to get advice from graphic design specialists, notation designers rarely do the same.

## 1.3  Current State of Research

The perceptual characteristics (visual appearance or *form*) of diagrams have been grossly understated by ISD researchers. While issues of semantics or *content* (what constructs to include in a notation) are treated as matters of substance, details of graphical syntax (how to visually represent these constructs) are treated as being of little or no consequence. Choice of graphical conventions is seen by researchers (like notation designers) as a matter of aesthetics or personal taste rather than effectiveness [14]. Research in diagrammatical reasoning suggests the exact opposite: the cognitive effectiveness of diagrams is primarily determined by their perceptual characteristics [19, 33]. Even slight changes in graphical representation can have dramatic impacts on understanding and problem solving performance. The extent to which diagrams exploit perceptual features largely explains why some diagrams are effective and others are not [19]. This suggests that the *form* of diagrams is just as important – if not more – than their *content*.

## 1.4  Objectives of this Paper

Most ISD diagrams do not communicate effectively and actually act as a *barrier* rather than an aid to user-developer communication [17, 28, 39]. Field studies show that end users understand ISD diagrams very poorly and that most developers don't even show diagrams to their users [13, 14, 28, 37]. The fault for this lies with educators, notation designers and researchers, who have largely ignored issues of graphical representation or treated them in an *ad hoc* way. The aim of this paper is to provide a scientific basis for the use of diagrams in IS development. We argue that ISD diagramming practice should be *evidence based*: decisions about what graphical conventions to use (language level) and layout of individual diagrams (sentence level) should be based on evidence about cognitive effectiveness rather than subjective notions of aesthetics. The major focus of this research is on improving the effectiveness of communication with non-specialists (end users) as this is most critical for improving for improving the quality of the IS development process.

# 2. THEORIES OF GRAPHICAL COMMUNICATION

In order to produce more cognitively effective diagrams, we need to consider two things [49]:

- The language of graphics: the techniques available for encoding information graphically. Clearly, the better our command of the language, the more effectively we will be able to communicate.
- Human graphical information processing: how diagrams are processed by the human mind. This is necessary to evaluate the cognitive effectiveness of alternative representations.

## 2.1 The Language of Graphics

The seminal work in the field of graphical communication is Jacques Bertin's *"Semiology of Graphics"* [5]. This is considered by many to be for graphic design what the periodic table is for chemistry. Bertin identified eight elementary *visual variables* which can be used to graphically encode information (Figure 1). These are categorised into *planar variables* (the two spatial dimensions) and *retinal variables* (features of the retinal image).

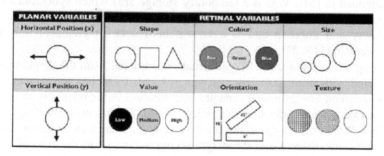

**Figure 1. Visual Variables [5]**

The set of visual variables define a "vocabulary" for graphical communication: a set of atomic building blocks that can be used to construct any graphical representation – similar to the way the elements of the periodic table can be used to construct any chemical compound. Different visual variables are suitable for encoding different types of information. For example, colour can be used to encode nominal data but not ordinal or ratio data because it is not psychologically ordered [18]. The choice of visual variables has a major impact on cognitive effectiveness as it affects both speed and accuracy of interpretation [9, 22, 50].

## 2.2   Human Graphical Information Processing

Figure 2 shows a model of human graphical information processing, which reflects current research in human cognition and visual perception. This consists of four major processing stages:

- Perceptual discrimination: features of the retinal image (i.e. visual variables) are detected, some serially, some in parallel, across the visual field (*feature integration*) [21, 41]. Based on this initial processing, the diagram is parsed into discrete elements based on common visual properties and separated from the background (*figure-ground segregation*) [30, 50].
- Perceptual configuration: diagram elements are grouped together (possibly recursively) based on their visual characteristics [30, 50]. The *Gestalt Laws of Perception* define a set of rules for how visual stimuli are organised into perceptual groups [46].

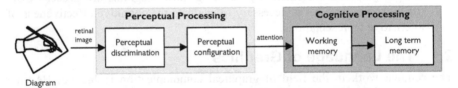

**Figure 2. Model of Graphical Information Processing**

- Working memory (WM): all or part of the processed image is brought into WM for active processing and interpretation under conscious control of attention. *Perceptual precedence* determines the order in which elements are attended to [51]. WM is a temporary storage area which synchronises rapid perceptual processes with slower cognitive processes. It has very limited capacity and duration and is a known bottleneck in graphical information processing [18, 22].
- Long term memory (LTM): information extracted from the diagram is integrated with prior knowledge stored in LTM. LTM is a permanent storage area which has unlimited capacity and duration but is relatively slow. There are two types of prior knowledge relevant to diagram understanding: *domain knowledge* (knowledge about the represented domain) and *notational knowledge* (knowledge about the diagramming notation). In the case of notation experts (i.e. IS developers), notational knowledge is likely to be encoded in a *diagram schema,* which largely automates the process of diagram interpreta-

tion [34]. Domain experts (i.e. end users) are unlikely to have such a schema as they interact with such diagrams infrequently and therefore interpretation will be much more error-prone and will require significant conscious effort.

Perceptual processes are automatic, pre-attentive, very fast and mostly executed in parallel while cognitive processes operate under conscious control of attention and are relatively slow, effortful and sequential. A major basis for the cognitive advantages of diagrams is that they shift some of the processing burden to the perceptual system, freeing up cognitive resources for other tasks [36].

# 3. PRINCIPLES FOR PRODUCING EFFECTIVE DIAGRAMS

In this section, we define a set of *evidence-based* principles for producing cognitively effective ISD diagrams. These are based on theoretical and empirical evidence from a wide range of disciplines including cartography, conceptual modelling, cognitive psychology, communication theory, computer graphics, diagrammatic reasoning, education, graphic design, graph drawing, human-computer interaction, information visualisation, linguistics, multimedia design, psychophysics, semiotics, statistics, technical writing, typography, visual perception and visual programming.

## 3.1 Discriminability: Diagram Elements should be Easy to See and Differentiate from one another

Perceptual discrimination is the first step in graphical information processing (Figure 2). Accurate discrimination of diagram elements is a necessary prerequisite for further processing. There are two aspects to discriminability [18]:

- *Absolute discriminability:* the ability to see diagram elements and separate them from the background.
- *Relative discriminability:* the ability to differentiate between different types of diagram elements.

Absolute discriminability is determined by three primary factors:

- Size: diagram elements (and also textual labels) need to be a certain minimum size to be seen and recognised correctly [48]. The optimal size of elements for human perception have been empirically established for both visual elements and text [2, 40].
- Contrast: according to the *Gestalt Figure-Ground principle*, the greater the contrast between diagram elements and the background, the more readily objects will be detected and recognised [30, 46]. Contrast can be achieved by using clearly different surface properties (*colour, texture or value*) between diagram elements and the background. Adequate contrast should also be established between textual labels and their background.
- Proximity: discernibility of diagram elements decreases with proximity of other elements [52]. This relates to the use of *white space*, which is one of

the major design elements in graphic design [47]. There is no empirical basis for choosing the optimal spacing between elements but for most types of ISD diagrams 1–1.5 shape widths provides adequate separation.

Relative discriminability is determined by the number and size of differences between symbols used to represent different constructs. The greater the perceptual variation between symbols used to represent different constructs, the faster and more accurately they will be recognised [51]. If differences are too subtle, errors in interpretation and ambiguity can result. In particular, requirements for discriminability are much higher for novices (end users) than for experts [7, 8].

## 3.2    Manageable Complexity: Diagrams should not Exceed Perceptual and Cognitive Limits

One of the most common mistakes in ISD diagramming practice is to show too much information on a single diagram. This results in "absurdly complex diagrams" that are a barrier rather than an aid to communication [17]. The reason for this is that the amount of information that can be effectively conveyed by a single diagram is limited by human perceptual and cognitive abilities:

- Perceptual limits: The ability to visually discriminate between diagram elements decreases with their number and proximity [23]. In general, the difficulty of discerning diagram elements increases quadratically with diagram size [31]. The root cause of discriminability problems with ISD diagrams (Principle 1) is excessive complexity.
- Cognitive limits: The number of diagram elements that can be comprehended at a time is limited by working memory capacity, which is believed to be "seven plus or minus two" concepts at a time [3, 21, 45]. When this is exceeded, a state of *cognitive overload* ensues and comprehension degrades rapidly [20, 26].

One of the most effective ways of reducing the complexity of large systems is to divide them into smaller subsystems or *modules*. This is called *decomposition* or *modularisation* [4]. In the context of diagrams, this means that large diagrams should be divided into perceptually and cognitively manageable "chunks" (seven plus or minus two elements per diagram). Experimental studies show that modularising ISD diagrams in this way improves end user understanding and verification accuracy by more than 50% [27].

## 3.3    Emphasis: The Relative Importance of Diagram Elements should be Clearly Shown

In most ISD diagrams, all elements look the same: there is no way of telling which are most important [17]. Such representations act as very poor information filters. Also, because there is no clear entry point or processing sequence, it makes them hard to access for novices and leads to inefficient and haphazard processing [6, 33]. The visual variables (Figure 2) can be used to create a clear perceptual precedence or visual hierarchy among diagram elements. The most effective visual variables for emphasis are those suitable for encoding *ordinal data* as emphasis defines a partial ordering over diagram elements. The most important concepts should be emphasised (*highlighted*) to bring them to the readers' attention, while less important or background elements should be de-emphasised (*lowlighted*) [52]. This defines a clear processing sequence which facilitates more efficient processing [6, 51]. Research in diagrammatic reasoning shows that directing attention to the most important concepts can dramatically improve understanding and problem-solving performance [6, 11, 52].

## 3.4 Cognitive Integration: When Multiple Diagrams are used, Explicit Mechanisms should be Included to Support Cognitive Integration

One of the unique problems with ISD diagrams compared to diagrams used in most other disciplines is that systems are typically represented using *multiple diagrams*. For example, UML consists of 13 different types of diagrams, each of which represents the system from a different perspective. The need to manage complexity (Principle #2) further exacerbates the problem by creating multiple diagrams of each type. This results in a complex network of diagrams that can be difficult to understand as a whole and navigate through. Using multiple diagrams places additional cognitive demands on the user to mentally integrate information from different diagrams and to keep track of where they are in the network of diagrams [38, 42]. For such representations to be cognitively effective, the diagramming notation must provide explicit mechanisms to support [16]:

- *Conceptual integration*: enabling the reader to integrate information from separate diagrams into a coherent mental representation of the problem.
- *Perceptual integration*: providing perceptual cues (orienting, contextual and directional information) to aid navigation between diagrams.

There are a range of mechanisms which can be used to achieve cognitive integration, such as summary diagrams [16], signposting [25] and spatial contiguity [44].

## 3.5 Perceptual Directness: Make use of Perceptually Direct Representations

*Perceptually direct* representations are representations whose interpretation is spontaneous or natural, in that their meaning can be extracted automatically by the perceptual system. Such representations are highly efficient as they offload interpretation effort from the cognitive system to the perceptual system: extracting meaning from the diagram becomes effort-free.

- Representation of constructs: *Icons* are symbols which perceptually resemble the objects they represent [32]. Using icons to represent constructs reduces cognitive load because they have built-in *mnemonics*: the association with the referent concept can be perceived directly, and does not have to be learnt [33]. Icons also make diagrams more visually appealing, speed up recognition and recall, and improve intelligibility to naïve users [7, 8].
- Representation of relationships: Perceptual directness also applies to representation of relationships among diagram elements. Certain spatial

configurations of diagram elements predispose people towards a particular interpretation even before the meaning of the elements is understood. For example, left to right arrangement of objects suggests causality or sequence while placing objects inside other objects suggests class membership [12, 48]. Diagramming notations can be designed to exploit these intuitively understood spatial arrangements to increase ease and accuracy of interpretation.

## 3.6    Structure: Organise Diagram Elements into Perceptual Groups

In most ISD diagrams, there is no clear structure or grouping among diagram elements. This leads to inefficient encoding in WM, as each diagram element must be encoded as a separate "chunk" [18]. The *Gestalt Laws of Perception* define a set of empirically validated principles for how the human perceptual system organises visual stimuli into perceptual units [46]. These can be used to group related diagram elements together and so facilitate *perceptual configuration* (Figure 3). In this way, This facilitates more efficient use of WM, as each group of elements can be encoded as a chunk rather than encoding each element separately [26]. This reduces cognitive load and frees up cognitive resources for other information processing tasks [10, 22]. Perceptual grouping provides both an alternative and a complement to decomposition (Principle 2). Organising diagram elements into groups expands the number of elements that can be shown on each diagram without exceeding cognitive limits [10]. This reduces the total number of diagrams required, which in turn reduces the need for cognitive integration (Principle 4).

## 3.7    Identification: Diagrams should be Clearly Labelled

Identification is an important concept in cartography [35] but is given little explicit attention in ISD diagramming practice. There are two aspects to identification [5]:

- External identification: this defines the correspondence between the diagram and the represented world. Each diagram should have a *title*, which should be clearly recognisable as such by its size and placement [18]. This should summarise the content of the diagram (the part of the referent domain it represents). Diagram elements (both nodes and links) should also be clearly labelled, using terminology familiar to domain experts to help trigger domain knowledge in LTM. Labels should be clearly grouped with their referent objects using Gestalt principles [15].
- Internal identification: this defines the correspondence between graphical conventions and their meaning. The *diagram type* should be clearly identified to trigger the appropriate diagram schema in LTM (if one exists) and reduce likelihood of misinterpretation. In addition, a *legend* or *key* should be included, summarising the graphical conventions used. This should be included within the frame of each diagram rather than on a separate sheet of paper or document to avoid problems of cognitive integration [25, 43, 44].

## 3.8   Visual Expressiveness: Use the Full Range of Visual Variables

Most ISD diagramming notations use a very limited graphical vocabulary and use only one of the eight available visual variables to encode information: shape. Shape is one of the least cognitively efficient variables as it can only be used to encode nominal data and is detected serially [23]. *Visual expressiveness* refers to the number of different visual variables used to encode information. Using multiple visual variables results in a perceptually enriched representation which uses multiple, parallel channels of communication. It also helps increase visual interest and attention. Using multiple visual variables to convey the same information (*redundant coding*) improves accuracy of communication and counteracts noise.

## 3.9   Graphic Simplicity: The Number of Different Graphical Conventions should be Limited

*Graphic complexity* is defined as the number of different graphical conventions used in a notation [28]. Experimental studies show that human ability to discriminate between perceptually distinct alternatives (*the span of absolute judgement*) is around six categories [26]. Most ISD diagramming notations currently in use exceed this significantly: for example, UML Class Diagrams have a graphic complexity of 14. One solution to this problem is increase the number of perceptual dimensions (i.e. visual variables) on which constructs differ. This percep has been shown empirically to increase human ability to discriminate between stimuli [26]. Another solution is *not* to show everything in graphical form: diagrams are useful for showing some types of information (e.g. structure, relationships) but not others (e.g. detailed business rules): some information can be more effectively represented in textual form [33].

# 4. CONCLUSION

This paper has described a set of principles for producing "good" diagrams, which are defined as diagrams that are cognitively effective (i.e. that communicate effectively). These principles are soundly based on theoretical and empirical evidence from a range of disciplines rather than on intuition, experience and convention like most principles used in ISD practice. The principles can be either applied at the level of diagramming notations (*language level*) or individual diagrams (*sentence level*). Some principles apply mainly at the language level, others apply mainly at the diagram level but most apply at both to at least some extent. In applying these principles to current ISD diagramming practices, the conclusion is that radical change is required to achieve effective user-developer communication.

## 4.1   Theoretical Significance

The theoretical contributions of this paper are as follows:
   (a)   It highlights the importance of the visual aspects (*form*) of ISD notations, which have been grossly understated in ISD research and practice.

(b)   It defines a *descriptive model* of how diagrams communicate, based on re-
      search in graphic design, cognition and visual perception. This provides a
      theoretical basis for evaluating the visual aspects of ISD notations which
      complements methods used to evaluate semantic aspects.

(c)   It defines a set of *prescriptive principles* for producing cognitively effec-
      tive diagrams. These define causal relationships between the perceptual
      characteristics of diagrams and efficiency and effectiveness of human in-
      formation processing. These help to increase our understanding of what
      makes ISD diagrams effective or ineffective and also represent theoretical
      propositions which can be empirically tested.

## 4.2   Practical Significance

The principles defined in this paper provide practical guidance for both designers
and users of ISD diagramming notations. Importantly, they are *not* abstract, theoretical principles but highly specific and operational principles, which could be
easily incorporated into current ISD practices. They can be used by ISD practitioners to produce diagrams that communicate more effectively with their customers.
They can also be used by ISD notation designers to develop diagramming notations that more effectively exploit human perceptual and cognitive capabilities.

# REFERENCES

1.    Ambler, S.W., *The Elements of UML 2.0 Style*. 2005, Cambridge, England:Cambridge
      University Press.
2.    Antes, J.R. and S.W. Mann, *Global-Local Precedence in Picture Processing*.
      Psychological Research, 1984. **46**(247-259).
3.    Baddeley, A. and G. Hitch, *Working Memory*, in *The Psychology of Learning and
      Motivation: Volume 8*, G.H. Bower, Editor. 1974, Academic Press: London.
4.    Baldwin, C.Y. and K.B. Clark, *Design Rules Volume 1: The Power of Modularity*.
      2000, Cambridge, Massachuesetts, USA: MIT Press.
5.    Bertin, J., *Semiology of Graphics: Diagrams, Networks, Maps*. 1983, Madison,
      Wisconsin, USA: University of Wisconsin Press.
6.    Blankenship, J. and D.F. Dansereau, *The Effect of Animated Node-Link Displays on
      Information Recall*. The Journal of Experimental Education, 2000. **68**(4): p. 293-308.
7.    Britton, C. and S. Jones, *The Untrained Eye: How Languages for Software Specification
      Support Understanding by Untrained Users*. Human Computer Interaction, 1999. **14**:
      p. 191-244.
8.    Britton, C., S. Jones, M. Kutar, M. Loomes, and B. Robinson. *Evaluating the Intelligibility
      of Diagrammatic Languages Used in the Specification of Software*. in *Proceedings of
      of the First International Conference on the Theory and Application of Diagrams
      (Diagrams 2000)*. 2000. Edinburgh, Scotland.
9.    Cleveland, W.S. and R. McGill, *Graphical Perception: Theory, Experimentation and
      Application to the Development of Graphical Methods*. Journal of the American
      Statistician Association, 1984. **79**(387): p. 531-554.
10.   Ericsson, K.A., W.G. Chase, and S. Faloon, *Acquisition of a Memory Skill*. Science,
      1980. **208**: p. 1181-1182.

11.  Grant, E.R. and M.J. Spivey. *Guiding Attention Produces Inferences in Diagram-Based Problem Solving*. in *First International Conference on the Theory and Application Application of Diagrams (Diagrams 2000)*. 2000. Edinburgh, Scotland.

12.  Gurr, C.A., *Effective Diagrammatic Communication: Syntactic, Semantic and Pragmatic Issues*. Journal of Visual Languages and Computing, 1999. **10**: p. 317-342.

13.  Hitchman, S., *Practitioner Perceptions On The Use Of Some Semantic Concepts In The Entity Relationship Model*. European Journal of Information Systems, 1995. **4**(1): p. 31-40.

14.  Hitchman, S. *The Details of Conceptual Modelling Notations are Important - A Comparison of Relationship Normative Language*. Communications of the AIS, 2002. **9**(10).

15.  Imhof, E., *Positioning Names on Maps*. The American Cartographer, 1975. **2**: p. 128-144.

16.  Kim, J., J. Hahn, and H. Hahn, *How Do We Understand a System with (So) Many Diagrams? Cognitive Integration Processes in Diagrammatic Reasoning*. Information Systems Research, 2000. **11**(3): p. 284-303.

17.  Kimball, R., *Is ER Modeling Hazardous to DSS?* DBMS Magazine, 1995.

18.  Kosslyn, S.M., *Understanding Charts And Graphs*. Applied Cognitive Psychology, 1989. **3**: p. 185-226.

19.  Larkin, J.H. and H.A. Simon, *Why a Diagram is (Sometimes) Worth Ten Thousand Words*. Cognitive Science, 1987. **11**(1).

20.  Lipowski, Z.J., *Sensory And Information Inputs Overload: Behavioural Effects*. Comprehensive Psychiatry, 1975. **16**(3): p. 105-124.

21.  Lohse, G.L., *A Cognitive Model for Understanding Graphical Perception*. Human-Computer Interaction, 1993. **8**(4): p. 353-388.

22.  Lohse, G.L., *The Role of Working Memory on Graphical Information Processing*. Behaviour and Information Technology, 1997. **16**(6): p. 297-308.

23.  Lohse, G.L., D. Min, and J.R. Olson, *Cognitive Evaluation of System Representation Diagrams*. Information & Management, 1995. **29**: p. 79-94.

24.  Mackinlay, J., *Automating the Design of Graphical Presentations of Relational Information*. ACM Transactions on Graphics, 1986. **5**(2): p. 110-141.

25.  Mayer, R.E. and R. Moreno, *Nine Ways to Reduce Cognitive Load in Multimedia Learning*. Educational Psychologist, 2003. **38**(1): p. 43-52.

26.  Miller, G.A., *The Magical Number Seven, Plus Or Minus Two: Some Limits On Our Capacity For Processing Information*. The Psychological Review, 1956. **63**: p. 81-97.

27.  Moody, D.L. *Complexity Effects On End User Understanding Of Data Models: An Experimental Comparison Of Large Data Model Representation Methods*. in *Proceedings of the Tenth European Conference on Information Systems (ECIS'2002)*. 2002. Gdansk, Poland.

28.  Nordbotten, J.C. and M.E. Crosby, *The Effect of Graphic Style on Data Model Interpretation*. Information Systems Journal, 1999. **9**(2): p. 139-156.

29.  OMG, *Unified Modeling Language Version 2.0: Superstructure*. 2005: Object Management Group (OMG).

30.  Palmer, S. and I. Rock, *Rethinking Perceptual Organisation: The Role of Uniform Connectedness*. Psychonomic Bulletin and Review, 1994. **1**(1): p. 29-55.

31.  Patrignani, M., *Visualization of Large Graphs*, in *Dottorato di Ricerca (Doctoral Dissertation), Ingegneria Informatica*. 2003, Università degli Studi di Roma: La Sapienza, Italy.

32.  Peirce, C.S., *Charles S. Peirce: The Essential Writings (Great Books in Philosophy)*, ed. E.C. Moore. 1998, Amherst, USA: Prometheus Books.

33.  Petre, M., *Why Looking Isn't Always Seeing: Readership Skills and Graphical Programming.* Communications of the ACM, 1995. **38**(6): p. 33-44.
34.  Pinker, S., *A Theory of Graph Comprehension*, in *Artificial Intelligence and the Future of Testing*, R. Freedle, Editor. 1990, Lawrence Erlbaum & Associates: Hillsdale, New Jersey, USA. p. 73-126.
35.  Robinson, A.H., J.L. Morrison, P.C. Muehrcke, A.J. Kimerling, and S.C. Guptill, *Elements of Cartography (6th Edition).* 1995, New York: Wiley.
36.  Scaife, M. and Y. Rogers, *External Cognition: How Do Graphical Representations Work?* International Journal of Human-Computer Studies, 1996. **45**: p. 185-213.
37.  Shanks, G.G., *The Challenges Of Strategic Data Planning In Practice: An Interpretive Case Study.* Journal of Strategic Information Systems, 1997. **6**(1): p. 69-90.
38.  Siau, K., *Informational and Computational Equivalence in Comparing Information Modelling Methods.* Journal of Database Management, 2004. **15**(1): p. 73-86.
39.  Tasker, D., *Worth 1,000 Words? Ha!* Business Rules Journal, 2002. **3**(11).
40.  Tinker, M.A., *Legibility of Print.* 1963, Ames, Iowa, USA: Iowa State University Press.
41.  Treisman, A. and G.A. Gelade, *A Feature Integration Theory of Attention.* Cognitive Psychology, 1980. **12**: p. 97-136.
42.  Verdi, M.P., J.T. Johnson, W.A. Stock, R.W. Kulhavy, and P. Whitman-Ahern, *Organized Spatial Displays And Texts: Effects Of Presentation Order And Display Type On Learning Outcomes.* The Journal of Experimental Education, 1997. **65**(4): p. 303-317.
43.  Wallgren, A., B. Wallgren, R. Persson, U. Jorner, and J.-A. Haaland, *Graphing Statistics & Data: Creating Better Charts.* 1996, London: Sage Publications.
44.  Watts-Perotti, J. and D.D. Woods, *How Experienced Users Avoid Getting Lost in Large Display Networks.* International Journal of Human-Computer Interaction, 1999. **11**(4): 169-299.
45.  Weber, R.A., *Are Attributes Entities? A Study Of Database Designers' Memory Structures.* Information Systems Research, 1996. **7**(2): p. 137-162.
46.  Wertheimer, M., *Laws of Organization in Perceptual Forms*, in *A Source Book of Gestalt Psychology*, W. Ellis, Editor. 1938, Routledge and Kegan Paul (originally published in 1923 in German as Untersuchungen zur Lehre von der Gestalt II, in Psycologische Forschung, 4, 301-350): London. p. 71-88.
47.  White, A.W., *The Elements of Graphic Design: Space, Unity, Page Architecture and Type.* 2002, New York: Allworth Press.
48.  Winn, W.D., *Encoding and Retrieval of Information in Maps and Diagrams.* IEEE Transactions on Professional Communication, 1990. **33**(3): p. 103-107.
49.  Winn, W.D., *A Theoretical Framework for Research on Learning from Graphics.* International Journal of Educational Research, 1990. **14**: p. 553-564.
50.  Winn, W.D., *Learning from Maps and Diagrams.* Educational Psychology Review, 1991. **3**: p. 211-247.
51.  Winn, W.D., *An Account of How Readers Search for Information in Diagrams.* Contemporary Educational Psychology, 1993. **18**: p. 162-185.
52.  Yeh, M. and C.D. Wickens, *Attention Filtering in the Design of Electronic Map Displays: A Comparison of Colour Coding, Intensity Coding and Decluttering Techniques.* Human Factors, 2001. **43**(4): p. 543-562.

# Searching The Deep Web: The WOW project

Domonkos Tikk, Zsolt T. Kardkovács, and Gábor Magyar

Dept. of Telecommunications and Media Informatics
Budapest University of Technology and Economics,
Budapest, Hungary
{tikk,kardkovacs,magyar}@tmit.bme.hu

## 1 Introduction

The amount of data available on the Internet is continuously and rapidly growing. It is a well-known fact that even the best search engines cannot index more than a relatively small fraction (15–30%) of entirety of data on the Internet, and due to the mentioned increase rate, this portion is solidly decreasing. The fraction of the indexed data is even smaller if one considers not only the easily indexable surface web, but also the so-called deep web (DW)[1].

Most of the information accessible through the net is organized and stored in structured databases, this content is termed as "deep web". The content of such databases is presented to the user as dynamic web pages being created to answer user's query, and thus standard search engines can never index and find them. Therefore, searching on the Internet today can be compared to dragging a net across the surface of the ocean. While a great deal may be caught in the net, there is still a wealth of information that is deep, and missed. Internet content is considerably more diverse and the volume certainly much larger than commonly understood.

The paper presents the results our project, called "In the Web of Words" (WOW), that aims to create a prototypical deep web search engine for Hungarian DW content. The content providers are contracted DW sites. The content is typically stored in relational databases. Another significant novelty of our approach is that it enables natural language querying. Consequently, one of the most crucial part of the system is the transformation of natural language questions to adequate SQL queries which are in accordance with schema and attribute convention of contracted partner databases. Thus the querying is performed in three steps: natural language question processing, context

---

[1] The deep web is also often called as "Invisible Web", "Cloaked Web" or "Hidden Web"

recognition, and SQL transformation. The paper delineates these components and the architecture of our system.

## 2 The importance of DW search

### 2.1 Change in web data storage

The notion of *deep web* refers to the information resources managed in structured (namely SQL), online searchable and accessible databases, as described in BrighPlanet's white paper [2]. DW is both qualitatively and quantitatively (see Subsection 2.2) different from the surface web. DW sources store the content in searchable databases that only produce results dynamically in response to direct requests initiated by the user. A direct query is a "one at a time" request, the result is created dynamically, therefore internet search engines cannot index it.

Let us investigate why dynamic web pages became a preferred way to present information on the web. In the earliest days of the Internet, there were relatively few documents and sites. It was a manageable task to post all documents as static pages. Because all pages were persistent and constantly available, they could be crawled easily by conventional search engines.

Sites that were required to manage tens to hundreds of documents could easily do so by posting fixed HTML pages within a static directory structure. In the mid 90s database technology was introduced to the Internet and since then, a true database orientation is becoming more and more relevant, especially for larger sites. It is now accepted practice that large data producers choose the Web as their preferred medium for commerce and information transfer. What has not been broadly appreciated, however, is that the means by which such data providers post the information is no longer through static pages but through database-driven designs.

As a consequence of the traditional model of crawling static Web pages, being today's paradigm for conventional search engines, no longer applies to the information content of the Internet. Serious information seekers can no longer neglect the importance or quality of deep Web information. Directed query technology is the only means to integrate deep and surface Web information.

### 2.2 Facts about the deep web

Let us investigate why it is important to incorporate DW access in the internet search engines, and how it can be elaborated. Studies about the internet [2, 4] show among other facts that

1. The size of the deep web is about 400 times larger than that of the surface web [2] that is accessible to traditional keyword-based search engines. The

---

[2] http://www.brightplanet.com

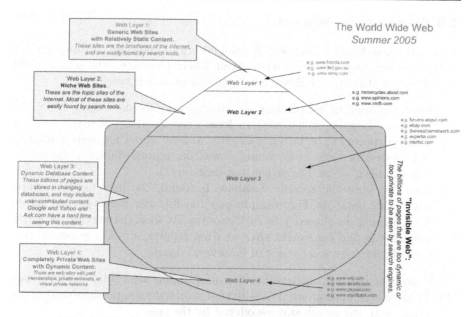

**Fig. 1.** The distribution of web in 2005 (figure is taken from [4])

deep web contains 7500 terabyte (TB) information, compared to the 19 TB information of the surface web.

2. The estimated number of static web pages is 50 billion, while the number of deep web pages is over 200 billion. The most popular web search engine, Google, indexes about 8.75 billion web pages (data from December 2005; [4], see also 1). Only about the 16% of the entire web is indexes by any of the search engines[3].

3. The size of DW is growing much faster than the one of surface web. DW is where new information appears the fastest on the web.

4. Deep web sites tend to be narrower and deeper than conventional surface web sites. DW sites typically contain topic specific databases, therefore the quality of the information stored on these sites is usually more adequate w.r.t. the given topic than the one accessible through conventional pages.

Traditional search engines create their catalogs based on crawling web pages that have to be static and linked to other pages. Therefore dynamic web pages, even though they have unique URLs, are not searchable by such engines [10]. However, it would be highly desirable to make the content of the deep web accessible to search engines, which can be normally accessed only through querying the search surface of the deep web sites.

---

[3] Estimation of Search Engine Watch; http://www.searchenginewatch.com

## 2.3 Searching the deep web

Currently, searching the deep web is quite laborious and time-consuming work, if the user has no prior information about where to search. The scenario DW search outlined in [4] as follows. The user has to search twice:

1. First, one need to use primary search engines (Google, Yahoo, MSN, A9, Vivisimo, Dogpile, AskJeeves) to locate the database of user's interest. This is expected to be be quite lengthy, at least about few tens of minutes (e.g. search for "jobs in honolulu", "weather reports dublin", "houses for sale winnipeg", "hard drive sales at best buy").
2. Secondly, once the specific database is found, the user need to search within that database. For example: one may find www.monster.com helpful for searching databased jobs in Honolulu. At www.theweathernetwork. com one can find the sought after weather reports, etc. The expected time for DW database searching can be several hours!

Hence, the user can retrieve his/her information need from the deep web, if s/he knows the appropriate DW site that stores the sought information and is familiar with the search surface offered by the site.

Deep web searchers—engines that focus on the content of DW sites—aim to bridge this gap between the user and deep web sites. The information that resides on deep web site can be efficiently accessed if the structure of the databases is known by the search engine. The current state-of-the-art of DW search facilities are rather listings of DW sites [3], especially for English users. In this work the currently known gateways to the deep web are listed: collections that contain up to a few hundreds of DW sites, and meta search engines that cover a few databases.

The build-up of a DW search site is more difficult than the creation of a large index database: the semantical correspondence between user queries and database contents also has to be captured and handled. Form based or other graphical interfaces are the best choices to retrieve information from a single database or to query web sites on a concrete topic. On the one hand, there are differences in structural design and in granularity of data between databases in a multi-database environment. That is why a form based search application needs to semantically restructure user input according to the target databases or it needs to reduce differences in a way. Both are hard tasks if the number of databases are not strongly limited, or if there is no agreement between the site owners. On the other hand, the number of attributes to be queried are not bounded in search engines. Without a strict limitation on the number of the topics, form based applications become unusable or impractical. For a more detailed analysis on the differences between NLIDBs, keyword and menu based search engines, see [1]. In the next, we argue for the importance of natural language querying in DW search, which is, in our opinion, the crucial key to the feasibility of DW search service.

## 2.4 Natural Language Querying

One of the bottlenecks of traditional search engines is that they keep keyword-based catalogued information about web pages; therefore they retrieve only the keywords from users' queries and display pages with matched ones. This matching method neglects important information granules of a natural language query, such as the focus of the query, the semantic information and linguistic connections between various terms, etc. Traditional searchers retrieve the same pages for *"When does the president of the United States visit Russia"* and *"Why does the president of Russia visit the United States"*, though the requested information is obviously quite different. Solutions that do not deal with the given morphosyntax of the sentence, e.g. Askjeeves[4], AnswerBus[5], Ionaut [6], also suffer from this problem.[7] These pieces of information could be very important particularly when DW search is concerned, because e.g. the interrogative is not a keyword-like information (the ideal result does not contain it), but it specifies the focus of the query. DWSEs communicate with DW sites by accessing the residing database using a querying language (e.g. SQL). In the retrieval of the proper answer of a question, hence, its focus should be encoded in the translated SQL query. The user expects different answer for the questions: *"When was J.F.K born"* or *"Where was J.F.K. born"*.

## 2.5 WOW project

In the remaining part of the paper we present the WOW project in details. Its main goal is to create a complex search service, which includes traditional, deep web and image search facilities. This paper concentrates on DW search of contracted partners' databases by means of natural language Hungarian queries. Although natural language processing is always language-dependent in certain respects, the paper focus on the non-language specific part of the operation. The inner interfaces of the system are designed to be applicable for arbitrary language, and the language-specific parts (e.g. syntactic parser, morphological parser) are kept in isolated modules and external tools in the system.

In the pilot phase of our project we intend to include only certain topics in the search space of our DW search engine, namely, certain fields of culture (books, movies & cinemas, plays & theaters). We have negotiated with selected databases's owners (a library, a digital data archive, and a cultural programme data provider) and worked out the key points and conditions of cooperation.

---

[4] http://www.askjeeves.com/

[5] http://www.answerbus.com/

[6] http://www.ionaut.com:8400/

[7] To test whether the solution is keyword based or not (even if the input is a NL question) try: "Who is the present King of France?" or "When visited the president of Russia the United States?"

## 3 System architecture

In the next we outline the system architecture of our natural language query driven DW search application. The system consists of five components depicted in Figure 2.

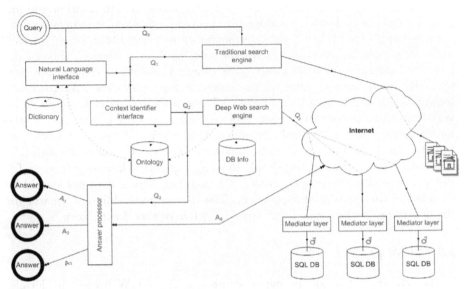

**Fig. 2.** The collaboration of main components of the DW search application

The input of the natural language (NL) module is the user's question[8]. The module performs syntactic parsing, more specifically, it specifies the morphological characteristics of each syntactically relevant unit (tokenization) of the sentence, and groups related units (bracketing). The output is either generated in a form of XML files that code the various linguistic structures appropriately, or for testing a tree-shaped graphical presentation a the parsed alternatives can also be chosen. Illustrating figures of NL module in our previous papers [8, 9] are generated by means of the latter option.

The context identifier (CI) determines the context(s) of the question and it creates a list of so-called CL (Context Language [8]) expressions. This transformation is performed on the basis of schema and attribute names that are related with the topics covered by the DW search service (see details in subsection 4.2).

The DW search engine (DWSE) stores the database (DB) information about partner DW sites. Based on the context of the query that is encoded in the CL expression(s), it determines databases where the CL expression should

---

[8] We equally use terms query and question referring to the natural language interrogative sentence typed in by the user.

be posted to. It also includes an SQL parser that translates CL expressions for local SQL queries. The word local here refers to the fact that the naming conventions of schemas and attributes in these SQL queries have local validity. Because each DW content provider has different database structures, and applies different terminology, DWSE uses its own one and the domestication of SQL queries for the mediator layer.

Mediator layer's role is to connect DWSE's central database and databases of DW content providers. It facilitates that database owners can provide the necessary and only the necessary information about their database, it ensures feasibility of querying, controls authority rights, and assures authenticity and answering facilities. The mediator layer transfers local SQL queries according to the naming convention and structure of the database of the deep site. The administrator of the database should fill in a form before the database is connected to DWSE; by this form the administrator can map the names of schemas and attributes of DWSE to the local convention. Finally, the appropriately transferred SQL queries are passed to the database of the deep web site and the answer is returned in the form of URLs.

The last component, the answer analyzer, orders the answer URLs and displays them to the user.

# 4 Description of components

## 4.1 NL module

The input questions should fulfill several requirements. The system accepts only simple (only one tensed verb is allowed), well-formulated and -spelled interrogative sentences starting with a question word from a given list. It is not designed to answer questions focusing on causality ("*Why did the Allies win WW2?*"), intension ("*Would you like a cup of coffee?*"), non-factual ("*How am I?*") information. The system's task is to answer questions based on information stored in partner's databases.

The module applies several tools for its operation: morphological parser[9], various databases storing the required lexical information (proper names, interrogatives, lists of some significant words, patterns for various fixed terms, such as dates, URLs etc.).

Figure 3 depicts main steps and the means of NL module.

NL module consists of two main steps, the tokenization and the syntactic parser. The former determines tokens of the sentence, and annotate them with morpho-syntactic information, the latter identifies and marks syntactic structures in the sentence.

---

[9] http://mokk.bme.hu/projects/szoszablya/index_html?set_language=en&cl= en

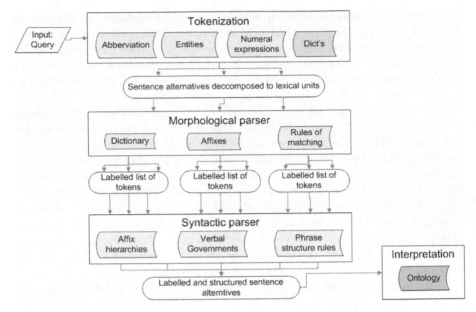

**Fig. 3.** Main steps and means of NL module

Tokenizer first identifies tokens (syntactically relevant units) of the sentence. Tokens are one-word or multi-word expressions whose internal structures are irrelevant w.r.t. the syntactic parsing of the sentence. Multi-word tokens are typically proper names (personal names, institution, proprietary and company names, titles, addresses, etc). As Hungarian is a highly agglutinative language where major semantic/syntactic relations are signalled by a series of "stackable" suffixes (see e.g. [6, 7]), the identification of tokens is a more complex task than simple pattern recognition and therefore requires the support of a morphological parser. This solution of subtask is reported in our paper [9]. The morphological parser has a second function at this phase: it assigns *part of speech* labels to tokens and provides their morphological analysis. This information stands as the basis of the subsequent bracketing phase. Another characteristics of the morphological system of the Hungarian language is that many morphologically complex word forms are ambiguous in terms of their morphological structure. Such ambiguous tokens are disambiguated in parsed alternatives. The detailed of the tokenizer can be found in [8].

The second part of the NL module groups related tokens in syntactic units. This task is executed by means of several sub-modules that are connected sequentially in the following order:

1. recognizer of adverbs and participles;
2. recognizer of adjective and noun groups;
3. recognizer of conjunctions (logical operators);

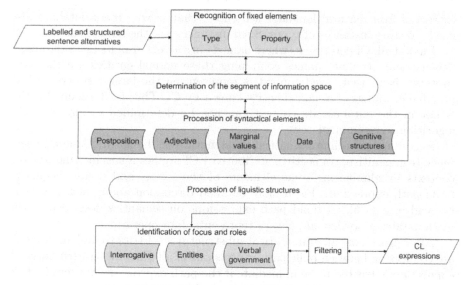

**Fig. 4.** Main steps of CI's algorithm

4. recognizer of possessive structures;

Each sub-module works based on the morphological information (stem [part of speech], suffixes) that is determined by the morphological parser and that is each token is annotated with. The sub-modules are executed iteratively until new grouping can be done in a cycle.

The output is generated in SADL (Syntax Analysis Description Language) developed by the WOW project[10].

## 4.2 The context identifier

The context identifier module (CI) gets sentence alternatives in SADL format as input. CI determines all possible key schema and attribute pairs (called contexts) for each alternative and it also translates the additional syntactically encoded information (if any) into database selection constraints. As a result CI outputs a set of SQL-like CL (Context Language) expressions which can be easily transformed into SQL queries. Figure 4 describes how CI works.

It is easy to see that SQL statements are a kind of path expression in databases. That is, one has to find a valid mapping of a SADL sentence to database path expressions. Since (relational) databases do not store information on the semantics of data one has to build a meta-database which defines which schemas (types) and attributes (properties) are used in database joins (associations). Property structure or other typological notations can not be

---

[10] Language definition in Bacchus-Naur Form is available at http://textmining.tmit.bme.hu/szavak/NL.output.bnf

extracted from natural language sentences, that is why meta-database also needs to store instances of types. Such instances are the named entities.

First of all, CI determines where named entities occur in its meta-database. Schema and attribute names containing these named entities are the fixed contexts. Note that, fixed context is representing the largest superset of all possible meanings of a named entity known by CI. That is, if a named entity is not in the database its context can not be determined in any way, the algorithm stops immediately.

According to each grammatical substructure of the natural language sentence (e.g. genitive, connective, attributive) CI applies a specific rule to fixed contexts by eliminating some elements of these sets, and it also begins to build path expressions. For a more detailed discussion about such rules can be read in e.g. [5]. CI build path expressions on semantics described in the meta-database, so they are always represents data operations.

After processing all grammatical substructures CI tries to find an immediate connection between built path expressions of all different substructures. A connection is treated to be immediate if the path expressions are terminating in the same schema or there exists a switching table in the meta-database between ends of path expressions. If a path expression can not be connected to another we eliminate it. Obviously, if all path expression of a substructure is eliminated then CI terminates by failure for this sentence. Nota Bene, if a syntactical ambiguity has no real sense at a semantical level, then it should terminate by failure at this point. That is, failure is not necessarily indicates lack of "knowledge".

On the other hand, if path expressions of different substructures are connected in all possible ways then it is left to determine for which attribute value the interrogative sentence refers, in other words, to determine the focus of the question. The focus identification is based on the verb, on the question tag and on the closest head of noun phrase of sentence, which is the subject or the object in the most cases. This triple uniquely identifies by verbal government a set of attributes of some schemas in the meta-database. We select those of them having an immediate connection to previously determined path expressions.

Finally, CI translates and outputs all non-eliminated path expression into SQL-like CL expressions. If there is no CL expressions left the processing terminates.

### 4.3 Connection with content providers: The Deep Web Search

The Deep Web Search Engine (DWSE) receives a set of SQL-like CL expressions and it extracts all schema and attribute name from these expressions to determine which content providers could answer the received queries. For this matter, one stores information on content providers' database structure. We called DB Info this store.

DWSE sends a message for each related content provider. The message contains an authentication and identification code for security reasons, a transaction id, a time-stamp, and a properly translated CL expression according to the content provider naming conventions. The message is caught by a provider-side mediator layer.

The tasks of the mediator layer are the joining of deep web site to the deep web searcher, authorization of queries, authentication, and assurance of answering. Its competence is restricted exclusively to tasks connected with querying; it neither stores data, nor starts processes.

The mediator layer is initialized by the administrator of DW site when the DW content provider is connected to WOW. Then the administrator selects topics of his/her site from a list, and determines the part of the database to be shared publicly via the deep web search engine. These data are registered in DB Info and used by the relevance identifier when selecting databases for question answering. DB Info can be updated on an administration interface.

The data transferred to the mediator layer consists of three parts: question ID, DWL query and authentication elements. After checking the authentication information of WOW and DW site, the mediator layer substitutes in DWL query the schema and attribute names to be in accordance to the naming convention of the given DW site. These information are provided by the DW site administrator when the mediator layer is initialized.

The answering is implemented analogously. The answer must contain the question ID, number of valid answers — if it does exceed the limit, the answers themselves, and finally the authentication elements.

The answer processor module collects and orders the incoming answers from different sources. Based upon our former investigations, data obtained from different sources are heterogenous: either records, set of records, or only a URL. Therefore, WOW returns to the user a page containing links to the answer pages of deep web sites. DW searcher is not competent in judging the soundness of DW sites' answers, therefore the answers are only grouped and ordered w.r.t. different aspects. The actual ordering method can be chosen by the user when customizing the user interface of WOW.

## 5 Conclusions

In this paper we argued for the importance of deep web search, because it deep web is the locality of huge amount of high quality well-organized data. We also shown that natural language querying is a crucial criteria in the design of a DWSE. The paper presented our WOW project, which includes a natural-question driven deep web search facility. The main part of the paper introduce the concept and the architecture of WOW's DWSE, and give a detailed description on the main components.

# References

1. I. Androustsopoulos, G. D. Ritchie, and P. Thanisch. Natural language interfaces to databases – an introduction. *Journal of Natural Language Engineering*, 1(1):29–81, 1995.
2. M. K. Bergman. The deep web: surfacing hidden value. *Journal of Electronic Publishing*, 7(1), August 2001. http://www.press.umich.edu/jep/07-01/bergman.html.
3. W. Boswell. Invisible web gateways-portals to the deep web, 2006. Web Search, http://websearch.about.com/od/invisibleweb/a/invisibleweb.htm.
4. P. Gil. What is "The Invisible Web"?, April, 2006. Internet for Beginners, http://netforbeginners.about.com/cs/secondaryweb1/a/secondaryweb.htm.
5. Zs. T. Kardkovács. On the transformation of sentences with genitive phrases to SQL statements. In *Proceedings of the $10^{th}$ International Conference on Applications of Natural Language to Information Systems (NLDB)*, volume 3513 of *Lecture Notes in Computer Science*, pages 10–20, Alicante, Spain, June 2005. Springer.
6. F. Kiefer, editor. *Structural Hungarian Grammar. Syntax.* Akadémiai Kiadó, Budapest, 1992. (In Hungarian; original title: Strukturális magyar nyelvtan. Mondattan.).
7. F. Kiefer, editor. *Structural Hungarian Grammar. Morphology.* Akadémiai Kiadó, Budapest, 2000. (In Hungarian; original title: Strukturális magyar nyelvtan. Morfológia.).
8. D. Tikk, Zs. T. Kardkovács, Z. Andriska, G. Magyar, A. Babarczy, and I. Szakadát. Natural language question processing for hungarian deep web searcher. In *Proc. of the IEEE International Conference on Computational Cybernetics (ICCC'04)*, pages 303–308, Vienna, Austria, August 2004.
9. D. Tikk, F. P. Szidarovszky, Zs. T. Kardkovács, and G. Magyar. Entity recognizer in Hungarian question processing. In S. Bandini and S. Manzoni, editors, *AI*IA 2005: Advances in Artificial Intelligence*, number 3673 in Lecture Notes in Artificial Intelligence, pages 535–546. Springer, Berlin–Heidelberg–New York, 2005. Proc. of 9th Congress of the Italian Association for Artificial Intelligence (AI*IA'05), 2005, Milano, Italy.
10. H. Winkler. Suchmaschinen. Metamedien im Internet? In B. Becker and M. Paetau, editors, *Virtualisierung des Sozialen*, pages 185–202. Frankfurt/NY, 1997. (In German; English translation: http://www.uni-paderborn.de/~timwinkler/suchm_e.html).

# Formal Grammars for Conformance Testing

Csaba V. Rotter

Nokia Hungary Kft, 1092 Budapest, Koztelek u. 6 csaba.rotter@nokia.com

**Summary.** Formal languages and especialy formal grammars are able to describe conformance testing. This paper is focused on the correlation between testing and regular grammars. We compare the standardized formal methods relation described in ISO standard [1][2] and formal grammars. We show that the implementation relation can be specified with distributing or inter-working grammars. Our goal is to demonstrate that formal grammars are able to describe communication protocols and they can be used also as a test notation. The attention is focused mainly on second part, where we show the importance of these grammars, because they can describe the test environment and the test suites of these protocols [3].

## 1.1 Introduction - Motivation

During the development phase of communicating systems with formal methods the major task is to compare the correctness of the implemented system to formal specification. If a formal specification exists a preliminary verification can be checked by existing tools [4], which tools are able to detect infinite loops and deadlocks. The reliability of implementation is ensured by checking the relation between the implementation and formal specification.

The motivation of this paper is to find a notation, which could be the same for the specification and for the test notation. This language can be an intermediate language (not human understandable) and the goal is to demonstrate that is able to describe the specification and the test notation also. In the conclusion part we will point to some further works which will analyze the possibility of generation of test cases from formal grammar description of protocols. For this generation purpose could be useful to use the same notation for both, the protocol specification and test specification. This paper proceeds as follows: Firstly we introduce the notion of conformance testing. Then, we show a correlation between the notation introduced and the formal grammars. In the main part we show how the grammars are related to each element of the test process. At the end after the conclusion we give an outlook to some further works.

## 1.2 Conformance Testing

Testing is a means to extract knowledge about a system by experimenting with it. The experimentation is carried out by executing test cases. The execution of a test case leads to an observation from which it can be concluded whether a system has a certain property or not. These basic concepts include the test architecture, test suite and the process of executing test cases. The test architecture consists of the environment where the test cases are executed against IUT (Implementation Under Test). The IUT is the implementation of that protocol, which we have to test.

The test system is the logically separated environment where the sending and receiving of test sequences are realized. The communication point between the tester and IUT is called PCO (Point of Control and Observation), which is also a key part of the test architecture connects the tester to test context. The test context is the system in which the IUT is embedded, and the "channel" on which IUT communicates with the tester. There is a strong relation between events that occur at PCO's and the events that occur at the IAP's (Implementation Access Point) which is the communication point between the test context and the IUT. The difference between the PCO and IAP is that PCO's are standardized by the test suite and they are logical points where the communication is realized but the IAP's are physically realized access points to IUT by the implementer specially for testing purposes.

The tester is the implementation of the test suite, it can be structured to lower or/and upper tester(LT/UT). The difference between the LT and UT is in there point of action. The LT is especially acts on the IUT's lower boundary trough the under-laying service and the UT's action to the IUT is realized typically from the upper interface of the IUT, it is the IUT's user. The formal language in which the test suite is expressed is called test notation. The test notation is denoted by TESTS. It means that a test suite(as a set of test cases) is an element of Powerset(TESTS).

A test case can be divided into three main parts. In the first part we have to set the IUT into the initial state, where the testing process could be started. For example if we have to test the disconnection of a protocol from information transfer state, firstly we have to bring it to this state(Information transfer state). This set up procedure is called test preamble. The second main part of a test case is the test body, where the test sequence is realized based on the test purpose. The third part after the test sequences we have to bring the IUT back to initial NULL state, for this we are using an other procedure called test postamble. This short test case introduction is necessary for the explanation of test case description grammars in later chapters.

## 1.3 Conformance Testing with Grammars

Before entering deeply into conformance relations to grammars we have to shortly present the principal things of formal theory of conformance testing.

Conformance involves defining whether an implementation is valid implementation of a given specification with respect to a certain correctness notion. It can be characterized by relations between models of implementation and specification or by satisfaction requirements by models of implementations. Two types of specifications are presented the parameterized specification and the instantiated specification. In parameterised specification the FDT (Formal Description Technique) allows to use parameters in a specification, but in the other case the formal parameters are instantiated with actual values. The set of instantiated specifications is denoted by SPECS. By the other hand the implementation consists of a combination of hardware and/or software. Implementation of any protocol can be done by different ways. The set of implementation is denoted as IMPS. It is assumed that any implementation $IUT \in IMPS$ can be modeled by an element $m_{IUT}$ in a formalism MODS (e.g. finite state machines, labeled transition systems, formal grammars...). The formalism MODS is used to model the behaviour of an implementation, may be the same as the formalism SPECS that is used for specification. If we are speaking about conformance we can distinguish two types, static conformance and dynamic conformance. Static conformance involves the correct instantiation of a parameterized specification. Dynamic conformance involves the permitted observable behaviour of an implementation based on the communication, which is described in specification. Dynamic conformance between an implementation and a specification is formally characterized by a relation between the model of the implementation and the specification. This is called implementation relation and is denoted by **imp**.

$$\mathbf{imp} \subseteq MODS \times SPECS$$

The formal language in which a test is described is called test notation and is denoted as TESTS. The test execution of a test suite $T \subseteq TESTS$ is running the implemented test case $t \in T$ in combination with the IUT. During the test execution is an observation handled in a domain of observations denoted by OBS.

$$verd_t : OBS \rightarrow \{pass, inconclusive, fail\} \tag{1.1}$$

The $verd_t$ is a direct mapping from domain of observations to pass, fail or inconclusive verdicts. The implementation under test IUT passes the test case $t$ if and only if the test execution of the IUT with $t$ leads an observation $O \in OBS$ to which $verd_t$ assigns a **pass** verdict.

$$IUT \quad \mathbf{passes} \quad t \iff verd_t = \mathbf{pass} \tag{1.2}$$

On the other hand, the process of executing a test suite means to consecutively executing each of test case which belongs to the test suite. For each single test case is assigned a verdict as in (1). An implementation under test IUT passes a test suite $T \subseteq TESTS$ if and only if passes all test cases in the test suite:

$$IUT \quad \textbf{passes} \quad T \iff \forall t \in T : IUT \quad \textbf{passes} \quad t$$

For the interpretation of test result a function has to be defined. The function $exec$ calculates the observations for models of IUT's ($m_{IUT}$) contained in a model of test context $C$. $C$ is also a function expressing formally the test context as the transformation of behaviour observed at the IAPs to behaviour observed at the PCOs. The subset of $MODS$ for which $verd(exec(t, C(m))) = pass$, is called *formal test purpose* $P_t$.

$$P_t = \{m \in MODS \mid verd_t \ (exec(t, C(m_{IUT}))) = pass\}$$

where the expression $exec(t, C(m_{IUT}))$ models the observation that is made by the test case t of the IUT modelled as $m_{IUT}$ in the context C. In the following chapters the test grammar rules will be demonstrated.

$$exec : \{T \times C(m_{IUT}) \ \rightarrow \ OBS\}$$

## 1.4 Test and Test System Description Language

After we have presented the basics on formal approach to conformance testing we have to present the idea how to describe the tests and the test system by the help of formal grammars. For this reason we show special grammar classes [5] and we show how the grammar system should be extend to be able to describe a test system. From the formal theory we know that a grammar is an ordered quadruple $G = (T, N, P, S)$, where T is the set of terminal symbols, N the set of non-terminal symbols, P the set of production rules and S is the starting point of the generation. If we can find a set of symbols from which the participants (tester and IUT) compose their sentences sent and we can construct the grammar containing the rules of correctly generating these sentences we can get the formal description of testing. Terminal elements are those which actually occur in sentences. All other symbols that are applied in the formulation of grammatical rules may be described as auxiliary or non-terminal elements. In the test execution there are many situations when we have to test a well defined state of the IUT and for this we have to bring the protocol in that state.

For this we are using test steps and we are using separate grammars $G_s$ which describe it's behaviour.

It is easy to observe that in a test suite it can be more than one test steps or $G_s$ in our case. Every messages in the protocol has more specific fields which could have different values in different protocol states. We can suppose that the message structure can be described also by help of other grammars $G_{mess}$. $G_{mess}$ is the union of all message grammars. We can observe that in the test system there are more grammars, which operate cooperating between each other. If we describe the whole test suite we have to define a grammar system which will handle all component grammars. The notion of cooperating distributed (CD) grammar systems is introduced in [5]. A CD grammar system is an (n+2)- tuple $\Gamma = (T, G_1, G_2, ..., G_n, S)$, where $G_i, i \in (1, n)$ are the component grammars, $T \in \bigcup_{i=1}^{n} T_i$ is the union of all terminal symbols used in component grammars, and $S \in \bigcup_{i=1}^{n} N_i = N$ is the starting point of derivation.

**Definition 1** *Let $\Gamma$ be a CD grammar system. Let $x, y \in V_i$. Then we write* $x \Longrightarrow_{G_i}^{k} y \iff \exists x_1, x_2, ... x_n$ *such that*

1. *$x = x_1$, $y = x_{k+1}$,*
2. *$x_j \Longrightarrow_{G_i} x_{k+1}$, i.e. $x_j = x_j' \cdot A_j \cdot x_i$", $x_{j+1} = x_j' \cdot w_j \cdot x_j$", $A_j \rightarrow w_j \in P_i$,* $1 \leq j \leq k$

Each grammar operates independently according to their separate operating rule, only the output of a grammar could be an input to other. Regarding to "live" of derivation rule we have to define a very important property of CD grammar systems.

**Definition 2** *Let $\Gamma$ be a CD grammar system.*

1. *For each $i \in \{1, ...., n\}$, the terminating derivation by the i-th component, denoted $\Longrightarrow_{G_i}^{t}$, is defined by: $x \Longrightarrow_{G_i}^{t} y$    iff $x \Longrightarrow_{G_i}^{*} y$ and there is no $z \in V^*$ with $y \Longrightarrow G_i z$*
2. *For each $i \in \{1, ...., n\}$, the k-steps derivation by the i-th component, denoted $\Longrightarrow_{G_i}^{=k}$, is defined by: $x \Longrightarrow_{G_i}^{=k} y$    iff there are $x_1, ..., x_{k+1} \in (N \cup T)^*$ such that $x = x_1, y = x_{k+1}$ and, for each $1 \leq j \leq k$, $x_j \Longrightarrow G_i x_j + 1$*
3. *For each $i \in \{1, ...., n\}$, the at most k-steps derivation by the i-th component, denoted $\Longrightarrow_{G_i}^{\leq k}$, is defined by: $x \Longrightarrow_{G_i}^{\leq k} y$    iff $x \Longrightarrow_{G_i}^{=k'} y$    for some $k' \leq k$*
4. *For each $i \in \{1, ...., n\}$, the at least k-steps derivation by the i-th component, denoted $\Longrightarrow_{G_i}^{\geq k}$, is defined by: $x \Longrightarrow_{G_i}^{\geq k} y$    iff $x \Longrightarrow_{G_i}^{=k'} y$    for some $k' \geq k$*

The normal * mode of derivation $\Longrightarrow_{G_i}^{t}$, describes the case where the agent performs its derivation rules as long as it wants. The t mode derivations corresponds to the strategy where the agent have to apply it's derivation rules while it can do it. The =k mode derivation corresponds to k direct derivation steps in succession using the rules of i-th component, which correspond the k-th derivation step. Then, the $\leq k$ derivation corresponds to a time limitation, the agent has to perform at most k derivations, and the $\geq t$ derivation mode is a minimal time of using the derivation rules, the agent has to perform at least k derivations. We can observe that in case of t mode derivation there is a result after using the derivation rules several times. This is important in case of using test steps in our test case, because there must be a successful output from any test step, which could result indifferent test verdict from the grammars point of view.

### 1.4.1 Grammar-Conformance relation

Let see now the relation between the above presented grammars and the test system. Here we are looking for a general relation between test components (IUT, UT, LT, etc...) In first approach we have two different grammars. One of them describes the implementation (imp) and the other describes the specification (spec).

$$G_{imp} = (T_{imp}, N_{imp}, P_{imp}, S_{imp}) \quad and \quad G_{spec} = (T_{spec}, N_{spec}, P_{spec}, S_{spec})$$

The T, N, P, and S are the respective set of terminal, set of non-terminal, set of production rules and the starting symbol.

A direct relation can be derived between this two grammars.

$$G_{imp} = G_{IUT} \subseteq G_{spec}$$

We are speaking about conformance testing when we are checking if the grammar $G_{IUT}$ satisfy the requirement of $G_{spec}$. If we are speaking about a test system we have to distinguish two main grammars, one which describes the protocol itself $G_{spec}$, the other one describes the communication sequence between the implementation under test and the tester.

Let see now the relation between grammars, verdicts and conformance relations, how the conformance relations can be explained with grammars. In order to have a formal grammar test description we have to introduce a set of terminal symbols, which will describe the verdict of a test case.

$$verds = \{pass, fail, inconclusive\}$$

The result of this equation we can define a test description grammar, which is able to describe one test case.

$$G_t = (T_t, N_t, P_t, S_t); \quad T_t \in T_{spec} + P_{t*}; \quad P_{t*} = P_t \rightarrow verds$$

**Definition 3** *Let G a grammar, which describe the test system and S(G) a sentence over G; this sentence should contain only terminal symbols*

Let now see the (2) "pass" equation using formal grammars.

$$G_{IUT} \quad passes \quad G_t \Leftrightarrow pass \in S(G_t)$$

By this way a test case is passes if and only if we can find the "pass" terminal symbol in the sentence generated by grammar $G_{IUT}$. This sentence is the sequence of terminal symbols corresponding to message exchange between tester and IUT.

## 1.4.2  WTP [9] with formal grammars

WTP is the transaction protocol in the WAP protocols. The Wireless Application Protocol (WAP) is an open, global standard empowering users of mobile
phones and wireless devices to access and instantly interact with Internet information and communication services. WAP is a major step in building the
wireless Internet. Providing Internet and Web-based services on a wireless
data network presents many challenges to service providers, application developers and handset manufacturers. The main purpose of WAP is to combine
the two emerging technologies, the Internet and wireless networking. Naturally the WAP capable mobile devices would offer not only the usual Internet
and wireless services but also the combination of them. Thus, this system
will provide such new facilities that will take a great influence on both technologies. For example call control with customized user interface or mobile
access of common Internet services like World Wide Web. Wireless Transaction Protocol (WTP) operates on the top of the datagram and security layer
and provides both reliable and unreliable service for the WTP user. Reliability is achieved through the use of unique transaction identifiers, acknowledgements, duplicate removal and retransmissions. Optionally WTP provides
user-to-user reliability, thus WTP user confirms every packet. WTP has to
cope with the special conditions of wireless environment, so it uses implicit
acknowledgements as much as possible and tries to minimize the number of
message retransmission due to the duplicate packets. WTP makes possible to
concatenate several messages into one Protocol Data Unit (PDU) and the last
acknowledgement may contain extra information related to the communication, for example performance measurements.

$$G_{WTPspec} = (T_{WTPspec}, N_{WTPspec}, P_{WTPspec}, S_{WTPspec});$$

In this case the $T_{WTPspec}$ is the terminals for WTP specification in the specified testing phase. These terminals are the protocol messages, service primitives and protocol data units. These are specified in WTP specification, and
describe an exact behaviour of the protocol. The $N_{WTPspec}$ is the non-terminal
symbols for WTP, which are the protocol states and each state after an event
has been processed by the WTP layer. Based on this knowladge let now see
a set of production rules for a small part of protocol behaviour. As a convention let use "!" sign before each message sent and "?" sign for every received
message.

In this section we are not intend to deep enter in WTP protocol functionality so the relations will not be explained from the protocol behaviours point
of view. The first relation is

$S_{WTPspec} = !Invoke1\,StartT\,NON_1$ where the Invoke1 is a terminal symbol
and describes an Invoke PDU of the protocol the StartT is a start timer T
event. $NON_1 = ?Abort1$ or $NON_1 = ?Result1\,NON_2$ here two alternatives
are presented as a response to the Invoke1 message. $NON_2 = TimeoutT$ or
$NON_2 = !Ack$ These rules describe a simple protocol operation but it can be

extended for the whole protocol, the whole behaviour can be described in this way. A more detailed grammar description of this protocol can be found on [3]

## 1.5 Test Cases and Formal Grammars

If we are entering deeper in the test architecture we have to analyze how the tests itself are described using grammars so how the relation among the terminal and non-terminal symbols inside the grammar $G_t$. We should start from the main definition of conformance testing. The main players in testing are the sent and received messages to/from the tester. This messages could be considered as terminal symbols if we are supposing that they will not be more divided. In a more practical situation the messages could be divided according to message containing fields. In this case the message itself is a non-terminal symbol and this symbol will be the result of a grammar, which describes the message. These situations could happen in case of multiple test cases when the sending message parameter can differ. These non-terminal symbols are not really non-terminal but also not terminal symbols. These could be named as preterminal symbols. In this case the test description grammar could be the following.

$$G_t = (T_t, N_t, P_t, S_t); \quad T_t = G_i{}^k F; \quad ,$$

where F is the set of fields of messages and $T_t$ are the preterminal symbols, which is derived from F in k-mode using rules described in grammar $G_i$. Each test case has its own rules of derivation, this derivation rules correspond to test purposes rules. It can be observed that a test case is composed from different interworking grammars. The output of a grammar is the input of other. Let now see the component grammars. One grammar is needed for each of the message $G_{mess}$, which plays in test sequence. Regarding to test case structure we should have a grammar, which describe the test preamble, $G_{pre}$ and an other, which describe the test postamble $G_{post}$ and of course we have not to forget the test sequence itself, let it denoted by $G_{purp}$ based on test purpose. There is a hierarchy of grammars defined by this way and it can be observed that as we are going upside in this hierarchy the grammar of one level includes the downlevel grammars. The test suite description grammar $G_{TS}$ is the reunion of all component test case grammars.

$$G_{TS} = \bigcup G_t, \quad G_t = \bigcap G_{step} + G_{purp}$$

The test case defining grammar is compound from some of test step defining grammars and from a grammar, which describe the test sequence. The test step defining grammar is a CD grammar system with a set of message describing grammar, an own set of non-terminal symbol and production rules.

$$G_{step} = (\bigcap G_{mess}, N_{step1}, ..., N_{stepN}, P_1, .., P_N, S), \ S \Longrightarrow_{G_{step}}^t$$

We can observe that the test suite can be described with a CD grammar system, where the component grammars corresponds to component units in the test suite. This could be very important in case when we want to generate the test sequences.

### 1.5.1 WTP test grammar

The WTP protocol is an Initiator-Responder protocol, in this case the testing procedure is th following. If we attend to test the Responder side of the protocol the tester have to behave az the initiator side and vice-versa. In the first case the main difference between the tester and initiator is that the tester has to show the verdict in an upper interface, and the tester must able to send and receive syntactically incorrect messages as well. If the test purpose is to test if the responder receives ready the Ack PDU for the Result PDU, we have to extend our protocol grammar with the fail verdicts in other leave on the protocol behaviour tree and with pass on the leave, which corresponds to test purpose. Let now see how the test grammars production rules are defined including test verdicts to the production rules.

$S_{WTPspec} = !Invoke1 StartT NON_1$ this is the same as in protocol description the StartT is a start timer T event. $NON_1 = ?Abort1(FAIL)$ or $NON_1 = ?Result1(PASS)NON_2$ here two alternatives are presented as a response to the Invoke1 message. $NON_2 = TimeoutT(FAIL)$ or $NON_2 = !AckPASS$, the verdicts (PASS), (FAIL), are preliminary verdicts, and the relation between preliminary verdict and final verdict is described in [7] A mapping between this test grammar and TTCN could be defined, this will be a transformation of this rules to table format

## 1.6 Further Works

The main reason of this work could serve for a test derivation from a standard protocol description language (ex. SDL ( Specification and Description Language [6])) to a standard test description language. The main problem is to find a conversion algorithm from for this test derivation. In this point we would like to present an idea how this conversion could be done. The idea is coming from the theory of DNA computing, using "Watson-Crick DOL systems" [8] for complementary state transitions. In this way in the grammar, which describes the specification a letter to letter endomorphism is defined. This means that we have to reduce or to extend our grammar to contain unambiguous input/output pairs. This endomorphism is referred to as the Watson-Crick morphism. The operational complementarities can be investigated in connection with generative process for words.

## 1.7 Conclusion

By this short introduction of testing and formal grammars we were trying to show the relation between grammars and conformance testing. We tried to present that the grammars are able to describe test systems. In case of generating test sequences these grammars could be an intermediate language of describing a test suite. In this way we would like to point to some further work where the test sequence generation is demonstrated, and an other important issue when we are using a standard description language (ex. Specification and Description Language SDL) to generate the source grammar for test derivation. In that way we can realize a test derivation from a standard description language to a test description language for example Tree and Tabular Combined Notation (TTCN)[7]. This grammar TTCN conversion were shown in [3].

## References

1. ISO/IEC JTC1/SC21, *Information Retrieval, Transfer and Management for OSI Framework: Formal Methods in Conformance Testing. Committee Draft CD 13245-1*, ISO, 1997.
2. ITU-T Recommendation Z-500(05/97) *Framework on formal methods in conformance testing*.
3. Csaba V. Rotter, Katalin Tarnay, *Formal Grammars in Protocol Testing*, Telecommunication Networks, 1999, pp. 303–308.
4. http://www.csr.ncl.ac.uk/projects/FME/InfRes/tools/name.html.
5. E. Csuhaj-Varju, J. Dassow, V. Mitrana, Gh. Paun, *Cooperation in Grammar Systems: similarity, universality, timing*, Acta Cybernetica, 4 (1993), 271-282.
6. ITU-T International Telecommunication Union Standard, *Z-100 Specification and Description Language*.
7. International Organization for Standardization, *ISO/IEC 9646-3, Tree and Tabular Combined Notation*.
8. Arto Salomaa, *Watson-Crick Walks and Roads on DOL Graphs*, Acta Cybernetica, 14 (1999), 179-192.
9. Wireless Transaction Protocol, Wapforum WTP standard, www.wapforum.org.

# Index

**A**

Activity based costing (ABC) model, 352
Activity based costing (ABC) system
    application of, 347
    data flow and architecture in, 349
    profitability of clients and suppliers, analysis
        of, 354–356
    project, steps of, 349, 350
    reason for applying and general architecture
        on, 348, 349
    stand-alone environment, development and
        implementation of model in, 350–354
Affective commitment, 316, 317, 319, 321
Agent behavior model, 71, 72
Agent interaction and internal design
    MOBMAS, 65
    P2P, 70–72, 73
Agent relationship diagram, 70, 73
Altruistic benefit, 248
American society for information management
    (SIM), 252
Apache, 447
*application* architecture, 288
Architecture design
    of MOBMAS, 65, 66
    of P2P, 74
Architecture of integrated information systems
    (ARIS), 134, 135
Atlas.ti software, 205
ATRIUM goal model
    for analysis of variability, 174
    mechanisms for, 170
Authorisation, digitally signed credentials for, 220
Automated obligation management system,
    222–223
Automation, and efficiency, 265
AVECON, 361
Average variance extracted (AVE), 451

**B**

B2B. *See* Business-to-business
'Back-end' developers, 216
Backus-naur form (BNF), 173
BBC WIL, 329
Behavior *vs.* technology, 127
Behavioral science, 128
    *vs.* design science, 132
Behavioral science research (BSR), 129

Billable hours, 309
Bologna declaration, 413
Bologna-Prague-Berlin-Bergen process, 413
Bottleneck metrics, 116–118
    average of, 123
    calculation of DF in, 117
    passive, estimating quality of experience with,
        115, 116
    on PIT, 116, 117
Bottleneck severity, function of, 119
Bottleneck(s)
    artificial, formation of download volumes
        after, 119
    definition and existence of, 116
    network, severity of, 116
BP model (ing)
    conceptual model from, receiving of, 33
    UML profile for, 141
Broker role, 337
BSR. *See* Behavioral science research
"BuildBehaviourModel", 441, 442
"BuildTestObjectives", 443
Business enabler, 268
Business information systems, requirements
    analysis of, 193
Business operations, reshaping of, stages in, 265,
    266
Business Process Modernisation (BPM), 372
Business processes, 161
    and object life cycles, discussion of differences
        between, 143
    design, important for correctness of, 139
    model, 34, 37
    phenomenon of, 141
Business reengineering, socio-technical design and,
    135, 136
Business-to-business (B2B) e-commerce (EC), 469,
    470

**C**

Capability Maturity Model (CMM), 412
Capability Maturity Model Integration (CMMI),
    359
Cardinality constraint, 6
Cartography, importance of identification in, 488
CASE tool-dependent part, for future DB and IS, 80
CDM. *See* Concept determination method
Cellulant, 330
Celtel, 327
Centre for Educational Leadership (CEL), 329

Client representatives, loyalty of, 209
Clients and suppliers, profitability analyses, 354–356
CMMI certification, 362
CMMI® model, 360
Co-ordination, 287
Code compiler, implementation of, 177
Committee of Sponsoring Organisations of the Treadway Commission (COSO), 412
Communicating systems, 505
Communication effectiveness, measurement of, 481
Communications, citizen-to-government, 227
Competing values model (CVM). *See also* specific models
    and systems characteristics and capabilities, 340
    for measuring organizational effectiveness, 336, 337
Competing values model (CVM). *See* Management Support Systems(MSS)
Complexity, of diagrams, 486
Comprehensive safety policy, implementation of, 259
Computation independent model (CIM), 25
Computer Supported Cooperative Work (CSCW) systems, 341
Computer-aided method engineering (CAME) tool, 99, 100
Concept determination method (CDM)
    for automatic schema and view integration, 85
    for linguistic conflicts, 81–84
Conceptual DB design, 40, 41
Conceptual model
    from BP model, receiving of, 33
    objects in, rules for structural consistency of, 149
    and MDA for ISD, 191
    modeling objects dynamics in, 139, 140
    in OO age, 140, 141
Conceptualization, 63, 65, 70
"Conference room pilot", 279
Conflict management, 337
Conformance testing, 506
    formal grammars for, 505
    with grammars, 506–508
Connection-type KCPM, notion of, 193
Consistency
    designing for, 42–44
    transaction, illustration of, 42
Context editor, 111
Context identifier (CI), 501, 502
Context language (CL), expression of, 498
Contextual approach
    for ISD and ME, 91

in method components, importance of, 93
    of method components, 90
Contextual integration, procedure of, 99
Contextual interface
    notions of, 93
    of method component, 92, 93, 99
    of method component, notion of, 99
Contextual method component, 90–93
Contextual method integration, 89, 90
    process and example of, 93
Contextual view, of method component, 91, 92
Continuance commitment, 316, 319, 321
Control Objectives for Information and Related Technology (COBIT), 411
Cookie-chain (CC) based discovery
    and networks, 182, 183
    of relation between internet users and real persons, 181, 182
Cookie-networks, 183
    comparison of creation and listing time of, 188
    experimental results of, 187, 188
    linked list for, 184, 185
    reversed tree for, 185
    theory of disjoint sets of, 183–185
Corex – Lean implementation, 390, 391
Corporate ICT infrastructure, consolidation and optimization of, 259
Corporate social responsbility, 367
Critical success factors (CSF) method, for MSS development, 335
CRM systems, 263
Cronbach's alpha, 244, 452
Cuneiform, 13

**D**

DA. *See* Dependency approach
Data processing, legal requirements on, 216
Data Track, 215
    by end-users, 224
    data processing, legal requirements on, 216
    functions for privacy protection
    data rectification and changing obligations, 221
    linkability computation function, 222–223
    logging, 219–220
    worried users, taking care of, 221–222
    PET requirements, architectural
    PRIME architecture, 217–218
    privacy policy, 220
    related work, 218–219
    user interface, 223–224
Data warehousing concept, implementation of, 259

Database (DB) consistency
  relational, advantage of, 459
  designing software components for, EM
    approach for, 37, 38, 45
Database (DB) design, 40
Database management system (DBMS)
  addresse of inconsistency by, 43
  data model of, 1
  for DB consistency, 38
  for existence of whole-part relationship, 10
  responsibility for transaction on, 44
Databases (DB)
  conceptual design of, 41
  future, CASE tool-dependent part for, 80
  implemented, definition of, 41
  in IS, use of, 37
  static description of, 44
DBMS. See Database management system
Decision Support Systems (DSS), 340
Decision-making, 287
Deep web (DW). See Web
  WOW project for searching of, 493, 494
Deep web search engine (DWSE), 498, 499
Delay factor (DF)
  average of, 123
  calculation of, 120–122
  for informative QoE metric, 122
  for networking service, calculation of, 117
  in function of elapsed time, values of, 120
'Delivered-feature' contracts, 310
Delphi technique, 252, 253
Denegability/satisfiability, in goal model, 169
Dependency approach (DA), 84–86
Design science
  and IS research, 129–131
  distinct perspectives on, 136
  in IS research, socio-technical perspectives on,
    127–129
  socio-technical reflection of, 131, 132
Design science research (DSR)
  and BSR, IS research approach for
    differentiation between, 129
  in IS, discussion of, 132
  processes of, 133
Design science thinking
  in IS, development of, 130
Design vs. behavioral science
  system in focus on, 132
Designing, for consistency, 42–44
Designing software components
  for DB consistency, EM approach for, 37, 38,
    45
DF. See Delay factor
Diagram elements

  relative importance of, 486, 487
  structure of, 488
Diagrams
  cognitive effectiveness of, prescriptive
    principles for, 490
  identification of, 488
  in ISD, cognitive effectiveness of, 481–483
  in ISD, use of, 483
  practical significance of, 490
  producing effective, principles for, 485–489
  theoretical significance of, 489, 490
Digital signatures, 218
Digitland enterprise, 280
Director role, of manager, 337
Director's process, in theatre production, 15
Discriminability, of diagrams, 485, 486
Disjoint sets
  of cookie-networks, theory of, 183–185
  use of LRT for, 186, 187
Distinctive competence, acquisition of, 267
Download volumes
  after artificial bottlenecks, formation of, 119
DSR. See Design science research
DSS systems, 263
DW. See Deep web
DW search, importance of, 494–497
Dynamic compilation techniques
  goal models by, configurable satisfiability
    propagation for, 167–168
Dynamic dependencies, in EM, 38, 39
Dynamic EM schemata, features of, 81
Dynamic KCPM schema, 81, 83
Dynamics, in conceptual models, 139

**E**

E-business portal
  for electronic invoicing for regional SMEs,
    469, 470
  in PMW, study of, 472–474
  methodology for, 475
E-commerce (EC). See also business-to-business
    (B2B)
  adoption and use of, 475
  advent of, 49
  B2B, 469, 470
  in e-invoicing, application of, 474, 475
  in SMEs, 471
E-Commerce (EC) adoption, in SMEs, 471, 472
E-government (electronic government), web design
  to improve trust, 227
E-government websites, usage in bilingual
  population, 228

E-government, paralingual web design to improve
    trust in
    alternative analytical calculations, 236
    analysis methods, 229–230
    grouping by language choice results
    Mann-Whitney U on, 230–232
    Spearman's rho on, 232–233
    Wilcoxon T test on, 233–235
    paralingual web pages
    readability of, 237
    usability of, 235
    research methodolgy, 229
    research question, 228–229
    Mann-Whitney U test on, 236
    Spearman's rho, 237
    Wilcoxon T test, 237
E-Invoice
    among SMEs, usage of, 472
    EC application in, 474, 475
    performance of, 478
E-learning
    emeging trends in university education, 412
    miniature but portable, 326
E-mail
    advantages of, 239
    definitions of variables, 242
    reading intention, influencing factors, 247
    willingness to forward, 248
E-mail marketing, study of, 239–240
    data analysis, 244–247
    implication of research results, 247–249
    rampancy of, 241
    research model and method, 241–244
EAS packages/implementation, 38
EC. See Electronic commerce
econet project, 413
Editor
    context, 111
    object type, 110
    opened model, main window of H2 toolset
        with, 110
Educational management information systems
    (EMIS), in Kenya, 330–334
Egocentrism, 205
Egoistical impulses, 209
Electronic commerce, 264
Electronic invoicing, for regional SMEs,
    e-business portal for, 469, 470
EM. See Enterprise modeling
"Embedded system", 264
EMIS. See educational management information
    systems
Enterprise application integration (EAI), 270
Enterprise architecture, 287

bottom-up initiative, 290–292
business perspectives of, 295
critical problems in, 288–289
research method, 289
stakeholders, selling project to, 293–296
value of, 289–290
focus, 291
frameworks and processes, evolution of, 292
issue affecting, 290
key benefits of, 294
"Eenterprise information systems" (EIS), 263, 271
business philosophy, 268, 269
business reshaping, 265, 266
distinct competence, 267, 268
ERP systems, 264, 265
levels of change, 266, 267
process management, 269, 270
systematic ways, 270
the IS field, 264
Enterprise modeling (EM) approach
hypernym and hyponym dependencies in, 85
and KCPM, comparison of, 80, 81
and KCPM, dealing with linguistic conflicts in,
    81–85
semantic dependencies, 80
static dependencies of, 84
views and schema, example of, 84
dependencies in, 38, 39
for designing software components for DB
    consistency, 37, 38, 45
in conceptual DB design, 42
integrated, advantage of, 41
integration rules of, 85
karlstad, 77, 79, 80
Enterprise ontology, 160
Enterprise resource planning (ERP) systems,
    263–265
Enterprise software, ability of, 154
Entity-relationship model (ERM)
for linguistic conflicts, 79
language, 105
notation, repository's data model in discussion
    of, 109
EPC. See Event-driven process chain
Enterprise Privacy Authorization Language
    (EPAL), 219
ERP (Enterprise Resource Planning)
implementation
    implications, 284, 285
    phases, 278, 279
    research data characteristics, 279, 280
    success factors, 276, 278, 283, 284
    relevance, 280–283
    works on, 275

ERP implementation phases, 278–283
  success factors importance across, 282
ERP package(s), 269, 279
  SAP or IFS, 280
ERP systems, investments in, 270
Error step, categories of, 440
ess/MSS, usefulness of, 341
EU data protection directive, 219
EU Data Protection Directive 95/46/EC, 216
Eudora, 326
European Credit Transfer and Accumulation
  System (ECTS system), 413
European Forum for Quality Management
  (EFQM), 359, 361, 363
European Quality Forum Model (EFQM), 368
Event-driven process chain (EPC), of ARIS, 135
Exploratory factor analysis (EFA), 244

**F**

Facilitator role, of manager, 337
File structure, 144, 145
File-sharing request, satisfy, 67
File-transfer process, carry out, 67
FireFox, 450
Fixed price, 306–308
  Suppliers' risk, 302, 303
Folk high school, case study in, 16–21
Formal description technique (FDT), specification
  of, 507
Free primary education (FPE), in Kenya, 328–330
Free Primary Education Support Programme
  (FPESP), 329

**G**

Global ontology, integration based on, 77
Goal model(s)
  ATRIUM, for analysis of variability, 174
  ATRIUM, mechanisms for, 170
  background for, 168–170
  by dynamic compilation techniques,
    configurable satisfiability propagation for,
    167–168
  exploitation of, 178
  for method components, 94–96
  integration of, 98
Goal modeling, for communication, 191
Goal Question Metrics (GQM), 366
Goal satisfaction, qualitative and quantitative
  approach for, 168
Gold plating, 304, 306, 309

Governance, definition of, 410
Grammar systems, cooperating distributed (CD),
  509
Grammar(s)
  conformance relation of, 510
  conformance testing with, 506–508
  formal, for conformance testing, 505
  formal, test cases and, 512, 513
  formal, WTP with, 511, 512
Graphic complexity, definition of, 489
Graphic design, principles of, 482
Graphical communication, theories of, 483, 485
Graphical information, human, process of, 484, 485
Graphical syntax, details of, 482
Graphics, language of, 483, 484
Grounded theory methodology, 300, 301
Group-oriented decision support (GDSS), 340
Gutenberg's printing press, 13

**H**

2HMD approach
  case study, 32–34
  formalization of, 27–32
  formalization using graph theory, 30–32
  formalized, application of, 35
2HMD. See Two-hemisphere model driven
Hierarchical modeling languages, definition of, 105
Hierarchies organigrams, creation of, 135
Hierarchy
  generalization and aggregation type of, 148
  of grammars, 512
Hierarchy level editor, 111
Higher education, knowledge management in. See
  Knowledge management
History manager, role of, 68, 69
Holistic approach
  for DB consistency, 37
  for designing databases, 42
Homonym conflicts, 84
Honesty-related ethical problems, 209
HP select identity, 221
Human graphical information, 484, 485
Human relations (HR) model, for measuring
  organizational effectiveness, 336
  ICT technoloies for, 341, 342
  managerial roles in, 337
Human resources management, 315
  approaches of, 317
  model of, 318
Human trustors, classification of, 51
Hypernym
  dependencies, in EM, 85

conflicts, DA for manual identification of, 84
Hyponym
    dependencies, in EM, 85
conflicts, DA for manual identification of, 84

**I**

IAP. *See* Implementation access point
IB meta data model, of integrated method
    components, 98
ICT technologies, for MSS subsystems, 341, 342
"Ideavirus marketing", 240
IF-THEN clauses, structure of, 84
IFS, 280
Imfundo, 329
Implementation access point (IAP)
    and PCO, difference between, 506
Inconsistency
    avoiding, 41–42
    by DBMS, addresse of, 43
    in view integration, identification and
        resolution of, 40, 42
Independent discipline *vs.* reference discipline
    in IS discipline, discussion of, 127
Individualism, 247
Industry projects, use of taxonomy in, 60
Industry-academia partnership
    benefits of both parties, 203
    forms of co-operation, 203
    moral problems in, 204
    accounting partners' objectives, 207
    competitors, avoidance of aiding, 205–206
    faced by client representatives, 206
    phenomenographic research design to study,
        204–205
    social responsibilities, fullfilling, 206–207
    students' efforts, benefiting from, 207
    students, effects of project on, 207–208
    practice and research, recommendations for,
        210
InfoCard, 219
Information acquisition, by personalization, 457
Information architecture, 288
"Information islands", 265
Information retriever, role of, 68, 69
Information retriever agent, class diagram for, 71
Information Services Procurement Library (ISPL),
    411
Information sharing, history of, 66
Information sharing ontology, 69, 72
    P2P application in, 71
Information system (IS) and management
    external dimension in different studies on, 208

key issues ordered by rated importance, 256,
    257
Information system (IS) mission, change in
    perception of, 255
Information system (IS) outsourcing, 259
Information system development (ISD), artistic
    engineering in, 21
Information systems (IS)
    conceptual design of, 41
    DB in, use of, 37
    design of, 132
    development of design science thinking in, 130
    directing and enacting, 13, 14
    discussion of DSR in, 132
    engineering of, 39
    future, CASE tool-dependent part for, 80
    implemented, use of, 41
    system theory for, 131
    web-based, for job offer acquisition, 461
    web-based, ontology-based user modeling for,
        457, 458
Information systems (IS) development practice, and
    contract type and pricing structure, study of, 299
    research method and setting, 300–302
    risk distribution and price level
    impact of behavior on, 306, 307
    impact of pricing structure choice on, 302,
        303, 308, 309
    impact on behavior, 303–306
    impact on pricing structure choice, 307, 308
Information systems (IS) domain
    determination of, 162
    for classification ofinteroperability issues, 160
Information systems (IS) failure, major categories
    of, 398, 399
Information systems (IS) management in
    companies in Slovenia, key issues in, 250, 251
    research approach, 252–254
    the research, 254, 255
    the results, 255–261
Information systems (IS) meta data model
    of goal model, 95
    of sequence diagramming technique, 94, 95
    of use case technique, 93, 94
Information systems (IS) research approach
    behavioral aspect of, 134
    cycle of, 131
    design science and, 129–131
    design science in, socio-technical perspectives
        on, 127–129
    notion of, 133
    for differentiation between BSR and DSR, 129
Information Systems Audit and Control Association
    (ISACA), 411

Information systems development (ISD), 397
    and software engineering, body of knowledge
        for, 159
    conceptual modeling and MDA for, 191
    conceptual modeling in, 111
    contextual approach for, 91
    diagrams in, cognitive effectiveness of,
        481–483
    implications for, 20, 21
    meta modeling in, 104, 105
    method components recognize aspects of, 91
    methods for, 89
    situational and evolutionary language
        adaptation in, framework for, 103, 104
    situational and evolutionary modeling
        language adaptation in, 106
    socio-technical aspects of, 107
Information systems development (ISD) method
    actions and actors in method components,
        relation of, 97
    context fragments of, 92
    deliverables in method components, contents
        of, 96, 97
    fragment of, 99
Information systems, tasks supported by, 287
Information technology (IT) artifacts
    analysis of, 136
    and socio-technical design, 133, 134
    facets of, 134
Information technology (IT) infrastructures, 162
Information Technology Infrastructure Library
    (ITIL), 411
Information-systems development, required skills
    for project mangers, 208
Innovator role, of manager, 337
Integrated method components
    IB meta data model of, 98
Integration, and cooperation, in business reshaping,
    265, 266
Integrity constraints, 6
Intellectual co-operation, 315
Inter-organisational collaboration, fundamentals of
    maintenance, 203
Interceptor, 217
Internal process (IP) model, for measuring
    organizational effectiveness, 336
    ICT technoloies for, 341, 342
    managerial roles in, 337
Internal validity, of trust decisions, 55, 56, 58
Internet
    applications trust in, survey of, 51
    wireless, WAP for building of, 511
Internet banking, 264

Internet data communications, important parts of
    privacy-friendliness in, 215
Internet users
    and real persons, CC based discovery of
        relation between, 181, 182
    global, 239
Interoperability
    collaborative ME platform for,
        155–157
    definition of, 154
    determination of, 162
Interoperability classes, 157–159
Interoperability classification framework,
    159–161
    for MCR, 153–155, 157
Interoperability domain
    determination of, 162
    for classification ofinteroperability issues, 160
Interoperability issues
    determination of, 162
    classification of, 157–161
    classification of, IS and interoperability
        domain for, 160
Interpret information
    specific enhancements to, 20
Investments
    and architecture, 289
    in ERP systems, 270
Investments in IT systems, factors influencing, 264
Investments, approaches to manage, 268
IS. See Information systems
ISD. See Information systems development
IT acceptance, models to explain, 449
IT artifacts, 264, 265
IT governance, 410–412
IT organisations, based on KM, objectives of,
    315
IT supported inter-organizational services. See
    Business-to-business (B2B) e-commerce (EC)
Itentia Movex, 267

J

J.J. Darboven Poland, 388–389
Jackson's theory
    for structural coherency, 148
Job offer acquisition
    ontology-based user model for, 460
    user model for, 461–465
    web-based IS for, 461
Job offer class
    selected object properties of, 463

K

Karlstad enterprise modeling (EM) approach, 79, 80
    for linguistic conflicts, 77
KCPM. *See* Klagenfurt conceptual predesign model
Kenya
    EMIS in, 330–334
    FPE in, 328–330
    mobile phone networks in, sophistication and
        agility of, 325, 327
    physical infrastructure, 327
    SEP in, 329, 330
Key resource teachers (KRTs), 329, 330
Klagenfurt conceptual predesign model (KCPM)
    and EM, comparison of, 80, 81
    and EM, dealing with linguistic conflicts in,
        81–85
    and OLIVANOVA, comparison between,
        194–196
    and OLIVANOVA, mapping process of,
        196–199
    development of, 192–194
    representation concept of, 191
Klagenfurt conceptual predesign model (KCPM)
    approach, 77–79
Klagenfurt conceptual predesign model (KCPM)
    schemata, 81, 83
Knowledge, creation and dissemination of, 321, 374
Knowledge Cube, 373, 375
Knowledge exploitation, 315
Knowledge management (KM)
    key success factors, 381
    in IT services, 381
    guidelines for development of, 378–379
    identification of business
        goal/objective, 372, 373
    identification of existing knowledge, 373, 374
    implementation issues, 380
    knowledge creation, 374
    knowledge sharing, 374, 375
    knowledge, measurement of, 376, 377
    Knowledge, utilization and retention of, 376
    and organisational commitment, relationship
        between, 314–315
    human resources management, model of, 317, 318
    in organisation, 315, 316
    organisational commitment and it's role in
        management
            affective/continuance/normative
                commitment, 319
            case study, 319–321

quality levels in organisation depending on,
    316, 317
issues in higher education, 371, 372
strategy, persuation of, 377–380
knowledge management (KM), in UK higher
    education, 371
    University of Wolverhampton, KM in IT
        services at, 372–377
Knowledge sharing, 318, 374, 375
Knowledge
    measurement of, 376, 377
    utilization and retention of, 376
KPMG, 269
kurtosis, 116, 117

L

Language
    entity-relationship model (ERM), 105
    in IS development, role of, 104
    natural, grammatical substructure of, 502
    natural, in DW search, query of, 497
    of graphics, 483, 484
    of ISD, diagrams form critical part of, 481
    test and test system description, 508, 509
Language adaptation
    situational and evolutionary
        framework for, 107
    in ISD, framework for, 103, 104
    meta modeling software for, repository of,
        108–110
Language editor, 110
Lifetime dependency (LD), 5, 6
Likert scale, 229
Linguistic conflicts
    future work of, 85
    in KCPM and EM, dealing with, 81–85
    recognition and resolution of, 77, 78
Linkability, evaluation functionality, 218
Linked list
    for cookie-networks, 184, 185
Linked reversed tree (LRT), 186, 187
    building time of, 188
    for management of web log entries, 181
"Linköping" model, for MPC systems, 270
"Live pilot", 279
Long term memory (LTM)
    in human graphical information processing,
        484
Loss based metric, 117, 118
LRT. *See* Linked reversed tree

## M

m-commerce (MC). *See also*
    E-commerce
    advent of, 49
Management information systems (MIS), 383
Management quality, 317
Management Support Systems (MSS)
    development methods
    critical success factors (CSF) method, 335
    strategic business objectives (SBO) method,
        335
    and CVM, 336, 337
    CVM-based approach, 338
    requirements, determination of, 339–343
    postulates on, 335
Management Support Systems (MSS) subsystems
    ICT technologies for, 341, 342
    MSS-HR, key capabilities of, 343
    MSS-IP, key capabilities of, 342, 343
    MSS-OS, key capabilities of, 343
    MSS-RG, key capabilities of, 343
Management, by processes and facts, 366
Managerial behavior, and cognition, requirements
    for, 339
Managerial roles, for organizational models, 337
Managers
    leadership qualities, 365, 366
Mann-Whitney U test, 230–232, 236
Manual information system
    analysis of, 21
    development of, 13
MAS
    by MOBMAS, development of, 64
    ontology in development of, role of, 64
MAS organization design
    of MOBMAS, 65
    of P2P, 69, 70
Material and production control (MPC) systems,
    "linköping" model for, 270
MCR. *See* Method chunk repositories
MDA. *See* Model driven architecture
ME. *See* Method engineering
Mentor role, of manager, 337
Meronym dependencies, in EM, 85
Meta data model
    IS, of goal model, 95
    IS, of sequence diagramming technique, 94,
        95
    IS, of use case technique, 93, 94
Meta modeling
    for situational and evolutionary modeling
        language adaptation, 106

in ISD, 104, 105
Meta modeling software, for situational and
    evolutionary language adaptation, repository of,
    108–110
Meta modeling tools, for modeling language
    adaptation, 104
Meta modeling toolset, for definition of languages,
    111
Meta rules, use of, 197
Metamodel, for requirements engineering, 170
Metamodel editor, 175
Metamodel elements, integration of, 168
Method application, situation-specific, 155
Method chunk repositories (MCR), 156
    interoperability classification framework for,
        153–155, 157
Method components
    contextual interface of, 92, 93
    contextual view of, 91, 92
    definition of, 90
    notion and categories of, 90, 91
    notion of contextual interface of, 99
    notions of, 93
    contextual approach of, 90, 99
    ISD actions in, relation of, 97
    purposes of, 96
Method construction, situation-specific, activity of,
    155
Method engineering (ME)
    component-based paradigm in, application of,
        92
    contextual approach for, 91
    strategies of, 89
Method engineering (ME) platform
    collaborative, architecture for, 155
    collaborative, for interoperability, 155–157
Method engineering (ME) tool
    computer-aided, use of, 99, 100
Method integration
    contextual, 89, 90
    contextual, process and example of, 93
    use of, 99
Methodology for ontology-based MASs
    (MOBMAS)
    activity of, 65
    analysis and design phases of, 67
    development process of, 74
    methodology of, 64–66
    on a P2P information sharing application, use
        of, 66
    P2P information sharing MAS by, design of,
        63, 64
    use of, 75
Minus technique algorithm, use of, 6

Mobile and wireless devices in education, emerging
    categories, 326
Mobile learning, 326
Mobile phone data communications, important
    parts of privacy-friendliness of, 215
MOBMAS. *See* Methodology for ontology-based
    MASs
Model driven approach, use of, 39
Model driven architecture (MDA)
    abstraction in framework of, levels of, 26
    and conceptual modeling for ISD, 191
    and requirements modeling, 191, 192
    graph theory in framework of, outlines of,
        25–27
    realization solutions for, 27
    transformations in framework of, realization
        levels of, 26
Model editor, 175
Modeling hierarchies, meta modeling tool for, 105
Modeling language
    for EM approach, 41
    proliferation of, 104
Modeling language adaptation
    situational and evolutionary
        framework for, 106–108
    in ISD, 106
    meta modeling for, 105, 106
Modeling language development and adaptation
    prototypical tool support for, 110, 111
Modeling languages
    adapting, alternatives of, 105
    design of, 103
Modeling object life cycles, with UML, 146–148
Modeling objects dynamics, in conceptual models,
    139, 140
MODPA (Mobile Design Patterns), 361
MODS formalism, use of, 507
Modularisation, 486
Monitor role, of manager, 337
Moral conflicts, 209
MORPHEUS, 175–177
Movie ontology, 68, 71, 72
Movie trailer resource ontology, 71, 72
MSS. *See* Management Support Systems
MSS-IP, key capabilities of, 342
MYSQL, 448
MySQL databases, construction of, 83

**N**

Narrative approach
    for theatre production, 21
Natural language (NL). *See* Language

Natural language (NL) module, 499–501
Navigational Development Techniques (NDT),
    423, 437
    practical applications of, 424–426
    grants management projects, 426, 427
    heritage management projects, 427, 428
    system to manage grade of handicap, 428
Network bottleneck
    severity of, 116
Network pseudonyms, use of, 215
Network services
    at different bottleneck, quality of, 119, 120
    simple throughput calculation for, 118
Networks, cookie-chains (CC) and, 182, 183
NIBA project, for treatment of German texts, 79
Non-ontological representations, in web-based IS,
    459–460
Normative commitment, 316, 317, 319, 321

**O**

Object life cycles
    and business professes, discussion of
        differences between, 143
    modeling, with UML, 146–148
Object relational database management systems
    (ORDBMS$_{SQLS}$)
    advantages of, 10
    features of, 2
    problems of, 3, 9
Object-oriented (OO) age
    conceptual modeling in, 140, 141
Object-relational database management systems
    (ORDBMS$_{TTM}$)
    in whole-part relationship, possible designs of,
        3, 4
    principles of, 2
    whole-part relationship in, 3
Object-relational databases, 1–3
Object's methods, conceptual meaning of, 141
Objects life cycles
    by structure diagram, description of, 141
    mutual consistency of, 140, 148–150
    process of, 142
    structural coherency of, 150
Objects *vs.* real world behavior, dynamics of,
    141–143
ObjectTypeDefinitions, 109
OLAP (On Line Analytical Processing), 342
OLIVANOVA, 194
    and KCPM, comparison between, 194–196
    and KCPM, mapping process of, 196–199
    for source code generation, 192

Ontological method, for analysis of interoperability, 154
Ontology
  and taxonomy of trust, 51, 52
  definition of, 77
  in MAS development, role of, 64
  information sharing, 69
  information sharing and movie, P2P application in, 71
  movie, 68
  representing user model by, 460, 461
  user model, 462–464
Ontology model
  construction of, 68
  use of, 74
OO. See Object-oriented
OOHDM, 424
Open source software (OSS), IT acceptance by FireFox users, 447
  conceptual models of users' acceptance of IT, 448–450
  data analysis and results, 451–453
  research method and survey design, 450–451
Open Source web browser, 447, 448
Open systems (OS) model, for measuring organizational effectiveness, 336
  ICT technoloies for, 341, 342
  managerial roles in, 337
Operationalization, 168, 169
Opportunistic behaviour, 301, 308
ORDBMS. See Object relational database management systems
Order line concept, dependencies of, 85
Organisation, depending on knowledge management, levels of quality in, 317
Organisational commitment, categories of, 316, 319
Organisational conflicts, in collaborative projects, key dimensions of, 208
Organizational effectiveness, 336
OROS modeler, 351
Outlook, 326

P

P2P. See Peer-to-peer
P3P (privacy preferences project), W3C platform for, 219
Packet interarrival times (PIT)
  on bottleneck metrics, 116, 117
  kurtosis average of, 123
Packet interarrival times (PIT) PDF, shape of, 123
Packet loss, by QoE metric, evaluation of, 118
Packet loss ratio (PLR), 122, 123

Partenership development, 367
Partial Least Squares (PLS), 451
PCO. See Point of control and observation
Pearson product moment coefficient, 246
Pedagogical issues, 17
Peer-to-peer (P2P)
  agent classes in, 74
  agent interaction design of, 72, 73
  agent internal design of, 70–72
  analysis, 67–69
  architecture design of, 74
  MAS organization design of, 69, 70
Peer-to-peer (P2P) information sharing MAS
  by MOBMAS, design of, 63, 64
  community-based, 66
  future work of, 74, 75
Perceptual directness, of diagrams, 487, 488
Perceptual limits cognitive and, of diagrams, 486
Petroglyphs, 13
PETs (Privacy-enhancing technologies). See Data track
Phenomenography, 204
Philanthropy, 210
php, 448
PISA project, 219
PIT. See Packet inter arrival times
Platform independent model (PIM), 25
  analogy of, 29
  in framework of MDA, development of, 27
  presentation of, 26
Platform specific model (PSM), 25
Playwright's process, in theatre production, 14
Plone, 448
Point of control and observation (PCO)
  and IAP, difference between, 506
Poland, ERP implementation projects in, 280
Portal meetingpoint wermland (PMW)
  e-business portal in, study of, 472–474
Portal role, 68, 69
PostgreSQL, 448
PRIME
  enhancing people's trust in, 222
  special activity on education, 224
PRIME (Privacy and Identity Management for Europe), 215
  system architecture, overview of, 216
PRIME middleware, 217
PRIME usability test, 221
Principal-agent theory, 301, 308
PRISM project, 329
Project Register for IT Services (PRITS), 375
Privacy-friendly data maintenance. See Data track
Probability distribution function (PDF)
  PIT, moment of, 116

PIT, shape of, 123
spike of, 117
Problem solving paradigm, 130
Producer role, of manager, 337
Product quality, 362
"Productivity paradox", 263
Profitability of customers, measurement of, 347
Profitability, as moral problem in industry-academia partnership, 209
Program structure, 144, 145
Project manager replacement, impact on project-in-progress, 397
implications for research and practice, 405
IT project managers' perceptions of critical success factors
the context perspective, 401, 402
the human perspective, 401
the management perspective, 400, 401
IT project managers' perceptions of impact of replacement, 403, 404
perceptions on replacement, 402, 403
projects and success factors, 398, 399
research, 399, 400
Propagation
of satisfiability/denegability in goal model, 169
sketched view of, 175
Propagation algorithm, 167, 168, 172
Propagation rules
qualitative, description of, 171
Prototypical software
for definition of languages, 111
Prototypical tool support
for modeling language development and adaptation, 110, 111
Pseudonymity, 218
Pseudonyms, 220
Python, 448

**Q**

Q-methodology, 255
ranking technique in implementation of, 253
Q-sort, 253
Quality of experience (QoE)
by passive measurements, methods determination of, 115
degradation cause of, 116
network-related, 115
Quality of experience (QoE) metric
evaluation of packet loss by, 118
informative, DF for, 122

Quality of service (QoS)
for network service, 123

**R**

Rational goal (RG) model, for measuring organizational effectiveness, 336
ICT technoloies for, 341, 342
managerial roles in, 337
Real persons
and internet users, CC based discovery of relation between, 181, 182
Real world vs. objects behavior
dynamics of, 141–143
Reference discipline vs. independent discipline
in IS discipline, discussion of, 127
Relational data model, 1
in TTM, describtion of, 8
revision of, 2
specification of, 10
Relvar constraint, 6
Relvars
complex data types in, use of, 2
values of, illustrations of, 3
virtual, relational expression of, 8
Repository, of meta modeling software, 108–110
Repository's schema, 109
Requirements modeling and MDA, 191, 192
Reversed tree
building time of, 188
for cookie-networks, 185
Rhetorical techniques
for transferring information, 21
use of, 17
Rigor vs. relevance, debate of, 127
Ripple effect, in EC, 476
Role diagram, 70
Rule editor, 176

**S**

Safaricom, 327
SAP, 280
SAP R/3, 267
Sarbanes-Oxley Act of 2002, 411
SAS ABM software, 351
Satisfiability/denegability, in goal model, 169
Schema integration
automatic, CDM for, 85
definitions of, 41
for linguistic conflicts, 77, 78

on storing and updating in sales system, 43
with CDM, steps for, 82–84
School empowerment programme (SEP), in Kenya, 329, 330
School-based teacher development program (SbTD), 329
Scrollable transaction track, 224
Security-related requirements, taxonomy for, 53
Self-centredness, as moral problem in industry-academia partnership, 208–209
SEMA!, 325, 330, 332, 334
Semiology of graphics, 483
Sequence diagramming technique
  for interaction between system and actors, 93, 94
  for method components, 93
  integration of, 98
  IS meta data model of, 94, 95
Service Level Agreements (SLAs), 415
Service oriented architecture (SOA), 270
SESCA Innovations, 361
  leadership and constancy of purpose, 365, 366
  corporate social responsbility, 367
  learning, innovation and improvement, 367
  management by processes and facts, 366
  partenership development, 367
  people development and involvement, 366, 367
  quality work, 362
  results and implications, 364, 365
SESCA Solutions, 361
SESCA technologies, 361
SEVECON Group, 361
Shareholder activism, 410
SIM cards, 328
Simulations, 224
Small and medium-sized enterprises (SMEs). See also SESCA Innovations
  ABC implementation in, obstacles for, 357
  barriers to EC adoption in, 471, 472
  case studies, 385–393
  e- business portal for electronic invoicing for, 469, 470
  EC in, 471
  principles of creation of, 383–385
  resource for, 473
  value-adding IT solutions for
SMEs. See Small and medium-sized enterprises
SMS messaging, 331
SMS text messages, 326
SMS text system, 327
SMS texting, 333
Social responsibilities, in business, 209–210

Socio-technical design
  analysis of, 136
  and business reengineering, 135, 136
  IT artifacts and, 133, 134
Software business
  sustainable growth in, models for, 360
Software component modeling, 39, 40
Software development
  inconsistency in, identification and resolution of, 42
Software development organization, management of, 359–361. See also SESCA Innovations
Software Engineering. See also Web engineering
  and ISD, body of knowledge for, 159
Software testing in industry, 435
Somers and Nelson's factors, 284
Spam, 248
Spearman's rho, 230, 232–233, 237
SPECS, formalism, use of, 507
SQL
  deficiencies and design of,1, 2
queries, domestication of, 499
State chart
  for description of object life cycles, 146, 150
  limitations of, 147, 148
  vs. structure diagram, 147
Static dependencies
  in EM, 38, 39, 80
  of EM, 84
Static KCPM schema, integration of, 79
Strategic business objectives (SBO) method, for MSS development, 335
Structural coherency
  for relationships between static and dynamic dimension of real world, 143–146
  Jackson's theory for, 148
  of objects life cycles, 150
Structure clash, 146
Structure diagram
  objects life cycles by, description of, 141
  vs. state chart, 147
sub Saharan Africa, 327
Supplier-customer relationships, theories of, 301
Supply-chain operations reference-model (SCOR), 269
Synonyms conflicts
  DA for manual identification of, 84
Syntactic elements, in EM, 39
Syntax analysis description language (SADL)
  by WOW project, development of, 501
System architecture, of natural language query in DW search, 498, 499
System development practice, impact of pricing structure on, 309

System task model, of P2P analysis, 67
System theory, for IS, 128, 131
System under test (SUT), 435
Systems development methods (SDM), 335
Systems integration, within and between
    organisations, 265

**T**

TAC Polska, 386–388
TAM. *See* Transitional auxiliary model
Task Technology Fit (TTF), 449
Taxonomy, 53, 54
    and ontologies of trust, 51, 52
    of other related types of requirements, 52, 53
    of trust-related requirements, 49, 50
    of trustor-related requirements, 56
    partial, of trustee-quality requirements, 58
Teacher advisory centre (TAC) tutors, 328
Teacher(s)
    interaction between, 17–20
    role of, 19
Technical architecture, 288, 293
Technology Acceptance Model (TAM),
    447, 449
Technology *vs.* behavior, discussion of, 127
Test objectives, automatic derivation of, 435
    case study, 439, 440
    state-of-the art, 436, 437
    test objectives, from use cases, 440
    behavioural model, building of, 440–443
    derivation of, 443, 444
    use cases, coverage of, 444, 445
    use case model and template for testing, 437,
        439
Test system description language, test
    and, 508, 509
Theatre production, core processes of
    actor's process in, 15
    audience's process in, 15, 16
    director's process in, 15
    playwright's process in, 14
Theatre productions
    development model for, 14–16
    development process of, 21
Theory of Planned Behaviour (TPB), 449
Theory of Reasoned Action (TRA), 239–241, 449
Thing type glossary, representation concept of, 193
Throughput
    calculation simple, for networking service, 118
    level in function of elapsed time, measurement
        of, 121
    measurement of, 123

    by packet level information, measurement
        of, 120
2 Toolset
    with opened model editor, main window of,
        110
Tokenization, 498, 499
Total Quality Management (TQM), 317, 359
Trade company, medium-sized
    ABC system for (*see* activity based costing
        system, for medium-sized trade company)
    profitability in, assessment of, 347, 348
Traffic properties, cumulated, analysis of, 122, 123
Transaction cost theory, 301
Transaction, planned, business value of, 52
Transformation
    and networking, in business reshaping, 265,
        266
    from TAM to collaboration diagram, 34
    model, in 2HMD approach, 32
    scheme of, 31
Transformation algorithms, 28
    2HMD, 30
    information of, 29, 30
Transitional auxiliary model (TAM)
    receiving of, 33, 34
    to collaboration diagram, transformation from,
        34
Trust
    between supplier and customer, 307
    in e-governance websites, 228
    notion of, 49
    taxonomies and ontologies of, 51, 52
Trust achievement, external validity of, 58
Trust decisions
    external validity of, 55, 56, 58
    feasibility of, 55, 56, 58
    requirements for quality of, 55
    validity or feasibility of, 55, 56, 58
Trust management
    reputation-based, classification of trust
        functions in, 51
    survey of field of, 52
Trust requirements
    category of, 57
    taxonomy of, 52
Trust-related requirements
    taxonomy of, 49, 50, 53
Trustee
    identity of, 52
    relationship between trustor, 51
    subtypes of quality requirements for, 58
Trustee-quality requirements, partial taxonomy of,
    58
Trustee-related requirements, 57–59

Trustor(s)
  human, classification of, 51
  kinds of requirements for, 56
Trustor-related requirements, 54–57
Tuning Educational Structures in Europe, 413
Tuplespace mechanism, 72
Two-hemisphere model driven (2HMD) approach, 27–29
  formalization of, using of graph theory in, 30–32
  transformation algorithms of, 30
  conceptual scheme of, 28
  for object-oriented software development, 27
  formalized, application of, 35
  formalized, case study in, 32–34
  model transformation in, 32
Typo3, 253

**U**

UI design, 219
Unified Modeling Language (UML), 192, 293
  architectural approaches for, 37
  diagrams, 436
  testing profile, 436
  architectural approaches for, 37
  for BP modeling, profile of, 141
  modeling object life cycles with, 146–148
  modeling objects dynamics in, possibilities of, 140
  propose of ontology in, 52
  use case model in, 93
Usability requirements, styles of, 53
Use case model, 438
  test objectives and template for testing, 437, 439
Use case technique
  for method components, 93
  integration of, 98
  IS meta data model of, 93, 94
Use cases
  coverage of, 444, 445
  test objectives from, 440
  behavioural model, building of, 440–443
  derivation of, 443, 444
User anonymous, 220
User characteristics, 458
User interface agents
  effector of, 74
  reflexive rule specification for, 72
User interface role, 69
User model
  domain-dependent part of, 464

  for job offer acquisition, 461–465
  representing, by ontology, 460, 461
  XML structure for, 466
User model ontology, 462–464
User model representation
  in web-based IS, 458–461
User modeling
  in web based IS, advantageous for, 467
  ontology-based, in web-based IS, 457, 458
  tools for, 464, 465
User-friendly modeling approaches
  for linguistic conflicts, 78
user's privacy awareness, function for raising of, 219
UWE, 424

**V**

Value-added services (VAS), 332
Value-adding IT solutions, for SMEs
  case studies, 385–393
  principles of creation of, 383–385
Variability analysis
  defining rules for, 174
Videoconferencing, 341
View integration
  automatic, CDM for, 85
  for linguistic conflicts, 77, 78
  in conceptual DB design, 41
  inconsistency in, identification and resolution of, 40, 42
Viral marketing, critical role player, 240
Virtual corporation, 410
Virtual Educational Space of Collaboration of Universities of Economics, in Poland, 413
Virtual organisation governance
  corporate vs. IT, 410–412
  virtual organization management theories, 409, 410
Virtual organization governance model, works essential for, 412
Virtual space of collaboration of universities of economics, 409
Virtual university architecture, 415
Virtual university governance, 412, 413
  contract management, 415, 416
  virtual education, standardization for, 416–418
  virtual university architecture, 415
  virtual university strategy management, 414, 415
Visual variables
  for graphical communication, 484

in graphics, 483
range of, 489

## W

W3C platform, for P3P, 219
WAP, 217. *See* Wireless application protocol
Web
  deep, facts about, 494, 495
  deep, searching of, 496
  deep, WOW project for searching of, 493, 494
  in 2005, distribution of, 495
Web content management system. *See* Typo3
Web data storage, change in, 494
Web design, paralingual, 227
Web EDI, 474
Web engineering, practical experiences in, 421–423
  global evaluation, 428–431
  NDT, 423
  practical applications of (*see* Navigational
    Development Techniques)
Web information, deep, quality of, 494
Web IS, development of, 107
Web log entries, LRT for management of, 181
Web of words (WOW) project, 497
  development of SADL by, 501
  for searching DW, 493, 494
Web search
  deep, connection with content providers for,
    502, 503
  deep, natural language query in, 497
  system architecture of, 498, 499
Web-based IS
  for job offer acquisition, 461
  ontology-based user modeling for, 457, 458
  user modeling in, advantageous for, 467
WebQ, 253
Whole-part relationship(s)
  DBMS for existence of, 10
  implementation of, design alternatives for, 4
  implementing properties of, 8

in object-relational databases, semantics of,
    1–3
  lifetime in, comparison of, 5, 6
  ORDBMS$_{TTM}$ in, possible designs of, 3, 4
  secondary characteristics of, 4
Wilcoxon T test, 230, 233–235, 237
Wireless application protocol (WAP)
  for building of wireless internet, 511
Wireless internet, WAP for building of, 511
Wireless transaction protocol (WTP)
  test grammar in, 513
  with formal grammars, 511, 512
Wolverhampton Online Learning Framework
  (WOLF), 376
Work environment quality, 317
Work flow, 269
Work practices in companies, levels of change for,
    266
Working memory (WM)
  in human graphical information processing,
    484
  use of, 488
World
  real, characteristics of, 140
  real, dynamics of, 139
  real, types of dynamics in, 142
World bank, FPESP in Kenya, 329
WOW. *See* Web of words
WTP. *See* Wireless transaction protocol

## X

XML, advantage of, 459

## Y

Yet another modeling approach (YAMA)
  syndrome, 104
  invention of, 111